CRITICAL SURVEY OF
Poetry

Fourth Edition

European Poets

CRITICAL SURVEY OF

Poetry

Fourth Edition

European Poets

Volume 1
Endre Ady—Jorge Guilléen

Editor, Fourth Edition
Rosemary M. Canfield Reisman
Charleston Southern University

SALEM PRESS
Pasadena, California
Hackensack, New Jersey

Editor in Chief: Dawn P. Dawson

Editorial Director: Christina J. Moose   *Research Supervisor:* Jeffry Jensen
Development Editor: Tracy Irons-Georges   *Research Assistant:* Keli Trousdale
Project Editor: Rowena Wildin   *Production Editor:* Andrea E. Miller
Manuscript Editor: Desiree Dreeuws   *Page Design:* James Hutson
Acquisitions Editor: Mark Rehn   *Layout:* Mary Overell
Editorial Assistant: Brett S. Weisberg   *Photo Editor:* Cynthia Breslin Beres

Cover photo: Petrarch (The Granger Collection, New York)

Some of the essays in this work, which have been updated, originally appeared in the following Salem Press publications, *Critical Survey of Poetry, English Language Series* (1983), *Critical Survey of Poetry: Foreign Language Series* (1984), *Critical Survey of Poetry, Supplement* (1987), *Critical Survey of Poetry, English Language Series, Revised Edition*, (1992; preceding volumes edited by Frank N. Magill), *Critical Survey of Poetry, Second Revised Edition* (2003; edited by Philip K. Jason).

∞ The paper used in these volumes conforms to the American National Standard for Permanence of Paper for Printed Library Materials, X39.48-1992 (R1997).

Library of Congress Cataloging-in-Publication Data

Critical survey of poetry. — 4th ed. / editor, Rosemary M. Canfield Reisman.

    v. cm.

Includes bibliographical references and index.

    ISBN 978-1-58765-582-1 (set : alk. paper) — ISBN 978-1-58765-756-6 (set : European poets : alk. paper) — ISBN 978-1-58765-757-3 (v. 1 : European poets : alk. paper) — ISBN 978-1-58765-758-0 (v. 2 : European poets : alk. paper) — ISBN 978-1-58765-759-7 (v. 3 : European poets : alk. paper)

1. Poetry—History and criticism—Dictionaries. 2. Poetry—Bio-bibliography. 3. Poets—Biography—Dictionaries. I. Reisman, Rosemary M. Canfield.

    PN1021.C7 2011

    809.1'003—dc22

2010045095

First Printing

PUBLISHER'S NOTE

European Poets is part of Salem Press's greatly expanded and redesigned *Critical Survey of Poetry* Series. The *Critical Survey of Poetry, Fourth Edition*, presents profiles of major poets, with sections on other literary forms, achievements, biography, general analysis, and analysis of the poet's most important poems or collections. Although the profiled authors may have written in other genres as well, sometimes to great acclaim, the focus of this set is on their most important works of poetry.

The *Critical Survey of Poetry* was originally published in 1983 and 1984 in separate English- and foreign-language series, a supplement in 1987, a revised English-language series in 1992, and a combined revised series in 2003. The *Fourth Edition* includes all poets from the previous edition and adds 145 new ones, covering 843 writers in total. The poets covered in this set represent more than 40 countries and their poetry dates from the eighth century B.C.E. to the present. The set also offers 72 informative overviews; 20 of these essays were added for this edition, including all the literary movement essays. In addition, seven resources are provided, two of them new. More than 500 photographs and portraits of poets have been included.

For the first time, the material in the *Critical Survey of Poetry* has been organized into five subsets by geography and essay type: a 4-volume subset on *American Poets*, a 3-volume subset on *British, Irish, and Commonwealth Poets*, a 3-volume subset on *European Poets*, a 1-volume subset on *World Poets*, and a 2-volume subset of *Topical Essays*. Each poet appears in only one subset. *Topical Essays* is organized under the categories "Poetry Around the World," "Literary Movements," and "Criticism and Theory." A *Cumulative Indexes* volume covering all five subsets is free with purchase of more than one subset.

EUROPEAN POETS

The 3-volume *European Poets* contains 188 poet profiles, arranged alphabetically. For this edition, 18 new essays have been added, and 6 have been significantly updated with analysis of recently published books or poems.

Each volume begins with a list of Contents for that volume, a Complete List of Contents covering the entire subset, and a Pronunciation Key. The poet essays follow in alphabetical order, divided among the three volumes. The third volume contains the Resources section, which features three tools for interpreting and understanding poetry: "Explicating Poetry," "Language and Linguistics," and "Glossary of Poetical Terms." The "Bibliography," "Guide to Online Resources," "Time Line," "Major Awards," and "Chronological List of Poets" provide guides for further research and additional information on European poets; comprehensive versions appear in *Topical Essays* and *Cumulative Indexes*. The "Guide to Online Resources" and "Time Line" were created for this edition.

European Poets contains a Geographical Index of Poets; a Categorized Index of Poets, in which poets are grouped by culture or group identity, literary movement, historical period, and poetic forms and themes; and a Subject Index. The *Critical Survey of Poetry* Series: Master List of Contents identifies poets profiled in *European Poets* as well as poets profiled in other *Critical Survey of Poetry* subsets. The *Cumulative Indexes* also contains comprehensive versions of the categorized, geographical, and subject indexes.

UPDATING THE ESSAYS

All parts of the essays in the previous edition were scrutinized for currency and accuracy: The authors' latest works of poetry were added to front-matter listings, other significant publications were added to back-matter listings, new translations were added to listings for foreign-language authors, and deceased authors' listings were rechecked for accuracy and currency. All essays' bibliographies—lists of sources for further consultation—were revised to provide readers with the latest information.

The 6 poet essays in *European Poets* that required updating by academic experts received similar and even fuller attention: All new publications were added to listings, then each section of text was reviewed to ensure that recently received major awards are noted, that new biographical details are incorporated for still-living authors, and that analysis of works includes recently published books or poems. The updating experts' names were added to essays. Those original articles identified by the editor, Rosemary M. Canfield Reisman, as not needing substantial updating were nevertheless reedited by Salem Press editors and checked for accuracy.

ONLINE ACCESS

Salem Press provides access to its award-winning content both in traditional, printed form and online. Any school or library that purchases *European Poets* is entitled to free, complimentary access to Salem's fully supported online version of the content. Features include a simple intuitive interface, user profile areas for students and patrons, sophisticated search functionality, and complete context, including appendixes. Access is available through a code printed on the inside cover of the first volume, and that access is unlimited and immediate. Our online customer service representatives, at (800) 221-1592, are happy to help with any questions. E-books are also available.

ORGANIZATION OF POET ESSAYS

The poet essays in *European Poets* vary in length, with none shorter than 2,000 words and most significantly longer. Poet essays are arranged alphabetically, under the name by which the poet is best known. The format of the essays is standardized to allow predictable and easy access to the types of information of interest to a variety of users. Each poet essay contains ready-reference top matter, including full birth and (where applicable) death data, any alternate names used by the poet, and a list of Principal Poetry, followed by the main text, which is divided into Other Literary Forms, Achievements, Biography, and Analysis. A list of Other Major Works, a Bibliography, and bylines complete the essay.

- *Principal poetry* lists the titles of the author's major collections of poetry in chronological order, by date of original appearance. Most of the poets in *European Poets* wrote in a language other than English. The foreign-language title is given in its entirely, fol-lowed by the first English publication and its date of publication, if a translation has been made.

- *Other literary forms* describes the author's work in other genres and notes whether the author is known primarily as a poet or has achieved equal or greater fame in another genre. If the poet's last name is unlikely to be familiar to most users, phonetic pronunciation is provided in parentheses after his or her name. A Pronunciation Key appears at the beginning of all volumes.

- *Achievements* lists honors, awards, and other tangible recognitions, as well as a summation of the writer's influence and contributions to poetry and literature, where appropriate.

- *Biography* provides a condensed biographical sketch with vital information from birth through (if applicable) death or the author's latest activities.

- *Analysis* presents an overview of the poet's themes, techniques, style, and development, leading into subsections on major poetry collections, poems, or aspects of the person's work as a poet. As an aid to students, those foreign-language titles that have not yet appeared in translation are followed by a "literal translation" in roman and lowercase letters in parentheses when these titles are mentioned in the text. If a collection of poems has been published in English, the English-language title is used in the text. Single poems that have not been translated are followed by a literal translation in parenthesis. Those that have been translated are referred to by their English-language title, although the original title, if known, is also provided.

- *Other major works* contains the poet's principal works in other genres, listed by genre and by year of publication within each genre. If the work has been translated into English, the date and title under which it was first translated are given.

- *Bibliography* lists secondary print sources for further study, annotated to assist users in evaluating focus and usefulness.

- *Byline* notes the original contributor of the essay. If the essay was updated, the name of the most recent updater appears in a separate line and previous updaters appear with the name of the original contributor.

APPENDIXES

The "Resources" section in volume 3 provides tools for further research and points of access to the wealth of information contained in *European Poets*.

- *Explicating Poetry* identifies the basics of versification, from meter to rhyme, in an attempt to demonstrate how sound, rhythm, and image fuse to support meaning.
- *Language and Linguistics* looks at the origins of language and at linguistics as a discipline, as well as how the features of a particular language affect the type of poetry created.
- *Glossary of Poetical Terms* is a lexicon of more than 150 literary terms pertinent to the study of poetry.
- *Bibliography* identifies general reference works and other secondary sources that pertain to European poets.
- *Guide to Online Resources*, new to this edition, provides Web sites pertaining to poetry and European poets.
- *Time Line*, new to this edition, lists major milestones and events in European poetry and literature in the order in which they occurred.
- *Major Awards* lists the recipients of major European poetry-specific awards and general awards where applicable to poets or poetry, from inception of the award to the present day.
- *Chronological List of Poets* lists all 188 poets covered in *European Poets* by year of birth, in chronological order.

INDEXES

The Geographical Index of Poets lists all poets covered in *European Poets* by country or region. The Categorized Index of Poets lists the poets profiled in *European Poets* by culture or group identity (such as Jewish culture, gay and lesbian culture, and women poets), literary movements (such as Dadism, Modernism, Surrealist poets, and Symbolist poets), historical periods (Spanish Golden Age and Hellenistic poets), and poetic forms and themes (such as political poets, religious poetry, epics, and visionary poetry). The *Critical Survey of Poetry* Series: Master List of Contents lists not only the poets profiled in *European Poets* but also those in other subsets, allowing users to find any poet covered in the complete series. The Subject Index lists all titles, authors, subgenres, and literary movements or terms that receive substantial discussion in *European Poets*. Listings for profiled poets are in bold face.

ACKNOWLEDGMENTS

Salem Press is grateful for the efforts of the original contributors of these essays and those of the outstanding academicians who took on the task of updating or writing new material for the set. Their names and affiliations are listed in the "Contributors" section that follows. Finally, we are indebted to our editor, Professor Rosemary M. Canfield Reisman of Charleston Southern University, for her development of the table of contents for the *Critical Survey of Poetry, Fourth Edition* and her advice on updating the original articles to make this comprehensive and thorough revised edition an indispensable tool for students, teachers, and general readers alike.

CONTRIBUTORS

Claude Abraham
University of California, Davis

Paul Acker
Brown University

Robert Acker
University of Montana

Sidney Alexander
Virginia Commonwealth University

Peter Baker
Southern Connecticut State University

Lowell A. Bangerter
University of Wyoming

James John Baran
Louisiana State University-Shreveport

Stanisław Barańczak
Harvard University

Theodore Baroody
American Psychological Foundation

Jean-Pierre Barricelli
University of California, Riverside

Enikő Molnár Basa
Library of Congress

Fiora A. Bassanese
University of Massachusetts, Boston

Walton Beacham
Beacham Publishing Corp.

Todd K. Bender
University of Wisconsin-Madison

Peter Bien
University of Massachusetts, Dartmouth

M. D. Birnbaum
University of California, Los Angeles

Nicholas Birns
Eugene Lang College, The New School

Franz G. Blaha
University of Nebraska-Lincoln

András Boros-Kazai
Beloit College

David Bromige
Sonoma State University

Joseph P. Byrne
Belmont University

Glauco Cambon
University of Connecticut

H. W. Carle
St. Joseph, Missouri

John Carpenter
University of Michigan

Joseph Carroll
Community College of Rhode Island

Francisco J. Cevallos
Orono, Maine

Carole A. Champagne
University of Maryland-Eastern Shore

Luisetta Elia Chomel
University of Houston

Peter Cocozzella
State University of New York at Binghamton

Steven E. Colburn
Largo, Florida

Robert Colucci
Pittsburgh, Pennsylvania

Victor Contoski
University of Kansas

Carrie Cowherd
Howard University

J. Madison Davis
Pennsylvania State College-Behrend College

Andonis Decavalles
Fairleigh Dickinson University

Mark DeStephano
Saint Peter's College

Lillian Doherty
University of Maryland

Desiree Dreeuws
Sunland, California

Clara Estow
University of Massachusetts

Welch D. Everman
University of Maine

Jack Ewing
Boise, Idaho

Christoph Eykman
Boston College

Robert Faggen
Claremont McKenna College

Rodney Farnsworth
Indiana University

Thomas R. Feller
Nashville, Tennessee

Daniel H. Garrison
Northwestern University

Katherine Gyékényesi Gatto
Richmond Heights, Ohio

Tasha Haas
University of Kansas

Donald P. Haase
Wayne State University

Steven L. Hale
Georgia Perimeter College

Shelley P. Haley
Howard University

Todd C. Hanlin
University of Arkansas

Robert Hauptman
St. Cloud State University

Sarah Hilbert
Pasadena, California

Ann R. Hill
Randolph-Macon Woman's College

Elizabeth A. Holtze
Metropolitan State College of Denver

Donald D. Hook
Trinity College

David Harrison Horton
Patten College

Tracy Irons-Georges
Glendale, California

Miglena Ivanova
Coastal Carolina University

Maura Ives
Texas A&M University

Karen Jaehne
Washington, D.C.

Juan Fernández Jiménez
Pennsylvania State University

Judith L. Johnston
Rider College

Irma M. Kashuba
Chestnut Hill College

Theodore L. Kassier
University of Texas-San Antonio

Jürgen Koppensteiner
University of Northern Iowa

Philip Krummrich
University of Georgia

Katherine C. Kurk
Northern Kentucky University

Rebecca Kuzins
Pasadena, California

Norris J. Lacy
University of Kansas

Carolina D. Lawson
Kent State University

John M. Lee
James Madison University

Raymond LePage
George Mason University

Marie-Noëlle D. Little
Clinton, New York

John D. Lyons
*University of Massachusetts,
Dartmouth*

Dennis McCormick
University of Montana

Magdalena Mączyńska
The Catholic University of America

David Maisel
Wellesley, Massachusetts

Richard Peter Martin
Princeton University

Anne Laura Mattrella
Southeastern University

Richard A. Mazzara
Oakland University

Laurence W. Mazzeno
Alvernia College

Michael R. Meyers
Pfeiffer University

Vasa D. Mihailovich
University of North Carolina

Leslie B. Mittleman
*California State University, Long
Beach*

Christina J. Moose
Pasadena, California

C. L. Mossberg
Lycoming College

Adriano Moz
Spring Hill College

Károly Nagy
Middlesex County College

Moses M. Nagy
University of Dallas

Caryn E. Neumann
Miami University of Ohio

Evelyn S. Newlyn
*Virginia Polytechnic Institute and
State University*

Hermine J. van Nuis
*Indiana University-Purdue
University, Fort Wayne*

David J. Parent
Normal, Illinois

John P. Pauls
Cincinnati, Ohio

La Verne Pauls
Cincinnati, Ohio

Margaret T. Peischl
Virginia Commonwealth University

Susan G. Polansky
Carnegie Mellon University

John Povey
University of California, Los Angeles

Verbie Lovorn Prevost
*University of Tennessee at
Chattanooga*

James Reece
University of Idaho

Sylvie L. F. Richards
Northwest Missouri State University

Helene M. Kastinger Riley
Clemson University

Joseph Rosenblum
Greensboro, North Carolina

Sven H. Rossel
University of Vienna

Norman Roth
University of Wisconsin

Victor Anthony Rudowski
Clemson University

Todd Samuelson
*Cushing Memorial Library &
Archives*

Minas Savvas
San Diego State University

Paul J. Schwartz
Grand Forks, North Dakota

Robert W. Scott
American University

Roberto Severino
Georgetown University

Jack Shreve
Allegany Community College

Thomas J. Sienkewicz
Monmouth College

Jean M. Snook
*Memorial University of
Newfoundland*

Janet L. Solberg
Kalamazoo College

Madison U. Sowell
Brigham Young University

Richard Spuler
Rice University

Kenneth A. Stackhouse
Virginia Commonwealth University

Tuula Stark
Hermosa Beach, California

Laura M. Stone
Milwaukee, Wisconsin

George Thaniel
University of Toronto

Rogelio A. de la Torre
Indiana University at South Bend

Thomas A. Van
University of Louisville

Gordon Walters
DePauw University

Shawncey Webb
Taylor University

David Allen White
United States Naval Academy

Michael Witkoski
University of South Carolina

Harry Zohn
Brandeis University

CONTENTS

COMPLETE LIST OF CONTENTS

VOLUME 1

VOLUME 2

VOLUME 3

RESOURCES

INDEXES

PRONUNCIATION KEY

To help users of the *Critical Survey of Poetry* pronounce unfamiliar names of profiled poets correctly, phonetic spellings using the character symbols listed below appear in parentheses immediately after the first mention of the poet's name in the narrative text. Stressed syllables are indicated in capital letters, and syllables are separated by hyphens.

VOWEL SOUNDS

Symbol	Spelled (Pronounced)
a	answer (AN-suhr), laugh (laf), sample (SAM-puhl), that (that)
ah	father (FAH-thur), hospital (HAHS-pih-tuhl)
aw	awful (AW-fuhl), caught (kawt)
ay	blaze (blayz), fade (fayd), waiter (WAYT-ur), weigh (way)
eh	bed (behd), head (hehd), said (sehd)
ee	believe (bee-LEEV), cedar (SEE-dur), leader (LEED-ur), liter (LEE-tur)
ew	boot (bewt), lose (lewz)
i	buy (bi), height (hit), lie (li), surprise (sur-PRIZ)
ih	bitter (BIH-tur), pill (pihl)
o	cotton (KO-tuhn), hot (hot)
oh	below (bee-LOH), coat (koht), note (noht), wholesome (HOHL-suhm)
oo	good (good), look (look)
ow	couch (kowch), how (how)
oy	boy (boy), coin (koyn)
uh	about (uh-BOWT), butter (BUH-tuhr), enough (ee-NUHF), other (UH-thur)

CONSONANT SOUNDS

Symbol	Spelled (Pronounced)
ch	beach (beech), chimp (chihmp)
g	beg (behg), disguise (dihs-GIZ), get (geht)
j	digit (DIH-juht), edge (ehj), jet (jeht)
k	cat (kat), kitten (KIH-tuhn), hex (hehks)
s	cellar (SEHL-ur), save (sayv), scent (sehnt)
sh	champagne (sham-PAYN), issue (IH-shew), shop (shop)
ur	birth (burth), disturb (dihs-TURB), earth (urth), letter (LEH-tur)
y	useful (YEWS-fuhl), young (yuhng)
z	business (BIHZ-nehs), zest (zehst)
zh	vision (VIH-zhuhn)

CRITICAL SURVEY OF
Poetry
Fourth Edition

European Poets

A

ENDRE ADY

Born: Érdmindszent, Austro-Hungarian Empire
(now Ady Endre, Romania); November 22, 1877
Died: Budapest, Hungary; January 27, 1919

PRINCIPAL POETRY

Versek, 1899

Még egyszer, 1903

Új versek, 1906 (*New Verses*, 1969)

Vér és arany, 1908 (*Blood and Gold*, 1969)

Az Illés szekerén, 1909 (*On Elijah's Chariot*, 1969)

A minden titkok verseiből, 1910 (*Of All Mysteries*, 1969)

Szeretném, ha szeretnének, 1910 (*Longing for Love*, 1969)

A menekülő élet, 1912 (*This Fugitive Life*, 1969)

A magunk szerelme, 1913 (*Love of Ourselves*, 1969)

Ki látott engem?, 1914 (*Who Sees Me?*, 1969)

A halottak élén, 1918 (*Leading the Dead*, 1969)

Margita élni akar, 1921

Az utolsó hajók, 1923 (*The Last Ships*, 1969)

Rövid dalok egyről és másról, 1923

Poems of Endre Ady, 1969 (includes *New Verses*, *Blood and Gold*, *On Elijah's Chariot*, *Longing for Love*, *Of All Mysteries*, *This Fugitive Life*, *Love of Ourselves*, *Who Sees Me?*, *Leading the Dead*, and *The Last Ships*)

OTHER LITERARY FORMS

Endre Ady (O-dee) was a journalist who wrote numerous articles, reports, reviews, criticisms, essays, and short stories for the press. These were collected after his death under the titles *Az új Hellász* (1920; new Hellas), *Levelek Párizsból* (1924; letters from Paris), *Párizsi noteszkönyve* (1924; Paris notebook), and *Ha hív az aczélhegyű ördög* (1927; if the steel-tipped devil calls). In his lifetime, Ady published *Vallomások és tanúlmányok* (1911; confessions and studies), contain-ing his important prose writings, both political and literary. Some of these writings are available in English translation in *The Explosive Country: A Selection of Articles and Studies, 1898-1916* (1977). His collections of short stories combine subjective, personal confession with a depiction of early twentieth century Hungary. They are *Sápadt emberek és történetek* (1907; pale men and stories), *Így is történhetik* (1910; it can happen thus also), *A tízmilliós Kleopátra és egyébb történetek* (1910; Cleopatra of the ten millions and other stories), *Új csapáson* (1913; on a new track), and *Muskétás tanár úr* (1913; Professor Muskétás). His letters have been published in *Ady Endre válogatott levelei* (1956; selected letters of Endre Ady), with an introduction by Béla György.

ACHIEVEMENTS

Endre Ady is one of Hungary's greatest lyric poets. Inspired by Western European models, primarily French, he created a new lyrical style that both shocked and inspired his contemporaries. At the same time, he revitalized indigenous Hungarian literary traditions, looking back to the seventeenth and eighteenth centuries rather than to the example of his immediate predecessors. His topics, too, were considered revolutionary: physical passion and erotic love, political and social reform. He remained, however, within the tradition of the great nineteenth century Hungarian poets who expressed the spirit of the nation in their works.

BIOGRAPHY

Endre Ady's heritage and birthplace had a profound influence on his poetry. His ancestry was the relatively poor nobility, or gentry, which on his mother's side also boasted a tradition of Calvinist ministers. In the small village of Érdmindszent, he came to know the peasantry intimately, for his own family's life differed little from theirs. His father wished him to enter the civil service, so he was educated with a view to obtaining a legal degree. The area in which Ady grew up (today Sălaj, Romania) is situated in the Partium, a region of eastern Hungary that had stormy ties to Transylvania during the sixteenth and seventeenth centuries, when that principality had been a bulwark of Hungarian autonomy and traditions while the rest of the country was under Turkish or Habsburg rule. The Partium was thus doubly a frontier area in whose Calvinist and *kuruc* (anti-Habsburg) traditions Ady saw justification for his own rebellious, individualistic nature. He was always proud of his ancestry and considered himself much more Magyar than many of his contemporaries with more mixed ethnic backgrounds.

After completing five elementary grades in his village, Ady was sent first to the Piarist school in Nagykároly, then to the Calvinist gymnasium at Zilah, which he regarded as his alma mater; he always fondly remembered his teachers there. Several of his classmates were later to become prominent among the more radical thinkers and politicians of the early years of the twentieth century. He also read voraciously, both earlier Hungarian literature and European naturalistic writers, and became acquainted with the works of Arthur Schopenhauer. After a brief period in law school in Debrecen and time spent as a legal clerk in Temesvár (Timisoara, Romania) and Zilah (Zălău), he realized that his true vocation was in journalism. He followed this career until his death.

Ady first worked in Debrecen, and in this period not only did his horizons widen, but his critical theses began to crystallize as well. "Life" and "truth" became important bywords for him, and he continued his readings: Auguste Comte, Herbert Spencer, Friedrich Nietzsche, Henrik Ibsen, Fyodor Dostoevski, and especially the late eighteenth century poet Mihály Csokonai Vitéz, a native of Debrecen. It was in Nagyvárad (today Oradea, Romania) that Ady became familiar with the life of a large city and the more cosmopolitan society it represented. He wrote for liberal papers, and for a while his political views agreed with the pro-government stance of such journals. In time, however, he became disillusioned with their reluctance to press for universal suffrage and other reforms affecting the poor and the national minorities. It was at this time that he became acquainted with *Huszadik század*, a progressive journal begun in 1900.

The years in Nagyvárad were also important in Ady's personal life and poetic development, for it was during this period that he met Adél Brüll, whom he was to immortalize as the Leda of his poems. This older, married woman (her married name was Diósi)—more experienced, more worldly, more cultured than he—was an important influence on his life. Their passionate and at times tempestuous love affair, which finally ended in 1912, is recorded in poems that were to revolutionize Hungarian love poetry. When Ady went to Paris as the foreign correspondent of his paper, Brüll was there, and his impressions of the French city were acquired under her tutelage. When he returned from the 1904 trip, he burst on the world with a new poetic style.

By 1905, Ady was working in Budapest for the liberal *Budapesti napló*. In numerous articles, he wrote of the need for radical reforms; independence from Austria was also debated. At this time, Ady turned his attention to the social problems that were destroying the country; in both his poetry and his prose writings, he championed the disenfranchised. The important journal *Nyugat* was started in 1908, and Ady soon became associated with it—all the more so as his increasingly radical views did not agree with the middle-of-the-road liberalism of the *Budapesti napló*.

When war broke out in 1914, Ady opposed Hungarian participation in the conflict, increasing his isolation from official political life. His antiwar poems were inspired by humanism and patriotism. The poor and the politically powerless suffered most heavily, Ady argued, and he believed that the war was being fought against Hungarian interests, purely for Austrian goals. During this time, Ady lived mostly in Érdmindszent and at Csucsa, the estate of Berta Boncza, whom he had met in 1914 and married the following year. Berta, the daughter of a well-to-do nobleman and prominent politician, was considerably younger than Ady; she had been attracted to him some time earlier, when she read his *Blood and Gold* while still in school in Switzerland. The poems written to her reflect a different mood from that of the Leda poems: The love is deeper and less intensely erotic. They project the hope that Csinszka (as Berta is called in the poems addressed to her) will preserve the thoughts and ideals of the poet. By this time, Ady was gravely ill with the syphilis that had been progressively destroying him since his Nagyvárad days.

The revolution that Ady had awaited came to Hungary in October of 1918. Ady went to Budapest, where the revolutionary government celebrated him, even though he had reservations about the Socialist system.

He also doubted whether the Karolyi government's courting of the Entente powers would bring any positive results. As it turned out, his instincts were right, and the Entente did little for Hungary. Ady died in January of 1919, spared the knowledge that Hungary's territory would be drastically reduced and that his own birthplace and home region would be awarded to Romania.

ANALYSIS

Endre Ady came from the deep center of the nation, and he sought to raise the nation to a new consciousness, just as János Arany and others had done before him. Ady was an innovator because the literary and political establishment had failed to grasp the need for change. Ady's "Hungarianness" is a central part of his work; he was intensely aware of his struggle "with Europe for Europe."

Ady never abandoned his native traditions. He built instead on folklore, the *kuruc* poetry of the eighteenth century, the folk-song-inspired lyrics of Mihály Csokonai Vitéz, and the revolutionary verse of the great national poet of nineteenth century Hungary, Sándor Petőfi. Ady also drew heavily on Hungarian Calvinism and the rich vernacular tradition of Protestant writings to create a highly personal modern style, animated by the tension between Hungarian and Western European influences. His great love poems to Leda and Csinszka, his poems on materialism and on national traditions—all incorporated European philosophies, preoccupations, and styles, reflecting the influence of Friedrich Nietzsche and Henri Bergson as well as of Charles Baudelaire and Paul Verlaine. Today, Ady is recognized as one of the most important of the generation of writers and thinkers who transformed the intellectual life of Hungary in the first decades of the twentieth century.

NEW VERSES

Ady's first two volumes of verse, *Versek* (poems) and *Még egyszer* (once more), did not attract great interest; they were relatively insignificant collections in the traditional vein. In 1906, however, Ady's own style emerged in *New Verses*. Here, he presented new subjects and new themes, new images and a fresh, new style. The emphasis in *New Verses*—an emphasis continued in Ady's next three collections—was on brevity and impact: short, concise lines; short poems packed with meaning; condensed language with multiple levels of reference. Many of the early poems develop a single metaphor. A very conscious innovator, Ady prefaced *New Verses* with a manifesto that identifies the tension that persists throughout his oeuvre: Hungary is a nation caught at the crossroads between East and West. While proudly claiming his descent from the conquering Hungarians of the ninth century, who came through the Eastern gate, he asks if *he* can break in from the *West* with "new songs of new times." Answering in a defiant affirmative, he states that, in spite of opposition by conservatives, these poems are "still victorious, still new and Hungarian."

TRANSFORMATIONS

After the burst of energy that characterized his style in the period from 1906 to 1909, Ady paused in mid-career to adopt a quieter style and grayer moods. His themes and concerns remained much the same, but there was a deepening of thought, and a more pessimistic note entered his poems. His concern for the fate of the country, particularly its ordinary citizens, grew as he saw policies that could only bring ruin being blindly followed by the political elite. His relationship with Brüll also cooled.

After 1914, during the war years, Ady's style underwent another transformation. His sentences became more complex as his verse became increasingly reflective, and he turned from softer, French-inspired tones to the somber and sublime style of the Bible and of sixteenth century Calvinist poetry. In this late poetry, Ady retained two themes from his earlier collection: patriotism, which broadened into humanitarianism, and love—no longer the unfulfilled and unsatisfying erotic encounters of earlier years but the deeper, more fulfilling passion of the Csinszka poems.

LEDA POEMS

Ady's poems can be organized thematically into four large groups (love, death, religion, patriotism), though there is considerable overlapping; also, some important minor themes are eventually subsumed into one or another of the major ones reflecting Ady's intellectual development. One of Ady's most enduring themes was romantic love. The Leda cycles, with their portrayal of destructive yet irresistible passion, reveal the influence of Baudelaire. These poems represented a break with Hungarian tradition in their emphasis on the physical aspects of love. Ady's poems to his wife, on the other hand, are more in the tradition of Petőfi, in which the emotional-spiritual content is on a par with the physical. It would be misleading, however, to dismiss the Leda poems as purely physical: Brüll offered Ady much more than physical excitement, and these poems reflect a world of shared ideas. They are more significant and generally more successful than the poems on fleeting alliances with insignificant partners.

"Félig csókolt csók" ("Half-Kissed Kiss"), from *New Verses*, and "Léda a kertben" ("Leda in the Garden"), from *Blood and Gold*, emphasize the intense desire that cannot be satisfied even in physical union. The "half-kissed kiss" is a metaphor for an erotic relationship that leaves the lovers still restless for fulfillment: "tomorrow, then perhaps tomorrow." Nature sympathizes with them in their eternal hunger, as an image from "Leda in the Garden" suggests: "even the poppy/ pities us, [itself] satisfied." Consummation, Ady suggests in "Héja nász az avaron" ("Kite-Wedding on the Loamy Earth"), can come only in death. In "A mi násznagyunk" ("Our Best Man"), Ady returns to this theme. There are also love poems of great tenderness in the Leda cycles, as "Add nekem a szemeidet" ("Give Me Your Eyes") illustrates. The beloved's eyes "always see him grand . . . always build, have mercy . . . see him in a better light," yet "they kill, burn, and desire." The poem, comprising four stanzas of three lines each, repeats the title line as the first line of each stanza and follows it with two rhymed lines. This *abb* tercet in anapestic meter echoes the lyrical mood and the melody of the words as well as the expansive ideas.

OF ALL MYSTERIES

The 1910 volume *Of All Mysteries* chronicles the waning of Ady's love for Brüll. This collection offers a virtual outline of Ady's characteristic themes, as is indeed suggested in the poem's motto: "youthful All vanquished, with the spear of Secrecy, Death in my heart: but my heart lives, and God lives." Here, Ady seems determined to hope in spite of disappointments. The Decadent pose of earlier poems is shed as the poet develops a real faith in humankind that culminates in the humanism of the war poems. Each of the six cycles in

Of All Mysteries is devoted to a "secret": of God, of love, of sorrow, of glory, of life, and of death. In the "Love" cycle, dedicated to Leda, the poem "A türelem bilincse" ("The Fetters of Patience") significantly refers to the "fetters" of their love in the past tense. Their whole life was fetters, yet the "kisses, exhaustions, flames, oaths" were all good fetters. The farewell becomes explicit in "Elbocsátó, szép üzenet" ("Dismissing, Beautiful Message"), where pity wins over the regretful remembrance of love.

LOVE POEMS

The poems of 1912 to 1914 show a man in search of love. In the final volumes, this love is found. "A Kalota partján" ("On the Banks of the Kalota") records the "security, summer, beauty and peace" brought to his life by Berta Boncza. The poem's two long free-verse stanzas depict a summer Sunday in which the peace and joy of the service and of the feast (Pentecost) mingle to overwhelm the poet, and the eyes of his beloved draw him into a magic circle.

DEATH

Ady saw life and death not as opposing forces but as two components of the same force. "Párizsban járt az ősz" ("Autumn Passed Through Paris") is a beautiful evocation, through the breath of autumn on a summer day, of the presence of death. Although death comes for all people, it need not be accepted passively, as Ady suggests in the melodic "A halál lovai" ("Death's Horsemen"). The riderless horse with the unclaimed saddle is always in the troop of death's horses, but "He before whom they stop/ Turns pale and sits into the saddle." The act is presented as voluntary. In "Hulla a búza-földön" ("Corpse on the Wheat-Field"), a corpse, forgotten on the snowy plain, will not have carnations, artemisia, and basil blooming on its grave, but "the victorious wheat-kernel" will win through; life will triumph.

RELIGIOUS POEMS

To some extent, Ady's God-fearing poems continue the life-death theme. They chronicle the same doubts and seek answers to the same questions. In time, Ady found the answers and the refuge, but as with John Donne, the struggle was a fierce one; indeed, Ady's love poems, much as in Donne's case, have a close and direct relationship to his religious verse. Although many of Ady's religious poems describe his struggle to achieve union with God, others reflect the peace of childlike faith. Ady seeks rest and forgiveness and creates powerful symbols to concretize these feelings.

In "A Sion-hegy alatt" ("Under Mount Sion"), he creates an image of God as a man in a huge bell coat inscribed with red letters, ringing for the dawn Mass. The figure is kindly yet sad; he cannot answer the poet's plea for simple, unquestioning faith. The poem is a poignant expression of the dilemma of modern humankind. In "Hiszek hitetlenül Istenben" ("I Believe, Unbelieving, in God"), Ady longs for belief in the great mystery of God, convinced that such faith will bring peace to his tormented soul.

The poems from the cycle "Esaias könyvének margójára" ("To the Margins of the Book of Isaiah"), often prefaced by biblical quotations that emphasize their prophetic intentions, transcend the personal religious quest and become pleas for the nation and for humanity. "Volt egy Jézus" ("There Was a Jesus") not only testifies to a personal acceptance of Jesus Christ but also proclaims the need for all humankind to heed his teachings on peace and brotherhood. "A szétszóródás elött" ("Before the Diaspora"), another poem with a biblical inspiration, scourges the nation for its sins, concluding with the powerful line: "And we were lost, for we lost ourselves."

PATRIOTIC POEMS

Many of Ady's poems can be classified as patriotic. This group, however, unites several different themes that were significant at different points in his career. Two important early threads are the "I" poems and the "money" poems. The I poems are more than personal lyrics; they present the speaker (the poet) as a representative of the nation. As such, they evolve into the patriotic poems in a fairly direct line. The money poems startled readers with their "nonpoetic" theme: Ady went beyond complaints against poverty to question the role of money in society at large.

THE KURUC THEME

An important thread in Ady's patriotic-revolutionary poetry is the use of the *kuruc* theme. *Kuruc* was the name applied to the supporters of Ferenc Rákóczi II, who had led a popular uprising against the Habsburgs in the eighteenth century. In Ady's vocabulary, the *kuruc* is the true but disenfranchised Hungarian, a fighter for national goals betrayed by his self-serving masters to Austrian interests. In the war years, Ady identified the *kuruc* with the common person everywhere, oppressed by political power plays.

"MAN IN INHUMANITY"

Ady's last poem, "Ember az embertelenségben" ("Man in Inhumanity"), was an appeal to humanity addressed to the victors of the war. He appealed, fruitlessly, to the Allies "not to tread too harshly" on Hungarian hearts. The nation sought reform, but suffered instead "War, the Horror." Defeated in a war fought against Hungarian sentiments and interests, Hungary paid for its all-too-recent union with Austria with the loss of much of its territory and millions of its citizens. Foreseeing this tragedy even before the war, Ady offered a poignant comment on its aftermath.

Although Ady was a very subjective poet, one of the first purely personal lyric voices in Hungarian poetry, he did not break with the national tradition of committed literature. Deeply influenced by Western European models, he transformed what he took by the force of his genius, exploiting the rich resources of the Hungarian tradition in the service of a powerfully modern vision. Thus, it is not surprising that Ady continues to inspire poets in Hungary today.

OTHER MAJOR WORKS

SHORT FICTION: *Sápadt emberek és történetek*, 1907; *Így is történhetik*, 1910; *A tízmilliós Kleopátra és egyébb történetek*, 1910; *Muskétás tanár úr*, 1913; *Új csapáson*, 1913.

NONFICTION: *Vallomások és tanúlmányok*, 1911; *Az új Hellász*, 1920; *Levelek Párizsból*, 1924; *Párizsi noteszkönyve*, 1924; *Ha hív az aczélhegyű ördög*, 1927; *Ady Endre válogatott levelei*, 1956; *The Explosive Country: A Selection of Articles and Studies, 1898-1916*, 1977.

BIBLIOGRAPHY

Bóka, Lazlo. "Endre Ady the Poet." *New Hungarian Quarterly* 3, no. 5 (January-March, 1962): 83-108. A biographical and critical study of Ady's life and work.

Cushing, G. F. Introduction to *The Explosive Country: A Selection of Articles and Studies, 1898-1916*, by

Endre Ady. Budapest: Corvina Press, 1977. Cushing offers some biographical insight into Ady's life.

Frigyesi, Judit. *Béla Bartók and Turn-of-the-Century Budapest*. Berkeley: University of California Press, 1998. A broad perspective on Bartók's art grounded in the social and cultural life of turn-of-the-century Hungary. Includes a discussion of Ady and his influence on Bartók.

Hanák, Péter. *The Garden and the Workshop: Essays on the Cultural History of Vienna and Budapest*. Princeton, N.J.: Princeton University Press, 1998. Ady is one of the central figures in his collection of essays. Deals with Ady's transition from journalism to poetry.

_____. *The Start of Endre Ady's Literary Career (1903-1905)*. Budapest: Akadémiai Kiadó, 1980. A brief study of Ady's early work, with bibliography.

Land, Thomas. "Endre Ady: Six Poems." *Contemporary Review* 279, no. 1627 (August, 2001): 100-105. Land briefly describes Ady's life, particularly his political activism, and translates six personal poems.

Nyerges, Anton N. Introduction to *Poems of Endre Ady*. Buffalo, N.Y.: Hungarian Cultural Foundation, 1969. Nyerges gives some biographic details of Ady's life.

Reményi, Joseph. *Hungarian Writers and Literature*. New Brunswick, N.J.: Rutgers University Press, 1964. A history and critical analysis of Hungarian literature including the works of Ady.

Enikő Molnár Basa

RAFAEL ALBERTI

Born: Puerto de Santa María, Spain; December 16, 1902

Died: Puerto de Santa María, Spain; October 28, 1999

PRINCIPAL POETRY

Marinero en tierra, 1925
La amante, 1926
El alba del alhelí, 1927
Cal y canto, 1929
Sobre los ángeles, 1929 (*Concerning the Angels*, 1967)
Consignas, 1933
Verte y no verte, 1935 (*To See You and Not to See You*, 1946)
Poesía, 1924-1938, 1940
Entre el clavel y la espada, 1941
Pleamar, 1944
A la pintura, 1945 (*To Painting*, 1997)
Retornos de lo vivo lejano, 1952
Baladas y canciones del Paraná, 1954 (*Ballads and Songs of the Parana*, 1988)
Poesías completas, 1961
Rafael Alberti: Selected Poems, 1966 (Ben Belitt, translator)
The Owl's Insomnia, 1973
Alberti tal cual, 1978

OTHER LITERARY FORMS

Although Rafael Alberti (ol-BEHR-tee) established his reputation almost entirely on the basis of his poetry, he became involved in drama after emigrating to Argentina, writing plays of his own and adapting Miguel de Cervantes' *El cerco de Numancia* (wr. 1585, pb. 1784; *Numantia: A Tragedy*, 1870) for the modern stage in 1944.

Alberti's most notable achievement in prose, a work of considerable interest for the student of his poetry, was his autobiography, *La arboleda perdida* (1942; *The Lost Grove*, 1976). In addition, he was a talented painter and supplied illustrations for some of his later volumes.

ACHIEVEMENTS

Rafael Alberti had at once the ill luck and the singular good fortune to flourish during Spain's second great literary boom. Despite his acknowledged worth, he was overshadowed by several of his contemporaries—in particular, by Federico García Lorca. Although Alberti's name is likely to come up in any discussion of the famous *generación del 27*, or Generation of '27, he generally languishes near the end of the list. On the other hand, the extraordinary atmosphere of the times did much to foster his talents; even among the giants, he earned acceptance and respect. He may occasionally have been lost in the crowd, but it was a worthy crowd.

His *Marinero en tierra* (sailor on dry land) won Spain's National Prize for Literature in 1925, and throughout his long career, his virtuosity never faltered. Always a difficult poet, he never gave the impression that his obscurity stemmed from incompetence. His political ideology—Alberti was the first of his circle to embrace communism openly—led him to covet the role of "poet of the streets," but Alberti will be remembered more for his poems of exile, which capture better than any others the poignant aftermath of the Spanish Civil War.

Ultimately, Alberti stands out as a survivor. Many of his great contemporaries died in the civil war or simply lapsed into a prolonged silence. Despite his wholehearted involvement in the conflict, Alberti managed to persevere after his side lost and to renew his career. He continued to publish at an imposing rate, took up new activities, and became a force in the burgeoning literary life of Latin America, as evidenced by his winning of the Cervantes Prize, the Spanish-speaking world's highest literary honor, in 1983. Consistent in his adherence to communism, he received the Lenin Prize for his political verse in 1965. Oddly enough, then, Alberti emerges as a constant—an enduring figure in a world of flux, a practicing poet of consistent excellence during six decades.

BIOGRAPHY

Rafael Alberti was born near Cádiz in Andalusia, and his nostalgia for that region pervades much of his work. His genteel family had fallen on hard times, and Alberti's schoolmates made him painfully aware of his inferior status. In 1917, the family moved to Madrid, where Alberti devoted himself to painting in the cubist manner, attaining some recognition. Illness forced him to retire to a sanatorium in the mountains—a stroke of luck, as it happened, for there he subsequently met such luminaries as García Lorca, Salvador Dalí, and Luis Buñuel and began seriously to write poetry. He won the National Prize for *Marinero en tierra* and thereby gained acceptance into the elite artistic circles of the day. Personal difficulties and an increasing awareness of the plight of his country moved Alberti to embrace

Rafael Alberti (Cover/Getty Images)

communism. In 1930, he married María Teresa León, also a writer, and together they founded the revolutionary journal *Octubre* in 1934.

Alberti's new political credo enabled him to travel extensively and to encounter writers and artists from all parts of Europe and the Americas. After participating actively in the civil war, he emigrated to Argentina in 1940. There, he began to write for the theater, gave numerous readings, and resumed painting. Hard work and fatherhood—his daughter Aitana was born in 1941— preserved Alberti from embittered paralysis, and his production of poetry never slackened. Indeed, many of his readers believe that he reached his peak in the late 1940's.

In 1964, Alberti moved to Rome, where he lived until 1977, when he was finally able to return to Spain, after almost thirty-eight years in exile. He was welcomed by more than three hundred communists carrying red flags as he stepped off the airliner. "I'm not coming with a clenched fist," he said, "but with an open hand." He enjoyed a resurgence of popularity after his return and proceeded to run for the Cortes, giving poetry readings instead of speeches, and won. Alberti resigned his seat after three months to devote himself to his art. He became a well-respected literary figure in his last two decades in Spain; the lost Andalusian had returned home. He died there on October 28, 1999, from a lung ailment; he was ninety-six years old.

ANALYSIS

Throughout his long career, Rafael Alberti proved to be a remarkably versatile poet. His facility of composition enabled him to shift smoothly from fixed forms to free verse, even within the confines of a single poem. Whether composing neomedieval lyrics, Baroque sonnets, or Surreal free verse, he always managed to be authentic. His deep emotions, sometimes obscured by his sheer virtuosity, found expression in all modes. His technical skill did not allow him to stagnate: Commentators on Alberti agree in their praise of his astonishing technical mastery. He might continue in the same vein for three volumes, but he would invariably break new ground in the fourth. His massive corpus of poetry comprises a remarkable array of styles, themes, and moods.

Although he was a natural poet with little formal training, Alberti always kept abreast of current developments in his art—indeed, he kept himself in the vanguard. He associated with the best and brightest of his time and participated in their movements. When the luminaries of Spain reevaluated Luis de Góngora y Argote, Alberti wrote accomplished neo-Baroque poetry; when Dalí and Buñuel were introducing Surrealism in Spanish art and film, Alberti adapted its principles to Spanish poetry; when most of the intellectuals of Spain were resisting General Franciso Franco and embracing communism, Alberti was the "poet of the streets." He remained withal a genuine and unique lyric voice. Even his political verses are not without poetic merit—an exception, to be sure. Alberti changed by adding and growing, never by discarding and replacing; thus, he became a richer talent with each new phase of his creative development.

Alberti's poetry is suffused with nostalgia. The circumstances of his life decreed that he should continually find himself longing for another time, a distant place, or a lost friend, and in his finest poems, he achieves an elegiac purity free of the obscurity and self-pity that mar his lesser works. From first to last, the sadness for things lost remains Alberti's great theme, one he explored more fully than any other poet of his generation.

Alberti was a poet who could grow without discarding his past. The youthful poet who composed marvelous lyrics persisted in the nostalgia of exile; the angry poet of the streets reasserted himself in diatribes against Yankee imperialism in Latin America. At ease in all forms and idioms, forever the Andalusian in exile, always growing in his art and his thought, Alberti wrote a staggering number of excellent poems. In the vast treasure trove of twentieth century Spanish poetry, he left a hoard of pearls and sapphires—hidden at times by the rubies and the emeralds, but worthy nevertheless.

MARINERO EN TIERRA

The doyens of Spanish letters received *Marinero en tierra* with immediate enthusiasm, and the young Alberti found himself a de facto member of the Generation of '27, eligible to rub elbows with all the significant writers of the day. Although Alberti seems to have been happy in the mid-1920's, his early volumes glow with poignant nostalgia for the sea and the coasts of his native Andalusia. He expresses his longing in exquisite lyrics in the medieval tradition. Ben Belitt, introducing his translations collected in *Selected Poems*, confesses that he could find no way to render these lyrics in English. They depend entirely on a native tradition, the vast trove of popular verses from Spain's turbulent Middle Ages. Alberti's genius is such that the poems have no savor of pedantry or preciosity. Luis Monguió, in his introduction to Belitt's translations, suggests that "it is far from unlikely that they are being sung in the provinces today by many in complete ignorance of their debt to Rafael Alberti." The notion is a tribute both to the poet and to the tradition he understood so well.

The verses themselves may seem enigmatic, but only because the modern reader is accustomed to probe so far beneath the surface. One of the best of them,

"Gimiendo" ("Groaning"), presents the plaint of a sailor who remembers that his shirt used to puff up in the wind whenever he saw the shore. The entire poem consists of only six brief lines; there is only one image, and only one point. That single image conveys a feeling close to the hearts of those born within smell of the sea—a need unfulfilled for Alberti. He speaks for all seafarers who are marooned inland, the sailors on land.

"Pradoluengo," an aubade in the same style, is only seven lines long and conveys an equally simple message. The beloved to whom the poem is addressed is told that the cocks are crowing, that "we need cross only river waters, not the sea," and is urged to get up and come along. With all the richness of the genre, Alberti hints at a wealth of erotic possibilities and natural splendors. Only William Butler Yeats, in modern English poetry, matches this exquisite simplicity and feeling for tradition.

CAL Y CANTO

As noted above, Alberti took a leading role in the Góngora tricentennial of 1927, and many of the poems in *Cal y canto* owe much to the Baroque model. Here, Alberti reveals a new facet of his technical mastery, particularly in his handling of the sonnet, perhaps the most difficult of forms. "Amaranta," a sonnet that frequently appears in anthologies, shows how completely Alberti was able to assimilate the poetics of Góngora and to adapt them to the twentieth century. The octave describes, in ornate and lavish terms, the beauty of Amaranta; as with Góngora, the very exuberance of the description disquiets the reader. Her breasts, for example, are polished "as with the tongue of a greyhound." The sestet conceals the scorpion sting so often found in Góngora's conclusions: Solitude, personified, settles like a glowing coal between Amaranta and her lover. In this poem, Alberti displays his affinity with Góngora in two respects: an absolute control of his idiom and an obscurity that has deprived both poets of numerous readers. As Alberti himself remarked in his autobiography, "this was painterly poetry—plastic, linear, profiled, confined."

CONCERNING THE ANGELS

Concerning the Angels differs sharply from Alberti's previous work. Bouts of depression and a loss of faith in his former ideals drove him to abandon nostalgia and to confront despair. Suddenly, all the joy and tender sorrow of his early work is gone, replaced by anguish and self-pity. The revolution in content corresponds to a rebellion in form: Free verse prevails as more appropriate to the poet's state of mind than any traditional order. Alberti does not despair utterly, as Monguió indicates, but the overall tone of the collection is negative.

"Tres recuerdos del cielo" ("Three Memories of Heaven"), a tribute to the great Romantic poet Gustavo Adolfo Bécquer, constitutes a noteworthy exception to the depressing tone of the volume. Here, Alberti displays the subtlety and tenderness that characterize his work at its most appealing. Evoking a condition of being before time existed, Alberti recaptures the tenuous delicacy of Bécquer, the sense of the ineffable. The meeting between the lovers, for example, takes place in a world of clouds and moonlight: "When you, seeing me in nothingness/ Invented the first word." Alberti imitates Bécquer masterfully, at the same time finding a new way to express his own nostalgia.

"Three Memories of Heaven," however, is atypical of the collection. Virtually all the other poems treat of "angels" and ultimately of a world turned to wormwood and gall. "El ángel desengañado" ("The Angel Undeceived") debunks the ideals of the younger Alberti, particularly in its desolate conclusion: "I'm going to sleep./ No one is waiting for me." "El ángel de carbón" ("Angel of Coals") ends no less grimly: "And that octopus, love, in the shadow:/ evil, so evil." Several of the poems offer a kind of hope, but it is a wan hope, scarcely better than despair. Like the T. S. Eliot of "The Hollow Men," however, Alberti maintains his poetic control, even with the world withering away around him.

TO SEE YOU AND NOT TO SEE YOU

Two pivotal events in Alberti's life helped him out of this quagmire: meeting his future wife and becoming a communist. The political commitment, while it did little to benefit his poetry, provided him with a set of beliefs to fill the void within. Of his proletarian verse, one can say only that it is no worse than most political poetry. Like his friend and contemporary Pablo Neruda, Alberti mistook a sincere political commitment for an artistic imperative; like Neruda, he eventually returned to more personal themes, although he never wholly abandoned doctrinaire verse.

Even at the height of his political activism, however, Alberti was capable of devoting his gifts to the elegy; the death of Ignacio Sánchez Mejías in the bullring moved him to write the sonnet series that makes up *To See You and Not to See You* in 1935. The same tragedy also inspired Federico García Lorca to compose one of the most famous poems in the Spanish language, "Llanto por Ignacio Sánchez Mejías" ("Lament for Ignacio Sánchez Mejías"). A comparison of the two poems reveals the radical differences between these two superficially similar poets. García Lorca chants compellingly, "At five in the afternoon," evoking the drama of the moment and the awful immediacy of the bull. Alberti reflects on the bull's calfhood, its callow charges as it grew into the engine of destruction that destroyed Sánchez Mejías. García Lorca goes on to convey, in muted tones, his sense of loss. Alberti expresses that sense of loss in terms of distance: As his friend dies in the bullring, Alberti is sailing toward Romania on the Black Sea. The memory of the journey becomes permanently associated with the loss of the friend and thus a redoubled source of nostalgia.

IN GARCÍA LORCA'S SHADOW

As usual, García Lorca enjoys the fame, and Alberti is lost in his shadow. No doubt García Lorca's elegy speaks more clearly and more movingly; it probably *is* better than its counterpart. Alberti himself admired the "Lament for Ignacio Sánchez Mejías" without reservation. The pattern, however, is only too familiar: Alberti, so like García Lorca in some ways, found himself outmatched at every turn while his friend and rival was still alive. Alberti wrote exquisite medieval lyrics, but García Lorca outdid him with the *Romancero gitano* (1928; *The Gypsy Ballads*, 1953). Alberti captured the essence of Andalusia, but the public identified Andalusia with García Lorca. Alberti wrote a noble and moving elegy for Ignacio Sánchez Mejías, but his rival composed such a marvelous lament that Alberti's has been neglected.

All this is not to imply conscious enmity between the two poets. Alberti had cause to envy his contemporary's fame, and his bitterness at playing a secondary role may have been reflected in *Concerning the Angels.*

Indeed, although Alberti gave many indications, in verse and prose, of his profound regard for García Lorca, his relationship with the poet of Granada represents an analogue to the dilemma of his literary life. The competition must have stimulated him, but, because his poetry was less accessible and less dramatic in its impact, he tended to be eclipsed. After the Spanish Civil War, Alberti emigrated to Argentina, mourning his slain and dispersed comrades, including García Lorca, who was senselessly gunned down at the outset of the hostilities. The war poems in the Alberti canon compare favorably with any on that subject, not least because his lively imagination enabled him to look beyond the slaughter.

ENTRE EL CLAVEL Y LA ESPADA

For all his faith, the poet soon found himself across the Atlantic, listening to reports of World War II, picking up the pieces. Somehow he managed to recover and to emerge greater than ever. A poem from his first collection published outside Spain, *Entre el clavel y la espada* (between sword and carnation), sounds the keynote of his renewed art:

> After this willful derangement, this harassed
> and necessitous grammar by whose haste I must live,
> let the virginal word come back to me whole and
>   meticulous,
> and the virginal verb, justly placed with its rigorous
>   adjective.

The poem, written in Spain, anticipates the purity of Alberti's poetry in exile. The poet forgot neither the horrors he had seen nor his love for his homeland.

Another elegy deserves mention in this context. Written after news of the death of the great poet Antonio Machado, "De los álamos y los sauces" (from poplar and willow) captures the plight of Alberti and his fellow exiles in but a few lines. The man in the poem is caught up "in the life of his distant dead and hears them in the air." Thus, Alberti returns grimly to his leitmotif, nostalgia.

RETORNOS DE LO VIVO LEJANO

With his return to his nostalgic leitmotif, Alberti reached his full potential as a poet during the 1940's and 1950's. He poured forth volume after volume of consistently high quality. *Retornos de lo vivo lejano* (returns of the far and the living), a book wholly devoted to his most serviceable theme, may well be the finest volume of his career. The poems are at once accessible and mysterious, full of meaning on the surface and suggestive of unfathomed depths.

"Retornos del amor en una noche de verano" ("Returns: A Summer Night's Love") recalls in wondrous imagery the breathlessness of a time long past. For example, two pairs of lips, as they press together, become a silent carnation. "Retornos de Chopin a través de unas manos ya idas" ("Returns: Chopin by Way of Hands Now Gone") evokes some of the poet's earliest memories of his family. After many years, the poet is reunited with his brothers by an act of imagination, supported by the memory of Frédéric Chopin's music as played by the poet's mother. This is the quintessential Alberti, the master craftsman and the longing man in one.

TO PAINTING

Amid the melancholy splendor of his poems of exile, Alberti distilled a curious volume entitled *To Painting*. In contrast to all that Alberti lost in exile, painting stands as a rediscovered treasure, and the Alberti of the early 1920's comes face to face with the middle-aged émigré. The collection includes sonnets on the tools of painting, both human and inanimate; free-verse meditations on the primary colors; and poems on various painters, each in a style reminiscent of the artist's own. Beyond its intrinsic value, the volume reveals much about the mutual attraction of the two arts.

"BALLAD OF THE LOST ANDALUSIAN"

A poem from *Ballads and Songs of the Parana*, deserves special mention. "Balada del Andaluz perdido" ("Ballad of the Lost Andalusian"), as much as any single poem, reflects Alberti's self-image as a poet in exile. Written in terse, unrhymed couplets, it tells of a wandering Andalusian who watches the olives grow "by the banks of a different river." Sitting alone, he provokes curious questions from the Argentine onlookers on the opposite bank of the river, but he remains a mystery to them. Not so to the reader, who understands the pathos of the riderless horses, the memory of hatred, the loneliness. The final question admits of no answer and in fact needs none: "What will he do there, what is left to be done/ on the opposite side of the river, alone?"

OTHER MAJOR WORKS

PLAYS: *El hombre deshabitado*, pb. 1930; *El trébol floride*, pb. 1940; *El adefesio*, pb. 1944; *El cerco de Numancia*, pr. 1944 (adaptation of Miguel de Cervantes' play).

NONFICTION: *La arboleda perdida*, 1942 (*The Lost Grove*, 1976).

BIBLIOGRAPHY

Gagen, Derek. "*Marinero en tierra*: Alberti's first 'Libro organico de poemas'?" *Modern Language Review* 88, no. 1 (January, 1993): 91. Alberti's *Marinero en tierra* is examined in detail.

Havard, Robert. *The Crucified Mind: Rafael Alberti and the Surrealist Ethos in Spain*. London: Tamesis Books, 2001. A biographical and historical study of the life and works of Alberti.

Herrmann, Gina. *Written in Red: The Communist Memoir in Spain*. Urbana: University of Illinois Press, 2009. This work examining memoirs of Communists in Spain contains a chapter on Maria Teresa León and Alberti.

Jiménez-Fajardo, Salvador. *Multiple Spaces: The Poetry of Rafael Alberti*. London: Tamesis Books, 1985. A critical analysis of Alberti's poetic works. Includes bibliographic references.

Manteiga, Robert C. *Poetry of Rafael Alberti: A Visual Approach*. London: Tamesis Books, 1978. A study of Alberti's literary style. Text is in English with poems in original Spanish. Includes bibliographic references.

Nantell, Judith. *Rafael Alberti's Poetry of the Thirties*. Athens: University of Georgia Press, 1986. This study puts Alberti's work in historical and social context by analyzing the influences from a turbulent decade in which civil war erupts, ignites a European conflagration, and ends in societal crises. The author discusses political poems that are not as memorable as his earlier works but deserve recognition for their artistic as well as social value.

Soufas, C. Christopher. *The Subject in Question: Early Contemporary Spanish Literature and Modernism*. Washington, D.C.: Catholic University of America Press, 2007. This overview of Spanish literature and modernism contains a chapter examining the poetry of Alberti and Luis Cernuda.

Ugarte, Michael. *Shifting Ground: Spanish Civil War Exile Literature*. Durham, N.C.: Duke University Press, 1989. Examination of the importance of Spanish exile literature during and after the civil war. The second section of the book explores the intellectual diaspora of the civil war, and an analysis of Alberti's *The Lost Grove* is featured prominently.

Philip Krummrich
Updated by Carole A. Champagne and Sarah Hilbert

Vicente Aleixandre

Born: Seville, Spain; April 26, 1898
Died: Madrid, Spain; December 14, 1984

Principal poetry

Ámbito, 1928
Espadas como labios, 1932 (*Swords as if Lips*, 1989)
La destrucción o el amor, 1935 (*Destruction or Love: A Selection*, 1976)
Pasión de la tierra, 1935, 1946
Sombra del paraíso, 1944 (*Shadow of Paradise*, 1987)
Mundo a solas, 1950 (*World Alone*, 1982)
Nacimiento último, 1953
Historia del corazón, 1954
Mis poemas mejores, 1956
Poesías completas, 1960
Picasso, 1961
En un vasto dominio, 1962
Presencias, 1965
Retratos con nombre, 1965
Poemas de la consumación, 1968
Poems, 1969
Poesía superrealista, 1971
Sonido de la guerra, 1972
Diálogos del conocimiento, 1974
The Caves of Night: Poems, 1976
Twenty Poems, 1977
A Longing for Light: Selected Poems of Vicente Aleixandre, 1979
A Bird of Paper: Poems of Vicente Aleixandre, 1981
Primeros poemas, 1985
Nuevos poemas varios, 1987
El mar negro, 1991
En gran noche: Últimos poemas, 1991
Noche cerrada, 1998

Other literary forms

Vicente Aleixandre (o-lehk-SON-dreh) published a great number of prologues, critical letters, memoirs, and evocations of friends and literary figures, many of them later included or rewritten for his major prose work, *Los encuentros* (1958; "the encounters"). Aleixandre also made several speeches on poetry and poets, later published in pamphlet or book form.

Achievements

After receiving the Nobel Prize in Literature in 1977, Vicente Aleixandre stated that the prize was "a response symbolic of the relation of a poet with all other men." In Aleixandre's own estimation, winning the Nobel was his only worthy achievement. All other influences on the development of poetry were insignificant compared with the poet's call to speak for his fellow humans.

The extent of Aleixandre's influence is considerable, however, even if he denied its importance. He was a member of the Royal Spanish Academy (1949), the Hispanic Society of America, the Academy of the Latin World, Paris, the Royal Academy of Fine Arts of San Telmo, Málaga, the Spanish American Academy of Bogotá, and the Academy of Arts and Sciences of Puerto Rico, and, as of 1972, an honorary fellow of the American Association of Spanish and Portuguese.

All these honors recognize Aleixandre's lifelong devotion to the production of a unified body of poetry. A member of the celebrated Generation of '27, which included Jorge Guillén, Pedro Salinas, Federico García Lorca, Rafael Alberti, and Gerardo Diego, Aleixandre was one of the central figures of Spanish Surrealism. Although influenced by André Breton and his circle, the Spanish Surrealists developed to a great extent independently of their French counterparts. While French Surrealism is significant for its worldwide impact on the arts, it produced a surprisingly small amount of lasting poetry. In contrast, Spanish Surrealism—both in Spain and, with notable local variations, in Latin America—constitutes one of the richest poetic traditions of the twentieth century, a tradition in which Aleixandre played a vital role.

BIOGRAPHY

Vicente Aleixandre Merlo was born on April 26, 1898, in Seville, Spain, the son of Cirilo Aleixandre Ballester, a railway engineer, and Elvira Merlo García de Pruneda, daughter of an upper-middle-class Andalusian family. Married in Madrid, Aleixandre's parents moved to Seville, the base for his father's travels with the Andalusian railway network. Four years after Aleixandre's birth, the family moved to Málaga, remaining there for seven years, spending their summers in a cottage on the beach at Pedregalejo a few miles from the city.

Aleixandre seems to have been very happy as a boy in Málaga, where he attended school, frequented the movie theater across the street from his house (he particularly liked the films of Max Linder), and read the Brothers Grimm and Hans Christian Andersen. Happy memories of Málaga and the nearby sea appear frequently in Aleixandre's poetry: He calls them "ciudad del paraíso" (city of paradise) and "mar del paraíso" (sea of paradise), respectively.

In 1911, the family moved to Madrid, where Aleixandre continued his studies at Teresiano School, but he found the strict requirements for the bachelor's degree tedious and preferred reading the books in his grandfather's library: classical and Romantic works and detective novels, especially those by Sir Arthur Conan Doyle. Aleixandre frequently visited the National Library, where he read novels and drama from Spain's Golden Age to the Generation of '98. During the summer of 1917, his friend Dámaso Alonso loaned him a volume by Rubén Darío, a book that, Aleixandre said, revealed to him the passion of his life—poetry. The next year, he discovered the works of Antonio Machado and Juan Ramón Jiménez, as well as the Romantic world of Gustavo Adolfo Bécquer, and his interest in poetry was firmly established.

At the age of fifteen, Aleixandre began to study law

and business administration, finishing the two programs in 1920. He became an assistant professor at the School of Commerce of Madrid and worked at night editing a journal of economics in which he published several articles on railroads. In 1921, he left his teaching post to work for the railway company, but when, in 1925, he suffered an attack of renal tuberculosis, he dropped all professional and social activities, dedicating himself to his poetry, reading, and traveling with his family through Portugal, France, England, and diverse regions of Spain.

Aleixandre's first poems appeared in *Revista de occidente* (journal of the West) in 1926, and two years later his first collection, *Ámbito* (ambit) was published. In 1929, he discovered Sigmund Freud, James Joyce, and Arthur Rimbaud, and, although he suffered a relapse into his tubercular condition in 1932, this period of his life was very productive, resulting in three collections published between 1932 and 1935.

After the removal of a diseased kidney in 1932, Aleixandre retired to Miraflores de la Sierra to convalesce, but in 1933, he returned to Madrid. Carlos Bousoño reports that during this year, Aleixandre read French translations of the German Romantic writers Ludwig Tieck and Novalis, as well as *Les Romantiques allemands* (1933; a translation of Ricarda Huch's *Blüthezeit der Romantik*, 1899; "the German Romantics"). He completed this new spiritual phase with the lyric poetry of William Shakespeare, John Keats, Percy Bysshe Shelley, and William Wordsworth. In 1934, Aleixandre's mother died, and he again traveled through England, France, and Switzerland. During the years of the Spanish Civil War (1936-1939), Aleixandre was isolated from political turmoil, spending much of the time in convalescence after renewed bouts of illness. The death of his father in 1939 brought him even closer to his sister Concepción.

Aleixandre's work reflects his psychological and physiological state as vitally passionate and chronically sick, and as a calm, patient, and creative man. His poetic production was sustained over a lifetime, although a great many years passed between his published collections. In his own words, "The poet dies only when the man dies. And then, his poetry lives forever."

ANALYSIS

In the work of Vicente Aleixandre's first period, the poet is interested primarily in terrible mythic elements of nature without people; he is chaotic, delirious, and grotesque. His is a kind of rebellion against the middle class that hems him in, but he is not yet aware that to save himself from its oppression he must transform his blind, ineffective rebellion into a conscious, efficient one. In his middle period, although Aleixandre continues to take refuge in myth to escape the horrible realities of the day, he faces them as he recalls his family and past, realizing that he cannot remain aloof from history, politics, and other realities when people believe in him. Finally, in his later work, the poet becomes academic, literary, cultured, and decorative. Gradually, finding historical and telluric man and his own dialectical reality, Aleixandre identifies with the public, and the amorous solidarity of the man and poet with all creation is complete.

The idea that love equals death is the leitmotif of almost all of Aleixandre's poetry; it appears most clearly in his recurring images of the sea. In addition to repressed sexuality, a neurotic and somewhat limited group of fantasies recur throughout his oeuvre, many of them associated with the sea. His early years in Málaga impressed the sea on his consciousness, so that it became for him a symbol of youth, equated in turn with innocence, happiness, and his mother (in psychoanalytic dream interpretation, the sea often symbolizes the mother). His desire to return and merge with that happiness and all it represents implies his death as an individual, as he is absorbed by a larger unit. Intrauterine life, being premortal (except to the Roman Catholic Church), is easily equated with postmortal life—life before birth equals life after death.

The sea occupies a high place in Aleixandre's poetic scale of values. Among the 336 poems of his *Poesías completas*, the sea appears 182 times; moreover, it is used as a central theme in sixteen poems. The sea, a recurring symbol or archetype that integrates all of Aleixandre's characteristic themes, represents primitive, instinctive life, true values lost by modern civilized humans and maintained by simple sea creatures, a constant interplay between Thanatos and Eros, and a variety of sensual, erotic states involving repressed

sexuality. Often Aleixandre juxtaposes the sea with images of forest, beach, teeth, tongue, birds, sun, moon, and breast. The sea in Aleixandre's poetry is pathognomonic in its psychological connotations, rooted in the painful dynamic of Aleixandre's own life, although at times it evokes a happy, innocent childhood, much as the gypsy symbolized the childhood of Federico García Lorca. Aleixandre disguises the relationship between the symbol and its meaning at unconscious levels; he distorts and represses it so that the symbols may lend themselves to many interpretations, which only psychoanalysis can fully reveal.

Indeed, a catharsis comparable to psychological analysis is accomplished by Aleixandre's poetry, except that here the patient ministers to himself; for example, unconscious forces account for the breast motif associated with the sea, one of Aleixandre's most constant neurotic projections. Throughout his poems, Aleixandre uses the sea as a surface on which to project his images, according to which it takes on various hues, colors, and attributes. It can be an "unstable sea," an "imperious sea," or a "contained sea," and it serves as the principal, though not the exclusive, vehicle for the projection of neurotic fantasies in which the poet employs symbols to convey meaning he might consciously wish to suppress. Aleixandre's sea imagery irrationally yet imaginatively challenges the reader's preconceptions, as the poet attempts deliberately or otherwise to recapture an unconscious knowledge and create a unity of perception.

Aleixandre's interest in Freudian analysis made him particularly receptive to Surrealism, yet he never accepted the "pure" Surrealism of Breton. Breton defined Surrealism as a psychic automatism through which he proposed to express the real functioning of thought without control by reason and beyond all aesthetic or moral norms, revealing the relationship between the real and the imaginary. For Breton, perception and representation are products of the dissociation of a single original faculty which the eidetic image recognizes and which is to be found in the primitive and the child. The distinction between the subjective and the objective lost its value as the poet sought to engage in a kind of automatic writing. Aleixandre rejected the notion of automatic writing, but in his preoccupation with the subconscious and his powerful, irrational imagery, he introduced Surrealism to Spanish poetry, where it found extremely fertile soil.

ÁMBITO

Ámbito, Aleixandre's first collection, is related to the much later volume, *Shadow of Paradise*. *Ámbito*, composed of seven sections and eight "Nights" (including an initial and final "Night" and one "Sea"), contains classical and Gongoristic forms—not unexpected at the time, since the collection was composed partly during the tercentenary of Luis de Góngora y Argote, when Baroque formalism ruled the day. Nature is everywhere; although there is a faint reflection of the cosmic force, the poet is largely descriptive and objective in a somewhat traditional way. Here, he contemplates nature, while in later works he would seek to possess it and be one with it. Written during his first serious illness, the book sensually examines the fleeting aspects of time. Within his own boundary—the limits of his sickroom, where he lived a solitary existence—he waxed both tender and uncontrollably passionate. However, *Ámbito*'s formal beauty, pleasure in the contemplation of nature, desire for perfection, and joy in life reflect both Juan Ramón Jiménez and Jorge Guillén more than the later Aleixandre. The poetry deals with the world of the senses, classic and cold at times but also warm and romantic. The elusive imagery resembles the reverberations of a musical instrument. The poet employs traditional ballad form instead of the free verse that he later came to use almost exclusively, and his ten- and six-syllable lines reveal his great sense of rhythm. In this volume of youthful love, Aleixandre delicately renders his love affair with nature, a love whose equations frequently resist logical interpretation.

SWORDS AS IF LIPS

Begun in the summer of 1929, Aleixandre's second collection, *Swords as if Lips*, concerns the central themes of life, death, and love—themes that the poet, in his moment of inspiration and suffering, views from a new perspective. An epigraph from Lord Byron, to the effect that the poet is "a babbler," serves notice that the volume eschews conventional "meaning." The work as originally presented was filled with poetic transpositions and capriciously arranged punctuation to help Aleixandre release what he considered his "interior

fire." His intention was not to induce a Surrealistic trance but to create a voluntary pattern of unusual images. Aleixandre, in his somewhat illogically and incoherently developed poetic structures, does not know exactly what theme he will develop. The diffuse emotion he creates in this confused and disturbed work gives rise to apparent indecision for the poet, which transfers to the reader. His liberty of form allows Aleixandre to cover a variety of subjects in a dream atmosphere that hovers between sensation and thought. *Swords as if Lips*, in its examination of reality, petrifies it—or, as one critic phrases it, indulges in the immobilization of the moment. Aleixandre's bittersweet imagery of dead roses, coals of silence (because they lack life-giving flame), and other signs of loss and decay suggests a desire to embrace the reality of death.

DESTRUCTION OR LOVE

If *Swords as if Lips*, despite its striking images, lacks imaginative coherence, Aleixandre's third collection, *Destruction or Love*, is an undisputed masterpiece. Here, in fifty-four poems divided into six parts, the poet offers a visionary transfiguration of the world in flux, a world of mystery and darkness whose basic fabric is erotic love. Aleixandre's universe is a place of cosmic and human passion, of frustrated and desperate clamor, and of unchained telluric forces that often prove fatal to humans, absorbing them and destroying them. In Aleixandre's vision, people can obtain love only by destroying themselves and fusing with the cosmos, for human love is fleeting, and a final fusion with the earth will prove to be the most enduring love of all. Aleixandre excludes the life beyond and salvation. Absorbed in the living unity of nature, he acclaims a love without religious connotations. Aleixandre stresses the idea that the unity of the world includes humanity's works and its civilization, but they remain peripheral to the primary, instinctive life. Perhaps love can save people from society's mask—for love fuses all things, animal, vegetable, and mineral, into one substance—but to achieve fusion, people must give up their limiting structures. Thus, the title of the volume is intended to signify not a choice between mutually exclusive alternatives (either destruction or love) but rather an identification (as when the subtitle of a book is introduced by the word "or").

In *Destruction or Love*, the animal and the vegetable worlds constantly interact with the thoughts and feelings of the poet. In virgin forests, ferocious beasts surround "man," who seeks fruitlessly to find himself, half glimpsing his salvation in an identification with nature in all its forms and thus affirming rather than denying love for all creation. Animals, the forest, and the sea live in intimate union with elementary forces of nature, and tender, small animals exist with large, destructive ones: the beetle and the scorpion with the cobra, the eagle, lions, and tigers. Thus, the tiger is an elastic fire of the forest, and the eagles resemble the ocean. Like other aspects of nature, such as the ocean, the moon, or the heavens, these animals may be virginal and innocent or terrible and destructive. In this vision of nature as a physical whole in which violence and love are complementary forces, everything attacks, destroys, and loves everything and, in so doing, loves, attacks, and destroys itself. Life is death. The limits between flora and fauna dissolve into a new unity; the sea's fish appear to be birds; foam is hair; a body becomes an ocean; a heart becomes a mountain; man may be metal or a lion. Like the mystic poets of old—who had to die in order to find eternal life—Aleixandre offers a mystic fusion or death with the sea and the maternal earth.

SHADOW OF PARADISE

Shadow of Paradise, begun in 1939 and finished in November, 1943, created a sensation among young poets even before its publication in book form; when it finally appeared in 1944, it won a wide and enthusiastic readership among the literary youth of the day. Here, Aleixandre returns to the innocent world of infancy, to a paradise beyond Original Sin and knowledge, to be one with the heavens and the creatures of the dawn. He evokes a Garden of Eden where he may find lost happiness to escape the evil world of humanity, its folly and malignity. The poet narcissistically reinvents his own reality, remembers it, or perhaps imaginatively recreates the world of childhood before the horrifying and inevitable loss of innocence. In his universe of serenity, order, and beauty, however, Aleixandre implies an awareness of the historical world, in which humans must play their role. The tension between paradise and history is always just beneath the surface.

Shadow of Paradise is divided into six parts. Of its fifty-two poems, only a dozen have a definite metric form, but through them all there are patterns of association among rhythms of different kinds. The verse lines are of varying length, including hendecasyllables, pentasyllables, hexameters, exciting combinations of anapestic lines, and irregular meters. Avoiding monotony in his rhythmical movements by means of this prodigality of expression, Aleixandre uses exclamations, interrogatives, and an almost musical progression of scales to form a polyphonic richness. His fetish for rhythmic simplicity extends to his use of adjectives, which he occasionally employs adverbially and, rarely, in double or triple combination. Often his naked nouns convey his precise tone or mood; on other occasions, for special effect, he ends a poetic line with a verb; infrequently, he employs gerundives experimentally.

HISTORIA DEL CORAZÓN

Of Aleixandre's later collections, the most important is *Historia del corazón* (history of the heart). Many underlying crosscurrents of thought and emotion can be found in this volume, but its central theme is the need for human solidarity and compassion for the victims of injustice. *Historia del corazón* reveals a dramatic change in Aleixandre's conception of humanity. Here, no longer creatures of telluric forces, humans are defined by the dolorous round of daily experience. Likewise, Aleixandre's conception of poetry has changed: The poet, a man, becomes all humans, destined to live and die, without the assurance of paradise or eternal life, in a world where death is always present. Nevertheless, the poet proclaims, it is not necessary to live desperate, solitary lives; he sings for all humankind of fleeting time, social love, and human solidarity. The poet recognizes that he is aging, but without despair, and empathizes with his neighbor, who must also stoically face the end.

OTHER MAJOR WORKS

SHORT FICTION: *Prosas completas*, 2002.

NONFICTION: *Los encuentros*, 1958; *Epistolario*, 1986 (with José Luis Cano).

CHILDREN'S LITERATURE: *Vicente Aleixandre para niños*, 1984 (illustrated by Concha Martinez).

MISCELLANEOUS: *Obras completas*, 1977 (2 volumes).

BIBLIOGRAPHY

Cabrera, Vicente, and Harriet Boyer, eds. *Critical Views on Vicente Aleixandre's Poetry*. Lincoln, Nebr.: Society of Spanish and Spanish-American Studies, 1979. Criticism and interpretation of Aleixandre's addresses, essays, lectures, and poetry. Includes selected poems in English translation.

Daydí-Tolson, Santiago. "Light in the Eyes: Visionary Poetry in Vicente Aleixandre." In *Contemporary Spanish Poetry: The Word and the World*, edited by Cecile West-Settle and Sylvia Sherno. Madison, N.J.: Fairleigh Dickinson University Press, 2005. Notes that the poet's work was filled with light and sensual descriptions of what he had observed, and that the poet's blindness in the 1970's severely affected his work.

_____, ed. *Vicente Aleixandre: A Critical Appraisal*. Ypsilanti, Mich.: Bilingual Press, 1981. A critical study of Aleixandre's work with a biographical introduction, extensively annotated bibliography, index, and Aleixandre's Nobel Prize acceptance lecture.

Harris, Derek. *Metal Butterflies and Poisonous Lights: The Language of Surrealism in Lorca, Alberti, Cernuda, and Aleixandre*. Anstruther, Fife, Scotland: La Sirena, 1998. History and criticism of Surrealism in Spanish literature, including the works of Aleixandre. Includes bibliography.

_____. "Prophet, Medium, Babbler: Voice and Identity in Vicente Aleixandre's Surrealist Poetry." In *Companion to Spanish Surrealism*, edited by Robert Havard. Rochester, N.Y.: Tamesis, 2004. Discusses Surrealism in Aleixandre's poems.

Ilie, P. *The Surrealist Mode in Spanish Literature*. Ann Arbor: University of Michigan Press, 1968. A study of Surrealism in Spanish literature. Includes bibliographic references.

Murphy, Daniel. *Vicente Aleixandre's Stream of Lyric Consciousness*. Lewisburg, Pa.: Bucknell University Press, 2001. Criticism and interpretation of Aleixandre's poetics, with bibliographical citations and index.

Schwartz, Kessel. *Vicente Aleixandre*. New York: Twayne, 1970. An introductory biography and critical analysis of selected works by Aleixandre.

Soufas, C. Christopher. *The Subject in Question: Early Contemporary Spanish Literature and Modernism*. Washington, D.C.: Catholic University of America Press, 2007. One chapter examines the geographies of presence in the poetry of Aleixandre and Jorge Guillén. Information on modernism in Spanish literature provides a context for understanding Aleixandre's works.

Richard A. Mazzara

ANACREON

Born: Teos, Ionia, Asia Minor (now Sigacik, Turkey); c. 571 B.C.E.
Died: Athens, Greece; c. 490 B.C.E.
Also known as: Anakreon

PRINCIPAL POETRY

Anacreon composed poems for oral performance, not posterity. He seems to have written no single book or collection of poems. For his complete poems in Greek, see *Poetae Melici Graeci*, 1962 (Denys Page, editor). The first English translation of Anacreon was *Anacreon Done into English out of the Original Greek*, 1683. Later translations include *The Odes of Anacreon*, 1928 (Erastus Richardson, translator), *Greek Lyric*, 1982 (David A. Campbell, translator), and *Anakreon: The Extant Fragments*, 1991 (Guy Davenport, translator).

OTHER LITERARY FORMS

Anacreon (uh-NAK-ree-uhn) is remembered only for his poetry.

ACHIEVEMENTS

Included in the Alexandrine canon of nine Greek lyric poets, Anacreon has influenced generations of poets since classical times, although it is difficult to measure his influence precisely with such fragmentary texts. The surviving fragments show that Anacreon set a high standard for sophisticated, polished, short poems written in a variety of meters. Although he appears to favor a combination of Glyconics and Pherecrateans in his extant verse, he is best known for the Anacreontic meter, an anaclastic Ionic dimeter to which he has given his name. He was probably most admired in antiquity for his love poems, his banquet poems, and his imagery and tropes, especially those dealing with Eros, which became standardized in later poetry.

Anacreon's style was copied by unknown Greek poets writing under his name; these spurious poems, usually called the Anacreonteia, survive in the *Palatine Anthology* and range in date from the Alexandrine period through late Byzantine times. The poetry of Horace and of other Roman lyric poets also shows conscious imitation of Anacreon, whose authentic works could still be read in Augustan Rome. Anacreon is better known in the modern world through the Anacreonteia than through his own works. The Anacreonteia, first printed in 1554, had a great influence on several European literary schools; on the French Renaissance poets Pierre de Ronsard and Rémy Belleau; on such Italian lyric poets of the seventeenth and eighteenth centuries as Gabriello Chiabrera and Jacopo Vittorelli; on such eighteenth century German poets as Friedrich von Hagedorn, Johann Gleim, and Johann Götz; and on the British and Irish poets Robert Herrick, William Oldys, and Thomas Moore. These poets, often called Anacreontics, either made free translations of the Greek Anacreonteia into their own languages or wrote original poetry in the meter and style known as Anacreontic.

BIOGRAPHY

Anacreon's poetry reflects the aristocratic Greek society of the sixth century B.C.E. in which he lived. His was a society endangered by Persian encroachments on Ionic Greece, as well as by internal political upheavals marked by the rise and fall of antiaristocratic tyrannies. Although little is known for certain about Anacreon's life, much can be conjectured from ancient citations and, to a lesser degree, from the remains of his own poetry.

Anacreon, son of Scythinus, was born in the Ionian city of Teos (now Sigacik, Turkey) about 571 B.C.E. Teos was seized by the Persian Harpagus soon after the fall of Sardis about 541 B.C.E. Many Teans, including

Anacreon, escaped Persian rule by fleeing to Abdera on the coast of Thrace; fragments 391 P. and 419 P. may refer to this traumatic period in Anacreon's life. Anacreon's Thracian period is obscure; only a few fragments, including 417 P., reflect his experiences there. Anacreon's poetic reputation, however, certainly grew from that time, for he was at some point invited to the court of the Samian tyrant, Polycrates (ruled 540 to c. 522 B.C.E.), to tutor Polycrates' son in music and poetry.

Polycrates' political policy on Samos included a patronage of the arts that brought to the island not only Anacreon but also the West Greek poet, Ibycus of Rhegium, known for his choral song. Although Anacreon remained in Samos until the death of Polycrates and is said by ancient sources to have made frequent reference to the tyrant in his poetry, only a few allusions to events in Samos (348 P., 353 P., and 426 P.) can be found in Anacreon's extant fragments. The surviving poetry suggests that Anacreon had little enthusiasm for political themes; he preferred to write about love and wine. Although Anacreon's love poetry was addressed primarily to young boys, this provides meager evidence for the poet's biography, since homoeroticism was a conventional poetic theme in his society (as in, for example, Sappho's works).

With the fall of Polycrates about 522 B.C.E., Anacreon was brought to Athens by the Pisistratid Hipparchus, who, like Polycrates, practiced a policy of art patronage under the tyranny of his brother Hippias. Anacreon remained in Athens for the rest of his life, except for a brief interlude in Thessaly about 512 B.C.E., caused by the fall of the Pisistratids.

As he grew older, Anacreon introduced the theme of old age into his poetry, often combining it with his favorite themes of love and wine. It was for this type of poetry that he was best known in the aristocratic Athenian society for which he wrote. Anacreon's personality came to be so closely associated with love and wine that long after his death he was remembered as a drunken, amorous old man. Indeed, this may account for the ancient tradition that Anacreon died as a result of choking on a grape pip. Whatever the actual cause, Anacreon died probably about 490 B.C.E., since the ancients say that he lived past the age of eighty and that he lived long enough to experience the poetry of Aeschylus.

ANALYSIS

The Greek poetic tradition in which Anacreon wrote was a particularly rich one, tracing its origins to the oral songs of the Homeric period. It was in many ways a conservative tradition. It restricted certain genres to specific meters, such as epic to hexameter and invective to iambic, and depended to a great extent on stock epithets, formulas, and vocabulary from Homeric epic. However, at the same time, it was a tradition that encouraged experimentation and novelty of expression. Thus, beginning in the late eighth century B.C.E., lyric poetry, distinguished by the use of the first person, blossomed, especially in the Greek cities of Ionia and Aeolia, and produced Archilochus, Sappho, and Alcaeus in the seventh century B.C.E. All these early lyric poets experimented with a poetic analysis of personal experience and emotion to which the late sixth century B.C.E. Anacreon was heir.

While accepting the traditional metrical types and continuing the lyric proclivity toward self-expression and introspection, Anacreon brought to this poetry not so much new emotions and feelings as the skill of a meticulous craftsman who chose his words carefully and knew when to inject exaggeration and humor for the proper effect. Anacreon enriched Greek lyric with the novelties of a poetic experimenter who constantly sought new imagery and approaches for old themes. Certainly the themes of love and wine that dominate Anacreon's extant poetry are, for the most part, traditional. What is significant about Anacreon is that he strove to express these themes in new contexts and succeeded so well that the novel imagery and contexts he introduced, especially in the realm of love poetry, have generally become the clichés of later generations of poets.

Anacreon (Library of Congress)

357 P.

Anacreon's goal of novelty in a traditional context is demonstrated in 357 P., a prayer to Dionysus. The prayer form had early been recognized to be well suited to lyric expression; these prayers are meant not for public ceremony but for private performance. Sappho's "Ode to Aphrodite" had already used the prayer poem in a love context with great success, and Anacreon may here be following Sappho. Anacreon's prayer is divided into two parts: the invocation, in which the deity is addressed and described; and the entreaty, or the request made to the god. Anacreon's invocation, striking in that it does not mention the god's name, identifies Dionysus only by his habitual companions and haunts. Dionysus is described as playing on the lofty mountaintops with Eros, nymphs, and Aphrodite. Novelty of expression is achieved by the use of new rather than stock epithets for Dionysus's companions. Although the epithet "subduer," which Anacreon invents for Eros, is never used again in Greek literature, the concept of Eros as a tamer of men, which Anacreon implies through this epithet, is one which becomes commonplace in later lyrics. Anacreon's descriptions of the nymphs as "blue-eyed" and Aphrodite as "rosy" are noteworthy both because these adjectives had never been applied to these deities before, and because they reflect another characteristic of Anacreon's style: a fondness for color contrasts. In a very few words, Anacreon is thus able to achieve a vivid, colorful, original description of Dionysus's world.

This formal invocation is followed by an equally formal entreaty. Anacreon maintains the solemnity of the prayer form here by employing standard expressions of entreaty: "I beseech you," "come kindly to us," and "hear our prayer." The climax to which the poem is leading is the specific request that the poet wants to make; the formality of structure and vocabulary suggests that the request is a serious one. However, the next phrase, "be a good counselor to Cleobulus," shows that Anacreon is not serious. Anacreon's word for "good counselor," *sumbulus*, creates a pun on Cleobulus's name which is difficult to miss, since both Cleobulus and *sumbulus* are placed at the beginning of their respective lines. The humor of this phrase shatters the solemn tone of the prayer and prepares for the surprise of the last two lines, where Anacreon finally reveals that he is actually praying to Dionysus not for some lofty request, but for aid in a homosexual love affair. The manipulation of the prayer form to suit a love theme is already found in Sappho, but without the change in tone developed here. Sappho maintains in her poem an intensity of emotion that is not found in Anacreon. By adding a pun at the point when he is introducing the love theme, Anacreon emphasizes not his intense emotions but his artistic skill, his ability to control his poem through the careful selection of words.

359 P.

Cleobulus is featured in several other poems, including 359 P., which again shows Anacreon's interest in form rather than emotions. This love poem is a sequence of three parallel statements about Anacreon's relationship with Cleobulus. Each line begins with Cleobulus's name used in a different case ending and

concludes with a different verb in the first person singular: "I love," "I am mad," and "I gaze." The grammatical trope is probably borrowed from Archilochus, who uses it in a political context. Anacreon's application of Archilochus's technique to love poetry reflects a de-emphasis of emotional intensity, which is suggested by the verbal sequence, through which Anacreon moves from mad love for Cleobulus to mere gazing at the beloved. "I gaze at Cleobulus" suggests a distance between lover and beloved that is not evident in "I love Cleobulus." Such distance is critical to Anacreon's poetic stance, which is based on careful word study.

358 P.

Another of Anacreon's poems, 358 P., demonstrates not only his use of special descriptive words but also his experimentation with new imagery. In this piece, Anacreon describes Eros's invitation to play ball with a girl from Lesbos. Anacreon may here be inventing the image of Eros as the "ballplayer," an image that was commonplace in later poets such as Apollonius and Meleager. The ball playing, possibly derived from Homer's *Odyssey* (c. 725 B.C.E.; English translation, 1614), in which Nausicaa plays ball with her servant girls, is a successful variation on the traditional Greek theme of apple tossing (as in the story of Atalanta). The play here is a double entendre. Anacreon's fondness for color contrasts, noted above, is evident in this poem as well, and with even more effect. Eros's ball is "purple," a rich and expensive color in the ancient world, while Anacreon transfers an epithet of Dionysus, "golden-haired," to Eros. The girl, too, is described with colors; she is the girl "with the motley slippers." The final, and perhaps most important, color reference is to Anacreon's white hair, implying that the girl rejects Anacreon because he is too old. This incompatibility of love with old age, a theme repeated in Anacreon's extant corpus, is emphasized by the contrast of colors developed in the poem.

Old age, however, is not the only motive for the girl's rejection of Anacreon. She is from Lesbos and gapes after some "other" (female). To the modern reader this situation suggests an association of the island of Lesbos with female homosexuality, which may not have been standard in Anacreon's day. Further, there is some ambiguity here, probably intentional, in the text. First, "female" is only grammatically understood and other nouns have been supplied, for example, "hair" (feminine in Greek), making the homosexuality theme more uncertain and, at the same time, enhancing the sexual double entendre. The epithet for Lesbos, "good to dwell in," is also ambiguous. Although derived from a standard Homeric epithet for the island, this word is employed here with a meaning that is difficult to establish. The solemn Homeric word may simply be used, as David A. Campbell suggests, to contrast with the more playful tone of the poem as a whole. C. M. Bowra argues in *Greek Lyric Poetry from Alcman to Simonides* (1961) that the epithet, transposed to the girl, may suggest that she comes from a prosperous family and can pick and choose her mates. Bowra has also suggested that this epithet is a subtle dig at Lesbos, "well-established" in its sexual habits. Any and all of these interpretations may be correct, for in this poem, where Eros is depicted as a tease, perhaps the poet, too, is a tease through his use of ambiguity. Once again Anacreon is more interested in his poetic expression than in his emotions. Such a poetic distance from his emotions permits him to deal with sexual passion and with the frustrations of old age in a distinctively humorous way.

376 P.

Anacreon also demonstrates a concern with novelty and effect. The fragment 376 P. combines two of the poet's favorite topics, love and wine, in the context of a traditional love theme: the spurned lover's desperate leap from the Leucadian Cliff. Anacreon uses this theme in a new way. The poet states that the climb onto the rock is being made "again," indicating that this particular leap is not a suicide, but rather a repeated occurrence. The emphasis is not on the despair of unrequited love, but on the loss of self-control caused by love. This helplessness is further stressed by the dive that the poet takes in the second line. Finally, the poet mentions that he makes the plunge "drunk with love." Inebriety may already have been associated with the traditional leap from the Leucadian Cliff, but Anacreon appears to have transposed the theme into a significant metaphor that was not there before and that has not left love poetry since. "To be drunk with love" is certainly a comical exaggeration that suits Anacreon's theme of loss of self-control and that underscores his evident mastery over his poetry.

396 P.

Wine and love are also combined in 396 P., in which the poet addresses the cupbearer, who played a role of honor at Greek drinking parties, and asks for water and wine, which the Greeks mixed before drinking, as well as a garland of flowers, another common trapping of a Greek drinking song. Anacreon, however, adds something new to the drinking song by introducing a love theme. "Bring me these things," he says, "that I may box with Eros." The boxing metaphor is apparently an invention of Anacreon, who may have used it at least once more (in 346 P.). Eros, who was represented as a youth in the sixth century B.C.E. and was not transformed into an infant until the Hellenistic period, is thus fitted by Anacreon with another apt metaphor, that of boxing, an image appropriate to Eros's pain-inflicting capabilities.

417 P.

A final selection, 417 P., shows Anacreon not creating new imagery but rather using an old image in a strikingly new fashion. For the first time, perhaps, a lyric poet may be creating an entire poem out of a single metaphor, a comparison of women with mares, which had appeared earlier in the choral poetry of Alcman. Ibycus, Anacreon's poetic associate on Samos, also used the racehorse image for the lover controlled by Eros. In 417 P., however, Anacreon reverses Ibycus's imagery by making the girl the wild mare and himself the potential rider. The vocabulary of the poem is a remarkable combination of words with amatory undertones, such as "reins" and "mounter," and of elevated epic phraseology, such as "stubbornly" and "think me in no way wise" and "around the limits of the course."

These few examples of the surviving fragments of Anacreon's poetry suggest what a great loss the disappearance of his corpus has been. They demonstrate his consummate skill as a lyric poet who could manipulate poetic themes, imagery, vocabulary, and even his emotions for poetic effect. The reader of Anacreon, tantalized by the few extant fragments, must appreciate the poet's ironic position within literary tradition. A playfully original and prolific innovator, Anacreon became an authoritative model for many later poets, and, despite the ravages of time, he remains a major figure in literature through imitation by others rather than by the weight of his own writings.

BIBLIOGRAPHY

Budelmann, Felix, ed. *The Cambridge Companion to Greek Lyric*. New York: Cambridge University Press, 2009. This volume on Greek lyric poetry examines this type of poetry in detail and contains a chapter on Anacreon and the Anacreontea.

Campbell, David A. *The Golden Lyre: The Themes of Greek Lyric Poets*. London: Duckworth, 1983. Comments about Anacreon's work are scattered throughout a book devoted to exploring Greek poets' writing about subjects such as love, athletics, politics, friendship, gods and heroes, life and death, and the arts. Provides excellent insight into the ways Anacreon's poetry parallels or diverges from the work of other classical lyricists.

Frankel, Hermann. *Early Greek Poetry and Philosophy*. Oxford, England: Basil Blackwell, 1975. A section on Anacreon is included in this extensive study of the development of Greek literature. Selected poems are examined to illustrate the musical qualities of Anacreon's poetry and highlight his technique.

Kirkwood, G. M. *Early Greek Monody: The History of a Poetic Type*. Ithaca, N.Y.: Cornell University Press, 1974. Treats Anacreon as a major writer in the tradition of monody. Illustrates differences between his work and that of earlier monodists, and describes his influence on later writers, especially the Latin poet Horace.

O'Brien, John. *Anacreon Redivivus: A Study of Anacreontic Translation in Mid-sixteenth Century France*. Ann Arbor: University of Michigan Press, 1995. Though concentrating on the work of scholars in only one century, this study provides useful insight into the ways Anacreon and his imitators have been read by later audiences. Carefully details the critical principles used by key translators who helped shape the canon of Anacreontic poetry in published form.

Rosenmeyer, Patricia A. *The Poetics of Imitation: Anacreon and the Anacreontic Tradition*. New York: Cambridge University Press, 1992. Discusses the influence of Anacreon on his contemporaries and examines the way Anacreontic imitators have been discovered, translated, and evaluated. Contains a chapter on the poet's life and work, explicating individual works and exploring major themes in his corpus. Also examines the concept of imitation as a poetic device in ancient poetry.

Thomas J. Sienkewicz
Updated by Laurence W. Mazzeno

GUILLAUME APOLLINAIRE

Born: Rome, Italy; August 26, 1880
Died: Paris, France; November 9, 1918
Also known as: Wilhelm Apollinaris; Guillelmus Apollinaris de Kostrowitzki

PRINCIPAL POETRY
Le Bestiaire, 1911 (*Bestiary*, 1978)
Alcools: Poèmes, 1898-1913, 1913 (*Alcools: Poems, 1898-1913*, 1964)
Calligrammes, 1918 (English translation, 1980)
Il y a, 1925
Le Guetteur mélancolique, 1952
Tendre comme le souvenir, 1952
Poèmes à Lou, 1955
Œuvres poétiques, 1956

OTHER LITERARY FORMS

Besides poetry, Guillaume Apollinaire (ah-pawl-ee-NEHR) wrote a number of prose works. Among the most significant of his short stories and novellas are *L'Enchanteur pourrissant* (1909; "the putrescent enchanter"), published by Henry Kahnweiler and illustrated with woodcuts by André Derain; *L'Hérésiarque et Cie.* (1910; *The Heresiarch and Co.*, 1965), a contender for the Prix Goncourt; and *Le Poète assassiné* (1916; *The Poet Assassinated*, 1923). They are contained in the Pléiade edition, *Œuvres en prose* (1977), edited by Michel Décaudin.

Apollinaire collaborated on numerous plays and

cinema scripts. His best-known individual works in these genres are two proto-Surrealist plays in verse: *Les Mamelles de Tirésias* (pr. 1917; *The Breasts of Tiresias*, 1961), first published in the magazine *SIC* in 1918, and *Couleur du temps* (the color of time; pr. 1918), which first appeared in the *Nouvelle Revue française* in 1920. They are available in the Pléiade edition of *Œuvres poétiques*. Apollinaire also published a great deal of art criticism and literary criticism in journals, newspapers, and other periodicals. In 1913, the articles published before that year were collected in *Peintres cubistes: Méditations esthétiques* (*The Cubist Painters: Aesthetic Meditations*, 1944). In 1918, *Mercure de France* published his famous manifesto "L'Esprit nouveau et les poètes" ("The New Spirit and the Poets"), which later appeared, along with many other articles, in *Chroniques d'art, 1902-1918* (1960), edited by L. C. Breunig. This collection has been translated into English as *Apollinaire on Art: Essays and Reviews, 1902-1918* (1972).

ACHIEVEMENTS

After Guillaume Apollinaire, French poetry was never the same again. Writing at the end of the long Symbolist tradition, a tradition very apparent in his early works, Apollinaire moved into a new perception of the world and of poetry. In the world of his mature verse, spatial and temporal relations are radically altered. Apollinaire's was one of the first voices in French poetry to attempt to articulate the profound discontinuity and disorientation in modern society. At the same time, however, his works reflect hope, frequently ecstatic, in the promise of the future.

Apollinaire's sense of radical discontinuity was reflected in his formal innovations, analyzed in considerable depth by Jean-Claude Chevalier in *Alcools d'Apollinaire* (1970). Immediately before the publication of *Alcools*, Apollinaire went through the volume and removed all punctuation, a device that he continued to use in most of his later works. His most notable poems, such as "Zone," "Liens" ("Chains"), and "Les Fenêtres" ("Windows"), use free verse with irregular rhyme and rhythm; his most startling works are the picture poems of *Calligrammes*, a form that he falsely claimed to have invented. They consist of verses arranged to give both a visual and an auditory effect in an effort to create simultaneity.

Like the cubists and other modern painters who sought to go beyond the traditional boundaries of space and time, Apollinaire desired to create the effect of simultaneity. This ambition is evident in "Zone," with its biographical, geographical, and historical discontinuity. In this single poem, the poet leaps from his pious childhood at the Collège Saint-Charles in Monaco to the wonders of modern aviation and back to the "herds" of buses "mooing" on the streets of Paris. Perhaps his most obvious achievement in simultaneity, though less profound, is in "Lundi rue Christine" ("Monday in Christine Street"), which records overheard bits of conversation in a "sinistre brasserie," a low-class café-restaurant that Apollinaire had frequented as early as 1903.

The friend and collaborator of many important painters during the exciting years in Paris just before World War I, Apollinaire began associating with artists when he met Pablo Picasso in 1904, after which he frequented the famous Bateau-Lavoir on the rue Ravignan with Max Jacob, André Derain, Maurice Vlaminck, Georges Braque, and others. After 1912, he moved into the world of art criticism, not always appreciated by the artists themselves, as critic Francis Steegmuller has noted. Not unrelated to this interest was Apollinaire's tumultuous liaison with Marie Laurencin from 1907 to 1912. He frequently inspired works and portraits by artists, including Laurencin, Henri Rousseau, and Picasso. Apollinaire's own works further testify to his links with painters: *Bestiary* was illustrated by Raoul Dufy, and "Windows" was the introductory poem to the catalog of the Robert Delaunay exhibit in 1912. His poems often parallel the work of the painters in their spirit of simultaneity; in their subjects, such as the *saltimbanques* of Picasso; and in their moods, such as those of Marc Chagall's dreamworld and inverted figures.

After 1916, Apollinaire became the *chef d'école*, the leader of a new generation of poets and painters. Among them were Pierre Reverdy, Philippe Soupault, Jean Cocteau, André Breton, and Tristan Tzara. His own works appeared in the most avant-garde journals: Reverdy's *Nord-Sud*, Picabia's *391*, and Albert Birot's

SIC. His lecture "The New Spirit and the Poets" called poets to a new prophetic vision, imploring them to create prodigies with their imagination like modern Merlins. Like Paul Claudel, Apollinaire regarded the poet as a creator. The modern poet, he believed, must use everything for his (or her) creation: new discoveries in science, in the subconscious and the dreamworld, and in the cinema and visual arts.

The Surrealists, in their desire to revolutionize art and literature, saw in Apollinaire their precursor. It was he who coined the word *surréaliste*, in the preface to his drama in verse *The Breasts of Tiresias*. In it, he explains that an equivalent is not always an imitation, even as the wheel, though intended to facilitate transportation, is not a reproduction of the leg. Apollinaire conveys his message with a lighthearted tone, employing incongruous rhythms, parody, and sexual imagery. This is essentially the technique he employs in his most avant-garde poetry, and *The Breasts of Tiresias* echoes poems from "Ondes" ("Waves," the first part of *Calligrammes*) such as "Zone," "Le Brasier" ("The Brazier"), "Les Fiançailles" ("The Betrothal"), and "Le Larron" ("The Thief"). Thus, Apollinaire indicated the path to follow in revolutionizing poetry, although much of his work was in some respects traditional. Like Victor Hugo, he served subsequent poets chiefly as a guide rather than as a model, but it was his "esprit nouveau" that gave considerable impetus to a new form of modern poetry.

BIOGRAPHY

Born in Rome on August 26, 1880, Guillaume Albert Wladimir Alexandre Apollinaire de Kostrowitzky was an illegitimate child; in "The Thief," he says that his "father was a sphinx and his mother a night." In reality, his mother was a Polish adventurer of noble ancestry, Angelique Kostrowicka, known in Paris mostly as "Olga." His father's identity has never been definitively ascertained. The most plausible supposition points to Francesco Flugi d'Aspermont, who was from a noble Italian family that included many prelates. This theory is based on the careful investigation of biographer Marcel Adéma. Apollinaire's mysterious and involved parentage haunted the poet throughout his life, leaving unmistakable marks on his character and works.

Apollinaire received his only formal education at the Collège of Saint-Charles in Monaco and the Collège Stanislas at Cannes, from 1890 to 1897, where he acquired a solid grounding in religious and secular knowledge. Although his Catholic training was to remain firmly implanted in his memory and is evident in his poetry, he moved away from any outward adherence to religious beliefs after 1897. In 1899, he arrived in Paris, his home for most of the next nineteen years of his life, and the center and inspiration of his literary activity. First, however, he made a significant trip to Germany's Rhineland in 1901, as tutor to Gabrielle, the daughter of the viscountess of Milhau. There, he met and fell in love with Annie Playden, Gabrielle's English governess. This ill-fated romance and the beauty of the Rhineland inspired many of Apollinaire's early poems, which were later published in *Alcools*.

Apollinaire's return to Paris coincided with the beginning of friendships with artists and writers such as André Salmon, Alfred Jarry, Max Jacob, and especially Picasso. In 1903, he began his collaboration on many periodicals, which he continued throughout his lifetime. Most of his prose and poetry was first published in such journals, many of which—such as *Le Festin d'Esope* and *La Revue immoraliste*—were of very short duration. His works appeared under several pseudonyms, of which "Apollinaire" was the most significant. Others included "Louise Lalame," "Lul," "Montade," and "Tyl." In 1907, he met Marie Laurencin, an artist, whose talent Apollinaire tended to exaggerate. Their liaison continued until 1912 and was an inspiration and a torment to both of them. During this period, Apollinaire was deeply marked by the false accusation that he was responsible for the theft of the *Mona Lisa* from the Louvre. A series of six poems in *Alcools*, "À la Santé" ("At the Santé") describes his brief stay in the prison of La Santé in Verlainian imagery.

The year 1912 marked Apollinaire's break with Laurencin and his definite espousal of modern art, of which he became a staunch proponent. During the two years preceding World War I, he gave lectures and wrote articles on modern art and prepared *Alcools* for publication. The beginning of the war, in 1914, was to Apollinaire a call to a mission. Although not a French citizen until the year 1916, he embraced with great enthusiasm his *métier de soldat* as an artilleryman and then as an infantryman, according an almost mystical dimension to his military service. His poetry of these first two years reveals the exaltation of war and the idealization of two women, "Lou" (Louise de Coligny-Châtillon) and Madeleine Pagès, to whom he was briefly engaged.

Wounded in the head in 1916, Apollinaire required surgery and was then discharged from the service. He returned to the world of literature and art with numerous articles, lectures, two plays, and a volume of poetry, *Calligrammes*. In May of 1918, he married Jacqueline Kolb ("Ruby"), the "jolie rousse" ("pretty redhead") of the last poem in *Calligrammes*. The marriage was of short duration, however, as Apollinaire died of Spanish influenza on November 9 of the same year.

ANALYSIS

In his poetic style, Guillaume Apollinaire might be characterized as the last of the Symbolists and the first of the moderns. He is considered a revolutionary and a destroyer, yet the bulk of his work shows a deep influence of traditional symbolism, especially biblical, legendary, and mythical. Very knowledgeable in Roman Catholic doctrine from his years with the Marianists at Monaco and Cannes, he uses extensive biblical imagery: Christ, the Virgin Mary, and the Holy Spirit in the form of a dove. Robert Couffignal has analyzed Apollinaire's religious imagery in detail and considers his comprehension of the Bible to be "a cascade of superficial weavings." Scott Bates sees the Last Judgment, with its apocalyptic implications, as central to Apollinaire's works. The concept of messianism and the advent of a new millennium is evident in both the early works and the war poems, which predict a new universe. In the Symbolist tradition, the poet is the seer of the new kingdom.

Many of Apollinaire's symbols are from the realm of legend and myth. Rosemonde, the idealized woman of the Middle Ages, is present in several poems, though she appears also as a prostitute. In "Merlin et la vielle femme" ("Merlin and the Old Woman"), the medieval seer foreshadows Apollinaire's vision of the future. Ancient mythology is the source for Orpheus, under

whose sign *Bestiary* is written. Orpheus is also the symbol of Christ and the poet, as is Hermès Trismègiste. Ancient Egypt appears in frequent references to the Nile, the Israelites in bondage, and Pharaoh, the image of the poet himself. The fantastic abounds in Apollinaire's works: ghosts, diabolic characters, and phantoms, as found, for example, in "La Maison des Morts" ("The House of the Dead") and especially in the short stories.

Much of Apollinaire's early symbolism is directed toward the quest for self-knowledge; his choice of the name Apollinaire is a clue to his search. Though it was

Guillaume Apollinaire (The Granger Collection, New York)

the name of his maternal grandfather and one of the names given to him at baptism, he seems to have chosen it for its reference to Apollo, the god of the sun. Indeed, solar imagery is central to his poetry, and the introductory poem of *Alcools*, "Zone," ends with the words "Soleil cou coupé" ("Sun cut throat"). Bates argues that the violent love-death relationship between the sun and night, with its corresponding symbolism, is as crucial to the interpretation of Apollinaire as it is to a reading of Gérard de Nerval or Stéphane Mallarmé. Along with love and death is death and resurrection. Apollinaire chooses the phoenix as a sign of rebirth and describes his own psychological and poetic resurrection in "The Brazier" and "The Betrothal," poems that he regarded as among his best. Fire seems to be his basic image, with its multiple meanings of passion, destruction, and purification.

Passion as a flame dominated Apollinaire's life and poetry. Of the many women whom he loved, five in particular incarnated his violent passion and appear in his work: Playden and Laurencin in *Alcools*; Lou, Madeleine, and Jacqueline in *Calligrammes* and in several series of poems published after his death. Apollinaire is capable of expressing tender, idealistic love, as in the "Aubade chantée à Lætare un an passé" ("Aubade Sung to Lætare a Year Ago") section of the "La Chanson du mal-aimé" ("The Song of the Poorly Loved") and in "La Jolie Rousse" ("The Pretty Redhead"), which closes *Calligrammes*. In most cases, Apollinaire is the *mal-aimé*, and as he himself says, he is much less the poorly beloved than the one who loves poorly. His first three loves ended violently; his last was concluded by his death. Thus, the death of love is as important as its first manifestation, which for him resembles the shells bursting in the war.

Autumn is the season of the death of love, wistfully expressed in such nostalgic works as "L'Adieu" ("The Farewell") and "Automne" ("Autumn"). Because the end of love usually involved deep suffering for him, the image of mutilation is not uncommon. The beloved in "The Song of the Poorly Loved" has a scar on her neck, and the mannequins in "L'Émigrant de Landor Road" ("The Emigrant from Landor Road") are decapitated, much like the sun in "Zone." Apollinaire perceives love in its erotic sense, and in many cases he resorts to ar-

cane symbolism, as in the seven swords in "The Song of the Poorly Loved." "Lul de Faltenin" ("Lul of Faltenin") is also typical, with its subtle erotic allusions. Such themes are more overt in Apollinaire's prose; indeed, Bates has compiled a glossary of erotic symbolism in the works of Apollinaire.

Apollinaire was both a lyric poet and a storyteller. In the lyric tradition, he writes of his emotions in images drawn from nature. His work is particularly rich in flora and fauna. *Bestiary* shows his familiarity with and affection for animals and his ability, like the fabulists, to see them as caricatures of people. *Alcools*, as the title indicates, often evokes grapes and wine; it also speaks of fir trees (in "Les Sapins") and falling leaves. "Zone" contains a catalog of birds, real and legendary. The Seine comes alive in Apollinaire's ever-popular "Le Pont Mirabeau" ("Mirabeau Bridge"). In *Calligrammes*, the poet often compares the explosion of shells to bursting buds.

Apollinaire was the author of many short stories, and he maintains a narrative flavor in his poetry. "The House of the Dead" was originally a short story, "L'Obituaire," and it reads like one. Many of the picture poems in *Calligrammes* tell a story; "Paysage" ("Landscape"), for example, portrays by means of typography a house, a tree, and two lovers, one of whom smokes a cigar that the reader can almost smell. Apollinaire's technique often involves improvisation, as in "Le Musicien de Saint-Merry" ("The Musician of Saint-Merry"). Although he claims almost total spontaneity, there are revised versions of many of his poems, and he frequently borrowed from himself, rearranging both lines and poems. In particular, Apollinaire tells stories of the modern city, imitating its new structures as Arthur Rimbaud did in his innovative patterns, and like Charles Baudelaire, Apollinaire peoples his verse with the forgotten and the poor, the prostitutes and the clowns.

Apollinaire had a remarkable sense of humor, displayed in frequent word-plays, burlesques, and parodies. The briefest example of his use of puns is the one-line poem "Chantre" ("Singer"): "Et l'unique cordeau des trompettes marines" ("and the single string of marine trumpets"). *Cordeau*, when read aloud, might be *cor d'eau*, or "horn of water," another version of a marine trumpet, as well as *corps d'eau* ("body of water") or even *cœur d'eau* ("heart of water"). The burlesque found in his short stories appears in poetry as dissonance, erotic puns, and irreverent parodies, such as in "Les Sept Epées" ("The Seven Swords") as well as in "The Thief," a poem that Bates interprets as parodying Christ. Apollinaire's lighthearted rhythm and obscure symbolism tend to prevent his verse from becoming offensive and convey a sense of freedom, discovery, and surprise.

BESTIARY

Bestiary is one of the most charming and accessible of Apollinaire's works. The idea for the poem probably came from Picasso in 1906, who was then doing woodcuts of animals. In 1908, Apollinaire published in a journal eighteen poems under the title "La Marchande des quatre saisons ou le bestiaire moderne" (the costermonger or the modern bestiary). When he prepared the final edition in 1911, with woodcuts by Raoul Dufy, he added twelve poems and replaced the merchant with Orpheus. According to mythology, Orpheus attracted wild beasts by playing on the lyre he had received from Mercury. He is the symbol of Gnosis and Neoplatonic Humanism and is also identified with Christ and poetry, in a mixture of mystical and sensual imagery.

Apollinaire himself wrote the notes to the volume and uses as its sign a δ (the Greek letter delta) pierced by a unicorn. He interprets it to mean the delta of the Nile and all the legendary and biblical symbols of ancient Egypt, also suggesting a *D* for Deplanche, the publisher, in addition to the obvious sexual symbolism. He added the motto "J'émerveille" ("I marvel"), thus giving a fantastic aura to the work. Roger Little sees in the volume a "delicious and malicious" wit, with metamorphoses, syncretism, pride in poetry, carnal love, and mysticism. Like all Apollinaire's early works, it is full of self-analysis. In "La Souris" ("The Mouse"), the poet speaks of his twenty-eight years as "mal-vécus" ("poorly spent").

The animals represent human foibles; the peacock, for example, displays both his best and, unbeknownst to him, his worst. They also speak of love: the serpent, the Sirens, the dove, and Orpheus himself. They point to God and things divine: the dove, the bull, or, again,

Orpheus. They speak of poetry: the horse, the tortoise, the elephant, and the caterpillar. For Apollinaire, poetry is a divine gift. He concludes his notes by observing that poets seek nothing but perfection, which is God himself. Poets, he says, have the right to expect after death the full knowledge of God, which is sublime beauty.

ALCOOLS

The most analyzed and the best known of Apollinaire's works is *Alcools*, a slender volume published in 1913 with the subtitle *Poèmes, 1898-1913*. A portrait of Apollinaire, an etching by Picasso, serves as the frontispiece. Apollinaire chose fifty-five of the many poems he had written from his eighteenth to his thirty-third year and assembled them in an order that has continued to fascinate and baffle critics. Michel Décaudin says that the order in *Alcools* is based entirely on the aesthetic and sentimental affinities felt by the author, or their discrete dissonances. Very few poems have dates, other than "Rhénanes" (September, 1901, to May, 1902) and "At the Santé" (September, 1911); nevertheless, critics have succeeded in dating many, though not all, of the poems.

The poems have several centers, though not all of those from one group appear together. More than twenty were inspired by Apollinaire's trip to the Rhineland in 1901, including the nine in the cycle "Rhénanes." Several of these poems and some others, such as "The Song of the Poorly Loved," "Annie," and "The Emigrant from Landor Road," refer to his unhappy love affair with Playden. These poems and an interview with her as Mrs. Postings in 1951 by Robert Goffin and LeRoy Breunig are the only sources of information about this significant period in Apollinaire's life. Three poems, "Mirabeau Bridge," "Marie," and "Cors de chasse" ("Hunting Horns"), scattered throughout the volume, refer to Laurencin.

The poems exhibit great variety in form, tone, and subject matter. They range from the one-line "Chantre" to the seven-part "The Song of the Poorly Loved," the longest in the collection. Most of them have regular rhyme and rhythm, but "Zone" and "Vendémiaire," the first and the last, give evidence of technical experimentation. The poems range from witty ("The Synagogue") to nostalgic ("Autumn," "Hunting Horns") and from

...

enigmatic ("The Brazier") to irreverent ("The Thief"). Critics have arranged them in various ways. Bates, for example, sees the volume as a "Dionysian-Apollonian dance of life in three major symbols: fire, shadow, alcools."

Apollinaire chose the beginning and concluding poems of the collection, "Zone" and "Vendémiaire," with great care. "Zone" is overtly autobiographical in a Romantic-Symbolist ambience, yet its instant leaps in space and time make it very modern. Also modern is the image of the city, where Apollinaire can see beauty in a poster, a traffic jam, and a group of frightened Jewish immigrants. The city is also the central focus in the concluding poem, "Vendémiaire" (the name given the month of vintage, September 22-October 21, in the revolutionary calendar), a hymn to the glory of Paris. The poet exuberantly proclaims his immortality and omnipresence: "I am drunk from having swallowed all the universe." Bates sees the end of the poem as a hymn to joy reminiscent of Walt Whitman and Friedrich Nietzsche.

The bizarre juxtapositions, the inner borrowings of lines from one poem to the next, and the absence of punctuation provoked various responses from critics. Cubists hailed Apollinaire as a great poet. Georges Duhamel, writing in the June 15, 1913, issue of *Mercure de France*, called the volume a junk shop. Critics such as Adéma, Décaudin, and Marie-Jeanne Durry analyze *Alcools* with depth and scholarship. They discover many platitudes and much mediocrity but find it redeemed by what Steegmuller identifies as a spirit of freedom.

CALLIGRAMMES

Intended as a sequel to *Alcools*, *Calligrammes* is much more unified than *Alcools*, yet its importance was seen only much later. It consists of six parts. The first part, "Waves," is the most innovative and was written before World War I in the frenzied stimulation of artistic activity in Paris. The other five contain poems inspired by the war and by the poet's love for Lou, Madeleine, and—in the final poem—his future wife, Jacqueline.

Philippe Renaud sees the difference between *Alcools* and "Waves" as one of nature rather than degree. Even the most enigmatic poems of *Alcools* follow a familiar

plan, he maintains, whereas in "Waves" the reader is in unfamiliar territory, disoriented in space and time. In "Waves" one feels both the insecurity and the indefiniteness that can only be called modern art. The introductory poem, "Chains," uses the elements recommended by Apollinaire in "The New Spirit and the Poets" yet remains anchored in the past. It leaps from the Tower of Babel to telegraph wires in disconcerting juxtapositions, speaking of humankind's eternal, frustrating quest for unity. In "The Windows," the window opens like an orange on Paris or in the tropics and flies on a rainbow across space and time.

Beginning with "Waves" and throughout *Calligrammes*, Apollinaire uses what he calls ideograms, or picture poems. They are the most attractive pieces in the book, though not necessarily the most original. They became excellent vehicles for the war poems, where brevity and wit are essential. The theme of war dominates the majority of poems in *Calligrammes*. The war excited Apollinaire, promising a new universe. He experienced exhilaration as he saw shells exploding, comparing them in the poem "Merveilles de la guerre" ("Wonders of War") to constellations, women's hair, dancers, and women in childbirth. He saw himself as the poet-hero, the omnipresent seer, the animator of the universe. In "La Tête étoilée" ("The Starry Head"), his wound was a crown of stars on his head.

Apollinaire was as dependent on love as he was on air, and he suffered greatly in the solitary trenches of France. His brief romance with Lou was intense and violent, as his pun on her name in "C'est Lou qu'on la nommait" ("They Called Her Lou") indicates; instead of "Lou," the word *loup* (which sounds the same in French but means "wolf") is used throughout the poem. In his poems to Madeleine, he devours images like a starving man. The anthology ends serenely as he addresses Jacqueline, "la jolie rousse," the woman destined to be his wife, as poetry was destined to be his life. This final poem is also his poetic testament, in which he bequeaths "vast and unknown kingdoms, new fires and the mystery of flowers to anyone willing to pick them."

OTHER MAJOR WORKS

LONG FICTION: *L'Enchanteur pourrissant*, 1909; *Le Poète assassiné*, 1916 (*The Poet Assassinated*, 1923).

SHORT FICTION: *L'Hérésiarque et Cie.*, 1910 (*The Heresiarch and Co.*, 1965).

PLAYS: *Les Mamelles de Tirésias*, pr. 1917 (*The Breasts of Tiresias*, 1961); *Couleur du temps*, pr. 1918; *Casanova*, pb. 1952.

NONFICTION: *Peintres cubistes: Méditations esthétiques*, 1913 (*The Cubist Painters: Aesthetic Meditations*, 1944); *Chroniques d'art, 1902-1918*, 1960 (*Apollinaire on Art: Essays and Reviews, 1902-1918*, 1972).

MISCELLANEOUS: *Œuvres complètes*, 1966 (8 volumes); *Œuvres en prose*, 1977 (Michel Décaudin, editor).

BIBLIOGRAPHY

Adéma, Marcel. *Apollinaire*. Translated by Denise Folliot. New York: Grove Press, 1955. This is the prime source of biographical material, the bible of scholars researching the poet and his epoch.

Bates, Scott. *Guillaume Apollinaire*. Rev. ed. Boston: Twayne, 1989. This book offers detailed erudite analyses of Apollinaire's major works and informed judgments on his place in French literature and in the development of art criticism. It emphasizes the importance to the entire world of Apollinaire's vision of a cultural millennium propelled by science and democracy and implemented by poetry. Included are a chronology, a twenty-six-page glossary of references, notes, and selected bibliographies of both primary and secondary sources.

Bohn, Willard. *The Aesthetics of Visual Poetry: 1914-1928*. New York: Cambridge University Press, 1986. Chapter 3, "Apollinaire's Plastic Imagination," reveals the lyric innovations that Apollinaire brought to visual poetry with *Calligrammes*: new forms, new content, multiple figures in a unified composition, a dual sign system used to express a simultaneity, and a difficulty of reading that mirrors the act of creation. Chapter 4, "Toward a Calligrammar," offers a sophisticated structural and statistical analysis of the calligrammes to demonstrate metonymy as the principal force binding the visual tropes, whereas metaphor and metonymy occur evenly in the verbal arena.

_____. *Apollinaire and the Faceless Man: The Creation and Evolution of a Modern Motif*. Rutherford, N.J.: Fairleigh Dickinson University Press, 1991. Traces the history of Apollinaire's faceless man motif as a symbol of the human condition, from its roots in the poem "Le Musicien de Saint-Mercy" to its dissemination to the arts community through the unproduced pantomime "A quelle heure un train partira-t-il pour Paris?"

_____. *Apollinaire and the International Avant-Garde*. Albany: State University of New York Press, 1997. Chronicles the early artistic and critical reception of Apollinaire in Europe, North America, and Latin America. Especially interesting is the discussion of Argentina, exported through the Ultraism of Jorge Luis Borges, and Apollinaire's place in the revolutionary circles of Mexico.

Cornelius, Nathalie Goodisman. *A Semiotic Analysis of Guillaume Apollinaire's Mythology in "Alcools."* New York: Peter Lang, 1995. Examines Apollinaire's use of linguistic and mythological fragmentation and reordering to mold his material into an entirely new system of signs that both encompasses and surpasses the old. Chapters give close semiotic readings of four poems: "Claire de lune," "Le Brasier," "Nuit rhëane," and "Vendémaine."

Couffignal, Robert. *Apollinaire*. Translated by Eda Mezer Levitine. Tuscaloosa: University of Alabama Press, 1975. This is a searching analysis of some of Apollinaire's best-known works, including "Zone," strictly from the Roman Catholic point of view. It traces his attitude toward religion from his childhood to his death. The book contains a chronology; translations of ten texts, both poems and prose, with the author's comments; a bibliographical note; and an index.

Matthews, Timothy. *Reading Apollinaire: Theories of Poetic Language*. New York: Manchester University Press, 1987. Uses a variety of historical, biographical, and stylistic approaches to offer an accessible point of entry into often difficult texts. Matthews's detailed discussion of *Alcools* focuses heavily on "L'Adieu" and "Automne malade," which allows for a reading that may be transferred to the rest of the book. His chapter "Poetry, Painting, and Theory" offers a solid historical background that leads directly into his examination of *Calligrammes*.

Shattuck, Roger. *The Banquet Years*. Rev. ed. New York: Vintage Books, 1968. In the two long chapters devoted to Apollinaire, "The Impresario of the Avant-garde" and "Painter-Poet," the author gives a year-by-year and at times even a month-by-month account of his life, loves, friends, employment, writings, and speeches. The tone is judicial, the critical judgments fair and balanced. Includes a bibliography and an index.

Steegmuller, Francis. *Apollinaire: Poet Among the Painters*. New York: Farrar, Straus, 1963. This is an exhaustive, extremely well-documented, unbiased, and highly readable biography. Contains a preface, translations, numerous photographs and illustrations, two appendixes, notes, and an index.

Irma M. Kashuba
Updated by David Harrison Horton

APOLLONIUS RHODIUS

Born: Alexandria or Naucratis, Egypt; between 295 and 260 B.C.E.
Died: Alexandria, Egypt; late third century B.C.E.
Also known as: Apollonius of Rhodes; Apollonii Rhodii

PRINCIPAL POETRY

Argonautica, third century B.C.E. (English translation, 1780)
Ktiseis, third century B.C.E.

OTHER LITERARY FORMS

Apollonius Rhodius (ahp-uh-LOH-nee-uhs ROH-dee-uhs) is credited with several works besides the *Argonautica*. A collection of epigrams passed under his name, but only one has survived. Besides these, he seems to have written a poem or group of poems called *Ktiseis*, dealing with the founding of the cities of Alexandria, Naucratis, Cnidos, Rhodes, and Caunus; in this work, Apollonius might well have been poaching on

Callimachus's preserve, since he wrote something similar. Apollonius also wrote philological works in prose, including *Against Zenodotos* (third century B.C.E.). A variety of other works are attributed to Apollonius, but it was not necessarily this Apollonius who wrote them, since the name was a common one.

ACHIEVEMENTS

Apollonius Rhodius's principal work, the *Argonautica*, which has survived in revised form, is a deliberate challenge to Callimachus's fundamental literary principle that poems should be short, for it fills four lengthy books with its 5,834 hexameter lines. It is a book of excellent stories told in good verse rather than a regular and unified epic poem, and its merit lies in its episodes, notably in the admirable recounting of the loves of Jason and Medea, which fills the third book and part of the fourth.

BIOGRAPHY

The birth of Apollonius Rhodius is placed by scholars at various times between 295 and 260 B.C.E., and the year of his death is equally uncertain. In fact, very little information about his life is available. There are two "lives" of Apollonius, both derived from an earlier biography that has been lost. In these accounts, Apollonius was the son of one Silleus (or Illeus) and was born either at Alexandria or Naucratis. Possibly, as has been suggested, he was born at Naucratis and reared in Alexandria.

Apollonius lived during the reign of the Ptolemies and apparently was a pupil of Callimachus, the literary dictator of the time, an author of frigid, learned poems and a few highly polished epigrams and the originator of the terse and generally true dictum that a big book is a big nuisance. Apollonius's opinions on the subject of lengthy poems were diametrically opposed to those of Callimachus and, hence, heretical. At a youthful age, the student-poet produced a long poem on the Argonautic expedition. It was a complete failure, and in his shame and distress, Apollonius left Alexandria and settled in Rhodes. There he revised and polished, and perhaps completed, his work. The Rhodians gave his book a far more favorable reception. He was given Rhodian citizenship, hence the surname Rhodius, and was held in high esteem. Years later, after the death of Callimachus, Apollonius returned to Alexandria to a better reception; indeed, one biographer reports that he followed Callimachus as head librarian there. He died in the late third century B.C.E. and was buried near his old foe.

This traditional account of the life of Apollonius has been questioned by modern scholarship. Callimachus may never have been head librarian at Alexandria or even the teacher of Apollonius. Indeed, Apollonius and Callimachus may have been near contemporaries and thus more likely to be literary opponents. Some scholars, for chronological reasons, deny the librarianship of Apollonius, but it is clearly asserted by his biographer, Suidas, and the arguments against it are not conclusive.

In spite of these uncertainties, it seems clear that Apollonius's quarrel with Callimachus was a crucial event in his life. This quarrel apparently arose from differences of literary aims and taste but degenerated into the bitterest sort of personal strife. There are references to the quarrel in the writings of both. Callimachus attacks Apollonius in a passage at the end of his *Hymn to Apollo* (third century B.C.E.), but he attacks Apollonius most vociferously in the *Ibis* (third century B.C.E.), which Ovid imitated or perhaps translated in his poem of the same name. On the part of Apollonius, there is a passage in the third book of the *Argonautica* that is of a polemical nature and that stands out from the context, as well as a savage epigram attacking Callimachus. There are not enough data to determine the chronological order of the attacks and counterattacks. The *Ibis* has been thought to mark the termination of the feud on the curious ground that it was impossible for the abuse to go further.

ANALYSIS

The chief characteristics of Alexandrianism, of which Callimachus was the leading proponent, were refinement in diction, precision of form and meter, erudition that often degenerated into pedantry and obscurity, and avoidance of the commonplace in subject, sentiment, and allusion. Apollonius Rhodius shares some of these traits, and he seems to have written the *Argonautica* out of bravado, to show that he could indeed write an epic poem. The influence of the age, how-

ever, was too strong. Instead of a unified epic, there is merely a series of episodes. In the four books of his *Argonautica*, Apollonius tells of the quest for the Golden Fleece and especially of Jason and Medea. The same story was known to Homer and certainly belonged in the repertory of old epic. It provided a splendid source of thrilling adventures and opportunities for excursions into the unknown, a literary device that varied the more straightforward episodes of epic. It demanded, however, a heroic sense of human worth and of perilous action, and this was precisely what Apollonius lacked. His Jason is the faintest of phantoms; he could hardly be otherwise, inasmuch as Apollonius lived in the metropolitan society of Alexandria and had little idea of how to depict a hero. There were other defects as well. Apollonius never forgot that he was an antiquarian and therefore he liberally garnished his poem with tidbits of erudite information. This is deadly not only to the flow of the narrative but also to the actual poetry. The delight in learning for its own sake was an especially Alexandrian characteristic. Literary allusions seeped into Alexandrian poetry without poets noticing how cumbersome and distracting they were. Apollonius must have thought such allusions gave richness and dignity to his story, but ultimately, they make it tedious and pedantic.

ARGONAUTICA

Not until the Hellenistic age and Apollonius's *Argonautica* was there a complete epic presentation of the Thessalian or Argonautic cycle of legends, among the oldest in Greek mythology. Poetry in all its forms had time and again turned to the legend of the Argonauts and the local history of the many places connected with it. Thus, Apollonius was faced with a rich tradition with many partly contradictory variants.

Apollonius's composition exhibits a systematic arrangement of the subject matter. The first two books describe the voyage to the land of Colchis, the third relates the adventures leading to the winning of the Golden Fleece, while the fourth tells of the dangers of the flight and the return home. The stress on details, however, is variously distributed; there are rapid transitions, but there are also passages over which Apollonius had lingered lovingly, typical of the rejection of symmetry and the tendency to variety found elsewhere in Alexandrian poetry.

BOOK 1

Although a proem with prayer formula is merely indicated at the beginning of book 1 and much of the preceding history is saved for later, the introductory passage offers an elaborate catalog of the Argonauts, geographically arranged in the manner of a circumnavigation and leading from the north of Greece to the east and west and then back to the north. The catalog tradition of ancient epic served as its model. The scenes of departure in Iolcus and on the beach at Pagasae are spun out in detail. Then follows the long series of stopping places and adventures on the way out, along the usual route to Colchis. For the voyage up to the treacherous passage through the Symplegades, which are thought to be at the entrance to the Pontus, the tradition had a number of effective, ready-made episodes on which Apollonius elaborated successfully. First is the landing in Lemnos, where the women, under a curse of Aphrodite, have killed their husbands. Now, however, they are glad to entertain the Argonauts. The result is a delectable sojourn from which Heracles has to call his companions to action. That is followed by the initiation into the mysteries at Samothrace and the adventures in Cyzicus. Here the Argonauts give the Doliones effective help against evil giants only to become involved, through a misunderstanding, in a bitterly regretted nocturnal battle with their friends.

The next stop on the coast of Propontis provides the setting for the Hylas episode. When Apollonius tells how the beautiful youth Hylas is dragged down into a pool by a nymph who has fallen in love with him, he does it very well, since his dramatic economy avoids any kind of false pathos, and the reader witnesses the nymph's ruthless determination as she puts her arms around the boy who is stooping to get water. Heracles seeks Hylas in the woods, and the Argonauts continue their voyage without him, since the sea-god Glaucus announces that the hero is destined to perform other deeds. This device eliminates from the narrative the greatest of the champions, beside whom the heroic Jason would pale by comparison.

BOOK 2

The story continues without a stop from book 1 to book 2, which begins with Pollux's boxing match with Amycus, a barbarian king. In Bithynia, the Argonauts come upon the blind king Phineus, who, in deep misery, is doing penance for some ancient offense. The winged sons of Boreas liberate him from the Harpies, the predatory storm spirits who rob him of every meal or defile it. As a reward, Phineus gives the Argonauts good advice for the rest of their voyage. The compositional significance of this preview is that it sums up the various minor episodes of the second half of the voyage. The passage through the Symplegades after a pigeon's test flight is depicted with dramatic power. Thereafter, the only sojourn worthy of mention is that on the island of Ares. There the Argonauts drive out the Stymphalian birds, and there they meet the sons of Phrixus. Their mother is Chalciope, Aeetes' daughter and the sister of Medea. Medea will play a significant role in the events in Colchis; thus, the meeting in the island of Ares provides a dramatic link between the description of the voyage and the winning of the Golden Fleece.

BOOK 3

Book 3 starts with a new proem and portrays the events in Colchis by means of a technique that often resolves the action into parallel strands. Medea's decisive intervention is first motivated in a scene in which the goddesses Hera and Athena enjoin Aphrodite to have Eros do his work. Independent from this motivation, however, Medea's awakening love, her hard struggle between loyalty to her father's house and passion for the handsome stranger, is presented as a drama full of tension with the girl's soul as the stage. Apollonius is at his best when he writes of love. What engages all his powers is not Jason's love for Medea (on which he leaves the reader uninstructed) but Medea's love for Jason, and it is this which makes book 3 of the *Argonautica* shine more brightly than the other three. Medea is still a girl, and she falls passionately in love at first sight. When she first sees Jason, he seems to her like Sirius rising from the ocean, and Apollonius, not without echoes of Sappho, describes how a mist covers Medea's eyes, her cheeks burn like fire, her knees are too weak to move, and she feels rooted to the earth. When, a little later, Medea helps him in his ordeals to win the Fleece, the light playing on his yellow hair makes her willing to tear the life out of her breast for him, and her heart melts like dew on roses in the morning. When their love is fulfilled, Medea is entirely absorbed in him, but when he plans to return to Greece and in his callous indifference is ready to leave her behind, the fierce side of her nature emerges, and she bursts into bitter remonstrances, chiding him for his ingratitude. If he really intends to desert her, she invokes disaster and vengeance on him and prays that the Furies will make him homeless. In this part of his poem, Apollonius tells one of the first surviving love stories in the world.

Alongside this love story runs a subplot concerning Chalciope, which leads to her intervention and to the decisive talk between the two sisters, Chalciope and Medea. The composition of book 3 is particularly careful. Developing in several stages, it progresses to the meeting of Medea and Jason, when he receives the magic ointment.

BOOK 4

Book 4, which begins with a brief invocation to the Muse, presents Apollonius with his most exciting challenge, to which he rises admirably. After receiving the magic ointment from Medea, Jason must yoke fire-breathing bulls, sow dragon's teeth, and destroy the armed men who spring out of them. Jason falls on the men like a shooting star, and the furrows are as filled with blood as runnels are with water. Apollonius presents the weird scene very vividly, capturing even the brilliant light shining from the armor and weapons. This struggle bears no resemblance to a Homeric battle, but, in its unearthly strangeness, is convincing and complete. Apollonius glories in strangeness for its own sake, and it is this quality that makes him a pioneer of the kind of poetry that deals with remote and unfamiliar themes. The rest of book 4 describes the homeward voyage, two high points being the murder of Absyrtus, who has gone in pursuit of his sister Medea, and the marriage of Jason and Medea in the land of the Phaeacians. One of the most enchanting aspects of mythic geography is the way the return of the Argonauts was modified as the knowledge of foreign countries and seas increased, newly discovered facts and ancient mythic elements forming various and often grotesque combinations. After a series of less-than-dangerous adventures, the Argonauts return to Colchis.

Apollonius's epic has numerous qualities that depend largely on the literary and historical background of the work. Some readers find it pedantic, unpoetic, or dry, while others—and especially in recent times—are able to appreciate the truly poetical qualities of the *Argonautica*. In the first place, it should be clearly understood that the intellectual world in which this epic originated was separated from that of Homer by an immeasurable distance. When older poets molded the history of the heroic past for their people, they claimed that their verses imbued true events with splendor and permanence. In these events, the gods were active everywhere; they were great spirits, inspiring faith and helpfully allying themselves with or wrathfully striking out at humankind. By Apollonius's time, the living belief had become mythology or was proceeding toward this condition. Hardly anything can be said about Apollonius's personal religious feelings, but his attitude to tradition cannot have been very different from that of Callimachus. Apollonius's *stylos* was guided both by an erudite interest in mythical tradition and by a delight in the unfading beauty of its creations. Both can be discerned in his verse.

COMPARISONS TO HOMER

The tremendous distance from Homer's world is in exciting contrast with the fact that numerous and essential elements of ancient epic remain preserved. In Apollonius, the gods also act, but the very nature of the great Olympian scene at the opening of book 3 reveals the ornamental character of such passages. With Hera, Athena, and Eros, a complete divine apparatus is developed, but Medea's love and its consequences are completely imaginable without it. Also, in the portrayal of the girl's emotional struggles, the poet can be recognized much more directly than in the conversations of the Olympians. Although in Homer, humankind's actions are determined simultaneously by its own impulses and by the influence of the gods, in Apollonius this duality of motivation has resulted in separate spheres of action. The divine plot takes place on an upper stage; its connection with earthly happenings is neither indissoluble nor irrevocably necessary.

Apollonius retains important formal elements of Homeric epic. Although he is sparing with metaphors, he uses similes with great frequency. Their free, Homeric spontaneity has been restricted in Apollonius in favor of a more direct bearing on the action, although the subject matter has been expanded in many directions. Illustrations of emotions by means of similes, found in the verse of Homer in rudimentary form, have been developed by Apollonius with great skill. Thus Medea's agitation and irresolution are elucidated by the image of the sun's ray, which is reflected onto a wall by the ruffled surface of water. Apollonius also uses stock scenes, but he keeps recurrent formulas to a minimum. This is connected with another, fundamentally important observation. Apollonius's language is largely based on that of Homer. This does not mean that Apollonius accepted the tradition without due reflection or that he imitated it naïvely. Rather, the linguistic resources he borrowed are given new effectiveness through constant, well-planned variation, sometimes even by means of a shifting of the meaning.

The Homeric legacy, which functions as a sort of framework for the *Argonautica* with regard to themes and style, contrasts with the poem's Alexandrian element. Apollonius is a realist, although the term is to be taken in its broadest sense. In the final analysis, this realism is connected with the altered attitude toward myths, with the awareness of their illusory nature. Apollonius may be granted poetic ability, and there may be much that is praiseworthy in his work, but he was not truly a poet filled with the Muse; time and again, the reader is struck by the cool objectivity with which he describes legendary events. This also explains the great care he takes with motivation and establishment of cohesion.

HELLENIST INFLUENCES

The poet frequently accounts for contemporary customs by seeking explanations in early history, and in this way he links his own time with the mythical past. A true Hellenist, Apollonius devoted much of his poem to etiological matters, interspersing the narrative of the voyage with a wealth of such stories.

As a portrayer of emotions, especially of those which Eros brings to the human soul, Apollonius belongs entirely within the sphere of Hellenistic poetry. It has already been pointed out that his highest achievement was his description of Medea's pangs and doubts. After the long-winded description of the outward voyage, which at times sinks to the level of a learned guide-

book, the realm of true poetry is entered. This is confirmed by the tremendous subsequent influence of book 3 in ancient literature. The characterization of Medea recalls Apollonius's predecessor Euripides in that the effective portrayal of individual emotion is more important than a finished portrait of a character. Medea the lovesick girl and Medea the great sorceress could not be readily combined in one description.

There is also an Alexandrian element in the many descriptions of nature that, in the traditional epic, would be unthinkable. Successful color effects are achieved in descriptions of seascapes, as in the sailing of the Argo when the dark flood foams under the beat of the oars, the men's armor flashes like fire in the morning light, and the long wake seems like a bright path in a green meadow. Apollonius also shares with the rest of Hellenistic art the discovery of children. The Eros of the celestial scenes of book 3, who in his day was a formidable god, has here been reduced to an ill-mannered boy. He is the epitome of the spoiled rascal who cheats his comrades at play and can be persuaded by his mother Aphrodite to perform a service only by means of an expensive present.

Apollonius cannot be characterized concisely. He proved himself to be a poet of considerable importance in several passages, but he was not completely successful in blending the rich epic tradition with his own creation. His fire was too weak to fuse all the heterogeneous elements into one whole.

OTHER MAJOR WORK

NONFICTION: *Against Zenodotos*, third century B.C.E.

BIBLIOGRAPHY

Albis, Robert V. *Poet and Audience in the "Argonautica" of Apollonius*. Lanham, Md.: Rowman and Littlefield, 1996. This short study of the poet's major work concentrates on the rhetorical position of the poet relative to his audience, with significant attention paid to poetic performance as a point of scholarly inquiry. In addition, Albis examines the figure of the poet and the inscribed audience in the poem.

Beye, Charles Rowan. *Ancient Epic Poetry: Homer, Apollonius, Virgil*. Ithaca, N.Y.: Cornell University

Press, 1993. The section on Apollonius examines his relationship to his literary patrons, including the Greek scholar Callimachus, and to the cultural milieu of ancient Alexandria. The study offers a significantly original interpretation of the *Argonautica* and counters ancient critical theories characterizing Apollonius's major work as both derivative and flawed.

Clauss, James Joseph. *The Best of the Argonauts: The Redefinition of the Epic Hero in Book One of Apollonius' "Argonautica."* Berkeley: University of California Press, 1993. This study presents the argument that Apollonius's major poem demonstrates a shift in the popular definition of heroism in ancient Greece, away from the notion of the protagonist as an autonomous superhero and toward later concepts of the protagonist as a tool of fate.

Harder, Annette, and Martijn Cuypers, eds. *Beginning from Apollo: Studies in Apollonius Rhodius and the Argonautic Tradition.* Dudley, Mass.: Peeters, 2005. This collection of papers from a colloquium in the Netherlands sheds light on Apollonius Rhodius's poetic works and the Argonautic tradition.

Hunter, Richard. *The "Argonautica" of Apollonius: Literary Studies.* New York: Cambridge University Press, 2004. Hunter places the *Argonautica* within its social and intellectual context. Topics include notions of heroism, eros and the suffering of Medea, the role of the divine, and the Ptolemaic context of the poem.

Hutchinson, G. O. *Hellenistic Poetry.* New York: Clarendon Press, 1988. This study adopts a necessarily broader view to position each of its subjects within the main currents of ancient Greek literature and culture and its impact on later Roman writers. The discussion of Apollonius Rhodius is fairly general.

Papanghelis, Theodore, and Antonios Renggkos. *Brill's Companion to Apollonius Rhodius.* 2d ed. Boston: Brill, 2008. An anthology of scholarly articles borrowing heavily from various literary theories, this work examines subjects such as Hellenistic poetry and genres such as epic poetry and includes character studies of Jason and Medea.

Shelley P. Haley
Updated by Michael R. Meyers

LOUIS ARAGON

Born: Paris, France; October 3, 1897
Died: Paris, France; December 24, 1982

PRINCIPAL POETRY

Feu de joie, 1920
Le Mouvement perpétuel, 1925
La Grande Gaîté, 1929
Persécuté persécuteur, 1931
Hourra l'Oural, 1934
Le Crève-coeur, 1941
Brocéliande, 1942
Les Yeux d'Elsa, 1942
En Français dans le texte, 1943
Le Musée grévin, 1943
La Diane française, 1945
Le Nouveau Crève-coeur, 1948
Les Yeux et la mémoire, 1954
Le Roman inachevé, 1956
Elsa, 1959
Les Poètes, 1960
Le Fou d'Elsa, 1963
Les Chambres, 1969
Aux abords de Rome, 1981
Les Adieux, et autres poèmes, 1982

OTHER LITERARY FORMS

Louis Aragon (ah-rah-GAWN) was one of the most prolific French authors of the twentieth century, and although lyric poetry was his first medium, to which he always returned as to a first love, he also produced many novels and volumes of essays. As a young man, he participated in the Surrealist movement, and his works of this period defy classification. In addition to the exercises known as automatic writing, which had a considerable impact on his mature style in both prose and poetry, he wrote a number of Surrealist narratives combining elements of the novel (such as description and dialogue) and the essay. The most important of these, *Le Paysan de Paris* (1926; *Nightwalker*, 1970), is a long meditation on the author's ramblings in his native city and on the "modern sense of the mythic" inspired by its streets, shops, and parks.

In the 1930's, after his espousal of the Communist cause, Aragon began a series of novels under the general title of *Le Monde réel* (1934-1944), which follow the tenets of Socialist Realism. These are historical novels dealing with the corruption of bourgeois society and the rise of Communism. His later novels, however, beginning with *La Semaine sainte* (1958; *Holy Week*, 1961), show greater freedom of form and lack the explicit "message" characteristic of Socialist Realism; these later works incorporate an ongoing meditation on the novel as a literary form and on its relation to history and biography.

An important characteristic of Aragon's style that cuts across all his works of fiction and poetry is the use of spoken language as a model: His sentences reproduce the rhythms of speech, full of parentheses, syntactic breaks, and interjections, and his diction, especially in prose, is heavily interlarded with slang. This trait is true to some extent even of his essays, although the latter tend to be more formal to both diction and rhetorical strategy. His nonfiction works are voluminous, for he was an active journalist for much of his life, producing reviews and essays on politics, literature, and the visual arts for a variety of Surrealist and then Communist publications.

ACHIEVEMENTS

Like most writers who have taken strong political stands, Louis Aragon was, during the course of his lifetime, the object of much praise and blame that had little to do with the literary value of his work. This was especially true of his series of novels, *Le Monde réel*, which was hailed by his fellow Communists as a masterpiece and criticized by most non-Communist reviewers as contrived and doctrinaire. He was, with André Breton, one of the leaders of the Surrealist movement; his poetry after the mid-1940's combined elements of Romanticism and modernism, but his style evolved in a direction of its own and cannot be identified with that of any one school.

After his Surrealist period, during which he wrote for an intellectual elite, Aragon sought to make his work accessible to a wider public and often succeeded. The height of his popularity was achieved in the 1940's, when his poems played an important role in the French Resistance: written in traditional meters and using rhyme, so that they might more easily be sung, they became rallying cries for French patriots abroad and in occupied France. (Many of Aragon's poems have, in fact, been set to music by writers of popular songs, including Léo Ferré and George Brassens.) Beginning in the late 1950's, Aragon's work became much less overtly political, which contributed to its acceptance by non-Communist critics. At the time of his death in 1982, Aragon was considered even by his political opponents as a leading man of letters. Writers of lesser stature have been elected to the French Academy, but Aragon never applied for membership, and it is hard to imagine such an ardent advocate of commoners, who used slang liberally in his own work, sitting in judgment on the purity of the French language.

For Aragon, who wrote his first "novel" at age six (and dictated a play to his aunt before he could write), writing was like breathing, a vital activity coextensive with living. He was a novelist whose eye (and ear) for telling detail never dulled, a poet whose lyric gifts did not diminish with age.

BIOGRAPHY

Until late in life, Louis Aragon was reticent about his childhood, and many biographical notices erroneously describe it as idyllic; in fact, his family (which consisted of his grandmother, mother, and two aunts) was obsessed with a concern for appearances that caused the boy considerable pain. The illegitimate son of a prominent political figure, Louis Andrieux, who chose the name Aragon for his son and acted as his legal guardian, Aragon was reared as his mother's younger brother, and although as a boy he guessed much of the truth, it was not until his twentieth year that he heard it from his mother (at the insistence of his father, who had previously insisted on her silence). Since his maternal grandfather had also deserted the family, his mother, Marguérite Toucas-Masillon, supported them all as best she could by painting china and running a boardinghouse. According to his biographer, Pierre Daix, the circumstances of Aragon's childhood left him with an instinctive sympathy for outsiders, especially women, and a great longing to be accepted as a full member of a group. This longing was first satisfied by his friendship with André Breton and later by Aragon's adherence to the Communist Party. (Indeed, his deep need to "belong" may help to account for his unswerving loyalty to the party throughout the Stalinist era.)

Breton, whom he met in 1917, introduced Aragon to the circle of poets and artists that was to form the nucleus of the Dadaist and Surrealist movements. Horrified by the carnage of World War I (which Aragon had observed firsthand as a medic), these young people at first embraced the negative impulse of Dada, an absurdist movement founded in Zurich by Tristan Tzara. Their aim was to unmask the moral bankruptcy of the society that had tolerated such a war. Realizing that a philosophy of simple negation was ultimately sterile, Breton and Aragon broke away from the Dadaists and began to pursue the interest in the subconscious, which led them to Surrealism. Through the technique of automatic writing, they tried to suppress the rational faculty, or "censor," which inhibited free expression of subconscious impulses.

Politically, the Surrealists were anarchists, but as they became increasingly convinced that profound social changes were necessary to free the imagination, a number of them, including Aragon, joined the French Communist Party. At about the same time (1928), Aragon met the Russian poet Vladimir Mayakovsky and his sister-in-law, the novelist Elsa Triolet, at the Coupole, a Paris café. As Aragon put it, describing his meeting with Elsa many years later, "We have been together ever since" (literally, "We have not left each other's side"). In Elsa, Aragon found the "woman of the future," who could be her husband's intellectual and social equal while sharing with him a love in which all the couple's aspirations were anchored. Aragon celebrated this love in countless poems spanning forty years; some of the most ecstatic were written when the two were in their sixties. Elsa introduced Aragon to Soviet Russia, which they visited together in the early 1930's; she also took part with him in the French Resistance during World War II, publishing clandestine newspapers and maintaining a network of antifascist intellectuals. Although he followed the "party line" and tried to rationalize the Soviet pact with the Nazis, Aragon was an ardent French patriot; he was decorated for bravery in both world wars and wrote hymns of

Louis Aragon (Library of Congress)

praise to the French "man (and woman) in the street," who became the heroes of the Resistance.

After the war, Aragon redoubled his activities on behalf of the Communist Party, serving as editor of the Communist newspaper *Ce Soir* and completing his six-volume novel *Les Communistes* (1949-1951). In 1954, he became a permanent member of the Central Committee of the French Communist Party, and in 1957, the Soviet Union awarded him its highest decoration, the Lenin Peace Prize. He was vilified by many of his fellow intellectuals in France for failing to criticize Stalin; not until 1966, during the much-publicized trial of two Soviet writers, Andrei Sinyavsky and Yuli Daniel, did he venture to speak out against the notion that there could be a "criminality of opinion." In 1968, he joined with the French Communist Party as a whole in condemning the Russian invasion of Czechoslovakia. Throughout his life, Aragon continued to produce a steady stream of poetry, fiction, and essays. His wife's death in 1970 was a terrible blow, but he survived it and went on to write several more books in the twelve years that were left to him.

ANALYSIS

Despite the length of Louis Aragon's poetic career and the perceptible evolution of his style in the course of six decades, there is a remarkable unity in the corpus of his poetry. This unity results from stylistic as well as thematic continuities, for even when he turned from free verse to more traditional metric forms, he managed to preserve the fluency of spoken language. In fact, his most highly structured verse has some of the qualities of stream-of-consciousness narrative. There are a variety of reasons for this. Aragon began to write as a very young boy and continued writing, steadily and copiously, throughout his life. As critic Hubert Juin has observed, Aragon never needed to keep a journal or diary because "his work itself was his journal," into which he poured his eager questions and reflections on what most closely concerned him.

This confessional impulse was reinforced and given direction in Aragon's Surrealist period by experiments with automatic writing, a technique adapted for literary use primarily by Breton and Philippe Soupault. By writing quickly without revising and by resisting the impulse to edit or censor the flow of words, the Surrealistis hoped to tap their subconscious minds and so to "save literature from rhetoric" (as Juin puts it). Literature was not all they hoped to save, moreover, for "rhetoric" had poisoned the social and political spheres as well; in liberating the subconscious, Aragon and his friends sought to break old and unjust patterns of thought and life. They also expected this powerful and hitherto untapped source to fuel the human imagination for the work of social renewal. Although Aragon repudiated the Surrealist attitude (which was basically anarchistic) when he embraced Communism as the pattern of the future, he never lost the stylistic freedom that automatic writing had fostered, nor did he become complacent about the "solution" he had found. Like his relationship with his wife, in which his hopes for the future were anchored, Aragon's Communism was a source of pain as well as of fulfillment: the deeper his love and commitment, the greater his vulnerability. Thus, poetry remained for him, as it had been in his youth, a form of questioning in which he explored the world and his relation to it.

There were, nevertheless, perceptible changes in Aragon's style during the course of his career. After the Dadaist and Surrealist periods, when he wrote mainly free verse (although there are metrically regular poems even in his early collections), Aragon turned to more traditional prosody—including rhyme—in the desire to make his verses singable. At the same time, he sought to renew and broaden the range of available rhymes by adopting new definitions of masculine and feminine rhyme based on pronunciation rather than on spelling. He also applied the notion of enjambment to rhyme, allowing not only the last syllable of a line but also the first letter or letters of the following line to count as constituent elements of a rhyme. Partly as a result of the conditions under which they were composed, Aragon's Resistance poems are for the most part short and self-contained, although *Le Musée grévin* (the wax museum) is a single long poem, and the pieces in *Brocéliande* are linked by allusions to the knights of the Arthurian cycle, whom Aragon saw as the symbolic counterparts of the Resistance fighters.

Aragon's postwar collections are more unified, and beginning with *Les Yeux et la mémoire* (eyes and memory), they might almost be described as book-length poems broken into short "chapters" of varying meters. Many of these "chapters," however, can stand alone as finished pieces; good examples are the love lyrics in *Le Fou d'Elsa* (Elsa's madman), some of which have been set to music, like the war poems, and the vignette from *Le Roman inachevé* (the unfinished romance) beginning "Marguerite, Madeleine, et Marie," which describes Aragon's mother and aunts—whom he thought of as his sisters—dressing for a dance. Within his longer sequences, Aragon skillfully uses shifts of meter to signal changes of mood and does not hesitate to lapse into prose when occasion warrants—for example, when, in *Le Roman inachevé*, he is suddenly overwhelmed by the weariness and pain of old age: "The verse breaks in my hands, my old hands, swollen and knotted with veins." Such disclaimers to the contrary, Aragon was never in greater control of his medium than in these poems of his old age, culminating in *Elsa, Le Fou d'Elsa*, and *Les Chambres* (the rooms). *Le Fou d'Elsa* is perhaps his greatest tour de force, a kind of epic (depicting the end of Muslim rule in Spain, with the fall of Granada in 1492) made up of hundreds of lyric pieces, along with some dialogue and prose commentary. As Juin has remarked, Aragon tends to alternate between two tones, the epic and the elegiac, and *Le Fou d'Elsa* is a perfect vehicle for both. The grand scale of the book gives full sweep to Aragon's epic vision of past and future regimes, while the inserted lyrics preserve the reduced scale proper to elegy.

To appreciate the texture of Aragon's poetry—his characteristic interweaving of image and theme, diction and syntax—it is necessary to examine a few of his poems in detail. Choosing one poem from each of the three distinct phases of his career (the Surrealist, Resistance, and postwar periods), all dealing with his central theme, the love of a woman, makes it possible to demonstrate both the continuities and the changes in his poetry during the greater part of his career. All three poems are in his elegiac vein, the mode easiest to examine at close range and the most fertile for Aragon. The occasional false notes in his verse tend to be struck when he assumes the triumphalist pose of the committed Marxist. When he speaks of his wife, his very excesses suggest a shattering sincerity, especially when the subject is separation, age, or death.

"POEM TO SHOUT IN THE RUINS"

"Poème à crier dans les ruines" ("Poem to Shout in the Ruins"), although addressed to a woman, is not addressed to Elsa, whom Aragon had yet to meet when it was written. The poem records the bitterness of an affair that has recently ended and from which the poet seems to have expected more than his lover did. Like most of Aragon's work, the poem is heavily autobiographical; the woman involved was American heir Nancy Cunard, with whom Aragon had lived for about a year, and the allusions to travel throughout the poem recall trips the couple had taken together. Although the poem opens with a passage that might be described as expository, and although it moves from particular details to a general observation and closes with a sort of reprise, it strikes the reader as more loosely organized than it actually is. This impression results from its rhythm being that of association—the train of thought created when a person dwells on a single topic for a sustained period of time. Because the topic is unhappy love and the bitterness of rejection, the process of association takes on an obsessive quality, and although

the resulting monologue is ostensibly addressed to the lover, the title suggests that neither she nor anyone else is expected to respond. The overall effect, then, is that of an interior monologue, and its power stems not from any cogency of argument (the "rhetoric" rejected by the Surrealists) but from the cumulative effects of obsessive repetition. Thus, the speaker's memories are evoked in a kind of litany ("I remember your shoulder/ I remember your elbow/ I remember your linen."); later, struck by the realization that memory implies the past tense, he piles up verbs in the *passé simple* (as in "Loved Was Came Caressed"), the tense used for completed action.

The lack of a rhetorical framework in the poem is paralleled by the absence of any central image or images. Although many arresting images appear, they are not linked in any design but remain isolated, reinforcing the sense of meaninglessness that has overwhelmed the speaker. The "little rented cars" and mirrors left unclaimed in a baggage room evoke the traveling the couple did together, which the speaker now sees as aimless. Some of the details given remain opaque because they have a private meaning that is not revealed ("Certain names are charged with a distant thunder"); others seem to be literary allusions, such as Mazeppa's ride (described in a poem by George Gordon, Lord Byron) and the bleeding trees, which to a reader who knows the works of Dante suggest that poet's "wood of the suicides." (Not until many years later did Aragon reveal that he had attempted suicide after the breakup with Cunard.)

The use of such arcane personal and literary allusions was a legacy of the Symbolist movement; as a young man, Aragon admired both Arthur Rimbaud and Stéphane Mallarmé, two of the most gifted Symbolists. The Surrealist approach to imagery evolved directly out of Symbolism in its more extreme forms, such as "Le Bateau ivre" ("The Drunken Boat") of Rimbaud and the *Chants de Maldoror* (1869) of Comte de Lautréamont. Despite its hopelessness, "Poem to Shout in the Ruins" conveys the almost hallucinatory power the Surrealists saw in imagery: its ability to charge ordinary things with mystery by appealing to the buried layers of the subconscious. "Familiar objects one by one were taking on . . . the ghostly look of escaped prisoners. . . ." The poem also suggests, however, that Aragon is not content merely to explore his subconscious; he hungers for a real connection to a real woman. In his desperate desire to prolong the liaison, he tries fitfully to make a "waltz" of the poem and asks the woman to join him, "since *something* must still connect us," in spitting on "what we have loved together." Despite its prevailing tone of negation and despair, the poem anticipates two central themes of Aragon's mature works: the belief that love between man and woman should be infinitely more than a source of casual gratification and the awareness of mortality (which the finality of parting suggests). This awareness is not morbid but tragic—the painful apprehension of death in a man whose loves and hopes were lavished on mortal existence.

"ELSA'S EYES"

"Les Yeux d'Elsa" ("Elsa's Eyes"), the opening poem in the collection of that name, is a good example of the metrically regular pieces Aragon produced in the 1940's (and continued to produce, together with free verse, until the end of his life). It is particularly characteristic in that, while each stanza has internal unity, the stanzas do not follow one another in a strictly necessary order; like those of a folk song or lyrical ballad, they offer a series of related insights or observations without logical or narrative progression. Many of Aragon's mature poems *do* exhibit such a progression (notably "Toi qui es la rose"—"You Who Are the Rose"), but in most cases it is subordinated to the kind of associative rhythm observed in "Poem to Shout in the Ruins."

The imagery of "Elsa's Eyes" is more unified than that of the earlier poem. Taking his wife's eyes as the point of departure, the poet offers a whole array of metaphors for their blueness (sky, ocean, wildflowers), brilliance (lightning, shooting stars), and depth (a well, far countries, and constellations). The last four stanzas are more closely linked than the preceding ones and culminate in an apocalyptic vision of Elsa's eyes surviving the end of the world. The poem as a whole, however, cannot be said to build to this climax; its power stems from the accumulation of images rather than from their arrangement. It should be noted that Aragon's Surrealist formation is still very much in evidence here, not only in the hallucinatory quality of his images but also in their obvious connection with subconscious desires and fears. The occasional obscurities are no longer the result of a deliberate use of private or literary allusions; Aragon was already writing with a wider public in mind. Nevertheless, he continued to evoke his own deepest desires and fears in language whose occasional ambiguity reflects the ambiguity of subconscious impulses.

A relatively new departure for Aragon in this period, the serious use of religious imagery, is reflected in the references to the Three Kings and the Mother of the Seven Sorrows in "Elsa's Eyes." Although reared a Catholic, Aragon became an atheist in his early youth and never professed any religious faith thereafter. During World War II, however, he was impressed by the courage of Christian resisters and acquired a certain respect for the faith that sustained them in the struggle against fascism. For his own part, Aragon began to use the vocabulary of traditional religion to extol his wife. Thus, for example, in "Elsa's Eyes," Elsa is described as the Mother of the Seven Sorrows, an epithet of the Virgin Mary; at the same time, Elsa is assimilated by natural forces and survives the cataclysm of the last stanza like a mysterious deity. This is partly attributable to Aragon's rediscovery, at about this time, of the courtly love tradition in French poetry, in which the lady becomes the immediate object of the knight's worship, whether as a mediatrix (who shows the way to God) or as a substitute for God himself. Repeatedly in Aragon's postwar poetry, Elsa is endowed with godlike qualities, until, in *Le Fou d'Elsa*, a virtual apotheosis takes place: The "holy fool" for whom the book is named (a Muslim, not a Christian) is convicted of heresy for worshiping a woman—Elsa—who will not be born for four centuries.

Whenever he was questioned on the subject, Aragon insisted that his aim was not a deification of Elsa but the replacement of the transcendent God of traditional religions with a "real" object, a woman of flesh and blood who could serve as his partner in building the future. Thus, Elsa's madman tells his judge, "I can say of her what I cannot say of God: She exists, because she *will be*." At the same time, the imagery of "Elsa's Eyes" clearly indicates that on some level there is an impulse of genuine worship, compounded of love, fear, and awe, in the poet's relation to his wife; he turned to the courtly tradition because it struck a deep chord in him. From the very first stanza, Elsa is identified with forces of nature, not all of which are benevolent: "Your eyes are so deep that in stooping to drink/ I saw all suns reflected there/ All desperate men throw themselves there to die." In most of the early stanzas, emphasis is laid on her grief (presumably over the effects of war), which only enhances her beauty, but the insistence on her eyes also suggests that, like God, she is all-seeing. Aragon himself often referred to his wife as his conscience, and Bernard Lecherbonnier has suggested in *Le Cycle d'Elsa* (1974) that the circumstances of Aragon's upbringing created in him, first in regard to his mother and later in regard to his wife, "an obsession with self-justification that permitted the myth of god-as-love to crystallize around the person, and in particular the eyes, of Elsa." Such an attitude is especially suggested by the final images of the poem, that of "Paradise regained and relost a hundred times" and that of Elsa's eyes shining over the sea after the final "shipwreck" of the universe.

"YOU WHO ARE THE ROSE"

An attitude of worship can also be seen in "You Who Are the Rose," from the collection *Elsa*, but it is tempered considerably by the vulnerability of the rose, the central image around which the poem is built. Its tight construction makes this a somewhat uncharacteristic poem for Aragon, yet his technique is still that of association and accumulation rather than logical or rhetorical development. As in "Poem to Shout in the Ruins," short syntactic units give the impression of spoken (indeed, in this poem, almost breathless) language. With an obsessiveness reminiscent of the earlier poem, the speaker worries over the flowering of the rose, which he fears will not bloom "this year" because of frost, drought, or "some subterranean sickness." The poem has a clear dramatic structure: The tension of waiting builds steadily, with periodic breaks or breathing spaces marked by the one-line refrain "*(de) la rose*," until the miraculous flowering takes place and is welcomed with a sort of prayer. The images that accumulate along the way, evoked by the poet in a kind of incantation designed to call forth the rose, are all subordinated to this central image of flowering, yet by their startling juxtaposition and suggestiveness, they clearly reflect Aragon's Surrealist background. Thus, the dormant plant is compared to "a cross contradicting the tomb," while two lines later its roots are "like an insinuating hand beneath the sheets caressing the sleeping thighs of winter." The use of alliteration is excessive—as when six words beginning with *gr-* appear in the space of three lines—and although this serves to emphasize the incantatory quality of the verse, to hostile critics it may look like simple bad taste. Hubert Juin, a friendly critic, freely acknowledges that a certain kind of bad taste is evident in Aragon; he ascribes it to the poet's "epic" orientation, his desire to include as much of the world as possible in his design, which precludes attention to every detail. It seems more to the point to recall that for the Surrealists, editing was a kind of dishonesty; by writing rapidly and not revising, they sought to lay bare what was most deeply buried in their psyches. What often saves Aragon from *préciosité*, or literary affectation, is the realism of this stream-of-consciousness technique. Caught up in the speaker's own anxiety or fantasy, the reader does not stop to criticize the occasional banalities and lapses of taste; he follows in the poet's wake, eager to see where the train of thought will lead.

The poignancy of "You Who Are the Rose," as of so many of Aragon's late poems, stems from the contrast between his exaggerated hopes—still virtually those of a young man—and the fact of old age, which threatens to deprive him of his wife and of his poetic voice. There is also, in some of his later work, a hint of sadness (although never of disillusionment) at the failure of Communism to fulfill its promise within his own lifetime. It is worth noting that in France the rose has long been associated with Socialist ideals; the poet's fear for his wife in "You Who Are the Rose" may be doubled by a tacit fear that the promise of Marxism will not be fulfilled. The two fears are related, moreover, because Aragon saw the harmony between husband and wife as the hope of the future, the cornerstone of a just and happy (Communist) society. His anguish is that of the idealist who rejects the possibility of transcendence: His "divinity" is mortal, like him. This helps to account for the fact that he continued to write with undiminished passion until the very end of his life, for poetry held out the only prospect of immortality in which he believed. The rose is mortal, but she has a name, and the poet can conjure with it (as his conclusion emphasizes: "O rose who are your being and your name"). What is more, Elsa Triolet was herself a writer, and in the preface to an edition combining her own and her husband's fiction, she described their mutually inspired work as the best possible memorial to their love. Aragon will probably be remembered primarily as the poet of Elsa—"Elsa's Madman," perhaps, in his anguished self-disclosure—but above all as Elsa's troubadour, an ecstatic love poet who insists on the possibility of earthly happiness because he has tasted it himself.

OTHER MAJOR WORKS

LONG FICTION: *Anicet: Ou, le panorama*, 1921; *Les Aventures de Télémaque*, 1922 (*The Adventures of Telemachus*, 1988); *Le Paysan de Paris*, 1926 (*Nightwalker*, 1970); *Les Cloches de Bâle*, 1934 (*The Bells of Basel*, 1936); *Le Monde réel*, 1934-1944 (includes *Les Cloches de Bâle*, 1934; *Les Beaux Quartiers*, 1936; *Les Voyageurs de l'impériale*, 1942; and *Aurélien*, 1944); *Les Beaux Quartiers*, 1936 (*Residential Quarter*, 1938); *Les Voyageurs de l'impériale*, 1942 (*The Century Was Young*, 1941); *Aurélien*, 1944 (English translation, 1947); *Les Communistes*, 1949-1951; *La Semaine sainte*, 1958 (*Holy Week*, 1961); *La Mise à mort*, 1965; *Blanche: Ou, L'oubli*, 1967; *Théâtre/roman*, 1974.

SHORT FICTION: *Servitude et grandeur de français*, 1945; *Le Mentir-vrai*, 1981.

NONFICTION: *Le Traité du style*, 1928; *Pour une réalisme socialiste*, 1935; *L'Homme communiste*, 1946, 1953; *Introduction aux littératures soviétiques*, 1956; *J'abats mon jeu*, 1959; *Les Deux Géants: Histoire parallèle des États-Unis et de l'U.R.S.S.*, 1962 (with André Maurois; 5 volumes; partial translation *A History of the U.S.S.R. from Lenin to Khrushchev*, 1964); *Entretiens avec Francis Crémieux*, 1964; *Écrits sur l'art moderne*, 1982.

BIBLIOGRAPHY

Adereth, M. *Aragon: The Resistance Poems*. London: Grant & Cutler, 1985. A brief critical guide to Aragon's poetry.

_____. *Elsa Triolet and Louis Aragon: An Introduction to Their Interwoven Lives and Works*. Lewiston, N.Y.: Edwin Mellen Press, 1994. An introductory biography of Triolet and Aragon and their lives together including critical analysis of their work and a bibliography.

Becker, Lucille Frackman. *Louis Aragon*. New York: Twayne, 1971. An introductory biography of Aragon and critical analysis of selected works. Includes bibliographic references.

Benfey, Christopher, and Karen Remmler, eds. *Artists, Intellectuals, and World War II: The Pontigny Encounters at Mount Holyoke College, 1942-1944*. Amherst: University of Massachusetts Press, 2006. Contains a chapter on Aragon, Gustave Cohen, and the poetry of the Resistance. Provides a general perspective on World War II literature.

Josephson, Hannah, and Malcolm Cowley, eds. *Aragon, Poet of the French Resistance*. New York: Duell, Sloan and Pearce, 1945. A study of Aragon's poetic works produced between 1939 and 1945.

Lillian Doherty

JÁNOS ARANY

Born: Nagyszalonta, Hungary (now Salonta, Romania); March 2, 1817
Died: Budapest, Hungary; October 22, 1882

PRINCIPAL POETRY

Toldi, 1847 (English translation, 1914)
Murány ostroma, 1848
Katalin, 1850
Összes muvei, 1851-1868
Nagyidai cigányok, 1852
Toldi estéje, 1854 (*Toldi's Eve*, 1914)
Kisebb költeményei, 1856
Buda halála, 1864 (*The Death of King Buda*, 1936)
Arany János összes költeményei, 1867
Toldi szerelme, 1879 (*Toldi's Love*, 1976)
Arany János összes munkái, 1884-1885
Epics of the Hungarian Plain, 1976

OTHER LITERARY FORMS

The criticism and studies in Hungarian literature of János Arany (OR-on-ee) are in the best tradition of scholarship and remain useful. His translations of several of William Shakespeare's plays and of Aristophanes' comedies are outstanding in the history of Hungarian translations.

ACHIEVEMENTS

János Arany contributed to Hungarian literature a poetic style and language—in fact, a poetic tradition—that united the best elements of native Hungarian verse, based to a large degree on folk song and folk poetry, with the learned traditions of Western Europe, particularly the traditions of the Enlightenment and of Romanticism. The result was a poetry that, while retaining its distinctively Hungarian character, joined the larger conversation of European literature.

BIOGRAPHY

János Arany was born the last child of György Arany and Sára Megyeri in Nagyszalonta, Hungary (now Salonta, Romania). Taught to read by his father, Arany began his studies in 1828 at Nagyszalonta. In 1831, he became a tutor at the school there, and in 1833, he transferred to the gymnasium (high school) at Debrecen on a scholarship. He took a leave of absence to serve as tutor in Kisujszállás for about a year, and in 1836, he left Debrecen without earning a degree. He settled in Nagyszalonta and became a teacher, later taking a post as notary. In 1840, he married Julianna Ercsey, the orphaned child of a lawyer. Their daughter, Juliska, was born in 1841, and their son, László, was born in 1844.

Although originally Arany had intended to give up his literary aspirations and devote his energies to building a secure future for his family, the friendship of István Szilágyi, who became rector at Nagyszalonta in 1842, drew him into the literary world. Arany had read widely in popular Hungarian literature since his childhood and had been introduced to earlier as well as contemporary Hungarian literature at Debrecen, but Szilágyi encouraged him to continue his studies of English and other foreign authors. Arany learned English to be able to read literary works in the original, and he

later translated from this language as well as from German, Greek, Italian, and other languages. In 1845, Arany's poem "Az elveszett alkótmany" (the lost constitution) won a literary prize. In 1847, his *Toldi* won even greater acclaim, and he became increasingly involved in the literary life of the country, as well as in the events leading up to the Revolution of 1848. He ran for a seat in parliament but was defeated; he also served as a soldier during the siege of Arad.

After the defeat of the Hungarians by the combined forces of the Austrian and Russian empires, Arany, like most of his contemporaries, spent several months in hiding and lost his teaching position. For a while, Count Lajos Tisza employed him as a tutor, and in 1851, he accepted a position as teacher in the gymnasium at Nagykörös. Arany never felt comfortable as a teacher, and in time the routine and the atmosphere of the small town depressed him. At first, however, there were brilliant colleagues who were similarly in hiding or exile during the years of terror, and he wrote a series of ballads, completed *Toldi's Eve* as well as several other narrative poems, and began the third poem of the Toldi trilogy, *Toldi's Love*. The notes for his lectures on Hungarian literature prepared at this time (never collected by him and published only after his death) show his sensitivity and the thorough critical and historical grasp he had of his subject.

In spite of his distance from the center of activity, Arany remained in close contact with literary developments. Recognition also came his way. On December 15, 1858, the Hungarian Academy of Sciences was allowed to resume its activity after a ten-year suspension, and Arany was elected a member. In his acceptance speech, he compared the epics of Miklós Zrinyi, a poet of the seventeenth century, with the work of Torquato Tasso. After repeated invitations by his friends to move to Budapest, Arany finally accepted the position of director of the Kisfaludy Társaság. In addition to administrative duties, he was active as an adviser and critic. He wrote a study on the Hungarian drama by József Katona, *Bánk bán* (pb. 1821), and helped prepare Imre Madách's *Az ember tragédiája* (pb. 1862; *The Tragedy of Man*, 1933) for publication. Increasingly accepted as the unofficial laureate of Hungarian literature, he became secretary of the Academy of Sciences in 1865. He continued writing, although he was unable to complete many projects. The major poem he worked on in this period was what he hoped would be a national epic, *The Death of King Buda*. It was, moreover, a period during which Arany was active as a translator, rendering Shakespeare, Aristophanes, and selections from many writers in other languages into Hungarian. He had the obligation to oversee the translation and publication of the complete works of Shakespeare and of Molière, as well as a comprehensive edition of Hungarian folk literature.

In 1879, Arany's third request for retirement was finally accepted by the academy. In his last years, he enjoyed a resurgence of lyric power and, despite his ill health, was able to finish some earlier projects, notably *Toldi's Love*. He published his *Prózai dolgozatai* (1879; prose essays) and was increasingly involved in linguistic studies.

Arany died on October 22, 1882, several days before the unveiling of the statue of his friend, the poet Sándor Petőfi, that still stands by the Danube in one of the city's old squares. Arany was laid out in state in the main chamber of the academy and was eulogized by the important critics and poets of his day. His role as one of the major figures in Hungarian poetry and literary criticism, as well as a sensitive and learned molder of the language, continues to be recognized to this day.

ANALYSIS

János Arany was not the only writer engaged in the literary development of Hungary, nor was he the first. He built on medieval, Renaissance, and Baroque traditions, and his goals were shared by many of his contemporaries. His individual contribution rests above all on his knowledgeable and sensitive use of folk elements, his ability to recognize and reject undue foreign influence while using foreign models to enrich his own work, and his unerring sense of the forms and rhythms best suited to the Hungarian language. His affinity with the folkloric tradition, as well as his recognition of its role in preserving Hungarian cultural traditions, enabled him to put into practice the theories and plans of the reform movement. As a teacher and critic, he was further able to explain and elucidate reformist goals. He not only used native words but also explained their ap-

propriateness and traced their history. He used meters based on folk song and wrote a thesis on Hungarian versification. Arguing that native themes and forms could equal the best in classical literature, he demonstrated this in his critical essays. Ever sensitive to literary developments abroad, he emphasized the need for literature to be realistic yet to avoid the excesses of naturalism; in his view, the poet should show not so much what is but rather its "heavenly counterpart."

"AZ ELVESZETT ALKÓTMANY"

In 1845, János Arany won the prize of the Kisfaludy Társaság with his mock-heroic epic, "Az elveszett alkótmany." He had begun writing it spontaneously and with no thought of publication, learning of the competition only when the poem was well under way. Although he was later to regret the unevenness and coarseness of the work, it deserves attention, for it shows Arany's use of supernatural machinery, which is rooted in Hungarian folklore and popular mythology—a device he borrowed from Mihály Vörösmarty and others but which Arany was to use effectively in later poems. His portrayal of the petty bickering between progressive and liberal political parties, no less than the high-handed and illegal actions of the party in power, indicates his political concerns. He suggests in the conclusion that only with a widening of the franchise, with the inclusion of all segments of the population in the political process can Hungarian institutions fulfill their proper role.

TOLDI

It was *Toldi*, however, that established Arany's literary reputation. As the enthusiastic Petőfi wrote, "Others receive the laurel leaf by leaf,/ For you an entire wreath must be given immediately." What Arany did was to create a folk-epic style that conveyed the life of the Hungarian Plain and the sense of history shared by the nation. Arany, who felt strongly that folk poetry should be the basis of the new national literary style, ennobled the genre by blending with it the qualities of the epic. Indebted to Petőfi's *János Vitéz* (1845; *János the Hero*, 1920), also a folk epic, which had appeared a year earlier, Arany nevertheless was responsible for innovations of his own. *Toldi* was written in the old narrative meter, the Hungarian Alexandrine or twelve-syllable hexameter line rather than in the simpler quatrain of the folk song. Arany's hero was an actual historical personage, while the poem's setting was based on the realistic verse chronicle by Péter Selymes Ilosvay; in contrast, Petőfi's *János the Hero* had a fairy-tale setting. In the handling of his sources and the characterization of his hero, Arany established the method he was to use in later poems.

Arany turns Ilosvay's sketchy tale about Miklós Toldi, a man of prodigious strength who won fame at the court of Lajos the Great (1342-1382), into a tightly organized poem in twelve cantos. Arany is careful to motivate each action and to fit each episode into his framework. Arany also concentrates on the hero's emergence as the king's champion rather than attempting to cover all his life. He deliberately refrains from beginning his poem in medias res and filling in background through digressions and backtracking, a method he believed would have been incompatible with the spirit of folk poetry.

The action of the poem covers nine days and falls into two sections: Cantos 1 through 6 relate the crime of Toldi and give the reason for his leaving home to seek the favor of the king, while cantos 7 through 12 show how this is accomplished. Several episodes are intertwined, but all serve to illustrate the development of the hero's character.

In the course of a few days, Toldi emerges as a loyal, brave, generous, faithful, and compassionate man who uses his great strength for good—whether working in the fields or fighting in the lists. Arany, through an examination of Toldi's actions as well as of his underlying motivations, makes his hero representative of that which is best in the Hungarian character. Arany also makes him a representative of the entire nation, not restricting his ties to any one class; noble by birth, yet close to the peasants and servants on the farm, he embodies Arany's political views as well. In contrast to the affected, treacherous György, who seems to be both a parasite and a tyrant on his own land, Toldi is equally at home with the servants and at the court of the king.

Idealized and simplified in some respects, the hero retains many very human qualities. He is despondent and brooding when disappointed, gives way to anger quickly, and almost gives up while hiding in the swamp. On the other hand, he can rejoice with abandon as he celebrates the arrival of a gift from his mother and the opportunity to earn respect and recognition.

Arany's portrayal of Hungarian qualities, of the soul of the nation, as it were, is not, however, restricted to Toldi. Arany captures the essence of Hungarian life in his description of the activities of the people, whether in the fields or in the city, working or enjoying a festival. By projecting familiar details of the nineteenth century onto his fourteenth century setting, Arany was able, moreover, to give the epic a realism and intimacy it would otherwise have lacked. Far from being false to the medieval setting or an oversimplification of life in Buda and the court, this projection carries Arany's message that in the past, Hungarian society was more unified: Distinctions of rank were not chasms.

Like the overall concept and style of the poem, its language and form are based on folk literature. Arany, well aware of the power of native words, used these deliberately. He wished to make his poetry easily understood and enjoyed by all, but he also sought to introduce the language of the people, no less than their poetry and song, into Hungarian literature. An active language reformer, he felt that the written Hungarian language could be revitalized only by absorbing the pure speech of the common person, still rich in archaic words, local dialect, and variety. The form of *Toldi* is also rooted in folk poetry, for the Hungarian Alexandrine was the traditional verse of earlier narrative poems. It echoes the patterns of Hungarian speech and, as Arany showed, is capable of a wide range. In this first epic, Arany used the traditional accented line, divided by a caesura. Later, he was to use both accented and quantitative feet to fit the form to the theme.

POETRY OF THE 1850'S

Arany was deeply affected by the failure of the War of Independence, yet the early 1850's was one of his richer periods, even though many of the poems of this time are expressions of despair and disappointment. He not only criticized the newly evolving political and social life but also questioned his own poetic style and creativity. In the two "Voitina levelei öccséhez" ("Voitina's Letters to His Brother"), he condemned the distortion of the folk style as well as the mere aping of foreign fashions, even as he himself sought the true possibilities of a popular national style. "Leteszem a lantot" ("I Lay Down the Lute"), an elegy for Petőfi, also expresses Arany's feeling that "he is no longer what he was,/ The better part has left him." No longer can he sing the hope of the future, nor can he even hope for the reward of immortality. The specter of the nation's death also haunted him in "Rachel" and "Rachel siralma" ("Rachael's Lament"). In "A nagyidai cigányok" ("The Gypsies of Nagyida"), he sought release from the disappointment and bitterness he felt at the failure of the revolution.

"FAMILY CIRCLE"

In his ballads and narrative poems, Arany continued to develop the folk style and to set his stories in a real time and place. He excelled in capturing the many moods of the life of the people, in painting intimate village scenes and establishing characterizations with a deft touch. A relatively short descriptive poem, "Családi kör" ("Family Circle"), illustrates this method in the compass of thirteen stanzas, but it was used no less effectively in the epics and the ballads. Arany describes a village evening, giving each element its due place while creating a domestic scene. As the village retires for the evening, the trees "nod," the bugs make a final sortie before becoming still, the frogs move "as if clods of earth had grown legs," and the bat and the owl take over their domain. He then moves closer to the farm to describe participants in the evening's activities: the cow, just milked, now feeding its calf; the playful cat; the inviting hearth guarded by the faithful dog; as well as the human inhabitants. A young girl is ironing her Sunday clothes; children listen to tales as they play or do their chores. A father returns from work and, putting his tools away, prepares for supper. Arany's attention to detail adds movement and drama to this still life; the father brings home from the fields a rabbit that the children immediately make their pet. As they sit down to the evening meal, a disabled veteran comes by, is welcomed as a member of the family, and yet is made to feel like an honored guest. After supper, he tells them stories of the war, and again it is through a comment here and there that the scenes are given dramatic tension. The father gently chides the young boy: The stranger's story is not fiction. The marriageable daughter asks about "her brother," yet the comment that she

will wait another year before marrying gives a clue that her relationship to the lost youth is something different: It would be unseemly to question a stranger about a lover. The final lines return the scene to the calm mood of the opening ones. Night has now completely fallen; the frame is complete. The family drama portrayed here is universal, while rooted nevertheless in the Hungarian village.

Within this seemingly simple poem, one that rivals Petőfi's "Szeptember végén" ("At the End of September") as a literary masterpiece, Arany creates a little gem of realistic description in which each detail has its place and in which each seems uncontrived and follows from the preceding one as if without artifice. Arany also comments obliquely on Hungarian life in the 1850's: The veteran tells tales of the War of Independence, and the daughter's lost "brother" is a casualty of the war, dead or in hiding from the Austrians. It is interesting that this quintessentially Hungarian poem was inspired by Robert Burns's "The Cotter's Saturday Night." Thus, it provides a good example of Arany's successful assimilation of Western European influences.

BALLADS

The ballad, a form that in Arany's hands was to reach a height unsurpassed by anyone in world literature, interested him throughout his life. He believed that the ballad, while remaining within the lyric sphere, achieved objectivity; such a blending of lyric emotion and objective setting was not possible in any other form. In range, the ballad allowed him to explore both historical incidents and psychological tragedies and even to blend the two. He was familiar with German and Scottish ballads and borrowed judiciously from these as well as from the Hungarian ballads of Transylvania. In vocabulary and form, he explored the possibilities of the language and metrical variations. In theme, he gave his readers a feeling for their history. By portraying Hungarian history through words and actions with which his audience could easily identify, he reinforced the unity and continuity of the nation.

Arany's earlier ballads, whether on historical themes or dealing with private tragedy, are less elaborate than the later ones. "Rákocziné" ("Rákoczi's Wife") is still in the direct folk-narrative style. "Rozgonyiné" ("Rozgonyi's Wife") also turns to a historical incident, the rescue of King Sigismund from battle by Cicelle Rozgonyi, but the emphasis is on the beauty and bravery of the lady who joins her husband in battle.

"TÖRÖK BÁLINT" AND "SZONDI'S TWO PAGES"

The Turkish wars provided Arany with much material. In "Török Bálint," he recounts the treachery of the Turks, who lure the champion of the widowed queen of Lajos II and her infant son into Turkish territory, then imprison the queen's protector in Constantinople. The ballad focuses on the complicated political maneuverings of Bálint Török and the treachery of the monk György. The story is told through innuendo and dialogue: how the queen was beset by both the Habsburgs and the Turks; Török's plan seemingly to unite with the Turks to gain victory; the suggestion that the monk betrayed him when he was invited to the Turkish camp after the victory; and how—while Török was ostensibly a guest of the Turks—the Turks took the city and drove out the queen and her infant son. Others are given honors by the sultan—Brother György is appointed governor—but the hero is imprisoned. Through this tale, Arany not only depicts the fall of Buda but also suggests the fateful division of the country, beset by both the Turks and the Habsburgs and forced to choose one or the other, or, as Bálint Török did, to try to play off one against the other.

"Szondi két apródja" ("Szondi's Two Pages") records the faithfulness of the pages who sing the deeds of their fallen master and refuse to leave his grave in spite of the promises and threats of the Turkish Ali. Interwoven with this song are the words of the Turkish messenger, who gradually loses his patience: All saw the battle, all recognize Szondi's heroism—but Ali will be angry if his offer is refused.

"THE WELSH BARDS"

In 1857, when Emperor Francis Joseph made a visit to Hungary and let it be known that he wished the poets to celebrate this event, Arany wrote "A walesi bardok" ("The Welsh Bards"). This ballad, based on a tradition that King Edward I of England had executed five hundred bards after his conquest of Wales, was a condemnation of the Habsburg ruler. Naturally, it was not published until later (1863), when the allusion was less obvious.

The ballad shows the influence of Scottish and medieval English models, which Arany had been studying for some time. The four-line stanza is in alternating iambic tetrameter and trimeter with an *abcb* rhyme scheme. Repetition and skillful variation are used both to move the narrative along and to paint the psychological mood. The scene is set with great economy, and the action is presented through dialogue. The opening lines, describing the triumphant march of the king, are repeated with significant variations at the beginning of each new section: "Edward the King, the English king/ Strides on his fallow horse/ Let's see, he says, just what the worth/ of the Welsh domains." He inquires about rivers and land and meadows ("Did the spilt patriot blood do it good?") and the people ("Are they happy . . . like the beast driven to the yoke?"). The courtiers assure him that all is well in words that echo the king's but with an ironic twist: "The people, the God-given people/ Are so happy here, Sire/ Its huts are silent, all silent/ Like so many barren graves."

The scene thus set in the first five stanzas is developed in the next section, which begins with the same two lines but intensifies the contrast between conqueror and conquered in the last two: "Edward the King, the English king/ Strides on his fallow horse/ Around him silence where'er he goes/ And a mute domain." The silence of the land puts its stamp on the banquet Edward holds that night, for the nobles sit in silence, and when Edward calls for song and toasts to celebrate his victory, "Words are choked, sound is suspended,/ Breath is caught" as an ancient bard rises. Arany presents three songs, or rather fragments of songs, for as each bard blesses the dead or curses Edward, he is sent to the stake. In the three songs, three different ages, three different styles are presented, symbolizing the united opposition of all. Edward flees the land, however, and in this final section, Arany gives the psychological retribution for the king's crime, which is not so much his conquest of the Welsh, but his presumption that the conquered should sing his praises: "Edward the King, the English king/ Gallops on his fallow steed,/ Around him burns earth and sky/ The entire Welsh domain." He is now fleeing a land that seems to be burning, yet it is only the fires of his own executioners. Nor does he find peace at home: All noise disturbs him, and drum, fife, and music will not drown out the curses of the Welsh banquet and the martyr-song of the five hundred.

CRIME AND THE SUPERNATURAL

Crime or sin upsets the balance of nature: It is this idea that lies at the heart of these ballads and dominates the series Arany wrote in 1877. In the late ballads, however, the scene is transferred to private life, and the crime itself becomes the focal point; the punishment often is more severe, and the role of the supernatural as a manifestation of spiritual disorder is more important. In "Éjfeli párbaj" ("Midnight Duel"), the Knight Bende's bride has been won in an unfair fight, and he has to duel with the ghost of his slain rival on three successive nights of the wedding festivities. Arany develops the mood gradually, from carefree joy to the bride's fear and the puzzling behavior of the host that forces the guests to leave. On the third night, Bende's guards watch as he hews and slashes the air, even killing some of them, thus fulfilling the ghostly foe's prediction that he will slay in the spirit, himself being a spirit. The interplay of the real and the imagined is at the core of the drama, as indeed it is in most of these ballads. Only the guilty see the supernatural forces, for these are projections of their own guilt and thus drive them mad.

In "Az ünneprontók" ("The Defilers of the Sabbath") and "Hídavatas" ("Bridge Dedication"), supernatural punishment is meted out to groups rather than to sinful individuals: Sunday revelers are forced by a demoniac bagpiper to perform a dance of death, and a procession of suicides jumps from a newly built bridge. It is interesting to contrast the concentration and technical skill achieved here with the style of certain earlier ballads of sin and retribution: "A Hamis tanú" ("The False Witness"), "Ágnes Asszony" ("The Woman Agnes"), and "Bor Vitéz." In these earlier ballads, Arany tends to exploit the supernatural for its own sake, although in "The Woman Agnes," the protagonist's punishment takes place in her own unbalanced mind.

"Tengeri hántás" ("Corn Husking") and "Vörös Rébék" ("Red Barbara") rely on folklore and superstition to create an eerie world in which human actions seem to be ruled by supernatural powers. In the first poem, the Halloween atmosphere of cornhusking and storytelling in the fields at night provides the background for a tale of illicit and tragic love. In the second, a snatch of a folk song serves as the leitmotif for a tale of infidelity and murder. "Tetemre hívás" ("Ordeal of the Bier") also has ancient beliefs at its core: A murdered youth begins to bleed in the presence of his lover, who, in a teasing mood, had given him the fatal dagger. While the narrative is relatively straightforward, the mood of intrigue and the grand medieval setting give the poem a mysterious quality. The climax, in which the girl suddenly goes mad with horror, achieves the surprising psychological realism of which the ballad form is capable.

THE DEATH OF KING BUDA

Throughout his life, Arany sought to create a popular national epic. The Toldi trilogy had not fulfilled these expectations fully, for it lacked the necessary historical component in the person of the central figure. The theme of the original settlement of Hungary would have been appropriate, but Arany found the historical and legendary material too limited. He projected events into an earlier period, that of the Hun conquest under the leadership of Attila. Originally, he planned a trilogy that would trace the fall of Attila and the fate of his son Csaba, who, according to legend, had led the remnant of Attila's forces back to their homeland, leaving a token force of Székelys in Transylvania. Their descendants later regained this patrimony and established the modern Hungarian state. Only the first poem, *The Death of King Buda*, was completed, but Arany did leave fragments of the other parts as well as several detailed outlines.

In *The Death of King Buda*, Arany united the archaic and the modern, the naïve and the sophisticated. He used a variety of sources and elements: Greek and Western history and legend, Eastern motifs in the tales and customs of the Huns, folklore, epic dreams and prophecies, even borrowings from the *Nibelungenlied* (c. 1200; English translation, 1848). All these elements contributed to the realism of the poem, which was reinforced by Arany's attention to psychological conflicts.

Formally and stylistically, Arany broke new poetic ground in *The Death of King Buda*. In its form, the poem presents yet another variation of the Hungarian Alexandrine: The twelve-syllable line is an accented one with a definite caesura, and while Arany maintains the hexameter, two of the accented feet in each half are significantly stronger than the third, so that the line seems shorter and closer to ballad and other meters of folk poetry. The occasional alliteration enhances the archaic quality of the verse, although the couplet rhyme is maintained. In diction, Arany again turned to popular speech and to the Hungarian literary heritage. The numerous footnotes show how consciously he used both popular expressions and archaic forms and how carefully he researched chronicle and legend for each detail—but also the sound reasons he had for departing from these sources in any respect.

LATE LYRICS

Arany's late lyrics, written mostly in 1877, are characterized by introspection and a peaceful acceptance of life, particularly of his old age and its infirmities. Originally intended only for himself, they are intensely personal yet reveal the same values that inform his more public poems. Whatever their point of departure, these late poems are about his love for his homeland (particularly the scenes of his youth on the Alföld) and the changes he had experienced over the years. They capture the mood of quiet meditation in forms that are as rich as any he had used.

"A tölgyek alatt" ("Under the Oaks") is a meditative lyric in which Arany recalls happy hours spent under oak trees in his childhood as he rests under the oaks at his retreat on St. Margit Island. The poem's dominant mood is quiet and resigned, yet it gathers a variety of colors and scenes ranging from childhood games to the sunsets of old age. "Vásárban" ("At the Market") also serves as a release for the poet's homesickness for the Hungarian Plain: A wagon from this region with its load of wheat reminds him of the activities, the sights, and the sounds of the harvest, in which he, too, once participated. He also expresses the hope that after many sorrowful years, the region—and the country—will see better times. Personal comment and a concern for his country, both the "smaller one" and the larger nation, mingle naturally in these poems, as do the poet's childhood memories and the concerns of his old age.

LEGACY

Drawn almost reluctantly into a literary career, Arany left a legacy rich in both creative and critical works. It has been said that if Hungary were suddenly to disappear, its history and life (at least through the nineteenth century) could be reconstructed from Arany's works. In many ways, he is a national poet. One reason that he is not better known abroad is that, aside from the difficulty of translating his rich language, it is difficult to convey the Hungarian scenes, ideas, moods, and emotions of his verse without an overabundance of notes and commentary. Nevertheless, Arany was a poet who dealt with universal themes and general human problems. While the setting of his poetry reflects what he knew best, the ideas come from his wide reading and perceptive studies of the Western tradition. His critical works and his own practice showed how native Hungarian themes and concerns could be integrated into the body of Western literature. When he is approached from this comparative perspective, Arany can offer his wealth to the non-Hungarian reader as readily as he has been inspiring Hungarian readers for generations.

OTHER MAJOR WORKS

NONFICTION: *Prózai dolgozatai*, 1879; *Zrinyi és Tasso*, 1885.

TRANSLATIONS: *A Szent-Iván éji alóm*, 1864 (of William Shakespeare's play *A Midsummer Night's Dream*); *Hamlet, dán királyfi*, 1867 (of Shakespeare's play *Hamlet*); *János király*, 1867 (of Shakespeare's play *King John*); *Aristophanes vígjátékai*, 1880 (of Aristophanes).

MISCELLANEOUS: *Arany János hátrahagyott iratai és levelezése*, 1887-1889.

BIBLIOGRAPHY

Adams, Bernard. "Janos Arany and 'The Bards of Wales.'" *Slavonic and East European Review* 77, no. 4 (October, 1999): 726-731. A critique of Arany's poem "The Bards of Wales," concluding that the tale of the massacre of Welsh bards by Edward I of England is traditional rather than historically accurate.

Basa, Enikő Molnár. *Hungarian Literature*. New York: Griffin House, 1993. This overview of Hungarian literature provides context on Arany's work.

Preminger, Alex, and T. V. F. Brogan, eds. *New Princeton Encyclopedia of Poetry and Poetics*. Princeton,

N.J.: Princeton University Press, 1993. Contains an informative section on Hungarian poetry.

Reményi, Jóseph. *Hungarian Writers and Literature.* New Brunswick, N.J.: Rutgers University Press, 1964. A history and critical study of Hungarian literature including the works of Arany. Includes bibliographic references.

Enikő Molnár Basa

ARCHILOCHUS

Born: Paros, Greece; c. 680 B.C.E.
Died: Paros(?), Greece; c. 640 B.C.E.
Also known as: Archilochos; Archilochus of Paros

PRINCIPAL POETRY

Archilochos, 1959 (Max Treu, editor)

OTHER LITERARY FORMS

Archilochus (or-KIHL-uh-kuhs) is remembered only for his poetry.

ACHIEVEMENTS

Archilochus was well known in antiquity as an innovator, especially in metrics. His metrical forms include iambic trimeter, elegiac couplets, trochaic tetrameter, epodes (poems in which a longer metrical unit is followed by a shorter one), and asynartete (verses consisting of two units having different rhythms). Although he is traditionally said to have been the inventor of iambic and epodic poetry, it is possible that poems in these meters were written earlier but failed to survive. Archilochus's technical innovations, rather, may be seen in the skilled combination of established meters in his epodes and asynartete. Archilochus writes mostly in an Ionic Greek, imbued with the language and especially the vocabulary of the epic tradition. In fact, he was frequently admired by the ancients for his successful imitation of Homer, and Homeric influence, on both theme and vocabulary, can be seen in Archilochus's surviving fragments. The view that Archilochus is an anti-Homeric poet, at least in his rejection of epic stan-

dards and values, is increasingly questioned today. Archilochus's elegiac poems generally reflect the martial or hortatory themes found in other Archaic Greek elegists, including Tyrtaeus and Theognis; elegy was not specifically associated with lament until the fifth century B.C.E. In general, Archilochus's poems are unbound by any rigid restriction of particular themes to particular meters. Not all his elegiacs are about war, and not all his iambics possess the invective or satirical mood to which that meter was restricted later in the Hellenistic period. Nearly all of Archilochus's poetry is written in the first person, and he has often been called the first European lyric poet. Modern scholars, however, are becoming increasingly convinced that Archilochus's invective poetry was part of an oral tradition of *iambus*, or Greek blame poetry, possibly cultic in origin and in performance and at least as old as the epic tradition, which used stock characters and the first-person persona in a conventional way. If this is true, Archilochus's "lyricism" in the modern sense of "expressing individual emotions" is much more formal and limited in scope than has heretofore been realized.

Archilochus's meters and style were imitated by later monodic Greek poets, including Alcaeus and Anacreon, but ancient admiration of Archilochus's skilled manipulation of meter was balanced by the poet's perhaps unjustified reputation for violent and abusive verse. The fifth century lyric poet Pindar himself criticized Archilochus for such violence in a Pythian ode. There is a suggestion that Archilochus was the butt of some later Greek comedy. Archilochus's poetry was evidently very influential on the iambics of the Hellenistic poet Callimachus, on the satirical poems of Catullus, and especially on the *Epodes* (c. 30 B.C.E.; English translation, 1638) of Horace. The poet was also the subject of several pieces in the *Palatine Anthology*. Archilochus's influence on more modern poets has been limited by the fragmentary preservation of his poetry.

BIOGRAPHY

A general biographical sketch of Archilochus can be drawn from the extant fragments, as well as from ancient sources that were clearly dependent for information on Archilochus's poetry. Particularly informative are several third and first century B.C.E. inscriptions that were found on Archilochus's native Paros and are usually called the *Monumentum Archilochium*. These inscriptions were mounted in a sanctuary of Archilochus, the Archilocheion, founded in the third century B.C.E., and are evidence of the poet's posthumous appeal to the inhabitants of his birthplace. Unfortunately, nearly all the available biographical information concerning Archilochus must be qualified by its ultimate poetic source. Although Archilochus does use the first-person persona and often provides apparent autobiographical information in his poetry, there is little that can be verified by independent sources. Modern scholars tend to argue that many of Archilochus's personal statements, especially in *iambus*, are actually conventions of the genre and provide little information about the life of the poet himself.

Even the dating of Archilochus is much debated. The poet's reference to a full eclipse of the sun in poem 74 D. suggests a date of either 711 or 648 B.C.E. The discovery in Thasos of the late seventh century tombstone of Archilochus's friend Glaucus (see, for example, poem 56 D.) makes the later period more likely for the poet's floruit. It is, therefore, probably safe to assume that Archilochus lived during the mid-seventh century B.C.E., perhaps from 680 to 640 B.C.E.

Traditionally, Archilochus is said to have been the son of Telesicles, a Parian aristocrat, and a slave woman, Enipo, but this bastard status may be a fictional poetic stance ("Enipo" may be derived from *enipe*, an epic word for "rebuke" or "invective"). It is fairly certain, however, that both Archilochus's life and his poetry reflect the history and rich Ionian tradition of Paros, the Aegean island on which he grew up. In the seventh century B.C.E., Paros organized a colony on the gold-rich island of Thasos, and it is probable that both Archilochus's father and the poet himself were involved in this venture. Mention of both islands occurs frequently in the surviving fragments. Archilochus's common martial themes mirror the military concerns of the Greek Archaic Age, when colonization and intense rivalry between city- and island-states led to frequent warfare. The tradition that Archilochus was a mercenary soldier may be a misinterpretation of his own poetry, but the evidence suggests that he was often called on to fight, both for Paros and Thasos, against the Thracians, Euboeans, and Naxians. He is said to have been killed in battle by a Naxian named Corax, but this name, too (which means "crow"), may be derived from the invective tradition. The bulk of Archilochus's extant fragments do not support the antimilitaristic sentiment that some have noted in such poems as "On My Shield," but rather suggest the patriotic sentiments of an Archaic Greek who knew his human weaknesses on the battlefield. Archilochus does not reject the martial world, but rather sees himself as a "soldier-poet."

The *Monumentum Archilochium* provides the mythic tale of how Archilochus as a boy met the Muses, who gave him a lyre in exchange for the cow that his father had sent him to sell. This etiology of Archilochus's poetic inspiration may have been derived from the poet's own work and is almost certainly an imitation of Hesiod's encounter with the Muses.

The best-known portion of Archilochus's poetry is concerned with his aborted engagement to Neobule, the daughter of Lycambes. According to tradition, Lycambes, said to have been an acquaintance of the poet's father, agreed to a match between Neobule and Archilochus. For unknown reasons, Lycambes later changed his mind, and Neobule married someone else. Much of Archilochus's invective poetry is directed against Lycambes and two of his daughters (the Lycambides), who are said to have hanged themselves as a result of the poet's bitter attacks. The entire Neobule story has by many scholars come to be considered spurious autobiographical material, despite the apparent confirmation of the tale suggested by a Hellenistic epitaph poem for the Lycambides. The suicide theme could be the result of the "killing-satire" tradition. In addition, the morphological relationship between Lyc-*amb*-es, i-*amb*-os, and dithyr-*amb*-os suggests to some modern scholars, including Martin West, that Lycambes and his daughters were not historical personages but rather stock characters in a traditional *iambus*, or blame poetry, possibly with some original cultic link with Dionysus and Demeter. The establishment of the Archilocheion sanctuary on Paros gives some confirmation of the poet's possible cultic connections.

ANALYSIS

Archilochus's poetry sprang from the rich oral poetic heritage of prehistoric and Archaic Greece, and especially of Ionia. It was influenced not only by the impersonal, formulaic, epic tradition ending with Homer, but also by a parallel oral tradition of more personal expression that led, beginning with Archilochus in the mid-seventh century B.C.E., to Greek iambic, elegiac, and lyric poetry. It is probable that the invective mood, animated dialogues, and vivid expression of personal feelings that fill Archilochus's poems were not inventions of the poet, but rather his inheritance from the iambic and elegiac traditions, which Archilochus utilized in his own distinctive, usually unorthodox, manner. Interaction between the epic and lyric traditions is particularly evident in Archilochus's poetry, in which the poet not only uses but also often semantically transforms Homeric words, epithets, and even scenes. Archilochus's poetry is filled with metaphors that are often derived from Homeric, martial sources, but which are abrupt and violent in their poetic context; the much-discussed metaphor of a woman taking a town by storm through her beauty is one example.

Archilochus can also be seen to use conventional themes in unconventional ways: for example, his "On My Shield," in which he revises traditional military values; his unorthodox *propemptikon* or "bon voyage" poem (fragment 79a D.), which is really a wish for an evil voyage for a personal enemy; and his seduction poetry, which has, at least once, in the *Cologne Epode*, an unconventional climax. His poetry also shows a fondness for animal fables in the tradition of Aesop; Archilochus uses these fables, often in unusual contexts, as brief metaphors or extended allegories. The biographical Archilochus may lie hidden behind the persona of his poetry, but the poetry itself reveals the talents of an original and unorthodox mind whose contributions to the Greek iambic and elegiac traditions are monumental. There may have been a lost "lyric" tradition before Archilochus, but through his personal, first-person poetry, a distinctive form of poetic expression developed that lies at the beginning of the European lyric tradition.

The fragments of Archilochus's work reveal a dynamic poetry that uses the vocabulary and themes of the oral epic and iambic traditions to create the impression of a personal voice on which modern lyric poetry is ultimately based. It is especially through his unconventional use of standard words and concepts that Archilochus's style develops its forceful and unexpected turns of thought and expression. Although critical discussion of Archilochus's life and poetry may never be free from the controversies occasioned by the lack of primary evidence, enough of his work survives to show his original contributions to the European poetic tradition, especially in the areas of metrical experimentation, iambic or invective poetry, and lyric or first-person expression.

FRAGMENT 67A D.

Fragment 67a D. is a trochaic tetrameter example of the hortatory poem usually expressed in elegiacs. It forms part of a thematic group in Archilochus's poetry on *tlesmosyne* or "endurance" (fragments 7 D., 68 D., and 58 D.). Significantly, this group is not bound to a particular meter and is composed of both elegiac and trochaic tetrameter. The exhortative theme is distinctive in 67a D. in that it is an introspective address to the poet's *thumos*, his "heart," rather than to another person (such as Glaucus in 68 D.). Address to one's own *thumos* and reflection on one's own state of mind are found in such epics as the *Odyssey* (c. 725 B.C.E.; English translation, 1614), but Archilochus's adaptation of this epic trope to the first-person persona reveals the ability to distance oneself from one's poetic persona, an ability that is essential to the lyric mode. In 67a D., Archilochus addresses his heart in a military or nautical context, as if his heart is under siege or at sea: "thrown into confusion" (*kukōmene*); "ward off" (*alexou*). The vocabulary is Homeric, but the context is original. The poet's advice to his heart is climaxed in lines 4 through 6 with a pair of parallel imperative phrases. The first pair, "don't in victory openly gloat" and "nor in defeat at home fall in grief," is balanced not only in sentiment but also in word order, where Greek participial references to victory (*nikṓ*) and defeat (*nikētheis*) are completed in meter and in sense by the imperative forms "gloat" (*agalleo*) and "grieve" (*odureo*). In the second pair of imperative phrases, the emphasis is not so much on the contradictory imperatives "rejoice" (*chaire*) and "give sorrow" (*aschala*) or on the objects of these actions, "good fortune" (*chartoisin*) and "evils" (*kakoisin*), but on the adverbial qualification of these commands at the beginning of the last line, "at least not excessively" (*mē liēn*). This plea for moderation in the expression of emotion was a traditional Archaic Greek sentiment, best known in the form of the Apollonian dictum "nothing in excess" (*mēden agan*), but Archilochus sums up this concept, in the rest of the last line, by a final imperative phrase semantically charged in a striking way: "Recognize what a rhythm of order controls human life."

Archilochus's use of *rhusmos*, an Ionic form of the Greek word *rhuthmos*, is ambiguous. The primary meaning of this word is "measure" or "order," but eventually the word developed a secondary meaning of flux, or change. Both meanings of the word may be operative in the poem and result in a paradoxical reading of the human situation: The order (*rhuthmos*) of human life is the constant change (*rhuthmos*) that Archilochus exhorts his heart to accept. Fragment 67a D. thus demonstrates Archilochus's original use of Homeric vocabulary and concepts as well as the hortatory mood of Greek elegy in a distinctive meter.

"ON MY SHIELD"

"On My Shield," composed of a pair of elegiac couplets, is Archilochus's best-known piece, in which he abandons his shield in battle. The shield, "untarnished by arms," that is, "brand-new," is left beside a bush where it is picked up by an enemy Saian (a Thracian). The poet's preference for saving his own life over keeping his shield (which he says he can always replace) has usually been interpreted as an outright rejection of epic, martial standards in favor of a more personal, self-centered attitude. Even in antiquity, this poem was contrasted with the Spartan woman's command to her man to return from battle "with his shield or on it," and Archilochus was known, derogatorily, as a *rhipsaspis*, or "shield-thrower," "deserter." Several later poets, including Alcaeus, Anacreon, and Horace, imitated this poem.

It should be noted, however, that, unlike some of his later imitators, Archilochus does not actually throw away his shield but rather hides it under a bush. Archilochus's act is not a frantic gesture in the midst of headlong flight but a calculated attempt to save his life

and, possibly, his shield. The sentiment is certainly different from the Homeric battle standard but only in emphasis. Archilochus, whose military adventures clearly speak through these lines, is not spurning martial values, but rather placing his emphasis on the preservation of life instead of gear.

The noble value that the shield possesses in epic (for example, the importance of the shield of Achilles in Homer's *Iliad*, c. 750 B.C.E.; English translation, 1611) is certainly undermined by Archilochus, who says of his shield that he can buy a "better one" (*ou kakiō*), but the underlying implication of this purchase is that Archilochus is prepared to enter battle again in the future. On the level of language, there appears to be a contrast in the poem between standard Homeric expressions and their unconventional contexts. The poet's lighthearted attitude toward the loss of his shield is reinforced in several ways. First, he uses the derogatory Homeric word *erretō* (to hell with it) in an emphatic position in reference to the shield. The epithet *amōmēton* (blameless), used for the lost shield, is also significant, for the poet's preference for a rare Homeric form of "blameless" instead of the more common epic form *amumona* is perhaps deliberately and comically unorthodox. Archilochus uses an even rarer form (*amōmon*) of this epithet in the *Cologne Epode*. Finally, the contrast between loss of shield and saving of life may be underscored by the possible phonological pun, unintelligible in translation, of *Saion* and *exesaosa*.

FRAGMENT 112 D.

Archilochus also expresses personal, unconventional views in an unconventional way in fragment 112 D., which is metrically an example of his asynartetic poems, using a combination of dactylic tetrameter, ithyphallic, and iambic trimeter catalectic. Here the poet is describing not a martial experience but an emotional one, but this personal theme is expressed in a vividly Homeric vocabulary: Eros (Passion), which in Archaic Greek poetry was still an emotion rather than the anthropomorphic mythological figure (Cupid) of later periods, is "coiled beneath the heart" of Archilochus. The word *elustheis* (coiled) verbally recalls the epic scenes in which Odysseus was coiled beneath the Cyclops's sheep and Priam at Achilles' feet. In the second line, "Eros pours a thick mist over the poet's eyes," the words "pour" (*echeuen*) and "mist" (*achlun*) both invoke epic passages where the mist of death pours over a dying warrior. The Homeric vocabulary thus implies a vivid metaphor for Eros, which has a deathlike grasp on the poet and is depicted, like death, as an external rather than an internal force. Archilochus continues this unconventional use of Homeric vocabulary in the last line, where Eros "steals the tender heart from his breast." Once again epic formulas for death are applied to Eros, but the epithet "tender" (*hapalas*) may be intentionally ambiguous; a secondary meaning of the word, "weak/feeble," is perhaps implied by Archilochus as a subtle transformation of the Homeric epithet into a significant expression of the poet's helplessness in the face of violent passion.

COLOGNE EPODE

A papyrus find that was published as the *Cologne Epode* in 1975, not only added forty precious lines to the corpus of Archilochus but also has greatly advanced knowledge of the poet's epodic and invective style. This epode, a composition of iambic trimeters, hemiepes, and iambic dimeter, is most easily accessible in this English translation by John Van Sickle. The papyrus, the beginning of which is lost, appears to pick up in the middle of a dialogue between a man and a woman. The conversation is being narrated by the man. Only the last four lines of the woman's speech survive. The bulk of the extant poem is devoted to the man's response, "point by point," to the woman. The general background is an attempted seduction in which the woman argues against and the man for immediate physical union. The poem climaxes in a narration of sexual activity, the precise nature of which has been greatly debated. (Full intercourse and "heavy petting" are the apparent choices of interpretation.) A similar use of dialogue within narrative is employed by Archilochus in another recent papyrus find, which is also a seduction scene. The narrative in the *Cologne Epode* demonstrates Archilochus's skilled use of a structure well suited to the tone of Ionian *iambus*, the genre of personal expression and ridicule in which the poet is here operating.

The world of Homer is not far to seek, in both the vocabulary and themes of the *Cologne Epode*. The use of the matronym "daughter of Amphimedo" is good

epic diction, and the phrase "I shall obey as you order" is another obvious example of Homeric phraseology. Thematically, the epode is a close iambic adaption of Hera's seduction of Zeus in the *Iliad*, book 14. The revelation in line 16 of the epode that Archilochus is probably talking to Neobule's sister makes the issue of autobiographical experience particularly pressing, but comparison of the epode to book 14 suggests that it is not so much the narration of a spontaneous and emotional event as it is an artistic, stylized variation of a Homeric seduction. The *Cologne Epode*, perhaps more than any other extant Archilochean fragment, suggests the presence of an artificial rather than an authentic first-person persona.

Formality is especially evident in the depiction of the woman in a bucolic setting and the contrasting use of images from several Archaic Greek professions and activities in an erotic context. Although Archilochus's adaptation of the bucolic setting from Homer is evidenced by the fact that both poems associate sexual union with wildly blooming flowers, Archilochus has integrated this association of the woman with the fertility of nature in a more basic way, into the very fiber of his vocabulary and imagery. The woman herself is described as "beautiful and tender" (*kalē tereina*), while her sister Neobule feels the brunt of Archilochus's invective in her description as a withered flower (*anthos d' aperruēke*). The final stage of this natural process is represented by the woman's late mother, Amphimedo, "who now is covered by the mouldering earth."

The concept and vocabulary, originally Homeric, is manipulated by Archilochus here into an unorthodox and subtle metaphor arguing in favor of the masculine demand of immediate sexual gratification. At the same time, the narrator disguises his eroticism behind references to various professions: rhetoric ("answering point by point"); architecture ("the coping stone" and "architrave"); navigation or horse racing ("I'll hold my course"); war ("reconnoitering"); wrestling ("seizing her"); and animal husbandry ("hasty bitch, blind pups"). The last reference, to an old Greek proverb, also underscores Archilochus's fondness for the use of animal fables as exempla. The proverb, arguing against hasty action, is a subtle ploy on the part of the narrator to disguise his own ambitions.

BIBLIOGRAPHY

Bartol, Krystyna. "Where Was Iambic Performed? Some Evidence from the Fourth Century B.C." *Classical Quarterly* 42, no. 1 (1992): 65. A discussion of the performance of iambic poetry in the fourth century B.C.E. Poems by Archilochus and Homer may have been presented during poetic competitions as suggested in a text by Heraclitus.

Burnett, Anne Pippin. *Three Archaic Poets: Archilochus, Alcaeus, Sappho*. London: Bristol Classical Press, 1998. Explores the paradoxical career of Archilochus as both a professional soldier and poet, the combination of "Ares and the Muses," as Burnett phrases it. This book also provides an even-handed view of Archilochus's use of obscenity in his poems. Burnett points out that during the time Archilochus was writing, obscenity was seen not as an end in itself but as part of ritual, verbal attacks on enemies. As such, Archilochus undoubtedly regarded his use of obscenity as a poet in the same way he considered his use of weapons as a warrior. Both were means to the same end: triumph over an adversary.

Davenport, Guy. Introduction to *Archilochos, Sappho, Alkman*. Berkeley: University of California Press, 1980. The placement of Archilochus among his contemporary poetic peers helps establish both his debt and contributions to the developing Greek poetic tradition. Davenport, who also translated and illustrated the selections in this volume, provides a brief but useful overview of Archilochus's place in early Greek literature, pointing out that "Archilochus is the second poet of the West" (after Homer). Because Davenport himself is both a creative writer and a scholar his translations tend to be more interesting than traditional, academic efforts.

Finglass, P. J., C. Collard, and N. J. Richardson, eds. *Hesperos: Studies in Ancient Greek Poetry Presented to M. L. West on His Seventieth Birthday*. New York: Oxford University Press, 2007. This collection of essays on ancient Greek poetry contains several essays that examine Archilochus's works and the time in which he lived.

Gerber, Douglas. Introduction to *Greek Iambic Poetry from the Seventh to the Fifth Centuries B.C.* Cambridge, Mass.: Harvard University Press, 1999. A solid essay that places Archilochus in the context of his times and his specific poetic genre. Gerber, who also provided the translations for the volume, offers a learned but accessible commentary on the techniques and methods of Greek verse of the period. Serving also as editor, Douglas has compiled a very useful volume.

Irwin, Elizabeth. "Biography, Fiction, and the Archilochaen Ainos." *Journal of Hellenic Studies* 118 (1998): 177-183. An examination of the historicity of characters in Archilochus's poetry. The question of the possible autobiographical nature of the poems remains open.

Rankin, H. D. *Archilochus of Peros*. Park Ridge, N.J.: Noyes Press, 1977. A good, in-depth review of the poet's career and achievements, with an emphasis on the themes and content of his verse. Rankin points out that Archilochus was the "first poet in our literary tradition to use sexuality in a conscious and deliberate way as a main theme in his poetry." Rankin's frank discussion of Archilochus's use of sexual themes and imagery helps the reader understand that the poet was not simply trying to shock the reader. In this and other areas, Rankin is especially helpful in his discussion of the role of poetry in Greek society of the time.

Will, Frederic. *Archilochos*. New York: Twayne, 1969. This volume provides a solid introduction to the study of the poet, his work, and his world. Because few of the basic facts known about the poet have changed—and little, in that sense, has been added—most of the material remains useful and can complement later works on Archilochus dealing more extensively with the interpretation of his work and his poetic techniques.

Thomas J. Sienkewicz
Updated by Michael Witkoski

LUDOVICO ARIOSTO

Born: Reggio Emilia, duchy of Modena (now in
    Italy); September 8, 1474
Died: Ferrara (now in Italy); July 6, 1533

PRINCIPAL POETRY

Orlando Furioso, 1516, 1521, 1532 (English
    translation, 1591)
Satire, pb. 1534 (wr. 1517-1525; *Ariosto's Satyres*,
    1608)
Cinque canti, 1545

OTHER LITERARY FORMS

Ludovico Ariosto (or-ee-AW-stoh) was an influential verse dramatist of his time, following the form of
the Latin comedies of Plautus and Terence and rigorously adhering to the unities of time and place, though
setting the plays in Ferrara and using the society of that
city for his plots. His plays include *La cassaria* (pr., pb.
1508; *The Coffer*, 1975; *I suppositi* (pr. 1509; *The Pretenders*, 1566), *Il negromante* (wr. 1520; *The Necromancer*, 1975), and *La Lena* (pr. 1528; *Lena*, 1975).
His final play, "I studenti," written in 1533, was completed posthumously by his brother Gabriele and retitled *La scolastica* (pb. 1547; *The Students*, 1975).

ACHIEVEMENTS

Ludovico Ariosto was one of the greatest Italian poets, his supreme achievement being the long poem *Orlando Furioso*. Many writers and thinkers of the Renaissance regarded *Orlando Furioso* as one of the
greatest works ever composed, and its influence lasted
well into the Romantic period, though it is little read today. Although Ariosto's patrons, the Este family, did
not fully recognize the importance of the poet who was
under their care, Ariosto's epic poem established a
proud, if fictitious, line of descent for the Estensi,
pleased the court at Ferrara, and spread Ariosto's name
across Europe; even bandits were said to hold him in
awe. *Orlando Furioso* captured the essence of Renaissance thought in its dynamic combination of classical
form, fantasy, chivalry, medieval romance, irony, morality, and style. Fiercely independent as an artist,
Ariosto obsessively wrote and rewrote his epic until it
became, along with the works of Michelangelo, Leonardo da Vinci, and Raphael, one of the supreme artistic expressions of the Italian Renaissance.

BIOGRAPHY

Ludovico Ariosto was the son of Niccolo Ariosto,
captain of the guard of Reggio Emilia, and vassal of the
duke of Ferrara. Niccolo was a stern father and a harsh
ruler who was hated by the people of Reggio Emilia. In
1484, he moved to Ferrara with his ten children and set
Ariosto to the study of law, despite the boy's inclination toward poetry. Ariosto resisted and was eventually
permitted to study literature with Gregorio de Spoleto,
until 1499, when Gregorio left for France as the tutor of
Francesco Sforza. Ariosto was fluent in Latin (Horace
became his favorite poet, exerting a significant influence on his later poetic forms and style), but as a result
of Gregorio's departure and subsequent events, he
never learned Greek, a failure that he regretted for the
rest of his life. His first poetry was in Latin and earned
the praise of Pietro Bembo, who urged him to continue
writing in Latin. Ariosto, however, with his taste for
simple things, preferred the vernacular and soon wrote
only in Italian.

In 1500, Ariosto's father died and the young man
was forced to take up the management of his mother's
dowry and put aside his studies to care for his four
brothers and five sisters. His dream of a simple life
filled with humanistic studies was shattered; he found
himself preoccupied with the banal tasks of finding positions for his younger brothers and administering the
estate, an experience on which he would comment bitterly in *Ariosto's Satyres*. In 1502, he wrote a long
Latin poem in honor of the marriage of Alfonso d'Este
to Lucrezia Borgia and was rewarded with a captaincy
in Reggio. He worked his way up to gentleman-in-
waiting to Cardinal Ippolito d'Este, the brother of Duke
Alfonso, and was sent on various diplomatic missions
for the Este family. In 1509, for example, he went to
Rome to seek the aid of Pope Julius II against Venice.
On two other occasions, he visited the pope, trying to
tighten the relationship between Julius and the Estensi,
who were allied by marriage to Louis XII of France.
Julius, however, became instrumental in driving the

French from Italy with the League of Cambrai. Indeed, Ariosto irritated Julius so much that the pope threatened to have him tossed into the Tiber; he was forced to flee over the Apennines with Duke Alfonso in order to escape the consequences of Julius's fury.

In 1513, Ariosto visited the new pope, Leo X, who had been his friend as a cardinal, expecting the pope to become his patron. Leo, however, was a Medici (son of Lorenzo de' Medici), and that family hated the Estensi, so Ariosto went home empty-handed. In the same year, on his way home from a diplomatic mission in Florence, he began a long romantic attachment to Alessandra Benucci. He had carried on a number of previous romances, several leading to the birth of illegitimate children. One son, Virginio, born in 1509 to Orsolina Catinelli, became Ariosto's favorite and resided with Ariosto until the old man's death, even after Ariosto married Alessandra.

In 1516, Ariosto completed his first version of *Orlando Furioso* and dedicated it to his unappreciative patron, Ippolito. (The cardinal coarsely asked Ariosto where he had come up with all that foolishness.) Ariosto was thoroughly disillusioned with his patron, who, he suspected, gave him his pension to compensate the poet only for his life-threatening duties as a diplomatic messenger and not at all for his poetry. Furthermore, Ariosto was irregularly paid. A year later, when Ippolito was appointed bishop of Budapest, Ariosto pleaded his ill health, the poor health of his mother, and a desire to continue with his studies and refused to accompany Ippolito to Hungary. The poet was not disappointed when the angry cardinal released him from his service and even denied him an interview. Ariosto proudly said that if the cardinal had imagined he was buying a slave for a miserable seventy-five crowns a year, he was mistaken and could withdraw the pension.

Ariosto entered the service of Duke Alfonso and became governor of Garfagnana, a wild area between the provinces of Modena and Lucca, claimed by the Luchesi, Pisans, and Florentines. It had surrendered to the Estensi, however, and though given only halfhearted support by the duke, Ariosto proved himself a capable, honest, and diligent administrator. His letters to the duke from his headquarters in Castelnuovo show that, despite his feeling of being in exile, he was a wise ruler in meting out justice, exacting tribute, and controlling the bandits. He was constantly called on to settle squabbles, feuds, and complaints and to coax one faction to make peace with another. There is a story of his having been captured by bandits and taken to their chieftain. When the bandit leader discovered that he was addressing the author of *Orlando Furioso*, he humbly apologized for his men's failure to show Ariosto the respect he deserved, a respect not shown even by his patrons. Ariosto did his best in extraordinarily difficult circumstances and was delighted when, after three years, he was allowed to return to Ferrara. One critic has observed that sending the gentle Ariosto to Garfagnana could be compared to Queen Victoria sending Tennyson to subdue a rebellion in Afghanistan; such were the absurdities of the patronage system.

Seeking a tranquil existence, Ariosto bought a vineyard in the Mirasole district with money he had set aside. He had always been frugal, and he built a small, simple house with a Latin motto on the facade: "Parva sed apta mihi, sed nulli obnoxia, sed non/ Sordida, parta

Ludovico Ariosto (Library of Congress)

meo sed tamen aere domus" (A little house, but enough for me; to none unfriendly, not unclean, and bought with my own money). Living with his son Virginio and his lame brother Gabriele, he was married to Alessandra Benucci (secretly, so that he could still collect his ecclesiastical income) and spent his time gardening, reading the Latin classics, writing comedies, and superintending their performance and the construction of a theater. He also made his third revision of *Orlando Furioso*, increasing the number of cantos from forty to forty-six. When this task was completed, he traveled to Mantua to present a copy to Emperor Charles V, to whom the Estensi had become allied after abandoning the French. Charles appreciated the arts; allegedly, he once stooped to pick up Titian's brush, and there was a rumor that he intended to crown Ariosto in a special ceremony. This never came about, however, and the poet died of tuberculosis a year after his trip to Mantua. He was buried in the church of San Benedetto, though his remains were later transferred to the Biblioteca Comunale of Ferrara.

The posthumous success of Ariosto's great epic was extraordinary. It went through 180 editions in the sixteenth century, often in expensive illustrated formats. It was translated into all the languages of Europe and imitated in all of them.

ANALYSIS

About 1494, Ludovico Ariosto began writing poetry, and, for about ten years, he wrote almost exclusively in Latin, primarily using the poetic forms of Catullus and Horace but influenced by many classical poets as well, including Albius Tibullus and Sextus Propertius. Although his verse in Latin is not equal in technical skill to that of Giovanni Pontano or Pietro Bembo, it has distinctive qualities, particularly its sincerity, which caused Bembo to urge Ariosto to continue writing in Latin. Ariosto's first published Latin ode, of 1494, is an Alcaic (the form most frequently employed by Horace), "Ad Philiroen" ("To Philiroe"). Written just as Charles VIII of France was about to invade Italy, it extols the blessings of peace and love. Catastrophe threatens, but it is good to lie under the trees gazing at Philiroe and listening to the murmur of a waterfall. Critic Francesco De Sanctis observes that Ariosto, in

his Latin verse, thinks, feels, and writes like Horace. Political upheavals are not worth worrying about as long as one can wander in the fields in pursuit of Lydia, Lycoris, Phyllis, Glaura, or any other woman given a Latin pseudonym.

In these lyrics, such as "De puella," "De Lydia," "De Iulia," "De Glycere et Lycori," "De Megilla," and "De catella puellae," one immediately perceives the personality of Ariosto and the general aspiration of artists in the Renaissance to transcend ordinary events for the higher realms of art. Despite his diplomatic career, Ariosto always preferred a simple existence in unpretentious surroundings, but not until late in his life was he able to settle in his little house near Ferrara, where he could spend his time on poetry and gardening. His preference for this type of life is apparent even in his earliest works. He found no satisfaction in the complexities of court and politics and attempted to achieve classical serenity in the pleasures of nature, love, and poetic form. It hardly mattered to him whether Italy was tyrannized by a French king or an Italian one: Slavery is slavery.

Despite Bembo's advice, Ariosto preferred to write in the vernacular, though his lyrics in Italian are a great deal less sensuous than are their Latin counterparts. Heavily influenced by Petrarch, the passions become Platonic, and the physicality of kisses and embraces is replaced by worshipful comparisons of the love object with divinity and the sun. Most of these poems are respectable but workmanlike imitations of Petrarch and are far from Ariosto's greatest work. The poet himself showed a great deal of indifference to the scattering of lyric poems he wrote throughout his life, never collecting and publishing them. He wrote in a number of forms: elegies, sonnets, canzones, madrigals, *capitoli*, and one eclogue. In the case of many poems ascribed to Ariosto, there are serious questions of authenticity. His most famous lyric poem is the sonnet "Non so s'io potro ben chiudere in rima" (I know not if I can ever close in rhyme), which touches on his falling in love with Alessandra in Florence on Saint John's Day as the accession of Leo X was being celebrated.

ORLANDO FURIOSO

Were it not for his great epic poem, *Orlando Furioso*, Ariosto would be regarded as no more than a minor poet whose lyrics influenced the French Pléiade and whose Roman-style comedies made a mark on Renaissance English drama through George Gascoigne, who adapted *The Pretenders* for the British stage in 1566, and William Shakespeare, who used part of it for the subplot of *The Taming of the Shrew* (pr. c. 1593-1594). *Orlando Furioso*, however, is one of the great works of the Renaissance, dwarfing the numerous romances of other writers of that period. It served as a model for Miguel de Cervantes' *El ingenioso hidalgo don Quixote de la Mancha* (1605, 1615; *The History of the Valorous and Wittie Knight-Errant, Don Quixote of the Mancha*, 1612-1620; better known as *Don Quixote de la Mancha*) and Edmund Spenser's *The Faerie Queene* (1590, 1596). It influenced Bernardo Tasso's *Amadigi* (1560) and Torquato Tasso's *Gerusalemme liberata* (1581; *Jerusalem Delivered*, 1600). Robert Greene wrote a play entitled *The History of Orlando Furioso* (pr. 1594), and Shakespeare's *Much Ado About Nothing* (pr. c. 1598-1599; pb. 1600) derives from an episode in Ariosto's epic. John Milton made some use of the poem, and *Orlando Furioso* left its mark on the Romantic period as well, particularly on the poetry of Lord Byron. Sir Walter Scott faithfully read through *Orlando Furioso* every year and relished the epithet bestowed on him by Byron, who called him "the Ariosto of the north." Though not widely read today, *Orlando Furioso* is nevertheless considered one of the masterpieces of the Italian Renaissance.

Ariosto's great poem began with his desire to complete the *Orlando innamorato* (1483, 1495; English translation, 1823) of the Homer of Ferrara, Matteo Maria Boiardo. The Orlando of Boiardo's poem is descended from the hero of the Carolingian epic *Chanson de Roland* (twelfth century; *The Song of Roland*, 1880). Boiardo merged the traditions of the Arthurian romance with those of the Carolingian, and in his hands Orlando becomes much more than a warrior battling Saracens. The love theme of Arthurian romance assumes a dominant role, as the title reveals. The epic is complex, with supernatural events, subplots, battles with infidels and dragons, strange people and islands, fairies, giants, and the rescues of fair maidens. In the latter part of the poem, Boiardo intended to have the Saracen knight Ruggiero convert and marry Brada-

mante and to make them the ancestors of the Este family. Boiardo, however, died in the same year the French invaded Italy, and his Ruggiero remains Muslim and unmarried.

In 1506, Ariosto began *Orlando Furioso* to complete Boiardo's epic, and over a lifetime of writing and revising, he proved himself the best Italian poet of the genre. As his predecessor had integrated the Carolingian and Arthurian traditions, so Ariosto added to them the classical tradition. Many critics have commented that the title of Ariosto's epic echoes Seneca's *Hercules furens* (first century C.E.). Ariosto's opening words, "I sing of knights and ladies, of love and arms, of courtly chivalry, of courageous deeds . . . ," are very close to the opening words of Vergil's *Aeneid* (c. 29-19 B.C.E.; English translation, 1553): "Of the arms and the man I sing." In fulfilling Boiardo's intention to establish an illustrious lineage for the Estensi, Ariosto was also paralleling Vergil's attempt to establish a great ancestry for Augustus Caesar. The following line, "I shall tell of the anger, the fiery rage of young Agramante their king . . . ," is reminiscent of the opening of Homer's *Iliad* (c. 750 B.C.E.; English translation, 1611) and the "wrath of Achilles." Critics have also noted the influence of Ovid, Lucan, and Statius on Ariosto's epic.

To summarize the story line of *Orlando Furioso* would take many pages. The poem is longer than Homer's *Iliad* (c. 750 B.C.E.; English translation, 1611) and *Odyssey* (c. 725 B.C.E.; English translation, 1614) combined, and simply cataloging its characters is a major task. Some critics have therefore asserted that the poem is episodic and lacks unity. Most, however, point to the story of Ruggiero and Bradamante as the central plot around which the themes revolve, although many episodes seem to have no explicit connection with the conflicts between duty and love which constantly interfere with their relationship. Bradamante refuses to marry Ruggiero unless he converts to Christianity, and Ruggiero hesitates to do so while his lord Agramante is in danger. Later, Ruggiero becomes the friend of Leo, the man Bradamante's father had chosen to be her husband, and, out of loyalty, agrees to fight Bradamante in disguise, as Charlemagne has proclaimed that only he who defeats Bradamante in combat may marry her.

Leo, however, asks Charlemagne to give his rights over her to Ruggiero (yet another act of selfless friendship and chivalry). As Ruggiero and Bradamante are being married, however, Rodomonte, a Muslim African king, calls Ruggiero an apostate, and they fight a duel. The poem ends with Rodomonte's condemned soul, in typical Renaissance style, blaspheming on its way to Hell.

Besides recounting the difficulties that Ruggiero and Bradamante must overcome in order to establish the Este line, *Orlando Furioso* tells the story of Orlando, driven to madness by his love for Angelica, daughter of the emperor of Cathay, who has been sent to destroy the court of Charlemagne. Despite the title of the poem, his story seems secondary to that of Ruggiero. After Angelica flees Paris, Orlando searches the world for her, like a knight of the Round Table in quest of the Holy Grail, encountering various adventures along the way but always one step behind her. He rescues a woman from being sacrificed to a monster, for example, just after Ruggiero has lifted Angelica off the same island by means of the hippogriff, a flying horse.

Midway through the epic, Orlando goes mad—God's punishment for abandoning the Christian armies—and rampages naked across France. He stumbles across Angelica as she is about to set sail, but because of his state, they do not recognize each other, and Angelica sails out of the poem. Orlando swims across the Strait of Gibraltar to Africa and does not recover his senses until another madman, Astolfo, travels with Saint John in Elijah's chariot of fire to the Moon, where all the things humankind has lost are collected. Astolfo recovers his own senses and puts Orlando's in a jar, so that he can transport them to Orlando. Restored, the knight devotes himself to the Christian cause and kills Agramante and several others in battles at Bizerta and Lipadusa.

This brief outline of the action of *Orlando Furioso* can give only a partial idea of the epic's complexity. The range of Ariosto's imagination is enormous, and that the poem manages to maintain any coherence at all, considering its myriad characters and supernatural intrusions, is testimony to Ariosto's genius. Besides being unified by its major plots, the poem is unified by its warning to Christendom that its internecine troubles can only increase the Islamic threat. The Turkish advance into Europe was stopped only in 1529, four years before Ariosto's death, when the siege of Vienna was abandoned. The poet did not live to see the Battle of Lepanto in 1571, which ended the Ottoman threat to Europe, and throughout his life, the Turks seemed to be growing in power, while Christians squabbled among themselves.

Many critics argue that *Orlando Furioso* is unified primarily by its style and tone rather than by its plot. With fantastic episodes occurring in every canto, Ariosto sustains the suspension of disbelief by deft use of details, imbuing scenes with the texture of familiar reality. He avoids the bombast and overt rhetorical flourishes that damage the style of so many epic poems of the period.

As De Sanctis points out, there are many tales concerning Ariosto's absentmindedness while composing the epic. It is said, for example, that he once walked halfway to Modena before remembering that he was still in his slippers. Few works of art in any age have been created with the intensity that Ariosto brought to *Orlando Furioso*. As his satires prove, Ariosto took the role of the artist very seriously. Art was his faith; religion, morality, and patriotism were secondary. Ariosto's incessant reworking of the poem shows his artistic obsession with finding the ideal form for his creation. Just as Dante had captured the essence of the end of the Middle Ages, so Ariosto synthesized the essence of the Renaissance, merging classical form with medieval romance and balancing the ironic detachment of a poetic craftsman with an earthy sense of reality.

Satire

Between 1517 and 1525, Ariosto wrote seven verse epistles in tercets, modeled after Horace's *Sermones* (35 b.c.e.). Published posthumously, as *Satire* (translated into English as *Ariosto's Satyres*), because of the real people and situations mentioned in them, these poems reveal much of what is known of Ariosto's personality. Written to friends and relatives such as Bembo and Ariosto's brothers Alessandro and Galazio, the satires are autobiographical and use his personal experiences and observations to make larger moral generalizations. The writer's need for independence is expressed, corruption in the Church and court is exposed, and the dangers of ambition are shown in an Aesop-like fable of a pumpkin that climbs a pear tree. Other poems express Ariosto's regrets at not having completed his education, his views on marriage, his love for the simple life, and his unhappiness at being separated from his family by his patrons' business.

Frequently witty, the satires lack the aristocratic sophistication of Horace and often seem rambling and coarse. Instead of offering incisive observations on human weakness and foolishness, Ariosto often seems to be using the satires as a device to release his pent-up frustrations with a world that will not leave him alone. Nevertheless, the satires do tell a reader much about the atmosphere of the Italian Renaissance, especially the obsessive scrambling for power among noble families.

OTHER MAJOR WORKS

PLAYS: *La cassaria*, pr., pb. 1508, 1530 (*The Coffer*, 1975); *I suppositi*, pr. 1509 (*The Pretenders*, 1566); *I studenti*, wr. 1519 (completed by Gabriele Ariosto as *La scolastica*, pb. 1547, and completed by Virginio Ariosto as *L'imperfetta*, pr. c. 1556; *The Students*, 1975); *La Lena*, pr. 1528 (*Lena*, 1975); *Il negromante*, pr., pb. 1529 (wr. 1520; *The Necromancer*, 1975); *The Comedies of Ariosto*, 1975.

BIBLIOGRAPHY

Ascoli, Albert R. *Ariosto's Bitter Harmony: Crisis and Evasion in the Italian Renaissance*. Princeton, N.J.: Princeton University Press, 1987. Ascoli's close reading of *Orlando Furioso* uncovers Ariosto's "poetics of concord and discord," the evasion of historical crises, and the relationship of this "text of crisis" to others of the genre.

Brand, C. P. *Ludovico Ariosto: A Preface to the "Orlando Furioso."* Edinburgh: Edinburgh University Press, 1974. An excellent overview of Ariosto's life and works. Contains full chapters on life, lyrics, satires, and dramas while concentrating on a thematic study of *Orlando Furioso*. Emphasizes the opposition of love and war. Contains brief bibliographies for each chapter and two indexes.

Carroll, Clare. *The "Orlando Furioso": A Stoic Comedy*. Tempe, Ariz.: MRTS, 1997. Analyzes the poem's stoic view of harmony through a dialectic of contradictory meanings (wisdom through madness,

juxtaposition of excess and restraint) and the balance of the poem's structure. The poem is envisioned as "a miniature animated cosmos," an organism ordered yet changing, accomplished through the imagery of circle, wheel, ring, and *tondo*.

Finucci, Valeria, ed. *Renaissance Transactions: Ariosto and Tasso*. Durham, N.C.: Duke University Press, 1999. Collection of six articles on *Orlando Furioso* by Ronald Martinez (Rinaldo's journey as epic and romance), Daniel Javitch (Ariosto's use of arms and love), Katherine Hoffmann (his juxtaposition of honor and avarice in the criticism of courtly society), Finucci (the problematic masculinity of Jocondo and Astolfo), Eric Nicholson (early theatrical adaptations), and Constance Jordan (the woman warrior Bradamante).

Griffin, Robert. *Ludovico Ariosto*. Boston: Twayne, 1974. Good introductory work on Ariosto, beginning with a chapter on his life and ending with a survey of criticism. Also contains chapters on lyrics, satires, dramas, and a thematic analysis of *Orlando Furioso*. Argues that the unity of the poem rests on man's inability to accept the will of fortune in a world beyond his limited comprehension. Contains chronology, notes, selected bibliography with brief annotations, and two indexes.

Javitch, Daniel. *Proclaiming a Classic: The Canonization of "Orlando Furioso."* Princeton, N.J.: Princeton University Press, 1991. Studies sixteenth century reception of the poem and how readers determined its literary value.

MacPhail, Eric. "Ariosto and the Prophetic Moment." *MLN* 116, no. 1 (January, 2001): 30-53. This essay, which looks at the historical context of Ariosto's epic poem, helps readers understand the times in which he wrote.

Wiggins, Peter De Sa. *Figures in Ariosto's Tapestry: Character and Design in the "Orlando Furioso."* Baltimore: The Johns Hopkins University Press, 1986. Agreeing with Galileo's early comments on the psychological consistency of Ariosto's characters and his exact knowledge of human nature, Wiggins suggests that their complex inner lives are universal human types. This invisible interior world, at odds with an exterior world of folly and depravity, is a major theme of the work. Excellent index and notes for each chapter.

_____. *The Satires of Ludovico Ariosto: A Renaissance Autobiography*. Athens: Ohio University Press, 1976. A bilingual text, using the Italian original edited by Cesare Segre with Wiggins' clear prose translations on the facing page. Each satire is placed in biographical and historical context with its own separate preface and notes. Argues that the narrator of the satires is an idealized poet courtier in typical situations rather than a factual mirror of Ariosto himself. Suggests that the satires share similarities with *Orlando Furioso*: the theme of illusion and reality, the ironic humor, and the use of a dramatic persona as narrator.

J. Madison Davis
Updated by Joseph P. Byrne

HANS ARP

Born: Strassburg, Germany (now Strasbourg, France); September 16, 1887
Died: Basel, Switzerland; June 7, 1966
Also known as: Jean Arp

PRINCIPAL POETRY

Die Wolkenpumpe, 1920
Der Pyramidenrock, 1924
Weisst du schwarzt du, 1930
Des taches dans le vide, 1937
Sciure de gamme, 1938
Muscheln und Schirme, 1939
Rire de coquille, 1944
Le Siège de l'air, 1946 (as Jean Arp)
On My Way: Poetry and Essays, 1912-1947, 1948
Auch das ist nur eine Wolke: Aus dem Jahren, 1920 bis 1950, 1951
Beharte Herzen, Könige vor der Sintflut, 1953
Wortraüme und schwarze Sterne, 1953
Auf einem Bein, 1955
Unsern ta{guml}lichen Traum, 1955
Le Voilier dans la forêt, 1957 (as Jean Arp)

Worte mit und ohne Anker, 1957
Mondsand, 1959
Vers le blanc infini, 1960 (as Jean Arp)
Sinnende Flammen, 1961
Gedichte, 1903-1939, 1963
L'Ange et la rose, 1965 (as Jean Arp)
Logbuch des Traumkapitäns, 1965
Jours effeuillés: Poèmes, Essais, Souvenirs, 1920-1965, 1966 (as Jean Arp; *Arp on Arp: Poems, Essays, Memories*, 1972)
Le Soleil recerclé, 1966 (as Jean Arp)
Gedichte, 1939-1957, 1974
Three Painter Poets, 1974

OTHER LITERARY FORMS

In addition to his large body of poetry, Hans Arp (orpt) wrote a substantial number of lyrical and polemical essays, in which the metaphysical basis of his thought is given its clearest and most systematic expression. These essays are collected in *On My Way* and *Dreams and Projects* (1952). Arp also wrote about his fellow artists in *Onze peintres vus par Arp* (1949), a collection that helps clarify the aesthetic values that influenced his own work as a plastic artist. Arp also published two works of fiction: *Le Blanc aux pieds de nègre* (1945), a collection of short stories, and *Tres inmensas novelas* (1935), short novels written in collaboration with the Chilean poet Vicente Huidobro.

ACHIEVEMENTS

Hans Arp actually has two reputations: one as a sculptor and painter of long-standing international fame, the other as a poet. Although his reputation as a plastic artist overshadowed his work as a poet during his lifetime, he is now recognized as an important and original contributor to the twentieth century literary avant-garde. As a literary artist, Arp is best known for his association with Dada and Surrealism. Together with Tristan Tzara, Hugo Ball, Richard Hülsenbeck, Marcel Janco, and Emmy Hennings, Arp was one of the earliest and most enthusiastic supporters of the Dada movement, which began in Zurich in February of 1916. In the 1950's and 1960's he erected sculptures for Harvard University, the University of Caracas, and the UNESCO Secretariat Building, the Brunswick

Technische Hochschule, and Bonn University Library. He also finished cement steles and walls for the Kunstgewerbeschule in Basel. In addition to these achievements, Arp is best known for sculptures such as *Owl's Dream* (1936), *Chinese Shadow* (1947), *Muse's Amphora* (1959), and *Shepherd's Clouds* (1953). In 1954, he won the international prize for sculpture at the Venice Biennale.

BIOGRAPHY

Hans Arp, also known as Jean Arp, was born in Strasbourg on September 16, 1887. At the time of his birth, Alsace-Lorraine, the region in which Strasbourg lies, belonged to Germany, although culturally it was tied to France, to which it presently belongs. Arp's bilingualism, his equal ease with both French and German, which was a product of the history of this region, helps to account for the confusion concerning his Christian name. As Arp explained it, when he wrote in French, he called himself Jean Arp; when he wrote in German, he called himself Hans Arp. In his view, neither name was a pseudonym—the change was made simply for convenience, as one shifts from speaking one language to the other according to the language of the auditor.

This mingled French and German heritage was also reflected in Arp's home and social environment. His father, Pierre Guillaume Arp, who operated a cigar and cigarette factory in Strasbourg, was of Danish descent. His mother, Josephine Köberlé Arp, was of French descent. At home, Arp recalled, French was spoken. In the state-operated primary and secondary schools he attended, however, standard High German was used, and taught, the Alsace-Lorraine being at the time under German annexation. With his friends he spoke the Alsatian vernacular, a dialect of different derivation from the standard German used in education and for official business.

Arp's first published poem appeared in 1902, when he was only fifteen. Like most of his earliest poetry, it was written in the Alsatian dialect, although only two years later he had completed, in standard High German, a manuscript volume of poems. This manuscript, entitled "Logbuch," was unfortunately mislaid by the publisher to whom it was sent. Three poems by Arp in Ger-

Hans Arp (©Hollaend/Keystone/CORBIS)

man did appear the same year, however, in *Das Neue Magazin*.

About 1904, Arp's involvement with the plastic arts began in earnest. He visited Paris for the first time, and for the next five years he studied art not only at Strasbourg but also in Weimar and Paris. In 1909, Arp, having served his artistic apprenticeship at various academies, moved with his family to Weggis, on the eastern shore of Lake Lucerne in Switzerland. In the five years Arp spent at Weggis, two important developments occurred. Isolated from the influences of the academies and their avant-garde faddishness, Arp began to develop the personal aesthetic he called concrete art, which was to influence the entire course of his career. In addition, he became acquainted with other artists who, like himself, were also pursuing personal aesthetics independent of the Paris academies. During this period, Arp exhibited his work with some of these artists, including Wassily Kandinsky and Paul Klee.

In 1914, Arp returned to Paris only to discover that war had been declared. Because his German money was suddenly valueless in France, and his German citizenship unwelcome, he promptly returned to neutral Zurich. To avoid the draft, he persuaded the authorities at the German consulate that he was mentally ill. In Zurich, Arp exhibited the abstract collages and tapestries that are the earliest examples of his work extant. In November of 1915, at an exhibition of his work with his friend and fellow artist Otto Van Rees, he met his future wife, Sophie Taeuber, an artist who was a native of Zurich.

In 1916, Arp and Taeuber participated in the activities of the newly formed Dada group, which met regularly at the Cabaret Voltaire. At this time, Arp produced bas-relief sculptures and woodcuts reflecting the developing aesthetic that he termed "concrete art." Unlike the earlier geometric productions of his abstract period, these reliefs and woodcuts were composed of asymmetrical curvilinear and bimorphic forms; they were, as Arp later explained, "direct creations," truly "concrete" art, not abstract representations of already existing forms. In 1921, Arp married Taeuber, and together they collaborated on cut-paper collages and other plastic works. Arp also returned to writing poetry, producing a great number of poems in German that were collected in *Die Wolkenpumpe, Der Pyramidenrock*, and *Weisst du schwartz du.*

After the demise of Dada in 1924, Arp formed an increasingly close association with the Surrealist movement, and in 1926, he settled permanently in the Paris suburb of Meudon. Arp's first poem written directly in French was published in 1933, in the Surrealists' journal *Le Surréalisme au service de la révolution*, and his first collection of poems in French, *Des taches dans le vide* (splotches in space), appeared in 1937. At this time, Arp also began to create the free-form sculptures that he called concretions, and that were to bring him international acclaim as a sculptor. He also began to experiment with a new type of "torn-paper" collage; his comments on these collages have often been linked to the Surrealist technique of automatic writing. From this time on, Arp published poetry in both French and German, often translating originals from one language into the other, and in the process frequently introducing substantial changes.

In 1940, with the outbreak of World War II, the Arps fled south from Paris to Grasse to escape the German occupation, later managing to reach Zurich, in neutral Switzerland, in 1942. It was there that Taeuber met with an accidental death on January 13, 1943, sending Arp into a deep depression that lingered for many years. Some of his most moving poems are beautiful evocations of Taeuber's transforming influence on his life.

After the war, Arp's growing fame as an important modern sculptor, as well as the increasing demand for exhibitions of his plastic works, allowed him to travel widely. During this period, he visited the United States, Mexico, Italy, Greece, Jordan, Israel, and Egypt.

In 1959, Arp married Marguerite Hagenbach, who had been a friend of Taeuber in Zurich and had long admired Arp's work. In the remaining seven years of his life, Arp and Hagenbach spent part of the year at their home in Meudon and the remainder at a second home near Locarno, in southern Switzerland. On June 7, 1966, Arp died at the age of seventy-eight, while away from home, in Basel.

ANALYSIS

Hans Arp was one of the founding members of the Dada movement, which had a broad impact on both art and literature in the early twentieth century. Dada's principal target was humanity's overestimation of reason. Its aim, Arp said, was "to destroy the reasonable deceptions of man," to expose "the fragility of life and human works" through the use of Dadaist humor, which would reveal "the natural and unreasonable order" of things. The poems of Arp's first collection, *Die Wolkenpumpe* (the cloud pump), date from this period, as does "Kaspar ist Tot" ("Kaspar Is Dead"), perhaps the most famous of all Dada poems. The Dada use of humor to reorient humanity's attitude toward the world was followed by Arp in these poems, where he began to develop his decidedly personal "Arpian humor."

Dada's critique of modern humanity, however, was not entirely destructive, despite the commonly held belief that it was a totally negative response to the world. Arp's own work is one of the best testaments to this fact. To rectify modern humanity's mistaken view of its place in the universe, Arp offered the notion of a concrete art that could transform both humankind and the world. His intention was "to save man from the most dangerous of follies: vanity . . . to simplify the life of man . . . to identify him with nature."

It was through his participation in the Dada group that Arp became acquainted with the Paris Surrealists, after he and his wife moved to the Paris suburb of Meudon in 1926, Arp frequently participated in Surrealist activities and contributed to their publications. Two important characteristics of Arp's poetry distinguish it, however, from the work of other Dada and Surrealist poets: his highly personal humor and the metaphysical philosophy that underlies all his mature work.

Arp's humor achieves its effect by combining opposites: the celestial with the terrestrial, the eternal with the transitory, the sublime with the mundane, among others. That which comes from above—the celestial, the eternal, the sublime—sustains and nourishes humanity, while that which comes from below—the terrestrial, the transitory, the mundane—confuses and intoxicates humanity. Thus, Arp's conception of humor is connected with his metaphysical philosophy, which aims to restore the lost balance of forces in humans. Arp uses humor in his work to destroy "the reasonable deceptions of man," which lead him to believe that he is "the summit of creation."

"KASPAR IS DEAD"

In Arp's view then, humor and metaphysics are not mutually exclusive, and elements of both are often present in a single work. A good example of this is the early poem "Kaspar Is Dead." The poem is written in the form of an elegy, and it begins, as is customary in the genre, with a lament for the dead. The poem then proceeds to describe the remarkable accomplishments of the deceased, which seem superhuman in character: "who will conceal the burning banner in the cloud's pigtail now . . . who will entice the idyllic deer out of the petrified bag . . . who will blow the noses of ships umbrellas beekeepers ozone-spindles and bone the pyramids." It seems as if some golden age has passed: The link between humanity and nature has been broken by the death of Kaspar. At this realization, the speaker resumes his lament, but this time it seems even more self-conscious, and it includes a note of facetiousness: "alas

alas alas our good kaspar is dead. goodness gracious me kaspar is dead." In the second half of the poem, the speaker turns to more generalized metaphysical speculation: "into what shape has your great wonderful soul migrated. are you a star now or a chain of water . . . or an udder of black light?" He despairs once again at the realization that, wherever he is and in whatever form, Kaspar can no longer reestablish for humankind the broken link between itself and nature. He has ceased to be human and has thus been liberated from the tragic condition of temporal consciousness that the speaker still suffers. The speaker concludes with resignation that it is humanity itself that is obligated to reestablish a proper relationship with nature; it cannot rely on anyone or anything else to do this for it, even such a heroic figure as Kaspar.

"I AM A HORSE"

One of Arp's most successful attacks on the reasonable deceptions of humanity is a poem of his early maturity, "Ich bin ein Pferd" (in French as "Je suis un cheval" and translated into English as "I Am a Horse"). It is not humankind itself that is under attack but humanity's vain rationality. The speaker of the poem is a reasoning horse, who resembles Jonathan Swift's Houyhnhnms. Investing a subhuman creature with the proud vanity of rational humanity creates an ironic situation reminiscent of the fable, in which talking animals are used to satirize particular forms of human folly. In this poem, however, it is the human beings who behave instinctively, emotionally, and impulsively—much to the disgust of the dignified horse, who observes the action from a detached perspective.

As the poem begins, the equine speaker is riding in a crowded passenger train, and "every seat is occupied by a lady with a man on her lap"—a most unpleasant sight to the snobbish, socially respectable horse. In addition to being crowded, the compartment is unbearably hot, and all the human passengers "eat nonstop." When the men suddenly begin to whine, unbuttoning the women's bodices and clutching their breasts, wanting to be suckled, the horse alone resists this primitive, uncivilized impulse, maintaining his proud composure. However, at the end of the poem, the detachment of the speaker, his feeling of superiority relative to the weak-willed humans with whom he shares the compartment, is revealed as a mere pose that disguises the same basic impulses behind the mask of rationality, for when he neighs loudly, "hnnnnn," he thinks proudly of "the six buttons of sex appeal" on his chest—"nicely aligned like the shiny buttons of a uniform." Through the agency of a reasoning horse, Arp presents a Dadaist fable which exposes the foolish vanity and isolation that has resulted from humanity's overestimation of its greatest creation—reason.

ARP'S WORLDVIEW

Arp's work consists of more than attacks on the reasonable deceptions of humanity and satires of his vain pride. Arp devoted a substantial portion of his mature work to communicating, in poetic images and symbols, his distinctive metaphysical philosophy, which has been called variously Platonic, Neoplatonic, Romantic, and Idealist. Arp's worldview eludes these categories; it is personal and intuitive in character, not critical and systematic.

When Arp spoke about the formation of his worldview, he associated it with two particular experiences. The first was the period of isolation he spent at Weggis, which gave him the opportunity to cast aside the aesthetic of abstraction and formulate his theory of concrete art. The second experience was his meeting Sophie Taeuber, whose work and life expressed in an intuitive way, free from self-consciousness, the reorientation of human values that Arp had been seeking.

"IN SPACE"

Arp's metaphysical beliefs, transformed into poetic images and symbols, appeared with increasing frequency in his poetry in the years following Taeuber's death. One of the best of these metaphysical poems is "Dans le vide" ("In Space"), a moving, imaginative elegy written after the death of Arp's friend and fellow artist, Theo van Doesburg. In this poem, death is treated as cause for celebration, not mourning. When the poem begins, the soul of Arp's beloved friend—after having sojourned for a time in the transitory material world below—is preparing to leap out into the unknown, the eternal realm of unbounded space above. The soul, freed from the physical body, realizes that death is a return home, not an exile. This is reinforced by the fact that he enters space, the Above, in the fetal position—which is also the crouch he assumes in order to leap into space.

Refusing to see this death as a loss, Arp focuses on the freedom his friend is now able to enjoy for the first time, as he is joyously liberated from the demands of others. Doesburg now knows neither honor nor dishonor, censure nor obligation; he dwells blissfully alone, in an eternal realm of light. Arp had already described this state of blissful eternal existence in a much earlier poem entitled "Il chante il chante" ("He Sings He Sings"). It is in later poems such as "In Space" that Arp reached the height of his powers as a highly distinctive, imaginative, and lyrical poet.

OTHER MAJOR WORKS

LONG FICTION: *Tres inmensas novelas*, 1935 (with Vicente Huidobro).

SHORT FICTION: *Le Blanc aux pieds de nègre*, 1945.

NONFICTION: *Onze peintres vus par Arp*, 1949; *Dreams and Projects*, 1952; *Collected French Writings*, 1974.

MISCELLANEOUS: *Gesammelte Gedichte*, 1963-1984 (3 volumes).

BIBLIOGRAPHY

Cathelin, Jean. *Jean Arp*. Translated by Enid York. New York: Grove Press, 1960. A short introduction to Arp's life and art, with many photographs of his artwork.

Fauchereau, Serge. *Hans Arp*. Translated by Kenneth Lyons. New York: Rizzoli, 1988. Biographical and critical introduction to Arp's artwork and poetry.

Jean, Marcel. Introduction to *Arp on Arp: Poems, Essays, Memories*, by Jean Arp. Translated by Joachim Neugroschel. New York: Viking, 1972. This introductory essay is an excellent summary of Arp's life and work, and the rest of the book consists of English translations of his collected French poetry and prose.

Last, Rex W. *German Dadaist Literature: Kurt Schwitters, Hugo Ball, Hans Arp*. New York: Twayne, 1973. This clear, thorough study of the three major German-speaking poets of the Dada movement helps to dispel the mistaken notion that it was mostly a French phenomenon after the Zurich period ended. Contains useful chronologies and succinct bibliographies.

_____. *Hans Arp: The Poet of Dadaism.* London: Wolff, 1969. Makes the criticism of Arp's poetry, most of which has been published in German, accessible to an English-speaking audience. The second half consists of translations of many of his German poems.

Lemoine, Serge. *Dada.* Translated by Charles Lynn Clark. New York: Universe Books, 1987. Introduction to Dadaism with biographical information on Arp and other artists. Includes bibliography.

Mortimer, Armine Kotin. "Jean Arp, Poet and Artist." *Dada/Surrealism* 7 (1977): 109-120. Explores the important symbiotic relationship between Arp's poetry and his visual art.

Motherwell, Robert, ed. *The Dada Painters and Poets.* 2d ed. Cambridge, Mass.: Harvard University Press, 1989. A collection of texts and illustrations by Arp and others in the Dada movement with a critical bibliography by Bernard Karpel.

Richter, Hans. *Dada: Art and Anti-Art.* Translated by David Britt. New York: Thames & Hudson, 1997. A historical and biographical account of Dada by one of the artists involved in the movement. Includes bibliographical references and index.

Rimbach, Guenther C. "Sense and Non-Sense in the Poetry of Jean Hans Arp." *German Quarterly* 37 (1963): 152-163. Argues that Arp is at root a religious poet and that the lack of reference to reality in his work is an attempt to come closer to God.

Steven E. Colburn

B

MIHÁLY BABITS

Born: Szekszárd, Hungary; November 26, 1883
Died: Budapest, Hungary; August 4, 1941

PRINCIPAL POETRY

Levelek Irisz koszorújából, 1909
Herceg, hátha megjön a tél is!, 1911
Recitativ, 1916
Pávatollak: Műfordítások, 1920
Jónás könyve, 1940
Hátrahagyott versei, 1941
Vlogatott művei, 1959
Összegyűjtött versei, 1963
21 poems = 21 vers, 1988

OTHER LITERARY FORMS

Although best known for his lyric poetry, Mihály Babits (BOB-ihts) was also among the outstanding essayists of modern Hungary, and his novels and short stories were important expressions of the Hungarian intellectuals' search for their place in a changing society. Equally familiar with the history of European and Hungarian culture, the formal and contextual problems of literature from Homer to the moderns, and the literary struggles of his own times, Babits wrote essays on topics ranging from Henri Bergson and Friedrich Nietzsche to folk literature. Especially revealing of his attitude toward the responsibility of creative artists is his 1928 essay, *Az írástudók árulása* (the treason of the intellectuals), which took its topic as well as its title from Julien Benda's *La Trahison des clercs* (1927). Babits's awareness of the intellectual and artistic ferment of the twentieth century is evidenced by the numerous reviews and critical essays he published.

Babits's novels and short stories are marked by the lyrical approach to prose characteristic of his generation. His short novel *A gólyakalfia* (1916; *The Nightmare*, 1966) is heavily garlanded with the Freudian trappings of the period, particularly with notions concerning dreams and split personalities. The novel *Timár Virgil fia* (1922; the son of Virgil Timár) is closer to the author's own experiences, as it deals with the life of a teacher-priest whose conflict with the urban world ends in tragic isolation, while *Kártyavár* (1923; house of cards) offers a repulsive picture of modern Budapest and its corrupting influence on human character. Babits's best novel is *Halálfiai* (1927; the condemned), an obituary-like tableau of his own generation, a Hungarian *Buddenbrooks* in which embezzlers, small-town curmudgeons, susceptible wives, and representatives of the emerging urban bourgeoisie are masterfully presented. *Elza pilóta vagy a tökéletes társadalom* (1933; Elza the pilot, or the perfect society) is a witty, stylistically elegant, though somewhat anemic utopian novel that takes place in "the forty-second year of the next war," and which is graced by an emphasis on two lasting human values: peace and decency.

Babits's translating activities began as mere philological excursions into other literatures, in part to satisfy his curiosity, and in part to assist him in finding his own voice. In time, however, he developed into one of the most significant modern Hungarian translators, with a range that included classical Greek drama and medieval Latin verse as well as the works of Dante, William Shakespeare, Johann Wolfgang von Goethe, George Meredith, Edgar Allan Poe, Oscar Wilde, and Charles Baudelaire. The impressionistic ease of Babits's early translations was replaced by a disciplined striving for precision and faithfulness.

It should be mentioned among the lasting contributions of Babits that, as the curator of the Baumgarten Foundation and as the editor of the journal *Nyugat*, he exercised great refining, moderating, and encouraging influence on his contemporaries and on younger generations of writers as well.

ACHIEVEMENTS

Mihály Babits, the lyric poet of "restless classicism," embodied the modern synthesis of the Hungarian spirit with the great European values. His only major award came in 1940, when he won the San Remo Prize from the Italian government for his translation of

Dante's *La divina commedia* (c. 1320, 3 volumes; *The Divine Comedy*, 1802). While his humanistic orientation and moral stand remained consistent throughout his life, the marginal nature of his background, combined with the events of his times, presented him with a weighty dilemma: His liberal erudition made him break with the provincialism of the late nineteenth century and urged him to lead his culture toward an acceptance of Western European trends, but his innate idealism made him lean toward conservatism and reinforced his view of literature as an "elite function," independent of any social utility. His writings represent the highest level of urban liberalism in Hungarian literature. Standing on the ground of a humanism that was declared anachronistic and unrealistic by many of his contemporaries, Babits defended the cultural values he considered timeless, against all onslaughts, from Right and Left alike. His experimentation with form and his meticulous craftsmanship enabled him to become one of the most accomplished masters of Hungarian literature. During his declining years, Babits became a living cultural symbol in his country: He dared to produce intellectual writings in an age when the cult of spontaneous life-energy was approaching its peak and young geniuses openly raged against the artistic validity of intellect.

BIOGRAPHY

Mihály Babits was born the only son of an intellectual Roman Catholic family. His father, a circuit judge, was assigned to Budapest and the city of Pécs before he died in 1898. Thus, young Babits became acquainted with various parts of Hungary but always considered Transdanubia (or, as he preferred to call it, Pannonia, after the ancient Roman territory) as his home region. From 1901, he studied at the University of Budapest, majoring in Hungarian and Latin. During his school years, he began to write poetry, and among his best friends he could count Dezső Kosztolányi and Gyula Juhász, who were also to become outstanding poets. After receiving his diploma in 1906, Babits taught in high schools in Szeged, in Fogaras (Transylvania), and in one of the workers' districts of Budapest. His poems were first published in 1902, and by 1908, he was one of the chief contributors to the new literary journal *Nyugat*. During the years preceding World War I, he published several volumes of poetry, read voraciously to acquire a broad European background, and began to translate the classics. He was opposed to the war from its beginning, and his pacifism became ever more outspoken. The nationalist press of the period attacked him, and one of his poems, "Fortissimo," provoked the confiscation of the journal in which it appeared.

Although decidedly apolitical, Babits welcomed the Revolution of 1918, seeing in it the end of Hungary's participation in the war and the birth of a national republic. As the revolution was quickly taken over by Hungary's handful of Bolsheviks, however, he became disappointed and aloof, even though the short-lived Republic of Councils appointed him professor of world literature at the University of Budapest. His acceptance of this position was harshly criticized in certain quarters during the subsequent years of counterrevolutionary backlash, but by that time his position as one of the central figures in Hungarian cultural life was established.

In 1921, Babits married Ilona Tanner, who (under the name Sophie Török) was herself an accomplished poet. At their summer home, in one of the most picturesque parts of Hungary, they entertained many of the country's best writers and poets. In 1927, Babits was appointed curator of the prestigious Baumgarten Foundation, which had as its aim the aiding of impoverished young writers and artists. This meant not only that his financial situation improved but also that he became perhaps the preeminent literary arbiter in the country— a role that was confirmed when he became the editor of *Nyugat*.

The 1930's brought a series of painful and destructive illnesses to Babits: first polyarthritis, later cancer of the larynx. The frail man underwent dangerous operations that proved to be only half successful. During the last years of his life, he was able to communicate only with the aid of his "talking notebooks." In spite of his illnesses, however, he remained active. In 1940, he was awarded the San Remo Prize by the Italian government for his translation of Dante's *The Divine Comedy* and subsequently he was elected a member of the Hungarian Academy of Sciences. He died of cancer in 1941.

ANALYSIS

The first volumes of the young Mihály Babits, *Levelek Irisz koszorújából* (leaves from Iris's wreath) and *Herceg, hátha megjön a tél is!* (prince, what if the winter comes?), contain poems representing the best of Hungarian fin de siècle aestheticism and secessionist tendencies. Babits rejected both the lyrical approach of his contemporaries—who, in the tradition of Hungarian populism, relied on the anecdotal retelling of subjective experiences—and the pathos of the neo-Romantics. The most frequent object of his early poetry is a cultural experience treated in an intellectualized manner; his own feelings appear only indirectly and in a highly generalized form. Another notable trait of Babits's youthful poetry is its playful richness and variety of tone. The poet refuses to reveal his feverish inner turmoil, his painful loneliness, and his internal conflict between thought and action. He hides behind a number of veils: now a scene from Hindu mythology, now a figure of the Roman Silver Age, now an episode from modern life—many worlds, many styles, many ways of looking at human existence. The poet's touch makes the rather ponderous Hungarian words dance in exciting configurations. Babits's verse can be read in a number of ways, not only because of the virtuoso arrangement of rhyme and rhythm but also because of the shimmering sound and sense of every word within the lines. Perhaps more than any of his Hungarian predecessors, Babits maintained a strong connection with the fine arts, not merely in his themes and images but also in his approach to literature. His stance as a craftsman was consciously chosen to distinguish himself from the multitude of spontaneous and pseudospontaneous versifiers.

Despite his experimental playfulness, Babits's poems are always thoughtful, often philosophical; they are also among the most eloquent expressions of the fin de siècle's characteristic moods: nostalgia, dissatisfaction, and a superstitious, almost mystical *Weltangst*. There are also powerful streaks of Satanism and sin consciousness in his poetry. This strain in Babits's work is not attributable to the poet's personal experience, for he led a quiet, almost ascetic life; rather, it can be viewed as an expression of "preventive guilt," resulting from the purity of his soul: While he recoiled from the touch of the vulgar, he was at the same time attracted by it.

Babits considered himself one of the last descendants of the great Hungarian poets of the nineteenth century and refused to bow to the "vulgar" democratism of his age. His sentences, therefore, remain among the weightiest in Hungarian literature; the poet crammed them with colorful and unusual words, arranged so that the reader is forced to read the lines rapidly, without relaxing his intellectual excitement. If they are to yield their full meaning, though, the sentences have to be broken down and dissolved, somewhat like those of the English sonneteers. As in the work of his great contemporary, Endre Ady, the sentences in Babits's verse have a larger function than simply conveying the idea: With their solidity or elusive airiness, their zigzagging speed or ponderous pace, they are meant to express the atmosphere and the emotional content of the poetic text.

There was a perceptible conflict between the young poet and the culture of Hungary under a dual monarchy, but this was scarcely manifested in writings of social or political content. The overwhelming presence of subjective elements, the almost total exclusion of reality, the adoration of the past, and an emphatic cultivation of Nietzschean individualism are all indicative of Babits's desire to evade having to deal with the present, even at the risk of becoming isolated.

WORLD WAR I

The years of World War I brought significant changes in Babits's poetry. "The cool glitter of classical contemplation" is gone from the poems written during this period. The style is now simpler and closer to everyday experience, while the poet's active pacifism also forced him to discontinue his flirtation with irrationalism. Babits remained immune to the radical fervor that infected many of his contemporaries, but his desire for peace was passionate and, at times, militant. After he claimed, in one of his poems, that he would rather shed blood for the little finger of his beloved than for any flag or cause, the nationalistic press of the period attacked him sharply. This did not stop the poet from repeating his cry for peace: "Let it end!" The signs pointing toward a great social upheaval in Hungary filled him with hope and enthusiasm: "The world is not a plaything! Here, one must see and create!" Soon, however, it became obvious that he viewed the events of 1919 (the "mud and blood of the revolution," in the words of a Hungarian historian) with increasing apprehension. Hope in the passing of the chaos permeates his writings after 1919, and, in a characteristically bitter image, he compares political ideologies to "slow-acting poisons."

POSTWAR CHANGES

In words as well as deeds, Babits put a distance between himself and public affairs during the post-World War I decades. "Fence in your property!" was his *ars poetica*; he sought to preserve his islandlike independence and remain aloof from politics, which interested him only as "a threatening force, which may seriously interfere with my life." Nevertheless, Babits's withdrawal into the shell of love (as represented by his 1921 marriage, and by the frequent get-togethers with a small circle of friends) cannot be classified as a frightened retreat. In stating his conviction that it is "better not to understand one's age and to be left behind" (repeated later as "noble souls do not pay obeisance to their immediate environments"), Babits remained consistent with his elitist conception of art. As the spiritual leader, later editor, of *Nyugat*, and as the curator of the prestigious Baumgarten Foundation, he remained uncompromising in upholding the highest artistic standards, and he refused to treat literature as a social force, or as a propaganda tool. At the same time, there were anticapitalist pieces among his poems ("The Mice of Babylon") and, realizing that the age of fin de siècle individualism was ended, he was enthusiastic about the rise of a socially and politically active neopopulist trend in Hungarian literature. Even his hitherto dormant nationalism was aroused, and in several poems he eloquently pleaded the cause of his nation.

The form of Babits's poetry now changed. The craftsman gave up strict rhyme and rhythm and assumed the freer style of expressionism, while his sentences became more puritanical, almost democratic in their spareness. He became more aware of the dominance of concrete experience, and registered this with sad resignation, because he could never become a vitalist. The main motive of his poems remains the primacy

and freedom of the human spirit over matter, a message he often conveyed with the resignation of a wounded combatant.

JÓNÁS KÖNYVE

With Europe shifting toward the right and the ascent of fascism, even Babits found it impossible to remain aloof. He was forced to take sides for moral and intellectual reasons. His condemnation of anything cheap, low-grade, and vulgar—which had made him lose faith in the Bolshevik experiment—was turned against the rising tide of another ideological madness, foreboding new horrors for his continent. He began to revise his views but had no time to complete this task; illness and suffering—which are the topics of several late works in Babits's oeuvre—sapped his energy during his final years. In *Jónás könyve* (the book of Jonah), a confessional allegory on the biblical theme, Babits appears chastened and repentant of his earlier idealism and aloofness: "The wicked find their cronies among the silent!" The most eloquent testimony of the poet, however, is perhaps best summed up in these lines from one of his essays:

> I still believe in human reason. I am still convinced that, as far as it reaches, it faithfully serves that which it cannot comprehend, . . . and that the poem will not suffer but improve if it is constructed by human intellect (as long as the Owner watches over the Architect!). Europe has experienced years of mindless horror: Let the age of reason come forth!

OTHER MAJOR WORKS

LONG FICTION: *A gólyakalfia*, 1916 (*The Nightmare*, 1966); *Timár Virgil fia*, 1922; *Kártyavár*, 1923; *Halálfiai*, 1927; *Elza pilóta vagy a tökéletes társadalom*, 1933.

NONFICTION: *Az írástudók árulása*, 1928; *Esszék, Danulmányok*, 1978 (2 volumes).

TRANSLATION: *Dante Romédiája*, 1913, 1920, 1923, 1939 (of Dante's *Divine Comedy*).

MISCELLANEOUS: *Összegyűjtött munkái*, 1937-1939 (collected works, including prose and poetry).

BIBLIOGRAPHY

Basa, Enikő Molnár, ed. *Hungarian Literature*. New York: Griffon House, 1993. A historical overview that provides some background to the life and work of Babits. Includes bibliographic references.

Czigány, Lóránt. *The Oxford History of Hungarian Literature from the Earliest Times to the Present*. Rev. ed. New York: Oxford University Press, 1986. A critical and historical overview of Hungarian literature. Includes bibliographic references and an index.

Lengyel, Balázs. "A Poet's Place: Mihály Babits." *New Hungarian Quarterly* 24, no. 90 (Summer, 1983). A brief critical study of the poetic works of Babits.

Remenyi, Joseph. "Mihály Babits." *World Literature Today* 63, no. 2 (Spring, 1989): 186. In his poetry, Babits reflects the introspective uneasiness of the modern man and his attempts to find meaning in a meaningless life.

András Boros-Kazai

INGEBORG BACHMANN

Born: Klagenfurt, Austria; June 25, 1926
Died: Rome, Italy; October 17, 1973

PRINCIPAL POETRY

Die gestundete Zeit, 1953
Anrufung des grossen Bären, 1956
Gedichte, Erzählungen, Hörspiel, Essays, 1964
Werke: In 4 Bänden, 1978
Die Gedichte, 1981
In the Storm of Roses: Selected Poems, 1986
Songs in Flight: The Collected Poems of Ingeborg Bachmann, 1994
Darkness Spoken: The Collected Poems, 2006

OTHER LITERARY FORMS

In addition to her poetry, Ingeborg Bachmann (BOK-mon) published two radio plays, three volumes of short stories, and a novel. Much of her prose concerns the role of women in search of their own identity. Bachmann also collaborated with the composer Hans Werner Henze, writing the librettos for his operas *Der Prinz von Homburg* (pb. 1960; the prince of Homburg)

and *Der junge Lord* (pb. 1965; *The Young Milford*, 1967). She was praised by critics as a librettist of great talent. Bachmann's other publications include essays in which she discusses her poetic theory.

ACHIEVEMENTS

Ingeborg Bachmann attracted and fascinated readers and critics alike during her short life and has continued to do so since her untimely death in 1973. Bachmann's work has been praised as great and pure poetry, and she has been compared with such towering figures of German poetry as Friedrich Gottlieb Klopstock, Friedrich Hölderlin, and Rainer Maria Rilke. At the same time, the critic Peter Demetz has charged that her verse is marred by a "gauche combination of high polish and utterly sentimental *Kitsch*," and her metaphors have been labeled vague, justifying almost any interpretation.

It cannot be denied that Bachmann's personality and her life, still shrouded in mystery, have attracted at least as much attention as her work. After her appearance in 1952 at a meeting of Gruppe 47 (group 47), an influential circle of postwar writers, followed in turn by a story about her in *Der Spiegel*, Germany's mass-circulation newsmagazine (similar to *Time* magazine), Bachmann could never rid herself of her image as a beautiful blond who had become, of all things, a writer—sensuous yet intellectual, a cosmopolite from a provincial town in Austria, succeeding in a world traditionally dominated by men. When, after her death, her colleagues Günter Grass, Uwe Johnson, and Max Frisch began writing about her, Bachmann, who had already become a legend of sorts, gained increasing recognition as a significant figure in postwar German literature.

Bachmann's appeal derived from a happy fusion of traditional and modern elements. The older generation of readers, reared on Hölderlin and Georg Trakl, appreciated her classical German, while the younger critics welcomed her linguistic experiments, controlled as they were, and what Demetz has called her "hard, dry poems in the manner of the older Brecht." It was, however, mainly because of their themes that Bachmann's poems struck the nerve of their time. In a period when Germans were busy reconstructing their country and enjoying the fresh fruits of the so-called economic miracle, she sent out warning signals of approaching doom. In imploring tones, she attempts to remind her readers that the end of time is near—the titles of her first two volumes, *Die gestundete Zeit* (borrowed time) and *Anrufung des grossen Bären* (evocation of the great bear), are such signals. The poems in these collections clearly define the situation: "Borrowed time, now recalled, grows visible on the horizon"; the "creature of cloudlike fur . . . with tired flanks, and the sharp, half-bared teeth stands threateningly in the sky." In the same breath, however, Bachmann exuberantly announces her readiness for life: "Nothing more beautiful under the sun than to be under the sun. . . ." Bachmann's combination of apocalyptic vision and lyrical affirmation compelled the attention of her generation.

Although Bachmann's poems must be understood as products of their time and seen in their historical and cultural context, they have universal and timeless appeal. Bachmann's existential concern, her warnings not to succumb to comfortable adjustment, and the unique poetic quality of her language will continue to capture the imagination of readers.

BIOGRAPHY

The daughter of a schoolteacher, Ingeborg Bachmann grew up in her native Klagenfurt, the capital city of Austria's southernmost province, Carinthia. If the fictional account of *Jugend in einer österreichischen Stadt* (1961; youth in an Austrian town) is any indication, Bachmann's childhood and youth were not particularly happy. Perhaps this accounts for her reticence concerning that period of her life. She does mention the traumatic days of March, 1938, when Adolf Hitler annexed Austria and the German army triumphantly marched into Klagenfurt with most of her countryfolk applauding enthusiastically. Otherwise, very little is known about Bachmann's life before the age of twenty-three.

Bachmann initially studied law but soon took up philosophy at the universities of Innsbruck, Graz, and Vienna. In 1950, she received her doctorate with a dissertation on the critical reception of Martin Heidegger's existential philosophy. In 1950 and 1951, she traveled to London and Paris. For two years, she was a

Ingeborg Bachmann (Courtesy, R. Piper)

member of the editorial staff of Radio Rot-Weiss-Rot, the American-sponsored radio station in Vienna. In 1952, she gave her first reading at a meeting of Gruppe 47.

After the success of her first two books of poetry, Bachmann chose to take up the life of a freelance writer, residing in Rome for many years. Her visit to the United States in 1955, at the invitation of Harvard University, provided the background for the American setting of her highly successful radio play, *Der gute Gott von Manhattan* (1958; the good god of Manhattan). From 1959 to 1960, Bachmann was the first guest lecturer in poetics at the University of Frankfurt. She was awarded many of the important literary prizes of her time, including the Great Austrian State Prize in 1968.

Bachmann died in 1973, following a somewhat mysterious fire in her Rome residence. Five years later, her collected works were published in four volumes by Piper Verlag in Munich. The tenth anniversary of her death sparked renewed interest in Bachmann and was the occasion for many symposia throughout the world on her work.

ANALYSIS

With love and joy, departure and death as her prevalent themes, it seems safe to say that Ingeborg Bachmann stays well within the conventions of poetry. Nor is her message novel; after all, the end of the world has been proclaimed many times before in poetry. Bachmann tells her readers solemnly that "the great cargo of the summer" is ready to be sent off and that they must all accept the inevitable end. Time is only borrowed, if one is to believe the ominous title of her first collection of poems. The titles of many of her poems are ciphers of farewell: "Ausfahrt" ("Departure"), "Fall ab, Herz" ("Fall Away, Heart"), "Das Spiel ist aus" ("The Game Is Over"), "Lieder auf der Flucht" ("Songs in Flight"). Indeed, Bachmann's poetry constitutes a "manual for farewells," as George Schoolfield has put it.

Images of night, darkness, ice, and shadow abound in Bachmann's verse. On closer inspection, however, one also discovers an entirely different set of images: warmth, summer, sunlight, plant growth. Although all these images may look conventional at first glance, one soon discovers that Bachmann has a very private mythological system and that most of her images have meaning only within that system. Many critics have attempted to decode Bachmann's verse; perhaps the most persuasive reading is that of Hans Egon Holthusen, who sees two basic attitudes reflected in Bachmann's poetry. One must agree with his diagnosis that there is a tension between hope and despair or joy and anguish in the fabric of nearly every poem by Bachmann.

DIE GESTUNDETE ZEIT

Bachmann's "dark" or "negative" images are ciphers for what Holthusen calls her "elegiac" consciousness (in contrast to her "panegyric" consciousness, as reflected in her "positive" imagery). Images of ice, snow, cold, or barren landscape represent restricting elements in life, such as the impossibility of communication between lovers. Particularly in her first volume, *Die gestundete Zeit*, Bachmann frequently writes about the coldness of time. The poem "Curriculum Vitae," for example, evokes a winter landscape. In it, life is imaged as a quest for a path laid between ice skeletons. Even in Bachmann's love poems, there are repeated images of snow, ice, and cold.

Such imagery must be related to Bachmann's worldview. Although there are those who see her poems as reflections of a blurry *Weltschmerz* trimmed in beautiful language, her pessimism was earned by experience and reflected a concrete historical situation. Bachmann herself protested frequently against the mere culinary enjoyment of her poetry. Rather, she wanted her poems to be understood as a reaction to the unprecedented horrors of World War II.

"EARLY NOON"

This intention is clear in "Früher Mittag" ("Early Noon"), a major poem of Bachmann's first collection. In this poem, there are numerous references to Germany's recent past. Having been offered a platter on which is displayed the German heart, Bachmann's lyrical traveler opens the heart, looks inside, and reflects on what he finds: Germany's misuse of idealism and its efforts to disguise the past with what George Schoolfield has called the "simple heartiness of the beer-garden." Fragments of a song by Franz Schubert and a poem by Johann Wolfgang von Goethe, cherished treasures of German musical and literary heritage, are interspersed with Bachmann's lines reminding the reader, all too painfully, of the aesthetic component of the German mind. In their context, these quotations sound like parodies, for Germany, in the poem, is a beheaded angel, and yesterday's hangmen drink from the golden goblet of Goethe's "Der König in Thule"—who, one must know, was "faithful unto the grave."

The message could not be lost on the German (or Austrian) reader of the poem. After all, loyalty was a key word with which many of Hitler's henchmen defended their actions. Later in the poem, Bachmann conjures up Fyodor Dostoevski's *Zapiski iz myortvogo doma* (1861-1862; *The House of the Dead*, 1881), provoking visions of Germany as a Siberian labor camp, with all the old jailers still in power—a not-so-subtle reminder that many of Germany's war criminals went free, had their civil rights and privileges restored, and even, in some cases, again enjoyed positions of power.

"Early Noon" clearly demonstrates that Bachmann did not wish to retreat into a realm of private memories or to hide behind fairy tales, as some critics have charged. On the contrary, it should be mentioned here that even many of her love poems are not as private as they may at first appear. Love, too, is shown as a victim of the modern age. Communication is no longer possible. The poem "Nebelland" ("Fog Land"), for example, is set in the winter. The lost lover is seen as a fish. The speaker is being driven away by ice floes, symbols of despair and desolation.

Although her poems can be related to their historical situation, Bachmann was not, strictly speaking, a political poet. Her methodological approach to language was based on her study of the philosopher Ludwig Wittgenstein. Attempting to discover the limits of human understanding, Bachmann, in "Early Noon," questions the effectiveness of the poetic word. "Where Germany's soil blackens the sky," she writes, "the cloud searches for words and fills the crater with silence. . . ." Silence, the ultimate vanishing point of a poem? In "Early Morning," Bachmann clings to the hope that the unspeakable may still be said. The poem concludes with these words: "The unutterable, gently uttered, goes over the land: it is already noon." As Schoolfield explains, "unutterable" is an abstract noun with two implications. Unspeakable crimes and unutterable beauty come to mind, and beyond these connotations lies a hint that there are problems the complexity of which defies expression.

It should be pointed out that Bachmann's skeptical attitude toward language reflects an Austrian tradition whose roots lie in the linguistic and philosophical dilemmas of the turn of the century. Hugo von Hofmannsthal, in his celebrated *Brief des Lord Chandos* (pb. as "Ein Brief" in 1902, pb. in book form in 1905; *Letter of Lord Chandos*, 1952), expressed his despair at the ineffectiveness of poetic language. In "Early Noon," an echo of the famous last sentence of Wittgenstein's "Logisch-philosophische Abhandlung" (1921; better known by the bilingual German and English edition title of *Tractatus Logico-Philosophicus*, 1922, 1961) can be heard: "What one cannot speak of, one must keep silent about."

"AUTUMN MANEUVERS"

Many of the poems in Bachmann's first collection read—in the apt formulation of George Schoolfield—like a *vade mecum* of instruction for dealing with a brief phase of European history. One such poem is "Herbst-

manöver" ("Autumn Maneuvers"). In it, Bachmann addresses German readers of the 1950's. They may find personal pleasures by traveling to the most exotic lands, but they will still be afflicted by twinges of guilt—guilt that they will not be able to dispel by claiming that they are not at home.

"BORROWED TIME"

Another such poem is "Die gestundete Zeit" ("Borrowed Time"). When time actually does run out and appears on the horizon, "your beloved," Bachmann writes, "sinks into the sand, which rises to her wandering hair, choking her into silence and finding her mortal, willing to part after each embrace." Once again, the imagery of this poem and its symbols, drawn from nature, should not be regarded as mere ornamentation but rather as integral elements in a "complex totality operating on the outer boundaries of meaning." Again, an individual is shown as being incapable of communication and falling into silence.

"EVOCATION OF THE GREAT BEAR"

One of Bachmann's best-known poems is "Anrufung des grossen Bären" ("Evocation of the Great Bear"). It has been anthologized many times and has provoked numerous interpretations. In spite of its fairy-tale-like introduction and atmosphere, it suggests many parallels with contemporary history.

In the first stanza, the image of a shaggy bear blends with that of the Ursa Major of the stars. The mighty old bear is about to break loose and destroy all those shepherds, representatives of humankind who have, maliciously or mischievously, invoked him, knowing full well that he would destroy them and their flock, thus bringing about their predicament. In the second stanza, the bear becomes a symbolic bear, and the earth itself becomes a pinecone with which he plays, testing it between his teeth, rolling it between the trees, and grabbing it with his paws—all this symbolizing humanity's precarious position. A warning follows in the last two stanzas: Contribute to the church and keep the blind man (who shows the bear at carnivals) happy, so that he will not let the beast loose. The bear could still crush all cones, all worlds that have fallen from the trees of the universe. Biblical parallels suggest themselves here: the story of the Last Judgment, the Fall of Man.

In the final analysis, no single interpretation is possible. The total effect of Bachmann's symbolic vocabulary in this poem is to leave the reader in doubt about its exact meaning.

THE VALUE OF POETRY

Bachmann's entire oeuvre can be interpreted as a transformation of inner conflict into art. In a speech of thanks to the donors of an award she received, Bachmann spoke in the following terms of the function of the poet:

> We extend our possibilities in the interplay between the impossible and the possible. It is important for us to create this tension, we grow on it, we look toward a goal, which becomes more distant the closer we get.

In this speech, Bachmann expresses a certain ambivalence about the role of the poet. She vacillates between a firm belief in the eternal value of poetry and poetic language and a sense of its ultimate futility. In the end, the latter prevailed, and she virtually gave up poetry. The few poems that Bachmann wrote after 1956 and published in various magazines all revolve around her doubts about the validity of poetic language. The final poem of her collection *Anrufung des grossen Bären*, titled "Ihr Worte," ends with two ambiguous lines that are indicative of her crisis: "Kein Sterbenswort, Ihr Worte!" ("not one more death-prone word, you words!").

Bachmann has been called a poet-thinker. As such, she made heavy demands on herself, and her work likewise demands much from her readers. Her readiness to confront, using exemplary lyric language, the issues of Germany's dark historical past as well as the universal problems of modern humanity has secured for her a permanent position among the great poets of German literature.

OTHER MAJOR WORKS

LONG FICTION: *Malina*, 1971 (English translation, 1989).

SHORT FICTION: *Das dreissigste Jahr*, 1961 (*The Thirtieth Year*, 1964); *Jugend in einer österreichischen Stadt*, 1961; *Simultan: Neue Erzählungen*, 1972 (*Three Paths to the Lake*, 1989).

PLAYS: *Der Prinz von Homburg*, pb. 1960 (libretto);

Der junge Lord, pb. 1965 (libretto; *The Young Milford*, 1967).

RADIO PLAYS: *Die Zikaden*, 1955; *Der gute Gott von Manhattan*, 1958.

MISCELLANEOUS: *Last Living Words: The Ingeborg Bachmann Reader*, 2005.

BIBLIOGRAPHY

Achberger, Karen. *Understanding Ingeborg Bachmann.* Columbia: University of South Carolina Press, 1995. The first biography of Bachmann in English offers interpretation of her poetry, radio plays, librettos, critical writings, and prose. Achberger is a leading critic and has published a number of articles on Bachmann.

Brinker-Gabler, Gisela, and Markus Zisselsberger, eds. *If We Had the Word: Ingeborg Bachmann, Views and Reviews.* Riverside, Calif.: Ariadne Press, 2004. This collection of essays was partly the result of a 1996 symposium on Bachmann. Provides analysis of Bachmann's poetry and major themes in her writing, such as death.

Brown, Hilary, ed. *Landmarks in German Women's Writing.* New York: Peter Lang, 2007. This work on prominent German women writers contains a chapter on Bachmann that analyzes her work and life.

Demetz, Peter. "Ingeborg Bachmann." In *Postwar German Literature: A Critical Introduction.* New York: Pegasus, 1970. A brief introduction to Bachmann's work.

Ezergailis, Inta. *Woman Writers: The Divided Self.* Bonn, Germany: H. Grundmann, 1982. Critical analysis of prose by Bachmann and other authors. Includes bibliographic references.

Gölz, Sabine I. *The Split Scene of Reading.* Atlantic Highlands, N.J.: Humanities Press, 1998. Criticism and interpretation of Bachmann and Franz Kafka's writing with an emphasis on the influence of Jacques Derrida and Friedrich Nietzsche. Includes an extensive bibliography.

Gudrun, Brokoph-Mauch, and Annette Daigger, eds. *Ingeborg Bachmann: Neue Richtungen in der Forschung?* Ingbert, Germany: Röhrig, 1995. A collection of critical essays on Bachmann in German with a section of essays in English.

Lennox, Sara. *Cemetery of the Murdered Daughters: Feminism, History, and Ingeborg Bachmann.* Amherst: University of Massachusetts Press, 2006. An analysis that relies on feminist criticism while at the same time positioning the works of Bachmann in their historical context.

Lyon, James K. "The Poetry of Ingeborg Bachmann: A Primeval Impulse in the Modern Wasteland." *German Life and Letters* 17 (April, 1964): 206-215. A critical analysis of selected poems by Bachmann.

Jürgen Koppensteiner

STANISŁAW BARAŃCZAK

Born: Poznań, Poland; November 13, 1946

PRINCIPAL POETRY

Koretka twarzy, 1968

Jednym tchem, 1970

Dziennik poranny: Wiersze 1967-1971, 1972

Ja wiem, że to niesłuszne: Wiersze z lat, 1975-1976, 1977

Sztuczne oddychanie, 1978

Where Did I Wake Up? The Poetry of Stanisław Barańczak, 1978 (translated by Frank Kujawinski)

Under My Own Roof: Verses for a New Apartment, 1980 (translated by Kujawinski)

Tryptyk z betonu, zmęczenia i śniegu, 1981

Wiersze prawie zebrane, 1981

Atlantyda i inne wiersze z lat, 1981-1986, 1986

Widokówka z tego świata: I inne rymy z lat, 1986-1988, 1988

The Weight of the Body: Selected Poems, 1989 (translated by Barańczak et al.)

159 wierszy, 1968-1988, 1990

Podróż zimowa: Wiersze do muzyki Franza Schuberta, 1994

Zimy i podróże, 1997

Chirurgiczna precyzja: Elegie i piosenki z lat, 1995-1997, 1998

Wiersze zebrane, 2006

OTHER LITERARY FORMS

Though Stanisław Barańczak (bo-RA-zhok) is principally known in his native Poland as a poet, he is also a prolific translator and essayist. In the English-speaking world, he may be best known for his translations of the 1996 Nobel Prize-winning poet Wisława Szymborska with his frequent collaborator Clare Cavanagh. He has also translated a large amount of English-language poetry into Polish to great acclaim; Cavanagh has acknowledged him as "perhaps the most gifted and prolific translator from English in the history of Polish literature." A translation of his book-length investigation of the writing of fellow Polish poet Zbigniew Herbert, *Uciekinier z Utopii: O poezji Zbigniewa Herberta* (1984; *A Fugitive from Utopia: The Poetry of Zbigniew Herbert*, 1987) was published by Harvard University Press. Several of his essays, which predominantly explore Eastern European writers and life under censorship, are collected in *Breathing Under Water and Other East European Essays* (1990).

ACHIEVEMENTS

Stanisław Barańczak received the Kościelski Foundation Prize in 1972, the Alfred Jurzykowski Foundation Literary Award in 1980, and the Terrence Des Prés Prize in 1989. His poetry collection *Chirurgiczna precyzja: Elegie i piosenki z lat, 1995-1997* (1998; surgical precision) won the influential Nike Literary Award (1999) for being the best book published in Poland in 1998. He also received a Guggenheim Fellowship in 1989 and a medal for meritorious service from his alma mater, Adam Mickiewicz University, in 1995. He is the recipient, with his cotranslator Cavanagh, of the 1996 PEN/Book-of-the-Month Club Translation Prize for *View with a Grain of Sand: Selected Poems* (1995), their translation of the poetry of Szymborska. In addition, he has played a significant role in introducing Polish poetry to a wide English-speaking audience through his tireless translations and criticism, following in the path of his predecessor Czesław Miłosz.

BIOGRAPHY

Stanisław Barańczak was born in 1946 in Poznań, where he remained as a student, studying Polish at Adam Mickiewicz University. His first collection of poetry, *Koretka twarzy* (proofreading the face), appeared in 1968, as Barańczak was pursuing his master's degree. Once he gained the degree in 1969, he began teaching Polish literature at the university; in 1974, after receiving his Ph.D., he was elevated to the position of assistant professor.

Barańczak's activity as a poet, editor, and critic were complemented by his leadership in political movements of the time, though he never separated the two impulses in his work and intellectual development. Cavanagh notes that its "fusion of poetry and politics . . . was the hallmark" of his generation of Polish poets, known as the New Wave or Generation of '68. The latter title refers to the riots in March of 1968, as students protested the suppression of a performance of *Dziady* (parts 2, 4, 1823, and 3, 1832; *Forefathers' Eve*, parts 2, 4, 1925, and 3, 1944-1946), a classic verse drama by the Polish national poet, Adam Mickiewicz. In 1976, Barańczak was instrumental in editing unauthorized literary journals such as *Zapis* and, in 1980, became a founding member of KOR (the Committee for the Defense of Workers), a group that solidified the connections between workers and intellectuals and would be instrumental in the foundation of the Polish trade union Solidarity.

These political activities led to the official blacklisting of Barańczak's works and, in 1977, the loss of his teaching position. During this period, Barańczak was unable to publish his writing through official channels, though some collections of his translations into Polish appeared in domestic publication; instead, he published in underground (*samizdat*) editions and through Polish émigré publishers, notably in France.

Though Barańczak's position at Adam Mickiewicz University was reinstated in 1980, largely because of the political impact of the Solidarity movement, he immigrated to the United States in 1981 to take a position at Harvard University, where he ultimately became the Alfred Jurzykowski Professor of Polish Language and Literature.

After his departure from Poland, Barańczak's translations from English to Polish and vice versa proliferated at a remarkable rate. He has translated into Polish the works of poets as diverse as William Shakespeare, the English Metaphysicals, Gerard Manley Hopkins,

Emily Dickinson, Robert Frost, W. H. Auden, and Seamus Heaney; in addition, he has translated into English and anthologized the works of Polish poets such as Jan Kochanowski, Szymborska, and various postwar poets.

ANALYSIS

One of the primary concerns of Stanisław Barańczak's early poetry is the perversion of language perpetrated by government systems, which seek to manipulate reality through ideologically charged "newspeak." The poet can effect the restoration of objective reality by attempting to point to the distinction between the distorted speech of official discourse and normal speech, with the unruly power of language and all its irrepressible contradictions. The act of reading a poem, through the social interaction of the reader and poet, allows the poet to return a measure of the complexity of language stripped of its ideological uses. As Barańczak notes in his introduction to *The Weight of the Body*, he began writing poetry in part to "restor[e] the original weight to the overabused words." In Barańczak's poems, this restoration is often achieved as the poem's speakers voice bureaucratic constructions and clichés, then use repetition, minor alterations, or the context of the poem to counteract the currents of official language.

Though his work has frequently been called political, Barańczak has noted in interviews that he prefers to be considered a public poet. Although his work contains a component of social commitment, it is not political poetry in the sense of being a topical response to current situations and injustices. According to Barańczak, the topical political poem is insufficiently complex because it fails to grapple with the problematic form of the poem's transmission: the language that has been contaminated by the very uses it argues against. Part of the complexity of Barańczak's poems arises in the self-scrutiny of their speakers, who not only voice an outward-pointing condemnation of the falsifications perpetrated by the state in all aspects of life, but also incorporate the self-recrimination of an individual who considers himself to be implicated in the same world he criticizes, partially through the language on which he relies. "The perfidy of modern totalitarianism," writes

Barańczak, "lies precisely in the fact that it imperceptibly blurs the difference between the oppressors and the oppressed, by involving the victim in the process of victimization." Perhaps the most profound, and difficult to observe, means by which this blurring occurs is through propaganda, which taints all language and caused Barańczak to note that for the New Wave poets, "the most interesting thing was not pure language but 'dirty' language, language spoiled and misused . . . that of mass media, of political speeches, of posters, things like that." The reason that the superficially political poem is insufficient is that it does not interrogate the language of its dissent, which operates on the ground belonging to its antagonists. A better solution, argues Barańczak, is for the poet to heighten and emphasize the vitality of the language he uses—or, as he puts it, simply to "write his poems well."

It is notable that a poet so concerned with language—its official degradation, which forces its users to become party to the manipulations of the state—is also recognized as being among the most linguistically resourceful poets of his generation. Barańczak's poetry is characterized by his virtuosic use of intricate poetic forms. Although this quality may be most pronounced in his later work, it is evident in his earliest collections as well. The complex elaboration of his versification is matched by involved, imaginative patterning of images and conceits, which give the impression of a searching, flexible intellect struggling through impediments to create a finished thought of monumental stability and beauty. In an essay about prison letters composed in response to totalitarian regimes of the twentieth century, Barańczak notes that "the chief wonder of art is that it thrives on overcoming difficulties. Being bound by countless rules immobilizes the author and sterilizes his expression only if he does not have much to say in the first place. . . . This is, in fact, the essence of all poetry."

THE WEIGHT OF THE BODY

The poems of *The Weight of the Body* are divided into two sections, corresponding to Barańczak's writing life in Poland and in the United States. Many of the early poems focus on the qualities of life under suppression, often presented through unexpected motifs. "The Three Magi," for example, compares the arrival of officers from the secret police to the visitation of the Magi on Epiphany, as the speaker—responding to his inevitable arrest with surprising detachment—muses about the "gold of their watches" and the "smoke from their cigarettes," which "fill the room with a fragrance like incense."

Although some of the poems respond to political events, even these poems are equally concerned with qualities of language. The first section of "The Restoration of Order"—a poetic sequence begun in December of 1981, written in response to General Wojciech Jaruzelski's imposing of martial law in an effort to suppress the Solidarity movement—contains the recurring phrase "according to unconfirmed reports," which introduces the dry tonalities of bureaucratic speech to the poem and also serves both to point to the irony of brutal suppression being characterized and diminished by such language and to heighten the reality of the exile's disengagement from "facts on the ground."

Many of the poems in the second section of the book are preoccupied with questions of what Barańczak calls "the invisible craft of exile" in the poem "Setting the Hand Brake." For example, "After Gloria Was Gone" is set during the aftermath of Hurricane Gloria and describes the banding together of the speaker's neighbors—each of whom appears to be a first-generation transplant, from Mrs. Aaron, who ". . . because she was blond,/ the nuns were willing to hide her . . ." to ". . . the new neighbor, what's his name,/ is it Nhu or Ngu. . . ." The only suitable response to the cataclysmic power of the hurricane, the poem suggests, is banding together in a community, though it is impossible to forget ". . . our pasts and futures which have been crossed out/ so many times. . . ."

Another common metaphor running through the collection involves the depiction of the failing body. At times, pain and bodily inadequacy are connected with interrogation or torture, which also serve as an analogue to the body politic that is being diagnosed. In a larger sense, however, these occurrences point to the despair an individual feels as an inherent part of the self betrays the rest. This complexity of image and concept emphasizes one of the essential qualities of Barańczak's writing: Its emphasis on human interaction and experience leads to its ability to be simultaneously concrete and allusive, political and metaphysical. According to the poet, "What political writing needs now is some sort of metaphysical dimension—not only the interest in horizontal or sociopolitical structures but also in some vertical dimension, which connects humanity with God, the universe, or whatever is eternal."

OTHER MAJOR WORKS

NONFICTION: *Ironia i harmonia*, 1973; *Etyka i poetyka*, 1979; *Ksiazki najgorsze, 1975-1980*, 1981; *Uciekinier z Utopii: O poezji Zbigniewa Herberta*, 1984 (*A Fugitive from Utopia: The Poetry of Zbigniew Herbert*, 1987); *Breathing Under Water and Other East European Essays*, 1990; *Tablica z macondo: Osiemnascie prob wytlumaczenia, po co i diaczego sie pisze*, 1990; *Poezja i duch uogolnienia: Wybor esejow, 1970-1995*, 1996.

TRANSLATIONS: *Spoiling Cannibals' Fun: Polish Poetry of the Last Two Decades of Communist Rule*, 1991 (edited and translated with Clare Cavanagh); *View with a Grain of Sand: Selected Poems*, 1995 (with Cavanagh; of Wisława Szymborska); *Laments*, 1995 (with Seamus Heaney; of Jan Kochanowski); *Poems New and Collected, 1957-1997*, 1998 (with Cavanagh; of Szymborska); *Monologue of a Dog: New Poems*, 2006 (with Cavanagh; of Szymborska).

BIBLIOGRAPHY

Barańczak, Stanisław. "A Conversation with Stanisław Barańczak." Interview by Daniel Bourne. *Artful Dodge* 12-13 (1985): 56-64. The poet treats issues of political suppression and censorship, the role of translation in his creative development, and the need of a metaphysical dimension in political writing.

Cavanagh, Clare. "The Art of Losing: Polish Poetry and Translation." *Partisan Review* 70, no. 2 (2003): 245-254. In discussing her philosophy and practice of translating, Cavanagh analyzes several of Barańczak's poems, tracing ways in which their work translating, together and separately, has influenced his poetry and incorporated new forms and voices into the tradition of Polish verse.

_____. "Setting the Handbrake: Baranczak's Poetics of Displacement." In *Living in Translation: Polish Writers in America*, edited by Halina Stephan. New York: Rodopi, 2003. Cavanagh argues that while many critics perceive a gap between Barańczak's politically engaged early work and his later "metaphysical" poetry, written after his immigration to the United States, a "distinct poetics of displacement" is visible in both his early and later poetry.

Kraszewski, Charles S. "Eschatological Imagery in the Early Verse of Stanisław Barańczak." *Polish Review* 46, no. 1 (2001): 43-61. An article exploring the apocalyptic language and imagery used by Barańczak from 1968 to 1980.

Serafin, Steven, ed. *Twentieth-Century Eastern European Writers: Third Series*. Vol. 232 in *Dictionary of Literary Biography*. Detroit: Gale Group, 2001. Contains a brief essay on Barańczak examining his life and works.

Todd Samuelson

CHARLES BAUDELAIRE

Born: Paris, France; April 9, 1821
Died: Paris, France; August 31, 1867

PRINCIPAL POETRY

Les Fleurs du mal, 1857, 1861, 1868 (*Flowers of Evil*, 1931)
Les Épaves, 1866
Petits Poèmes en prose, 1869 (also known as *Le Spleen de Paris*; *Poems in Prose*, 1905, also known as *Paris Spleen, 1869*, 1947)
Complete Poems, 2002

OTHER LITERARY FORMS

Collections of essays by Charles Baudelaire (bohd-uh-LEHR) on literature, art, aesthetics, and drugs appeared under the titles *Les Paradis artificiels* (1860; *Artificial Paradises*, 1996), *Curiosités esthétiques* (1868), and *L'Art romantique* (1868). Baudelaire also published translations of several volumes of the prose works of Edgar Allan Poe. The most convenient edition of most of his works is the Pléiade edition, *Œuvres complètes* (1868-1870, 1961), edited by Yves Le Dantec and Claude Pichois.

ACHIEVEMENTS

Although Charles Baudelaire is sometimes grouped with the Symbolists, a movement that constituted itself more than a decade after his death, he himself neither belonged to nor founded a school. It is probably fair, however, to designate him as one of the earliest exponents of modernism. He constantly sought, in both literature and painting, works that expressed a beauty specific to the reality of the moment, even if that reality was unpleasant or bizarre. His corrosive irony, his suggestive understatement of the metaphoric sense of his images, and his aggressive use of material drawn from the prosaic side of life have had a lasting success and influence. Movements as diverse as Symbolism, Dadaism, and the Italian neorealist cinema have claimed descent from his work.

BIOGRAPHY

Charles Pierre Baudelaire was born in Paris on April 9, 1821. His father, Joseph-François Baudelaire, was of modest origin but well educated, for he attended seminary and became a priest before the Revolution. Well connected, he became preceptor to the children of the duke of Choiseul-Praslin and, as a painter, was personally acquainted with Enlightenment figures such as Condorcet and Cabanis. After the Revolution, having left the priesthood, he worked on the administrative staff of the French senate. Caroline Archenbaut-Defayis, Baudelaire's mother, was thirty-four years younger than his father. Widowed, she remarried when her son was six years old. Baudelaire's stepfather, Jacques Aupick, was a career military officer who had Baudelaire placed in a series of boarding schools, first in Lyons, when the child was nine, and then in Paris, at the age of fifteen. The choice of schools permitted Baudelaire to be near his mother as the Aupick household moved in response to the officer's promotions.

As an adolescent, Baudelaire was friendly, religious, and studious. He won prizes in Latin verse composition (one of the poems in *Flowers of Evil* is in Latin). He seems to have had few serious disputes with his stepfather until after obtaining the *baccalauréat* in

1839. After that, however, the now successful general became progressively the object of Baudelaire's dislike and even hatred. Disapproving of the young man's friends and conduct, the general sent him on a long boat trip toward India, but Baudelaire, once embarked, refused to go farther than Mauritius. When Baudelaire reached legal majority in 1842, he broke with the Aupicks and lived prodigally on the money he inherited from his father. The life of ease of the young literary dandy lasted only two years, however, for the Aupicks had Baudelaire placed under conservatorship in 1844 on the grounds that he was incapable of managing his money. This deprivation of his full personal freedom had a devastating effect on Baudelaire, who attempted suicide the following year. Upon his recovery, he apparently resolved to write copiously and seriously, contributing to various reviews, especially *L'Artiste* and *Le Corsaire-Satan*.

Baudelaire was widely acquainted with important Romantic authors, including Charles Sainte-Beuve, Théophile Gautier, Victor Hugo, Gérard de Nerval, Théodore de Banville, Petrus Borel (the Wolf-man), and Champfleury. He was also close to the active painters of his day and spent much of his time in their studios. His essays on expositions and on individual artists, especially Eugène Delacroix and Constantin Guys, actually occupy twice as many pages in the complete works as his literary criticism. More intermittently, Baudelaire was involved in the political life of his day, staffing the barricades in the 1848 Revolution and distributing political tracts. His love of order, or rather his aspiration to order and hatred of disorder, kept him from fitting into the revolutionary cause, and his hatred of the bourgeoisie prevented him from siding with the conservatives.

By 1845, Baudelaire was already announcing a forthcoming volume of poetry, under the title "Les Lesbiennes." In 1848, he claimed to be working on a volume called "Les Limbes." Finally, in 1855, he settled on the title *Flowers of Evil*. When it appeared in 1857, the collection provoked a scandal that led to the prosecution of the poet and the publisher. Six of the poems were suppressed, and the poet was fined.

The death of General Aupick a few months before the appearance of *Flowers of Evil* led Baudelaire to a

Charles Baudelaire (Library of Congress)

reconciliation with his mother. Although he never succeeded in putting his life in what he called order, living within his means and avoiding debts, his attempt to heal his rift with his respectable middle-class origins may explain the increasingly Christian and even Catholic orientation of his ideas in the last decade of his life. In 1866, while visiting Brussels, Baudelaire was stricken with partial paralysis and became aphasic. He died in Paris after more than a year of suffering.

ANALYSIS

Although Charles Baudelaire was close to the major Romantic artists and poets, his work announced something new and difficult to describe. Baudelaire did not introduce a fundamentally new aesthetic principle but made important changes in the proportions of idealism and realism, formal beauty and attention to ideas, social commitment and alienation from society—all categories through which the Romantic poets had expressed their conception of literary art. More than most Romantics, he wrote poetry based on the ugliness of urban life and drew an intense beauty from the prosaic and the un-

speakable. Although major Romantics, including Hugo, had broken down many restrictions on subjects that could be treated in poetry, Baudelaire went further, choosing such topics as crime, disease, and prostitution as his points of departure. Although many Romantics suggest a transcendent redemptive quality in art, a spiritual enlightenment that gives readers a kind of religious or social pathway to liberation, Baudelaire tantalizes the reader with religious hope but then pulls it away, suggesting that all hope is in the moment of artistic insight and not in the real future.

The image of the poet as prophet or spiritually superior dreamer, typical of Hugo or Alfred de Vigny, flickers occasionally through Baudelaire's work, but it generally yields to an image of the poet as a sensitive and marginal individual whose only superiority to his contemporaries is his consciousness of his corruption and decadence, something Baudelaire expressed as "conscience [or consciousness] in the midst of evil." Baudelaire thus prepared the way for the Decadent poets, and for those poets of the twentieth century who conceived of their work as primarily individual and not social. In this regard, it is significant that Baudelaire introduced Edgar Allan Poe to the French. Poe subsequently came to be a major influence on Stéphane Mallarmé and Paul Valéry and even played a role in contemporary French psychoanalysis.

In terms of poetic form, Baudelaire's major innovation was undoubtedly in the prose poem, which existed before him but achieved status as a major form principally through *Paris Spleen, 1869.* In his verse, Baudelaire often used the highly restrictive "fixed forms" with their set repetition of certain verses, such as the *pantoum*, in which the second and fourth verses of one stanza become the first and third of the following four-verse unit. Such forms were common among the Romantics, but Baudelaire's combination of this formal perfection with surprising and even shocking subjects produces a dissonant and unforgettable music. Baudelaire thus avoids the pitfalls of the school of art for art's sake, which he denounced for its exclusive attachment to surface beauty.

FLOWERS OF EVIL

Baudelaire insisted that *Flowers of Evil* should be read as a structured whole and not as a random collection of verse. Whatever one may think about the authority of such claims, the six major divisions of the book, beginning with the longest section, eighty-five poems, titled "Spleen et idéal" ("Spleen and Ideal"), and ending with the six poems of "La Mort" ("Death"), seem to outline a thematic and perhaps even chronological passage from aspirations toward a transcendence of pain, suffering, and evil (in the earliest section) through the exploration of various kinds of intoxication or escape—glimpsed in the sections "Le Vin" ("Wine"), "Flowers of Evil," and "Révolte" ("Rebellion")—only to end in death, seen itself as a form of escape from the disappointments or boredom of this world.

"TO THE READER"

Throughout *Flowers of Evil*, a major theme is the uncovering of humanity's own contradictions, hypocrisies, desires, and crimes: all the aspects of life and fantasy that the respectable middle class hides. In the very first poem of the book, "Au lecteur" ("To the Reader"), Baudelaire establishes an unusual relationship with his public. The poem begins with a list of vices—stupidity, error, sin, and stinginess—but instead of reproaching humanity and urging the reader to reform, the poet finishes the sentence with an independent clause containing a remarkable simile: "We feed our nice remorse,/ As beggars nourish their lice." Over this humanity presides the Devil, described two stanzas later as the magician, not Hermes but Satan Trismegistus (three-times great), who turns the rich metal of the will into vapor like an alchemist working backward. Building toward what will apparently be a crescendo of vice, Baudelaire, in stanza 7, lists sins that humanity would commit if people had the courage (such as rape, poisoning, stabbing, and arson) and then points to a still greater vice, which he names only three stanzas later in the conclusion: boredom (*ennui*). In the poem's striking concluding lines, Baudelaire claims that the reader knows this "delicate monster," and then calls the reader "Hypocritical reader, my likeness, my brother!"

This strange poem, borrowing so much of its vocabulary and rhetoric from the tradition of religious exhortation, does not choose between good and evil. Instead, it promotes a third term into what is usually a simple dilemma: Boredom, as the greatest of vices, is an aesthetic concept that replaces traditional moral concepts of evil as that which must be avoided at all costs, a vice that "could swallow the world in a yawn." In religious verse, the address to the reader as a brother is part of a call, first to recognize a common weakness and, second, to repent. Baudelaire does make an avowal of similarity but calls for an aesthetic rather than an ethical response.

"BEACONS"

The largest part of *Flowers of Evil* evokes a struggle against boredom through the artistic use of the ugliness of everyday life and ordinary, even abject, passions. The poem "Les Phares" ("Beacons") is an enumeration of eight great painters, including Peter Paul Rubens, Rembrandt, and Michelangelo, not as a celebration of human greatness but as a testimony to human sentiment and sensation, predominantly in the negative. Rubens is described, for example, as a "Pillow of fresh flesh where one cannot love" and Rembrandt as a "sad hospital full of murmuring." The last three stanzas seem at first to point to a religious purpose in this art that depicts a swarming, nightmare-ridden humanity, for Baudelaire uses terms from religion: malediction, blasphemy, *Te Deum*. Humankind's art is called a "divine opium," but this drug is not offered upward as incense to the Deity. It is, rather, an opium for human hearts. The purpose of art is ambiguous in this conclusion, for it is the best testimony to human dignity but is destined to die at the edge of God's eternity. In the historical context of French Romanticism, this vision of art serves at least to set Baudelaire apart from the partisans of art for art's sake, a movement that Baudelaire himself called the plastic school. Clearly, the visual beauty of the paintings alluded to is not their primary characteristic in "Beacons." These works of art are great because of their representative quality and for the tension between their beauty and the suffering on which they are based.

"A CARCASS"

The paradoxical search for an art that draws its beauty from ugliness and suffering appears in a spectacular way in another of the early poems of *Flowers of Evil*, titled "Une Charogne" ("A Carcass"). Baudelaire's particular delight in the shocking combination of refined form with a crude and repugnant subject is noticeable in the very organization of the stanzas. There are twelve units of four lines each: The first and third lines of each stanza are rhyming Alexandrines (twelve-syllable lines), while the second and fourth lines are rhyming octosyllables. This division imposes a rhythm that heightens the contrast between refined gentleness and sickening sensations. As a whole, the poem is a monologue addressed to a person or character whom the speaker calls "my soul." Although there is a certain ambiguity about the significance of the term (it could represent a division of the self into two parts, a common Baudelairean theme), the poet's "soul" assumes the role of a woman to whom he speaks in words of endearment. He also recalls, however, the discovery, one summer morning, of a carcass lying near a pathway.

The poem's opening stanza illustrates the way in which a tension is created between contrasting tones. The first two lines are addressed to the soul in terms that allow one to expect some pretty image, something that would fit the context of a beautiful, mild summer morning. The end of the second Alexandrine, however, names the object: a "foul carcass." The discovery occurs as the speaker and his soul are coming around a bend in the path (*détour*), which parallels the transition from the first half of the stanza to the somewhat startling second half. The next eight stanzas continue to tell about the discovery of this cadaver in a tone that alternates, sometimes within stanzas and sometimes from one stanza to the next, between a distant aesthetic contemplation and a crude and immediate repulsion. The fourth stanza starts with a presentation of the point of view of the sky witnessing the "blossoming" of the carcass as if it were a flower, while the next two lines ("The stench was so strong that you thought you would faint on the grass") take a distinctly human point of view, even rather sadistically delighting in the soul's weakness. The speaker's reaction is represented as quite different, much closer to that attributed to the sky. In stanza 7, he compares the sounds coming from the carcass, eaten by organisms of decomposition, to flowing water and wind and to the sound of grain being winnowed. Not only does this comparison permit the poet to find beauty in ugliness, but it also permits him to pay homage to the bucolic poetry of the Renaissance (ex-

emplified in such poems as Joachim du Bellay's "D'un vanneur de blé aux vents" ("From a Winnower to the Winds"), showing that classical themes can be presented in a thoroughly modern way.

In the following stanza, the speaker's drift continues from a purely aesthetic contemplation of the object to a comparison of the carcass to an artist's preliminary sketch in the artist's memory. This reverie is broken off in the ninth stanza by the return to the supposed summer morning scene and the recollection that a dog was waiting for the couple to leave so that he could get the "meat."

The last three stanzas are quite different, for they depart from the scene, which is in the past, and look forward to the future of the speaker's beloved "soul," foreseeing the time when she will be like that carcass. However, even in this section (a form of *envoi*, a traditional closing message to the addressee of a poem), the alteration of tone continues. In the tenth stanza, where the speaker declares "You will be like this filth," he still continues to refer to her as "my angel and my passion." This contrast leads toward the final stanza in which Baudelaire, again recalling the poetry of the French Renaissance, proclaims the immortality of his poetry ("I have kept the form and divine essence/ Of my decomposed loves") in contrast to the fleshly mortality of his "soul," his beloved.

It is impossible to assert that this conclusion is a straightforward poetic doctrine. Perhaps the poet, after having cast the "soul" in the paradoxical role of decomposition, is exercising a final irony toward his own poetry. In any case, it is clear that "A Carcass" represents Baudelaire's reworking of traditional texts from classical and Renaissance tradition. His way of using the tradition sets him apart from those Romantics he called the pagan school, who preferred to assume the posture of outright return to pre-Christian belief by denying historical evolution. One reason Baudelaire objected to this position was that he himself possessed a deeply tormented Christian character, described by some as Jansenist (that is, as belonging to the most severe, pessimistic, and ascetic form of seventeenth and eighteenth century French Catholicism), penetrated by the sense of sin and guilt. He could not imagine a simple return to classical "innocence." Baudelaire also had an acute sense of the passage of time and of historical change. In calling the work of the neopagans "a disgusting and useless pastiche," he was implicitly drawing attention to his own use of antiquity in a resolutely modernist manner, one that did not copy the ancients but assimilated their ideas into a representation of the reality of modern life.

"THE SWAN"

The poignancy that Baudelaire achieves with such an approach can be seen in his "Le Cygne" ("The Swan"), dedicated, like two other poems in the section "Tableaux parisiens" ("Parisian Pictures"), to Hugo, a deep believer in the historical movement of poetry. "The Swan" is divided into two numbered parts, one of seven and the other of six stanzas. In the first section, the speaker begins by addressing the legendary figure Andromache, the Trojan Hector's widow, captive in the city of Epirus. The Parisian speaker's memory, he says, has been made pregnant by the thought of the "lying Simoïs swelled by your tears." This allusion to the legends of Troy is the key to understanding the rest of the first part of the poem, most of which seems merely to tell of an event in the speaker's own life, an event without apparent connection with Andromache. He was walking across the new Carrousel Square when he recalled a menagerie that once stood on that spot. A swan had escaped from its cage and was bathing its wings in the dust of a gutter.

The allusion to Andromache is now clearer, for the "lying" Simoïs was a replica in Epirus of the small river that once flowed at the foot of the walls of Troy. In an attempt to make the widow happier, her captors had constructed this imitation, described by Baudelaire as "lying" because it is not only false but also actively and disappointingly deceitful. It can never replace the Simoïs but can only remind Andromache of the discrepancy between past and present. In the second part of the poem, Baudelaire explains the multiple analogy that had been left implicit in the first part. Returning to the present (the first part had been composed of three chronological layers: the legendary past of Andromache, the moment when the speaker saw the swan, and the approximate present in which he recollects the swan), he exclaims, "Paris changes! but nothing in my melancholy/ Has moved!"

What had seemed in the first part to be a comparison only between the widow and the swan now includes the speaker. Each of the three has an immovable memory on the inside—the speaker compares his to rocks—which cannot match the mutable outside world. This dissonance between mind and world is expressed not only in the image of the swan but also, more subtly and pathetically, in the temporal organization of the poem. Between the time he saw the swan and the time of the creation of the poem, the swan has vanished and the old carrousel has been changed into the new. The chronological layering of the text has the same function as the simile. Furthermore, the changes in Paris, composed of monumental constructions of carved stone, give the city an ironic and metaphoric significance. Monuments, like the palace of the Louvre near which the menagerie stood, are usually associated with memory. They are meant to last longer than individuals. Here, however, the city represents change. Baudelaire has thus united a commonplace of certain Romantic poets (the indifference of nature to humankind's suffering) with a classical poetry of cities (Troy, Epirus, Rome) to produce a thoroughly modern poetic idiom.

The conclusion of "The Swan" continues the interplay of literary allusion, for it opens still further the analogy involving Andromache, the swan, and the poet to include an African woman exiled in a northern climate, sailors, captives, and the conquered. There is a decidedly epic quality to this expansion of the analogy to include vast numbers of modern exiles. Baudelaire did not, unlike many Romantics, believe in long poems, and he seems here to be condensing the grandeur of the epic into the brevity of the personal lyric. The many components of this epic analogy, stretching from Andromache to the suggestively open-ended last line ("Of captives, of the conquered . . . of still others!"), are reminiscent of the multiple symbolic figures (the artists) of "Beacons." With this latter poem, "The Swan" also shares the vision of suffering as a defining characteristic of life, for exiles "Suck at the breast of Sorrow as if she were a good wolf." This image is a way of tying in the Roman epic of Romulus and Remus while emphasizing the voluntary or consoling aspect of pain and suffering.

SUFFERING

Suffering, inflicted on others or on oneself, is a frequent theme in *Flowers of Evil* and is linked to learning and self-awareness. In "Heautontimoroumenos" (a Greek term for "the executioner of oneself," borrowed from a comedy of Terence), the speaker declares himself a "dissonance in the divine symphony" on account of the irony that eats away at him. In the most remarkable stanza, he declares in part, "I am the wound and the knife!/ I am the blow and the cheek!" In the poem immediately following, "L'Irrémédiable" ("The Irreparable"), after briefly tracing the fall of an ideal being from Heaven into Hell, Baudelaire evokes a "Somber and clear tête-à-tête/ A heart become its own mirror!" This division of the self into two sides, each looking at the other, is then described metaphorically as a "Well of truth, clear and black/ Where a pale star trembles." Although, here, knowledge is stressed more than the pain that is so fiercely displayed in "Heautontimoroumenos," pain must be the outcome of self-examination in this "well of truth" because the inward discovery is the sentiment of a fall from a higher state, an "irreparable" decadence. However, there is a tension here between the claim to total clarity and the image of the well, for the latter promises depths that can never be coextensive with the mirroring surface. Working back from this tension, one can see that the whole poem is full of terms for depth, darkness, and entrapment. The lucidity toward which the poem tends will never be complete, for consciousness can only discover the extent, apparently infinite, of its deprivation.

"THE TRIP"

The concluding note of *Flowers of Evil*, the section called "Death," is a reminder of this perpetual quest for new discovery, even at the price of horror. In fact, the last stanza of the concluding poem, "Le Voyage" ("The Trip"), is based on the concept of depth that had already appeared in "The Irreparable": "Plunge into the deeps of the abyss, Hell or Heaven, that difference/ Into the depth of the Unknown to find something *new*!" Here the preoccupation with boredom as supreme evil in "To the Reader" appears coupled with the themes of knowledge and discovery that constitute much of the other sections. "The Trip" is a kind of summary in dialogue of *Flowers of Evil*, beginning with the childlike hope of

discovery in the exploration of the real world. When asked later what they discovered, the travelers say that no city they discovered was ever as interesting as the cities they imagined in the shapes of clouds. Then, in passages that seem to recall the "Parisian Pictures," "Wine," and "Rebellion," the world of human sin is sketched out as a monotonous mirror in which humankind sees its own image, "An oasis of horror in a desert of boredom!" The only hope is in death itself, addressed in the last two stanzas as a ship's captain. He alone holds out a balm for people's boredom, which itself results from an unresolvable tension between the aspirations of the heart and the outside world, ostensibly a mirror but actually an incomplete reflection because it can capture only actions and not intentions.

PARIS SPLEEN, 1869

Baudelaire's collection of prose poems, *Paris Spleen, 1869*, is thematically similar to *Flowers of Evil*. The prose pieces, however, have greater means to establish a situation for the poetic speaker and to accumulate aspects of life that seem "realistic" but serve ultimately to reveal figurative meanings in the most ordinary surroundings, a process sometimes called "correspondences" after the title of one of Baudelaire's verse poems. Frequently, as in "Le Gâteau" ("The Cake"), Baudelaire dramatically alters the situation of the poetic speaker so that he is not a representative of dissatisfaction with the world but an amazed spectator of the subjectivity of desire. In "The Cake," a traveler finds himself in a country where his plain bread is called "cake," unleashing a fratricidal war for its possession. In "Le Joujou du pauvre" ("The Poor Child's Plaything"), he discovers two children playing on opposite sides of a fence. One child is rich and has a meticulously crafted doll while the other holds his toy in a little cage. It is a living rat. Although these texts include elements of diction, characterization, and setting typical of fiction in the realist or naturalist vein, Baudelaire always suggests a larger significance that makes the scene or incident figurative. In "The Poor Child's Plaything," the fence between the children is referred to as a symbolic barrier, and the rat is described as a toy drawn from life itself. Baudelaire specifies the metaphoric meaning much less in the prose poems than in his verse.

One can, however, easily view the rat as a synecdoche for Baudelaire's aesthetic, based on drawing beauty from those aspects of life that are most repulsive.

OTHER MAJOR WORKS

LONG FICTION: *La Fanfarlo*, 1847.

NONFICTION: *Les Paradis artificiels*, 1860 (partial translation as *Artificial Paradises: On Hashish and Wine as a Means of Expanding Individuality*, 1971; also as *Artificial Paradises*, 1996); *L'Art romantique*, 1868; *Curiosités esthétiques*, 1868; *Mon cœur mis à nu*, 1887 (*My Heart Laid Bare*, 1950); *The Letters of Baudelaire*, 1927; *My Heart Laid Bare, and Other Prose Writings*, 1951; *Baudelaire on Poe*, 1952; *The Mirror of Art*, 1955; *Intimate Journals*, 1957; *Beaudelaire as Literary Critic: Selected Essays*, 1964; *The Painter of Modern Life, and Other Essays*, 1964; *Art in Paris, 1845-1862: Salons and Other Exhibitions*, 1965.

TRANSLATIONS: *Histoires extraordinaires*, 1856 (of Edgar Allan Poe's short stories); *Nouvelles Histoires extraordinaires*, 1857 (of Poe's short stories); *Aventures d'Arthur Gordon Pym*, 1858 (of Poe's novel); *Eureka*, 1864 (of Poe's poem); *Histoires grotesques et sérieuses*, 1864 (of Poe's short stories).

MISCELLANEOUS: *Œuvres complètes*, 1868-1870, 1961.

BIBLIOGRAPHY

Blood, Susan. *Baudelaire and the Aesthetics of Bad Faith*. Stanford, Calif.: Stanford University Press, 1997. Examines the role of Baudelaire in the history of modernism and the development of the modernist consciousness. Detailed analysis of the poetry, especially its relationship to Baudelaire's writings on caricature and the problem of its "secret architecture." Also examines the nature of Baudelaire's symbolism.

Evans, Margery A. *Baudelaire and Intertextuality*. New York: Cambridge University Press, 1993. Study of *Paris Spleen, 1869* that validates its reassessment as a work that rivals the success of *Flowers of Evil*. Sees these prose poems as hybrid works that set themselves up for comparison with the novel as much as with lyric poetry.

Hyslop, Lois Boe. *Charles Baudelaire Revisited*. New York: Twayne, 1992. Useful and uncomplicated general introduction to the life and work of Baudelaire. Sees Baudelaire as transforming his emotional torment into aesthetic form, and as finding both beauty and spiritual revelations within the dark side of modernity. Discusses *Paris Spleen, 1869* and *Flowers of Evil* as major works and pays much attention to Baudelaire's theories of art. Includes a chronology and bibliography.

Leakey, F. W. *Baudelaire: "Les Fleurs du mal."* New York: Cambridge University Press, 1992. Thorough, appreciative, and thoughtful introduction to *Flowers of Evil*, with particular attention to the sociopolitical context in which the poems were written. Includes a detailed discussion of individual poems and a bibliography.

Lloyd, Rosemary. *Baudelaire's World*. Ithaca, N.Y.: Cornell University Press, 2002. A biography of the poet that examines the world in which he lived.

Thompson, William J., ed. *Understanding "Les Fleurs du mal."* Nashville: Vanderbilt University Press, 1997. Collection of sixteen essays on *Flowers of Evil*, with the purpose of giving students a clear, scholarly introduction to the poems. Each essay selects one particular poem for detailed discussion, and the analysis may be theoretical or textual. Essays represent a variety of critical perspectives, including feminist, Jungian, sociopolitical, and structuralist.

John D. Lyons

SAMUEL BECKETT

Born: Foxrock, near Dublin, Ireland; April 13, 1906
Died: Paris, France; December 22, 1989

PRINCIPAL POETRY

Whoroscope, 1930
Echo's Bones and Other Precipitates, 1935
Poems in English, 1961
Collected Poems in English and French, 1977

OTHER LITERARY FORMS

Samuel Beckett is far better known for his fiction and plays than for his poetry, even though it was as a poet that he began his writing career. In fact, Beckett explored almost every literary form, writing in English and in French. His early fiction, the collection of stories *More Pricks than Kicks* (1934) and the novels *Murphy* (1938) and *Watt* (1953), was written originally in English, but his best-known fiction, including the trilogy of *Molloy* (1951; English translation, 1955), *Malone meurt* (1951; *Malone Dies*, 1956), and *L'Innommable* (1953; *The Unnamable*, 1958), and *Comment c'est* (1961; *How It Is*, 1964) and *Le Dèpeupleur* (1971; *The Lost Ones*, 1972) were written and published originally in French. From the beginning, Beckett's greatest strength was as an innovator, writing prose works that do not seem to fit easily into traditional categories but instead extend the possibilities of contemporary fiction and have had a profound influence on the writers who have followed him.

Beckett was also a writer of plays, and when his name is mentioned, most people think of *En attendant Godot* (pb. 1952; *Waiting for Godot*, 1954). This difficult theatrical work met with astounding success on stages throughout the world, and it is still Beckett's best-known and most-discussed piece. Other works for the stage, *"Fin de partie," suivi de "Acte sans paroles"* (pr., pb. 1957; music by John Beckett; *Endgame: A Play in One Act, Followed by Act Without Words: A Mime for One Player*, 1958); *Krapp's Last Tape* (pr., pb. 1958), *Happy Days* (pr., pb. 1961), and *Rockaby* (pr., pb. 1981), to name only a few, have extended the possibilities of live theater. His *Collected Shorter Plays* was published in 1984.

Never content to restrict himself to a single medium, Beckett demonstrated that radio and television can serve as vehicles for serious drama with radio plays such as *All That Fall* (1957), *Cascando* (1963), and *Words and Music* (1962), and television scripts such as *Eh Joe* (1966; *Dis Joe*, 1967). Beckett also wrote the screenplay for the short movie *Film* (1965), produced and directed by Alan Schneider and starring Buster Keaton. Like the novels and the plays, these works for the mass media tapped new possibilities and pointed out new directions for younger writers.

Early in his career, Beckett also showed that he was a brilliant critic of the arts, writing on the fiction of James Joyce and Marcel Proust and on the paintings of his longtime friend Bram van Velde. In addition to translating his own works, he has translated those of other writers, including Robert Pinget, Paul Éluard, Alain Bosquet, and Sebastien Chamfort from the French and *An Anthology of Mexican Poetry* (1958) from the Spanish. His English version of Arthur Rimbaud's "Le Bateau ivre" (The Drunken Boat), done in the 1930's but lost for many years and rediscovered and published for the first time only in the 1977 *Collected Poems in English and French*, is masterful, but his best-known translation is of Guillaume Apollinaire's "Zone" (1972), a long poem that addresses many of Beckett's own themes and opens with a line that could well characterize Beckett's efforts in all forms: "In the end you are weary of this ancient world."

ACHIEVEMENTS

When the Swedish Academy selected Samuel Beckett to receive the Nobel Prize in Literature in 1969, the award only confirmed what critics and readers had known for some time: that he is one of the most important literary figures of the late twentieth century. Few authors in the history of literature have attracted as much critical attention as Beckett, and with good reason; he is both an important figure in his own right and a transitional thinker whose writings mark the end of modernism and the beginning of a new sensibility, postmodernism. The modernists of the early twentieth century—James Joyce, W. H. Auden, Virginia Woolf, Marcel Proust, and others—were stunned by the absurdity of their world. Previous generations had filled that world with philosophical, religious, and political meanings, but their orderly vision of reality no longer seemed to apply to life in the early twentieth century. The modernists lacked the faith of their forebears; they had experienced the chaos of the modern world with its potential for global war and the destruction of civilization, and they believed that the order of reality was a fiction, that life was unknowable. In response to their doubts, they turned literature in on itself, separating it from life, creating an art for its own sake. These writers trusted in language to create new meanings, new knowledge, and a separate, artistic human universe.

As a young man, Beckett also experienced this sense of absurdity and meaninglessness in the modern world, but unlike his modernist predecessors, he could not even muster faith in his art or in language. Thus, although Joyce could revel in the possibilities and textures of the written word, Beckett could not. Instead, he reduced his fictions, his plays, and his poems to the barest elements, and throughout his career, he tried to rejoin art and life in his own way. For the premodernists, art imitated the world beyond the human mind. The modernists rejected this idea of imitation, and so did Beckett. Instead, his art reflects the inner world, the world of the human voice, the only world human beings can ever really experience. In the premodern era, art was successful if it depicted some truth about the world. For the modernists, art succeeded only on its own terms, regardless of the world beyond the scope of the arts. For Beckett, art never succeeds. It is a necessary failure that never manages to link the inner mind to outer reality. As such, art is an exercise in courage, foredoomed to failure, like human life itself. Human beings are human beings not because they can give meaning to the world or because they can retreat into aesthetics but because they can recognize that their world is meaningless and that their lives are leading them only toward death; yet they must continue to live and strive. As a philosopher of failure, Beckett was the first thinker of the postmodern age.

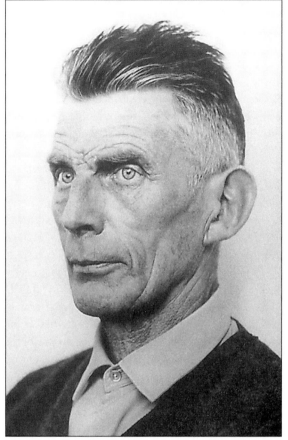

Samuel Beckett (©The Nobel Foundation)

BIOGRAPHY

Samuel Barclay Beckett grew up in a suburb of Dublin, Ireland, a Protestant in a Catholic country and therefore something of an exile in his own land. He attended Trinity College in Dublin, where he discovered his talent for languages and studied English, French, and Italian. He taught for two terms at Campbell College in Belfast and then, in 1928, traveled to Paris, where he lectured in English at the ècole Normale Supèrieure. It was during this tenure that he met his countryman James Joyce. Beckett returned to Ireland to teach four terms at Trinity College, but in 1932, after much consideration and anguish, he left the teaching profession for good, convinced that he could not survive as a writer in academe. For the next five years, he wandered through Europe, and in 1937, he settled in Paris permanently. It was in Paris that Beckett died in 1989, at the age of eighty-three.

There were probably many reasons for Beckett's self-imposed exile and for his decision to write in a language not his by birth, but surely one reason was the influence of Joyce, who recommended exile for artists. It would be difficult to overestimate the effect that Joyce had on Beckett's life and work. In the late 1930's, the younger Irishman was an intimate member of Joyce's inner circle. He worked on a translation of Joyce's "Anna Livia Plurabelle" into French, took dictation for his friend, wrote a critical study of Joyce's writings, ran errands for the Irish master, and even attracted the romantic interest of Joyce's daughter, Lucia. Apparently, Joyce thought a great deal of Beckett, and Beckett looked on Joyce as a consummate master, so that it is possible he decided to write in French to avoid the language that, in his own mind, Joyce had all but exhausted.

As Beckett grew older and developed as a writer, Joyce's influence began to weaken, and in many ways, Beckett's later style—spare, flat, reduced to the barest elements—is the antithesis of Joyce's rich, punning, heavily textured prose. Beckett also rejected Joyce's "Irishness" in favor of characters and settings without specific nationality or history. In the early poetry, however, the influence of Joyce and Ireland is still strong, and, in fact, it was in his poems that Beckett first began to work through Joyce's voice and to discover his own.

ANALYSIS

Whoroscope was Samuel Beckett's first major publication. It is a long poem, written originally in English, and published in book form by Hours Press after winning a prize offered by the publisher for the best poem on the subject of time. The first-person narrator of the work is René Descartes, the seventeenth century French philosopher, mathematician, and scientist, and the poem is so full of obscure allusions to his life and times that, at the publisher's request, Beckett added a page and a half of notes to the ninety-eight-line piece. In fact, the notes are almost as interesting as the poem itself, and, without them, it is unlikely that the average reader would even recognize Descartes as the speaker.

WHOROSCOPE

Whoroscope is an important poem not only because it marked Beckett's official entry into the literary world but also because it introduced the basic themes that continued to occupy him as a writer and thinker. Clearly, Beckett himself recognized this fact, because he chose to keep this early work intact in the subsequent collections of his poetry, *Poems in English* and *Collected Poems in English and French*, which include all the works discussed here. In many ways, *Whoroscope* is quite unlike the author's later writings. The structure of the piece is open, without rhyme or regular meter. The poem shows the influence of the French surrealists in its associative juxtaposition of images, but the influence of Joyce is also apparent in the punning title and in the body of the text.

On first reading, it is not at all obvious that this is a poem about time. From the opening line, Descartes rambles on, apparently at random, about various events in his life, without respect for chronology or even historical accuracy. In the closing section, it becomes clear that the philosopher is on his deathbed and that his ramblings are the result of illness and fever. In a sense, his life is flashing before his eyes. He is trying to grasp the fullness of time at the moment of his death, and a closer reading shows that the sequence of memories is not random at all but associative, each a memory leading to the next—not in chronological order but in the order dictated by Descartes's subjective thought process.

In fact, the poem is very much about time—the time of a man's life and the attempt to recapture lost time in the instant before time runs out. The Joycean influence in Descartes's stream-of-consciousness narrative is evident, but it is also obvious that Beckett has learned a great deal from Marcel Proust's *À la recherche du temps perdu* (1913-1927; *Remembrance of Things Past*, 1922-1931), which the young Beckett knew well—so well, in fact, that in 1931 he published *Proust*, a book-length study of this French masterwork.

Whoroscope, then, is about time as the great destroyer, time that eats up a man's life and leads only to death. It is important to remember, however, that this poem is about the lifetime of a particular man, Descartes, and there is good reason for Beckett's choice of this philosopher as his narrator. Like Beckett himself, Descartes was a transitional figure, the founder of modern philosophy and the opponent of Aristotelian scholasticism. He and his contemporaries initiated a new age in Western civilization, and in his poem, Beckett pays tribute to other great thinkers such as Galileo and Francis Bacon, who directed Western thought into the era of science and rationalism.

Descartes was a great builder, but he was also a great destroyer of the philosophies of the past, and in the poem, he speaks with pride of "throwing/ Jesuits out of the skylight." He devoted his life to the development of a new system of thought, but, in so doing, he also undermined the Aristotelian metaphysics that had served as the basis of European philosophy for centuries. Ironically, while Descartes was destroying his predecessors, the time of his own life was destroying him.

This is one of the key themes of Beckett's work: the fact that death comes to all living things, without reason, without justice, regardless of whether one is innocent or guilty. As Beckett writes in a later, untitled poem, humanity lives "the space of a door/ that opens and shuts." Humans are born to die; they are dying even in the womb, losing time from the moment of conception, and there is nothing that can stop or even delay this process. Each person's life cancels itself, moment by moment.

The historical Descartes died while in the service of Queen Christina of Sweden, who forced the aging philosopher to call on her at five o'clock each morning although he had been in the habit of staying in bed until midday all his life. This change in his routine, coupled with the northern weather, led to his final illness. In the poem, the fictional Descartes refers to Queen Christina as "Rahab of the snows." Rahab was a biblical harlot mentioned in *La divina commedia* (c. 1320, 3 volumes; *The Divine Comedy*, 1802) of Dante (whom Beckett has called the only poet), and so it would seem that the queen is the "whore" of the title. In his notes to the poem, Beckett points out that Descartes kept his birthday a secret so that no astrologer could cast his horoscope. The philosopher was opposed to such mysticism, not only because it was unscientific but also because he felt that many people let their entire lives be dictated by astrology; he even knew of two young men who had allowed themselves to die simply because their horoscopes had predicted death for them. With this knowledge, the Joycean pun of the title becomes clear. Queen Christina, the harlot, has cast Descartes's death, which was present from the moment of his birth. His "whoroscope" is her prediction of his inevitable end.

This theme of the inevitability of death, of death as a necessary function of birth, runs through the poem in the form of a recurring motif. Again in the notes, Beckett explains that Descartes liked his morning omelette to be made from eggs that had been hatched from eight to ten days—that is, eggs in which the embryo was partially developed. Time and again in the poem he asks about his morning eggs: "How long did she womb it, the feathery one? . . . How rich she smells,/ this abortion of a fledgling!"

For Beckett, the egg is the symbol of the fetus conceived only to die, its brief span of life lived out in the instant between nonexistence and nonexistence. The time of the egg is the time of the philosopher as well. As with all human beings, Descartes is dying before he has even really lived, and like the fledgling in the egg, he is dying for no purpose, simply because that is the way things are.

Beckett explored the themes of the inevitability of death and the meaninglessness of life time and again in his works, but he has always coupled these themes with another: the necessity of going on, of raging against the inevitable, of refusing to accept humanity's fate. In the poem "Serena III," he insists that human beings must "keep on the move/ keep on the move," and in *Whoroscope*, he depicts Descartes first as angry, cursing his fate, then as begging for another chance at a life he has never managed to understand, a "second/ starless inscrutable hour." There is no reason for him to go on, and yet, as a human being, he must.

For Beckett, humans must die, but they must also live and think and speak, as Descartes does, even to the last possible instant. They must live in their own inner world, which is always dying, and they must also live in the outer world, which will live on after them and which, therefore, is not theirs. This theme of the conflict between the inner and the outer worlds that runs through Beckett's later work is present in *Whoroscope* as well. The very structure of the poem, which follows the philosopher's associative thinking, places the narrative within Descartes's inner mind, though in the end it moves to the outer world, to "Christina the ripper" and to her court physician, Weulles, who is attending to Descartes in his last moments. In his inner world, Descartes is alive and reliving his past, but it is the outer world that is leading him to inevitable death. Descartes devoted his life to trying to understand the outer world, but the very foundation of his thought, the dictum *Cogito, ergo sum* ("I think, therefore I am") trapped him within his own subjectivity, and generations of later philosophers have tried to understand how one can move from the certainty of the *cogito* to the world beyond which is not oneself. The *cogito*, the single point of certainty in the Cartesian philosophy of doubt, is the fulcrum of modern Western philosophy, and yet it restricts thinkers to their own inner worlds, to what Beckett calls, in his poem "The Vulture," "the sky/ of my skull."

For Beckett, it is impossible for humanity to come to know the world beyond the skull, that very world in which people must live and die. In the play *Endgame*, the characters Hamm and Clov live within a skull-like structure; Hamm is blind, and Clov can see the world only through two eyelike windows that restrict his vision. In the short novel *The Lost Ones*, an entire society lives and passes away within a huge white dome, a skull. In *Whoroscope*, Descartes can know his inner world, but the outer world remains "inscrutable." He knows that he thinks and, therefore, that he is, but he does not know why. He wants to know the truth and to speak it, but the *cogito* cannot lead him to knowledge of the outer world. In the poem, he mentions Saint Augustine, who also sought a single point of certainty in a world in which everything was open to question and found that the only thing he could be sure of was that he could be deceived. The Descartes of the poem states the Augustinian dictum as "Fallor, ergo sum!" ("I am deceived, therefore I am"). At the moment of death, this certainty seems truer to the philosopher than his own *cogito*. To be a human is to be deceived, to fail, and, for a human being, courage is the courage to fail. Humans are human only insofar as they know that failure is inevitable and yet keep going in spite of that knowledge.

ECHO'S BONES AND OTHER PRECIPITATES

Another important Beckett theme surfaces only briefly in *Whoroscope* but becomes the main focus of the author's second collection of poems, *Echo's Bones and Other Precipitates*: the theme of the impossibility of love in the face of absurdity and death. For Beckett, love is another of humankind's basic needs, as important as the quest for meaning, and as futile. The Descartes poem touched on the theme only briefly, in the philosopher's memory of a little cross-eyed girl who was his childhood playmate and who reminds him of his only daughter, Francine, who died of scarlet fever at the age of six. The implication is that love always ends, if not now, then later; and, like the rest of life, love is both essential and hopeless, necessary and frightening. Knowing that love is impossible, pretending that it is not, humanity loves, and that love is the source of human pain but also of human life.

The poems of *Echo's Bones and Other Precipitates* differ from *Whoroscope* not only because they focus on love but also because the narrator is not a fictional version of a historical character but the author himself. The title of the collection comes from Ovid's *Metamorphoses* (c. 8 C.E.; English translation, 1567), from the story of Echo, who, after being spurned by Narcissus, lets herself wither away until only her bones and voice remain. The connection between Ovid's tale and Beckett's theme of love is clear, but the story of Echo also provides the poet with two of his favorite images: the inevitability of death and the survival of the voice.

Most of the titles and forms of the poems in this collection are based on the songs of the troubadours, which Beckett knew well and which attracted him no doubt because they were songs of love and, often, of loss, and also because the troubadours were usually wanderers and exiles, like Beckett himself and like the narrators of most of these poems. The work "Enueg I" draws its title from the traditional Provençal lament or complaint, and as might be expected, it is a complaint of love. In the poem, the narrator leaves the nursing home where his beloved is dying of tuberculosis ("Exeo in a spasm/ tired of my darling's red sputum") and wanders through Dublin, traveling in a wide circle. He finds that the world is full of images of death ("a dying barge," "the stillborn evening," "the tattered sky like an ink of pestilence") and that he cannot forget his beloved or the fate of their love. Of course, these signs of death are not really present in the outer world; they reflect the narrator's inner life, the only life he can know, and, like Descartes, he rages against what he knows to be true as his own blood forms a "clot of anger."

There is no romance in Beckett's lament, only the all-encompassing awareness of mortality. Love and romance are like "the silk of the seas and the arctic flowers/ that do not exist," figments of the imagination that lose all sense of reality in the face of "the banner of meat bleeding."

The narrator keeps moving, however, and throughout the poem he has contact with others, with a small boy and "a wearish old man," an archetypal Beckett character, "scuttling along between a crutch and a stick,/ his stump caught up horribly, like a claw, under his breech, smoking." These meetings show the continuing possibility of human contact, even in a dying world; they also make clear the need for going on even in the face of futility. Perhaps the others, like the narrator, are also moving in circles, but circular movement is still movement, and even the old man, crippled and in pain, does not remain motionless, does not give up.

"Sanies I" is also modeled on a Provençal form; the title is derived from a Latin term meaning "morbid discharge." For Beckett, writing is such a discharge, a residue, a "precipitate." It is a by-product of living and dying, but it is also that which remains, like Echo's voice.

Like the narrator of "Enueg I," the narrator of "Sanies I" is a wanderer in the process of completing a circle; in this case, he is returning home to Ireland after traveling in Europe, apparently in Germany, for his speech is full of Germanic terms. Like later Beckett protagonists, he rides a bicycle, and he describes himself as "a Ritter," a German knight, and, therefore, a somewhat ironic hero, though perhaps the only kind of hero who remains in the postmodern age: the hero who keeps moving. He has been wandering for a long time, and he says that he is "müüüüüüüide now." The German "müde" means "tired," but the extended "ü" sound also gives a sense of boredom, an essential element in most of Beckett's work. Clearly, the narrator is both tired and bored, and, as a result, he is "bound for home like a good boy." Thinking about home and his parents, he recalls his birth and longs for that sweet oblivion of the womb: "Ah to be back in the caul now with no trusts/ no fingers no spoilt love."

This is a key passage. "The caul" to which the narrator would like to return is a fetal membrane covering the head, and according to folklore, the child who is born with a caul is born to good luck. The implication here, however, is that the best of luck is never to have been born at all and, therefore, to have avoided "trusts" and "spoilt loves," those exercises in futility. The unborn child also has "no fingers," and one without fingers cannot, and therefore need not, travel on a bicycle as the narrator does. Even better, one without fingers cannot write, no matter how strongly he might feel the need to do so.

Of course, the narrator no longer has the option of not being born. He is "tired now hair ebbing gums ebb-ing ebbing home," and yet he approaches his hometown like a "Stürmer," German slang for "lady-killer." It would seem that, despite his "spoilt loves," he is prepared for love again, and indeed, he sees his beloved waiting for him. "I see main verb at last/ her whom alone in the accusative/ I have dismounted to love." In German, the "main verb" comes at the end of the sentence, and in this sentence that word is "love." At the last moment, however, the narrator sends the girl away ("get along with you now"), refusing to make the mistake his parents made by bringing another being into the world. Although one cannot return to the peace of the womb, one can at least refuse to pass on the curse of life to another.

If "Sanies I" is about nonexistence in the womb (the Cartesian egg), and if "Enueg I" is about nonexistence in the tomb, the title poem of the collection brings these two notions together. "Echo's Bones" is a short lyric that restates Beckett's key themes in capsule form. The first word of the poem is "asylum," a reference to the womb, but this is an "asylum under my tread," a shelter underground, a tomb. Like those in the womb, those in the tomb are beyond the confusions and pains of living now that they have run the gauntlet of life, "the gantelope of sense and nonsense." Only now, in death, are they free to be themselves, "taken by the maggots for what they are," and what they are is fleshless bone, without love or dreams and without the need to keep striving. The title of the poem, however, is a reminder that something more than bone remains: the voice. The words may be only a "morbid discharge," but, like Echo's voice, they survive.

"SOMETHING THERE"

Leaping ahead four decades to "Something There," a poem composed in 1974, the reader finds that the author's voice has changed, although his key themes remain. Here the lines are short and direct, flat and prosaic. There are no obscure allusions, no Joycean puns. The "something there" of the title is "something outside/ the head," and this contrast of inner and outer worlds returns the reader to *Whoroscope* and to the Cartesian dilemma of subjectivity that cannot reach beyond itself. The poem tries to reach that "something" in the only way it can, through words, but "at the faint sound so brief/ it is gone." The reality beyond the inner mind disappears as soon as the words of the mind try to grasp it, and so language, in the end, describes only the inner world, which becomes something like a womb and a tomb in the midst of life. The inner world is not life, and although humanity cannot reach beyond its inner self to comprehend the "something outside/ the head," still it must try to do so, and the sign of its failure is language, the voice that always remains.

One can argue that Beckett's view of existence is largely negative. However, it is important to remember that he was influenced greatly by the medieval theologians who argued that truth, in the person of God, is beyond positive statement and that humankind can know the truth only in the negative, by describing what it is not. Beckett seems to have taken the same approach. It is true that he wrote about the curse of life, but he did so beautifully, raging against the inevitability of silence. The beauty of his work is the beauty of the human will to live in the face of death. Beckett sings the praises of those who say, with the nameless, formless, faceless narrator of *The Unnamable*, "I can't go on, I'll go on."

OTHER MAJOR WORKS

LONG FICTION: *Murphy*, 1938; *Malone meurt*, 1951 (*Malone Dies*, 1956); *Molloy*, 1951 (English translation, 1955); *L'Innommable*, 1953 (*The Unnamable*, 1958); *Watt*, 1953; *Comment c'est*, 1961 (*How It Is*, 1964); *Mercier et Camier*, 1970 (*Mercier and Camier*, 1974); *Le Dépeupleur*, 1971 (*The Lost Ones*, 1972); *Company*, 1980; *Mal vu mal dit*, 1981 (*Ill Seen Ill Said*, 1981); *Worstward Ho*, 1983.

SHORT FICTION: *More Pricks than Kicks*, 1934; *Nouvelles et textes pour rien*, 1955 (*Stories and Texts for Nothing*, 1967); *No's Knife: Prose, 1947-1966*, 1967; *First Love, and Other Shorts*, 1974; *Pour finir encore et autres foirades*, 1976 (*Fizzles*, 1976; also known as *For to Yet Again*, 1976); *Four Novellas*, 1977 (also known as *The Expelled, and Other Novellas*, 1980); *Collected Short Prose*, 1991.

PLAYS: *En attendant Godot*, pb. 1952 (*Waiting for Godot*, 1954); *"Fin de partie," suivi de "Acte sans paroles,"* pr., pb. 1957 (music by John Beckett; *"Endgame: A Play in One Act," Followed by "Act Without Words: A Mime for One Player,"* 1958); *Krapp's Last Tape*, pr., pb. 1958; *Act Without Words II*, pr., pb. 1960 (one-act mime); *Happy Days*, pr., pb. 1961; *Play*, pr., pb. 1963 (English translation, 1964); *Come and Go: Dramaticule*, pr., pb. 1965 (one scene; English translation, 1967); *Not I*, pr. 1972; *Ends and Odds*, pb. 1976; *Footfalls*, pr., pb. 1976; *That Time*, pr., pb. 1976; *A Piece of Monologue*, pr., pb. 1979; *Ohio Impromptu*, pr., pb. 1981; *Rockaby*, pr., pb. 1981; *Catastrophe*, pr. 1982; *Company*, pr. 1983; *Plays*, pb. 1984; *Complete Dramatic Works*, 1986; *Eleutheria*, pb. 1995.

SCREENPLAY: *Film*, 1965.

TELEPLAYS: *Eh Joe*, 1966 (*Dis Joe*, 1967); *Tryst*, 1976; *Shades*, 1977; *Quad*, 1981.

RADIO PLAYS: *All That Fall*, 1957, 1968; *Embers*, 1959; *Words and Music*, 1962 (music by John Beckett); *Cascando*, 1963 (music by Marcel Mihalovici).

NONFICTION: *Proust*, 1931; *The Letters of Samuel Beckett: Vol. 1, 1929-1940*, 2009 (Martha Dow Fehsenfeld and Lois More Overbeck, editors).

TRANSLATION: *An Anthology of Mexican Poetry*, 1958 (Octavio Paz, editor).

MISCELLANEOUS: *I Can't Go On, I'll Go On: A Selection from Samuel Beckett's Work*, 1976 (Richard Seaver, editor).

BIBLIOGRAPHY

Bair, Deirdre. *Samuel Beckett: A Biography*. 1978. Reprint. New York: Simon & Schuster, 1993. Although Beckett was often reluctant to talk about himself, he cooperated with Bair. It is the fullest, most helpful version of his life in print, and to know his life is to understand his art. The criticism of the specific texts is often limited, but Bair is very good at putting the work in conjunction with Beckett's very odd life.

Birkett, Jennifer, and Kate Ince, eds. *Samuel Beckett*. New York: Longman, 2000. A collection of criticism of Beckett's works. Bibliography and index.

Brater, Enoch. *The Essential Samuel Beckett: An Illustrated Biography*. New York: Thames & Hudson, 2003. A general biography of Beckett that provides information on how his life affected his works.

Carey, Phyllis, and Ed Jewinski, eds. *Re: Joyce'n Beckett*. New York: Fordham University Press, 1992. This collection of essays examines the relationship between Joyce and Beckett.

Cronin, Anthony. *Samuel Beckett: The Last Modernist*.

New York: HarperCollins, 1996. A fully documented and detailed biography of Beckett, describing his involvement in the Paris literary scene, his response to winning the Nobel Prize, and his overall literary career.

Kenner, Hugh. *Reader's Guide to Samuel Beckett.* Syracuse, N.Y.: Syracuse University Press, 1996. Kenner, a well-known commentator on Beckett, places Beckett in the Irish tradition and assesses his part in the movement of experimental literature.

Knowlson, James. *Damned to Fame: The Life of Samuel Beckett.* New York: Simon & Schuster, 1996. A comprehensive biography with much new material, detailed notes, and bibliography.

McDonald, Ronan. *Samuel Beckett: The Life and the Work.* Dublin: Dublin Stationery Office, 2005. A general biography of Beckett that looks at his literary works.

Pattie, David. *The Complete Critical Guide to Samuel Beckett.* New York: Routledge, 2000. A reference volume that combines biographical information with critical analysis of Beckett's literary works. Bibliography and index.

Pilling, John, ed. *The Cambridge Companion to Beckett.* New York: Cambridge University Press, 1994. A comprehensive reference work that provides considerable information about the life and works of Beckett. Bibliography and indexes.

Welch D. Everman

GUSTAVO ADOLFO BÉCQUER

Born: Seville, Spain; February 17, 1836
Died: Madrid, Spain; December 22, 1870

PRINCIPAL POETRY

Rimas, 1871 (*Poems,* 1891; better known as *The Rhymes,* 1898)

OTHER LITERARY FORMS

Although the fame of Gustavo Adolfo Bécquer (BEHK-ur) rests mainly on his only volume of poetry,

The Rhymes, he was also a notable prose writer. Bécquer demonstrated his talent at an early age with the publication of *Historia de los templos de España* (1857; a history of Spain's temples), an ambitious project of which only the first volume, a study of the churches of Toledo, was completed. Posterity has recognized the greater value of a variety of prose works that appeared in Madrid's newspapers and magazines during Bécquer's lifetime. Outstanding among these works are the newspaper letters published under the heading *Cartas desde mi celda* (1864; *From My Cell,* 1924). They were written from Veruela's monastery in Aragón, where the author had gone to seek relief for his failing health. In these "letters," Bécquer pours out his moral biography, revealing himself to be a religious man who is both aware of the problems of his surroundings and sensitive to the legends and traditions he hears from shepherds and rovers in the northeast of Spain.

Also of great importance among Bécquer's prose works are the four *Cartas literarias a una mujer* (1860-1861; *Letters to an Unknown Woman,* 1924) and the prologue to the book *La Soledad* (1861) by his friend Augusto Ferrán. In these works, Bécquer expresses his ideas about love, literature in general, and, above all, poetry. In his prologue to Ferrán's book, Bécquer categorizes his own poetic production as the kind that is "natural, brief, dry, that which germinates in the soul like an electric spark, touches the feelings with a word and flees. . . ."

Bécquer's most celebrated prose works were his more than twenty legends, *Leyendas* (1858-1864; partial translation in *Terrible Tales: Spanish,* 1891; also in *Romantic Legends of Spain,* 1909). The themes of these prose tales do not differ substantially from those of the tales in verse typical of the Romantic movement in Spain and throughout Europe; they reveal a taste for the macabre, medieval settings, and exotic lore. What differentiates Bécquer's legends from the verse narratives and plays of the Duque de Rivas and José Zorrilla y Moral is their greater emphasis on the mysterious, the uncanny, and the supernatural.

ACHIEVEMENTS

Gustavo Adolfo Bécquer achieved fame only after his death. Although in his last years he was beginning to be recognized as a good journalist and an excellent prose writer, he was virtually unknown as a poet; only a handful of his poems were published during his lifetime.

Bécquer's recognition as a poet began with the publication of *The Rhymes* one year after his death. By 1881, when the third edition of his poems was published, Bécquer was acknowledged as an important poet, and his fame was spreading throughout the Hispanic world. Since that time, Bécquer's reputation has grown steadily; his verse has achieved both critical acclaim and an extraordinary popular appeal. Indeed, after Miguel de Cervantes's *El ingenioso hidalgo don Quixote de la Mancha* (1605, 1615; *The History of the Valorous and Wittie Knight-Errant, Don Quixote of the Mancha*, 1612-1620; better known as *Don Quixote de la Mancha*), no literary work has had as many editions in Spanish as Bécquer's *The Rhymes*. Since the poet's death, no Spanish poem has touched as many hearts or has been recited and memorized as often as "Rime of the Swallows" and no poet has surpassed Bécquer's influence on Hispanic poetry. All the movements, groups, and poetic generations that have come after Bécquer in Hispanic literature have been indebted, directly or indirectly, to his innovations.

BIOGRAPHY

Gustavo Adolfo Bécquer was born in Seville, in the south of Spain, on February 17, 1836, the son of José María Domínguez Insausti, a painter, and Joaquina Bastida Vargas. The surname Bécquer had come to Spain from Flanders during the seventeenth century as Becker. Although the direct line of the name had ended with the poet's great-grandmother, the whole family was still known as the Bécquers. One month before young Bécquer turned five, his father died, and four years later his mother also died, leaving Bécquer and his seven brothers to the responsibility of their surviving relatives. While under the care of his mother's uncle, Don Juan de Vargas, Bécquer began to study at the Colegio de San Telmo in Seville to become a sea pilot. When this school was closed a short time later, he went to live with his godmother, Doña Manuela Monchay. It was decided that Bécquer should take up his late father's profession, and he began to study painting at the

school of the Sevillian artist Antonio Cabral Bajarano. Bécquer devoted his free time to reading in his godmother's library, where he developed his preference for Horace and for the Spanish Romantic Zorrilla and where he became fond of literary studies in general.

Bécquer also studied painting with his uncle Joaquín Domínguez Bécquer. Nevertheless, his interest in literature had continued to grow, and when his uncle expressed doubts about Bécquer's potential to become a great artist, Bécquer decided, in 1854—against his godmother's advice—to go to Madrid and seek his fortune as a writer.

If in Seville Bécquer had found little happiness, he found even less in Madrid, where he always had economic difficulties and where he was soon diagnosed as having tuberculosis, the sickness that would take him to an early grave. Bécquer quickly ran out of the little money he had brought from Seville, and when he could no longer pay rent in the boardinghouse of Doña Soledad, she generously allowed him to continue residing there anyway. During his early years in Madrid, he worked in collaboration with various friends, turning out translations from French and writing original dramas and *zarzuelas* (musicals). These pieces for the stage, largely hackwork, did not command good payment, and some were not even produced. Needing to find another source of income, Bécquer obtained an insignificant position as a public servant, but he was soon fired, after being caught during working hours drawing a picture of William Shakespeare's Ophelia. In those days, he also contributed to a number of Madrid's newspapers and magazines, and he even tried, unsuccessfully, to found some new ones. These activities neither produced sufficient income for a comfortable life nor contributed to Bécquer's fame, since his works were often published without his name.

In the year 1858, Bécquer began to publish his "legends" in the newspapers of Madrid; in the same year, he met Julia Espín, a beautiful girl who later became an opera singer. It is said that, although Bécquer's love for this girl was unrequited, she inspired many of the entries in *The Rhymes*. It was at this time that Bécquer experienced his first health crisis. In 1859, a poem later included in *The Rhymes* was published under the title "Imitación de Byron" ("Imitation of Byron"); it was the first of fifteen of *The Rhymes* that appeared in Madrid periodicals during Bécquer's lifetime.

In 1860, Bécquer began publishing *Letters to an Unknown Woman* in serial form and met Casta Esteban Navarro, his doctor's daughter, whom Bécquer married the following year; the marriage would eventually produce two sons. In that same year, Bécquer's brother, Valeriano, a notable painter, came with his two children to live in Madrid and soon moved in with the poet and his wife. Throughout his married life, the poet and his wife spent several periods near Soria, where his father-in-law had a house. Between 1863 and 1864, Bécquer spent eight months living in the monastery of Veruela, where he wrote the letters in *From My Cell*. On several occasions, Bécquer and his brother Valeriano took long trips to various parts of Spain, during which the artist would paint typical local scenes while the writer would take notes for his own works or would write articles for newspapers.

The year 1864 marked a change in Bécquer's life. He was appointed to a higher civil-service position with a better salary, but a change in the government caused him to lose the job a year later. Soon, however, yet another change in the government resulted in his reappointment to the job, where he worked until 1868, when the revolution that dethroned Isabella II took place. In the same year, Bécquer separated from his wife. Taking his two children, he went to live with his brother Valeriano in Toledo, where he supposedly wrote the last poems for *The Rhymes*. A year later, they all returned to Madrid, and Bécquer resumed his journalistic work for the newspaper *La ilustración de Madrid*, where he was appointed editor in 1870. In September of that year, Valeriano died, and almost immediately Bécquer's wife repentantly returned to live with him and their children. Soon, the poet's health declined, and he died on December 22, 1870, at the age of thirty-four.

After Bécquer's death, his friend appointed a committee to publish his works. The committee collected his prose works that had appeared in the periodicals of Madrid and published them with the seventy-six poems from the manuscript of *The Rhymes*. This first edition of Bécquer's works was published in 1871, one year after his death.

ANALYSIS

The poems that made Gustavo Adolfo Bécquer famous, and that make up practically his entire production, are those included in *The Rhymes*. Only eight or ten other poems have been found, almost all juvenilia and not of high quality. When Bécquer's friends published the first edition of his works in 1871, *The Rhymes* consisted of seventy-six untitled poems as well as the previously published prose works. Another manuscript of the collection was later found, containing three more poems, for a total of seventy-nine. The discovery and publication of other poems raised the number to ninety-four, but later it was proved that many of the new poems actually had been written by Bécquer's contemporaries or had been fraudulently attributed to him.

The single most important influence on Bécquer's poetry was Heinrich Heine, whose impact on Bécquer is universally acknowledged. In addition, critics have pointed out a wide variety of other influences, ranging from Lord Byron and Edgar Allan Poe to the German poets Johann Wolfgang von Goethe, Friedrich Schiller, and Anastasius Grün (pseudonym of Anton Alexander, count of Auersperg) and the Spanish poets Eulogio Florentino Sanz (the translator of Heine into Spanish), José María de Larrea, and his friend Ferrán. Nevertheless, Bécquer's poetic genius was so powerful that he was capable of fusing these influences with that of the popular Andalusian tradition to create his own distinctive style.

The most important characteristics of Bécquer's poetry are its simplicity and its suggestive, ethereal inwardness. It should be noted that the great majority of his poems are very short; his verse lines are generally short as well, and he prefers assonance to rhyme. Bécquer's language is elegant but simple, lacking exotic and high-sounding words, and he uses a minimum of rhetorical techniques. His preference for suggestion rather than explicit statement is reflected in his frequent use of incorporeal motifs such as waves of light, the vibration of air, murmurs, thoughts, clouds, and sounds. Anecdotes are absent from his poetry, except for some extremely short ones that are indispensable to the communication of emotions. Nature appears in his poems impressionistically, mirroring the poet's interior drama. Above all, Bécquer is an eminently subjective poet who uses his poetry to express his inner feelings with almost complete indifference to the objective reality of the world.

The above-mentioned characteristics, as well as others, place Bécquer as a precursor of the Symbolist movement. Traditionally, he has been considered a late Romantic, and to a certain extent this classification is correct. In Bécquer's poetry, it is easy to observe the cult of the individual, the exaggerated sensitivity, the centering of the world on the subjectivity of the poet—all typical of the Romantic movement. Nevertheless, these characteristics appear in Bécquer in conjunction with others that typify the Symbolism of Stéphane Mallarmé, Paul Verlaine, and Arthur Rimbaud. For Bécquer, emotions or feelings are the true object of poetry. Feelings cannot be expressed with exact and precise words, and to represent his interior world, the poet must rely on suggestion and evocative symbolism. In the first poem in *The Rhymes*, Bécquer says that he would like to express the "gigantic and strange hymnal" that he knows, by "taming the rebel, and miserly language,/ with words that are at the same time/ sighs and laughs, colors and notes." In these lines, it can be seen that Bécquer conceived of the possibility of the correspondence of sensations, also typical of Symbolism. For him, as for the Symbolists, there is an ideal, absolute, and perfect world, of which the familiar physical world is an imperfect representation, significant not for itself but only for the impressions of a higher reality that it conveys. Finally, Bécquer, like the Symbolists, made frequent allusions to music and struggled to make his language as musical as possible.

THE RHYMES

In the manuscript of *The Rhymes*, the poems do not follow a chronological order; indeed, they seem to follow no logical order at all. The most widely accepted critical opinion is that, having lost the original manuscript (which he gave to a friend for publication right before the revolution of 1868), Bécquer had to reconstruct the collection from memory, adding some new poems. It is speculated that in the new copy, the majority of the poems appear in the order in which the poet remembered them, interspersed with those newly created. In any case, when Bécquer's friends decided to publish his works, they rearranged the poems, placing them in the order in which they have appeared in all their subsequent publications.

The sequence imposed on the poems, justifiably or not, gives the collection a "plot." Early poems in the sequence reflect the enthusiasm of a young poet who seeks to explain the mystery of his art and who discovers the mysterious connections between poetry and love. In later poems, however, celebration of love gives way to disillusionment with the beloved. In the final poems in the sequence, the poet is increasingly preoccupied with death.

Thus, with few exceptions, the poems collected in *The Rhymes* can be divided into four sequential groups. The first group consists of poems that consider the poet per se and the nature of poetry; the second, of poems dealing with love; the third, of poems expressing disillusionment with love; and the fourth, of poems dealing with anguish and death.

Included in the first group are poems 1 through 8—except for poem 6 (a pathetic description of Shakespeare's Ophelia)—and poem 21. In poems 2 and 5, Bécquer focuses his attention on the poet per se, trying to explain what it means to be a poet and to describe the intimate nature of the poetic spirit. In the first of these two poems, Bécquer employs a series of similes to define himself both as a poet and as a human being. To suggest the narrow limits of humans' control over their own destiny, Bécquer imagines himself to be an arrow, a dry leaf, a wave, and a ray of light, saying in the last stanza that he is crossing the world "by accident," "without thinking/ where I am coming from nor where/ my steps will take me." In poem 5, Bécquer portrays the poet as a vase containing the poetic spirit, described as an "unknown essence," a "mysterious perfume." Throughout the poem, Bécquer tries to determine the nature of that spirit. He identifies it in another series of beautiful similes in which the objects of comparison are almost always immaterial and vague, with the clouds, the waking of a star, the blue of the sea, a note from a lute, and so on. This poem introduces an important idea in Bécquer's poetics: Poetry is the marvelous reduction of ideas and feelings to words and verbal forms. The poetic spirit is described as the "bridge that crosses the abyss," as "the unknown stair/ that connects heaven and earth," and as "the invisible/ ring that holds together/ the world of forms with the world of ideas."

The remaining poems of the first group attempt to explain the mystery of poetry. Poem 1 declares that poetry is "a hymn" that cannot be confined by words and that the poet can communicate fully only with his beloved. Here again, one notes the identification of poetry with feelings and the insistence that feelings cannot be explained but can be communicated only emotionally. These same notions lie behind the succinct affirmation of poem 21, repeated by countless lovers of the Hispanic world since it was first published: Bécquer answers his beloved's question, "What is poetry?" with the simple statement, "Poetry is you."

The second group of poems, those dealing with love, includes poems 9 through 29, except for 21 (already placed in the first group) and 26 (which is closely related to the poems in the third group). Some of these poems can be considered as a series of gallant phrases forming beautiful madrigals appropriate for address to young ladies. Among them are poem 12, written to a green-eyed girl; poem 13 (the first of Bécquer's poems to have appeared in a newspaper, titled "Imitation of Byron"), composed for a blue-eyed girl; and poem 19, addressed to a girl who has the purity of a white lily. Some of the poems in this group have the charm, brevity, and sparkling shine of the *coplas* (ballads) from the Andalusian region; among these are poems 17 and 20.

In almost all the remaining poems of the second group, Bécquer appears as the poet of love, but of love as a superior and absolute feeling. Poems 9 and 10 show the universality of love. The former attempts to present all of nature as loving, and the latter describes how everything is transformed when love passes by. In poems 11 and 15, Bécquer realizes that love and the beloved for whom he searches are ideal entities of an absolute perfection and beauty that cannot exist in tangible reality. In the first of these two poems, two girls appear, one brunette and the other blond, and each in turn asks the poet if it is she for whom he is looking, to which he answers no. Then comes an unreal girl, "a vague ghost made of mist and light," incorporeal and intangible, who is incapable of loving him; immediately, the poet shows his preference for this ethereal figure, crying "Oh come, come you!" In poem 15, the ideal beloved is a "curled ribbon of light foam," a "sonorous rumor/ of a golden harp," and the poet runs madly after her, "after a shadow/ after the fervent daughter/ of a vision."

The beloved becomes corporeal in only a few poems of the second group. In poem 14, the poet sees "two eyes, yours, nothing else," and he feels that they irresistibly attract him. In poem 18, the entire physical woman appears "fatigued by the dancing" and "leaning on my arm," and in poem 29, the poet and his beloved are reading the episode of Paolo and Francesca in Dante's *La divina commedia* (c. 1320; *The Divine Comedy*, 1802) when suddenly they turn their heads at the same time: "our eyes met/ and a kiss was heard." Finally, in this second group, there is a poem that expresses the realization of love. In a typical series of incorporeal images, Bécquer says that his and his beloved's souls are "two red tongues of fire" that reunite and "form only one flame," "two notes that the hand pulls at the same time from the lute," "two streams of vapor" that join to form only "one white cloud," "two ideas born at the same time," and "two echoes that fuse with one another."

The third group of poems in *The Rhymes*, those expressing disillusionment with love, includes poems 30 through 51 as well as poem 26. Although in these poems Bécquer continues talking about love, the ideal and sublime love of the poet has decayed, ending in failure and producing great disappointment, disenchantment, and sorrow. Bécquer speaks scornfully of feminine inconstancy in a few poems, but without the note of sarcasm characteristic of Heine. In Bécquer, sorrow produces only a fine irony, which at times leads him to insinuate that women are valuable only for their physical beauty. In poem 34, after describing in detail the beauty of a woman, the poet faces the fact that she is "stupid." Bécquer resolves this conflict by saying that, as long as she stays quiet, her intelligence is of no concern to him, since "what she does not say, will always be of greater value/ than what any other woman could tell me." Similarly, in poem 39, the poet enumerates the character flaws of a woman, only to end up stressing his preference for physical beauty by saying, "but . . ./ she is so beautiful!"

The most interesting and intense poems of this third

group are those in which the poet expresses his sorrow at the failure of his love. Some of them also seem to be the most autobiographical, although the impression given by the poems of *The Rhymes* is that all of them were the result of experiences lived by their author. Poem 41 appears to allude to the incompatibility between Bécquer and his wife, although it could refer to another woman. Its three brief stanzas present the poet and his beloved as opposing forces: the hurricane and the tower, the ocean and the rock, the beautiful girl and the haughty man. In each instance, the conclusion is the desolate phrase, "it could not be." The next poem, number 42, describes the moment when "a loyal friend" tells the poet a piece of "news" not mentioned in the poem. The last lines, in which the poet expresses his gratitude, would seem rather prosaic if the author had not earlier shown the intensity of his sorrow by saying, "then I understood why one cries,/ and then I understood why one kills."

The fourth and last group of poems in *The Rhymes*, those preoccupied with anguish and death, includes poems 52 through 76. In general, the poems of this group seem to be more detached from autobiographical experience, less charged with emotional intensity. Perhaps for this very reason, they are pervaded by a haunting lyricism.

One of the most famous poems ever written in Spanish is poem 53, the "Rime of the Swallows," which has been read and memorized by one generation after another. The poem expresses the brevity and the irreversibility of life and the unique value of every experience. The poet admits that the "dark swallows will return," but not "those that learned our names," "those . . . will not return!" He acknowledges that there will be flowers again on the honeysuckle tree, but not "those decorated with dew/ whose drops we used to see trembling," "those . . . will not return!" Finally, he concedes that "the fervent words of love/ will sound again in your ears," but "as I have loved you, . . . do not deceive yourself/ nobody will love you like that!

The last poems in the collection are dominated by the theme of death. When the poet asks himself about his origin and his end in poem 66, he ends his expression of radical loneliness by affirming that his grave will be "where forgetfulness lives." In poem 71, he

hears a voice calling him in his sleep, and he concludes that "somebody/ whom I loved has died!" In another of his most famous poems, which is also the longest in the book, Bécquer describes the funeral of a girl, repeating at the end of each stanza, "my God, how lonely stay the dead!" The same experience may have inspired poem 74. In poem 74, it seems that he sees a dead woman, and at the spectacle of death his soul is filled with "a fervent desire": "as the abyss attracts, that mystery/ was dragging me towards itself." At the same time, the angels that are engraved on the door seem to speak to him: "the threshold of this door only God trespasses." In poem 74, which concludes the volume, Bécquer again describes the funeral of a woman and expresses his own wish to rest from the struggles of life: "oh what love so quiet that of death/ what sleep so calm that of the sepulchre."

Other major works

short fiction: *Leyendas*, 1858-1864 (serial; partial translation in *Terrible Tales: Spanish*, 1891; also in *Romantic Legends of Spain*, 1909).

nonfiction: *Historia de los templos de España*, 1857; *Cartas literarias a una mujer*, 1860-1861 (serial; *Letters to an Unknown Woman*, 1924); *Cartas desde mi celda*, 1864 (*From My Cell*, 1924).

miscellaneous: *Obras*, 1871; *Legends, Tales, and Poems*, 1907; *The Infinite Passion: Being the Celebrated "Rimas" and the "Letters to an Unknown Woman,"* 1924 (includes *Rimas*, *Letters to an Unknown Woman*, and *From My Cell*); *Legends and Letters*, 1995.

Bibliography

Bécquer, Gustavo Adolfo. *Collected Poems (Rimas)*. Translated by Michael Smith. Exeter, England: Shearsman Books, 2007. This bilingual work is a modern translation of *The Rhymes*, with an informative introduction by the translator.

Bynum, B. Brant. *The Romantic Imagination in the Works of Gustavo Adolfo Bécquer*. Chapel Hill: University of North Carolina Press, 1993. Interpretation of Bécquer's work with an introduction to Romanticism and an extensive bibliography.

Havard, Robert. *From Romanticism to Surrealism:*

Seven Spanish Poets. Totowa, N.J.: Barnes & Noble, 1988. Brief biography and critical analysis of Spanish poets of the nineteenth and twentieth centuries. Includes bibliographic references.

Mayhew, Jonathan. "Jorge Guillén and the Insufficiency of Poetic Language." *PMLA* 106 (October, 1991). Discusses the skepticism of Bécquer and other poets regarding the capacity of language to convey the poets' experiences.

Silver, Philip W. *Ruin and Restitution: Reinterpreting Romanticism in Spain*. Nashville, Tenn.: Vanderbilt University Press, 1997. Examines Bécquer and Luis Cernuda and their works in terms of Romanticism.

Rogelio A. de la Torre

PIETRO BEMBO

Born: Venice (now in Italy); May 20, 1470
Died: Rome (now in Italy); January 18, 1547

PRINCIPAL POETRY

Gli Asolani, 1505 (includes poems and prose; English translation, 1954)
Rime per festa carnascialesca, 1507
Rime, 1530
Carmina, 1533
Opere, 1729
Lyric Poetry, 2005 (Mary P. Chatfield, editor and translator)

OTHER LITERARY FORMS

Pietro Bembo (BEHM-boh) wrote a range of non-fiction titles, many of which presented literary criticism, including *De Aetna* (1496), *De imitatione* (1514), *Prose della volgar lingua* (1525), *De Guidobaldo liber* (1530; also known as *De Urbini ducibus*), and *Epistolae familiares libri VII* (1552).

ACHIEVEMENTS

The influence of Pietro Bembo on his contemporaries and on the Italian language far outstripped his talent as a writer. The literary dictator of Italy for more than fifty years, he was dubbed the foster father of the Italian language, and authors whose names are more familiar than his sent him their manuscripts for corrections and improvements. Bembo did not fail to partake of the best his era had to offer. He lived in the Florence of Lorenzo de' Medici, the Venice of Aldus Manutius, and the Rome of Pope Leo X. Bellini and Titian painted portraits of him. He was a friend of Lucrezia Borgia, Isabella d'Este, Raphael, Poliziano, Ludovico Ariosto, Desiderius Erasmus, and Pietro Aretino, and both friend and literary mentor to Gaspara Stampa, Vittoria Colonna, and Veronica Gambara. Giangiorgio Trissino, Colonna, and Ariosto, among many others, wrote sonnets to him. He wrote two of the most famous essays of his century and the best Petrarchan verse.

Bembo is credited with having heterosexualized the concept of Platonic love. For the ancient Greeks, Platonic love was not love between the sexes but a philosophical idea based on heroic friendship, and what was so called by the Neoplatonists was still essentially the same as, for example, the relationship of Marsilio Ficino and Guido Cavalcanti, or of Giovanni Pico della Mirandola and Girolamo Benivieni. The Neoplatonic idealism that inspired Bembo and his style of balanced moderation determined an important pattern in the Renaissance poetry of several countries until the early Baroque.

Bembo restored Petrarchanism to its original luster and form by providing an unmistakably elegant standard by which the excesses of such conceitful poets as Il Chariteo, Antonio Tebaldeo, Serafino Aquilano, and Panfilo Sasso (who stressed the obvious and inferior elements of Petrarch's poetry rather than its deeper and less readily imitable perfections) could be judged as inferior. The prose style of *Gli Asolani* is equally elegant. Bembo was always an imitator, but he could judge better than others who and which elements were worthiest of imitation. As his poetry is modeled after Petrarch, his prose is modeled on the classicizing prose of Giovanni Boccaccio. The Italian of *Gli Asolani* is indeed a new classic language, as if its author had been writing in Latin.

If readers did not become familiar with the Neoplatonism, the revised Petrarchanism, and the lapidary stylistics of Bembo from *Gli Asolani*, they read the words put into his mouth in the fourth book of Baldassar Castiglione's *Il libro del cortegiano* (1528; *The Book of the Courtier*, 1561), a work of deeper insight than Bembo's, and his name was subsequently associated with all the characteristics that Castiglione attributed to him. Bembo, who is present in all the dialogues of *The Book of the Courtier*, assumes a leading role when the Duchess asks him to expound on what kind of love is appropriate for a courtier. Despite what his American translator Rudolph B. Gottfried calls the raillery and worldliness apparent in *Gli Asolani*, Bembo waxes almost mystical as he defines the Neoplatonic doctrine of love for Castiglione. He speaks of the divine origin of beauty, the distinction between the worlds of sense and intellect, and the various steps by which sensual love for a woman is finally transformed into spiritual love for God.

Perhaps Bembo at the age of fifty-eight simply allowed himself to appear more Platonic than he had been in his earlier years. The fifty *Rime per festa carnascialesca* that he composed for the Carnival at Urbino in 1507 (reworked by the Spaniard Juan Boscán in his own long poem, *Octava rima*, omitting certain stanzas whose licentiousness was unsuited to Spanish taste) urge Duchess Isabella Gonzaga and her sister-in-law Emilia Pia not to deny themselves the joys of love and are anything but Platonic. Even in *Gli Asolani*, published some twenty years before *The Book of the Courtier*, Perottino's attack on, and Gismondo's eulogy of, earthly love are more convincing than Lavinello's shorter Platonic resolution of the problem in book 3. While Castiglione uses some of the same arguments that are advanced in *Gli Asolani*, he also adds material that makes Bembo more Platonic than he appears in his own works; indeed, Bembo's Platonism in *Gli Asolani* is more literary than philosophical. The fact remains, however, that without Bembo, the finer art of Castiglione might never have emerged.

BIOGRAPHY

Pietro Bembo, the son of Venetian vice doge and senator Bernardo Bembo and his wife, Elena Morosina, was born in Venice in 1470. Bembo acquired a more thorough knowledge of Tuscan than would have otherwise been possible, because his father, a member of

Ficino's Academy, took him to Florence when he was eight years old. Proud of the boy's facility with languages, his father sent him to Messina to study under Constantine Lascaris in 1492. Bembo stayed in Sicily for two years, years of intense study that he fondly remembered all his life. Later, he studied philosophy at Padua under Pietro Pomponazzi, for whom Bembo would later intercede to save him from condemnation by the Lateran Council.

In 1498, Bembo's father went to Ferrara as Venetian coruler and took Pietro with him, hoping to acquaint him at long last with affairs of state. There he became intimate with Jacopo Sadoleto and Ercole Strozzi, and was appreciated by Duke Ercole of Ferrara. When Duke Ercole's son and heir Alfonso married Lucrezia Borgia in 1502, Bembo became friendly with her as well, and there developed between the two of them a deep friendship that may or may not have been Platonic.

On leaving Ferrara, Bembo returned to Venice, where he helped the printer Aldus Manutius form a learned academy and, in 1501, prepared for him the text of Petrarch's *Rerum vulgarium fragmenta* (1470; also known as *Canzoniere*; *Rhymes*, 1976), as well as the first Aldine copy of *La divina commedia* (c. 1320; *The Divine Comedy*, 1802), published under the title *Terza rima* in 1502. Bembo and Aldus are credited with establishing the use of the apostrophe, the period, and the comma in modern printing.

Tall and handsome, witty and learned, a writer of verse in three languages (Italian, Latin, and Greek), Bembo was in his prime when he moved to Urbino in 1506. Until 1511, he was a member of the court circle of Urbino, which, under Duke Guidobaldo Montefeltro and his wife, Elisabetta Gonzaga, rivaled Ferrara in social, artistic, and literary brilliance and which included such figures as the dramatist Bernardo Bibbiena, Giuliano de' Medici, Ottaviano Fregoso (later doge of Genoa), Louis of Canossa (later papal nuncio to France), and sundry other poets, musicians, and visitors. It was this refined circle that Castiglione idealized in *The Book of the Courtier*, and it was to Bembo that he gave the most distinguished role in the dialogue to discourse on the nature of Platonic love.

In 1512, Bembo accompanied Giuliano de' Medici

to Rome, and when Giuliano's brother became Pope Leo X in 1513, Bembo was given duties as Leo's secretary, a post he shared with his old friend and fellow student Sadoleto. Bembo was precisely the man to make Leo's life more agreeable by flattering his superficial tastes and by directing the faculties of his highly cultured mind to frivolous, if intellectual, amusements. The position afforded Bembo the opportunity to display his greatest talent, composing papal documents and letters in very polished Latin. It was also during these papal years that Bembo was most aggressively Ciceronian in his controversy with Poliziano and Erasmus.

In 1519, Bembo's debt-ridden father died, and Bembo left the Vatican to spend most of the next year between Venice and Padua. In April, 1521, wearied after nearly thirty years of continual court life, harried by illness, and depressed by the deaths of many of his good friends in Rome the previous year (Raphael, the banker Agostino Chigi, and Bibbiena had all died in 1520), he resigned his secretaryship and retired to his villa Noniamo near Padua. There, he entertained himself collecting manuscripts (his library, particularly rich in the works of the Provençal poets and Petrarch, passed after his death to Urbino and thence to the Vatican), experimenting with horticulture, and following the example of Horace and Vergil in appreciating the charms of country life. He was living with Morosina (Ambrogia della Torre), whom he had met in Rome in 1513 when she was barely sixteen (his ecclesiastical responsibilities and aspirations had precluded marriage), and was much concerned with the education of their three children, Lucilio, Torquato, and Elena. In 1530, he was appointed historiographer of the Venetian Republic, succeeding Andreas Navigero, and later, librarian of St. Mark's.

After the death of his beloved Morosina in August, 1535, Bembo embraced a more austere life, gave up his classical interests, and devoted himself to scriptural and patristic readings. Pope Paul III made him a cardinal in 1539, when he was sixty-nine years of age. In 1541, he was given the bishopric of Gubbio, where he moved in 1543. In 1544, he was given the rich see of Bergamo, but he never moved there. During these last years of life, Bembo seems to have taken great interest

Pietro Bembo (The Granger Collection, New York)

in the reforming views of Cardinal Pole and Vittoria Colonna at Viterbo—so much so that after his death, his name was found on the list of suspects of the Roman Inquisition.

In March of 1544, Bembo moved back to Rome, where he lived until his death in 1547 after a fall from his horse. He was buried in the Church of the Minerva between Popes Leo X and Clement VII. Olimpia Morata wrote the following words for him in Greek: "Bembo is no more. . . . He dies, and with him, disappears the splendid genius of eloquence; Cicero seems to have passed away a second time into the dark shadows."

ANALYSIS

Pietro Bembo's poems were borrowed, translated, and clearly plagiarized by subsequent generations of European writers. Among Italian poets, his greatest disciple was Giovanni Della Casa. In England, Sir Thomas Wyatt paraphrased "Voi me poneste in foco" ("Lady, You've Set Me All Afire") from *Gli Asolani*, representing it as his own work, and Thomas Lodge included translations from Bembo in his *Phillis with* the Tragical Complaynt of Elstred (1593). Because the principles of scansion are the same in Italian as in Spanish, Spanish poets such as Bartolomé de Torres Naharro, Boscán, and Luis de Léon were especially avid imitators of Bembo's verse, and Bembo's poem "Quand'io penso al martire" ("Madrigal") found its way into no less a work than Miguel de Cervantes's *El ingenioso hidalgo don Quixote de la Mancha* (1605, 1615; *The History of the Valorous and Wittie Knight-Errant, Don Quixote of the Mancha*, 1612-1620; better known as *Don Quixote de la Mancha*). Francisco de Sá de Miranda, who spent time in Italy in the 1520's and became acquainted with Bembo, introduced Petrarchan imagery in Portugal and ultimately influenced the style of Luis de Camões. The epitaph Bembo wrote for Jacopo Sannazzaro, "De sacro cineri flores. Hic ille Maroni/ Syncerus, musa proximus ut tumulo" ("give to the sacred ashes flowers. Here Maro/ in Muse Sincerus neighbors as in tomb") was copied on Edmund Spenser's tomb in Westminster Abbey.

As a native Venetian and an affiliate of the papal court who endorsed the Florentine dialect, Bembo did not see himself as a pacesetter. He had observed that the majority of older exemplary writers were native Tuscans, but he mistakenly considered himself the successor of such non-Tuscan writers as Pietro de Crescenzi and Guido delle Colonne of Messina. Actually, their works had been composed in Latin and translated anonymously by Tuscan scribes. It was not until the decision of Jacopo Sannazzaro, a Neopolitan, to write his highly successful *Arcadia* (1504) in Tuscan that the precedent of the Tuscan dialect as a vehicle for non-Tuscan writers was set. In the wake of Sannazzaro, Bembo proclaimed the preeminence of fourteenth century Tuscan; his views prevailed, and the influence of his prescriptive attitude on the subsequent development of Italian literature can hardly be exaggerated. Ariosto, for example, undertook a massive revision of *Orlando Furioso* (1516, 1521, 1532; English translation, 1591) after the appearance of Bembo's *Prose della volgar lingua*. Ariosto attempted to bring his Italian closer to the precepts of Bembo by doubling consonants, modifying his use of the article (*il* for *el, lo* before impure *s*), and revising verb forms. In a letter to Bembo dated February 23, 1531, Ariosto announced his intention of coming to Padua to consult him on stylistic matters. Ariosto gave Bembo a permanent tribute in the body of his masterpiece:

> I see Pietro Bembo here,
> Him who our pure and dulcet speech set free
> From the base vulgar usage, and made clear
> By his example what it ought to be.

GLI ASOLANI

Gli Asolani is a treatise on love in three books, with sixteen poems (canzones, canzonets, and one double sestina) interspersed in the text. The canzonets do not qualify as madrigals, even by Bembo's own broad definition in *Prose della volgar lingua*, but in *Italian Poets of the Renaissance* (1971), Joseph Tusiani nevertheless gives to one of them, "Quand'io penso al martire," the title "Madrigal." The treatise takes its name from the Castello d'Asolo, belonging to Caterina Cornaro, the former queen of Cyprus, in the mountains north of Venice, which also served as the poetic inspiration of Robert Browning, who made it the scene of *Pippa Passes* (pb. 1841) and finished there the collection of lyrics titled *Asolando* (1889). Bembo wrote the treatise between 1497 and 1502, recast the work in 1503 and 1504, and published it in 1505, with a dedication to Lucrezia Borgia. The three principal speakers are three young Venetian gentlemen, Perottino, Gismondo, and Lavinello, and their ladies, Lisa, Sabinetta, and Berenice, all members of the court under fictitious names. Praises of the Asolan circle run through the work, and the picture of the six novices, sauntering through shade and sunlight under the vines of a leafy pergola or seated on the grass listening to a deftly stroked lute, retains its freshness even for the modern reader.

The discussion revolves around the question of whether love is a good or a bad thing. Gismondo maintains that it is good, and Perottino counters that it is bad with an argument that occupies the entire first book. Berenice refuses to accept his conclusion, whereupon Perottino recites a list of love's casualties (Pyramus and Thisbe, Murrha and Byblis, Medea, Tarquin) and supports his argument by singing songs of his own composition. Perottino's tale of sighs and wretchedness is also punctuated with questions on punning etymologies, such as the relationship of *amare* ("to love") and *amaro* ("bitter"), *donna* ("lady") and *danno* ("damage"), *giovani* ("young men") and *giovano* ("they help").

One of the poems he recites, translated by Tusiani as "Madrigal," is "Quand'io penso al martire," which traces how the lover is forced by Love to stand before the sea of bitterness, where, once facing death, he is so happy to be relieved of his first burden that he feels like living again. In another, which Perottino recites in a voice "which would move stones," "Lady, You've Set Me All Afire," the poet admits that he is not as angry at the lady who caused his discomfort as he is at Love and at himself for allowing himself to be in Love's thrall.

In book 2, Gismondo refutes the arguments of Perottino, concluding that love is not only good but also the source of all that is good in life. In the canzonet "Non si vedrà giammai stanca né sazia" (oh love, my lord, faint and forworn this pen), Gismondo thanks Love for leading him to seek the skies and for giving his speech a sweet music. It is to Love that the poet owes his happy life and his pure and joyous thoughts.

On the third afternoon, the queen and some other guests join the six, and Lavinello assumes a conciliatory position between Perottino and Gismondo, arguing that love can be good if it is worthy love of a good object; that love is evil if it is love of an evil object and evil as well if it is unworthy love of a good object. Love is the search for beauty, and beauty, physical or mental, is a grace, which derives from good proportion, compatibility, and harmony of the various elements. Halfway through Lavinello's argument and after he recites three poems, he introduces a conversation he claims to have had with a hermit that morning. If love is to be good, the hermit tells Lavinello, it must arise from true beauty, beauty that is divine and immortal.

All in all, *Gli Asolani* has little that is original. From Petrarch, Bembo derived the first and second books and the first half of the third book, while the hermit's conversation is mainly from Dante; despite the Neoplatonic label attached to Bembo, only a few tidbits are borrowed from Platonic theory. Although some of its individual passages are beautiful, on the whole the work holds little appeal for the modern reader. Bembo makes no attempt to develop an independent philosophy apart from Ficino's theory of Platonism, nor does

he, except in the second book, try to relate it to practical problems, regarding it as a thing beautiful in itself, a charming abstraction shining in its distant and rarefied air.

RIME

The poetry in *Rime* is thoroughly Petrarchan in form (sonnets, canzones, *ballate*), phrasing (eyes brighter than the sun, the calming smile, the ivory hands), imagery (love as the impious lord, the lover as the ship battered by the storm, the song of birds expressive of the pain of love), and content (the request to God for the power to resist love, lamentation for the ruthlessness of love, regret for allowing oneself to be caught by love). Bembo's poetry demonstrates a more refined taste than that of earlier imitators of Petrarch, but it still lacks originality by modern standards. Bembo's most famous sonnet, "Crin d'oro crespo" ("A Curly Hair of Gold"), is a catalog of his lady's attributes that ends with a line taken almost verbatim from Petrarch: "Grazie, ch'a poche il ciel largo destina" ("Graces that on few women heaven freely bestows").

While Petrarch was keenly and painfully aware of both the transitory nature of human existence and the profane power of love to deflect people from their true devotion to God, these themes did not particularly interest Bembo. There is some religious poetry among his sonnets, but it is rather facile; indeed, Bembo wrote to the duchess of Urbino on March 20, 1504, that the thought of heavenly things had never occupied him much and did not occupy him then at all. He is supposed to have undergone a conversion after the death of Morosina, but until then he had blithely accumulated ecclesiastical benefits without in the least renouncing earthly pleasures. In his sonnet, "O Sol, di cui questo bel sol è raggio" (oh sun, of whom this beautiful sun is a glimmer), written probably in 1538, he asks God to look on his soul, "to sweep away the ancient fog," and to keep his soul safe from the injuries of the world. In "Signor, quella pietà, che ti constrinse" (Lord, that mercy which bound you), the reader is impressed with the familiarity that Bembo affects in order to bargain for his salvation, which may be due to the earlier date of its composition (1510). In "Signor, che per giovar si chiama Giove" (Lord, who for your help, are called Jove), written in 1528, he plays flippantly on the similarity of the verb *giovare* ("to help") and the name of the pagan deity *Giove* (Jove).

OCCASIONAL POEMS

Bembo wrote many occasional poems, such as to celebrate the birth of a friend's son or to celebrate the exploits of an unidentified "conqueror of Naples." He had a knack for converting an ordinary incident into a subtle vignette. In "Ove romita e stanca si sedea" (where tired and alone she sat), the poet, like a thief burning with hope and fear, surprises his beloved as she is lost in thought and perhaps even talking to herself. She is mildly upset that he has seen her so absorbed, and he is possessed by tenderness to have seen her so. His elegies on the death of persons dear to him are counted among his best poems; unlike so many of his Petrarchan exercises, they do not lack spontaneous emotion. "Donna, di cui begli occhi alto diletto" (lady, whose beautiful eyes gave such delight) is one of his many sonnets on the death of his mistress Morosina, and "Adunque m'hai tu pur, in sul fiorire" ("On the Death of His Brother") was penned in memory of his brother Carlo, who died at the age of thirty-two in 1503.

LATIN POEMS

Bembo also wrote Latin poetry. His hexameter poem "Benacus" is a description of Lago di Garda, and he also wrote epitaphs in Latin for many of his contemporaries. In his epitaph for Poliziano, whose death in 1494 followed close on that of his patron, Lorenzo de Medici, Bembo tells how death struck him while he wept, breaking his heartstrings in the middle of his sighs, and dubs him in the last line as "master of the Ausonian [Italian] lyre." Two elegiac poems, "Priapus" and "Faunus ad nympheum flumen," are remarkable for their pagan approach to morality; his masterpiece in elegiac meter is "De Galeso et Maximo," about a boy, Galesus, who wrongs his master, Maximus, who, as the epigraph explains, is a great man in Rome and may possibly represent Pope Leo X himself. When Maximus is confronted with the boy's misdeed, the boy does not apologize but rather runs to clasp the neck of his angry master, raining kisses on him. Bembo concludes: "Still doubting, Maximus? Change place with me:/ Gladly I'd bear such infidelity."

The influence of Bembo was so strong that an entire half century (1500-1550) is designated by many critics as the Bembist period. His support of the vernacular as the equal of Latin, and his support of the Florentine dialect over competing dialects, determined in no small way the course of Italian literature. As a poet, he refurbished the Petrarchan tradition, and he was instrumental in the spread of Neoplatonism. While it is true that his influence on literature was out of proportion to the value of his literary output, Bembo inspired a fierce loyalty in his contemporaries, and his precepts commanded a vigorous authority long after his death.

OTHER MAJOR WORKS

NONFICTION: *De Aetna*, 1496; *De imitatione*, 1514; *Prose della volgar lingua*, 1525; *De Guidobaldo liber*, 1530 (also known as *De Urbini ducibus*); *De Virgilii Culice et Terentii fabulis*, 1530; *Epistolarum Leonis X nomine scriptarum libri XVI*, 1535; *Lettere*, 1548-1553 (4 volumes); *Rerum Venetarum historiae libri XII*, 1551 (*History of Venice*, 2007); *Epistolae familiares libri VII*, 1552.

MISCELLANEOUS: *Gli Asolani*, 1505 (includes prose and poetry; English translation, 1954); *Prose e rime di Pietro Bembo*, 1960 (prose and poetry).

BIBLIOGRAPHY

Brand, Peter, and Lino Pertile, eds. *The Cambridge History of Italian Literature*. New York: Cambridge University Press, 1999. In "Bembo and the Classicist Tradition," Anthony Oldcorn sketches the broad influence of Bembo on the likes of Michelangelo, Della Casa, Torquato Tasso, and contemporary women poets, such as Gaspara Stampa. Presents Bembo's establishment of *bembismo* and the debate it sparked.

Kidwell, Carol. *Pietro Bembo: Lover, Linguist, Cardinal*. Ithaca, N.Y.: McGill-Queen's University Press, 2004. Examines the life of Bembo, his multiple roles, and his literary works.

McLaughlin, Martin L. *Literary Imitation in the Italian Renaissance: The Theory and Practice of Literary Imitation from Dante to Bembo*. Oxford, England: Clarendon Press, 1995. The final chapter outlines the 1512 literary dispute between Bembo and Pico della Mirandola. McLaughlin examines Bembo's defense of strict Ciceronian formalism, in opposition to eclectic or syncretic developments in Latin or the vernacular, and his "literary credo," which is applicable to all his subsequent critical work.

Raffini, Christine. *Marsiglio Ficino, Pietro Bembo, Baldassare Castiglione: Philosophical, Aesthetic, and Political Approaches in Renaissance Platonism.* New York: Peter Lang, 1998. This is a short, chronological treatment of Bembo's life and major works with an emphasis on his impact on contemporary poets and scholars. Platonism is treated but lightly.

Robb, Nesca A. *Neoplatonism in the Italian Renaissance.* London: Allen & Unwin, 1935. In the chapter on the *trattato d'amore*, Robb analyses *Gli Ascolani* as a Neoplatonic treatise on love in a courtly setting and a prototype of its genre.

Wilkins, Ernest H. *A History of Italian Literature.* Rev. ed. Cambridge, Mass.: Harvard University Press, 1974. Wilkins's short chapter on Bembo places him squarely in the tumultuous years of the early sixteenth century. His life and major works are discussed chronologically, if briefly, and his later influence is asserted.

Jack Shreve

GOTTFRIED BENN

Born: Mansfeld, Germany; May 2, 1886
Died: Berlin, East Germany (now in Germany); August 7, 1956

PRINCIPAL POETRY

Morgue, und andere Gedichte, 1912
Söhne, 1913
Fleisch, 1917
Schutt, 1924
Betäubung, 1925
Spaltung, 1925
Gesammelte Gedichte, 1927
Ausgewählte Gedichte, 1911-1936, 1936
Gedichte, 1936
Zweiundzwanzig Gedichte, 1943

Statische Gedichte, 1948
Trunkene Flut, 1949
Fragmente, 1951
Destillationen, 1953
Aprèslude, 1955
Gesammelte Gedichte, 1956
Primal Vision, 1958
Primäre Tage, Gedichte und Fragmente aus dem Nachlass, 1958
Gedichte aus dem Nachlass, 1960
Gottfried Benn: Selected Poems, 1970
Gottfried Benn: The Unreconstructed Expressionist, 1972
Sämtliche Gedichte, 1998

OTHER LITERARY FORMS

Gottfried Benn (behn) was primarily a poet, but he did write some significant works in other genres, most notably a collection of novellas, *Gehirne* (1916; *Brains*, 1972); a novel, *Roman des Phänotyp* (1944; novel of the phenotype); the essay *Goethe und die Naturwissenschaften* (1949; Goethe and the natural sciences); his autobiography, *Doppelleben* (1950; *Double Life*, 2002); and a theoretical treatise, *Probleme der Lyrik* (1951; problems of lyric poetry). His writings also include other prose and dramatic works.

ACHIEVEMENTS

No other German poet exemplifies as fully as Gottfried Benn the emergence of the modern tradition within postwar German literature. His radical aesthetic as well as his political affiliations have made Benn a controversial figure. He was the "phenotype" of his age—that is, the exemplary representation of the intellectual and spiritual condition of his times. As such, Benn can be viewed as not only a remarkable poet but also an important figure of twentieth century German *Geistesgeschichte*.

Benn's early work (until about 1920) was known only to a relatively small circle of readers. Indeed, it was only after World War II, in the last decade of his life, that Benn achieved fame. His achievements were acknowledged in 1951, when he was awarded the Georg Büchner Prize in literature. For years prior to this time, Benn had been blacklisted, as it were, as a result of his short-lived infatuation with Nazism. Because of the public commentary to which he had been subjected, Benn was reluctant to reenter public life. He did publish again, however, and in the years before his death a generation of poets in search of a tradition flocked around him like disciples around a master.

The years of Nazi control had yielded a vast wasteland in German literature. Indeed, the historical events of the twentieth century, in particular as they affected Germany, intensified the general philosophical disorientation of the immediate postwar period. Marxism was no real alternative for the West; existentialism prevailed instead, based in large measure on the writings of Martin Heidegger and Jean-Paul Sartre. In this context, Benn's theory of art as a metaphysical act had considerable authority. For postwar poets in search of a new way of writing, Benn provided a transition from the various offshoots of French Symbolism and German expressionism to contemporary modernism.

BIOGRAPHY

Gottfried Benn was born on May 2, 1886, the son of a Protestant minister. He studied philosophy and theology at the University of Marburg and later studied medicine at the University of Berlin. He completed his medical degree in 1910 and was awarded first prize for his thesis on the etiology of epilepsy in puberty. Benn worked as a pathologist and serologist in Berlin, where he became friends with several expressionist poets, the most important of whom was Else Lasker-Schüler. Benn also set up medical practice in Berlin, and his first volume of poetry, *Morgue und andere Gedichte* (morgue, and other poems), clearly shows the influence of his scientific and medical training: The cold and unforgiving objectivity and precision of medical and surgical technique inform these poems, with their shocking portrayal of brutality and morbidity.

In 1914, Benn traveled briefly to the United States. Upon his return, he was drafted into the military medical corps, serving as an officer in Belgium before returning to Berlin in 1917. These years, contrary to what one might expect, were extremely productive for Benn as a writer, and he later noted that during the following years, on the whole relatively uneventful for him, he constantly drew for inspiration on his experiences in Belgium.

In 1933, Benn filled the position of which Heinrich Mann had been relieved, section president of the Prussian Academy. Later, Benn became director for the department of literature. In April of the same year, he gave a radio talk, "Der neue Staat und die Intellektuellen" ("The New State and the Intellectuals"), clearly in response to a letter from Klaus Mann, the son of Thomas Mann, who wrote from the south of France. It is true that Benn initially embraced National Socialism in 1933. He greeted the political doctrines of the Nazis as a means for overcoming the stagnation and nihilism of Western civilization, but he soon regretted his participation and withdrew into silence.

In 1935, Benn left Berlin and headed for Hannover. It was Benn's early poetry that gave rise to the debate on expressionism carried in the émigré paper *Das Wort*, printed in Moscow. In the ensuing years,

Gottfried Benn (Getty Images)

Benn had a run-in with W. Willrich, a party loyalist who labeled Benn a "cultural Bolshevist" and tried to have Benn effectively "removed" from public life. Ironically, only the intervention of Heinrich Himmler himself stayed Willrich's attempts. Benn remained in the army medical service from 1935 until the end of the war. After 1948, he enjoyed a new phase of poetic creativity, and his poetry eventually achieved recognition throughout Europe.

ANALYSIS

Both poetically and existentially, Gottfried Benn resided at the crossroads of two significant traditions. At the turn of the century, the natural sciences exercised a substantial "claim to truth" and provided influential paradigms of thought. For many of Benn's generation, however, scientific study had entered a rapid phase of entropy—it was seen no longer to answer questions meaningfully from the humanist point of view. In fact, one could even say that the "scientific approach" was seen by many to "explain" the universe inadequately, precisely because it did not pose the right questions. In Germany, the most significant manifestation of this dissatisfaction with the scientific paradigm took place under the rubric of "expressionism," which in many respects carried on the tradition of German Romanticism. The tension exemplified in the conflict between Benn's scientific training and his early intoxication with expressionism came to play an important role in the development of his aesthetic theory and poetry.

A concept basic to Benn's thought was his conviction that humankind necessarily "suffered consciousness." He attributed this suffering to modern overintellectualization: "The brain is our fate, our consignment and our curse." The modern consciousness fragments the totality of the world into its conceptual categories; reality is divided past meaningful comprehension; and the loss of humans' capacity to perceive relationships points ineluctably in the direction of nihilistic resignation. During the years from 1921 to 1932, Benn studied the works of Johann Wolfgang von Goethe, Friedrich Nietzsche, Oswald Spengler, Carl Jung, Ernst Troeltsch, and Gotthold Ephraim Lessing, and through his study of prehistory, paleontology, and myth, he developed his own notions of art, reality, and the self.

In Benn's conceptual framework, the inner space once occupied by the premodern sense of harmony and totality is now filled with a kind of nostalgic longing. By somehow penetrating and deactivating the rational consciousness, Benn hoped to return (momentarily) to archetypal, primal, and prelogical experience. Benn identified this act as "hyperemic metaphysics"—that is, an intensified state of perception (such as that induced by intoxication, dream visions, or hallucinations), which he then applied exponentially to derive his "hyperemic theory of the poetic," or primal moments of poetic creativity.

It is necessary to see how Benn viewed the creative process to understand his poetry. According to Benn, the creative process required first "an inarticulate, creative nucleus, a psychic substance"; second, words familiar to the poet that "stand at his disposal" and are "suited to him personally"; and third, a "thread of Ariadne, which leads him with absolute certainty out of this bipolar tension"—that is, the tension between the psychic substance and the "word." This amalgam constitutes the basic creative situation for Benn.

"BEAUTIFUL YOUTH"

One of his first poems, "Schöne Jugend" ("Beautiful Youth"), perhaps best illustrates Benn's early cynicism. The poem describes the dissection of the body of a young (and possibly at one time "beautiful") girl, whose decomposed mouth and esophagus are perfunctorily noted, as is the nest of young rats discovered beneath the diaphragm, "one little sister" of which lay dead while the others lived off the liver and kidneys— "drank the cold blood and had/ spent here a beautiful youth." A quick death awaits the rats: "They were thrown all together in the water. Ah, how their little snouts did squeal!" It becomes obvious that the "beautiful youth" to which the title refers is not that of the young girl, as the reader is intended to assume, but rather of the rats.

"ONE WORD"

A good example of Benn's preoccupation with the capacity of language to "fascinate," and in so doing to give momentary vision to meaning within meaninglessness (form from chaos), is his poem "Ein Wort" ("One Word"). This poem is about the fact that words and sentences can be transmuted into *chiffres*, from which rise life and meaning. The effect can be such as to halt the sun and silence the spheres, as everything focuses for the moment on the primal catalyst, the single word. The word, however, is transitory, brilliant but short-lived, and already in the second and last strophe of this brief poem it is gone, leaving behind it the self and the world once again apart and distinct, alone in the dark, empty space surrounding them. Perhaps this paraphrase of Benn's poem gives an idea of how Benn viewed the magic of the poetic word, its unique ability to stand (and consequently place the reader/listener) outside the "normal" conceptual categories of time and space. It communicates truth as a bolt of lightning momentarily illuminating the sky.

"LOST SELF"

The radical dissolution of meaning with the evaporation of the word's spellbinding aura aligns with Benn's view of the disintegration of reality in general. Nowhere are the consequences of this loss of reality for the individual given more poignant expression than in Benn's poem "Verlorenes Ich" ("Lost Self"). Benn applies the terminology of modern science as an explanation of the radical alienation of the modern self. The strictly scientific explanation of the universe does not adequately explain the vicissitudes of human existence. Benn does not envision a return to a previous form of existence since that is an impossibility, nor does he seek refuge in a Christian answer, positing God as the source of an otherwise incomprehensible universe. Neither, however, is his stance one of resignation or of art for art's sake, even though he is often reproached for both. Instead, his predicament always centers on the struggle for human meaning and significance. The solution to this existential dilemma, he finds, is manifested in the intellectual and spiritual acts that human beings can perform, among these the creative act of giving form. "The artist," wrote Benn, "is the only one who copes with things, who decides their destiny."

"DEPARTURE"

It is true that Benn felt that all good poetry is "addressed to no one," and that he expressly refuted the possibility of poetry having any public function. To castigate Benn for an unconscionable aestheticism, though, would not be accurate or just. He does not cast aside the question of ethical responsibility; if he did, one would not expect to find such an obsession with what constitutes the essence of humanity, above all with the existential-poetic confrontation with Being. To explore this problem further, it is illuminating to consider a highly autobiographical poem by Benn, "Abschied" ("Departure"), contained originally in a cycle of poems Benn referred to as "Biographische Gedichte" ("Biographical Poems") and first published in *Zweiundzwanzig Gedichte* (twenty-two poems). Formally, the poem is a classic example of artistic control: four strophes of eight lines each in iambic pentameter, with alternating feminine and masculine rhymes in an *ababcdcd* scheme. Structurally, the poem constitutes a tightly organized unit: Its formal principles interact with its themes—namely, the schizophrenic existence of the persona and the acknowledged taking leave from the old Self.

The topos of parting (*Abschied*) is itself an interesting one within German poetry; one may recall the significant example of Goethe's "Willkommen und Abschied" ("Welcome and Farewell"). Benn's poem, however, does not deal with the separation of two individuals—two lovers, for example. Instead, it describes a separation of the persona, a division of the Self into a former "You" and a present "I." The You represents the part of the individual that belongs to a world of the past, while the I attempts to grasp and develop within the poem the process of alienation to which it has been subjected. The first strophe outlines the relationship of the former to the present Self by employing a series of metaphors, while the second strophe probes the cause of the schism and relates the sole recourse as perceived by the persona. The link between past and present—memory—becomes the topic of the third strophe, and finally the poem moves toward a further degree of estrangement, concluding with a note of sadness and melancholy typical of Benn.

The subject of each independent clause in the first strophe is the pronoun "you," and initially it is the active subject, while the "I" remains the passive object. The relationship is established via a metaphor: "You fill me as does blood the fresh wound,/ and run down its dark path." The image of the wound operates on the physical plane to suggest impairment, disease, decay.

Later, in the third strophe, this physical affliction is seen to be present on a psychological plane as well. The adjective describing the wound, "fresh," can be read two ways. On one hand, it accentuates the grotesque nature of the wound by showing it in its first moments when blood flows most freely. On the other hand, "fresh" can suggest "recent." The reader is thus made privy to the suffering of the persona as it takes place. The metaphor of the wound encompasses the first two lines of the poem. The dark trace of the blood is more than merely graphic realism; it evokes an aura of mysterious origin. Blood is the life-sustaining fluid, and its escape from the wound enacts the kind of exposure that the "deep self" of the persona endures. Its dark hue contrasts with the "day of minutiae," the "heavenly light" of the third strophe, and "a high light" in the third line of the last strophe. Its opaqueness suggests obscurity and impregnability. The persona's flight into silence at the end of the second strophe ("you must take your silence, travel downward/ to night and sorrow and the roses late") gives image to the inexpressibility of the "deep self."

The night setting maintains the motif of darkness found in the "dark path" on the second line. The hour corresponds to dusk and evinces the twilight of the former self, the You. The atmosphere of darkness surrounding the You continues to dominate, although it retreats for the moment with the appearance of roses in the following line. While this imagery is initially perplexing (because it does not seem to cooperate with the earlier metaphor of the wound), under the assumption that the You represents a former state of naïve harmony and quietude, the rose will be seen to bloom now only with difficulty, indicating the suffering connected with the memory of the persona's previous unified existence.

In the second strophe, the self-reflection intensifies, resulting in a kind of linguistic breakdown: The abstract nouns lack contact with reality and no longer illustrate the tendency toward analogous thought, as in the first five lines; no finite verb appears from lines 6 to 8, leaving the explication static and ineffective. Significantly, it is the second strophe which introduces the idea of alienation. Its cause is seen as the absence of a homogeneous reality, as a craze of pluralities (Benn

speaks of "realities"). Resistance against this disembodying centrifugal force is sustained within the act of composing the poem itself, in the creative act that circles around the "deep self" in an attempt to describe it with more accuracy than simple, or even scientific, language can yield. "The form *is* the poem," Benn wrote elsewhere, stating the crux of his aesthetic.

In spite of the alienation from the "deep self," it is only this region that can satisfy the needs of the persona. This part of the Self, however, is (linguistically) impregnable, and silence represents the only alternative. The poem ends as "a last day" (Benn's own advancing age), which "plays its game, and feels its light and without/ memory goes down—everything is said." Such a poetic stance is rooted in the modernist poetic tradition. Benn acknowledges that no word or sign can now reveal that for which he searches; they are but symbols of the essential thing.

Had the persona no memory of itself, then no tension or conflict would result. The plague of consciousness is such, however, that it disrupts the fluidity of expression. This is represented throughout the poem by frequent dashes, colons, and question marks. Sentences and thoughts are left incomplete, fragmented; punctuation replaces words and becomes itself a frustrated sign or symbol of the inexpressible. The "deep self" evades all intellectualization.

In his epoch-making address, *Probleme der Lyrik*, Benn postulated that

> not one of even the great poets of our time has left behind more than six or eight complete poems. The rest may be interesting from the point of view of biography and the author's development, but only a few are content in themselves, illuminating from within themselves, full of lasting fascination—and so, for these six poems, [there are] thirty to fifty years of asceticism, suffering, and struggle.

Even according to Benn's own stringent definitions, he deserves to be acknowledged as a great poet.

OTHER MAJOR WORKS

LONG FICTION: *Roman des Phänotyp*, 1944; *Die Stimme hinter dem Vorhang*, 1952 (*The Voice Behind the Screen*, 1996).

SHORT FICTION: *Gehirne*, 1916 (*Brains*, 1972); *Provoziertes Leben: Eine Auswahl aus den Prosaschriften*, 1955.

NONFICTION: *Fazit der Perspektiven*, 1930; *Nach dem Nihilismus*, 1932; *Der neue Staat und die Intellektuellen*, 1933; *Kunst und Macht*, 1943; *Goethe und die Naturwissenschaften*, 1949; *Doppelleben*, 1950 (*Double Life*, 2002); *Essays*, 1951; *Probleme der Lyrik*, 1951.

MISCELLANEOUS: *Die gesammelten Schriften*, 1922; *Gesammelte Prosa*, 1928; *Ausdruckswelt: Essays and Aphorismen*, 1949; *Frühe Prosa und Reden*, 1950; *Gesammelte Werke in vier Bänden*, 1958-1960 (4 volumes).

BIBLIOGRAPHY

Alter, Reinhard. *Gottfried Benn: The Artist and Politics (1910-1934)*. Bern, Switzerland: Herbert Lang, 1976. A biography including the history of German politics and literature in Benn's time.

Dierick, Augustinus Petrus. *Gottfried Benn and His Critics: Major Interpretations, 1912-1992*. Columbia, S.C.: Camden House, 1992. Critical interpretation and history by an expert in German expressionist literature. Includes an exhaustive bibliography.

Donahue, Neil H., ed. *A Companion to the Literature of German Expressionism*. Rochester, N.Y.: Camden House, 2005. Chapter on expressionist poetry discusses Benn.

Powell, Larson. *The Technological Unconscious in German Modernist Literature: Nature in Rilke, Benn, Brecht, and Döblin*. Rochester, N.Y.: Camden House, 2008. Examines the works of Benn, Bertolt Brecht, Rainer Maria Rilke, and Alfred Döblin, with attention to the role of nature. Contains a chapter on Benn.

Ray, Susan. *Beyond Nihilism: Gottfried Benn's Postmodernist Poetics*. New York: P. Lang, 2003. Ray analyzes Benn's poetry, placing him with the postmodern poets.

Roche, Mark William. *Gottfried Benn's Static*. Chapel Hill: University of North Carolina Press, 1991. Intellectual and historical interpretation of Benn's poetry with bibliography and index.

Travers, Martin. *The Poetry of Gottfried Benn: Text and Selfhood*. Studies in Modern German Literature 106. New York: P. Lang, 2007. Examines the question of self in Benn's poetry.

Richard Spuler

THOMAS BERNHARD

Born: Heerlen, the Netherlands; February 9 or 10, 1931
Died: Gmunden, Austria; February 12, 1989

PRINCIPAL POETRY
Auf der Erde und in der Hölle, 1957
In hora mortis, 1957 (English translation, 2006)
Unter dem Eisen des Mondes, 1958
Die Irren-die Häftlinge, 1962
Contemporary German Poetry, 1964 (includes selections of his poetry in English translation)

OTHER LITERARY FORMS

The reputation of Thomas Bernhard (BEHRN-hort) rests primarily on his fiction and his memoirs. His first novel, *Frost* (1963; English translation, 2006), won critical acclaim, and his subsequent novels, novellas, and stories brought him most of the significant literary prizes awarded in the German-speaking world. Among Bernhard's novels are *Verstörung* (1967; *Gargoyles*, 1970; literally translated, "derangement"); *Das Kalkwerk* (1970; *The Lime Works*, 1973); and *Korrektur* (1975; *Correction*, 1979). Bernhard's memoirs, regarded by many critics as semifictional, present autobiographical material in the monomaniacal voice of his fictional narrators. This ongoing sequence includes *Die Ursache: Eine Andeutung* (1975; *An Indication of the Cause*, 1985), *Der Keller: Eine Entziehung* (1976; *The Cellar: An Escape*, 1985), *Der Atem: Eine Entscheidung* (1978; *Breath: A Decision*, 1985), *Die Kälte: Eine Isolation* (1981; *In the Cold*, 1985), *Ein Kind* (1982; *A Child*, 1985), and *Wittgensteins Neffe: Eine Freundschaft* (1982; *Wittgenstein's Nephew: A Friendship*, 1986).

The premiere of Bernhard's first play, *Ein Fest für*

Boris (pr., pb. 1970; *A Party for Boris*, 1990), created a small sensation, and since then many of his plays have been produced, some of them at the Salzburg Festival; among them are *Die Macht der Gewohnheit* (pr., pb. 1974; *The Force of Habit*, 1976) and *Über allen Gipfeln ist Ruh: Ein deutscher Dichterag um 1980* (pb. 1981; *Over All the Mountain Tops*, 2004).

ACHIEVEMENTS

Critic George Steiner has described Thomas Bernhard as "the most original, concentrated novelist writing in German." The locution "writing in German" is significant, for Bernhard's achievements must be seen in the context of the Austrian literary tradition. Bernhard occupies a special position in contemporary Austrian literature. Unlike most Austrian writers of recent fame, he did not belong to a group, such as the Wiener Gruppe or the group at the Forum Stadtpark in Graz, nor could he be identified with any of the prevailing literary factions. However, if Bernhard was a nonconformist—in his personal life as well as in his writing—he was nevertheless a typical Austrian author, rooted in the Austrian literary tradition, despite the fact that he rejected "Austria" as a political and ethnic abstraction and even blamed it for much of his existential anguish. This distinctively Austrian tradition is characterized by several features, the foremost of which is a morbid preoccupation with death, and in particular with suicide.

Another facet of this tradition can be traced to the Baroque period and manifests itself as an inclination to give form preference over substance—to value the way something is expressed more highly than what is said. Other Baroque contributions to the Austrian tradition clearly visible in Bernhard's work are the memento mori theme and the typically Austrian response to this reminder of the imminence of death, the carpe diem motif. Another Baroque ingredient is the recurring metaphor of the *theatrum mundi*—the notion that the world is a stage on which all humans must perform their roles. It is no accident that Bernhard has increasingly devoted himself to the theater in the 1970's and 1980's and that critics have noted in his works affinities with Hugo von Hofmannsthal and Franz Kafka.

Austrian literature has a long tradition of complaining about the conservative artistic attitudes of the Austrians and about the narrowness of the country's intellectual life. This complaint, which is surely not exclusively Austrian, appears in the works and in the private utterances of Wolfgang Amadeus Mozart, Franz Grillparzer, Sigmund Freud, and Arthur Schnitzler, to name only a few, and a frighteningly large number of Austrian artists and intellectuals were driven to suicide or into exile by this feeling of rejection and claustrophobia. Bernhard expresses this notion with obsessive force in many of his works. He did not grant interviews and lived in virtual isolation on a farm in a secluded valley, rejecting most involvement in the social life of the Austrian literary scene.

Finally, Bernhard is firmly entrenched in an Austrian tradition of language skepticism associated with Hofmannsthal, Ludwig Wittgenstein, and Theodore Mauthner. Bernhard's entire oeuvre is informed by a profound distrust of language as an efficacious artistic or communicative tool. The influence of Wittgenstein, most explicit in the novel *Correction*, in which one of the characters is modeled after him, and in the memoir *Wittgenstein's Nephew*, is of particular significance in Bernhard's development. Bernhard treats Wittgenstein with a mixture of reverence and savage irony, and the philosopher's ideas are implicit in all Bernhard's works. One of the key phrases in *Gargoyles* is an implicit response to the famous aphorism that concludes Wittgenstein's *Tractatus Logico-Philosophicus* (1922, 1961); Bernhard writes: "The words we use really do not exist any longer. . . . But it is also no longer possible to be completely silent." Bernhard shares this belief with many contemporary Austrian writers, including Peter Handke.

Although Bernhard's verse is not his most significant contribution to Austrian literature—four slim volumes containing some 150 poems are an insufficient basis for such a claim—it did provide Bernhard with an early testing ground for his literary talent. Critics so far have not paid much attention to Bernhard, the poet, although this neglect is not justified. At their worst, the poems are a youthful testimony to early poetic influences and to eclectic readings in nineteenth century European philosophy. At their best, they are lyrical precursors of Bernhard's fiction, foreshadowing the linguistic experiments of his early prose and introducing the themes of his mature work, such as death, the desertion of God, impotence in the face of suffering, the world as prison and insane asylum, rural decay, urban decadence, and the impossibility of communication. Bernhard's poetry is sure to be given increased critical attention.

BIOGRAPHY

Biographical data, particularly of Nicolaas Thomas Bernhard's early life, must be considered with some caution, as many of these "facts" have been excerpted from the author's autobiographical writings and from a letter to the editor of an anthology, published in 1954—a letter that Bernhard had not intended to make public.

Bernhard was born on February 9 or 10, 1931, the illegitimate son of an Austrian carpenter. Bernhard's mother was the daughter of an eccentric Austrian writer, Johannes Freumbichler. In the strictly Catholic, rural Austrian environment, an illegitimate birth would have created quite a stir, and so Bernhard was born in a convent near Maastrich, the Netherlands, where his mother had to remain in service to defray the cost of the birth of her son. Much of Bernhard's childhood was spent with his maternal grandparents near Salzburg. He formed a strong attachment to his grandfather, who became the dominating personal and intellectual influence of his early life, as described in Bernhard's memoir, *A Child*. In Freumbichler's house, the young Bernhard met Ödön von Horvath and Carl Zuckmayer; Zuckmayer later wrote encouraging and thoughtful reviews of the young man's first volumes of poetry. Bernhard's grandfather, who had received the highest Austrian literary award, mainly for his novel *Philomena Ellenhub* (1937), was an avid reader of the German writers and philosophers of the later nineteenth century and was particularly fond of Michel Eyquem de Montaigne. Bernhard claimed to have read Arthur Schopenhauer in Freumbichler's study and to have discovered then for the first time "the impossibility of saying the truth and the inability of transcending human existence."

In 1938, Bernhard's family—his mother was then married to a man who was not Bernhard's father—moved to Traunstein, Bavaria, where the boy had his first music lessons. Music has played an important part in Bernhard's life; much of his literary vocabulary is taken from musical terminology, and he speaks in terms of the theory of musical composition when he discusses the structure of some of his works. In 1943, the boy was sent to a Nazi-sympathizing boarding school in Salzburg. After the war, the school was taken over by the Roman Catholic Church, but Bernhard claims not to have noticed any difference. In his memoir *An Indication of the Cause*, he deals extensively with this depressing period in his life.

In 1946, Bernhard's family was forced to leave Germany and moved to Salzburg. Soon after that, Bernhard quit school and apprenticed himself to a grocery merchant. His relationship with his stepfather deteriorated, and finally the working conditions in the wet storage cellar of his employer (described in his memoir *The Cellar*) caused Bernhard to contract first pleurisy and then a severe lung disease. The next four years, a hellish period described in the memoirs *Breath* and *In the Cold*, were spent being shuttled between hospitals and sanatoriums; in 1949, Bernhard's grandfather was taken to the same hospital where the young man himself lay in a bathroom in the section for the terminally ill. During the following year, both Bernhard's grandfather and his mother died, and he also learned that his natural father had died in 1943 in the turmoil of the war. It was at this time, while confined to the bed of a hospital for pulmonary diseases, that Bernhard began to write. He is convinced that this activity prevented him from succumbing to insanity or suicide and eventually cured him of his illness.

In 1951, Bernhard received a scholarship to attend the music academy in Vienna, but since the stipend covered only his tuition, he was forced to work as garbage collector, luggage porter, and attendant to a seventy-year-old insane woman whom he cared for until her death. He often slept in railroad cars and in abandoned air-raid shelters; his move to the Mozarteum in Salzburg in 1952 was a welcome change. At the Mozarteum, he did considerable acting and directing in addition to his musical studies and earned his way by working for a local newspaper, mainly as a court reporter and an art critic. In the period from 1952 to 1956,

Bernhard also submitted his first poems and short stories to various publishers and to literary contests, but
with no success. In 1955 and 1956, he interrupted his
studies at the Mozarteum to travel around Europe; he
graduated in 1957 after completing a thesis on Antonin
Artaud and Bertolt Brecht. In that year, Bernhard also
published his first two volumes of poetry, followed by
his third collection in 1958. During the next five years,
he tried to make his living as a freelance writer in Vienna and Carinthia; he traveled frequently and also
spent a short time as librarian at the Austrian Cultural
Institute in London.

Discouraged by his continuous failure to gain recognition as a writer—again and again his submissions
did not find favor with the judges of literary contests
awarding prestigious and lucrative prizes—Bernhard
decided to emigrate to South Africa. Allegedly on the
very day he was ready to embark from Venice, he received notice that his first novel, *Frost*, had been accepted for publication. Official recognition and prizes
followed in rapid succession, most notably the Austrian State Prize in 1968, when he shocked the dignita-
ies with his polemical acceptance speech. He died in
Gmunden, Austria, on February 12, 1989.

ANALYSIS

Thomas Bernhard's biography offers a temptation
to the critical reader of his work. It is easy to conclude—as many critics have—that his chaotic, parent-
less childhood, the rootless life of his adolescence, the
loss of all those he loved, and his own near-fatal illness
are the direct causes of the grim worldview expressed
in his novels and plays, and are responsible for the melancholy tone of his poems. Such a view is contradicted
by the fact that Bernhard's journalistic work, which is
chronologically closest to the period from 1950 to
1952, the most depressing years of his life, shows few
traces of this pervasive pessimism. The articles and reviews of that time are full of praise for contemporary
artists; they speak of the regenerative beauty of the
Salzburg region and comment favorably on the value of
regional Austrian culture. The tone of these articles is
low-key, often a little sad, but still full of joie de vivre
compared with that of his early poems, which appeared
in 1957. Further study of Bernhard's life and his pub-

Thomas Bernhard (Hulton Archive/Getty Images)

lished and unpublished work of the years from 1950
to 1957 is needed to explain the struggling author's
change in outlook.

AUF DER ERDE UND IN DER HÖLLE

Bernhard's first collection of poems, *Auf der Erde
und in der Hölle* (on Earth and in Hell), was published
in 1957 in an edition of one thousand. It contains
seventy-one poems grouped into five thematic sections; many of these poems have since been included in
anthologies of contemporary German and Austrian poetry. Bernhard himself claims to have been influenced
mainly by Walt Whitman, Georg Trakl, and Charles-
Pierre Péguy—the latter supplies the motto for the
volume—but one also hears echoes of Paul Celan and
Charles Baudelaire, as well as of William Blake's more
hellish visions. "Der Tag der Gesichter" appears as a
separate poem before the first section and sets the tone
for the entire volume: The "Earth" and the "Hell" of the
title are not to be understood as separate locations but as
identical places. The poet acknowledges his complicity
in the decay, suffering, and death that are all around
him. He anticipates shudderingly the apocalyptic "day
of visions" when he will be shown Hell, reproduced for

the reader in the following seventy poems. It is Earth as Inferno that the poet sees. *Auf der Erde und in der Hölle* offers a vision of Hell without any glimpses of Heaven. The five sections of the volume systematically deny any relief from this view and reject any traditional redemptive imagery.

The journey through Hell—the reluctant reader is led by the guilt-ridden poet—begins in the traditional "dark wood," the rural region of Bernhard's ancestors. There is no pastoral tranquility, however, in this "other world behind the trees." This area has changed drastically since the time of the poet's great-grandfather. Now, there is decay, despair, and other harbingers of death in the form of frost, crows, and blackbirds. The black farm soil prophesies a wintry death; schnapps, fame, and love are insufficient anesthesia for loneliness and the sense of complicity in the sad state of the world. What is the poet to do, cast out from this destroyed Eden into the night? The brave front he puts up at times—as in the great poem "Crows," which ends with the line "But I am not afraid"—cannot be maintained for long, and he crosses the river to find "another world."

There, he finds the "burnt-out cities" of the second section—Vienna, Paris, Venice, Chioggia—cities that one can no longer shore against one's ruins. Wherever the journey leads, the poet encounters night, death, the pale, unapproachable ghosts of his ancestors, and anterooms to Hell. Attempts at cleansing through penitence on Ash Wednesday (Bernhard knows T. S. Eliot very well) are ineffectual.

In the last section, "Rückkehr in eine Liebe," the poet expresses the wish to be able to return to his "love," represented by his rural village, the memory of his parents, and nature, but even the first poem of the section, "Yeats war nicht dabei," indicates that he cannot go home again. The fields do not accept his name, the trees withdraw their roots, and no one offers him a bed and a jug with drink.

Auf der Erde und in der Hölle is a remarkable first collection of poems. Clearly, there are literary debts, but Zuckmayer's judgment, that these poems show the mark of the great modern artists and originate from the same artistic background as the music of Béla Bartók, is accurate.

In hora mortis

Bernhard's second collection of poems, *In hora mortis*, also appeared in 1957. The title is taken from the Latin text of the "Hail Mary," in which the Holy Virgin is asked to intercede for all sinners in the hour of death. The volume, much slimmer than *Auf der Erde und in der Hölle*, is dedicated to "my only and true friend G. L. whom I met at the right moment." "G. L." is almost certainly the young Austrian composer Gerhard Lampersberg, who had apparently taken in the despondent writer for some time between 1957 and 1959. Bernhard always speaks in negative terms of the Roman Catholic Church and of religion, but it appears that the time he spent in a Catholic boarding school left him with the wish to come to terms with that facet of his childhood. It is even more likely that his self-confessed interest in Blaise Pascal's *Pensées* (1670; English translation, 1688) and his early acquaintance with the writings of Schopenhauer and Montaigne are responsible for the persistent religious stratum in his early work.

In hora mortis has the structure of a prayer—it is quite possible that Pascal's "Prayer in Sickness" is the model—and employs frequent direct appeals to "my God" and "my Lord." These appeals are not always submissive in tone; the first line of the collection, "Wild grows the flower of my anger," indicates the mood of the poet. Rebellion, outrage, and disappointment in an elusive God dominates the early parts of the volume; later, the tone changes to hopelessness and to the Schopenhauer-like recognition that redemption is only possible when the rebellious will to live has been subdued. It can be assumed that the poetic experience in this slim volume closely parallels Bernhard's wrestling for a spiritual and intellectual position during the time of his near-fatal illness.

In these poems, Bernhard does not as closely identify himself with his literary models as in *Auf der Erde und in der Hölle*. His poetry here approaches that of his contemporaries Ingeborg Bachmann, Christine Busta, and Christine Lavant in its imperious appeals to a *Dieu absconditi*. Bernhard's early verse depicts a desolate universe through which humankind is condemned to wander aimlessly, incapable of bringing any relief to the universal suffering, unable to stop the general decay, but also unable to resign itself completely to this condition. The language is emotional, the imagery flowery, and the tone still echoes the plaintive cries of the expressionists. Bernhard's next collection of poems, however, published in 1958, marked a transition from subjective lyrical expressionism to the maniacal "objectivity" of his prose.

UNTER DEM EISEN DES MONDES

In *Unter dem Eisen des Mondes* (under the iron of the moon), Bernhard broke completely with his poetic models. The fifty-seven untitled poems in this volume severely reduce the use of the first person in an attempt to objectify the lyrical "I" of *Auf der Erde und in der Hölle* and *In hora mortis*. The title is taken from Georg Büchner's play *Woyzeck* (1879; English translation, 1927), from the scene in which the protagonist is about to stab his fiancé; to her observation, "How red the moon rises!" He replies with the words "like a bloody blade" (*Eisen*).

This bloody moon casts a grim light; there is not even the elusive hope for redemption still expressed in *In hora mortis*, nor the faint prospect of a "return to love." Images are no longer used as objective correlatives of the poet's subjective feelings but take on a physical and metaphysical reality of their own. The reader can no longer escape by rejecting Bernhard's night visions as sentimental exaggerations of a paranoid, tortured soul but must deal with an intellectual position. The symbolism of the four seasons that runs through the whole volume further serves this purpose.

Unter dem Eisen des Mondes was the penultimate step in Bernhard's development from lyric poet to novelist. The symbolic code of these poems and their syntactic structure anticipates the forms of his early prose, particularly of his first novel, *Frost*. Apart from some poems published in the magazine *Akzente* in 1968, but probably written before 1963, Bernhard published only one more, very small volume of poetry before abandoning verse after the success of his first novel.

Published in 1962 by a small Klagenfurt publisher in an edition of only 120 copies, *Die Irren-die Häftlinge* (the madmen, the prisoners) does not appear in many Bernhard bibliographies. The critic Manfred Mixner considers it the last and most important stage of Bernhard's early creative period. The left-hand pages of this collection contain "Die Irren," a poem of fifteen stanzas; on the right-hand pages appears "Die Häftlinge," a poem of twenty-two stanzas. Both are interrupted by aphoristic prose sentences that appear to be quotations, but no source is indicated. Some of these sentences seem like remarks by a distant observer concerning the "madmen" and "prisoners" who are the subjects of these two long poems.

Madmen and prisoners (their prisons are often metaphorical) are the central characters of Bernhard's novels and plays. In his later work, Bernhard reiterates his conviction that the human condition is best defined as incarceration. Most of his characters are trapped by the narrowness of their physical, cultural, or geographical prisons. Only "insane" people are sensitive enough to recognize the inevitability of their fate as prisoners, from which they try to find relief in interminable cascades of tautological ruminations. The "sane" people live as animals, unthinking, trapped in lies and clichés.

DIE IRREN-DIE HÄFTLINGE

In *Die Irren-die Häftlinge*, Bernhard anticipates the recurring themes of his prose. The madmen are anonymous, deprived of their individuality by being addressed only by the symptoms of their condition. Their fate is not presented from their subjective standpoint as lyrical narrators; instead, they are viewed by an impersonal observer who registers their hate, their torture, and their indignation as if seen through the peephole of their cells and who punctuates his observations with aphorisms on rationality. With this virtually forgotten volume, Bernhard found the logical transition from poetry to the novel; he abandoned the emotive stance of the lyrical "I" and assumed the role of an omniscient, clinical observer who presents the twitchings of his tortured madmen and prisoners in the manner of a painstakingly arranged medical report.

The small but growing number of Bernhard scholars have devoted themselves almost exclusively to his fiction, his memoirs, and his plays, neglecting his journalism and paying scant attention to his poetry. Bernhard's verse deserves to be read for its own considerable achievements rather than as a mere preface to his fiction.

OTHER MAJOR WORKS

LONG FICTION: *Frost*, 1963 (English translation, 2006); *Verstörung*, 1967 (*Gargoyles*, 1970); *Das Kalkwerk*, 1970 (*The Lime Works*, 1973); *Korrektur*, 1975 (*Correction*, 1979); *Ja*, 1978 (*Yes*, 1991); *Die Billigesser*, 1980 (*The Cheap-eaters*, 1990); *Beton*, 1982 (*Concrete*, 1984); *Der Untergeher*, 1983 (*The Loser*, 1991); *Holzfällen: Eine Erregung*, 1984 (*Wood-cutters*, 1987; also as *Cutting Timber: An Imitation*, 1988); *Alte Meister*, 1985 (*Old Masters*, 1989); *Aus-löschung: Ein Zerfall*, 1986 (*Extinction*, 1995); *In der Höhe: Rettungsversuch, Unsinn*, 1989 (*On the Mountain: Rescue Attempt, Nonsense*, 1991).

SHORT FICTION: *Amras*, 1964 (English translation, 2003); *Prosa*, 1967 (*Prose*, 2010); *Ungenach*, 1968; *An der Baumgrenze: Erzählungen*, 1969; *Ereignisse*, 1969; *Watten: Ein Nachlass*, 1969 (*Playing Watten*, 2003); *Gehen*, 1971 (*Walking*, 2003); *Midland in Stilfs: Drei Erzählungen*, 1971; *Der Stimmenimitator*, 1978 (*The Voice Imitator*, 1997); *Three Novellas*, 2003 (includes *Amras*, *Playing Watten*, and *Walking*).

PLAYS: *Der Rosen der Einöde*, pb. 1959 (libretto); *Ein Fest für Boris*, pr., pb. 1970 (*A Party for Boris*, 1990); *Der Ignorant und der Wahnsinnige*, pr., pb. 1972; *Die Jagdgesellschaft*, pr., pb. 1974; *Die Macht der Gewohnheit*, pr., pb. 1974 (*The Force of Habit*, 1976); *Der Präsident*, pr., pb. 1975 (*The President*, 1982); *Die Berühmten*, pr., pb. 1976; *Minetti: Ein Porträt des Künstlers als alter Mann*, pr. 1976; *Immanuel Kant*, pr., pb. 1978; *Vor dem Ruhestand*, pb. 1979 (*Eve of Retirement*, 1982); *Der Weltverbesserer*, pb. 1979 (*The World-Fixer*, 2005); *Am Ziel*, pr., pb. 1981; *Über allen Gipfeln ist Ruh: Ein deutscher Dichtertag um 1980*, pb. 1981 (*Over All the Mountain Tops*, 2004); *Der Schein trügt*, pb. 1983 (*Appearances Are Deceiving*, 1983); *Ritter, Dene, Voss*, pb. 1984 (English translation, 1990); *Der Theatermacher*, pb. 1984 (*Histrionics*, 1990); *Elisabeth II*, pb. 1987; *Heldenplatz*, pr., pb. 1988; *Histrionics: Three Plays*, 1990.

SCREENPLAY: *Der Italiener*, 1971.

NONFICTION: *Die Ursache: Eine Andeutung*, 1975 (*An Indication of the Cause*, 1985); *Der Keller: Eine Entziehung*, 1976 (*The Cellar: An Escape*, 1985); *Der Atem: Eine Entscheidung*, 1978 (*Breath: A Decision*, 1985); *Die Kälte: Eine Isolation*, 1981 (*In the Cold*, 1985); *Ein Kind*, 1982 (*A Child*, 1985); *Wittgensteins Neffe: Eine Freundschaft*, 1982 (*Wittgenstein's Nephew: A Friendship*, 1986); *Gathering Evidence*, 1985 (English translations of five works, *An Indication of the Cause*, *The Cellar*, *Breath*, *In the Cold*, and *A Child*).

BIBLIOGRAPHY

Cousineau, Thomas J. *Three-Part Inventions: The Novels of Thomas Bernhard*. Newark: University of Delaware Press, 2008. Although this work focuses on Bernhard's novels, it does describe his development as a writer.

Dierick, A. P. "Thomas Bernhard's Austria: Neurosis, Symbol, or Expedient?" *Modern Austrian Literature* 12, no. 1 (1979). Explores the relationship of Bernhard's works to the sociopolitical climate of Austria.

Dowden, Stephen D., and James N. Hardin, eds. *Understanding Thomas Bernhard*. Columbia: University of South Carolina Press, 1991. Part of the series Understanding Modern European and Latin American Literature. Explores the themes and approaches of Bernhard. Bibliography and index.

Honegger, Gitta. *Thomas Bernhard: The Making of an Austrian*. New Haven, Conn.: Yale University Press, 2001. The first comprehensive biography of Bernhard in English, it examines the complex connections of Bernhard's work with Austria's twentieth century geographical, political, and cultural landscape.

Konzett, Matthias. *The Rhetoric of National Dissent in Thomas Bernhard, Peter Handke, and Elfriede Jelinek*. New York: Camden House, 2000. Examines how these writers expose and dismantle conventions of communal consensus that work to derail the development of multicultural awareness and identity.

_____, ed. *A Companion to the Works of Thomas Bernhard*. Rochester, N.Y.: Camden House, 2002. Contains essays on Bernhard's writings, including some on his poems.

Martin, Charles W. *The Nihilism of Thomas Bernhard: The Portrayal of Existential and Social Problems in His Prose Works*. Atlanta: Rodopi, 1995. Examines the nihilistic basis of Bernhard's writing and traces developments in the author's writing. Bibliography and index.

"Thomas Bernhard." *Artforum* 8, no. 3 (Fall, 2001): 17-24. Provides profile of Bernhard, a time line of important events in his life, a reader's guide to his work, and excerpts from several pieces.

Franz G. Blaha

WOLF BIERMANN

Born: Hamburg, Germany; November 15, 1936

PRINCIPAL POETRY

Die Drahtharfe: Balladen, Gedichte, Lieder, 1965
    (*The Wire Harp: Ballads, Poems, Songs*, 1968)
Mit Marx- und Engelszungen: Gedichte, Balladen,
    Lieder, 1968
Deutschland: Ein Wintermärchen, 1972
Für meine Genossen: Hetzlieder, Gedichte,
    Balladen, 1972
Nachlass I, 1977
Poems and Ballads, 1977
Preussischer Ikarus: Lieder, Balladen, Gedichte,
    Prosa, 1978
Verdrehte Welt—das seh' ich gerne: Lieder,
    Balladen, Gedichte, Prosa, 1982
Alle Lieder, 1991
Alle Gedichte, 1995
Paradies uff Erden: Ein Berliner Bilderbogen, 1999
Heimat: Neue Gedichte, 2006

OTHER LITERARY FORMS

Most of the published work of Wolf Biermann (BEER-mon) consists of poems and songs. This fact reflects his conviction that poetry, especially song, provides the most appropriate and effective means of conveying the intensely personal and political content of his work. Biermann's other writings reinforce this strong political emphasis. These writings include several collections of essays, university lectures on the writing of poetry and songs, children's books, and a

play. The play *Der Dra-Dra: Die grosse Drachentöterschau in acht Akten mit Musik* (1970; the dra-dra: the great dragon-killer show in eight acts with music), is an adaptation of the fairy-tale comedy *Drakon* (1943; *The Dragon*, 1963) by the Russian playwright Yevgeny Schwartz and concerns the fate of a city-state ruled by a dragon. In Biermann's hands, it becomes a political parable about the specter of Stalinism in Eastern Europe. In addition, Biermann has translated numerous poems and songs by other poets into German, most notably the long Yiddish poem on the fate of the Jews of Eastern Europe by the Polish-Jewish writer Yitzak Katzenelson, *Grosser Gesang vom ausgerotteten jüdischen Volk* (1994; great song of the exterminated Jewish people).

ACHIEVEMENTS

Wolf Biermann is perhaps the best-known living German-language poet. The success of his books—*The Wire Harp* became a best-selling book of German poetry in the postwar era—and the popularity of his more than twenty recordings provide ample evidence of this.

Several factors have contributed to Biermann's renown. There is, first, the political controversy which has surrounded him since he first fell into disfavor with cultural authorities in East Germany in the early 1960's. While his problems with the party bureaucracy led very quickly to an absolute publication and performance ban in the East, his identification with opposition forces in East Germany served to increase his notoriety, particularly in the West. It is ironic that, although Biermann's work was never to reach a large audience in the socialist East—depending as it did upon the circulation of underground manuscripts and tapes—his poetry and recordings were widely distributed and discussed in capitalist West Germany. Not surprisingly, Biermann's outspoken and often uncomfortable political views kept him in the public eye during much of his thirteen years of western "exile" and continued to do so after the reunification of Germany in 1990.

Another factor has played an even more central role in Biermann's popularity as a poet. He is a people's poet in every sense of the word, a fact reflected in the everyday language, themes, and imagery of his poetry. His preference for simple, traditional forms, such as the

German folk song and the ballad, and his use of music as a vehicle for his texts have enhanced the strong populist appeal of his work.

Biermann's strong identification with the traditions of the German folk song and the political song places him somewhat outside the mainstream of contemporary German-language poetry, with its greater emphasis on sophisticated aesthetic and literary values. Nevertheless, the strength and vitality of Biermann's language and imagery effectively rebut the notion that the populist orientation of his work lessens its significance in any way, and his poems are clearly among the most provocative being written in Germany today.

Biermann has been awarded numerous prizes including Germany's most prestigious literary prize in the Georg Büchner Prize in 1991. Other major prizes include the Berlin Art Prize for Literature (the Theodor Fontane Prize) in 1969, the Jacques Offenbach Prize of the City of Cologne (for his achievement as a composer and performer of the contemporary political song) in 1974, the Friedrich Hölderlin Prize of the City of Homburg in 1989, the Eduard Mörike Prize in 1991, the Heinrich Heine Prize of the City of Düsseldorf in 1993, and the National Prize of the German National Foundation in 1998.

BIOGRAPHY

Wolf Biermann (born Karl Wolf Biermann) comes from a Communist, working-class family tradition. His father, Dagobert Biermann, a Jewish worker on the Hamburg docks, joined the Communist Party in 1921 and was active in the antifascist resistance of the early and mid-1930's. Arrested in 1937 for his role in sabotaging arms shipments to Francisco Franco's Spain, he was sent in 1942 to Auschwitz, where he was put to death in 1943. Although Biermann hardly knew his father, he was reared by his mother and grandmother, both active Communists, in the spirit and image of the elder Biermann. This legacy of political activism and Communism would have a profound effect upon Biermann's life.

In the spirit of his father, Biermann left his native Hamburg in 1953 to join in the socialist experiment under way in East Germany. There, he finished his high school education and, from 1955 to 1957, studied polit-ical economy at Humboldt University in East Berlin. In 1957, he interrupted his studies to take a position as a dramatic assistant at Bertolt Brecht's theater, the Berliner Ensemble. Although Brecht had died the previous year, this experience with his work was of great importance in Biermann's development. During this period, too, he met Brecht's friend and collaborator, the composer Hanns Eisler, whose musical influence is readily apparent in Biermann's songs.

The years from 1960 to 1964 represent a particularly significant period in Biermann's life. He had returned to the university in 1959 to study philosophy and mathematics, but his studies were gradually replaced by an ever-greater emphasis upon his artistic interests. In 1960, at the relatively late age of twenty-three, he began to write and compose his first songs. The songs written after the building of the Berlin Wall in 1961 concentrated more and more upon the discrepancy between the promise and the reality of socialism in East Germany and quickly drew the attention of cultural authorities.

In 1961-1962, Biermann helped to found the Berlin Worker and Student Theater and wrote his first dramatic effort for its scheduled opening. His unpublished play *Berliner Brautgang*, a love story set amid the political tensions of the newly divided city, was never performed. Before its premiere, the theater was closed by authorities, and Biermann was placed under a performance ban. The ban was lifted again in 1963, but Biermann was excluded from the Socialist Unity Party, in which he had been a candidate for membership.

During a brief period of relative cultural freedom in 1964, Biermann began to make a name for himself as a writer and performer of political songs. He was allowed to undertake a concert tour of West Germany, which established his reputation there as one of East Germany's leading young poets and which led to the 1965 publication in the West of his first book of poems, issued by a leftist publishing house. This brief cultural thaw, however, ended for Biermann as abruptly as it had begun; at the Eleventh Party Congress in 1965, his poetry was attacked for its "dangerous" subjectivity and its "anti-Communist" slant, and he was placed under a second absolute publication and performance ban.

For the next eleven years, Biermann lived as a "non-person" in his homeland: There was no possibility for public discussion or performance of his work, much less publication; he was under constant surveillance; and his friends were subjected to various forms of official intimidation. Surprisingly, during this period he was allowed to continue to publish and record his work for release in the West. His reputation grew as he, together with his close friend, the physicist and philosopher Robert Havemann, became the focus and primary symbols of intellectual opposition in East Germany.

As early as 1972, Biermann was offered the chance to emigrate to the West, but he was adamant in his refusal to leave his chosen land. Unexpectedly, Biermann was allowed in 1976 to accept an invitation from West German unionists for a concert tour of several major cities. Following the first concert, in Cologne, he was notified that his East German citizenship had been revoked and that he would not be allowed to return home. This calculated move by the Communist Party resulted in an unprecedented protest among artists and intellectuals in the East and had far-reaching consequences for elements of the opposition there. Over the next several years, numerous East German writers and artists chose or were forced to emigrate to the West. For many of those who remained, Biermann's expatriation served to solidify and unite their opposition to the East German regime.

Following his expatriation in 1976, Bierman steadfastly resisted the attempts in the West to cast him in the role of an anti-Communist dissident. While affirming his preference for socialism and the East German homeland now closed to him, he began immediately to immerse himself in the political and social reality of his new home. The dislocation of being "exiled" in the West, which often severely interrupted the work of other East German writers who later came to West Germany, seemed to have little effect on Biermann. Indeed, the thirteen years of western "exile" (1977-1990) brought an increase in artistic productivity, as evidenced in several new volumes of poetry and songs, new recordings, and a busy concert schedule throughout Germany, Western Europe, and Scandinavia. In 1983, Biermann also spent three months in the United States as a guest professor at Ohio State University.

Despite this public notoriety and success, the early and mid-1980's was a period of profound artistic and personal crisis for Biermann. In 1980, he retreated from the demands of his public life and concert schedule and spent the majority of the next one and one-half years in relative isolation in Paris. From the distance of Paris, he struggled to understand better his new German-German identity as a poet-singer who was at home in both the East and the West yet fully at home in neither. This period of artistic self-questioning was followed by the traumatic collapse of his marriage. In keeping with the intensely personal nature of his work, this personal crisis occupied a central place in the poetry, songs, and concerts of the mid-1980's.

The fall of the Berlin Wall in 1989 and German reunification the following year ushered in a new phase in Biermann's biography. As the poet who perhaps more than any other had come to personify divided Germany, he now took up a prominent position in the public discussion of Germany and its future. His return to East Germany in December of 1989 to give a concert in Leipzig was a media event, and the concert was carried by both East and West German television. Throughout the early 1990's, Biermann was seen and heard from—especially in articles for newspapers—on a regular basis.

Biermann's essays reflect his return to a public involvement with political issues. Typically outspoken and unconventional, they contain some of the most stimulating contributions to the public discussion of German unity, the legacy of the former East Germany, and the issues raised by the Gulf War. From 1992 to 1995, Biermann lectured on the writing of poetry and song as a guest professor at the Heinrich Heine University in Düsseldorf, and in 1997-1998, he returned to Berlin for one year as a fellow at the prestigious Wissenschaftskolleg.

Although free to resettle in Berlin after German reunification in 1990, Biermann chose to remain in Hamburg, the city of his father, together with his second wife, Pamela Biermann.

ANALYSIS

Wolf Biermann is a political poet. He follows in the tradition of François Villon, Heinrich Heine, Kurt Tucholsky, and Brecht, with whom he shares both an acute political awareness and a biting, aggressive wit.

As with these forerunners, art, life, and politics are virtually inseparable in Biermann's work. He is, as one collection of critical essays refers to him in its title, a "Liedermacher und Sozialist," both a "maker of songs" and a dedicated socialist; his poetry records with great feeling his own political struggle as a socialist poet and his personal political fate as a renegade and exile.

Biermann's connection with the tradition of Heine and Brecht is apparent. He is the prototypical "troublesome" poet, unwanted and rejected by his homeland—a homeland that he "loves" and "hates" in nearly equal degrees. In a recurring image in his early poetry, Biermann portrays himself as the embattled but unrelenting poet caught in the no-man's-land between East and West, as the poet balanced precariously on the Wall—neither understood nor at home in either Germany. He is torn as Germany itself is torn, not between socialism and capitalism—for his political position as a socialist is clear—but torn by the disparity between Germany's promise and its reality. He is both the victim and the uncompromising critic of this disparity, which is given concrete form in his poetry in the image of the Berlin Wall.

This intense intermingling of the personal with the political is central to all of Biermann's poetry and provides the key to its understanding. One cannot separate the poetry from the man and his experience, or hope to understand it fully outside the political and historical context of his personal struggle. Although his poems and songs display a rich variety of themes, Biermann's central concerns may be summarized under three broad headings: Germany's fascist legacy, division, and reunification; the unfulfilled promise of socialism; and the poet's celebration of life despite its many contradictions. As these themes suggest, the poetry often exhibits an antithetical structure built upon the contradictions and antagonisms which Biermann perceives around him—antagonisms between the real and the possible, between that which exists and that which remains to be done, and ultimately between the forces of quiescence, stagnation, and death and those of life. The conflict expressed in the major themes is mirrored in Biermann's own mixed feelings regarding the world around him. These reactions are expressed in a broad range of tones, from anger and bitterness to ecstatic celebration. Biermann's poems are alternately sad and accusatory, aggressive and subdued, but there remains in them always a determined optimism and a fundamental affirmation of life.

THE WIRE HARP

Biermann's first collection of poetry, *The Wire Harp*, introduces many of the central themes and formal hallmarks of his work. His preference for a simple lyrical style and for everyday rather than literary language is clearly demonstrated here, as is his reliance upon traditional lyrical forms and rhymed verse. He reacts in these poems both to the broader world—as in his critically optimistic picture of socialism in the "Buckower Balladen" ("Buckow Ballads") and in his indictment of American racism in "Ballade von dem Briefträger William L. Moore" ("Ballad of the Letter-Carrier William L. Moore")—and to the more immediate personal world of his loves, his joys, and his sorrows, as illustrated in the Berlin poems of this volume. Included under the heading "Portraits" are tributes to both Brecht and Eisler, as well as the well-known "Ballade auf den Dichter François Villon" ("Ballad on the Poet François Villon"). Here, Biermann celebrates the rude and drunken Frenchman with whom he so obviously identifies. He, like his "brother" Villon, is always in trouble with the authorities, and he never tires of ridiculing their petty fears. In this poem, Biermann is at his provocative best, and he revels in the impudent, mocking tone of his great predecessor.

In the group of poems titled "Beschwichtigungen und Revisionen" ("Reassurances and Revisions"), Biermann addresses his ambivalent relationship to the Communist Party. He alternately asserts his role as the critical outsider in "Rücksichtslose Schimpferei" ("Reckless Abuse") and affirms his solidarity of purpose with his comrades in "An die alten Genossen" ("To the Old Comrades"). These poems characteristically illustrate Biermann's defiant subjectivity and his refusal to accept the party's demand for artistic and political conformity. In the poem "Tischrede des Dichters" ("The Poet's Table Speech"), Biermann presents his criticisms by means of a simple culinary metaphor: He complains that his comrades reject his rich and varied cuisine, preferring instead their bland "single-course dinner of happiness." The tone of the poem is assertive and yet conciliatory as Biermann defends his role as critic and argues for greater artistic tolerance.

MIT MARX-UND ENGELSZUNGEN

In the poems and songs of his second collection, *Mit Marx- und Engelszungen* (with the tongues of Marx and Engels—or angels), Biermann continues his attack upon the blandness of officially sanctioned literature. There is, however, a discernible difference in tone in these poems. Although the poet's voice is no less insistent here, the tone has become more earnest and betrays some hint of the bitterness and frustration which have come of Biermann's prolonged isolation. In the love songs included in this volume, Biermann celebrates life and love, combining traditional images of spring and hope with good-humored earthiness. The poems express the poet's hope against the background of his personal political struggle, and they represent an attempt to counteract his growing sadness.

In one of the last songs in the collection, Biermann finds the source of this sadness in the deep division of Germany itself. He concludes his poem "Es senkt das deutsche Dunkel" ("The German Darkness Falls") with the paradoxical assertion that, though he lives in the "better half" of this divided land, he feels "double the pain." This doubly intense pain is the pain of hopes betrayed, a theme which comes to play an ever-greater role in his work.

DEUTSCHLAND

The idea for Biermann's long narrative poem *Deutschland: Ein Wintermärchen* (Germany, a winter's tale) was taken from Heine's verse satire of the same title, which appeared in 1844. Biermann's poem was written in 1965 shortly after a visit to his native Hamburg, where he had stopped during his Western concert tour the year before. Biermann uses the occasion of his trip, as Heine had done more than one hundred years earlier, to reflect satirically upon Germany's current political "misery" as mirrored in the country's political division. He has retained both the tone and the simple folk-song verse (four-line stanzas rhyming *abab*) of the original, and he consciously imitates and parallels Heine's masterpiece at every turn.

The return to this "foreign" homeland evokes a mixed response in Biermann. Though he views the "German question" from the perspective of a socialist, critical of Western capitalism, he does not gloss over the heritage of Stalinism in Eastern Europe. He concludes his "winter's tale" with the important programmatic poem "Gesang für meine Genossen" ("Song for My Comrades"), which summarizes the political focus of his entire work, a work he characterizes here as "das Lied von der verratenen Revolution" (the song of the revolution betrayed). The poem illustrates a central paradox of Biermann's work: the fact that he devastatingly criticizes that which he loves. The party is the object of simultaneously his love and his hate, for it represents both the future hope of socialism and its dogmatic inflexibility and bureaucratic stagnation.

FÜR MEINE GENOSSEN

The poetry of Biermann's third collection, *Für meine Genossen* (for my comrades), documents the "crimes" of which he was accused in East Germany. Organized under five headings corresponding to sections of the East German penal code, the poems are presented as evidence of his "misdemeanors," "slander," "agitation," and "irresponsibility," but also of the "extenuating circumstances." Biermann defends his "crimes" by placing them in the context in which he prefers to view them: Each section of the collection begins with an appropriately "heretical" quotation from Karl Marx, Vladimir Ilich Lenin, or Rosa Luxemburg that supports Biermann's view of revolutionary art and its function in socialist society.

The poems and songs of *Für meine Genossen* continue in the vein of Biermann's earlier collections. The theme of betrayal—the betrayal of the revolution by the party, and the betrayal of hope by the friends who have given up the fight—is especially prominent and is recorded in emotions ranging from impatience and anger to profound sorrow. The melancholy undertone, present to some extent in the earlier poetry, is more pronounced here, and the songs have lost much of the playfulness of the early years. The ballad, in Biermann's view a proper instrument of "agitation," maintains its formal preeminence in his work, but is complemented here by highly self-conscious and reflective poems that expand his range of expression.

PREUSSISCHER IKARUS

Biermann's experimentation with new forms and themes alongside the old is carried a step further in the book *Preussischer Ikarus* (Prussian Icarus). This volume was published after Biermann's expatriation in 1976 and includes both poems written in the East and others written in and from the perspective of his Western exile. Together with the familiar East German motifs of the earlier collections, there are a variety of new, specifically Western themes. Biermann responds here not only to the problem of his exile but also to the Western German political scene—to the misdirected terrorism of the Baader-Meinhof era and the disarray and ineffectiveness of the West German Left.

The title for the collection is taken from the poem "Ballade vom preussischer Ikarus" (ballad of the Prussian Icarus), which closes the first half of the book. In the poem, Biermann projects himself into the role of a modern Icarus weighed down by the heavy iron wings of Prussian tradition—a tradition of authoritarianism and unquestioning obedience that continues to throttle the socialist revolution in the East. The West, however, offers Biermann no solace; the poems that close the second half of the volume portray the ostensibly "free" and "democratic" West as merely the other side of the same German coin.

VERDREHTE WELT

In *Verdrehte Welt* (world turned on its head), a collection of poems, songs, and ballads, Biermann struggles to find his bearings in the West. As in *Preussischer Ikarus*, political themes remain in the forefront and many of the poems address topical issues: labor unrest and the 1980 elections in West Germany, environmental concerns, and the suppression of the Solidarity movement in Poland. The poetry dealing with Poland is significant in Biermann's work for the clear break with Communism that it signals. It is a difficult emotional step for the poet, who in the poem "Schuften" (scoundrels) dreams of wrestling with the ghost of his father over his public critique of Communism's failure.

Despite Biermann's continuing political engagement, the poetry of *Verdrehte Welt* betrays a more complicated and less ideological view of the world, one that admits to not having all the answers. The long poem "À Paris" (in Paris) describes Biermann's attempt to come to terms with his new western identity. He is no longer the socialist "dragon-slayer" of old, a role that his western exile denies him; but neither is he at home in the in-

consequential leftist "ghetto" to which the western media would assign him. From the healing distance of Paris, Biermann learns to accept a dual German identity outside the confining pull of ideology. From this position, he is able again to write from his life experience rather than merely in response to the issues of the day. Biermann's most compelling poetry arises where personal experience and political reality intersect for him. Thus, for example, the apparently private, family poem "Willkommenslied für Marie" (song of welcome for Marie), written at the birth of his daughter, reflects both the father's joy at her birth and his consciousness of a threatening world, with its "forest of weapons" and its ruined environment, that imperils her future.

AFFENFELS UND BARRIKADE

Affenfels und Barrikade (1986) is Biermann's most personal and least political book. It clearly carries the mark of the collapse of his marriage, which affects both the tone and the content of the poems and songs. The title of this mixed-genre collection contains Biermann's ironic assessment of human life on the planet, determined by human beings' animal nature—captured in the image of the "Affenfels" (monkey rock) of human, especially sexual, relations—and by human attempts, inspired by human reason, to change and improve it—symbolized in the "Barrikade," that is, the political barricades on which the battles for change are fought. In contrast to the earlier collections, these poems and songs reveal an unsure and less assertive, even at times a despairing, poet.

The collection opens with the song "Pardon" (pardon me!), a clever account of his contented discontent living in the West. Each of the poet's claims to be doing fine in his new life in the West is immediately contradicted (Pardon!) by a qualifying addition. Thus he sings that he is "living still"—well, he really meant to say, he is "not yet dead"; he has everything he needs—well, come to think of it, he is actually in dire need. In this manner, Biermann announces a central theme of the collection: learning to live in this less-than-perfect and often contradictory world.

In the long poem "Vom Lesen in den Innereien" (reading in my innards), Biermann offers a self-critical assessment of his first ten years in West Germany. His experience in this time, both personal and political, has freed him from many of the illusions with which he arrived ten years earlier. Communism in Eastern Europe is "dead," incapable of the reform he had agitated for in his early work; similarly, he no longer places much hope in the ability of art and poetry to bring about change in the world. Rummaging through his "innards," he derides his utopian optimism of earlier days and refers to his present-day role in the West as an "artist for hire," a "dragon-slayer armed with a lyre" who is astounded to find that the dragon (money and capitalism) has come to reside in him. In the West, he, like other poets, finds himself asking of his poetry, "Will it sell?" when in the East he used to ask, "Will it be banned?" Despite this new tone of self-doubt, the poem ends with an affirmation of the path he has taken and must continue to follow. He will continue to walk in the footsteps of his father and of the Jewish and Communist dead of his father's generation who will not allow him to escape their grasp and the responsibility it holds for him. Thus the poem ends with the repeated refrain, "I'm on my way," a way from which he cannot be deterred, neither by the "applause of my enemies" nor by the "hate of my friends."

PARADIES UFF ERDEN

Nearly fourteen years transpired between the publication of *Affenfels und Barrikade* and the release of *Paradies uff Erden* (paradise on Earth) in 1999. Relatively few new songs and poems appear in either of the two compilations of poetry that Biermann issued in the early and mid-1990's, a fact that reflects his high-profile participation in various public debates during these years. As suggested by its subtitle, meaning "a Berlin picture album," the new collection consists almost entirely of poems and songs about Berlin. Almost all of them were written in 1997 and 1998, during a year that Biermann spent at Berlin's Wissenschaftskolleg, where he had planned to continue his work on the translation of William Shakespeare's sonnets. Instead, he found himself drawn out into the city, the eastern half of which had been his home from 1953 until 1976. As Biermann writes in the afterword, the book represents his retaking possession of his beloved second home, a claim that is reinforced by the many poems in which present and past, personal and political history intersect for him in Berlin.

Partly because of the more reflective, even occasionally nostalgic tone of some of the poems, *Paradies uff Erden* displays a literary quality somewhat at odds with Biermann's rough-edged image as a political poet. This is not to say that the firebrand poet is absent here; under the heading "Pasquille," Biermann delivers more of his trademark attacks on the stupidity he finds around him. In the song "Journaille" (yellow press), for example, he is on the offensive against the irresponsible German boulevard press and its smear tactics, while in another, "Einem Hirten ins Gebetbuch" (into a shepherd's prayer-book), he attacks the wrongheaded logic of a Lutheran pastor-politician's proposal to destroy the files that the former East German state security agency kept on its citizens. In other poems, however, a different tone emerges. In "Güterbahnh of Grunewald" (Grunewald freight yard), the poet invites an aged Holocaust survivor and friend from Israel to return to the scene of the crime, to Berlin and the freight yard from which many of Berlin's Jews began their journey to the Nazi death camps; it is not perfect here, he argues, but in the reunified country, the Germans have made progress in confronting their past. Returning to his old neighborhood in East Berlin, he is struck now, for the first time, by the absence of Jews in what before World War II had been the hub of Jewish life in Berlin. This and other absurdities are to be found "Im Steinbruch der Zeit" (in the quarry of time) as this poem is titled; understanding them is crucial to Germany's future, for "the future will be decided/ in the struggle over the past."

Despite Berlin's central place in his life and memory, Biermann takes leave of the city in the poem "Adieu, Berlin." His absence, however, will not keep him from getting involved in the affairs of the new "Berlin Republic." In an image reminiscent of his early poetry, he portrays himself as the crowing cock-rooster who can make any "dung-heap," regardless of its location, into the "center of this world." The more reflective tone of the Berlin poems and songs may signal yet another transition in Biermann's career, one that ushers in a more literary and less public phase in his poetry and writing.

HEIMAT

In *Heimat* (homeland), Biermann has created poems that deal with a theme that can be found in all his works, despite the changes in his life and circumstances. This theme is his search for a homeland, which seems always to elude him. The journey of this Jew, Communist, and German from Hamburg and back represents both a geographical journey and a trip in search of himself. In this work, critic Peter Thompson suggests that Biermann is more interested in defending the state of Israel than in defending Communism.

OTHER MAJOR WORKS

PLAY: *Der Dra-Dra: Die grosse Drachentöterschau in acht Akten mit Musik*, pb. 1970.

NONFICTION: *Klartexte im Getümmel: 13 Jahre im Westen*, 1990; *Über das Geld und andere Herzensdinge: Prosaische Versuche über Deutschland*, 1991; *Der Sturz des Dädalus: Oder, Eizes für die Eingeborenen der Fidschi-Inseln über den IM Judas Ischariot und den Kuddelmuddel in Deutschland seit dem Golfkrieg*, 1992; *Wie man Verse macht und Lieder: Eine Poetik in acht Gängen*, 1997; *Die Ausbürgerung: Anfang vom Ende der DDR*, 2001; *Über Deutschland unter Deutschen: Essays*, 2002.

TRANSLATIONS: *Berichte aus dem sozialistischen Lager*, 1972; *Grosser Gesang vom ausgerotteten jüdischen Volk*, 1994 (of Yitzak Katzenelson's poem).

CHILDREN'S LITERATURE: *Das Märchen vom kleinen Herrn Moritz*, 1972; *Das Märchen von dem Mädchen mit dem Holzhein*, 1979.

MISCELLANEOUS: *Affenfels und Barrikade: Gedichte, Lieder, Balladen*, 1986.

BIBLIOGRAPHY

Flores, John. "Wolf Biermann." In *Poetry in East Germany: Adjustments, Visions, and Provocations, 1945-1970*. New Haven, Conn.: Yale University Press, 1971. An introduction to Biermann and his early poetry in English; includes several translations of Biermann's poems and songs.

Rosellini, Jay. *Wolf Biermann*. Munich: C. H. Beck, 1992. One of the most comprehensive studies of Biermann's work. Includes a detailed account of Biermann's life and its relation to his poetry up to the end of 1991.

Stamp Miller, G. Ann. *The Cultural Politics of the German Democratic Republic: The Voices of Wolf Biermann, Christa Wolf, and Heiner Müller*. Boca Raton, Fla.: BrownWalker Press, 2004. Examines the influence that Biermann, Christa Wolf, and Heiner Müller had on the cultural politics of East Germany.

Thompson, Peter. "Wolf Biermann: Die Heimat ist weit." In *Protest Song in East and West Germany Since the 1960's*, edited by David Robb. Rochester, N.Y.: Camden House, 2007. Thompson provides an extensive discussion of Biermann's poetry, focusing on the 2006 collection *Heimat*. He traces Biermann's search for a homeland throughout his works.

James Reece
Updated by Reece

JOHANNES BOBROWSKI

Born: Tilsit, East Prussia (now Sovetsk, Russia); April 9, 1917
Died: East Berlin, East Germany (now Berlin, Germany); September 2, 1965

PRINCIPAL POETRY

Sarmatische Zeit, 1961
Schattenland Ströme, 1962
Shadow Land: Selected Poems, 1966
Wetterzeichen, 1966
Im Windgesträuch, 1970
The White Mirror, 1993

OTHER LITERARY FORMS

Although Johannes Bobrowski (bawd-ROW-skee) is remembered primarily for his poetry, he did publish two critically acclaimed experimental novels: *Levins Mühle: 34 Sätze über meinen Grossvater* (1964; *Levin's Mill: Thirty-four Statements About My Grandfather*, 1970) and *Litauische Klaviere* (1966; Lithuanian pianos). He also wrote several short stories, which are collected in the following volumes: *Boehlendorff, und andere Erzählungen* (1965; Boehlendorff, and other stories), *Mäusefest, und andere Erzählungen*

(1965; festival of the mice, and other stories), and *Der Mahner* (1967; *I Taste Bitterness*, 1970). Working as a reader at an East German publishing house, he had the opportunity to edit books by others, including collections of legends and poetry. Recordings of several of his poems are available.

ACHIEVEMENTS

Johannes Bobrowski belonged to that generation of East German poets who matured late artistically, since their creative development was interrupted by the events of World War II and the founding of a new state. When Bobrowski finally published his first slender volumes in the early 1960's, they caused a great deal of excitement in both East and West Germany, for he was recognized as a major talent. His thematic concerns were new and provocative, and his unique style, based in part on classical German modes yet stripped to the bare linguistic essentials, was rich in metaphor and allegory. For his poetic accomplishments, he was awarded the prestigious prize of the Group 47 in 1962, a prize given only to the most promising new authors in the German-speaking world. In the same year, he won the Alma-Johanna-Koenig Prize in Vienna. For his novel *Levin's Mill*, he was awarded the Heinrich Mann Prize of the East Berlin Academy of the Arts and the international Charles Veillon Prize from Switzerland, both in 1965. He was posthumously granted the East German F. C. Weiskopf Prize in 1967.

Together with Erich Arendt and Peter Huchel, Bobrowski is credited with giving a new direction and inspiration to East German poetry, which until his time was bogged down in the principles of Socialist Realism and the Brechtian tradition. Bobrowski showed his own generation and younger, emerging poets that artistic integrity and genuine creativity and diversity were possible within the framework of a socialist state. He also called attention to the great classical German heritage, which had been largely forgotten in the postwar years, and to the most recent developments in West German and foreign poetry. About ten years later, in the early 1970's, his name was again invoked by younger authors in East Germany who sought a new means of aesthetic expression. Although Bobrowski was notably absent from literary anthologies and histories in

East Germany immediately after his death, he later was given a place of honor in the literary canon there and is recognized as a humanitarian author who strove for socialist ideals. In West Germany, more emphasis is placed on an appreciation of his style. He is often mentioned in connection with Günter Eich and Paul Celan, who, like Bobrowski, employed a reduced and concentrated lexical inventory, to the point of being hermetic or even opaque, and who at the same time did not shy away from combining mythological elements with autobiographical and contemporary references.

BIOGRAPHY

Johannes Bobrowski was born in a German town in East Prussia, not far from Lithuania; his father was a German railroad employee of Polish descent. Bobrowski spent his childhood in the small village of Mozischken and frequently visited his grandparents on their farm in the country. It was at this time that he learned much about the culture and history of the Slavic peoples who lived across the border. In 1928, the family moved to Königsberg (later called Kaliningrad), where Bobrowski attended a college-preparatory high school. In school, he was particularly attracted to the disciplines of music and painting; one of his teachers there was the writer Ernst Wiechert. In 1937, the family moved again, this time to Berlin, where Bobrowski began to study art history.

In 1939, Bobrowski was conscripted into military service. During World War II, he served as a soldier in France, Poland, and northern Russia, but he was also a member of the Bekennende Kirche (the Confessing Church), a Protestant resistance group. He was taken prisoner of war in 1945 and remained in Russian captivity until 1949; he was held in the regions of the Don and middle Volga Rivers and did forced labor as a coal miner. He returned to East Berlin in 1949, and in 1950, he began working as a reader at the publishing house Union Verlag, affiliated with the Lutheran Church. He remained there until his death, resulting from complications after an appendicitis operation, in 1965.

Bobrowski began writing poetry in 1941, when he was stationed at Lake Ilmen, and a few of his poems were published in the "inner emigration" magazine *Das innere Reich*. He did not write much again until the

Johannes Bobrowski (©Lufti Özkök)

early 1950's. His first poems after the war appeared in 1954 in the East German literary magazine *Sinn und Form*, which was edited by his friend Peter Huchel. Bobrowski continued to write sporadically after this literary debut, but he did not feel that his style had matured sufficiently until the early 1960's, when he published his first two volumes of poetry. He completed work on *Wetterzeichen* (signs of the weather), but it did not appear until after his death. *Im Windgesträuch* (in the wind bushes), appeared in 1970, containing poems of lesser quality which were written between 1953 and 1964.

ANALYSIS

Many of Johannes Bobrowski's poems, as he often stated, have as their central theme the relationship between the Germans and their neighbors to the East, the Slavic peoples. Because he grew up along the river Memel, where these two cultures merge, Bobrowski was particularly sensitive to this issue. From the days of the Order of the Teutonic Knights in the Middle Ages, the Germans had treated these people very badly, and the history of their relations is marred by war, repres-

sion, and murder. Bobrowski the poet recalls these atrocities, lest contemporary Germans forget to atone for their past misdeeds.

SARMATIA POEMS

To accomplish this goal, Bobrowski uses the concept of Sarmatia, a vague term applied by ancient historians and geographers to the area that he has in mind—namely, the territory between Finland and southern Russia from the Baltic to the Black Sea. He populates his Sarmatia with a host of various personages: ancient gods, legendary figures, and historical personalities. Bobrowski thus creates a mythology of sorts to come to terms with the German past, but it is not a well-defined mythology, and one can discern its full richness only by studying his poems as a totality.

Thus, when one reads about the ancient gods Perkun and Pikoll in "Pruzzische Elegie" ("Prussian Elegy"), about the great Lithuanian ruler Wilna in "Anruf" ("Appeal") or in "Wilna," about the legendary sunken city of Kiteshgorod in "Erzählung" ("Story"), or about Russian writer Isaac Babel in "Holunderblüte" ("Elderblossom"), one confronts only one aspect of Bobrowski's poetic world. History is treated as myth and myth as history. The reader must be willing to mingle and combine past and present, the real and the fictional, to form a coherent concept of the historical development Bobrowski has in mind.

LAYERS OF HISTORY

This historical dimension of Bobrowski's poetry offers a key to understanding his works. His poems contain five intertwined temporal layers: ancient times, in which the Slavic or Sarmatian tribes were free to determine their own existence and live in close harmony with nature; past centuries of conflict with the German invaders; the horrors of World War II, which Bobrowski had personally experienced; the present time, in which one must rectify old wrongs; and a future era, in which all men will live in communion with one another. It is often difficult to separate these layers, particularly when the reader finds many confusing temporal references within a single poem, yet this very ambiguity accounts for the richness of Bobrowski's verse; the various layers illuminate one another and promote an understanding of historical and cultural processes.

Moreover, these poems transcend their historical

occasion, offering profound general insights into man's inhumanity to man on a global scale and forcefully arguing the need for reconciliation and the end of barbarism. They can thus be read and appreciated by people from various cultural backgrounds and different eras. This rich philosophical content of the poems also explains how Bobrowski, as a Christian non-Marxist, was able to survive and publish in East Germany. He was seen as a seer or prophet who pointed out the errors of the past and the way to achieve the future brotherhood of all men—one of the proclaimed goals of the communist state. In a manner similar to the historical process he was describing, Bobrowski's poetry underwent a noticeable thematic development or progression: His first poems are concerned primarily with the fantastic landscape of Sarmatia; later poems include historical events and persons from the recent and distant past; and finally, Bobrowski arrives at a discussion of the problems of contemporary Berlin.

HONOR AND REMEMBRANCE

Not all Bobrowski poems deal with Sarmatia. A few treat the themes of love and death, not with any specificity, but in general philosophical terms. Two other categories, however, must be discussed in greater detail. The first contains poems written in honor or in memory of other artists with whom Bobrowski feels some affinity, such as François Villon, Joseph Conrad, Dylan Thomas, Marc Chagall, Johann Georg Hamann, Friedrich Gottlieb Klopstock, Gertrud Kolmar, Friedrich Hölderlin, Else Lasker-Schüler, Nelly Sachs, Wolfgang Amadeus Mozart, Johann Sebastian Bach, Christian Domelaitis, and Jakob Michael Reinhold Lenz. These "portrait poems" are not biographical or artistic summaries, but rather impressions of the artists or their lives. Bobrowski merely takes one aspect or feature of the artist and explains why he admires it or considers it important for his work. Thus, in the poem "An Klopstock" ("To Klopstock"), Bobrowski praises Klopstock's notion that one must recall the past and atone for former transgressions. (Bobrowski considered Klopstock to be his "taskmaster," both stylistically and thematically.) In "Hamann," he praises the eighteenth century poet for collecting and preserving ancient tales and legends. (Bobrowski was greatly influenced by Hamann while still in school and felt that

Hamann's life's goals were similar to his own. He had been collecting material for years for a monograph on Hamann but was unable to complete it because of his premature death.) In the poems "Else Lasker-Schüler" and "An Nelly Sachs" ("To Nelly Sachs"), Bobrowski points to the suffering these poets endured because they were Jewish, a suffering similar to that of the Jews living in Sarmatia. Bobrowski shared with all these artists a deep humanistic commitment to others and a concern for suffering in the world.

"ALWAYS TO BE NAMED" AND "LANGUAGE"

Another significant category of Bobrowski's poems, though by no means large, could be termed metapoetry. In these poems, Bobrowski describes his concept of poetic language and poetic communication. Two of these poems are especially paradigmatic: "Immer zu benennen" ("Always to Be Named") and "Sprache" ("Language"). Here, Bobrowski shows that he believes in an almost mystical relationship between the word and the thing named, that the word somehow captures the spirit of the thing or the person to which it refers. This idea plays an important role in Bobrowski's mythology, for objects, particularly from nature, take on a new significance: They become part of humans, part of their past and their relationships to others. Thus, to advance into the future, not only history but also words and nature are important, as words and nature enable people to communicate with one another and prepare themselves for what is to come. This is for Bobrowski the highest sense of poetry—it speaks to readers on several levels and raises their degree of consciousness. Poetry does not, Bobrowski claims, move the reader to bold political or social acts.

NATURE AS SYMBOL

Because of his emphasis on humanity's relationship to nature through language, and because he believed that humanity's harmony with nature, which was somehow lost in the past, must be regained to save the human race, Bobrowski's work has often been referred to as nature poetry. This description is valid only to a certain extent. It is true that Bobrowski does employ a great number of recurring nature motifs in his poetry, most frequently rivers, birds, trees, fish, stones, wolves, light, and darkness. These motifs, however, are not an evocation of nature per se. They do not merely conjure up the beauty of landscapes to be admired and enjoyed, but rather they function as symbols within the overriding thematics of the poem. Although they have varying connotations, Bobrowski generally uses these motifs to connect human beings to nature and to show how humans are part of the natural historical process. The objects of nature remain constant throughout historical change, says Bobrowski, and so, too, does the human soul. If people can rid themselves of the barbarous acts of war and violence and return to their primeval natural state, they will have reached their ultimate goal. This strong concern for the human and communal element is what sets Bobrowski's poems apart from traditional nature poetry.

POETIC MINIMALISM

Bobrowski's symbolic treatment of nature is only one aspect of his laconic style. The most striking feature of his poetry is the reduction of the linguistic material to an extreme minimum. Frequently, lines consist of merely a word or two each, and the length of the line is very irregular. Bobrowski often employs sentence fragments consisting of a single word, and longer syntactic units are usually broken up into several lines, interrupting the semantic flow.

The breaking of the poem into small phrases gives primacy to the individual word and lends the poetic message an aspect far different from what it would possess were it written in prose or even conventional poetic style. The free rhythms are sometimes fairly regular, so that the reader is often reminded of the odes and elegies of previous centuries. Bobrowski's concentrated and abbreviated style demands the active participation of the reader, who must fill in the missing material and make the appropriate associations and connections, a process similar to that through which one tries to remember events of the distant past. Such a difficult procedure tends at times to weaken the thematic impact of the poem, but as Fritz Minde points out in an article on Bobrowski, the poems can indeed be decoded with the help of published biographical and historical material; their difficult construction mimics the deformed and incoherent structure of reality.

STRUCTURE

In *Poetry in East Germany* (1971), John Flores suggests a method by which this decoding can be performed. He believes that most of Bobrowski's poems have three parts or stages. In the first, or introductory, part, the author relies chiefly on nouns, employed in an uncertain, staccato fashion. He is setting the mood for the poem by using the naming process described above. The reader is uncertain and somewhat confused. In the second stage, spatial and temporal connections begin to appear. The style is more reflective and narrative, and nouns are linked with verbs. The thematic thrust of the poem begins to take shape. In the final stage, the staccato mode is reintroduced, but here the verb prevails. The author unleashes his thoughts and ideas in a torrent of words. These thoughts have been building in intensity throughout the poem, and they all come together in the end in a desperate cry for recognition.

LEGACY

The difficult and cryptic nature of many of Bobrowski's poems raises the question of his place in literary history. Was he a true member of the avant-garde, a forerunner of or participant in the reductive "linguistic" movement of contemporary German poetry? No, he did not use language as a collection of building blocks devoid of meaning. Instead, he can be seen as part of the movement toward radical reduction of language that began around 1910 with the expressionists in Germany and that insisted on a language free of all Decadent cultural encrustations. Such a purification of language became all the more necessary after the abuses of the Nazi years. At the same time, however, Bobrowski went beyond this essentially negative program, offering in his verse substantive arguments in favor of a new and better world.

OTHER MAJOR WORKS

LONG FICTION: *Levins Mühle: 34 Sätze über meinen Grossvater*, 1964 (*Levin's Mill: Thirty-four Statements About My Grandfather*, 1970); *Litauische Klaviere*, 1966.

SHORT FICTION: *Boehlendorff, und andere Erzählungen*, 1965; *Mäusefest, und andere Erzählungen*, 1965; *Der Mahner*, 1967 (*I Taste Bitterness*, 1970).

BIBLIOGRAPHY

Bridgwater, Patrick. "The Poetry of Johannes Bobrowski." *Forum for Modern Language Studies* 2 (1966): 320-334. A critical study of Bobrowski's poetic works.

Flores, John. *Poetry in East Germany: Adjustments, Visions, and Provocations, 1945-1970.* New Haven, Conn.: Yale University Press, 1971. A history and critical analysis of poetry in postwar East Germany including the works of Bobrowski during this period. Includes bibliographic references.

Glenn, Jerry. "An Introduction to the Poetry of Johannes Bobrowski." *Germanic Review* 41 (1966): 45-56. A brief critical assessment of Bobrowski's poetic works.

Keith-Smith, Brian. *Johannes Bobrowski.* London: Wolff, 1970. Introductory biography with selected poetry and prose in English translation. Includes bibliography.

O'Doherty, Paul. *The Portrayal of Jews in GDR Prose Fiction.* Atlanta: Rodopi, 1997. Contains a short section on Bobrowski's depiction of Jews in his prose work. While it does not discuss the poetry, it does shed light on who Bobrowski was and the times in which he lived.

Scrase, David. *Understanding Johannes Bobrowski.* Columbia: University of South Carolina Press, 1995. Critical interpretation and brief biography by a specialist in German and Austrian art and literature. Includes bibliography.

Wieczorek, John P. *Between Sarmatia and Socialism: The Life and Works of Johannes Bobrowski.* Atlanta: Rodopi, 1999. Examines the chronological development of Bobrowski's Sarmatian works and places them within the context of a biography of his career.

Robert Acker

GIOVANNI BOCCACCIO

Born: Florence or Certaldo (now in Italy); June or July, 1313

Died: Certaldo (now in Italy); December 21, 1375

PRINCIPAL POETRY

Rime, c. 1330-1340

La caccia di Diana, c. 1334

Il filostrato, c. 1335 (*The Filostrato,* 1873)

Il filocolo, c. 1336 (*Labor of Love,* 1566)

Teseida delle nozze d'Emilia, 1339-1341 (*The Book of Theseus,* 1974)

Comedia delle ninfe fiorentine, 1341-1342

Il ninfale d'Ameto, 1341-1342 (also known as *Commedia delle ninfe*)

L'amorosa visione, 1342-1343 (English translation, 1986)

Elegia di Madonna Fiammetta, 1343-1344 (*Amorous Fiammetta,* 1587, better known as *The Elegy of Lady Fiammetta*)

Il ninfale fiesolano, 1344-1346 (*The Nymph of Fiesole,* 1597)

Buccolicum carmen, c. 1351-1366 (*Boccaccio's Olympia,* 1913)

OTHER LITERARY FORMS

Although Giovanni Boccaccio (boh-KOCH-ee-oh) was an excellent poet, his long-lived literary reputation is founded on his prose works. As a scholar and humanist, he wrote long encyclopedic works, including genealogies of the pagan Greek and Roman gods, geographies, and biographies of famous men and women from history, myth, and legend. *De casibus virorum illustrium* (1355-1374; *The Fall of Princes,* 1431-1438) as well as *De mulieribus claris* (c. 1361-1375; *Concerning Famous Women,* 1943) were influential in Geoffrey Chaucer's composition of "The Monk's Tale" in *The Canterbury Tales* (1387-1400). One of his most curious prose works, *Corbaccio* (c. 1355; *The Corbaccio,* 1975), is a long vernacular work, misogynistic in its theme, that parodies the conventions of the medieval dream-vision genre.

It is Boccaccio's *Decameron: O, Prencipe Galeotto* (1349-1351; *The Decameron,* 1620) that reveals his literary genius and narrative gift. Set during the Black Death, this large prose work consists of an outer narrative frame describing the effects of the plague on the city of Florence and the subsequent flight of three young men and seven women to the countryside, where they tell a hundred tales to amuse one another and pass the time. Often labeled the "mercantile epic," *The Decameron,* with its focus on the vices and virtues of everyday life, is decidedly Renaissance in its outlook and tone.

ACHIEVEMENTS

Giovanni Boccaccio, along with his friend and fellow humanist Petrarch, can be classified as one of the architects of the Italian Renaissance. Boccaccio, Petrarch, and Dante are the crown jewels of fourteenth century Italian poetry. Boccaccio was both a scholar and a poet, and his writings in Latin and Italian took inspiration and delight in the classical past and his contemporary world. While he was instrumental in encouraging the reading and translating of ancient Greek literature, he also continued the tradition started by Dante of promoting vernacular Italian as a worthy vehicle for great poetry and prose. Read in the original or translated into a variety of languages, his works were instrumental in spreading Renaissance values and ideas throughout Europe. His prose and poetry were foundational and inspirational for later poets and writers, including Chaucer, Christine de Pizan, Ludovico Ariosto, William Shakespeare, and Miguel de Cervantes. Boccaccio is also credited with popularizing the ottava rima; this verse form, used in his long poetic narratives, would become the mainstay for epic poetry written in Italian for centuries.

BIOGRAPHY

Giovanni Boccaccio was born in 1313, in Florence or Certaldo, as the illegitimate son of Boccaccino di Chellino and an unknown mother. His father, a fairly well-to-do merchant banker for the Bardi banking family, made his home in the village of Certaldo some twenty miles southwest of Florence. Despite the circumstance of Boccaccio's birth, his father recognized his son's legitimacy by 1320 and sought an education for him. By the age of seven, Boccaccio had had his first taste of Latin verse, in particular that of Ovid and Vergil. His father, however, hoped for his son to follow him in his career as a merchant-banker, and by the time Boccaccio was fourteen, he was brought or sent to Naples to be apprenticed as a merchant in one of the banking houses operated by the Bardi family.

At the time, Naples was a cultural, artistic, and intellectual center, and it fed the young Boccaccio's passion for literature more than it incited any pecuniary interests. His position within the banking industry allowed him access to a broad social and cultural spectrum.

Giovanni Boccaccio (Library of Congress)

Boccaccio frequented the royal libraries in Naples and became acquainted with some of the age's greatest Humanist scholars, jurists, artists, and theologians. They introduced him to the great poetic traditions of the ancient world and his own time, including the poetry of his future friend and fellow poet, Petrarch. Eventually, Boccaccio abandoned his father's profession for a literary career and began composing his own poetry. It is during this time that he is supposed to have met and fallen in love with Fiammetta, a woman whose beauty and charm would inspire his poetry throughout his life. Although there has been speculation over her true identity, most scholars maintain she was a fictitious but convenient muse for the poet.

In 1341, Boccaccio returned to Florence and immersed himself further in his study of the classics and poetic composition. For much of his adult life, his literary pursuits were supported by his public role as ambassador for Florence. This position would take him to the courts of Rome, and Lombardy and even to the papal court of Urban V in Avignon.

In 1348, Boccaccio, along with the entire city of

Florence, experienced the Black Death. It would claim the lives of his father and stepmother and, by some reports, more than a third of his community. Shortly thereafter, he began his most ambitious work, *The Decameron*, which uses the devastation of Florence by the plague as the starting point and narrative frame for the telling of his hundred prose tales. In 1350, he met Petrarch, and their lifelong friendship began. Although he never married, Boccaccio fathered at least five children, none of whom survived beyond adolescence.

Boccaccio's later life was fruitful both artistically and in terms of scholarship. He wrote the satire *The Corbaccio* and spent much of his time studying ancient texts and writing his encyclopedic works. For all of his work, he was held in high esteem by contemporary poets, Humanists, and scholars, and he would meet with many of them when he could. At this stage in his life, his mind turned to more spiritual matters, and he possibly took minor religious orders. Sometime after the death of his friend Petrarch in 1374, Boccaccio's health began to deteriorate. He suffered from gout and scabies, both made worse by obesity. He remained in Certaldo, and on December 21, 1375, at the age of sixty-two, he died.

ANALYSIS

Although Giovanni Boccaccio is a foundational figure in Renaissance Humanism and literature, his life and work are, nevertheless, an outgrowth of the literary and cultural sensibilities of the late medieval period. Like Dante, whose works he admired tremendously, he chose to write in the vernacular and employ the *dolce stil nuovo*, "the sweet new style," which emphasized personal introspection on matters of love and relied on a vocabulary of accepted metaphors and symbols to express the fruit of that introspection. In addition, his devotion to his muse, Fiammetta, and the poetry and prose she inspired reflect the tendency of contemporary poets to spiritualize the older courtly love traditions that originated in the writings of the twelfth century writer Andreas Cappellanus and the poetry of the troubadours and medieval romance poets. To this late medieval tradition, however, Boccaccio brought a burgeoning Renaissance way of thinking, as seen in his passion for the ideals, literary models, and narrative texts of the classical world. Specifically, his long narrative poems reflect a conscious imitation of epic and have for their subject matter classical myth and heroic tradition; he also wrote eclogues, *Boccaccio's Olympia*, in Latin in imitation of Vergil.

In his narrative poetry, Boccaccio frequently explores the conflict between love and fortune and how each tests the lovers involved. Two of the most important in this genre are *The Filostrato* and *The Book of Theseus*.

THE FILOSTRATO

Boccaccio based *The Filostrato* on the twelfth century *Le Roman de Troie* (the romance of Troy) by Benoît de Sainte-Maure. In this work, Boccaccio creates a complex poem of love, passion, and intrigue divided into eight cantos. The poem is set against the famed Trojan War, and the main character Troilo, a prince in the house of King Priam of Troy and a great warrior in the ongoing battle with the Greeks, is smitten with love for Criseida, a young widow whose father, Calchas, has defected to the Greek side. Her cousin Pandaro, a friend of Troilo, discovers his friend's love and orchestrates a meeting and later romantic trysts. The vicissitudes of war interrupt their love, however, as Calchas arranges to have his daughter returned to him. Though Troilo and Criseida swear fidelity and plan for a swift reunion, Criseida is soon courted by the Greek Diomede and abandons Troilo, whose pain and sorrow at the loss of his love can find no solace. His subsequent death on the battlefield is the only thing that relieves him of his emotional pain. Throughout the poem, Troilo's quick and complete surrender to an overwhelming and seemingly boundless love for Criseida is contrasted with her slow and deliberate yielding to the advances made on his behalf by Pandaro.

For Troilo, love is an overwhelming emotion that afflicts the will; it possesses him and renders him completely helpless in either working to fulfill his desires or extricating himself from them. Not so for Criseida, as she rules the relationship and to a great degree her own heart. She chooses to love Troilo and does so fully, but she is quite capable of leaving him behind when the circumstances of her life change. Ultimately, the poem presents how those who love deeply are subject to the whims of a fickle universe that brings lovers together and ultimately separates them. The proem to the text suggests that the theme and events reflect Boccaccio's own love affairs, although literary historians have long debated how much of the poem is infused with autobiographical details. *The Filostrato* would eventually serve as the source for Chaucer's *Troilus and Criseyde* (1382), which in turn would be the source for Shakespeare's *Troilus and Cressida* (pr. c. 1601-1602).

THE BOOK OF THESEUS

Set in ancient Greece, *The Book of Theseus*, a twelve-canto poem, is Boccaccio's attempt to write a poem in Italian that is consciously modeled on the classical epics of Vergil and Statius. Like his *The Filostrato*, it fuses the subjects of classical heroic poetry with a courtly love tradition. The plot of the narrative relates how Teseo (Theseus) conquers the Amazons, marries their queen, Ippolita (Hippolyta), and then returns to his homeland. After defeating Thebes in battle, Teseo takes two Thebans prisoner, the cousins Arcita and Palemone. While imprisoned, the two catch sight of Emilia, Ippolita's sister, and are immediately smitten with love for her. Eventually their freedom is gained, and with Teseo's approval, they compete in a tournament for Emilia's hand in marriage. All three pray to the gods for intervention to resolve the conflict and receive answers. Mars intercedes on behalf of Palemone, who wins the battle and Emilia for his bride. Shortly thereafter, Venus, on behalf of Arcita, strikes down Palemone. After Palemone's funeral, Emilia and Arcita are married.

Interestingly, the poem presents the matters of love and war as situations that paradoxically allow human beings to achieve the highest expressions of their virtues, such as loyalty, bravery, piety, and compassion, while at the same time engaging in acts of war and in brutal conflict. In the end, Boccaccio balances the turmoil and strife that both war and love can bring to the world with the balance and order of the world as ordained and maintained by the gods. Teseo is the human counterpart of the gods, as he too is a source of order, wisdom, virtue, and power.

Over the years, critics have debated Boccaccio's success in reviving the classical epic in *The Book of Theseus*. For some, his ambition and hopes for the work as epic were not matched by his poetic abilities. They claim that the poem, rather than achieving the lofty se-

riousness of epic narrative, instead tends toward the melodramatic and that the plot is stretched to meet the required twelve cantos necessary for an epic. Nevertheless, Chaucer found the work to be intriguing enough to use its plot, characters, and passages as the basis for "The Knight's Tale" in *The Canterbury Tales*.

OTHER MAJOR WORKS

SHORT FICTION: *Decameron: O, Prencipe Galeotto*, 1349-1351 (*The Decameron*, 1620).

NONFICTION: *Il filocolo*, 1338; *Genealogia deorum gentilium*, c. 1350-1375; *Trattatello in laude di Dante*, 1351, 1360, 1373 (*Life of Dante*, 1898); *Corbaccio*, c. 1355 (*The Corbaccio*, 1975); *De casibus virorum illustrium*, 1355-1374 (*The Fall of Princes*, 1431-1438); *De montibus, silvis, fontibus lacubus, fluminibus, stagnis seu paludibus, et de nominbus maris*, c. 1355-1374; *De mulieribus claris*, c. 1361-1375 (*Concerning Famous Women*, 1943); *Esposizioni sopra la Commedia di Dante*, 1373-1374.

BIBLIOGRAPHY

Bergin, Thomas Goddard. *Boccaccio*. New York: Viking Press, 1981. This is a good introduction to the life of the poet and is a thorough critical study of all of his works.

Boitani, Piero. *Chaucer and Boccaccio*. Oxford, England: Society for the Study of Mediaeval Languages and Literature, 1977. Most students of English literature will come to Boccaccio's works through Geoffrey Chaucer. This is an excellent critical study of the literary connection between the poets.

Branca, Vittore. *Boccaccio: The Man and His Works*. Translated by Richard Monges and Dennis McAuliffe. New York: New York University Press, 1976. This English-language biography is a respected source and is frequently referenced by critics.

Stillinger, Thomas, and F. Regina Psaki, eds. *Boccaccio and Feminist Criticism*. Chapel Hill, N.C.: Annali d'Italianistica, 2006. The most recent trend in Boccaccio scholarship has been to examine his depiction of women. The essays contained in this work examine both his poetry and his prose in regard to feminism.

Joseph Carroll

MATTEO MARIA BOIARDO

Born: Scandiano, Papal States (now in Italy); May,
1440 or 1441
Died: Reggio nell' Emilia, Papal States (now in
Italy); December 19, 1494

PRINCIPAL POETRY

Pastoralia, 1464 (English translation, 1996)
Trionfi, c. 1468
Carmina de laudibus Estensium, c. 1463
Epigrammata, c. 1475
Orlando innamorato, 1483-1495 (English
    translation, 1823)
Rime, 1499 (English translation, 1835)
Amorum libri tres, 1499 (English translation,
    1993)

OTHER LITERARY FORMS

Though poetry—primarily Petrarchan sonnets,
tercets, eclogues, and ottava rima—was his forte,
Matteo Maria Boiardo (boh-YOR-doh) experimented
freely with different forms of writing throughout his
lively career. He translated such classical prose works
as Xenophon's *Ellēnika* (date unknown; also known as
Helenica; History of the Affairs of Greece, 1685) and
Lucius Apuleius's *Metamorphoses* (second century;
The Golden Ass, 1566), though he concentrated more
on story than style or accuracy. Late in life, in response
to a renewed local interest in the comedies of Terence
and Plautus, Boiardo attempted to write for the theater,
producing his only known play, *Il Timone* (pb. c. 1487),
which is considered inferior to his other work.

ACHIEVEMENTS

Matteo Maria Boiardo's major accomplishment, the
work for which he is best remembered, is his massive—
more than four-thousand-stanza-long—yet uncom-
pleted epic, *Orlando Innamorato*. A complex poem
with hundreds of named characters, composed over
the last two decades of the author's life, *Orlando
innamorato* gathers several subject threads. The legends of Charlemagne and King Arthur are intertwined
with myths and Renaissance sensibilities to produce an

idealized, imaginary world wherein loyalty and betrayal, chivalry and dishonor, and romantic love and
human lust are explored. Boiardo's unfinished masterpiece, a Renaissance fantasy-thriller best seller, would
inspire a sequel early in the following century from a
more accomplished poet: the *Orlando furioso* (1516,
1521, 1532; English translation, 1591) of Ludovico
Ariosto.

A secondary but perhaps longer-lasting achievement is Boiardo's invention of what became the modern Tarot. Working off a fifty-six-card deck of playing
cards introduced into Italy in the early fifteenth century, the poet added twenty-two trumps (later called the
major arcana) and appended brief poetic descriptions to
produce the seventy-eight-card deck that would in succeeding centuries be used to divine fortunes.

BIOGRAPHY

Matteo Maria Boiardo was born in 1440 or 1441 at
the family castle in Scandiano, near Reggio in the
Emilia Romagna region of northern Italy. He was the
eldest of five children and the only son of Giovanni
Boiardo and Lucia Strozzi, sister of poet Tito Ves-
pasiano Strozzi. Boiardo's grandfather, Feltrino Boiardo, count of Scandiano, was a major influence on the
young poet's life. A knight who had served the duke of
Ferrara, Niccolò III d'Este, during the late Crusades,
Boiardo's grandfather was a well-educated courtier
who had written poetry and executed translations from
classical literature. Boiardo would follow in his grandfather's footsteps with great success.

Boiardo's grandfather brought the young Boiardo
into the d'Este court during the reign of Niccolò's successor Leonello (ruled 1441-1450), providing him with
the opportunity to receive an excellent education. In
Ferrara, Boiardo, as a member of the nobility, was privately tutored, allowed access to the well-stocked
d'Este library, introduced to scholars, and exposed to
chivalric traditions, including jousting tournaments.
Boiardo's grandfather, after Giovanni Boiardo's death
around 1451, arranged for his grandson to inherit his title. When Boiardo's grandfather died in 1456, the title
passed first to Boiardo's uncle, Giulio Ascanio Boiardo. When his uncle died in 1460, Boiardo duly became count of Scandiano during the reign of Duke

Borso d'Este (ruled 1450-1471) and afterward divided his time between his home and Ferrara.

Boiardo, a witty and learned individual, was a popular presence at the courts of both Borso and his successor, Ercole d'Este (ruled 1471-1505), who made Ferrara one of Europe's most distinguished and fashionable centers of art and science during the late fifteenth century. Boiardo contributed to the milieu through his literary abilities, composing courtly love sonnets in the manner of Petrarch and translating excerpts from Greek and Latin classics for the entertainment of the dukes and their retinue. Because of his charm and talent, Boiardo was summoned to participate at important events, for which he sometimes wrote celebratory verse. Some of his love poems may have been completed for the wedding of Ippolita Sforza. His *Trionfi*—tercets written on fifty-six playing cards and twenty-two trumps that were precursors to modern Tarot decks—were probably composed in advance of the reception that accompanied the marriage of Borso's sister Bianca to Boiardo's cousin Galeotta Pico della Mirandola in 1468. His *Carmina de laudibus Estensium*, written for Ercole's investiture, compared that newly created duke of Ferrara, Modena, and Reggio to the mythological Hercules. His romantic *Armorum libri tres* was inspired by his unrequited love for Antonia Caprara before his marriage in the early 1470's to Taddea Gonzaga, daughter of the count of Novellara, by whom Boiardo fathered a son, Camillo, and several daughters.

As a member of one of the most trusted families during the intrigue-filled Renaissance in Italy, Boiardo was granted a stipend in the mid-1470's. In 1480, when Boiardo was already engaged in writing *Orlando Innamorato*, Duke Ercole appointed Boiardo governor of Modena. During his three-year tenure, he contended with plague, famine, and revolt before leaving the post early in 1483 to protect Scandiano during a war with Venice. In 1487, the year that Boiardo had the first two books of *Orlando Innamorato* privately published, Ercole named Boiardo governor of Reggio, and he remained at that post until his death in 1494. Though much of his written work was reprinted or anthologized posthumously in Italy throughout the following century, Boiardo fell into obscurity until the nineteenth century, when he was rediscovered.

ANALYSIS

As much as any of his better-known Italian contemporaries—Leonardo da Vinci, members of the Medici and Sforza families, Christopher Columbus, and Niccolò Machiavelli—Matteo Maria Boiardo was also a Renaissance man. Like those more famous names, he too was a product of and a contributor to an age of discovery that dragged the world from the medieval into the modern age. Boiardo's relative obscurity is more a result of his operation within a smaller sphere of influence than of his talent. His venue was the duchy of Ferrara, an enclave bordered to the south by the powerful Republic of Florence and the Papal States, and to the north by the Republic of Venice and the territories of the Milanese and Genoese city-states.

Boiardo was fortunately situated in both place and in time. Born just after the Gutenberg press was introduced, he was physically in the path of the first wave of scientific and intellectual inquiry called the Renaissance, which originated in Florence about 1400 and swept through Italy and the rest of Europe.

Steeped in the available literature of his era, Boiardo began writing in his late teens. Like authors from any epoch, he drew on past works for inspiration. He began by imitating Petrarch, writing sonnets of unrequited love in the traditional octave/sestet form. Once he had perfected the technique, he moved on to whatever attracted his eager mind, producing works to entertain the elite and discriminating court of Ferrara. Boiardo was successively caught up in the rediscovery of classical Greek and Latin thought and style, captivated by a popular card game, and enamored of drama. In the fullness of time, he took existing materials, reshaped and reinvented them, and made them his own, in the process becoming a consummate storyteller in verse, the unofficial poet laureate of Ferrara.

TRIONFI

Introduced into northern Italy around 1425, playing cards—called *trionfi* (triumphs, or trumps) because higher-numbered cards triumphed over lesser cards—quickly became a favorite aristocratic pastime at court functions. It is probable that gambling on the turns of cards took place from the outset. Early decks, consisting of four suits of either thirteen or fourteen cards, were produced for especially happy occasions such as weddings, military victories, and festivals.

In the 1460's, Boiardo significantly changed the concept of playing cards, essentially inventing a new game that came to be known as the Tarot. He composed eighty poems for *Trionfi*: introductory and concluding sonnets explaining the nature of the game, and seventy-eight tercets (three-line poems) to accompany each card from a fifty-six-card deck, plus twenty-two trump cards. Boiardo changed suits and symbols of minor cards to match the four passions of which he wrote: love (arrows), hope (chalices), jealousy (eyes), and fear (batons); each card contained a pithy, poetic statement about the particular emotion in question. To these, Boiardo added twenty-two special cards (such as Reason, World, Grace, Anger, and Perseverance), illustrating the particular quality with an example from Greek mythology; the poet was the first to introduce the concept of the wild card by inserting the Fool (Joker) into his deck.

The first seventy-eight-card deck designed to Boiardo's scheme was produced around the time of his death; examples of these five-hundred-year-old cards still exist. It is not known precisely when the original game of chance segued to a method of fortune-telling. However, in the modern Tarot, Boiardo's seventy-eight-card structure has been retained. Though his simplistic poetry has been eliminated to allow greater freedom of interpretation for card readers, much of the symbolism he initially alluded to remains, and many of the twenty-two trumps of the major arcana still bear the names or ideas he attached to them.

ORLANDO INNAMORATO

The work with which Boiardo is most closely identified, *Orlando Innamorato*, offered his audiences something for every taste, from erotic love (for the ladies) to the mayhem of battle (for the lords). A sprawling romantic epic in regular octaves of *ababcc* structure, the poem was probably read aloud at court functions as a particular section was finished, in serialized fashion like a medieval version of a modern soap opera. Written late in Boiardo's career—and a work still in progress at his death—*Orlando Innamorato* demonstrates both the author's wide-ranging learning and his maturity as a poet.

The epic presents an alternative universe: an imaginary age based partly on historical events and partly on legend and mythology, all held together and enhanced by the poet's skill. At the core of the story is the love of the knight Orlando (the Italian version of Roland, from *Chanson de Roland*, twelfth century; *The Song of Roland*, 1880) for the exotic Angelica of Cathay. Thwarting that love are two major conflicts: the Siege of Paris, pitting Orlando's king, Charlemagne, against the invading Saracens, and the Siege of Albracca, matching Angelica's father, the king of Cathay, against marauding Tartars. Further complicating the issue are scores of secondary characters on all sides, whose allegiances shift back and forth. As if that were not enough, Orlando, his friends, and rivals experience dozens of encounters with giants and dwarves, enchanted groves, magical swords, love potions, dragons, griffins, and a host of other fantastic dangers that keep tension and audience interest high. Whenever the plot drags, Boiardo brings in a damsel on a palfrey with a new tale of woe and a quest to pursue, or confronts the hero with an antagonist to present a fresh challenge. If all else fails, the poet resorts to cliffhangers: He leaves a protagonist in peril and cuts to a previous scene where a different character is in jeopardy.

Echoes of many earlier works are present in *Orlando Innamorato*. Elements from the Arthurian legends, the saga of El Cid, Geoffrey Chaucer's *The Canterbury Tales* (1387-1400), Giovanni Boccacio's *Decameron: O, Prencipe Galeotto* (1349-1351; *The Decameron*, 1620), Dante's *La divina commedia* (c. 1320; *The Divine Comedy*, 1802), and Homer's *Odyssey* (c. 725 B.C.E.; English translation, 1614) present intriguing subplots. Boiardo also references current events, working in compliments to the Este family and news about a war between Ferrara and Venice. The composite result is the colorful, wistful *Orlando Innamorato*, a unique paean to an idealized chivalrous age when the concepts of loyalty and honor, truth and the quest still mattered.

OTHER MAJOR WORKS
PLAY: *Il Timone*, pb. c. 1487.
NONFICTION: *Di viris illustribus*, 1485.
TRANSLATION: *Istoria Imperiale*, c. 1475 (of Ricobaldo of Ferrara's *Chronicon Imperatorum*).
MISCELLANEOUS: *Eclogues*, c. 1464.

BIBLIOGRAPHY

Boiardo, Matteo Maria. *Orlando Innamorato*. Translated by Charles Stanley Ross. West Lafayette, Ind.: Parlor Press, 2004. A newly revised and unabridged translation of the epic for a general audience, complete with summaries of events to assist reader understanding and appreciation.

Cavallo, Jo Ann. *The Romance Epics of Boiardo, Ariosto, and Tasso: From Public Duty to Private Pleasure*. Toronto: University of Toronto Press, 2004. This study compares and contrasts the political motivations and treatments of subject matter of the three major epic romance poets of the Italian Renaissance: Boiardo, Ludovico Ariosto, and Torquato Tasso.

Dean, Trevor. *Land and Power in Late Medieval Ferrara: The Rule of the Este, 1350-1450*. New York: Cambridge University Press, 2002. Provides a detailed study of the rise of the wealthy Este family, members of which would exert considerable political authority in and around the northern Italian cities of Ferrera, Reggio, and Modena during the time Boiardo flourished at their courts.

Huson, Paul. *Mystical Origins of the Tarot: From Ancient Roots to Modern Usage*. Rochester, Vt.: Destiny Books, 2004. This profusely illustrated volume traces the symbolical and metaphorical origins of Tarot cards from their purported beginning in ancient Persia through their introduction into Europe in the early fifteenth century to their use in modern times, encompassing Boiardo's contributions to the lore of the cards.

Molinaro, Julius A. *Matteo Maria Boiardo: A Bibliography of Works and Criticism from 1487-1980*. Ottawa, Ont.: Canadian Federation for the Humanities, 1984. A compact but invaluable resource, this book traces the history of the publication of Boiardo's works in various languages and describes the literary reactions at the time.

Jack Ewing

NICOLAS BOILEAU-DESPRÉAUX

Born: Paris, France; November 11, 1636
Died: Paris, France; March 13, 1711
Also known as: N. Boileau-Despréau; Monsieur Despréau

PRINCIPAL POETRY

Les Satires, 1666-1711 (12 volumes; *Satires*, 1711-1713)
Les Épîtres, 1669-1698 (12 volumes; English translation, 1711-1713)
L'Art poétique, 1674 (*The Art of Poetry*, 1683)
Le Lutrin, 1674, 1683 (partial English translation, 1682)
Ode du sieur D*** sur la prise de Namur, 1693

OTHER LITERARY FORMS

Nicolas Boileau-Despréaux (bwaw-LOH day-pray-OH) published an extensive selection of his letters to both friends and antagonists, as well as *Dialogue des héros de roman* (1688; *The Heroes of Romances*, 1713), a highly critical assessment of the novel form, of which Boileau disapproved. Boileau also translated the ancient critic Longinus's treatise on the sublime into French as *Traité du sublime*, bringing it back into the mainstream of European literary tradition. His letters, composed in a highly literary style and envisioned as published documents, are an important part of his oeuvre. Most interesting to the student of literature and criticism is his correspondence with Charles Perrault, who stood for the "modern" side, as Boileau did for the "ancient," in the famous Quarrel of the Ancients and Moderns that preoccupied the French cultural scene in the latter half of the seventeenth century.

ACHIEVEMENTS

Though Pierre Corneille produced greater imaginative work, Nicolas Boileau-Despréaux was the most commanding of the seventeenth century French neoclassical critics. His prescriptions on art were connected with the perceived good of the state, for he was a favorite of King Louis XIV, probably the most powerful and authoritarian monarch Christian Europe had yet seen. Boileau, indeed, epitomized the base of the king's support, which was not the aristocracy, whose privileges the king curtailed, but the solid middle class, who saw a career at court as a way to rise in society.

BIOGRAPHY

Nicolas Boileau-Despréaux was born and raised in Paris and was intended for the church, but by the age of twenty, he had instead pursued the study of law. By 1666, with the publication of part of his *Satires*, he had established himself as a bright young star in the French literary firmament. The year 1674 was something of an annus mirabilis for Boileau, as he not only produced *Le Lutrin* and *The Art of Poetry*, his two major works of poetry, but also published his translation of the ancient critic Longinus's *Peri hypsous* (first century C.E.; *On the Sublime*, 1652), which, in the long term, became his greatest legacy to European literature. In 1677, he was named historiographer to the king, and he increasingly put his life at court and his responsibilities to that social milieu ahead of his writing. Increasing deafness and the lingering effects of a botched surgery performed on his back in his youth hindered him in his later years, although he remained revered by younger writers.

If Boileau at times seems like the mouthpiece of an authoritarian ruler, it can also be said that he possessed the verve and sense of individual assurance to keep up with the demands of an often petulant monarch and an often capricious and intrigue-ridden court.

ANALYSIS

The satire at once seems an inevitable genre for someone of Nicolas Boileau-Despréaux's opinions and temperament, yet an interesting choice for a young poet starting off his literary career. Boileau was writing in an age when the development of a poet's work was expected to conform to the *rota vergilii*, or wheel of Vergil: Vergil had started off writing pastoral poems, then wrote georgics (poems dealing with agriculture), and finally his great epic, the *Aeneid* (c. 29-19 B.C.E.; English translation, 1553). Satire was a somewhat wayward choice, but Boileau

had a combination of the confidence of the young, the moxie of someone not born to power and wealth and thus lacking culturally sown social inhibitions, and the moral fervor of someone whose standard of taste would not permit him to sit silently while bad writing by others was overpraised. All these elements combined to render Boileau the epitome of the enfant terrible, the abrasive newcomer whose elders both are shocked by and swoon over him.

The *Satires* of Boileau are not just monologic screeds but also little playlets, involving personified allegorical figures such as Raison (reason) and Esprit (spirit), as well as beast-fable personas such as the donkey who narrates satire VII. Structurally, they are among his most complex works, with many small jokes and flourishes adding to their intricacy.

LE LUTRIN

Le Lutrin (the lectern) was also an unusual choice for Boileau. This satire of two Catholic clerics quarrel-

Nicolas Boileau-Despréaux (Hulton Archive/Getty Images)

ing over where to place a lectern in a church was not an attack on Catholicism as such, although liberal-leaning English commentators such as John Dennis mistakenly interpreted it as such. What Boileau intended was to make fun of two serious men of responsibility quibbling over such a trivial matter. *Le Lutrin* is a mock epic like Alexander Pope's *The Rape of the Lock* (1712, 1714), because it both satirizes people for quarreling over trifles and implies that the traditional contexts for epic antagonism are often little more than such trifles. However, Boileau is not out to burlesque the entire idea of epic. He merely wants to explore the poetic effect of taking the well-developed form of epic and training it on a trivial subject. Boileau imparts a wry lesson in incongruity that has a poetically self-conscious and experimental aspect.

THE ART OF POETRY

Boileau's major poem, *The Art of Poetry*, was published in the same year as the bulk of *Le Lutrin*. It is a didactic poem in four books explicitly modeled on the work of the Latin poet Horace in the first century B.C.E. Boileau both provides general rules for the art of poetry and exemplifies them, using the characteristic meter and diction of the mode. When he is critiquing inept poetic procedures, or those he sees as such, he mimics them himself, demonstrating that he knows where of he speaks.

The mission of *The Art of Poetry* is twofold. One aim is to set abiding rules for the writing of literature, or to reiterate those the tradition had already espoused. In many ways, Boileau is repeating long-established critical precepts; however, he no doubt felt that they needed to be displayed to each new generation, given what he saw as the literary culture's tendency toward mediocrity and complacency. For this firm critical stance, Boileau was known as "the legislator of Parnassus" (the mountain where the mythical Nine Muses were said to dwell).

The poem has another aim, however: It is a partisan document that seeks to position Boileau vis-à-vis older poets who were his rivals (and whom he hoped to dislodge) and who were less interested than Boileau in securing the good graces of the royal court. As in the *Satires*, in which writers not studied in modern times are denigrated in favor of such still well-known figures as Jean Racine and Corneille, Boileau's taste has stood the test of time. However, many of the writers he dislikes

are clearly, for him, diminished by their Protestantism or their insufficient royalism. Despite the dignity and serenity of both his prose and his imaginative outlook, Boileau did let his judgment at times be affected by partisanism. Boileau has some of the "young conservatism" often seen in those who seek to rise in society against an entrenched elite and yet still affirm the society's codified values. For example, most of his criticisms of writers whom he finds inadequate or incompetent are of older contemporaries, people whom he could conceivably hope to dislodge and who in any event were probably in decline. He disliked Marc-Antoine Girard, sieur de Saint-Amant, whose biblical epic *Moïse sauvé* (1653) was at the time thought likely to become the major French contribution to the epic tradition. Boileau, a pious Catholic, also disliked some writers for religious reasons, such as the Huguenot (Protestant) poet Guillaume de Salluste, seigneur du Bartas. There is thus a tactical, opportunistic element in his work, though that can most likely be said of anybody who writes about contemporaries because of the unavoidable jealousy or self-interest involved. It is for this reason that most ancient and medieval treatises preoccupied themselves with writers who were safely in the past.

Boileau, though, was too intellectually imposing and had too much good sense to be just a literary courtier. He loved the classics because they were the best works he knew, not just because of their literary standing. His exacting standards proved beneficial in that they crystallized what neoclassical criticism actually aspired to do instead of simply ventilating its slogans. His position in the Quarrel of the Ancients and Moderns was determinedly on the ancient side (Boileau's great rival in literary life was his opposite number in this quarrel, the fairy-tale writer and wit Perrault). Boileau, indeed, had the contemporary scene on his mind a great deal. In *The Art of Poetry*, he spends time on recent and contemporary writers as well as the classics. He displays a striking sensitivity to language, seeing "Childebrand" as a name unfit to be honored by treatment in poetic meter.

TRAITÉ DU SUBLIME

Boileau was also influential in a very different way, as he translated Longinus, rescued him from obscurity, and put "the sublime" on the modern literary map. Most immediately, he probably was motivated by reasons different from those that inspired later followers of the sublime. The majesty of Louis XIV aspired to dignity beyond the merely stately; the levels of awe and vastness that Longinus evoked may have been thought the only truly adequate backdrop for the aura of the king. Longinus himself was no revolutionary, generally subscribing to the mainstream hierarchies and evaluations of his time. Boileau believed that Longinus was identifiable with Cassius Longinus, the third century political figure, an identification that later scholars disproved. In reviving Longinus, Boileau introduced a new vocabulary into criticism that was eventually to upend the stranglehold of the very neoclassical prescriptions he so eloquently affirmed.

Boileau discerns a sense of proportion in Longinus, commending the splendor-filled beginning of Georges de Scudéry's epic *Alaric: Ou, Rome vaincue* (1654), "I sing the conqueror of the conquerors of the earth," but also saying that, in any other context, this line would have been over the top by a wide margin and is somewhat so even here. Boileau's classicism helps him understand the importance of tone and structure with regard to the sublime. The sublime cannot be put simply anywhere and still operate as the sublime; it has to be deployed discerningly and with an awareness of proportion, which is far more Aristotelian than the image usually presented of Longinus.

The greatest advocate of established truths was also the seventeenth century critic who most opened the way for their eventual overthrow. Boileau was revived by later classicists such as Ferdinand Brunetière, but his spirit was larger than the use they made of him.

OTHER MAJOR WORKS

NONFICTION: *Discours sur la satire*, 1668; *Dissertation sur Jaconde*, 1669; *Épître IX*, 1683 (wr. c. 1675); *Dialogue des héros de roman*, 1688 (*The Heroes of Romances*, 1713); *Réflexions sur Longin*, 1694 (preface to *Œuvres diverses*, 1701); *Selected Criticism*, 1965.

TRANSLATION: *Traité du sublime*, 1674 (of Longinus's *On the Sublime*).

MISCELLANEOUS: *The Works of Monsieur Boileau, Made English by Several Hands*, 1711-1713 (3 volumes).

BIBLIOGRAPHY

Corum, Robert. *Reading Boileau: An Integrative Study of the Early Satires*. West Lafayette, Ind.: Purdue University Press, 1998. A specialized study of the *Satires*, going into great depth on their structure and meaning.

Delahanty, Ann, "Mapping the Aesthetic Mind: John Dennis and Nicolas Boileau." *Journal of the History of Ideas* 68, no. 2 (April, 2007): 233-253. Compares Boileau to an English critic of the same period who was much more liberal, politically and aesthetically, than Boileau; Delahanty, though, stresses the commonalities of outlook between the two writers.

Peters, Jeffrey N. "Boileau's Nerve: Or, The Poetics of Masculinity." *Esprit Créateur* 43, no. 3 (Fall, 2003): 26-36. An innovative look at Boileau in the context of gender studies.

Pocock, Gordon. *Boileau and the Nature of Neoclassicism*. New York: Cambridge University Press, 1980. Still the best standard account of Boileau in the context of the aesthetic theories of his age; especially good on the connection with the theories of Longinus.

Weinbrot, Howard. *Menippean Satire Reconsidered: From Antiquity to the Eighteenth Century*. Baltimore: The Johns Hopkins University Press, 2005. Though Boileau's satires were of the more traditional Horatian or Juvenalian kind rather than the more idea-oriented Menippean variety that Weinbrot considered, Weinbrot mentions Boileau frequently as a key figure in the literary history of satire.

Wood, Allen G. *Literary Satire and Theory: A Study of Horace, Boileau, and Pope*. New York: Garland, 1985. The best available study of Boileau within the tradition that he cherished and did so much to promulgate.

Wygant, Amy. "Boileau and the Sound of Satirze." *Forum for Modern Language Studies* 31, no. 2 (1995): 128-139. The most in-depth look at Boileau's formal aspects, it is notable in seeing his satiric practice as more subversive than is usually the case.

Nicholas Birns

YVES BONNEFOY

Born: Tours, France; June 24, 1923

PRINCIPAL POETRY

Traité du pianiste, 1946
Anti-Platon, 1947
Du mouvement et de l'immobilité de Douve, 1953
    (*On the Motion and Immobility of Douve*, 1968)
Hier régnant désert, 1958
Pierre écrite, 1965 (*Words in Stone*, 1976)
Selected Poems, 1968
Dans le leurre du seuil, 1975 (*The Lure of the
    Threshold*, 1985)
L'Ordalie, 1975
Rue traversière, 1977
Trois remarques sur la couleur, 1977
Poèmes, 1978
Poems, 1959-1975, 1985
Things Dying, Things Newborn: Selected Poems,
    1985
Ce qui fut sans lumière, 1987 (*In the Shadow's
    Light*, 1991)
Début et fin de la neige, 1991
Early Poems, 1947-1959, 1991
New and Selected Poems, 1995
Le Cœur-espace, 2001
Les Planches courbes, 2001 (*The Curved Planks*,
    2006)

OTHER LITERARY FORMS

Yves Bonnefoy (BAWN-foy) has distinguished himself in the fields of art criticism and literary criticism. He is also renowned for his translations of William Shakespeare's plays into French. His essays on art span the entire range from Byzantine to contemporary, from studies of the Renaissance and the Baroque to such works as Bonnefoy's *Alberto Giacometti: Biographie d'une œuvre* (1991; *Alberto Giacometti: A Biography of His Work*, 1991), on the twentieth century Italian sculptor. Bonnefoy is not simply an academic critic; some of his most moving prose writing is that which ties the experience of the artist to the interior experience of the imaginative writer. In *L'Arrière-pays*

(1972; the back country), for example, he combines insightful discussions of classical Renaissance paintings with meditations on the sources of inspiration he draws from his own childhood. The title (which brings to mind *arrière-plan*, the background in a painting) allows for an extended meditation on the figures in the backgrounds of classic paintings and the feeling of well-being that Bonnefoy has experienced in his childhood and in his many travels.

This interior experience is Bonnefoy's major focus in his literary criticism as well, from the essays in *L'Improbable et autres essais* (1959, 1980; "The Improbable" and other essays) to the monograph *Rimbaud par luimême* (1961; *Rimbaud*, 1973) to the collections *Le Nuage rouge* (1977; the red cloud) and *La Présence et l'image* (1983; the presence of the image). Bonnefoy returns again and again to the idea that the images a poet uses, while in some sense unreal, are able to lead the reader to what he calls the "true place" of poetry. Thus the line "Ô Saisons, ô châteaux" (oh seasons, oh castles), which begins the famous poem by Rimbaud, becomes for Bonnefoy both a utopian dream and a reality that can be reached through language.

The philosophical issues that the poet locates in his artistic and literary researches are, in turn, fed back into his poetry, with the result that the poetry and the critical works come to mirror each other's concerns. His collection of lectures, *Lieux et destins de l'image: Un Cours de poétique au Collège de France, 1981-1993* (1999) is a compilation of his poetics.

ACHIEVEMENTS

Yves Bonnefoy is one of the most highly admired poets to reach maturity in France in the post-World War II period, and many would identify him as the most important French poet-intellectual at the turn of the twenty-first century. His early work had the character of being challenging and even hermetic, but it struck a chord with a whole generation of readers and poets. His poetry has always maintained the quality of being highly meditated and serious in purpose. While his preoccupations are philosophical—death, the existence of the loved one, the place of truth—his poetic language is highly imaged and moves equally in the realms of beauty and truth.

The close association Bonnefoy has always maintained with visual artists who are his contemporaries has given him a high prominence in the art world as well. Though he maintains a teaching position in literature, he has tended more and more in his later career to pursue his interests in art and the theory of culture. His writings on art are prized both for what they say about individual artists and for the high level of reflection they bring to the subject of creativity.

Bonnefoy's nomination to the chair of comparative studies of the poetic function at the Collège de France in 1981 confirmed his position as one of France's leading poets and intellectual figures. A regular affiliation with Yale University and visiting professorships at other American universities ensured Bonnefoy's prominence among American academic circles as well; he was awarded an honorary doctorate by the University of Chicago in 1988. He was also honored, in 1992, with an exhibition of his manuscripts and other documents at the Bibliothèque Nationale, Paris. His many other awards include the Grand Prix de Poésie from the French Academy (1981), the Grand Prix Société des Gens de Lettres (1987), the Bennett Award from *Hudson Review* (1988), the Bourse Goncourt (1991), the Prix Balzac (1995), the Prix Del Duca (1995), the Prix National de Poésie (1996), the Masaoka Shiki International Haiku Grand Prize (2000), and the Franz Kafka Prize in 2007.

BIOGRAPHY

Yves Bonnefoy was born on June 24, 1923, in Tours, France. His mother was a nurse and later a schoolteacher; his father died when Bonnefoy was thirteen. His early life was divided between the working-class surroundings of Tours and the rural home of his maternal grandfather, a schoolteacher and natural intellectual who had a great influence on the boy, and in many ways, Bonnefoy considered his grandparents' home his own true home. He studied in Tours and at the University of Poitiers, primarily chemistry and mathematics.

Yves Bonnefoy (©Sophie Bassouls/Sygma/CORBIS)

Bonnefoy moved to Paris in 1943 to continue his scientific studies, but once there he found that his interests moved more toward poetry and philosophy. He sought out what remained of the Surrealist group—André Breton in particular—and although his formal association with it was brief, he formed many important friendships with young artists and poets, including Egyptian francophone Surrealist Georges Henin. Bonnefoy married, edited a review, and studied widely different subjects, eventually taking a degree by writing a thesis on Charles Baudelaire and Søren Kierkegaard. This combined interest in poetry and philosophy has remained with him during his entire career.

Bonnefoy accepted jobs in Paris as a mathematics and science teacher, escaping the draft for "compulsory labor" during World War II because the war ended before he was called. During this time, he was reading the poetry of Paul Éluard, whose influence, according to Bonnefoy, "tempered the influences of Baudelaire and [Paul] Valéry." In politics, he was a Trotskyite, and having broken away from Breton's influence, he and friends edited a journal, *La Revolution, la nuit*. He was poor during these years and benefited from his sister's influence as a secretary at the Sorbonne in that she found him a job there, which allowed him to attend lectures and apply for research grants. These, in turn, allowed him to travel. He began to publish his poems and art criticism as well. Subsequently, he earned a living teaching at universities, both in France and in the United States, becoming a professor of comparative poetics and department chair at the Collège de France in 1981.

In 1981, at the inauguration ceremony of his being named a department chair at the Collège de France, his highly publicized lecture "La Présence et l'image" (presence and the image) became a major statement for his particular style of intermixing philosophy and literature. Throughout his working career, Bonnefoy has traveled widely, especially in pursuing his growing interest in art, art history, and the theory of culture. He is recognized as one of the most important poets of his generation. In 2001, he published a collection of early Surrealist texts, *Le Cœur-espace* (heart space), and a new collection of poetry, *The Curved Planks*. In 2005, *The Curved Planks* was included among the texts of the *baccalauréat*. He published his work on Francisco de

Goya's paintings *Goya, les peintures noires*, in 2006. Bonnefoy examines the relationship between prose and poetry in *La Longue Chaîne de l'ancre* (2008; the anchor's long chain).

Analysis

From the beginning of his poetic career, Yves Bonnefoy's work has sounded the note of a serious pursuit of the truths that language reveals. His early divergence from the later figures of the Surrealist movement in France seems to have been provoked by what he perceived as a lack of purpose in their pursuits. For Bonnefoy, poetic language, above all, is a place or a function that grants access to the truths of existence. The path to those truths may of necessity be a difficult one, but once one is on that path, there can be no turning back. Bonnefoy is a highly original and engaging writer of criticism exploring these issues, but it has always been in his poetry that he has sought to discover their ground.

Anti-Platon

The early works *Anti-Platon* (against Plato) and *On the Motion and Immobility of Douve* introduce his poetry of high seriousness and announce a break from Surrealist practice. If Bonnefoy declares early his stance, it is to restore the real dimension of experience, this object here and now, against any sort of Platonic ideal. By extension, the importance of this real object leads Bonnefoy to examine the importance of this real life, here and now, in its affective dimension. Perhaps paradoxically, the importance of life emerges fully only when one confronts the actual death of someone. The poems in the second collection take up this theme; they are also the poems that established Bonnefoy as one of the most important poets of his generation.

On the Motion and Immobility of Douve

The figure of Douve in Bonnefoy's second collection, *On the Motion and Immobility of Douve*, is based on a young girl of his acquaintance who died a sudden and tragic death. (He gives her name only in a later collection.) As the form in the poems alternates between highly organized quatrains and looser prose-poem utterances, so the investigation in the poems moves between the image of the dead young woman and death in general. As the sequence progresses, the speaker seeks to discover his own destiny based on an identification with the words of the young woman. In this work, death is present in the form of a person who is no longer there. She is troubling, however, because she poses the question of existence, of essence, of being. It is by means of this questioning that the poet discovers his own means of expression. More even than the torment of mourning, there seems to emerge the injunction to silence as the most accurate means of representing death.

There is a progression, then, in the poems of this collection as far as the identification of the poet with the figure of the dead woman by means of her speech. When she speaks in the first part of the collection, it is in the past tense, and she speaks of natural forces, wind and cold. The poet-speaker sees her, however, and as a result there is a separation, the separation of death. The only way to overcome this separation is by the identification involved in speaking. Changing to the present tense, the speaker says, "Douve je parle en toi" ("Douve, I speak in you"):

> Et si grand soit le froid qui monte de ton être,
> Si brûlant soit le gel de notre intimité,
> Douve, je parle en toi; et je t'enserre
> Dans l'acte de connaître et de nommer.

> (And though great cold rises in your being,
> However burning the frost of our intimacy
> Douve, I speak in you; and I enshroud you
> In the act of knowing and of naming.)

This is one of the strong moments of identification and the beginning of poetic creation, as Bonnefoy describes it in his essay "The Act and the Place of Poetry": "So Dante who has lost her, will *name* Beatrice." Over against the natural forces that are imaged here as present because of her death, the act of naming and of knowing restores a certain presence to the lost loved one. Even so, this is a first stage: Far from being consoling, it leads the poet to the point of anguish.

The central part of the collection, "Douve parle" (Douve speaks), begins with this identification in speaking, "ce cri sur moi vient de moi" ("this cry above me comes from me"). Paradoxically, in the series of poems bearing the title "Douve speaks," she finishes by saying: "Que le verbe s'éteigne" ("Let the verb be extinguished"). That which one must recognize in oneself as death surpasses the function of speech. The poet enters this region of contradiction when he says: "Je parle dans ton sang" ("I speak in your blood").

This progression reaches its completion in the injunction, which the figure of the woman makes to the speaker, to remain silent. The poem that begins "Mais que se taise" ("but that one be silent") requires silence above all of the one "Qui parle pour moi" ("who speaks for me"). In the following poems, she is even more direct, saying simply, "Tais-toi" ("remain silent; shut up"). The speaker finds himself in a place of radical transformations, during a time of anguish and of struggle: "Quand la lumière enfin s'est faite vent et nuit" ("When the light at last has become wind and night"). The figure of the dead woman has led the speaker to a privileged place of being, where the poet not only recognizes himself in his own expression but also is faced with his own anguish, his authentic attitude toward death.

HIER RÉGNANT DÉSERT

The collected edition of Bonnefoy's poetry *Poèmes* of 1978 added three important collections to the earlier work, *Hier régnant désert* (yesterday the desert reigning), *Words in Stone*, and *The Lure of the Threshold*. These collections continue to explore the areas mapped out by Bonnefoy's earlier work. The tone is serious and the subject matter highly philosophical. Death is a constant presence and is confronted continually for what it tells about existence. In *Hier régnant désert*, Bonnefoy returns again to the Douve figure, although here, at least in one poem, she is named—Kathleen Ferrier. The same contradictions between a conflicted natural universe and a tragic sense of human destiny are confronted again in the elemental terms: face, voice. Whereas to see an image of the dead young woman leads to separation, an identification with her voice allows the poet to discover his own utterance. As he says in "À la voix de Kathleen Ferrier" ("to the voice of Kathleen Ferrier"):

> Je célèbre la voix mêlée de couleur grise
> Qui hésite aux lointains du chant qui s'est perdu
> Comme si au delà de toute forme pure
> Tremblât un autre chant et le seul absolu.

> (I celebrate the voice mixed with grey color
> Which hesitates in the sung distances of what is lost
> As if beyond every pure form
> Trembled another song and the only absolute.)

This poem is more insistently philosophical than any examined hereto. The voice that is celebrated seems to have lost all contact with the merely human as it moves toward the realms of pure being.

WORDS IN STONE

Even the poems ostensibly concerned with inanimate objects bear their burden of existence, as does this short poem from *Words in Stone*, "Une Pierre" (a stone):

> Il désirait, sans connaître,
> Il a péri, sans avoir.
> Arbres, fumées,
> Toutes lignes de vent et de déception
> Furent son gîte.
> Infiniment
> Il n'a étreint que sa mort.
>
> (It desired, without knowing
> It perished, without having.
> Trees, smoke,
> All lines of wind and of deception
> Were its shelter
> Infinitely
> It only grasped its death.)

This deceptively simple poem about a stone carries a weight of thought and image balanced off in a skillful suspension. It may or may not carry direct reference to Jean-Paul Sartre's existential philosophy, which affirmed the stone's interiority and self-identity over time while denying these same inherent qualities to the human subject. Bonnefoy's turn on the idea here is to introject the tragic sense into the simple being of the stone. Bereft of the human qualities of knowing or having, it was at one with nature and alone to face death.

POÈMES

Bonnefoy's later poems in *Poèmes* trace a dialectic between the tragic sense of human destiny, as presented in Douve's words, and the introjected tragedy of nature examined in the poem from *Words in Stone*. The difference in the later works is in their form. From the short, often highly formal, verse of his early career, Bonnefoy here moves to a more expanded utterance. Though the poems are longer, however, there is a greater degree of fragmentation. It is as though the silence that was so important thematically in the speech of Douve has been refigured in the form of the poem itself. From the highly wrought, lapidary form of the early work has emerged a laconic style, hinting at what the speaker cannot say.

Into the atmosphere of charged philosophical speculation—in effect, a dialogue between being and nonbeing—Bonnefoy brings a new element of disjunction and, ultimately, of mystery, as in these lines from "Deux Barques" (two boats): "Étoiles, répandues./ Le ciel, un lit défait, une naissance." ("Stars, spread out./ The sky, an unmade bed, a birth.") The traditional analysis of metaphor in terms of "tenor" and "vehicle" becomes very difficult with lines such as these. How is one to decide what is the content of the statement and what is the rhetorical trapping? Here the stars could be the vehicle for an image having as its content the beginning of human life. In like manner, the heavens could be the content and the bed an image to describe the appearance of stars, with birth as an added metaphorical element. As this example makes clear, Bonnefoy's long meditations on the power of language to investigate the central issues of existence remain as intense in his later work as in his earlier poetry.

In all of Bonnefoy's work, an extremely restricted vocabulary is used to describe the conflicts between nature and human existence. Words such as "stone" and "fire," "wind" and "star," take on an elemental sense rather than being merely descriptive. These word elements are placed in the context of laconic statements, each statement offering but a hint of the overall movement in the poem. This overall movement in turn is established through the cumulative force of these elemental images placed into disjunctive and often contradictory sequences. Almost always, a mood of high seriousness is the result. The simplest language thus becomes a language of tragic dimensions. The elemental forces at work in the poem's image sequences reflect directly on the human dimension of existence. Bonnefoy places hard demands on the conceptual capabilities of his readers. He is clearly uninterested in easy sentiment or pleasing verses. His poetry presents a continual invitation to join in the struggle out of which the truths of existence emerge.

In the final poem of this collection, "L'Épars, l'indivisible" (the sparse, the indivisible), an anaphoric repetition is utilized, with the first word of most stanzas being "Oui" (yes). Under the general structuring principle of affirmation, the seemingly most opposite elements are joined. One section reads simply: "Oui, par la mort,/ Oui, par la vie sans fin" ("Yes, through death,/ Yes, through life without end"). Affirming opposites in this manner runs the risk of affirming nothing, but again the cumulative effect of the contradictions is to lead to a synthesis of values. Two sections later, the speaker states: "Oui, par même l'erreur,/ Qui va,// Oui, par le bonheur simple, la voix brisée." ("Yes, even through error,/ Which passes,// Yes, through simple happiness, the broken voice.") Bonnefoy does not seek easy resolution or unexamined pleasures. When he speaks of happiness in the same breath with a broken voice, however, the force of the image goes beyond the conceptual setting up of paradoxes. Happiness that leads to a broken voice is happiness that carries with it a strong emotion and the force of personal history. These deceptively simple images are weighted with complex and achieved emotion.

The figure of Bonnefoy the poet is closely allied to that of Bonnefoy the thinker. His researches into art, literature, and the sources of creativity in life history have always been motivated by a search for truth that can then find form and be expressed in his poetry. This is not to say that reading Bonnefoy's poetry is the equivalent of reading his essays and criticism or that the philosophical underpinnings of the works are presented in a predigested or easily digestible form. His highly imaged poems show a consistent concern for poetic image and emotion. As a result, the reality they possess is one that adds to experience. The highly wrought, imaginatively charged poems of Bonnefoy reveal the common origins of thinking and of poetry. By posing the central questions of existence, they are timeless. They are also of a pressing timeliness in that they recall the reader to being in the present.

LE CŒUR-ESPACE

Surrealism has played an important role in Bonnefoy's poetry, initially as a guide to poetical expression and subsequently as a point of departure into a poetical expression that rejects much of Surrealism. Surrealism fascinated Bonnefoy as a young poet because it proposed to dissolve the barrier between the conscious and unconscious and to make known the true reality. Surrealism, however, with its automatic writing and its lack of control of language in creation of images and its reliance on the imagined, soon began to lose its authenticity as poetical expression for him. Bonnefoy has stated that *Le Cœur-espace*, while still Surrealist in its form and content, was the poetical writing that freed him from the confines of Surrealism. While writing the text, he discovered what he refers to as a rhythm in the images that played a greater role in revealing the true than the images themselves. For Bonnefoy, language moved beyond the function of merely a tool for expressing image to become the object of his poetical questioning and expression.

Le Cœur-espace is a poetry dominated by images that in the Surrealist tradition hope to reveal that which is true, the reality beyond the reality of everyday life. Written in 1945, when Europe was in the middle of the destruction of World War II, the poetry's imagery is harsh and unsettling. It relies on fantasy and imagination. The poet is in a garden, he cries out in pain as death's branches claw his face. The gray stars of midday reign anguish on him. Appearing is a poor woman with a Gorgon head and carrying a child. Other images include pikes of wind, the earth deforming a frozen face in mirrors, and the terrible silence of the garden. These images contrast sharply with those found in Bonnefoy's later poetry.

THE CURVED PLANKS

The Curved Planks takes its name from the récit or short story "The Curved Planks" included in the collection. In this short tale, written in a repetitive, almost staccato language, Bonnefoy recounts the passage of the child to adulthood and the void that develops as the individual moves from the presence of childhood to that of adulthood. The passeur (ferryman) as the inevitable flow of time and change in a mortal's life transfers his passenger from one shore of the river to the other, from childhood to adulthood. Bonnefoy also anchors human existence in the terrestrial. The ferryman explains to the child that to be a father, one must have a house, and that he (the ferryman) is not real, but only the ferryman, the symbol or metaphor of passage.

However, while the human being cannot actually physically return to the past, the events of the past can be taken into the mind or subconscious and relived as memories or dreams. The poems of "La Pluie d'eté" ("Summer Rain") and "La Maison natale" ("The House Where I Was Born") treat past experiences of the poet as memories recalled or awakened in dreams. Images of water predominate in the poems. Just as water carries the child from childhood to adulthood in "The Curved Planks," water invades and transforms the childhood home of the poems of "The House Where I was Born." In "Summer Rain," water in the form of rain refreshes human beings: it gives brilliance and translucence to objects. Water and rain become transparent veils which alter sensory perception.

"Jeter les pierres" ("Throwing Stones"), the final group of texts of *The Curved Planks* is composed of three texts that have totally abandoned traditional poetic form for the prose form of the story or essay. However, the language of the texts is neither narrative nor explanatory in the traditional sense. It is a language of images, the language of poetry. This relationship between prose and poetry becomes one of the major areas of Bonnefoy's further research into language as means and as object.

The poems also reaffirm Bonnefoy's beliefs in the mortality of the human being, of his close ties to the earth. The poems collected under the title "Que ce monde demeure!" ("Let This World Endure!") both through their imagery and the rhythm of their verse witness the poet's joy in the terrestrial, in being and being part of the earth. Throughout the collection, the rhythm of the language plays an important role. The poetical strength of the images comes as much from their rhythm as from their portent.

LA LONGUE CHAÎNE DE L'ANCRE

La Longue chaîne de l'ancre contains a mix of genres. It addresses Bonnefoy's research and further development of his poetics after the publication of *The Curved Planks*. The major theme of the collection is the relationship between poetry and prose. He treats both the place and the act of poetry, two fields of investigation that have been of concern to him during his entire involvement with language and writing. He examines the relationship of poetry to the language of the short story and to that of theater, both of which are prose writing. Bonnefoy's language in both the "prose" writ-

ings and the poems is carried along by a rhythm that makes it fluid and enlarges the concept of the poetic such that poetry and prose subconsciously become one language.

Bonnefoy continues to employ simple images drawn from that which surrounds the human being, and this reiterates the importance of presence. He uses an image of wheel tracks in wet earth that shine slightly to define the act of writing poetry. However, for Bonnefoy, the place of poetry, of thought, of creativity remains in the subconscious. There life and thought meet. In his imagery of the anchor, its chain, and the boat to which it is attached, he attests that the boat cannot anchor in the earth for it desires and seeks another space that is the realm of dream or subconscious. The long anchor chain anchors the human spirit or consciousness in the subconscious. It is that which makes poetry, writing, painting, or any act of creativity more than merely descriptive.

OTHER MAJOR WORKS

NONFICTION: *Peintures murales de la France gothique*, 1954; *L'Improbable et autres essais*, 1959, 1980; *Rimbaud par luimême*, 1961 (*Rimbaud*, 1973); *La Seconde Simplicité*, 1961; *Miró*, 1964 (English translation, 1967); *La Poésie française et le principe d'identité*, 1967; *Un Rêve fait à Mantoue*, 1967; *Rome 1630: L'Horizon du premier baroque*, 1970; *L'Arrière-pays*, 1972; *Le Nuage rouge*, 1977; *Entretiens sur la poésie*, 1981; *La Présence et l'image*, 1983; *La Vérité de Parole*, 1988; *The Act and the Place of Poetry: Selected Essays*, 1989; *Alberto Giacometti: Biographie d'une œuvre*, 1991 (*Alberto Giacometti: A Biography of His Work*, 1991); *La Vie errante, suivi de Une autre Époque de l'écriture*, 1993; *Dessin, couleur, et lumière*, 1995; *The Lure and the Truth of Painting: Selected Essays on Art*, 1995; *Théâtre et poésie: Shakespeare et Yeats*, 1998; *Lieux et destins de l'image: Un Cours de poétique au Collège de France, 1981-1993*, 1999; *La Communauté des traducteurs*, 2000; *Le Poète et le flot mouvant des multitudes: Paris pour Nerval et pour Baudelaire*, 2003; *Shakespeare and the French Poet*, 2004; *Le Secret de la pénultième*, 2005; *Goya, les peintures noires*, 2006; *La Stratégie de l'éingme: Piero dela Francesca, la Flagellation du Christ*, 2006; *Ce qui alarma Paul Celan*, 2007; *Le Grand espace*, 2008.

TRANSLATIONS: *Une Chemise de nuit de flanelle*, 1951 (of Leonora Carrington); *1 Henri IV, Jules César, Hamlet, Le Conte d'hiver, Vénus et Adonis, Le Viol de Lucrèce*, 1957-1960 (6 volumes; of William Shakespeare); *Le Roi Lear, Roméo et Juliette, Macbeth*, 1965-1983 (5 volumes; of Shakespeare); *La Tempête*, 1997 (of Shakespeare).

EDITED TEXTS: *Dictionnaire des mythologies et des religions des sociétés traditionnelles et du monde antique*, 1981 (*Mythologies*, 1991); *Greek and Egyptian Mythologies*, 1992; *Roman and European Mythologies*, 1992; *American, African, and Old European Mythologies*, 1993; *Asian Mythologies*, 1993.

MISCELLANEOUS: *La Longue Chaîne de l'ancre*, 2008 (includes poems and short stories).

BIBLIOGRAPHY

Caws, Mary Ann. *Yves Bonnefoy*. Boston: Twayne, 1984. A book-length work in English that introduces Bonnefoy's life and works to students. Bibliography.

Greene, Robert W. *Searching for Presence: Yves Bonnefoy's Writing on Art*. Amsterdam: Rodopi, 2004. Although focused on Bonnefoy's art criticism, the text deals with the notion of presence, which is also one of the main concerns of his poetics.

Grosholz, Emily. "Song, Rain, Snow: Translating the Poetry of Yves Bonnefoy." *Hudson Review* 61, no. 4 (Winter, 2009): 625-644. Examines the process of translation, presenting translations of several of his poems as examples.

Lawler, James. "'La Neige Piétinée est la seule rose': Poetry and Truth in Yves Bonnefoy." *L'Esprit Créateur* 32, no. 2 (Summer, 1992): 43-53. Analysis of Bonnefoy's work.

Naughton, John T. *The Poetics of Yves Bonnefoy*. Chicago: University of Chicago Press, 1984. One of the few book-length studies in English devoted to Bonnefoy's poetics. Naughton's notes provide detailed information. Includes a bibliography of works by and about the poet and an index of names and titles.

Petterson, James. *Postwar Figures of "L'Ephémère": Yves Bonnefoy, Louis-René de Forêts, Jacques Dupin, André Du Bouchet*. Lewisburg, Pa.: Bucknell University Press, 2000. Discusses Bonnefoy

and other postwar poets associated with the journal *L'Ephémère* (1966-1972) and looks at poetry's ties to history, politics, and philosophy.

Peter Baker; Gordon Walters; Christina J. Moose
Updated by Shawncey Webb

BERTOLT BRECHT

Born: Augsburg, Germany; February 10, 1898
Died: East Berlin, East Germany (now Berlin, Germany); August 14, 1956

PRINCIPAL POETRY

Hauspostille, 1927, 1951 (*Manual of Piety*, 1966)
Lieder, Gedichte, Chöre, 1934 (*Songs, Poems, Choruses*, 1976)
Svendborger Gedichte, 1939 (*Svendborg Poems*, 1976)
Selected Poems, 1947
Hundert Gedichte, 1951 (*A Hundred Poems*, 1976)
Gedichte und Lieder, 1956 (*Poems and Songs*, 1976)
Gedichte, 1960-1965 (9 volumes)
Bertolt Brecht: Poems, 1913-1956, 1976 (includes *Buckower Elegies*)
Bad Time for Poetry: 152 Poems and Songs, 1995

OTHER LITERARY FORMS

A prolific writer, Bertolt Brecht (brehkt) experimented with several literary forms and subjected nearly everything he wrote to painstaking revision. He first became known as a dramatist when he won the distinguished Kleist Prize in 1922 for his plays *Baal* (pb. 1922; English translation, 1963), *Trommeln in der Nacht* (pr., pb. 1922; *Drums in the Night*, 1961), and *Im Dickicht der Städte* (pr. 1923; *In the Jungle of Cities*, 1961), and he remains perhaps best known for plays such as *Mutter Courage und ihre Kinder* (pr. 1941; *Mother Courage and Her Children*, 1941) and his groundbreaking operas *Die Dreigroschenoper* (pr. 1928; *The Threepenny Opera*, 1949) and *Aufstieg und Fall der Stadt Mahagonny* (pb. 1929; *Rise and Fall of* the City of Mahagonny, 1957). His longer prose works include the novels *Der Dreigroschenroman* (1934; *The Threepenny Novel*, 1937, 1956) and *Die Geschäfte des Herrn Julius Caesar* (1956; the affairs of Mr. Julius Caesar). Brecht also wrote about eighty short stories, as well as essays in his *Arbeitsjournal* (1938-1955, 1973; *Bertolt Brecht Journals*, 1993).

ACHIEVEMENTS

Just as he would have it, Bertolt Brecht remains a controversial figure. His literary works, his politics, and his biography spark disagreement, but one thing is clear: Brecht belongs among the great writers of the twentieth century and certainly among the great modern poets. When Brecht died, Lion Feuchtwanger praised him as the only originator of the German language in the twentieth century.

Brecht was a bit of a showman (he was immediately recognizable in Berlin with his leather jacket, his proletarian cap, and his nickel-rimmed glasses), but he was always more interested in what people thought of his work than in what they thought of him. Eric Bentley, for example, has called Brecht's *Manual of Piety* "one of the best of all books of modern poems." Brecht's initial success on the stage in 1922, the year in which he won the Kleist Prize, was echoed in 1928 with the sensational premiere of *The Threepenny Opera* in Berlin. He received a National Institute of Arts and Letters Award in 1948. Toward the end of his life, Brecht was awarded the East German National Prize (1951), the highest distinction conferred by the German Democratic Republic on one of its citizens. In 1954, he became vice president of the East German Academy of Arts. One year before his death, he traveled to Moscow to accept the Stalin Peace Prize.

Without a doubt, Brecht is best known for his concept of the epic theater and his staging and acting technique of *Verfremdung* (alienation). He sought the intellectual rather than the emotional engagement of the audience, and his propensity for didactic structure rather than sentimental discourse is evident in his poetry as well. Brecht embraced Karl Marx's thesis that "it is not a matter of interpreting the world, but of changing it." His anti-Aristotelian theater concentrated on the factual and sober depiction of human and social

conflicts, but with humorous alienation and alienating humor. To do serious theater today without acknowledging Brecht in some way is nearly impossible.

An assessment of Brecht's achievements cannot overlook his relation to literary tradition. Brecht "borrowed" freely from his predecessors, and he frequently chose the forms of parody or satire to make his readers aware of historical change and social contradictions. His candid speech did not always win favor: Because of his antiwar poem "Legende vom toten Soldaten" ("Legend of the Dead Soldier"), which was appended to his play *Drums in the Night*, Brecht was high on the Nazis' list of undesirables. It must be ranked among Brecht's accomplishments that, with his pen, he fought doggedly against the forces of evil and injustice that he saw embodied in the figure of Adolf Hitler and in the Nazi regime. The intensity and range of Brecht's voice as an essayist and dramatist have long been recognized; in contrast, because of the publication history of his poetry, it is only since Brecht's death that the power and scope of his lyric voice have begun to be appreciated.

BIOGRAPHY

Eugen Bertolt Friedrich Brecht was born into a comfortable middle-class home. His father, the manager of a paper factory, was Catholic; his mother, Protestant. Brecht was reared in the Lutheran faith. Before long, he turned strongly against religion, but the language of Martin Luther's translation of the Bible continued to influence Brecht throughout his life. A local Augsburg newspaper carried his first poems and essays in 1914, under the pen name "Berthold Eugen." Brecht dropped the mask in 1916 with the publication of his poem "Das Lied der Eisenbahntruppe von Fort Donald" ("Song of the Fort Donald Railroad Gang"), in the same local paper.

A restless and arrogant student ("I did not succeed in being of any appreciable help to my teachers"), Brecht enrolled in the University of Munich in 1917. There, he claimed to study medicine (as his father wished) and learned to play the guitar (less to his father's liking, no doubt). He completed a brief term of military service in 1918 as a medical orderly in a hospital for patients suffering from venereal disease. (It was in this year that Brecht wrote the "Legend of the Dead

Soldier.") In Munich, Brecht soon became more interested in the local cabarets than in the study of medicine. He especially enjoyed the comedian Karl Valentin, who, along with Frank Wedekind, became an important influence on Brecht's literary development. He turned increasingly to literature and began taking seminars at the university with Professor Arthur Kutscher in 1918; he wrote the first version of *Baal* between March and June of the same year. Brecht traveled to Berlin in 1920; the city impressed him, but he returned to Munich after failing to make substantial literary contacts.

Brecht was to make one more trip to Berlin before finally moving there in 1924. From then until 1933, he spent his time in the capital and cultural center of Germany. In 1926, he first became acquainted with the writings of Marx; in its profound impact on his work, Brecht's discovery of Marx could be compared to Friedrich Schiller's reading of Immanuel Kant. At the time, Brecht was working on the play "Wheat" (to be staged by Erwin Piscator), and he wanted to understand how the exchange market worked. In the short run, his effort proved futile: "From every point of view," he wrote, "the grain market remained one impenetrable jungle." The consequences of his study, however, were far-reaching. His planned drama was never completed. Instead, he began to read Marx intensely: "It was only then that my own jumbled practical experiences and impressions came clearly into focus." Brecht's conversion to the principles of communism had begun. What followed in its literary wake were the operas and several strongly didactic plays in the early 1930's. Brecht, the eminent political poet, wisely left Germany on February 28, 1933, the day after the burning of the Reichstag. Several years of exile ensued.

"Changing countries more often than shoes," as Brecht reflected once, he eventually found his way to a place near Svendborg in Denmark, after traveling through Prague, Zurich, Lugano, and Paris. In Denmark, Brecht was—for the time being, anyway—relatively settled. Still, he remained acutely sensitive toward "escape routes" (images of doors are frequent in the poetry of his exile). He traveled to Moscow and New York in 1935, to London in 1936, and to Paris in the next year. With the threat of Nazi invasion looming large, Brecht left Denmark for Sweden in 1939 and settled near Stockholm. Before long, this sanctuary, too, appeared endangered by the Nazis. Brecht fled to the United States in 1941.

Brecht's life in exile, coupled with his fascination for the exotic, drew him in particular to the Chinese poet, Bai Juyi (Po Chü-i), whose work he had come to know through the translation of Arthur Waley. In the United States, Brecht was particularly conscious of his displacement; having settled in Santa Monica near Hollywood, he never felt comfortable in the "tinsel town." His productivity slackened somewhat during his American years, though he collaborated with artists of the stature of Fritz Lang and Charles Laughton. On October 30, 1947, the day after he appeared before the House Un-American Activities Committee, Brecht flew to Paris and shortly thereafter moved to Switzerland.

Brecht's second wife, the accomplished actress Helene Weigel, was an Austrian citizen, and it is most likely for this reason that Brecht acquired Austrian citizenship as well, even though he finally settled in East Berlin in 1949. There, until his death in 1956, Brecht

Bertolt Brecht (The Granger Collection, New York)

worked with the Berlin Ensemble. Meanwhile, his Austrian citizenship allowed his work to remain accessible to all the German-speaking countries (Brecht was also shrewd about the business and politics of publication). As he wished, Brecht's death was noted with a quiet ceremony. He lies buried in an old cemetery not far from his apartment, near the graves of Georg Wilhelm Friedrich Hegel and Johann Gottlieb Fichte.

ANALYSIS

It is important to note that Bertolt Brecht's creativity as a poet resulted less from any inclination toward introspection than from his desire to communicate with others. Against the prevailing tone of German poetry in the 1920's, at least as it was represented by Rainer Maria Rilke, Hugo von Hofmannsthal, and Stefan George, Brecht's poetic voice startled and shocked his readers. "These poems [of Rilke and others] tell ordinary people nothing, sometimes comprehensibly, sometimes incomprehensibly," he wrote in his youth. One of Brecht's main objections to this style of poetry was that its sense of artistic order hid rather than disclosed the chaos he saw in modern life. For this reason, Brecht eventually came to see rhyme and rhythm as obstructive and to prefer "Rhymeless Verse with Irregular Rhythms," as the title of an essay in 1939 reads. As basic to Brecht's poems as their consideration of the reader is his notion of functionality. He first articulated this concept in 1927 when asked to judge a poetry contest that had brought more than four hundred entries. Brecht read them all and awarded no prize. Instead, he acknowledged an unsubmitted poem from a little-known writer, appreciating its simplicity, its engaging choice of topics, its melodiousness, and its documentary value. The notion that "all great poems have the value of documents" was central to Brecht's thought. Writing poetry was, for Brecht, no "mere expression," but a "social function of a wholly contradictory and alterable kind, conditioned by history and in turn conditioning it."

Brecht wrote his poems in, as he called it, "a kind of Basic German." His sensitivity for the "gestic" power of language was nurtured by his fondness for Luther's Bible (the term Brecht uses, *Gestus*, is difficult to render adequately in English: John Willet identifies it with "gesture" and "gist," attitude and point). At the root of Brecht's poetry, indeed all his work, are the notions of clarity ("The truth is concrete" was Brecht's favorite maxim from Hegel) and functionality. Form, of which Brecht was a master and not a slave, was a means toward an end, that being enlightenment. In tracing Brecht's poetic development, one can see how the forms and motifs change against the backdrop of these guiding concepts.

One attribute of the term "gestic" is that of performance. Brecht was always concerned with delivery (it is central to his theory of the epic theater), and his early poetry is characterized by its close links with song. Indeed, most of Brecht's early poems were written to be accompanied by the guitar. Verse and melody often came about simultaneously, the rhythm of the words combining with the flow of the song. It is not surprising that Brecht's early poems acknowledge such traditional forms as legends, ballads, and chronicles. He was aware that no poet who considered himself important was composing ballads at that time, and this fact, too, may have intrigued the young iconoclast. What drew Brecht to these older poetic forms was their attention to adventure, to nature, and to the role of the heroic individual. Brecht rejuvenated a tired literary tradition by turning to the works of François Villon and Rudyard Kipling. Brecht's ballads mark a decisive turning point in the history of that genre.

"SONG OF THE FORT DONALD RAILROAD GANG"

"Song of the Fort Donald Railroad Gang," written in 1916, exhibits Brecht's youthful keenness for the frontier spirit. It relates the struggle and demise of a railroad crew laying track in the wilderness of Ohio. The portrayal of nature as rugged and indifferent marks a distinct switch for Brecht from the mediocre war poems he had been writing earlier. A common denominator, however, was the element of destructive force. This poem leads, step by inevitable step, through six strophes toward the culminating catastrophe. Initially, nature tolerates the intruders, who can be seen as pilgrims of modern progress pitted against the dense forests, "forever soulless." With the onset of torrential rains, the tolerance of nature becomes indifference, but the railroad gang forges on. Striking up a song within a song, they take to singing in the night to keep themselves awake and posted of the dangers posed by the downpour and the swelling waters. For them, escape is not an option. Death simply comes, and comes simply, leaving only the echo of their melody: "The trains scream rushing over them alongside Lake Erie/ And the wind at that spot sings a stupid melody." A stupid melody? What has happened to these modern "heroes"? There are no modern heroes, Brecht answers—and this in the poetic form that traditionally extols them. Brecht debunks their melody, uses the ballad to put an end to the balladesque hero. Death and nature prevail.

"REMEMBERING MARIE A."

Death and nature, along with murder and love, are the elemental themes distinguishing Brecht's early poems. He was wont to treat these perennial subjects, though, in nontraditional ways. He does this with great effect in what is ostensibly a love poem, "Erinnerung an die Maria A." ("Remembering Marie A."), written in 1920 and later included in *Manual of Piety*. It is more lyrical than the balladesque forms Brecht had already mastered, but it does not get lost in sentimentality. Instead, Brecht achieves a parody of the melancholy youth remembering an early love, and in its attitude it is quintessential Brecht. What the speaker in the poem actually recalls is less his "love so pale and silent/ As if she were a dream that must not fade," than it is "a cloud my eyes dwelt long upon/ It was quite white and very high above us/ Then I looked up, and found that it had gone." Not even the woman's face remains present for Brecht's persona, only her kiss, and "As for the kiss, I'd long ago forgot it/ But for the cloud that floated in the sky." The idyllic atmosphere of the first strophe turns out to be nothing but cliché.

What Brecht does with the element of time in this poem is essential to its overall effect. He establishes an internal relationship on three levels: first, the love affair, located in the past; second, the passage of time, the forgetting that wastes all memory; and third, the making present, by means of the cloud, that September day long ago. The tension Brecht succeeds in creating between these different levels has ironic consequences. For one, his use of verb tenses renders as present what is actually narrated in the past tense, while the grammatical past tense functions on the level of present

time. The hierarchy of experiences is also switched: the backdrop of nature, the embodiment of everything transitory, can be remembered, while the primary experience (or what convention dictates should be the primary experience)—namely, the relationship between the lovers—falls prey to bad memory. Ultimately, it is a poem about the inconstancy of feeling and the mistrust between people that renders meaningful and lasting relationships problematic. It treats an old theme originally; where others write poems directed toward those lovers in the present, those passed away, those absent, or even those expected in the future, Brecht writes of the lover forgotten.

"OF POOR B. B."

"I, Bertolt Brecht, came out of the black forests." So begins Brecht's famous autobiographical poem, "Vom armen B. B." ("Of Poor B. B."), first written in 1922 and later revised when he was preparing *Manual of Piety* for publication. It was composed when Brecht's feet were mostly in Augsburg and Munich, but his mind was mostly in Berlin. The poem marks a turning point for Brecht. He leaves behind the ballad form and takes up the theme of the city. Nature in the raw yields to the irrepressible life of the big city, although neither locus is ever idealized. Written literally while under way (apparently on a train to Berlin), the poem is about where one feels at home, "one" in this instance being no one but Brecht himself. "In the asphalt city I'm at home," he admits, and he goes on to describe the daily routine of city dwellers, situating himself in their midst: "I put on/ A hard hat because that's what they do./ I say: they are animals with a quite peculiar smell/ And I say: does it matter? I am too." The poem is full of cynicism and despair. The poet admits that he is undependable and remains convinced that all that will remain of the cities is what passed through them—that is, the wind: "And after us there will come: nothing worth talking about." Thematically, the change of emphasis in "Of Poor B. B." prepares the way for later poems. Formally, the delivery of the poem depends less on melody (song) and relies instead on the premise of conversation between poet and reader.

"IN DARK TIMES"

Brecht's poems of the 1930's reveal a heightened awareness of the function of the poet with regard to his readership. He had made this point quite polemically already in 1927 as the judge of the poetry contest noted above. The poem, he claimed, had functional value. Looking for the functional lyric caused Brecht to seek a new style and idiom. The often-quoted poem "In finsteren Zeiten" ("In Dark Times"), written in 1937 during Brecht's exile in Denmark, attests his self-conscious task as responsible poet. Brecht imagines what people will later say about these "dark times." "They won't say: when the child skimmed a flat stone across the rapids/ But: when the great wars were being prepared for." History, in other words, will ride along on the backs of the little people—as Brecht makes clear in "Fragen eines lesenden Arbeiters" ("Questions from a Worker Who Reads")—but what remain visible are only the "great powers." In the face of this adversity, Brecht remarks with chagrin: "However, they won't say: the times were dark/ Rather: why were their poets silent?"

"BAD TIME FOR POETRY"

Brecht refused to be silent. His "Schlechte Zeit für Lyrik" ("Bad Time for Poetry"), written in 1939, is a personally revealing poem about his own internal struggle to reconcile aesthetic demands with demands of social responsibility: "In my poetry a rhyme/ Would seem to me almost insolent." Still, as Brecht wrote in his essay on poetry and logic, also from the 1930's, "we cannot get along without the concept of beauty." The poem "Bad Time for Poetry" thus concludes:

> Inside me contend
> Delight at the apple tree in blossom
> And horror at the house-painter's speeches.
> But only the second
> Drives me to my desk.

Brecht seldom mentioned Hitler by name, preferring to call him only "the house-painter," ridiculing Hitler's artistic pretentions.

"LEGEND OF THE ORIGIN OF THE BOOK TAO-TÊ-CHING ON LAO-TZÛ'S ROAD INTO EXILE"

To appreciate Brecht's aesthetic sensitivities, one must realize that he saw the felicitous poem as one in which "feeling and reason work together in total harmony." For Brecht, too, there was no distinction between learning and pleasure, and thus a didactic poem

was also cause for aesthetic pleasure. The sensual pleasure derived from knowledge is an important aspect of the title figure of Brecht's play *Leben des Galilei* (pr. 1943; *The Life of Galileo*, 1960). What to do with knowledge and wisdom was another question that, for Brecht, followed inevitably. He answered it in his poem "Legende von der Entstehung des Buches Taoteking" ("Legend of the Origin of the Book Tao-Tê-Ching on Lao-tzû's Road into Exile") written in 1938 and included in the *Svendborg Poems*.

This poem is a highly successful combination of Brecht's earlier fascination with legends, the balladesque narrative, and the aesthetics of functional poetry. It relates the journey of Laozi (Lao Tzu), "seventy and getting brittle," from his country, where "goodness had been weakening a little/ And the wickedness was gaining ground anew" (a topic of immediate interest to the exile Brecht). Brecht does not puzzle over Laozi's decision to leave; it is not even an issue. He states simply, "So he buckled his shoe." (One recalls Brecht's line that he had "changed countries more often than shoes.") Laozi needs little for the journey: books, pipe, and bread (note here the relation between knowledge and sensual pleasure). After four days, he and the boy accompanying him come across a customs official at the border: "'What valuables have you to declare here?'/ And the boy leading the ox explained: 'The old man taught'/ Nothing at all, in short." The customs official, however, is intrigued by the boy's modest assertion that the old man "'learned how quite soft water, by attrition/ Over the years will grind strong rocks away./ In other words, that hardness must lose the day.'" The official shouts to them before they are able to move on and requires them to dictate what it was the old man had to say about the water: "'I'm not at all important/ Who wins or loses interests me, though./ If you've found out, say so.'" The old man obliges him ("'Those who ask questions deserve answers'"), and he and the boy settle down for a week, the customs man providing them with food. When the dictation is finally done, "the boy handed over what they'd written./ Eighty-one sayings." This is the wisdom of Laozi, for which posterity has been grateful, but Brecht is quick to point out that "the honor should not be restricted/ To the sage whose name is clearly writ./ For a wise man's wisdom needs to be extracted./ So the customs man deserves his bit./ It was he who called for it."

Brecht's return to rhyme in this poem is consistent with its ballad form. Where rhyme no longer sufficed for what was to be said, Brecht applied his theory of rhymeless verse with irregular rhythms. He had already used this style occasionally in the 1920's but mastered it fully in the poetry of the 1930's and 1940's; the form corresponded to Brecht's perception of a society at odds with itself, and it dominated his later lyrical writings.

BUCKOWER ELEGIES

Brecht's later poetry tends to be at once more intimate and more epigrammatic than his earlier work. This late style is best illustrated in his last group of poems, the *Buckower Elegien* (*Buckower Elegies*), written in 1953. The poems are concise evidence of Brecht's fascination with the fragmentary nature of the lyric, which he viewed as an appeal to the reader. Many of the poems mimic the open form of the riddle, with a strong central image, as in "Der Radwechsel" ("Changing the Wheel"). In six brief lines, Brecht observes how a driver changes a wheel. He voices his own dissatisfaction with his course in life ("I do not like the place I have come from./ I do not like the place I am going to"). Brecht characteristically leaves this poem open toward the future: "Why with impatience do I/ Watch him changing the wheel?"

The critic Joachim Müller has written that

> In all its phases and in all its forms, Brecht's poetry is neither exclusively subjective confession, nor simply an agitator's call to arms; every confession becomes an appeal to human activity, and every appeal, however it may alienate us by its satire or its polemics, springs from the deep emotion of a rational heart that sees all conditions in the world dialectically and that always sides with what is human against every inhumanity.

OTHER MAJOR WORKS

LONG FICTION: *Der Dreigroschenroman*, 1934 (*The Threepenny Novel*, 1937, 1956); *Die Geschäfte des Herrn Julius Caesar*, 1956.

SHORT FICTION: *Geschichten vom Herrn Keuner*, 1930, 1958 (*Stories of Mr. Keuner*, 2001); *Kalendergeschichten*, 1948 (*Tales from the Calendar*, 1961);

Me-ti: Buch der Wendungen, 1965; *Prosa*, 1965 (5 volumes); *Bertolt Brecht Short Stories, 1921-1946*, 1983 (translation of *Geschichten*, volume 11 of *Gesammelte Werke*); *Collected Stories*, 1998.

PLAYS: *Baal*, pb. 1922 (English translation, 1963); *Trommeln in der Nacht*, pr., pb. 1922 (wr. 1919-1920; *Drums in the Night*, 1961); *Im Dickicht der Städte*, pr. 1923 (*In the Jungle of Cities*, 1960); *Leben Eduards des Zweiten von England*, pr., pb. 1924 (with Lion Feuchtwanger; based on Christopher Marlowe's play *Edward II*; *Edward II*, 1966); *Die Hochzeit*, pr. 1926 (wr. 1919; pb. 1953 as *Die Kleinbürgerhochzeit*; *The Wedding*, 1970); *Mann ist Mann*, pr. 1926 (*A Man's a Man*, 1961); *Die Dreigroschenoper*, pr. 1928 (libretto; based on John Gay's play *The Beggar's Opera*; *The Threepenny Opera*, 1949); *Aufstieg und Fall der Stadt Mahagonny*, pb. 1929 (libretto; *Rise and Fall of the City of Mahagonny*, 1957); *Das Badener Lehrstück vom Einverständnis*, pr. 1929 (*The Didactic Play of Baden: On Consent*, 1960); *Happy End*, pr. 1929 (libretto; lyrics with Elisabeth Hauptmann; English translation, 1972); *Der Jasager*, pr. 1930 (based on the Japanese Nō play *Taniko*; *He Who Said Yes*, 1946); *Die Massnahme*, pr. 1930 (libretto; *The Measures Taken*, 1960); *Die heilige Johanna der Schlachthöfe*, pb. 1931 (radio play; pr. 1959, staged; *St. Joan of the Stockyards*, 1956); *Der Neinsager*, pb. 1931 (*He Who Said No*, 1946); *Die Mutter*, pr., pb. 1932 (based on Maxim Gorky's novel *Mat*; *The Mother*, 1965); *Die Sieben Todsünden der Kleinbürger*, pr. 1933 (cantata; *The Seven Deadly Sins*, 1961); *Die Rundköpfe und die Spitzköpfe*, pr. 1935 (based on William Shakespeare's play *Measure for Measure*; *The Roundheads and the Peakheads*, 1937); *Die Ausnahme und die Regel*, pb. 1937 (wr. 1930; *The Exception and the Rule*, 1954); *Die Gewehre der Frau Carrar*, pr., pb. 1937 (*Señora Carrar's Rifles*, 1938); *Furcht und Elend des dritten Reiches*, pr. 1938 (in French; pr. 1945, in English; pb. 1945, in German; *The Private Life of the Master Race*, 1944); *Die Horatier und die Kuriatier*, pb. 1938 (wr. 1934; *The Horatians and the Curiatians*, 1947); *Mutter Courage und ihre Kinder*, pr. 1941 (based on Hans Jakob Christoffel von Grimmelshausen's *Der abenteuerliche Simplicissimus*; *Mother Courage and Her Children*, 1941); *Der gute Mensch von Sezuan*, pr.

1943 (wr. 1938-1940; *The Good Woman of Setzuan*, 1948); *Leben des Galilei*, pr. 1943 (first version wr. 1938-1939; second version, in English, wr. 1945-1947, pr. 1947; third version, in German, pr., pb. 1955, revised pb. 1957; *The Life of Galileo*, 1947; better known as *Galileo*); *Die Antigone des Sophokles*, pr., pb. 1948 (*Sophocles' Antigone*, 1990); *Herr Puntila und sein Knecht, Matti*, pr. 1948 (wr. 1940; *Mr. Puntila and His Hired Man, Matti*, 1976); *Der kaukasische Kreidekreis*, pr. 1948 (wr. 1944-1945, in English; pb. 1949 in German; based on Li Hsing-dao's play *The Circle of Chalk*; *The Caucasian Chalk Circle*, 1948); *Der Hofmeister*, pr. 1950 (adaptation of Jacob Lenz's *Der Hofmeister*; *The Tutor*, 1972); *Der Prozess der Jeanne d'Arc zu Rouen, 1431*, pr. 1952 (based on Anna Seghers' radio play; *The Trial of Jeanne d'Arc at Rouen, 1431*, 1972); *Don Juan*, pr. 1953 (adaptation of Molière's play; English translation, 1972); *Die Gesichte der Simone Machard*, pb. 1956 (wr. 1941-1943; with Feuchtwanger; *The Visions of Simone Machard*, 1961); *Pauken und Trompeten*, pb. 1956 (adaptation of George Farquhar's *The Recruiting Officer*; *Trumpets and Drums*, 1972); *Die Tage der Commune*, pr. 1956 (wr. 1948-1949; based on Nordahl Grieg's *Nederlaget*; *The Days of the Commune*, 1971); *Der aufhaltsame Aufstieg des Arturo Ui*, pb. 1957 (wr. 1941; *The Resistible Rise of Arturo Ui*, 1972); *Schweyk im zweiten Weltkrieg*, pr. 1957 (wr. 1941-1943, in Polish; pb. 1957 in German; based on Jaroslav Hašek's novel *Osudy dobrého vojáka Švejka za svetove války*; *Schweyk in the Second World War*, 1975); *Coriolan*, pb. 1959 (wr. 1952-1953; adaptation of William Shakespeare's play *Coriolanus*; *Coriolanus*, 1972); *Turandot: Oder, Der Kongress der Weisswäscher*, pr. 1970 (wr. 1950-1954).

SCREENPLAYS: *Kuhle Wampe*, 1932 (English translation, 1933); *Hangmen Also Die*, 1943; *Das Lied der Ströme*, 1954; *Herr Puntila und sein Knecht, Matti*, 1955.

RADIO PLAYS: *Der Ozeanflug*, pr., pb. 1929 (radio play; *The Flight of the Lindberghs*, 1930); *Das Verhör des Lukullus*, pr. 1940 (radio play; *The Trial of Lucullus*, 1943).

NONFICTION: *Der Messingkauf*, 1937-1951 (*The Messingkauf Dialogues*, 1965); *Arbeitsjournal*, 1938-1955, 1973 (3 volumes; *Bertolt Brecht Journals*, 1993); *Kleines Organon für das Theater*, 1948 (*A Little Organum for the Theater*, 1951); *Schriften zum Theater*, 1963-1964 (7 volumes); *Brecht on Theatre*, 1964; *Autobiographische Aufzeichnungen, 1920-1954*, 1975 (partial translation *Diaries, 1920-1922*, 1979); *Letters*, 1990; *Brecht on Film and Radio*, 2000.

MISCELLANEOUS: *Gesammelte Werke*, 1967 (20 volumes).

BIBLIOGRAPHY

Bartram, Graham, and Anthony Waine, eds. *Brecht in Perspective*. London: Longman, 1982. Thirteen excellent essays by highly qualified scholars. The topics range from German drama before Brecht through Brecht's manifold innovations to Brecht's legacy for German and English playwrights. Indispensable reading for understanding the broader context of his works.

Dickson, Keith A. *Towards Utopia: A Study of Brecht*. Oxford, England: Clarendon Press, 1978. Places Brecht's works in the context of literary, philosophical, social, and political history. German quotations are translated at the end of the book.

Giles, Steve, and Rodney Livingstone, eds. *Bertolt Brecht: Centenary Essays*. Atlanta: Rodopi, 1998. A collection of essays on Brecht written one hundred years after his birth. Bibliography.

Hayman, Ronald. *Brecht: A Biography*. London: Weidenfeld and Nicolson, 1983. A lengthy, dispassionately objective biography with many interesting details. Hayman skillfully integrates the facts of Brecht's private life with the discussion of his works. Opens with a chronology and a list of performances.

Martin, Carol, and Henry Bial. *Brecht Sourcebook*. New York: Routledge, 2000. Collection of protean essays in three sections: Brecht's key theories, his theories in practice, and, most successful, the adoption of his ideas internationally.

Mews, Siegfried, ed. *A Bertolt Brecht Reference Companion*. Westport, Conn.: Greenwood Press, 1997. An indispensable guide for the student of Brecht. Includes bibliographical references and an index.

Speirs, Ronald, ed. *Brecht's Poetry of Political Exile*.

New York: Cambridge University Press, 2000. A collection of essays that examine the poetry Brecht wrote while in exile from Germany during World War II.

Thomson, Peter, and Glendyr Sacks, eds. *The Cambridge Companion to Brecht*. New York: Cambridge University Press, 1994. This extensive reference work contains a wealth of information on Brecht. Part of the Cambridge Companions to Literature series. Bibliography and index.

Willett, John. *Brecht in Context: Comparative Approaches*. Rev. ed. London: Methuen, 1998. A comparative analysis of the works of Brecht. Bibliography and index.

Richard Spuler

ANDRÉ BRETON

Born: Tinchebray, France; February 19, 1896
Died: Paris, France; September 28, 1966

PRINCIPAL POETRY

Mont de piété, 1919
Clair de terre, 1923
L'Union libre, 1931 (*Free Union*, 1982)
Le Revolver à cheveux blancs, 1932
L'Air de l'eau, 1934
Fata Morgana, 1941 (English translation, 1982)
Pleine marge, 1943
Young Cherry Trees Secured Against Hares, 1946
Ode à Charles Fourier, 1947 (*Ode to Charles Fourier*, 1970)
Poèmes, 1948
Poésie et autre, 1960
Selected Poems, 1969
Poems of André Breton, 1982 (includes *Free Union* and *Fata Morgana*, among other selected poems)

OTHER LITERARY FORMS

André Breton (bruh-TOHN) published many experimental works during his career, some of which were written in collaboration with friends. *Les Champs magnétiques* (1921; *The Magnetic Fields*, 1985), the first Surrealist text to employ the technique of what came to be called automatic writing, was done with Philippe Soupault. *L'Immaculée Conception* (1930; immaculate conception), an attempt to simulate the thought processes of various types of insanity, was written with Paul Éluard. Among the basic Surrealist documents were several works by Breton alone, such as *Poisson soluble* (1924; soluble fish) and *Les Vases communicants* (1932; *Communicating Vessels*, 1990), which mixed lyrical elements with philosophical speculations cast in the form of prose, as well as the numerous polemical manifestos such as *Manifeste du surréalisme* (1924; *Manifesto of Surrealism*, 1969) and *Second Manifeste du surréalisme* (1930; *Second Manifesto of Surrealism*, 1969). Breton's numerous essays were also collected in three volumes: *Les Pas perdus* (1924; the lost steps), *Point du jour* (1934; *Break of Day*, 1999), and *Perspective cavalière* (1970). Convenient selections from Breton's prose in English translation have appeared in *Les Manifestes du surréalisme* (1955; *Manifestoes of Surrealism*, 1969), translated by Richard Seaver and Helen R. Lane, and *What Is Surrealism? Selected Writings* (1978), edited by Franklin Rosemont.

ACHIEVEMENTS

Above all, André Breton will be remembered as the founder and leader of the Surrealist movement. Of all the avant-garde movements that rocked the foundations of the arts at the beginning of the twentieth century, Surrealism has had perhaps the greatest and longest-lived impact. Surrealism, created in Paris in 1924 by Breton and a small group of friends, was the last inheritor of a long series of "isms," including Dadaism, German expressionism, French and Spanish cubism, Italian Futurism, and Anglo-American Imagism and Vorticism, which attempted to transform the conception of the world through artistic innovation. Under the leadership of Breton, Surrealism became the most mature expression of this developing sensibility, not only because of its relatively well developed underlying philosophy—which was both far-reaching and systematic in nature—but also because it eventually came to have the greatest international scope of all these movements and because it stimulated the production of a vast body of work of great diversity in all the major artistic genres—poetry, fiction, drama, philosophy, painting, sculpture, and film.

BIOGRAPHY

André Breton was born on February 19, 1896, in Tinchebray, a small inland town in the old French province of Normandy. The family soon moved, however, to the fishing port of Lorient, in Brittany, on the Atlantic coast of France. This seaside environment was particularly important later in the poet's life. When Breton first began to write in 1914, his highly imaginative lyrical poems expressed the wondrous abundance of nature and were often filled with images of sea life and other details evoking the maritime setting of his youth—which contrasted sharply with his life in Paris.

Breton was an only child, and his parents seemingly had an unusually strong influence on his personality. His father, who was a merchant, seems almost a prototype of the complacent, self-satisfied bourgeois that the Surrealists were later to attack as the epitome of the so-

cial conformity they rejected. Breton's mother, whom he described as straitlaced, puritanical, and harsh in her response to any suggestion of impropriety, must have also been responsible, to a large degree, for his later hatred of restraint and his provocative attitude toward anything he considered conventional.

Being the only child of a comfortably situated family, Breton had much attention lavished on him, and naturally, his parents had great ambitions for him. He attended school in Paris from 1907 until his graduation in 1912, entering the Sorbonne in 1913 to study medicine. This contact with medicine was also important for the later development of the poet and is reflected in Breton's diverse poetic vocabulary. Even more important, however, was the experience that resulted when Breton was sent to work at the neurological center of the hospital at Nantes during World War I instead of into combat. Breton's experiences as a medical assistant during the war—first at Nantes and later at the psychiatric center at Saint-Dizier, to which he was transferred in 1917—introduced the young, impressionable poet to the bizarre aberrations of mental illness.

During this period, Breton was exposed not only to the diverse forms of mental illness from which the soldiers suffered but also to the theories on which the practical measures used to treat them were based. Among the most important of these theories were those of Jean-Martin Charcot, Sigmund Freud, and Pierre Janet, each of which contributed an important element to the formulation of Breton's view of the operation, structure, and purpose of the human mind. From Charcot's work, Breton learned of the unlocking of the will through the use of hypnosis and saw some of the dramatic cures it was able to effect. From Freud's work, he learned about the existence of the unconscious, its role in determining mental health, and the method of dream interpretation by which one could reveal its secrets to the dreamer. From Janet's work, he learned about the existence of "psychic automatism" and the means by which it might be evoked—which eventually resulted in his own experiments with automatic writing.

These influences were reflected in three im-

André Breton (Roger Viollet/Getty Images)

portant ways in Breton's later work. First, they resulted in the two important prose experiments in automatic writing that he produced: *The Magnetic Fields*, written with Philippe Soupault, and *Poisson soluble*, which Breton created alone. The second product of his wartime experience was the novel *Nadja* (1928; English translation, 1960), which describes the encounter of an autobiographical persona with a mysterious woman who suffers a bizarre and debilitating psychosis. The third product of these influences was *L'Immaculée Conception*, a series of writings undertaken with Paul Éluard, with the purpose of simulating, in verbal form, the thought processes of various types of insanity.

Following the war, Breton came under the influence of Dadaism, which by then had moved its base of operation from Zurich to Paris. The heyday of Dada in Paris was brief, however, lasting from January of 1920 until July of 1923. In the meantime, beginning in May of 1921, Breton and some of his friends were forming a new group whose optimistic attitude toward life, experiments with new methods of literary composition, and increasingly systematic philosophical orientation was in marked contrast to Dada's attitude of nihilistic despair. Breton later called this period the intuitive phase of Surrealism, a phase that extended from May of 1921 until October of 1924, when the first *Manifesto of Surrealism* was published. The publication of this first manifesto established, in an explicit way, a new aesthetic and a profoundly optimistic, imaginative conception of the world which its author, Breton, named Surrealism. The intense period of Surrealist creative activity, which began at that time and continued unabated until the appearance of the *Second Manifesto of Surrealism* in 1930, Breton was later to call the reasoning phase of Surrealism. This period culminated in the appearance of *Communicating Vessels*, a series of lyrical philosophical discourses expressing in mature, fully developed form the central ideas of the Surrealist philosophy and aesthetic.

The period following 1930, the year of the second manifesto, was characterized by two developments. One of these was the Surrealists' increasing involvement with the Communist International movement. The second development was, in a direct sense, an outgrowth of the first, for it was also during this period that

Surrealism was disseminated on a worldwide scale and gained adherents outside Western Europe in many places where it was seen as the artistic concomitant of Marxist revolutionary philosophy. This period, which might be called, with some small injustice, the dogmatic phase of Surrealism, lasted until the outbreak of World War II. In 1941, Breton left France and lived for five years in New York. When he returned to Paris in 1946, Surrealism was effectively dead, although with those few friends of the original group who still remained, and with the growing support of countless other self-acknowledged "Surrealists" in many other countries where their dream had been carried, Breton lived on as the universally acknowledged magus of Surrealism until his death on September 28, 1966, in Paris.

ANALYSIS

André Breton's poetry forms a relatively small though important part of his total literary output, being dwarfed in quantity by his lengthy experiments in prose and his numerous polemical writings. His poetry, from the first published collection, *Mont de piété* (mount of piety), to his last major poetic work, *Ode to Charles Fourier*, shows a remarkable consistency of style. As a poet, Breton is best known for his remarkable imagery—which, at its best, expresses the powerful ability of the imagination to reconcile basic human drives and desires with the material conditions of reality and, at its worst, lapses into bizarre forms of irrationality that are incomprehensible to all but the poet himself.

In general terms, Breton's poetic imagery is characterized by comparisons that yoke together extremely disparate objects; by the sudden, sometimes violent shifting of context as the poet moves from one image to the next; and by an extremely indirect method of expressing comparisons between objects. It is these three qualities, above all, that give his poetic imagery the appearance of being spontaneous rather than deliberate. As critics have shown, however, much to Breton's credit as a poet, this initial impression is a misleading one.

Breton's imagery is reinforced by other prominent aspects of his style, one of which might be called devices of syntactic derangement. These devices range from the use of simple paradoxes involving logical and semantic contradictions, to syntactic ambiguity involving multiple or imprecise grammatical modification, to much more unsettling contradictions of reference—where the referent of a speech act is left unidentified, is deliberately misidentified, or is made ambiguous.

One other important element of Breton's style that helps support the dramatic effect of his poetic images on his readers is his diction, which is characterized by two principal traits. The first of these is the extremely wide range of his vocabulary, which frequently includes the use of words from anatomical, zoological, botanical, and technical contexts that are unfamiliar to most readers of poetry. The second important trait of his diction is the tendency to use words in specialized, atypical ways that emphasize (and often create) their figurative meanings over their denotations. These qualities have two important effects on Breton's work: The first helps make possible his imagery of violent contrasts, and the second is, to a large degree, responsible for the great difficulty his readers and translators encounter searching for paraphrasable or translatable meaning in his work.

Another element of Breton's style is his use of recurring themes and symbolic motifs, such as the revolver as a synecdochic image for rebellion or revolt of any kind. These recurring thematic and symbolic elements in Breton's work can frequently be used as contextual clues for interpreting his most difficult works.

The poetry of Breton expresses three key ideas—the liberating power of the imagination, the transformation of the material world into a utopian state, and the exploration of human potentiality through love—which recur, with increasing elaboration, throughout the course of his work and constitute the essence of his Surrealist vision.

POWER OF IMAGINATION

Breton's faith in the liberating power of the human imagination, although suggested and influenced by his contact with modern psychoanalytic thought, especially that of Freud on the operations of the unconscious, goes far beyond the notion of simply releasing the bound or "repressed" energies that is the therapeutic basis of psychoanalytic practice. For Breton, the unconscious is not an enclosed inner space, or reservoir, of trapped energy; it is, rather, the way out of the every-

day world of material reality into the realm of the surreal. According to the Surrealists, this realm—where human reason and imagination no longer struggle against each other but function in harmony—is the ultimate reality, and each person's goal in life is to seek out continually the signs of this reality, which, when directly experienced, is capable of transforming the life of the person. Although Breton envisioned the realm of the surreal as accessible to all men who seek it, it was especially important for the artist, whose goal was to capture the fleeting traces of *le merveilleux* (the marvelous) in his writing.

The Surrealists recommended a number of different methods for attaining this experience. Two, in particular, are frequently used and referred to in Breton's work: the surrendering of the person to the *hasard objectif* ("objective chance") of the universe, and the evocation of the "primary processes" of the unconscious through such procedures as automatic writing. The first of these methods is illustrated well in "Au regard des divinités" ("In the Eyes of the Gods"), one of Breton's early poems from *Clair de terre* (the light of Earth):

> Shortly before midnight near the landing-stage
> If a dishevelled woman follows you, pay no attention.
> It's the blue. You need fear nothing of the blue.
> There'll be a tall blonde vase in a tree.
> The spire of the village of melted colors
> Will be your landmark. Take it easy,
> Remember. The dark geyser that hurls fern-tips
> Towards the sky greet
> Greets you.

This poem reads like, and in fact is intended to be, a set of instructions for encountering the marvelous through the technique of objective chance.

Breton's other primary technique for evoking the marvelous—using the unfettered association of ideas in the unconscious to produce automatic writing—is illustrated by "Au beau demi-jour" ("In the Lovely Half-light"), a poem from *L'Air de l'eau* (air of the water):

> In the lovely half-light of 1934
> The air was a splendid rose the colour of red mullet
> And the forest when I made ready to enter it
> Began with a tree that had cigarette-paper leaves
> For I was waiting for you. . . .

UTOPIAN IDEAL

Breton believed not only in the power of the creative imagination to transform the life of individuals but also in the possibility of transforming society itself into a Socialist utopia, and he came to believe that the Communist International movement was a means to that end. Breton's association with the Communist Party, which began about 1930, was an increasingly divisive force among the French Surrealists. Many who were willing to accept Surrealism's aesthetic and philosophical premises did not believe that this view of life could ever transform the material world of nations and societies. Breton saw this resistance against political involvement as an indication of insufficient commitment, while those who resisted engagement countered by emphasizing the restrictive nature of the Communist Party, its repressive disciplinary practices, and its hostility to artistic activity that did not directly further the interests of the party itself. Regardless of the problems it created for him, Breton never gave up this utopian faith, as the choice of subject for his last major poetic work, *Ode to Charles Fourier*, makes clear.

TRANSFORMATIVE POWER OF LOVE

The third key idea that informs Breton's poetry is one that, like his belief in the liberating power of the imagination, was shared by many of the Surrealists: the belief that romantic love was the means by which humans might establish an enduring link between the mundane world of material reality and the limitless, eternal world of surreality. At times, the mere presence of the beloved is enough to evoke such a response, and some of Breton's most moving poetry deals with this experience. The idea is expressed in two principal forms in Breton's love poetry. The first is the belief in woman as muse: The beloved becomes the source of contact with the realm of surreality, where, Breton's friend Paul Éluard (the greatest of the Surrealist love poets) wrote, "all transformations are possible." This belief is clearly expressed in two of Breton's best poems: the famous "catalog-poem" "Free Union," which celebrates the magical connection between the poet's beloved and the unspoiled world of nature, and "Fata Morgana," which celebrates the ecstatic elation of the poet at the advent of a new love. The second form taken by this belief in the magical power of love is the equation of poetic creation itself with sexual love, as in "Sur la route de San Romano" ("On the Road to San Romano"): "Poetry is made in a bed like love/ Its rumpled sheets are the dawn of things."

It was these three ideas—together with the support of countless writers, scattered across the world, who identified themselves with the Surrealist ideal—that sustained Breton throughout a career that lasted more than fifty years. Although Breton died in 1966, the beliefs that he helped to formulate and that he expressed so brilliantly in his own poetry continue to exist.

OTHER MAJOR WORKS

LONG FICTION: *Nadja*, 1928 (English translation, 1960).

NONFICTION: *Les Champs magnétiques*, 1921 (with Philippe Soupault; *The Magnetic Fields*, 1985); *Manifeste du surréalisme*, 1924 (*Manifesto of Surrealism*, 1969); *Les Pas perdus*, 1924; *Poisson soluble*, 1924; *Légitime Défense*, 1926; *Le Surréalisme et la peinture*, 1928, 1945, 1965; *L'Immaculée Conception*, 1930 (with Paul Éluard); *Second Manifeste du surréalisme*, 1930 (*Second Manifesto of Surrealism*, 1969); *Les Vases communicants*, 1932 (*Communicating Vessels*, 1990); *Point du jour*, 1934 (*Break of Day*, 1999); *Qu'est-ce que le surréalisme?*, 1934 (*What Is Surrealism?*, 1936); *L'Amour fou*, 1937 (*Mad Love*, 1987); *Prolégomènes à un troisième manifeste du surréalisme ou non*, 1942 (*Prolegomena to a Third Surrealist Manifesto or Not*, 1969); *Arcane 17*, 1944 (*Arcanum*, 1994); *Situation du surréalisme entre les deux guerres*, 1945; *Les Manifestes du surréalisme*, 1955 (*Manifestoes of Surrealism*, 1969); *Perspective cavalière*, 1970; *What Is Surrealism? Selected Writings*, 1978.

BIBLIOGRAPHY

Aspley, Keith. *Surrealism: The Road to the Absolute*. 3d ed. Chicago: University of Chicago Press, 1986. Updated with a new introduction. A critical history of Surrealist literature.

Balakian, Anna. *André Breton: Magus of Surrealism*. New York: Oxford University Press, 1971. A biography by an expert in Surrealist art and literature.

Benedikt, Michael. *The Poetry of Surrealism: An An-

thology. Boston: Little, Brown, 1975. With introduction, critical notes, and translations.

Breton, André. *Conversations: The Autobiography of Surrealism*. Translated and with an introduction by Mark Polizzotti. New York: Paragon House, 1993. Collection of interviews with Breton.

Carrouges, Michel. *André Breton and the Basic Concepts of Surrealism*. Tuscaloosa: University of Alabama Press, 1974. Biography and an introduction to Surrealism with bibliographic references.

Caws, Mary Ann. *André Breton*. Rev. ed. New York: Twayne, 1996. Caws provides practical analysis of individual works. The French is ably translated into readable English.

Petterson, James. *Poetry Proscribed: Twentieth-Century (Re)visions of the Trials of Poetry in France*. Lewisburg, Pa.: Bucknell University Press, 2008. Examines the relationship among poetry, politics, and culture in France, with a chapter on Breton.

Polizzotti, Mark. *Revolution of the Mind: The Life of André Breton*. New York: Farrar, Straus and Giroux, 1995. A thorough biography of the artist and poet highlighting his lifelong adherence to Surrealist principles even at the expense of personal relationships. With an extensive bibliography and index.

Steven E. Colburn

BREYTEN BREYTENBACH

Born: Bonnievale, South Africa; September 16, 1939

PRINCIPAL POETRY

Die ysterkoei moet sweet, 1964
Die huis van die dowe, 1967
Kouevuur, 1969
Lotus, 1970
Oorblyfsels: Uit die pelgrim se verse na 'n tydelike, 1970
Skryt: Om 'n sinkende skip blou te verg, 1972 (*Sinking Ship Blues*, 1977)

Met ander woorde: Vrugte van die droomvan stilte, 1973
'N Seisoen in die Paradys, 1976 (poetry and prose; *A Season in Paradise*, 1980)
Voetskrif, 1976
Blomskryf, 1977
And Death as White as Words: An Anthology of the Poetry of Breyten Breytenbach, 1978 (A. J. Coetzee, editor)
In Africa Even the Flies Are Happy: Selected Poems, 1964-1977, 1978
Eklips: Die Derde bundel van die ongedanste dans, 1983
Buffalo Bill: Panem et circenses, 1984
YK, 1984
Soos die so, 1990
Nege landskappe van ons tye bemaak aan 'n beminde, 1993
Lady One: 99 Liefdesgedigte, 2000 (*Lady One: Of Love and Other Poems*, 2002)
Die toneelstuk: 'N belydenis in twee bedrywe, 2001
Ysterkoei-blues: Versamelde gedigte, 1964-1975, 2001
Windcatcher: New and Selected Poems, 1964-2006, 2007
Oorblyfsel: Op reis in gesprek met Magmoed Darwiesj = Voice Over: The Nomadic Conversation with Mahmoud Darwish, 2009

OTHER LITERARY FORMS

In addition to his poetry, Breyten Breytenbach (BRI-tuhn-bahk) has written the short stories *Katastrofes* (1964; catastrophes) and *De boom achter de maan* (1974; the tree behind the moon), the biographical *A Season in Paradise* and *The True Confessions of an Albino Terrorist* (1983), a record of his prison experiences. This last, his best-known work, describes his decision to return to South Africa with the intention of establishing a revolutionary organization. The ideas are presented indirectly: Instead of the simple diary chronology, as might be anticipated, he devises a complex literary structure. A series of interrogations and confessions, made to an impersonal, elusive, but threatening figure, Mr. Interrogator, are interrupted by "inserts," which act as a kind of chorus providing lyrical speculation and philosophic debate among the evidence of the persecution he was suffering. Breytenbach makes his most defiant challenge to the regime with subtle literary technique rather than blatant accusation.

ACHIEVEMENTS

Breyten Breytenbach's distinction occurs at two levels. The fact that he writes his poetry in Afrikaans has limited his audience outside South Africa. His immense reputation within that country derives from the same fact. He was part of the so-called Sestiger movement of the 1960's, which revolutionized Afrikaans literature. For the first time, Afrikaans was made to describe radical attitudes that horrified the Afrikaner establishment, whose puritanism and reactionary beliefs had until then controlled all literary expression. Understandably, conventional social attitudes made his work highly controversial. The old with anger, the young with excitement, saw Breytenbach as a literary iconoclast who broke the controls that had traditionally restricted both form and subject of Afrikaans poetry and who linked Afrikaner concerns with the dangerously experimental, outspoken, and often-censored writings being published in English, the language of those who had traditionally sought to extirpate the culture of the Afrikaner "volk."

All of his work has provoked bitter attack and equally violent counterattack. For every critic who denounced the blasphemy and radicalism of his work, others praised his originality that liberated the Afrikaans language from a narrow and bigoted orthodoxy. Internationally, his poetry is known in translation, but he is far more renowned as a political figure, as a fighter against apartheid. His prison memoirs, *The True Confessions of an Albino Terrorist*, have been accepted as an important addition to the literary condemnations of the Pretoria regime.

His literary honors are many. He was awarded the APB Literary Prize for *Die ysterkoei moet sweet*, and the Afrikaans Press Corps Prize for *Die ysterkoei moet sweet* and *Katastrofes*, both in 1964. He won the South African Central News Agency prizes in 1967 for *Die huis van die dowe*, in 1969 for *Kouevuur*, and in 1970 for *Lotus*. He received the Lucie B. and C. W. Van der Hoogt prize from the Society of Netherlands Literature

(1972) for *Sinking Ship Blues*, the Reina Prinsen-Geerling Prize (1972) for *Die huise van die dowe*, a prize from the Perskor newspaper group (1976) for *Voetskrif*, the Pris des Sept (1977), the Hertzog Prize from South African Academy of Science and Arts (1984, 1999, 2008), the Rapport Prize for Literature from the Afrikaans newspaper *Rapport* (1986) for *YK*, the Jacobus van Looy Prize (1995), the Alan Paton Award for literature (1996), and the Max Jacob Prize (2009) for the French version of *Voice Over*.

BIOGRAPHY

Breyten Breytenbach was born in a conservative small town, Bonnievale, on the western side of Cape Town to a distinguished Afrikaner family. He entered the then-unsegregated Cape Town University to study painting. The opportunity, for him, was revolutionary. For the first time, Breytenbach met Africans as equals, mixed with left-wing student groups, and delighted in his intellectual freedom and his escape from the narrowness and racism of his upbringing. He became a member of the radical African National Congress. In 1960, at the age of twenty-one, he left South Africa. In

Breyten Breytenbach (©Jerry Bauer)

1962, he settled in Paris, completing his liberation, or revolt, from his family and race.

In 1962, he married Yolande Ngo Thi Hoang Lien, a French woman of Vietnamese descent, which was forbidden by South African law. He had no choice but to remain in Paris, where he worked as an artist. He was prevented from returning with his wife even to accept the national prizes that were being awarded his work. A brief visit was arranged in 1972, during which his wife stayed across the border in independent and unsegregated Swaziland. This discrimination and rejection fostered his resentment. In 1975, he decided on active involvement and made plans almost as bizarre in practice as they were optimistic in intention. He returned to South Africa on a forged French passport to set up a revolutionary organization for whites called Okhela, which would use sabotage and guerrilla action to overthrow the government.

There is still some confusion about Breytenbach's true motives and expectations. Given his wide fame, his attempt at disguise was ludicrous. He was arrested and charged under the Terrorism Act. His unexpected apologies to the court allowed him to escape a potential death penalty, but he was sentenced to nine years' imprisonment for terrorism. Frequent international appeals effected his release in 1982, and he returned to Paris, where he continued his writing and involvement with movements opposed to apartheid. In 1990, apartheid began to be dismantled.

Breytenbach spent the 1990's writing a number of fiction and nonfiction titles, many of which explore the politics of the postapartheid era of South Africa, as well as two memoirs. Breytenbach's work as a painter increased, with a number of one-man exhibitions held at the South African Association of Arts in Cape Town and at the UNISA Art Gallery in Pretoria, and in France, the Netherlands, Sweden, and Germany. He also cofounded the Gorée Foundation on the Gorée Islands off the coast of Senegal, which helps promote democratic unity on the African continent. In 2000, he was appointed a visiting professor in the University of Cape Town's School of Humanities, an appointment that lasted for three years. He also dedicated part of his time to his continuing work with the University of New York, serving in the Graduate School of Creative Writing. In the winter of his life, Breytenbach became a wanderer, dividing his time between France, Spain, Senegal, and New York City.

ANALYSIS

The poetry of Breyten Breytenbach is both highly personal and highly public. This paradox is explained by his intense emotional involvement with the society in which he was born, a society that was condemned universally for its racism and bigotry. His sensitivity to this relationship readily leads self-expression into public posture. He was constantly antagonistic to apartheid, yet he realized that he was inevitably a part of it. The consequent dilemma may begin to explain the moods of near suicidal despair and depression that are found in his more intimate poems. Brought up among cosmic cruelties, it must have seemed to him that the opportunity for any individual to find separate solace was as delusive as it was reprehensible. That admission contains within it one of the reasons for the constant emotional tension encountered in his revealing verse.

Another way in which Breytenbach's work may be considered personal is the close link it has with his actual experience. The sequence of his poems follows the events that were occurring in his life as an exile and a political prisoner. By exploring and confronting the anxieties he faced as a human being, he indicates that his responses are based on political conviction but have a deeper psychological origin than radical activism. Breytenbach defies and rejects apartheid in his writing through introspective self-analysis, rather than through a more open and formal stand. There is an almost neurotic emotion that commands the efflorescence of extraordinarily violent language and metaphor, but it affects only the poetic surface. By implication, as much as by direct statement, there clearly remains an underlying political stance in Breytenbach's poetry. Breytenbach denounces the South African regime with an anger that derives some of its intensity from his own sense of personal affront as well as his predetermined and principled political beliefs. The man is the poet and the poet is a political activist. The paradox provokes a revealing duality of aims between poet as artist and poet as spokesperson. This divergence has preoccupied both writers and critics in the twentieth century and beyond. The essential elements of the controversy have never been convincingly resolved. What is the proper role of a poet who exists under an oppressive regime? Does the urge toward declamatory affirmation make poetry mere propaganda? Jean-Paul Sartre's famous essay "What Is Literature?" explores this issue with typical acuity. Does moral and political commitment minimize the expression of the more universal human truths which many believe constitute the ultimate reason for poetry? Breytenbach's work both explores and exemplifies this dilemma. These are the issues that must be considered as one examines the volumes of poetry that have come from his pen. Across his career, these ideas have confirmed his development as a writer and signaled his commitent to revolution.

DIE YSTERKOEI MOET SWEET

Breytenbach's earliest poetry, collected in *Die ysterkoei moet sweet* (the iron cow must sweat), gives immediate early evidence of his capacity for a striking vigor of imagery. His language is extravagant and unexpected. Expressions such as "blood like peaches in syrup," "people are biting at each other's gullets," and "spiky Jesus stands out on a cross," from a single poem, exhibit his evocative originality. At the center of his use of language is a vividly confident assurance remarkable in so youthful a poet. His effusive self-confidence is particularly apparent in comparison to the formality and polished moderation of the poets of the Afrikaner establishment. In spite of this verbal virility, the mood that Breytenbach's brilliant language expresses is curiously negative. There are hints of suicide. "I am not yet ready/ for I must still learn how to die." He emphasizes death often enough to suggest that some psychological imbalance, almost a neurosis, exists within the poet even in his earlier years. There is fear, also, as if he realized the conclusions of his combative attitudes. "But keep Pain far from Me o Lord/ That others may bear it/ Be taken away into custody,/ Shattered/ Stoned/ Suspended/ Lashed. . . ."

All is not gloom, however; there is also a gentle deprecatory irony: "Ladies and gentlemen allow me to introduce you to Breyten Breytenbach," begins one poem, which concludes with a comment so infinitely more poignant, given our knowledge of his future:

"Look he is harmless, have mercy upon him." Perhaps he was not. Certainly, no one did.

The later poems in this volume are written from Paris after his departure from South Africa, occasioned partly by political constraints, but more by his desire to explore the cosmopolitan world beyond the margins of Cape Town. Quickly there is an awareness of disillusion, albeit he proclaimed his satisfaction. "I can't complain," and "I'm happy here." Away from his country, freed from its constant social tensions that rapidly became his own, he has a new freedom of choice. It is precisely that luxury, however, that requires him to determine what he will do with such a dramatic opportunity. For a South African, the relief of exile is always attended by some guilt. The decision can be interpreted as cowardly escape or as bold defiance. In this new context of liberation, Breytenbach must ask himself those unanswerable questions: "What were your grand resolutions?/ or is your existence only a matter of compromise?/ what are you looking for here/ without the excuse of being young . . . and what are you planning to do?" South Africa refuses to be wished away. The recognition of distance more acutely induces memory. In contrast to Paris, "somewhere the aloes are shining/ somewhere some are smelling fresh guavas." (Aloes are the floral symbol of South Africa.) The mood is sad and fretful. Escape does not constitute solution "because other worlds and other possibilities exist you know."

Only in some of the later poems dedicated to his new wife does any happier note appear: "I press my nose in the bouquet of your neck/ how ripe how intoxicating its fragrance the smell of life/ you live." Even so intense an intimacy is laced with an insistent bitterness of spirit. "You are a butterfly of trembling light/ and inside you already your carcase is nibbling."

DIE HUIS VAN DIE DOWE

Similarly, the second collection, *Die huis van die dowe* (the house of the deaf), though intended to celebrate love, expresses Breytenbach's persistent self-doubt: "Pain bruises us all to a more intimate shade—/ . . . which can never heal, the dreams." The bitterness of the words suggests that the freedom that Breytenbach so eagerly sought by departure has proved geographic rather than spiritual. "No restful eye/ and no rest or surrender or cellars or the cool of sleep." His agitation is both personal and professional. There are insistent expressions of concern about his poetry; inspiration seems to be weakening without the violent indignation that the daily experience of South Africa provided. He realizes that there has begun to be a separation between his life and his work. He observes that "My fire has slaked/ I must stand to one side." More vulgarly, "My arsehole is full of myself," a crudely worded but significant condemnation since, unlike more circumspect poets, he deplores an introspective style. The intention to escape from the constrictions of self was to determine his decision to play a public role as an activist, rather than as a poet-spokesperson.

SENSE OF ISOLATION

Breytenbach soon began to achieve some international recognition, but this publicity did not fulfill him, since it seemed totally remote from his indigenous commitment to South Africa. Success only increased his sense of painful isolation. "I'm a globe-trotter . . . as thirsty as ever" and "from a lot of travelling/ the heart grows mute and waterlogged." No political condemnation of his country will drive away his exile's longing. Of his own city, Cape Town, he writes, "that's how I love you/ as I have dreamed of you . . ./ my cape, godcape, lovecape, capeheart . . . Fairest cape in all the world."

His urge toward verse remains strong, though its effect seems constantly tainted even while he uses it to sustain his personal and ardent life. "Give me a pen/ so that I can sing/ that life is not in vain." Perhaps he presents his own reflection in a poem he dedicated to Yousef Omar, and recognizes the same emotions and the same fate: "His heart is a clot of fear/ the man is not a hero/ he knows he'll have to hang/ for he is stupid/ and wanted to believe." One might hope that Breytenbach's disillusionment is not so comprehensive, but his doubts persist in his private life. He yearns for love: "Give me a love/ like the love I want to give to you," while suggesting that desire is equivocal.

KOUEVUUR

Breytenbach explores his anxieties further in his *Kouevuur* (coldfire-gangrene). Some of these poems show the beginnings of disintegration in both form and statement. Burning with an inner bitterness, he finds himself giving others the advice he should have taken to his own heart: "Above all watch out for the slimy black paw paw/ of bitterness, black child—/ he that eats of it dies on bayonets." He might well have deliberated on this truth. In this collection, passionate lyric poems are matched by violent expressions of self-condemnation. His political work distracts him from poetry, and yet at the same time, its obligations tease him with the more shocking thought that writing may no longer be considered an adequate response to South African circumstances. He is increasingly aware of how separated he has become from his country. "You ask me how it is living in exile, my friend/ What can I say?/ that I'm too young for bitter protest/ and too old for wisdom and acceptance/ of my destiny."

Acceptance of destiny was gradually invading Breytenbach's thoughts, but his unexpected reversal of the anticipated attitudes of youth and age display the convolutions of his present moods. Return was legally forbidden with a "non-European" wife, and therefore his marriage required that he express his gradual recognition of the permanence of exile (which he somewhat casually chose as a young man) and its painful results: "Yes, but that I now also know the rooms of loneliness/ the desecration of dreams, the remains of memories." The "if" in the following line indicates both admission and anxiety: "I've been thinking if I ever come back." He realizes that there are the outward changes, that he will appear, "wearing a top hat/ a smart suit . . . new Italian shoes for the occasion," garb that defines his new European citizenship. He can only hope that "ma knows it's me all the same." He can still write lyrically of his love, of the happiness that it has brought. "I love you/ you lead me through gardens/ through all the mansions of the sun . . ./ love is sweeter than figs." Or even more tenderly, "sleep my little love/ sleep well sleep dark/ wet as sugar in coffee/ be happy in your dreams." Love is a pleasure that provides no resolution of his confusion. Old age is seen not as a conclusion but as a period of harmony and calm. It provides comfort in allowing escape from the obligations of action that he and others had imposed, and permits abdication from oppressive responsibility: "That's the answer, to be an old man, a naked/ treedweller, too old to climb down."

LOTUS

The *Lotus* collection is specifically addressed to his wife. There are lines of unusual exhilaration and intensity. "For my love travels along with you/ my love must stay with you like an angel." However, such elevated emotions are not entirely convincing. More typical is the ambivalent self-flagellation of the following lines: "I'm in love with my loneliness/ because I'm alone/ . . . Two things I have to say:/ I'm alone, but I love you."

OORBLYFSELS

In *Oorblyfsels: Uit die pelgrim se verse na 'n tydelike*, Breytenbach's increasing emotional disgust spills over. His psychological dismay urges him toward greater political assertiveness. He describes himself with shame as "I, a white African featherless fowl." He turns upon his entire race, equating whiteness with evil, blaming whites for his own cursed Afrikaner inheritance: "whitedom." "The white man knows only the sun/ knows nothing of black or man." This judgment exacerbates his ferocious inner conflicts. It requires that he accept connection with the atrocity he perceives and condemns, but from which he cannot free himself. No matter his protestations of racial neutrality, he is one of them. His admission of this is more angry than sad, "I am German/ I am cruel/ I am white, I steal." It becomes an inverse communion with his soul. It is a kind of litany of social condemnation in which, in color terms, he must include himself.

SINKING SHIP BLUES

By the time the even more belligerent *Sinking Ship Blues* was written, the political accusations are more apparent than the introspective anxieties that provide their source. It is South Africa that Breytenbach has in mind when he describes, from a different coast, how "the ocean washes like blood against the land/ I stand on my knees where the hearts are laid down/ sand in my throat like grievances that cannot be stomached." His inspection is factual; his response has become pathological. He contemplates with increased awareness what Africa has suffered, comprehending that in his own country "to live black is a political crime." He also contemplates how Africa might survive: "Africa so often pillaged, purified, burnt!/ Africa stands in the sign of fire and flame." His hatred for his country intensifies. He excoriates it mercilessly as "this is hell with

God." He roundly condemns its people, seeing them as villains "lugging an attache case with shares and gold in one hand/ and a sjambok [whip] in the other." It would be far simpler if such denegration could remain purely political, but inevitably he incorporates the same scathing attitudes into his more intimate analyses. The fact that the regime survives increases his sense of incompetence and inadequacy. Gloomily he reports on his present state: "You grow less agile, more compliant/ . . . yet death walks in your body . . . and by the time you want to smash the day with your fist/ and say: look my people are rising up! . . . you've forgotten the silences of the language." He expresses his failure as a poet, a lover, and as a revolutionary: "I fold the dead of that/ which we/ called love/ in chalk dark words/ bury it here/ within this paper/ that a God should fill the gaps." It is clear that only some defiant and unequivocal action will satisfy his needs, but that action would not cure his heart's malaise.

MET ANDER WOORDE

Ironically, South Africa's liberation would not affect Breytenbach's own. It is this despairing admission that permeates the 1973 collection *Met ander woorde* (in other words). Poetry can provide no adequate means of resolving the racial and social impasse of South Africa. In this book, he more openly announces his intention for more explicit assaults on the system. "Now that death/ begins to seek out the eyes/ a single burning purpose remains/ to grow stronger towards the end/ you feel you are bound to yourself/ by an underground movement." However, is he, the poet-artist, the person capable of carrying out such deliberate service? Can an intellectual become a functioning revolutionary? In a self-deprecatory way, Breytenbach offers himself some disguised advice in a wry and comic metaphor: "When the canopy of sky tears/ then all the stars fall out:/ you know you can't let a drunk man work on the roof."

In spite of this warning, his determination to transmute his art and philosophy into action drove him to the deeds that resulted in arrest, trial, and conviction. His incarceration did not free his spirit from his recognition of racial guilt. The fact that he had so demonstrably and publicly suffered in the cause of revolution did not purge him of his association from Afrikaner history.

Given what he was, or more accurately, what he thought himself to be, there were no acts he could perform that would satisfy him nor assuage his inner despair. Even Afrikaans, the language that he had done so much to vivify, seems to be the vehicle in which the oppression is expressed: "We ourselves are aged./ Our language is a grey reservist a hundred years old and more." The Afrikaans language defines the racist system, "For we are Christ's executioners./ . . . We bring you the grammar of violence/ and the syntax of destruction."

A few poems survived his incarceration, though many were lost and stolen. Some are personal, for the painful imposition of extended solitary confinement necessitated an introspection that opened up vistas of self-awareness impossible during the cosmopolitan distractions of his Paris exile. Part of this discovery is expressed in purely physical terms. "I feel the apples of decay in my chest/ and in my wrists the jolt of trains./ Now—after how many months of solitary confinement?"

THE TRUE CONFESSIONS OF AN ALBINO TERRORIST

At the conclusion of *The True Confessions of an Albino Terrorist* are thirteen poems that record his last days in jail and his liberation. He tries to write but thinks little of his efforts: "A man has made himself a poem/ for his birthday the sixteenth of the ninth—/ o, no not a fancy affair with room and rhyme/ and rhythm and iambs and stuff. . . ." He can rejoice in the memories that fill the long hours of his confinement. They are sometimes recalled with irony: "Do you remember when we were dogs/ you and I?" Other moments are recollected more poignantly, "He will remember—/ mornings before daybreak." Memory is reinforced by the arrival of a letter, "word from outside." He tells, "I fled to your letter, to read/ that the small orange tree is a mass of white blossoms." This ordinary world becomes richer and more exotic when set against the one he inhabits where, "in the middle of the night/ the voice of those/ to be hanged within days/ rise up already sounding thin."

Finally, there is the bliss of release. "I arrive on this first day already glistening bright/ among angel choirs." Then the return to the haven of Paris, where he writes one of the few expressions of unalloyed delight

to be found in his poetry: "Listen to that same wind calling/ through the old old Paris streets/ you're the one I love and I'm feeling so good." The final couplet has a fine ring, so positive in contrast to his earlier anxieties. He still speaks of death, but his attitude is now devil-may-care: "Burn, burn with me love—to hell with decay to live is to live, and while alive to die anyway."

WINDCATCHER

Windcatcher, which won the 2008 Hertzog Prize, is essentially a capstone collection of Breytenbach's poems. The works draw from his time in France, his imprisonment in South Africa, and his life as an exile who wanders the globe. In his usual extravagant language, Breytenbach writes about living in Dar-es-Salaam, Amsterdam, Paris, and Vancouver as well as the United States. The poems, particularly the later ones, serve as defense of the value of this art form. In "New York, September 12, 2001," he wonders if poetry has enough power to help him rise above the horror of the terrorist attacks on the World Trade Center on September 11. The poem represents Breytenbach's belief that poetry in barbaric times can be classified into literal effect and into larger consciousness.

The wide span of time covered by the works makes it easy to see Breytenbach's progression as a poet. The earlier works reflect rage at the injustices of the world, while the later ones reflect a sad recognition that such horrors will persist. In "Isla Negra," written in the early 1970's, Breytenbach writes of the assassination of Chile's Salvador Allende, "the rise and fall of a thousand years/ shall not wipe out the footsteps of those killed here." By 2000, Breytenbach no longer possesses such optimism. He writes of the dreamer who sobs in his sleep.

The later poems do not focus as much on politics but instead explore the intimacy of everyday. In "Self-Portrait," Breytenbach briefly notes that "Nelson Mandela does not count me/ among his close hangers-on." He stresses his ordinariness and his sexuality as well as his acceptance of the passage of time. He writes about growing old, about forgetting, and about "dark remembrances." In "Pre-Word," he declares that "the world is no longer about/ the long dance of life with wife." Death is coming closer to Breytenbach and it is not a visitor that he fears.

OTHER MAJOR WORKS

LONG FICTION: *Mouroir: Bespieëlende notas van 'n roman*, 1983 (*Mouroir: Mirrornotes of a Novel*, 1984); *Memory of Snow and Dust*, 1989.

SHORT FICTION: *Katastrofes*, 1964; *Om te vlieg 'n opstel in vyf ledemate en 'n ode*, 1971; *De boom achter de maan*, 1974; *Die miernes swel op*, 1980; *All One Horse: Fiction and Images*, 2008.

NONFICTION: *The True Confessions of an Albino Terrorist*, 1983; *End Papers: Essays, Letters, Articles of Faith, Workbook Notes*, 1986; *Boek: Dryfpunt*, 1987; *Terugkeer naar het paradijs: Een afrikaans dagboek*, 1993 (*Return to Paradise*, 1993); *The Memory of Birds in Times of Revolution*, 1996; *Dog Heart: A Memoir*, 1999; *Intimate Stranger: A Writing Book*, 2009.

MISCELLANEOUS: *Judas Eye and Self-Portrait/Deathwatch*, 1988.

BIBLIOGRAPHY

Breytenbach, Breyten. *Dog Heart: A Memoir*. New York: Harcourt Brace, 1999. A violent yet eloquent memoir of the African National Congress activist and author that explores the fusion of violence and gentleness, turbulence and dignity.

Brink, André. Introduction to *A Season in Paradise*, by Breyten Breytenbach. Translated by Rike Vaughn. New York: Persea Books, 1980. Provides a useful overview of Breytenbach's early development.

Cope, Jack. *The Adversary Within: Dissident Writers in Afrikaans*. Atlantic Highlands, N.J.: Humanities Press, 1982. A historical and critical analysis of Afrikaans literature in the twentieth century, written during apartheid.

Coullie, Judith Lutge, and J. U. Jacobs, eds. *A.K.A. Breyten Breytenbach: Critical Approaches to His Writings and Paintings*. New York: Rodopi, 2004. Explores the links between Breytenbach's embrace of Zen Buddhism and his writings, the relationship between his poetry and paintings, and unexamined heterosexism in his works.

Golz, Hans-Georg. *Staring at Variations: The Concept of "Self" in Breyten Breytenbach's "Mouroir: Mirrornotes of a Novel."* New York: P. Lang, 1995. Analyzes *Mouroir* at length.

Lewis, Simon. "Tradurre e Tradire: The Treason and Translation of Breyten Breytenbach." *Poetics Today* 22, no. 2 (June, 2001): 435-452. Argues that Breytenbach's use of the English language to write his prison memoir, *The True Confessions of an Albino Terrorist*, represented a kind of linguistic treason consistent with his treason against the apartheid state.

Mateer, John. "Breyten Breytenbach: The Wise Fool and Ars Poetica." *Westerly* 26 (Winter, 2001): 84-99. Discusses the imagery of violence and use of language in Breytenbach's poetry.

Sanders, Mark. *Complicities: The Intellectual and Apartheid*. Durham, N.C.: Duke University Press, 2002. A literary and historical exploration of the role of intellectuals, including Breytenbach, in South African apartheid and argues that to some degree, ideological complicity on the part of intellectuals is unavoidable. Also looks at Jacques Derrida, Jean-Paul Sartre, and Frantz Fanon in analyzing political writings.

Schalkwyk, David. "Confession and Solidarity in the Prison Writing of Breyten Breytenbach and Jeremy Cronin." *Research in African Literatures* 25, no. 1 (Spring, 1994). A discussion of *The True Confessions of an Albino Terrorist*.

Weschler, Lawrence. *Calamities of Exile: Three Nonfiction Novellas*. Chicago: University of Chicago Press, 1998. Includes a brief biography of Breytenbach.

John Povey
Updated by Caryn E. Neumann

C

PEDRO CALDERÓN DE LA BARCA

Born: Madrid, Spain; January 17, 1600
Died: Madrid, Spain; May 25, 1681

PRINCIPAL POETRY

Psalle et sile, 1741
Poesías, 1845
Obra lírica, 1943
Sus mejores poesías, 1954
*Poesías líricas en las obras dramáticas de
    Calderón*, 1964
Los sonetos de Calderón en sus obras dramáticas,
    1974

OTHER LITERARY FORMS

Pedro Calderón de la Barca (kol-day-ROHN day lo-BOR-ko) is known primarily as a verse dramatist, an occupation to which he was dedicated during his entire life. He wrote more than one hundred plays, most of which were published during his life or soon after his death. Some of the better known include *Amor, honor, y poder* (1623; love, honor, and power); *El sitio de Breda* (pr. 1625; the siege of Breda); *El príncipe constante* (pr. 1629; *The Constant Prince*, 1853); *La dama duende* (pr., pb. 1936; *The Phantom Lady*, 1664); *Casa con dos puertas, mala es de guardar* (pr., pb. 1936; *A House with Two Doors Is Difficult to Guard*, 1737); *La devoción de la cruz* (pb. 1634; *Devotion to the Cross*, 1832); *Los cabellos de Absalón* (pb. 1684; *The Crown of Absalom*, 1993); *La vida es sueño* (pr. 1635; *Life Is a Dream*, 1830); *El mayor encanto, amor* (pr. 1635; *Love, the Greatest Enchantment*, 1870); *A secreto agravio, secreta venganza* (pb. 1637; *Secret Vengeance for Secret Insult*, 1961); *El mágico prodigioso* (pr. 1637; *The Wonder-Working Magician*, 1959); *El alcalde de Zalamea* (pr. 1643; *The Mayor of Zalamea*, 1885); *El médico de su honra* (pb. 1637; *The Surgeon of His Honor*, 1853); *El pintor de su deshonra* (pb. 1650; *The Painter of His Dishonor*, 1853); *La hija del aire, Parte I* (pr. 1653; *The Daughter of the Air, Part I* 1831); and *La hija del aire, Parte II* (pr. 1653; *The Daughter of the Air, Part II*, 1831).

ACHIEVEMENTS

Pedro Calderón de la Barca lived during Spain's Golden Age, his death marking the end of that most productive period of Spanish letters. He was known as a poet and dramatist in his teens, and in his early twenties, he took several poems to the poetic jousts held in 1620 and 1622 to commemorate the beatification and canonization of Saint Isidro. He was awarded a prize in the second contest, and Lope de Vega Carpio, who was the organizer of the two events, praised the young poet highly on both occasions. Indeed, throughout his life, Calderón continued to write lyric poetry, the great bulk of which, however, is incorporated into his plays. His first dated play, *Amor, honor, y poder* is from 1623, and subsequently he established himself so well in the theatrical scene that, when Lope de Vega died in 1635, Calderón became the official court dramatist, a position he held until his death. Calderón proved a worthy successor of Lope de Vega, for he wrote more than two hundred dramatic pieces, a total second only to that of Lope de Vega. Calderón produced several masterpieces, including *Life Is a Dream*, one of the great works of Spain's Golden Age. In addition, he was the supreme master of the *auto*, or Eucharist play, a dramatic form which he refined and improved progressively and to which he was dedicated almost exclusively during the last years of his life.

BIOGRAPHY

Pedro Calderón de la Barca was born in Madrid into a family of some nobility. His father, Diego Calderón de la Barca, came from the valley of Carriedo, in the mountains of Santander, and was a secretary to the treasury board under Philip II and Philip III. Calderón's mother, Ana María de Henao, was from a noble family of the Low Countries that had moved to Spain long before. Calderón was their third child.

Soon after Calderón was born, his family moved to Valladolid, following the transfer of the court, and there the boy learned his first letters. When the court returned permanently to Madrid, and with it his family, Calderón, then nine years old, was placed in the Colegio Imperial of the Jesuits, where he studied Latin and the humanities for five years.

Calderón's mother died in 1610, and his father married Juana Freyre four years later, only to die himself the following year. His death was followed by a bitter and costly lawsuit between Juana and the Calderón children, ending favorably for Juana. Calderón had entered the University of Alcalá de Henares in 1614, but, after his father's death, he transferred to the University of Salamanca to be under the supervision of his uncle. In Salamanca, he studied canon law and theology, planning to become a priest and take charge of a chaplaincy endowed by his maternal grandfather. Calderón abandoned his studies in 1620, however, and returned to Madrid, where for some time he led a turbulent life. He and his brothers, Diego and José, were engaged in a fight that resulted in the murder of Diego de Velasco. The father of Velasco demanded retribution, and the Calderón brothers settled the case by paying six hundred ducats (a substantial sum in those days).

While in Salamanca, Calderón had started writing poetry and drama; in Madrid, he entered the poetic competitions of 1620 and 1622, organized to celebrate the beatification and canonization of Saint Isidro. Calderón's entries won the praise of Lope de Vega, judge of the contests and editor of its proceedings. The works that Calderón presented to these jousts are of interest not only because they are his earliest extant poems but also because they are among his few surviving nondramatic poems.

The next few years took Calderón away from Spain. He enlisted in the Spanish army and went to Northern Italy and to Flanders, where he probably witnessed the defeat that the Spaniards inflicted on the Flemish, an event that he dramatized so well in *El sitio de Breda*. The poet returned to Madrid around 1625, and soon afterward he entered the service of Duke Frías. From that time on, Calderón fully committed himself to the theater, constantly writing new plays and staging them with all the available machinery and scenery. According to Pérez de Montalbán, Calderón had written many dramas by 1632—all of which had been performed successfully—as well as a substantial body of lyric verse.

Consequently, he was enjoying an enviable reputation as a poet.

About that time, the dramatist was involved in another unhappy event. Pedro de Villegas wounded one of Calderón's brothers very seriously, and in pursuit of Villegas, Calderón, accompanied by some police officers, violated the sanctity of the Trinitarians' convent. The entire court reacted negatively to this event, including Lope de Vega, who protested violently because his daughter Marcela was in the convent. Calderón was reprimanded for his actions, but nothing more, and he even made fun of the affair in *The Constant Prince*. His popularity was already larger than the gravity of his actions, and, therefore, he came out of it unscathed.

In 1635, the Retiro Gardens and Palaces were opened with great festivities, and Calderón's play, *Love, the Greatest Enchantment*, was staged for the occasion. Lope de Vega died that same year, and Calderón became officially attached to the court, furnishing dramas for the exclusive entertainment of the Royal Palace. In recognition of his services, King Philip IV made Calderón a knight of the Order of Santiago in

Pedro Calderón de la Barca (Library of Congress)

1637. As such, he participated in the liberation of Fuenterrabía that same year, and with the army of Count Duke Olivares, he took part in the pacification of Catalonia, serving loyally and courageously until 1642, in recognition of which he was awarded a monthly pension of thirty gold crowns.

The war of Catalonia made an impact on Calderón, aggravated by the fact that his brother José lost his life in the conflict. Nevertheless, he went back to Madrid and continued his occupation as court dramatist, increasingly enjoying the favor of the king, who put in his hands the arrangement of the festivities for the arrival of the new Queen, Mariana de Austria, in 1649.

During these years, Calderón, about whose intimate life little is known, fathered a son out of wedlock. This son, born around 1647, died before reaching adulthood, while his mother died soon after his birth. Calderón, who had been contemplating the idea for some time, determined to become a priest. He was ordained in 1651, and two years later, Philip IV appointed him to the chaplaincy of the New Kings in the Cathedral of Toledo. Calderón moved to that city, but he kept in contact with Madrid, supplying the court with new plays and *autos* on a regular basis. While in Toledo, and inspired by the inscription of the cathedral's choir, he wrote the poem *Psalle et sile* (sing and be silent), an unusually self-revealing work.

Calderón returned to Madrid in 1663 as the chaplain of honor to Philip IV, who had created that position to ensure Calderón's presence in the court. Later that year, Calderón joined the Natural Priests of Madrid, and he became head of the congregation afterward, remaining in that position until his death. He led a quiet life during that time, dedicated to his priestly duties and restricting his literary activity to the writing of Eucharist plays and an occasional drama for the court. He still enjoyed an immense popularity, and his plays were staged frequently. Three volumes of his *Partes* (1636-1684; collected plays) appeared during this period (two had been published in 1636 and 1637), although he disowned four dramas of the last volume and one of the Eucharist plays. Preparation was under way to publish his entire dramatic production, a task that was undertaken by Juan de Vera Tassis after Calderón's death.

Calderón died on May 25, 1681; his death marked the end of the Golden Age of Spanish literature. Following his desires, the dramatist was buried during a simple ceremony, but a gorgeous one took place a few days later to satisfy the many admirers who wanted to pay homage to the playwright for the last time.

ANALYSIS

There are extant only about thirty nondramatic poems by Pedro Calderón de la Barca. Most of them are short poems, composed for a particular occasion, usually in praise of someone in whose collection they would appear.

USE OF SONNETS

As he did in his plays, Calderón employed a variety of verse forms in his nondramatic poems, but the sonnet is the prevalent form. The sonnet had been an important part of Spanish poetry since Juan Boscán and Garcilaso de la Vega assimilated the Italian poetic form into Castilian verse, but it was losing popularity during Calderón's time, as he observes in one of his plays, *Antes que todo es mi dama* (pb. 1662; my lady comes before everything else). Fifteen of Calderón's nondramatic poems are sonnets; added to the sonnets that he included in his dramatic works and the one inserted in the longer poem *Psalle et sile*, they make a total of eighty-six sonnets, collected in a single volume by Rafael Osuna in 1974.

Calderón's sonnets reflect the main poetic currents of his times; Gongorism and *conceptismo* are both present, with a preference for the latter. In general, Calderón's sonnets reveal the poet's desire for a poetry of geometric perfection, evident in the parallel constructions, the *enumeratio* of concepts and *recopilación* or recapitulation of them in the final line, and other rhetorical techniques. They are also filled with the rich imagery that the poet uses in all his literary production. The nondramatic sonnets are, in general, less convincing than those found in the plays, given their occasional character, but some of them are well constructed and worthy of praise. Among these are the sonnet dedicated to Saint Isidro, beautiful in its simplicity; the one written in honor of Saint Teresa de Ávila, which shows a fervent respect for the reformer of the Carmelitans; the one inserted in *Psalle et sile*, which hails the Cathedral of Toledo as a symbol of faith; and the one praising

King Philip IV's hunting skills, the best of all, according to Osuna.

USE OF ROMANCE VERSE

Another poetic form that Calderón used with great skill is the romance. He gives a particular lightness to this traditional verse form, making the poem flow with ease, always adapting it appropriately to the theme he is poeticizing. In this meter, Calderón wrote his only two extant love poems, an ascetic composition, and a self-portrait in verse that reveals his comic genius. This last is, unfortunately, incomplete, yet the 173 lines of the fragment are rich in wit. Calderón first describes his physical appearance—not forgetting any part of his body—in a very unflattering manner. He proceeds to tell the reader about his studies in Salamanca, referring to his mother's desire that he become a priest, his dedication to the theater, and his days as a soldier, adding jokingly that none of these occupations enabled him to find a decent woman who would marry him. The poet, however, does not let this situation affect him, for he has learned that, "as a philosopher says, it makes good sense to adapt to the times." Based on this thinking, he involves himself with two women because he prefers two ugly maids to a beautiful lady. The poem ends abruptly in an argument against Plato's concept of love. The sarcastic tone of the opening lines informs the entire composition; for example, when referring to his lack of responsibility, the poet observes that his peccadilloes are excused by everyone because he is a Salamanca graduate. The tone of the poem is far from Calderón's characteristic sobriety, although it is possible that he wrote other poems of this nature that have not survived. Because of the reference to the time he spent in the army, the poem must have been written sometime between 1625 and 1637, for he became very disappointed with the reality of war during the Catalonian uprising.

"DÉCIMA"

It is in his serious compositions that Calderón shows his best abilities as a poet. In them, as in some of his philosophical plays, Calderón is preoccupied with the reality of death. The best poem of this type is "Décimas a la muerte" ("Decima"), the tone of which is reminiscent of Jorge Manrique's *Coplas por la muerte de su padre* (1492; *Ode*, 1823), although it is less impressive than that fifteenth century masterpiece. Its themes include the brevity of life; the justice of death, which ends every man's life equally; and the *ubi sunt* topos. Absent from it is the theme of fame, so strong in Manrique and present elsewhere in Calderón's works. Here, the poet is deeply pessimistic: "Everything resolves to nothingness,/ all comes from dirt, and dirt becomes,/ and thus it ends where it began." This sense of pessimism is heightened by the fact that there is only a vague reference to eternal life at the end of the poem. The emphasis is placed on the "end" of everything and the absurdity of life, on a pervasive lack of meaning.

A similar attitude is expressed in another poem, "Lágrimas que vierte un alma arrepentida" (1672; tears of a repentant soul). Written in Calderón's old age, "Lágrimas que vierte un alma arrepentida" reveals his strong religious sentiments. The poet presents himself with humility, declaring that he is a sinner, full of vices, and asks God to forgive him. The poem is an expression of love for Christ; it recalls Saint Teresa of Ávila and the anonymous "Soneto a Cristo crucificado" ("Sonnet to Christ Crucified").

PSALLE ET SILE

Calderón's longest poem is *Psalle et sile*, written in Toledo while the poet was in charge of the chaplaincy of the New Kings (1653-1663). The 525-line poem was inspired by the words inscribed at the entrance of the cathedral's choir. Calderón tries to explain the meaning of the inscription, which, because of its location, implies a request or command to those who enter the choir. How is it possible to sing and be silent at the same time? The poet praises silence as the greatest moderation and as the language of God, with whom one can communicate only in the silence of one's soul. Calderón adds, however, that "he who speaks with propriety does not break silence." To speak with propriety, one has to concentrate on the subject of the conversation. In the same manner, one needs to concentrate when conversing with God, which can be done only by meditating. If one is immersed in meditation, then one is speaking the language of God—that is, one is truly silent. At the same time, one could sing songs without interrupting the mental conversation with God. Following this reasoning, it is possible to sing and to be silent simultaneously, utterly absorbed in spiritual communication with God.

OTHER MAJOR WORKS

PLAYS: *Amor, honor y poder*, pr. 1623; *El sitio de Breda*, pr. 1625; *El príncipe constante*, pr. 1629 (*The Constant Prince*, 1853); *La devoción de la cruz*, pb. 1634 (*The Devotion to the Cross*, 1832); *El mayor encanto, amor*, pr. 1635 (*Love, the Greatest Enchantment*, 1870); *La vida es sueño*, pr. 1635 (*Life Is a Dream*, 1830); *Casa con dos puertas, mala es de guardar*, pr., pb. 1636 (wr. 1629; *House with Two Doors Is Difficult to Guard*, 1737); *La dama duende*, pr., pb. 1636 (wr. 1629; *The Phantom Lady*, 1664); *A secreto agravio, secreta venganza*, pb. 1637 (*Secret Vengeance for Secret Insult*, 1961); *El mágico prodigioso*, pr. 1637 (*The Wonder-Working Magician*, 1959); *El médico de su honra*, pb. 1637 (*The Surgeon of His Honor*, 1853); *El alcalde de Zalamea*, pr. 1643 (*The Mayor of Zalamea*, 1853); *El gran teatro del mundo*, pr. 1649 (wr. 1635; *The Great Theater of the World*, 1856); *El pintor de su deshonra*, pb. 1650 (wr. 1640-1642; *The Painter of His Dishonor*, 1853); *La hija del aire, Parte I*, pr. 1653 (*The Daughter of the Air, Part I*, 1831); *La hija del aire, Parte II*, pr. 1653 (*The Daughter of the Air, Part II*, 1831); *El laurel de Apolo*, pr. 1659; *La púrpura de la rosa*, pr. 1660; *Antes que todo es mi dama*, pb. 1662; *Hado y divisa de Leonido y Marfisa*, pr. 1680; *La Estatua de Prometeo*, pb. 1683 (wr. 1669); *Los cabellos de Absalón*, pb. 1684 (wr. c. 1634; *The Crown of Absalom*, 1993); *Eco y Narciso*, pr. 1688 (wr. 1661).

BIBLIOGRAPHY

Acker, Thomas S. *The Baroque Vortex: Velázquez, Calderón, and Gracián Under Philip IV.* New York: Peter Lang, 2000. This comparative study places Calderón in both a literary and historical context. Contains bibliographical references.

Aycock, Wendell M., and Sydney P. Cravens, eds. *Calderón de la Barca at the Tercentenary: Comparative Views.* Lubbock: Interdepartmental Committee on Comparative Literature, Texas Tech University, 1982. An important collection of papers on the three-hundredth anniversary of Calderón's death. The essayists concentrate on comparing some of Calderón's contributions with other artistic impulses, such as German Idealist philosophy, Euripides, Mexican cleric characters, and William Shakespeare.

Cascardi, Anthony J. *The Limits of Illusion: A Critical Study of Calderón.* New York: Cambridge University Press, 2005. Valuable for the breadth and variety of its inquiry. Includes an index.

Hesse, Everett W. *Calderón de la Barca.* Boston: Twayne, 1967. Treats the Spanish theater of the Golden Age, the political and social arena, the structure of Calderón's work, the works in which he excelled, and Calderón's critical reception. Selected bibliography and index.

Maraniss, James E. *On Calderón.* Columbia: University of Missouri Press, 1978. Stresses Calderón's sense of "order triumphant" and moves through the canon examing the plays. Gives a sense of who the poet was.

Rupp, Stephen James. *Allegories of Kingship: Calderón and the Anti-Machiavellian Tradition.* University Park: Pennsylvania State University Press, 1996. An examination of Calderón's portrayal of the monarchy in literature and of his political and social views. Bibliography and index.

Suscavage, Charlene E. *Calderón: The Imagery of Tragedy.* New York: Peter Lang, 1991. Although concerned with the plays, focuses on Calderón's language and figures of speech. Bibliographical references.

Wardropper, Bruce W., ed. *Critical Essays on the Theatre of Calderón.* New York: New York University Press, 1965. Essays on Calderón's themes, characters, structure, political viewpoint, and theoretical perspectives. The opening article, by A. A. Parker, is a good summary of the justifications for ranking Calderón among the great writers of a great literary age.

Juan Fernández Jiménez

CALLIMACHUS

Born: Cyrene, North Africa (now Shaḥḥāt, Libya);
c. 305 B.C.E.
Died: Alexandria, Egypt; c. 240 B.C.E.
Also known as: Kallimachos

PRINCIPAL POETRY

Aitiōn, n.d. (*Aetia*, 1958)
Ekalē, n.d. (*Hecale*, 1958)
Epigrammata, n.d. (*Epigrams*, 1793)
Hymni, n.d. (*Hymns*, 1755)
Iamboi, n.d. (*Iambi*, 1958)
Lock of Berenice, 1755

OTHER LITERARY FORMS

Callimachus (kuh-LIHM-uh-kuhs) was a scholar and literary critic as well as a poet and wrote prose monographs on subjects as diverse as the names of tribes, rare words, barbarian customs, and marvelous occurrences throughout the world. Unfortunately, none of the prose is extant.

ACHIEVEMENTS

Callimachus is the preeminent Alexandrian poet, the most daring, technically skilled, and prolific among the writers practicing their art in that Hellenized Egyptian city during the third century B.C.E. Like his contemporaries Theocritus and Apollonius Rhodius, Callimachus wrote allusive, learned, yet dramatic poetry; unlike these two fellow Alexandrians, however, he seems to have deliberately mined the widest variety of genres. Moreover, he alone among the poets whose work survives from this period crafted and refined throughout his career a poetic dogma, a highly developed notion of what a poem should be. In this, one could compare him to Ezra Pound among modern poets, continually urging his colleagues to "make it new" and exerting a powerful influence on subsequent generations of poets. Callimachus, who was also like Pound in being a scholar of poetry, renewed the Greek poetic tradition in two ways: He cultivated forms that had fallen into disuse (such as the hymnic), and he infused traditionally nonpersonal poetry with allusions to his own time and condition. A hymn, for example, could become a vehicle for praise of the patron monarch Ptolemy and for pronouncements on style, while purporting to praise Zeus or Apollo; a funerary epigram might be turned in the poet's hands to serve as a sophisticated joke.

It was Callimachus's achievement to compose poetry that satisfied a discerning, restricted audience—the royal court at Alexandria and other scholar-poets—without becoming hopelessly obscure or dated. Instead, his poetry in all genres usually attains the ideal he set: Lightness of tone is wedded to brevity, urbane manner, erudite content, and exclusive allusions. That these qualities were prized in poetry is evidenced by the many papyrus fragments later discovered to contain works by Callimachus—far more than those of any other author, including the very popular Euripides. Ironically, this "exclusive" poet obtained a far-from-exclusive audience, perhaps because his verse challenged the reader as it simultaneously offered rare pleasures. His influence extended even beyond the Greek-speaking lands; the verse of the Roman poets Quintus Ennius, Catullus, Horace, Vergil, and Sextus Propertius, and the poetic stance that each assumes, would be unthinkable without the example of Callimachus.

In turn, from the poets writing during the reign of the Emperor Augustus, the English "Augustans" inherited the Callimachean poetic ideal; Alexander Pope's *The Rape of the Lock* (1712, 1714) echoes the Alexandrian poet's *Lock of Berenice*, although Pope added the mock-epic tone. Indeed, Callimachean aesthetic principles are so much a part of the European literary tradition that they may be taken for granted. Whenever a new poetic movement (Imagism, for example) challenges outworn canons of taste, jettisons tedious narrative, and turns instead to highly crafted "small" verse forms, the creators of the new poetry are treading the path first cleared by the Alexandrian poet.

BIOGRAPHY

Callimachus was not a native Alexandrian; he grew up and seems to have begun composing poetry in Cyrene, a Greek city of North Africa. From a commentary on a lost portion of his long poem, the *Aetia*, it appears that Callimachus represented himself as once dreaming that he was transported from his boyhood home in Libya to Mount Helicon, the place on the mainland of Greece which was considered the traditional home of the Muses. He thus alludes to an early initiation into his art.

Neither his date of birth nor his parentage is known, but Callimachus's family apparently prided itself on being descended from Battus, the legendary eighth century B.C.E. founder of Cyrene. From this assumption, it may be deduced that his education was that of an aristocrat. On moving to Alexandria, however, which was one of the main cultural centers of Hellenistic Greek civilization, Callimachus was initially a marginal figure; family connections did not help. He held the position of schoolmaster in the suburb of Eleusis, which was not a lucrative job. Several of his epigrams that mention his poverty have been thought to date from this period (c. 280-270 B.C.E.); nevertheless, it should be remembered that the topic of poverty (*penia*) was a convention in Greek literature as early as Hesiod (fl. 700 B.C.E.), a poet whom Callimachus admired and imitated. When, therefore, the poet addresses a lover in Epigram 34 M., "You know that my hands are empty of wealth . . . ," and proceeds to beg affection, the words are most likely those of a persona rather than of the poet himself.

At some later point, Callimachus received an appointment to the great library at Alexandria, perhaps after an introduction to Ptolemy II Philadelphus, the library's royal patron (who ruled from 285 to 246 B.C.E.). Callimachus's groundbreaking compilation of the 120-volume *Pinakes* (tablets), a catalog of the library's hundred thousand or so papyrus scrolls of Greek literature, entailed far more than merely listing titles, involving him in decisions about genre, authorship, authors' biographies, and the arrangement of sections within each work. This extensive piece of literary history provided the poet with a wealth of material—often obscure—from which to fashion learned verse.

Despite his important contributions there, Callimachus was never appointed head of the library. Some controversy may have been involved, as literary infighting was surely a part of his life, but the details of his arguments with various contemporaries remain vague. Ancient commentators mention a feud between Callimachus and Apollonius Rhodius, the author of the epic *Argonautica* (third century B.C.E.; English translation, 1780). Callimachus's preference for brevity and disdain for pseudo-Homeric epic apparently prevailed for a time: Apollonius is said to have left, humbled, to live on the island of Rhodes. Callimachus's *Ibis*, now lost, a piece of darkly worded invective that Ovid later imitated, may have hastened its victim's departure from Alexandria. Other personal enemies apparently were attacked through allusions in the revised prologue of the *Aetia*.

Although much of his poetry continues such artistic debates, several of Callimachus's poems might best be understood in a different light—as responses to occasions at the royal court that demanded expression on the part of an "attached" poet. The *Lock of Berenice*, for example, commemorates an actual event, the dedication of a wife's lock of hair to petition the gods for the safe return of her husband, Ptolemy III, as he departed for war in 247 B.C.E. (This is the only datable poem extant.) Again, court happenings might be alluded to in that portion of the *Hymns to Zeus* that mentions Zeus's rule over his older brothers; the entire composition may be an elaborate, half-veiled praise of Callimachus's patron. It is surely not a real hymn meant for ritual recitation. Unfortunately, nothing is known of the poet's relation with the royal family other than that their patronage extended until his death at an advanced age. This social situation in its broader implications must be kept in mind: What appears to be Callimachean allusive indirection often might have resulted from politic discretion.

ANALYSIS

Because the legacy of Callimachus lies so much in his theory of style, it is best, first, to examine several of his extended metaphors describing the ideal style; then his major works can be evaluated according to his own aesthetic standards.

EPIGRAM 30 M.

In most cases, Callimachus's pronouncements about poetry are blended skillfully with other topics. Epigram 30 M. is a good example. The seven-line poem builds on the poet's exclusive tastes:

I hate a cyclical poem, take no delight in the road
That carries many to and fro. I detest
A lover that wanders, nor do I drink from a well;
All held in common I abhor. . . .

Then the poet dramatically changes tack. What began as a literary manifesto ends abruptly as a bitter personal love poem:

Lysaniē, you are beautiful, beautiful . . .
But before Echo speaks this, someone says
"Another possesses him."

The reader is left in suspense, yet he could eventually conclude that the poet, true to his lonely principle in life as in art, is here abandoning the one thing he does not hate.

The long, undistinguished epic poems, called cyclic because they complete the Trojan War myth cycle, represent for Callimachus all that one should avoid in verse. Even though his *Hymn to Apollo* uses the centuries-old Homeric meter and epic diction, the poem in praise of the god is startlingly fresh and compresses details of geography, ritual, history, and myth into a dramatic framework. The final lines, which express Callimachus's aversion for the epic form, are spoken by the god of poetry himself, using the images of Epigram 30 M. again—wide thoroughfares and water. To "Envy" (Callimachus's unnamed detractors), whispering in Apollo's ear like a court sycophant about the hateful poet "who does not sing as many things as the sea" (that is, vast epics), the god replies with a kick. He cites the filthiness of the "great stream" Euphrates; in an oracular tone, he says that Demeter's shrine is watered by "bees" (priestesses of the goddess) that carry water only from pure, undefiled streams. Envy is thus defeated.

Purity of water, insectlike artisanship—these are metaphors for Callimachus's light, unencumbered verse. The two images are combined once more in the combative prologue to the "collected poems" edition of the *Aetia*. After acknowledging the objection that he has not written "one long poem," Callimachus again uses the dramatic mask of Apollo to defend his own application of *techne* (skill) rather than bulk and big noises: As a youth, he saw the god, who instructed the poet to "nourish a slender Muse," to imitate the cicada. Callimachus's final prayer to become "the light one, the winged," living on dew, takes on a more personal note, for now he desires the insect's levity to shake off burdensome old age.

AETIA

How does Callimachus in his verse attain this cicada-like freedom of expression? The *Aetia* itself can show. Although nearly half the length of Homer's *Iliad* (c. 750 B.C.E.; English translation, 1611) when extant in full, this was certainly not "one long poem" but rather an episodic meandering through every sort of Greek ritual lore, a poem that explained (like the poet's prose works) curious customs—why the Parians, for example, sacrifice without flute music, or why the Lindians honor Heracles with blasphemy. A scholar's poem, the *Aetia* has the dramatist's voice behind its narrative, choosing exact details and often breaking into direct speech. Here Callimachus's novel narrative technique appears to be built on deliberate random changes of topic, like the flitting of an industrious insect.

The story of Acontius and Cydippe, one of the longer, completely separable stories within the *Aetia*, illuminates the Callimachean method very well. An introduction, sprinkled allusively with obscure proper names, relates the legendary beauty of this pair of lovers and tells how Acontius by means of an inscribed apple contrived to bind Cydippe on oath to love him, so that her attempts to marry others are all divinely thwarted. Then the poet focuses on one such attempt at marriage with another. Seeming to lose the narrative thread, however, he begins to describe the history of the ritual prenuptial sleep that Cydippe and her husband-to-be must take; but the poet breaks off: "Hold back, shameless soul, you dog!" Such rituals are too holy to tell; "having much knowledge is bad for one who does not control the tongue," he says. Clearly, the aposiopesis (falling silent) technique is employed only to show off, in elegant manner, a vast erudition, and at the same time it is a technique that prevents the reader from being bored with the extraneous details of the digression. Finally, the poet makes his transition to another topic by a surprising bibliographical reference, an unheard-of device in serious epic poems: "Cean, your clan, the Acontiadae, dwell in honored numbers at Iulis still. This love-match we heard from old Xenomedes, who set down once the entire island in a mythological history." At one stroke, the scholar-poet gives the *aetion* (cause) that he set out to tell—the origin of this clan—and turns his narrative to other Cean myths with a librarian's remark.

The levity of Callimachus can be appreciated in other ways; it is not merely narrative flightiness. Indeed, he sometimes employs old conventions for the sake of elaborate jokes. A few of his epigrams have their origin in this technique. There were generic social precedents for these short poems: the inscription-verses on tombs and on dedicated shrine offerings. The poet subverts both. A four-line poem poses as a tombstone epitaph to commemorate a youth who allegedly was putting garlands on his stepmother's tomb ("thinking now that she had changed life and her nature as well") when the woman's *stēlē* toppled and killed him. The last line is both traditional in its address to passersby, and humorous: "O step-sons, shun even a step-mother's grave." In imitation of a dedicatory object, Callimachus wrote another poem that plays on the similarity in Greek between the word for sea and the word for salt. Like a shipwrecked sailor who traditionally offered an oar or clothing to the gods who saved him from drowning, the speaker, Eudemus, in Epigram 48 M. dedicates his saltcellar: Now he has become rich and no longer eats frugally and so is "saved from the salt."

EPIGRAM 2 M.

Lest it be thought that the poet only plays, one other epigram might be mentioned to acknowledge the elegiac strain and the ability to evoke intense feeling also to be found in Callimachus. Perhaps his most famous short poem, Epigram 2 M., is that addressed to Heraclitus:

> Someone told me of your death, Heraclitus, and put me
> In tears; I remembered the many times we both
> By conversing put the sun to sleep. . . .

Although his friend has been "ashes long since now," Callimachus in recalling him affirms the love of the art of poetry that the two friends shared:

> But your nightingales are still alive;
> Hades, who snatches all, will not put hand on them.

The light touch—of tone, as in many epigrams, of allusiveness and narrative pace, as in the *Aetia*—character-

izes Callimachus's approach to other genres as well. Never satisfied with remaining at work in any single verse form, he seems to have intended to appropriate all, even writing tragedy and comedy (now lost). Doubtless this approach was criticized by his contemporaries as evidence of a lack of staying power; it was scorned as *polyeideia* (writing in many forms). Today, one sees this method as the prime virtue of Callimachean art. Three other works—*Iambi, Hymns,* and *Hecale*—show the advantages Callimachus derived from this stylistic tenet.

IAMBI

The thirteen poems of the *Iambi* present a much modulated form of the invective traditionally associated with the genre of poetry written in this meter as practiced by Archilochus and Hipponax in Archaic Greece. Attacks on personal enemies are replaced in these compositions by a mild correction of received opinion: The true story of a well-known proverb occupies Iambus 11 T., and similar antiquarian interests take up the description of statues, the origin of a footrace on Aegina, the reason that sows are slaughtered in a certain Aphrodite cult. These *Iambi* show Callimachus, as in the *Aetia*, crossing prose genres of historiography and mythology with disused poetic forms to create something new. In the few *Iambi* that mention contemporaries, the names in question are tangential to the poem. Thus, Iambus 2 T. relates one of Aesop's fables about the way in which animals lost their voices to men; only at the end does the poet intrude: "Eudemus, therefore, has a dog's voice, Philton a donkey's. . . ." Such a technique, distancing the original purpose of the iambic form, allows Callimachus to expand its range. He adapts it thereby to the changed social conditions of the third century B.C.E., in which the cosmopolitan court, rather than the tightly knit city-state, is the intended audience.

HYMNS AND HECALE

The *Hymns* and *Hecale*, finally, allow Callimachus's light handling to be traced through two interrelated effects. First, there is once again generic innovation; second, the innovation is tied to narrative methods of compressing, arranging, and ordering point of view, all of which are new.

The hymn, since the time of Homer, was a narrative

commemorating the deeds of a particular divinity; it was framed by praises of the god. Callimachus, however, in the *Hymn to Apollo* and other hymns re-creates dramatically the god's epiphany at his shrine. The poem adopts a second-person narrator, rather than the more distant, epic-sounding, third-person narration. Immediately noticeable, too, is the way in which Callimachus allies poetry with secret and holy ritual: to hear the poem, one must be an initiate, like the worshipers of Apollo. It is not far from such poetry to the Roman lyricist Horace's claim to be "priest of the Muses."

The *Hecale*, on the other hand, rather than being a reworking of a very old genre, is a completely new form, the *epyllion*, which arose in the Alexandrian period of Greek literature. Who invented this form is not known with certainty. Theocritus wrote several; Callimachus may simply have perfected the use of this form. The purpose of the "little epic" is not to tell all the deeds of a hero, for that ambition would require the scope of the detested "cyclic" poem. Instead, only one, often little-known episode in the life of a hero, one with plenty of local-color possibilities, is selected. In the case of the *Hecale*, it is Theseus's capture of a destructive bull that has been ravaging Marathon, near Athens. The scale of the narrative is further reduced by the poet's intense focus on the events of the night before the heroic feat, rather than on the deed itself. Theseus's visit to the rustic hut of an old woman named Hecale, the simple supper she prepares for him, their conversation—all are described in painstakingly realistic detail. There is pathos (the hero returns later to find the woman has died), erudition (the origin of the Hecale-feasts is explained), and a good deal of stylistic tour de force (into the "heroic" hexameter the poet fits the words "bread-box," "baking oven," and other commonplace terms). Although most of the poem survives in fragments, it was intact and widely imitated from Vergil's time to the thirteenth century. Fragmentary as the *Hecale* remains, it is nevertheless a fitting testament to its author's lifelong urge to distill, renew, and perpetuate essential and lively poetry.

OTHER MAJOR WORK

NONFICTION: *Pinakes*, n.d.

BIBLIOGRAPHY

Bing, Peter. *The Well-Read Muse: Past and Present in Callimachus and the Hellenistic Poets*. Rev. ed. Ann Arbor: Michigan Classical Press, 2008. An examination of Callimachus's poetry and its themes along with the works of other Hellenistic poets.

Blum, Rudolph. *Kallimachos: The Alexandrian Library and the Origins of Bibliography*. Translated by Hans H. Wellisch. Madison: University of Wisconsin Press, 1991. In his study of the Alexandrian Library, Blum argues that Callimachus, the second director of the library, was the inventor of two essential scholarly tools: the library catalog and the biobibliographical reference work.

Cameron, Alan. *Callimachus and His Critics*. Princeton, N.J.: Princeton University Press, 1995. A wide-ranging survey of Callimachus's literary reputation over the centuries, noting that his elaborate verbal precision has become his hallmark. Cameron shows how, and to some extent why, Callimachus worked so diligently to achieve that literary effect.

Ferguson, John. *Callimachus*. Boston: Twayne, 1980. This general survey of Callimachus is interesting and thorough. Ferguson pieces together fragments of gossip to make a coherent life of Callimachus, and he includes the fragments of the poems. Callimachus' social and cultural background is treated. Ferguson compares Callimachus with T. S. Eliot. Contains an excellent bibliography.

Gutzwiller, Kathryn. *Poetic Garlands: Hellenistic Epigrams in Context*. Berkeley: University of California Press, 1998. Although it concentrates most of its attention on Callimachus's *Epigrammata*, this work goes beyond that to look at the poetic convention of the epigram in the larger realm of classical literature.

Harder, M. A., R. F. Regtuit, and G. C. Wakker, eds. *Callimachus II*. Dudley, Mass.: Peeters, 2004. Literary criticism and analysis of Callimachus that arose as part of the sixth Gröningen Workshop on Hellenistic poetry.

Hollis, A. S. Introduction to *Callimachus' "Hecale."* Oxford, England: Clarendon Press, 1990. The *Hecale*, Callimachus's retelling of the story of how the Athenian hero Theseus tamed the bull of Marathon, was the poet's effort to show that he too was capable of crafting epic verse. Hollis places this key work of Callimachus into both the poet's canon and the Western poetic tradition, helping to explain its importance and enduring achievements.

Hunter, Richard. *The Shadow of Callimachus: Studies in the Reception of Hellenistic Poetry at Rome*. New York: Cambridge University Press, 2006. Examines the influence of Greek poetry on the Romans, focusing on the works of Callimachus.

Kerkhecker, Arnd. *Callimachus' Book of Iambi*. New York: Oxford University Press, 1999. An extended discussion of Callimachus's collected Iambi, arguably one of the earliest surviving Greek "books of poetry."

Williams, Frederick. "Callimachus and the Supranormal." In *Hellenistica Gronigana: Proceedings of the Gröningen Workshops on Hellenistic Poetry*, edited by Annette Harder. Gröningen, Germany: Egbert Forster, 1993. Because Callimachus can be as much noted for his works based on myths and legends as for his lyric poetry, this study provides an interesting and useful review of how the poet deploys the supranormal world and events in his works.

Richard Peter Martin

LUÍS DE CAMÕES

Born: Lisbon, Portugal; c. 1524
Died: Lisbon, Portugal; June 10, 1580
Also known as: Luís de Camoëns

PRINCIPAL POETRY

Os Lusíadas, 1572 (*The Lusiads*, 1655)
Cancioneiro, 1580
Rimas, 1595 (*The Lyrides*, 1803, 1884)
Selected Sonnets, 2005
The Collected Lyric Poems of Luís de Camões, 2008 (Landeg White, translator)

OTHER LITERARY FORMS

Although Luís de Camões (kuh-MOYNSH) does not seem to have tried to compete with his great compa-

triot, the dramatist Gil Vicente, Camões did write three short *autos* (short plays). *Enfatriões* (pr. 1540; amphytrions), an adaptation of Plautus's comedy, was probably staged in 1540 as a scholar's exercise or for an academic celebration at Coimbra University. The *Auto del-Rei Seleuco* (pr. 1542; the play of King Seleuco), based on Plutarch, was performed in the home of Estácio da Fonseca, one of the king's officials, perhaps on the occasion of a wedding, very likely in 1542 during the poet's sojourn in Lisbon and at court. Finally, *Filodemo*, the longest, most classical, and most mature of Camões's plays, was presented in Goa in 1555 to honor the newly appointed governor of India, Francisco Barreto.

ACHIEVEMENTS

No Iberian lyric poet has been more successful than Luís de Camões in the expression of feeling. Indeed, he represents all Peninsular poetry at its peak. Lord Byron, whose inspiration introduced new emotion into literature, admired the authenticity of Camões's lyricism and understood the human truth in his verse. In all his work, Camões was able to combine native Portuguese traditions with the classical influences and with the vital spirit of the Renaissance.

Camões is probably best known for his epic poem, *The Lusiads*. The focal point in this work is not Vasco da Gama, realistically characterized as the uncultivated captain that he was, but the Portuguese conquistadores as a whole—who, in the tradition of their ancestors, set out to create the vast Portuguese Empire for themselves and posterity. Although Camões wrote his propaganda to glorify the nation at its peak, he recognized the weakness of the imperial structure for the future. Such objectivity regarding the empire—and the honesty to express his views to the king, to whom he dedicated his poem—bespeak Camões's faith in the best principles of the Renaissance and his confidence in himself as the poet most representative of his time.

BIOGRAPHY

Although he has had many biographers, little is known for certain of the adventuresome life of Luís Vaz de Camões, who represented so well in his life and works the Renaissance man and the Portuguese conquistador. The son of Simão Vas de Camões and Ana de Macedo or Sá, Camões was possibly related, through his paternal grandmother, to Vasco da Gama, as well as to other Portuguese notables dating as far back as 1370. Camões was a gentleman, then, although always of scant financial resources. It is clear, too, that he possessed a vast erudition. Because of the quantity and quality of Camões's learning, it is likely that he studied at Coimbra University and therefore that he was born in Coimbra, as he probably would have been too poor to move there from Lisbon.

With some reputation as well as noble birth, Camões went to Lisbon between 1542 and 1545, to frequent the court and enjoy the greater activity of the capital. His enjoyment was short-lived, unfortunately, for in 1546 or 1547, he was banished to Ribatejo because of his passion for a lady of the court whose parents did not approve. It is known that during the years from 1547 to 1549, Camões was in Ceuta, Morocco, winning his spurs as a proper young nobleman but losing an eye, probably in combat with the Moors. In 1549, he was back in Lisbon, where he led a bohemian existence until 1553, when, in a brawl, he injured his adversary so seriously that he was jailed.

Camões was released only on the condition that he depart for India, which he did on March 7, 1553, after having been enlisted as a soldier for three years. His ship, the splendid *São Bento*, commanded by Fernão Alvares Cabral, capsized at the Cape of Good Hope but arrived at Goa in September, 1554. Despite his constant involvement in numerous military expeditions, Camões wrote regularly, presenting his short play *Filodemo* to the governor of India, Francisco Barreto, on the occasion of his installation in 1555. In 1556, the poet was in Macao, perhaps in the capacity of the governor's "officer for deceased and absentees," perhaps in prison for embezzlement, perhaps composing portions of *The Lusiads*. Internal evidence does reveal that, shipwrecked near the mouth of the Mecon River on his return to Goa, Camões swam to safety with his epic poem, although his Chinese sweetheart, Dinamene, drowned. Back in Goa in 1559 or 1560, he was imprisoned for debt.

After sixteen difficult years in Asia, the weary poet decided in 1568 to return to Portugal with Pero Barreto

Luís de Camões (Library of Congress)

Rolim, who, for an unknown reason, left Camões, without resources, in Mozambique. There Camões remained until 1569, when the well-known chronicler Diogo do Couto rescued him and took him back to Lisbon on the *Santa Fé* in 1569 or 1570. Camões had all but completed his great epic as his country was about to engage in the bloody Battle of Alcácer-Quibir (1578). The Inquisition's approval to publish *The Lusiads* was signed by King Sebastian on September 24, 1571, and two editions, one authentic, the other plagiarized, appeared in 1572. Pensioned by the king, the greatest of Portuguese poets struggled to survive—but probably without the rumored need to beg—until his death in 1580.

ANALYSIS

During his lifetime, Luís de Camões never published his complete works. Many of his lyric poems were circulated as *separata* from admirer to admirer; many others were printed in the collective *cancioneiros* (songbooks), both during his day and posthumously.

Those that the poet had collected in his personal *Parnaso* (Parnassus) were stolen from him. The first complete collection of Camões's lyrics appeared under the editorship of Fernão Rodrigues Lobo Soropita in Lisbon in 1595; the first critical edition, prepared by José Maria Rodriques and Alfonso Lopes Vieira, did not appear until 1932.

Camões's life was a continual *via dolorosa*, filled with love but also with sorrow and disaster. It was a life that taught him the entire gamut of tragic emotions, which his destiny called him to express in his lyrics. With very rare exceptions, Camões's songs, odes, elegies, *redondilhas*, and sonnets are composed of the passion and anguish caused him by his misadventures throughout a considerable part of the then vast Portuguese Empire and transmitted by him directly and sincerely to his sensitive readers of all times. It is not surprising that such an unfortunate lyric poet should so ably and faithfully interpret the human heart. He does not move the reader with sensuous images or brilliant technique alone. Constantly transformed and vibrant in his pain, Camões pours the wealth of his own varied experiences and tormented soul into each well-constructed stanza. Seldom capable of stirring the reader with their cold, almost inert poetics, Sá de Miranda, António Ferreira, and other contemporary poets pale before Camões, whose language is clear, grave, profound, dramatic, moving, and always harmonious.

Many were the women loved by Camões. Chief among them were Isabel Tavares, or "Belisa," the cousin whom he won in his youth in Coimbra; Catarina de Ataíde, or "Natércia," a lady of the court on whose account he was banished; Dinamene, the Chinese slave girl lost at sea; and Barbara, another slave woman about whom little is known. Although he treats other themes, often combining those of Portuguese tradition and those of the Renaissance, Camões's lyrics center on love—as do those of the great Petrarch, whom he emulated, cited, and sometimes paraphrased. Indeed, the Italian poet's influence was keenly felt by virtually all European lyric poets in the fifteenth and sixteenth centuries—in the Platonic transformation of erotic love, beyond the grave as well as in life, and in the quality of his imagery and mellifluous rhythms. Not only does

Camões represent the apotheosis of the angelic beloved—framing her in all the attributes of incorruptible grace and revering her with feelings of purest chastity—but also portrays all nature as sharing in the poet's joy or anguish. Further, Camões uses metric forms—sonnets, songs, tercets, sestinas, and decasyllables—identical to those of Petrarch. The latter, however, was conscious of having made Laura's name famous through his work, whereas Camões's convulsive passion and pain seem more genuinely felt, more dramatic, and more human.

Platonism transformed Camões's emotion, tenderly sublimating it. Apart from Petrarch, Camões knew something of Plato's idealism, as may be seen in the *redondilhas maiores* beginning "Sobolos os rios que vão" ("Over the Rivers That Flow"). Written in despair when the poet was still in Goa or Mozambique, this long poem quivers with his painful longing for home and inner peace: Suffering the evils of Babylon, Camões weeps and moans nostalgically for the joys of Zion and glimpses the Promised Land. It may be said that Camões was more comprehensive than Petrarch in the matter of form, for he excelled in the traditional *redondilha* of the *cancioneiros* and in the inventions of the Renaissance alike. Doubtless first influenced by the graceful verse of Sá de Miranda, as were all the contemporary practitioners of the Italian style in Portugal, Camões learned as well, not only directly from Petrarch and Jacopo Sannazzaro (not to mention Vergil) but also from the Spanish Italianate poets Juan Boscán and Garcilaso de la Vega. Ultimately, Camões rivaled Dante and Petrarch in the sonnet and song of Sicilian origin. Moreover, no lyric poet in Portuguese before or since has achieved Camões's transparency, plasticity, harmony, and taste in language, whether in the expression of abstract thought, concrete nature, or personal feeling.

The Lusiads

Although it is Camões's lyric poetry that holds the greater interest for today's reader, it is *The Lusiads* that made its author universally famous. The idea of creating an epic poem concerning Portuguese expansion had existed from the fifteenth century, both in and out of Portugal. The Italian Humanist Poliziano, whose work later inspired Camões to a degree, had offered his services to João II to sing of his deeds in Latin verse. In the prologue to the *Cancioneiro general* (1516; general songbook), Garcia de Resende laments that the accomplishments of the Portuguese have not been properly glorified. Despite his repeated aversion to the military life on land and sea, Ferreira encouraged his colleagues to write such an epic, and he himself attempted the epic style in several odes. This aspiration on the part of the Humanists was related to their ambition to revive the classical genres, including the epic; the voyages of the Portuguese could easily be compared to those of Ulysses and Aeneas.

Camões, too, sought to meet the challenge of the Homeric model that so engaged other Humanists. The maritime setting of the *Odyssey* (c. 725 B.C.E.; English translation, 1614) and other ancient poems was indeed appropriate for the central theme of a Portuguese epic, as was the nationalism of the *Aeneid* (c. 29-19 B.C.E.; English translation, 1553) for the official ideology of the Portuguese expansion, according to which the nation was fulfilling a divine mandate by extending both the empire and the faith. In the midst of wars between Protestants and Catholics—not to mention between rulers of the same religion, such as Charles V and Francis I—and above all in the face of the Turkish onslaught in the Mediterranean, the Lusitanians accepted their sacred mission as had the Crusaders before them.

It is unknown precisely when the young Camões set about writing *The Lusiads*, although it was probably composed between 1545 and 1570, but there is evidence in his collection of lyric poetry of early intentions to glorify the great deeds of his people. Camões's title, signifying "the Portuguese" (descended, according to legend, from Luso, a companion of Bacchus), incorporated a term created and used in several works by André de Resende, a scholar famous throughout Europe and a consummate Humanist. *The Lusiads*, first published in 1572, comprises ten cantos of ottava rima; the lengths of the cantos vary, ranging from eighty-seven stanzas (canto 7) to 156 stanzas (canto 10).

The poet begins by explaining the subject, invoking the Muses of the Tagus to grant him the proper sublime tone and flowing, grandiloquent style, and dedicating the poem to King Sebastian. The remainder of the work is divided between two main story lines, the first relating the history of Portugal prior to King Manuel (cantos 3, 4, and 8) and the second, the voyage of Vasco da Gama to India (cantos 1, 2, 5, 7, 9, and 10). Imitating Vergil, who has Aeneas narrate the history of his people and his own nautical adventures to Dido, Camões imagines Vasco and Paul da Gama telling different parts of their story to other characters. With this device, it was possible for Camões to introduce the historical narratives of the Lusos, ancient and modern, derived from the nationalistic works of João de Barros, into the description of the extraordinary voyage of Vasco da Gama, based on several written accounts as well as oral tradition, and at the same time maintain the structural balance of the poem. Thus, the history of past heroes seems related to that of current ones, with no interruption in the logical sequence of the action. The poem concludes with a sorrowful, poignant censure of the nation's decadence and with the poet's firm exhortation to the king to conquer Morocco.

Da Gama's voyage was insufficient to give artistic unity to the poem, however, for a work of art requires unity of action—that is, the convergence of the events in a dramatic situation and its denouement. Camões found no plot in the voyage, only a chronological sequence of events. Moreover, human characters and passions are indispensable in motivating the action of a narrative poem. Camões, however, failed to find these qualities in his historical figures—so much so that his characters more often resemble statues in a procession than human beings. It is perhaps for these reasons that, in keeping with the rules of the genre and, once more, with Vergil as his chief model, Camões invented a mythological plot of impassioned gods. The psychological interest, then, does not reside in the difficulties and complications of da Gama's voyage but in the rivalry between Venus, patron of the Portuguese, and Bacchus, who is their enemy. This rivalry accounts for the obstacles that the fleet encounters on the eastern coast of Africa (the fictitious storm occurring at the end rather than the beginning of the trip) and for the intrigues that create enemies for the Portuguese. Disguised, Bacchus makes trouble for the protagonists, provokes mistrust of the newcomers, and stirs up the gods of the sea to unleash the storm against them. On the other hand, Venus intercedes on their behalf with

Jupiter, who enlists the nymphs to weaken the efforts of the sea gods.

In general, the gods are more human than the humans, and the action depends on and revolves about them. The poet, however, strives for a realistic interpretation, at least within the realm of Christian miracle. The contacts between the gods and humans take place in dreams or through incarnations. Furthermore, the gods could be interpreted as angelic, demonic, or astrological forces—all very acceptable to the poet's contemporaries. At the end of the poem, the mythological fiction dissipates, and on the Isle of Love, the sea nymphs grant the returning sailors every favor, even immortality. Da Gama replaces Adamastor and Neptune as the lover of Thetis, who herself declares the use of mythology allegorical.

As a Humanist, Camões combined a reverence for the classical world with the passionate exploratory spirit characteristic of the Renaissance. Thus, his epic is a compendium of lore—geographical, nautical, and otherwise—much of which he acquired at first hand on his far-flung travels.

Indeed, the vigor of the Renaissance is consistently reflected in Camões's brilliant verse. Certain episodes reveal his genius in the dramatic description of the concrete. His accounts of the Battle of Aljubarroto (canto 4) and of the tourney of the Twelve English Peers (canto 6) are extraordinarily vivid portrayals of war. The poignant assassination of Inês de Castro (canto 3) is a scene worthy of Euripides, while the Old Man of Restelo, weeping and cursing at da Gama's departure (canto 6), and Adamastor, threatening the Lusitanian heroes and sobbing at the disappearance of the beautiful nymph (canto 5), are pathetic figures drawn with the realistic power of Dante. The furious waves and ominous winds (canto 6) and the "bloodsucking" waterspout (canto 5) are remarkable in their exact representational qualities, rivaling the naturalism of Albrecht Dürer or Michelangelo. Finally, the Isle of Love (canto 9) is a typical scene of pagan sensuality that depicts most vividly the voluptuousness to which the men of the Renaissance were so susceptible.

At the same time, Camões excelled in making his form follow his function. Many of his concise formulas have become engraved in the collective memory of the Portuguese people. Despite transpositions and other syntactical liberties modeled on Latin and despite an excess of mythological allusions, Camões's phrases are usually clear and precise. The prodigious sense of rhythm characteristic of his verse is sometimes adapted to the movement and sounds of battle, with much onomatopoeia, sometimes to the tedious calm of the doldrums on the equator, sometimes to the aroused ardor of desire, sometimes to the crystalline lyricism of Venus's island paradise. Coupled with a capacity for picturesque imagery, these devices make Camões the foremost exponent of the sensuous Renaissance.

The explicit ideological content of *The Lusiads* is of much less interest today than its artistic realization. The notion of Portugal as a model for the disunited Christian nations of Europe, already expressed by Gil Vicente and others, was perhaps advanced more eloquently and strikingly by Camões. That Portugal represented Western culture as opposed to the barbarism of the rest of the world, however, is not borne out by the bloodthirsty tale of Portuguese history as told by the poet. The noble warriors of *The Lusiads* faithfully reflect the ideology of the class to which Camões himself belonged. His sword in one hand and his pen in the other, he expressed a way of life—aristocratic, warlike, and highly individualistic.

Camões's influence on the Baroque period, which in some respects he foreshadowed, was substantial. The term "poet" was said to be synonymous with his name. Editions of his lyric poetry began to appear immediately following his death, and new editions of the lyrics and *The Lusiads* were published throughout the seventeenth century—so enthusiastically that many works were incorrectly attributed to Camões. Biographies, commentaries, and criticism soon followed. Camões's first editors, André de Resende and Soropita, were his first disciples in the lyric as well, and because of Camões's prestige at court, Francisco de Portugal, more an imitator than a genuine poet, enjoyed considerable favor. As for narrative or didactic epics in Portuguese, more than thirty were composed between 1572 and 1656 alone, each exploiting different aspects of Camões's work and attempting to resolve the problems of the genre; as the Portuguese ideology of expansion deteriorated, the epic became a historical novel in verse. Although the importance of *The Lusiads* remains great, Camões's influence as a lyric poet has been more fruitful.

OTHER MAJOR WORKS

PLAYS: *Enfatriões*, pr. 1540; *Auto del-Rei Seleuco*, pr. 1542; *Filodemo*, pr. 1555.

BIBLIOGRAPHY

Camões, Luís de. *The Lusiads*. Translated by Landeg White. New York: Oxford University Press, 2008. Translation of Camões's famous work, with an introduction that looks at his life and provides some analysis of the poem.

Gil, Fernando, and Helder Macedo. *The Traveling Eye: Retrospection, Vision, and Prophecy in the Portuguese Renaissance*. Dartmouth: University of Massachusetts Press, 2009. Discussion of the Portuguese Renaissance centers on *The Lusiads*.

Hart, Jack. "*The Lusiads*." In *Masterplots*. 4th ed. Edited by Laurence W. Mazzeno. Pasadena, Calif.: Salem Press, 2011. A comprehensive plot summary and literary analysis of *The Lusiads*.

Monteiro, George. *The Presence of Camões: Influences on the Literature of England, America, and Southern Africa*. Lexington: University Press of Kentucky, 1996. An introduction to Camões and an investigation of his influence on a number of writers. Includes bibliographic references and an index.

Nicolopulos, James. *The Poetics of Empire in the Indies: Prophecy and Imitation in "La araucana" and "Os lusíadas."* University Park: Pennsylvania State University Press, 2000. An investigation of literary representations of sixteenth century Iberian colonialism and imperialism. Camões's poem *The Lusiads* is interpreted.

O'Halloran, Colin M. *History and Heroes in the "Lusiads": A Commemorative Essay on Camoëns*. Lisbon: Executive Commission of the Fourth Centenary of the Publication of The Lusiads, 1974. A short book examining the use Camões made of the history of Portugal in the creation of the heroes and kings in his poem. Discusses the poem as a record of and tribute to Portugal's national drive to conquer new lands and convert the people there. It is interesting and accessible, but all quotes from the poem are in Portuguese.

Ouden, Maria Den. *Notions of Patriotism and Images of Women: A "New" Reading of the "Lusiads."* Haamstede, the Netherlands: Author, 2002. Examines the representation of women in Camões's poem.

Richard A. Mazzara

GIOSUÈ CARDUCCI

Born: Val di Castello, Duchy of Lucca (now in Italy); July 27, 1835
Died: Bologna, Italy; February 16, 1907
Also known as: Enotrio Romano

PRINCIPAL POETRY

Rime, 1857
Juvenilia, 1863
Giambi, 1867 (also known as *Giambi ed epodi*, 1882)
Levia gravia, 1868
Decennalia, 1871
Poesie, 1871
Nuove poesie, 1872
Odi barbare, 1877 (*Barbarian Odes*, 1939)
Nuove odi barbare, 1882 (*New Barbarian Odes*, 1939)
Ca ira, 1883
Rime nouve, 1887 (*Rime nouve of Carducci*, 1916; *The New Lyrics*, 1942)
Rime e ritmi, 1899 (*The Lyrics and Rhythms*, 1942)
Terze odi barbare, 1889 (*Third Barbarian Odes*, 1939)
A Selection of His Poems, 1913
A Selection from the Poems, 1921
The Barbarian Odes of Giosuè Carducci, 1939, 1950 (includes *Barbarian Odes*, *New Barbarian Odes*, and *Third Barbarian Odes*)
Selected Verse, 1994

OTHER LITERARY FORMS

Giosuè Carducci (kor-DEWT-chee) had a long career as a scholarly critic as well as a poet and also combined the two activities. He wrote many volumes of literary history and criticism and edited several editions of Italian authors, including Petrarch and Politian. His two volumes on Giuseppe Parini have been called "the most impressive monument of his indefatigable industry." The major fault in his prose, as in his poetry, is a tendency toward bombast, though at his best he was the finest essayist of his time. Often asked to speak on public occasions, he displayed disciplined classical eloquence, speaking on Vergil, Dante, Petrarch, Giovanni Boccaccio, Alessandro Manzoni, and Giacomo Leopardi. His greatest speech, delivered in Bologna on June 4, 1882, was his extemporaneous eulogy for Giuseppe Garibaldi, who had died two days previously: "Per la morte di Giuseppe Garibaldi" (on the death of Giuseppe Garibaldi). All his nonfiction, as well as his poetry, is collected in his complete works, *Opere complete* (1940).

ACHIEVEMENTS

The first Italian to win the Nobel Prize in Literature, which he received in 1906, Giosuè Carducci synthesized two great literary traditions to create a distinctive, original body of work. Although he came to maturity in the Romantic era, Carducci adhered to and helped maintain the values of the classical tradition; indeed, he became the outstanding exponent of the classicism which lay beneath the surface of Romanticism throughout the seventeenth century. Unlike his contemporaries, who looked nostalgically back to the Middle Ages, Carducci turned his attention toward ancient Rome and Greece. His fusion of a classical aesthetic with essentially Romantic sentiments exerted a powerful influence, particularly in the last decades of the century. Poets such as Enrico Panzacchi, Lorenzo Stecchetti, Giovanni Marradi, and Severino Ferrari were all part of Carducci's circle. Both for his influence and for his work, Carducci is recognized as the major Italian poet of the late 1800's.

BIOGRAPHY

Giosuè Carducci was born to Michele Carducci and Ildegonda Celli in Val di Castello, a small town near Viareggio, in Tuscany. Carducci's father, a physician, was greatly affected by the patriotism which would lead to the Risorgimento. An active Carbonaro (a member of a secret society seeking the unification of Italy), he was confined for a year in Volterra because of his participation in the Revolution of 1831. When Carducci was three, his family moved to Bolgheri, in the wild and desolate Maremma region south of Pisa. Maremma, with its Etruscan tombs, became the emotional landscape of Carducci's later poetry, appearing in such poems as "Idillio maremmano" ("Maremma Idyll") and "Traversando la Maremma Toscano" ("Crossing the Tuscan Maremma"). Carducci's mother reared him on the tragedies of Vittorio Alfieri, a writer in the French neoclassical style who had sought to revive the national spirit of Italy. For his part, Carducci's father attempted to impart to his son his own fervent enthusiasm for the writings of Manzoni, but Carducci, always an independent thinker, never acquired a taste for Manzoni. The boy was also taught Latin by his father and delighted in the works of Vergil and other ancient authors. He avidly read Roman history and anything dealing with the French Revolution. His first verse, satirical in nature, was written in 1846.

In 1848, the Carduccis were obliged to move when the attempt at independence failed. The threat of violence became too great for Carducci's father, and the family relocated first to Laiatico, then to Florence. Carducci went to religious schools until 1852, and was influenced by his rhetoric teacher, Father Geremia Barsottini, who had translated into prose all the odes of Horace. The boy became further impassioned in the cause of Italian reunification and discovered the works of Ugo Foscolo and Giuseppe Mazzini. After completing his education, Carducci followed his wandering father to Celle on Mount Amiata but soon after won a scholarship to the Normal School of Pisa. In 1855, he published his first book, *L'arpa del populo*, an anthology, and a year later he received his doctoral degree and a certification for teaching. He took a position as a rhetoric teacher in a secondary school at the *ginnasio* in San Miniato al Tedesco.

With several friends, among them Giuseppe Chiarini, Carducci founded a literary society, Amici Pedanti, a group that was essentially anti-Romantic and anti-

Catholic. They believed that Italy's only hope for the future was in the revival of the classical, pagan spirit of the ancient world, which was emphasized as still existing in the Italian land and blood. Such opinions naturally provoked violent objections, both from Romantics and from those who favored the status quo. Carducci freely and ferociously responded in prose to the attacks many times. His first collection of poetry, *Rime*, appeared in July, 1857.

Although Carducci won a competition for the chair of Greek in a secondary school in Arezzo, the granducal government did not approve his appointment, so in 1857, he returned to Florence and eked out a living by giving private lessons. In November, his depression became worse when his brother Dante killed himself for unknown reasons. A year later, Carducci's father died, and Carducci became the head of his impoverished family. In 1858, he moved his mother and brother Walfredo into a very poor house in Florence, continuing his private lessons and editing the texts of the Bibliotechina Diamante of publisher Gaspare Barbèra. Together with Barbèra, he founded a short-lived periodical, *Il poliziano*. Despite his financial situation, Carducci married Elvira Menicucci in March, 1859.

With the union of Tuscany and Italy, Carducci's fortunes turned for the better. First, he was offered the chair of Greek in the secondary school of Pistoia, where he remained for nearly a year; then, the minister of education, Terenzio Mamiani, appointed him to the chair of Italian Eloquence at the University of Bologna. Carducci was somewhat ambivalent toward his professorial role and its traditional philological orientation and fretted about its effect on his poetry, but the position allowed him to deepen his acquaintance with the classics and with the literature of other nations. His political views also changed. Under Victor Emmanuel II, Carducci had been an idealistic monarchist in support of the union of Italy, but after Garibaldi was wounded and captured by government troops at Aspromonte in 1862, Carducci allied himself with the democratic republicans and became more pronouncedly Jacobin and anti-Catholic, venting his intense feelings in aggressive poetry.

Carducci published his *Giambi* (iambics; later *Giambi ed epodi*), a collection of polemical poems, under the pseudonym Enotrio Romano; the poems reveal Carducci's affinities with Victor Hugo and Heinrich Heine. "Inno a Satana" ("Hymn to Satan") was in a similar vein and became one of his most famous poems, though his work suffered in quality as he became more vituperative. By 1872, however, he had begun to control his polemical instincts, and some of his finest poems, later collected in *The New Lyrics*, were written in the 1870's. *Barbarian Odes*, begun in 1873, became his most influential work.

Indeed, following the publication of the collection *Barbarian Odes*, Carducci became an object of adulation for younger poets throughout Italy. Periodicals such as *Fanfulla della Domenica*, *Cronaca bizantina*, and *Domenica letteraria* helped spread his fame. *New Barbarian Odes* solidified his reputation, and he assumed the role of national poet.

In part, Carducci's position as a leader of young Italian poets was the result of the efforts of Angelo Sommaruga, who had founded *Cronaca bizantina* to encourage native Italian writing and gathered newcomers such as Marradi, Matilde Serao, Edoardo Scarfoglio, Guido Magnoni, and Gabriele D'Annunzio for

Giosuè Carducci (Library of Congress)

its pages. Sommaruga sought out Carducci to give credibility to the group, and Sommaruga's encouragement spurred Carducci to intense activity in verse and prose. During this period, Carducci's political and philosophical views shifted; he resigned himself to the monarchy and acquired a more religious attitude, with some appreciation of the Roman Catholic Church's mission, though he remained fundamentally anticlerical.

The last two decades of Carducci's life were filled with misery. In 1885, he became ill. Five years later, he was made a senator, but in 1899, a stroke paralyzed his hand and nearly deprived him of speech. He continued working, despite the setbacks, publishing his last volume of poetry in 1899 and collecting his works from 1850 to 1900. In 1904, he resigned from teaching. He received the Nobel Prize in Literature the year before he died.

ANALYSIS

When granting Giosuè Carducci the 1906 Nobel Prize in Literature, the Swedish Academy stated that the award was given "not only in consideration of his deep learning and critical research, but above all as a tribute to the creative energy, freshness of style, and lyrical force which characterize his poetic masterpieces." Carducci's works are exceptional in their synthesis of literary qualities often seen as opposites. Though his life coincided with the height of Romanticism in Italy, he took the classical mode as his paradigm of artistic creation. This might have made him a curious anachronism, but his passion and his agility with classical form kept his works free of the servility that mars much neoclassical poetry. Carducci had too great a heart to let formal considerations neuter him and too much poetic skill not to exploit the opportunities of form.

Indeed, Carducci's great learning gave him the ability to scrutinize his own work, to evaluate and revise it with a living sense of literary history. Full of the passions of the Risorgimento and the nationalism of the new Italian state, he nevertheless viewed his work as part of a long historical tradition; whatever the Romans had been in essence was still in the Italian landscape, soil, and blood. Though Italy had drifted from the unity and glory of its past, it was always possible to restore

those qualities, which were not dead but merely submerged. Classicism thus became a way of restoring to the Italian nation and people their rightful identity and heritage. Carducci himself wrote:

> Great poetry aspires ceaselessly to the past and proceeds from the past. The dead are infinitely more numerous than the living, and the spaces of time under the Triumph of Death are incomparably more immense and more tranquil than the brief moment agitated by the phenomenon of life.

JUVENILIA

Carducci collected his earliest poetry (that written between 1850 and 1860, including that published in *Rime*) in *Juvenilia*. In these early poems, the young Carducci was searching for his voice, but he had already adopted many of the values which inform his mature work. *Juvenilia* reveals a familiarity with Greek and Latin models as well as with Italian poetry; the values that antedate Romanticism are stressed, along with a natural humanism free of the sentimentality and egotistic aberrations of Romanticism. *Juvenilia* is highly patriotic in tone and often violently anti-Catholic because of the Church's opposition to the reunification of Italy. Carducci revives the memory of ancient poetry and pagan strength by saluting the ancient gods; he praises ancient Greece, "Mother Rome," and "free human genius." He reminds Italy of the greatness of Rome and the heroic example of the French Revolution. He salutes the heroes of Italian unity, such as Garibaldi, Mazzini, and Victor Emmanuel II, the latter in a joyous celebration of the imminent war with Austria in 1859. Many of the poems are violently emotional: Carducci attacks those whom he perceives as the enemies of Italy and plunges into depression over the contemporary state of the country and its people.

One of Carducci's most famous and controversial poems was "Hymn to Satan." Later in his life, the poet would disavow the poem and call it "vulgar sing-song," but he stood defiantly behind it when it was published, astounding the public and causing great outrage at the University of Bologna and elsewhere. The critic Querico Filopanti, for example, asserted that it was not a poem at all but an intellectual orgy. In it, Carducci gives full vent to his anticlerical feelings, seeking to shock Italians out of their spiritual apathy. Satan becomes the symbol of nature and reason: He is Lucifer, carrier of light, enemy of asceticism and of a Church which denies the natural rights of human beings. Free thought, progress, and physical vitality are Satan's promises. Curiously, the poem praises Girolamo Savonarola for his defiance, ignoring the religious reformer's own asceticism. Carducci's Satan has been likened to Charles Baudelaire's in *Les Fleurs du mal* (1857, 1861, 1868; *Flowers of Evil*, 1909), but a more fruitful comparison can be drawn with the English Romantics' interpretation of John Milton's Satan in *Paradise Lost* (1667, 1674) as a Romantic hero. Carducci's Satan is clearly more Promethean than Satanic.

LEVIA GRAVIA AND GIAMBI ED EPODI

Levia gravia (light and heavy) has a tone of somberness and bitter disappointment, reflecting the events of the 1860's. During this time, the conquest of Rome was delayed, the disaster at Aspromonte occurred, and Carducci himself was drifting from his belief in the monarchy. The largely political inspiration and the tendentiousness which characterize *Levia gravia* also mar *Giambi ed epodi*, in which Carducci's combative nature overcomes his sense of poetry. "Canto dell'amore" ("Song of Love"), the last poem in *Giambi ed epodi*, provides a departure from this combativeness and reveals a depth greater than that of many of his earlier works. Most of this collection simply attacks and satirizes Pope Pius IX and the problems of the newly formed Italian government. "Song of Love," however, expresses a simple, robust view of life. Looking from Perugia, where the fortress of Paolina (a symbol of tyranny razed by the people in 1860) once stood, the poet is filled with the beauty of spring and lifted above the level of ordinary human struggle. The song of love fills him. The ancient Etruscans and Romans and foreign invaders of the Umbrian plain are evoked as symbolic of the ongoing cycles of nature. The poet even invites his enemy the pope to drink a glass of wine to liberty with him. He hears a chant rising from the hills, the voice of people of the past saying, "Too much we hated, suffering. So love!/Holy and fair the world shall be always."

NUOVE POESIE

Some critics, such as Eugenio Donadoni, remark on the gracefulness of images and rhythms in *Levia gravia*

and date Carducci's beginnings as a major poet from this volume. Others, however, would delay his "arrival" as a major poet to the more mature *Nuove poesie*, four years later. One notable poem from the latter is "I poeti di parte bianca" ("Poets of the White Faction"), which makes reference to the factions in Dante's Florence and evokes that moment in history as well as the poetry of the fourteenth century. "Francesco Petrarca" celebrates the great sonneteer and speaks of raising an altar to him in the deep, green woods, combining Carducci's sense of landscape with his love for the tradition of Italian poetry.

BARBARIAN ODES, NEW BARBARIAN ODES, AND THIRD BARBARIAN ODES

At the center of Carducci's oeuvre is the highly influential and original sequence comprising *Barbarian Odes*, *New Barbarian Odes*, and *Third Barbarian Odes*. "I hate the outworn meters," Carducci proclaimed, and he began to adapt such classical forms as the Alcaic, the Asclepiadean, and the Sapphic, all commonly used by Horace.

Carducci's adaptations of classical meters are extraordinarily successful; the demanding requirements of the ancient forms are satisfied gracefully and unobtrusively. When, late in life, he returned to modern forms, the musicality and facility of his verse were markedly enhanced.

Among the most successful poems of the *Barbarian Odes* is the pensive love poem "Alla stazione in una mattinata d'autunno" ("To the Station on an Autumn Morning"), in which Carducci evokes the melancholy feeling of the autumn season. "Miramar," the title of which is derived from the name of the castle near Trieste from which Maximilian began his voyage to Mexico, also conveys a tragic, pensive mood, using vivid natural imagery of the Adriatic Sea in the context of the story of the ill-fated Emperor Maximilian of Mexico. "Alla fonti del Clitunno" ("At the Sources of the Clitumnus"), a protest against Christianity, lacks the sharp edge of Carducci's earlier poems on the same topic. The poet celebrates the peasants who live along the quiet river, condemns the fanatic humility of medieval life, and hails the fecund vitality of Italy, mother of crops, laws, arts, and industry. "Presso l'urna di P. B. Shelley" ("Near the Urn of P. B. Shelley") is one of

Carducci's many poems making reference to great persons, living or dead. Written in elegiac distichs (a dactylic hexameter followed by a pentameter), the poem portrays a faraway island where mythical and literary figures meet. Siegfried and Achilles walk along the sea; Roland and Hector sit together under a tree; Lear tells his story to Oedipus. Ophelia and Iphigenia, Cordelia and Antigone, Durendala and Andromache, Helen and Iseult, Lady Macbeth and Clytemnestra are paired. Shelley, the only modern poet present, has been brought to the island by Sophocles. The narrator speaks: "The present hour is in vain; it but strikes and flees;/ only in the past is beauty, only in death is truth." Like many classicists, Carducci believed that it is possible to cheat death only by the immortality of art.

THE LYRICS AND RHYTHMS

In *The Lyrics and Rhythms*, his final book of poetry, Carducci abandoned the classical meters of *Barbarian Odes* and returned to modern forms. Many of the poems in this volume were composed in the Alps and have a clear, wide-ranging vision, as if written in imitation of the clear, broad expanses visible from the mountains. Standing on the "mount of centuries," the poet looks deeply into the past in order to see the future. The landscape is rich with associations from his memory, from history, from ancient myth and legend. The tone of the collection is generally solemn, as if Carducci, who had been obsessed with death since his brother's suicide and the death of his infant son, were contemplating his own end. In the gravity of its tone and the sweep of its vision, this last book of poems offers a fitting valediction.

OTHER MAJOR WORKS

EDITED TEXT: *L'arpa del populo*, 1855.

MISCELLANEOUS: *Opere*, 1889-1909 (includes prose and poetry); *Opere complete*, 1940 (30 volumes; includes all his prose and poetry).

BIBLIOGRAPHY

Bailey, John Cann. *Carducci*. Oxford, England: Clarendon Press, 1926. A brief biographical and critical study of Carducci.

Brand, Peter, and Lino Pertile, eds. *The Cambridge History of Italian Literature*. Rev. ed. New York: Cambridge University Press, 1999. Contains a short discussion of Carducci and classicism. Includes bibliographical references and index.

Carducci, Giosuè. *Selected Verse*. Translated and edited by David H. Higgins. Warminster, England: Aris & Phillips, 1994. The introduction and commentary to this collection of Carducci's verse provide information on his life and poetic works.

Scalia, S. Eugene. *Carducci: His Critics and Translators in England and America, 1881-1932*. New York: S. F. Vanni, 1937. A history of the critical reception of Carducci's work in England and America. Includes bibliographic references.

Sherby, Louise S., ed. *The Who's Who of Nobel Prize Winners, 1901-2000*. 4th ed. Westport, Conn.: Oryx Press, 2002. Contains a short entry on Carducci, a prize recipient.

Williams, Orlo. *Giosuè Carducci*. 1914. Reprint. Whitefish, Mont.: Kessinger, 2008. A short biography of Carducci. Includes bibliographic references.

J. Madison Davis

ROSALÍA DE CASTRO

Born: Santiago de Compostela, Spain; February 24, 1837

Died: Padrón, Spain; July 15, 1885

PRINCIPAL POETRY

La flor, 1857

A mi madre, 1863

Cantares gallegos, 1863

Follas novas, 1880

En las orillas del Sar, 1884 (*Beside the River Sar*, 1937)

Obras completas, 1909-1911 (4 volumes)

Poems, 1964

Poems, 1991

OTHER LITERARY FORMS

Rosalía de Castro (KOS-troh) was a novelist as well as a poet. Her five novels—*La hija del mar* (1859;

Daughter of the Sea, 1995), *Flavio* (1861), *Ruinas* (1866; ruins), *El caballero de las botas azules* (1867; the knight with the blue boots), and *El primer loco* (1881; the first madman)—span the transition from Romanticism to realism. Although Castro herself put considerable stock in her novels, she is remembered only for her poetry.

ACHIEVEMENTS

Rosalía de Castro has been called Spain's foremost woman poet; Gerald Brenan has gone further, asserting that if she had written more in Spanish than in her native Galician dialect, she would be recognized as the greatest woman poet of modern times. Her unabashedly heart-throbbing lyrics are saved from mawkishness by her disciplined style. Castro's poetry, along with that of Gustavo Adolfo Bécquer, is the most representative of Spanish poetry at the time of its transition from Romanticism to the modern lyric. Some critics believe that she interacted with Bécquer—that in fact she lent him in 1857 a copy of Gérard de Nerval's translation of Heinrich Heine's *Tragödien, nebst einem lyrischen Intermezzo* (1823; *Tragedies, Together with Lyric Intermezzo*, 1905), a book said to have influenced Bécquer. It was not until the second decade of the twentieth century, when Azorín (José Martínez Ruiz) and Miguel de Unamuno y Jugo recommended her to the public, that her reputation as a poet became assured. Later, even poet Luis Cernuda, who found her work uneven and sentimental, recognized the rare timelessness of her observations. Antonio Machado borrowed images from her poetry, Juan Ramón Jiménez referred to her as "our Rosalía," and Gerardo Diego used her name as a metaphor in his own poetry. Her Galician poetry inspired Federico García Lorca to write his own "poemas gallegos," including a "Canzón de cuna pra Rosalía Castro, morta" ("Lullaby for the Late Rosalía de Castro").

With her contemporaries Manuel Curros Enríquez (who wrote an elegy for her) and Eduardo Pondal, Castro made up a triad of Galician poets who effected a renaissance of their provincial literature. Using the folk songs of Galicia as her models, she bonded modern Spanish poetry to oral forms that would have otherwise been lost. She led the way for subsequent poets to utilize folk tradition, and her work tolled the death knell for urban Romanticism. Modernist poets availed themselves of the revolutionary meters used by Castro (her ennea-syllabic verse in *La flor*—the flower—predates the so-called innovations of Rubén Darío), and her use of free verse heralded the boldness of contemporary poetry.

To a remarkable extent, Castro's Galician and Spanish poetry has been accepted into English-language anthologies of world verse, especially in those of women's poetry (such as *A Book of Women Poets: From Antiquity to Now*, rev. ed., 1992).

BIOGRAPHY

Rosalía de Castro was born in Santiago de Compostela in 1837, the child of María Teresa de la Cruz de Castro y Abadía. Her mother, who came from a once-wealthy family, was thirty-three when Rosalía was born; her father, Jose Martínez Viojo, was thirty-nine and a priest. Although her father could not acknowledge Rosalía as his daughter, he may have taken some interest in her welfare. Rosalía was brought up by Francisca Martínez, who, despite her surname, does not appear to have been the priest's sister. By 1853, Rosalía was living with her real mother, and there developed between them a deep bond. In Rosalía's eyes, her mother sanctified whatever sin she may have committed by reaffirming her obligation to her daughter in defiance of a hypocritical society.

A precocious child, Castro was writing verses by the age of eleven, and by the age of sixteen she could play the guitar and the piano, had developed a fine contralto voice, and could draw well and read French. She read the foreign classics in translation and was fond of Lord Byron, Heinrich Heine, Edgar Allan Poe, and E. T. A. Hoffmann. Judging from the spelling errors in hand-written manuscripts of her poetry, however, her formal education may not have been extensive.

As a teenager, Castro was taken from Padrón to Santiago, where she attended school and where she participated in the city's cultural life. At a young people's cultural society, she met Aurelio Aguirre, one of the most representative figures of the Romantic movement in Galicia, a man who was later to be the model of Flavio in her novel of the same name, and who dedicated to her a work called "Improvisation"—apparently an attempt to console her for the discrepancy between her enchanting poetry and her less than enchanting physical appearance. Perhaps it is too facile to attribute the characteristic wistfulness of her poetry to a failed love affair, but it has been suggested that the lost love recalled in her poems and her fiction was Aurelio Aguirre. Among the poems not included in her own collections but included in *Obras completas* is an elegy for Aguirre.

In 1856, Castro went to Madrid, where she stayed at the home of a relative. It is generally said that she went "on family business," but it is possible she left home with the idea of becoming an actress in Madrid. Exposed to the cultural life of the Spanish capital, she devoted herself to writing and was able to meet other contemporary writers. In 1857, her first book of poetry *La flor* appeared and was favorably reviewed by Manuel Murguía in *La Iberia*. According to Murguía, he was not acquainted with the young author, but this is rather unlikely, not only because some of his comments presuppose a direct knowledge of Castro's personality, but also because he, too, had recently come from Galicia and, in fact, was Aguirre's best friend. Castro and Murguía were married in Madrid on October 10, 1858. Murguía, like Aguirre a Galician of Basque descent, was a journalist and historian destined to be honored in Galicia for his role in promoting regionalist literature. The couple had seven children. Their first child, a daughter, was born in 1859; their second child, also a daughter, was not born until ten years later. One of the twins Castro bore in 1871, Ovidio, was an accomplished painter of Galician landscapes but died young. Her youngest son died in his second year as the result of a fall, and her youngest daughter was stillborn in 1877.

In 1862, Castro's beloved mother died, and Castro honored her with a privately printed collection of poems, *A mi madre* (to my mother) of limited literary value but elegiac and emotional.

It remains unclear what kind of a marriage Castro had with Murguía. Gerald Brenan believes that Murguía, envious of his wife's talents, mistreated her; it is certain that Murguía destroyed his wife's correspondence after her death. Castro scholar Marina Mayoral, on the other hand, prefers to see in Murguía—who survived his wife by thirty-eight years and wrote lovingly and abundantly about her—one of the few mainstays of Castro's sad life. Despite the fulfillment of children and the security of family life, she was frequently bored, and in both her poetry and her fiction, she mourned lost happiness.

It is important, however, not to exaggerate the pathetic nature of Castro's life. She loved the arts and took great pleasure from her endeavors in the fields of music, drawing, and acting. She was a great success when she acted in Antonio Gil y Zárate's play *Rosamunda* (1839), and for the greater part of her life she enjoyed exchanging ideas with her friends. Her daughter Gala, who lived until 1964, was especially concerned that her mother not be remembered as morose. As Victoriano García Martí points out, people who are authentically sorrowful often develop a profound love of humankind and achieve a different kind of contentment. This was especially true of Castro, and after her death a legend grew concerning her generosity to others, endowing her with a kind of saintliness.

Between 1859 and 1870, the couple lived in Madrid and Simancas, where Murguía had a position as a government historian, and they traveled extensively throughout Spain. To Castro, any terrain that was not green, damp, and lush like her native Galicia was disappointing; thus, she disliked most of the rest of Spain. She became so consumed with nostalgia for her native land that she began her *Cantares gallegos* (Galician songs), written in Galician but given a Spanish title. In the 1870's, Murguía held positions in Galicia, and Castro spent much of her time at Padron, which she considered home. Having suffered from vague ill health all her life, she withdrew completely from society in her last decade; she died of uterine cancer in 1885. In the moments before her death, she received the Sacraments, recited her favorite prayers, and begged her children to destroy her unpublished manuscripts. With her last breath, she asked that the window be opened, for she wished to see the ocean—which in fact was not visible from her home.

Castro was buried near her mother in the peaceful cemetery of Adina in Padron, a place whose enchantment she had evoked in *Follas novas* (new leaves). On the very day of her death, accolades began to arrive, and as a result of the homage paid her in death, her remains were moved in 1891 to a marble tomb in the Convent of Santo Domingo de Bonaval in Santiago. In 1917, her compatriots, together with an organization of Galician emigrants in America, organized a campaign to raise a statue to their poet in the Paseo de la Herradura in Santiago, looking toward Padron. According to biographer Kathleen Kulp-Hill, this statue is faithful to portraits and descriptions of Castro. The figure is seated in a calm, pensive attitude, projecting an aura of strength and warmth.

ANALYSIS

As Frédéric Mistral is to Provence and Joan Maragall to Catalonia, Rosalía de Castro is to Galicia, the northwest corner of the Iberian peninsula, linked politically with Spain but tied ethnically, linguistically, and temperamentally with Portugal. When Castro was nine years old, there was an unsuccessful insurrection in Galicia against the Spanish government. The unpleasant memory of the savage reprisals undertaken by the government may help explain her strong hostility toward Castile and Castilians, as in the lines, "May God grant, Castilians,/ Castilians whom I abhor,/ that rather the Galicians should die,/ than to go to you for bread."

Santiago de Compostela, Castro's birthplace, possesses the bones of Saint James the Apostle, for which reason Galicia became in the Middle Ages the third most holy shrine in Christendom (after Jerusalem and Rome). The steady stream of pilgrims traveling to Galicia from all parts of Europe made Santiago a medieval cultural center, and in the thirteenth century, Galician became the language of lyrical poetry throughout the Iberian peninsula. The Galician *jograles* (minstrels) sang characteristically of melancholy (designated in Spanish by its Galician and Portuguese name, *saudades*), as in, for example, their *cantigas de amigo*, the songs of women whose lovers were absent, either away at sea or fighting the Moors in Portugal. After the thirteenth century, however, there was an eclipse of Galician poetry, and it was not until the nineteenth century that an interest in the poetic potential of the Galician language was reawakened.

The poetry of Castro flows from line to line in a musical sequence and does not, as Gerald Brenan observes, condense well into a single epithet or phrase. She was not fond of metaphors but rather relied heavily on repetition—in such lines as ("Breezes breezes, little breezes/ breezes of the land I come from")—and contrast—as in "To them those frosts/ are the promise of early flowers;/ To me they are silent workers/ weaving my winding sheet." In her earlier poems, she sometimes used the *leixa-pren*, a special feature of the medieval *cantigas de amigo*, whereby each new stanza begins with an echo from the last line of the previous stanza. Her diction is almost colloquial, her syntax uninverted (except in her earliest poetry and in some of her later poetry), and her adjectives are always the least ornamental possible. There abound words for the lushness of Galicia, names of animals and birds, and especially of trees (such as the oaks sacred to the ancient Celts of Galicia; giant chestnuts; and the cedars of "our own" Lebanon). In her somber moods, she draws repeatedly on Spanish adjectives such as *torvo* (grim), *amargo* (bitter), and *triste* (sad), and uses verbs such as *anonadar* (to destroy), *agostar* (to wither up as in August), *hostigar* (to scourge), while she uses words such as *guarida* (lair), *nido* (nest), and *egida* (aegis) to express the security and coziness of home in Galicia. Galician, more than Spanish, is a nasal language (for example, Galician *min*, "my," as opposed to Spanish *mí*), and Castro uses its humming nasals as a tool to craft more sharply the gloom she suffers on Earth, as in the line "Pra min i-en min mesma moras" (for me and in myself you live), rom "Cando penso que to fuche" (when I think that you have gone), in *Follas novas*.

"I USED TO HAVE A NAIL"

One remarkable poem that reveals Castro's attitude toward sorrow is "Una-ha vez tiven un cravo" ("I Used to Have a Nail") in *Follas novas*. This painful nail, whether made of gold, iron, or love, leads the poet, weeping like Mary Magdalen, to entreat God to effect a miracle for its removal. When at last she gathers the courage to pluck it out, the void it leaves is something like a longing for the old pain. Some critics have speculated that without an abundant supply of sorrow for her to sublimate into poetry, Castro felt lost. This contradictory hunger for suffering cannot be reduced to the level of a personal neurosis, for it reflects the ideals of traditional Christianity. Castro believed that thistles, though harsh to the flesh, mark the road to heaven, and in "Yo en mi lecho de abrojos" ("I on My Bed of Thistles," from *Beside the River Sar*), avowedly preferred her destiny to a "bed of roses and feathers," which have been known to "envenom and corrupt."

RELIGION AND SUPERSTITION

Castro was conventionally religious; she needed God and sought him everywhere, and she fought herself for her faith, as Unamuno did. There are biblical references in her poetry, as well as her marginally Christian *sombras* ("shades"), the souls of persons no longer living whom Castro "invokes" from time to time and who respond by intervening in the lives of the living. She also draws on Galician lore concerning the supernatural world. Witches (*meigas, lurpias*), warlocks (*meigos*), and elves (*trasgos*) inhabit her forests, and the safety of the unwary nocturnal traveler may be jeopardized by the Host of Souls in Torment. In "Dios bendiga todo, nena" ("God Blesses Everything, Child," from *Cantares gallegos*), an old woman warns a young girl of the dangers of the world, whereupon the girl declares her intention never to leave her village without scapularies, holy medals, and amulets to protect her from witches. The fine line between religion and superstition is typified in "Soberba" ("Foolish Pride") in *Follas novas*, where a family frightened by a storm tries to placate God with candles, olive leaves, and prayers, and by scouring from their personal slates offenses that might have incurred his wrath. Nor is the imagery of the supernatural always to be taken literally. In an aubade, Castro has the heroine address her lover affectionately as "warlock" while he prepares to leave her bed, and elsewhere employs the same word to create a metaphor for sorrow: "N' hay peor meiga que un-ha gran pena" (there is no worse demon than a great sorrow).

CANTARES GALLEGOS

Castro's first important book of poems was *Cantares gallegos*. In the prologue to this volume, she acknowledges the inspiration of *El libro de los cantares* by Antonio de Trueba, published the previous year, and apologizes for her shortcomings as a poet, claiming that her only schooling was that of "our poor country folk." The poems are dedicated to Fernan Caballero (Cecilia

Böhl de Faber), the pioneer of the realistic novel in Spain, who won Castro's appreciation with her unprejudiced portrayal of Galicians. Working without a grammar, Castro apologizes for her Galician; indeed, it is not a pure dialect unaffected by Castilian influence, and lexical and orthographic inconsistencies abound. She attempted to imitate modern Portuguese in her use of diacritical marks, contractions, and elisions, and included a short glossary of Galician words for the sake of her Castilian readers.

Castro's usual procedure was to begin her poems with a popular couplet and then to elaborate it into a ballad. Her masterpiece is perhaps "Airiños, airiños, aires" ("Breezes, Breezes, Little Breezes") in which she portrays the nostalgia of a Galician emigrant, playing upon the dual meaning of *airiños* as "little breezes" and "little songs." Everywhere this unfortunate emigrant turns in the strange country of her destination, people peer curiously at her, and she longs for the sweet breezes of home, those "quitadoiriños de penas" ("takers-away of sorrow") that enchant the woods and caress the land. Similarly as Galician poetry inspired the Castilian lyric of the fifteenth and sixteenth centuries, this poem influenced the revival of Spanish poetry that began thirty years after Castro's death. The *Romancero gitano, 1924-1927* (1928; *The Gypsy Ballads of García Lorca*, 1951, 1953) of Federico García Lorca, for example, with its themes and repetitions derived from folk tradition, owes much to this poem.

In "Pasa rio, pasa rio" ("Pass by, River, Pass By"), a disconsolate lover weeps tears into the ocean in hope that they may reach her beloved in Brazil, where he has had to emigrate. The plight of the Galician emigrant forced to leave his homeland because of economic necessity troubled Castro deeply. There are many poems of praise for Galicia, such as "Cómo chove mihudiño" ("How the Rain Is Falling Lightly"), in which she describes Padrón, lulled by the river where the trees are shady, and reminisces about the great house owned by her humanitarian grandfather. She dares to ask the Sun of Italy if it has seen "more green, more roses,/ bluer sky or softer colors/ where foam stripes your gulfs with whiteness"; and is reminded by a wandering cloud of the sad shade of her mother wandering lonely in the spheres before she goes to glory.

FOLLAS NOVAS

The poems of *Follas novas* are meant to be read and reflected upon, as opposed to the folk poems of *Cantares gallegos* with their marked oral quality. The 139 poems of *Follas novas* are more subjective and personal and bleaker than those of the earlier book, which radiate innocence and hope; they are also more innovative in form: Castro employed varying line lengths with metrical combinations then regarded as inappropriate for Spanish verse, such as combinations of eight with ten or eleven syllables or eight with fourteen. Dedicated to the Society for the Welfare of Galicians in Havana, the book was published simultaneously in Havana and Madrid in 1880. In her prologue, Castro expresses her concern for the suffering of Galicians in distant lands, and she also asserts her artistic independence as a woman. Certainly the successive deaths of her two youngest children within three months of each other in 1876-1877 did much to intensify her tragic sense of life, but many of the poems in this collection were written as long as ten years before the publication date.

Here, Castro's poetry is no longer concerned with aubades but rather with the departures of lovers and their separation. Love is no longer hopeful but rather furtive and anxious. In "¿Que lle digo?" ("What Should I Tell Her?") the emigrant may be plagued by *saudades* for his homeland but may wax cynical about love as well: "Antona is there, but I have Rosa here." The landscape of Galicia is always in the background, but is no longer decorative and is now interwoven with more complex emotions. Death is seen as a cure for the disease of life, and the poet asks God why suicide must be deemed a crime.

Although she occasionally dedicated her poems to worthy persons (such as her husband and Ventura Ruíz de Aguilera), Castro did not often exalt either historical figures or living persons in her poetry. One notable exception, written in classical form, is her elegy on the tomb of Sir John Moore, the affable British general who led a retreat to Corunna that ended in the British victory over the Napoleonic forces there in 1809, but which cost Moore his life. *Follas novas* also includes a translation into Galician of the poem "Armonias d'a tarde" (harmonies of the afternoon), by Ventura Ruíz de Aguilera, a contemporary poet who drew on the folk motifs of the Salamanca area.

BESIDE THE RIVER SAR

As a result of complaints made by her Galician readers that some of her material was scandalous, Castro vowed never again to write in Galician, and it is to this decision and the Spanish poems of her last collection, *Beside the River Sar*, that she owes her prominence in Spanish literature. Not all the critics, however, proclaim the superiority of these poems. Gerald Brenan, who prefers the softer, more tender tone of her Galician verse, finds the aloofness of her Castilian poems chilling. Many of the poems collected in *Beside the River Sar* were written between 1878 and 1884 and were published in periodicals, some as distant as *La nación española* of Buenos Aires. These late poems reflect a greater concern with ideas; they are characterized by unusual combinations of lines and broken rhythms, with lines of as many as sixteen or eighteen syllables, and by a syntactical complexity not previously seen in Castro's work.

In *Beside the River Sar*, Galicia is no longer a focal point, assuming instead the role of a backdrop, and the folk element is even less in evidence. Castro continues to excel in nature poetry, displaying in "Los robles" ("The Oaks") a distinctly modern concern for ecology when she protests the wasteful destruction of trees in Galicia with an almost druidic reverence for arboreal vitality. The River Sar of the title, the beloved river of her homeland, is a symbol for the flowing of life toward its unknown and unknowable destination.

In what is possibly her most frequently anthologized poem, "Dicen que no hablan las plantas" ("They Say That Plants Do Not Speak"), Castro asserts the importance that natural phenomena such as plants, brooks, and birds have for her. Although it seems that these natural phenomena view her as a "madwoman" because of her outlandish dreams, she exhorts them not to poke fun at her, because without those dreams, she would lack the wherewithal to admire the beauty that they themselves so generously display.

In her valorization of dreams (*sueños* or *ensueños*) and her refusal to accept the pathetic constraints by which humankind is necessarily bound, Castro prefigures the concerns of the Generation of '98, of poets

195

such as Unamuno, Machado, and Azorín. Nevertheless, she must acknowledge that dreams can lead to folly, as they do in the poignant "La canción que oyó en sueños el viejo" ("The Song Which the Old Man Heard in His Dreams"), in which an old man, designated crazy in the poem, feels his blood pump and surge as his youthful passions return when in truth he should be reckoning with "infallible death" and "implacable old age."

In *Beside the River Sar*, the winter, symbolic of despair and the end of life in Castro's earlier work, is friendly, a herald, in fact, of spring, and is "a thousand times welcome." Even the desert of Castile, anathema in her earlier poetry and so drastically opposed to the lushness of Galicia, assumes a positive guise, coming to represent the realm beyond carnal suffering, lit by "another light more vivid than that of the golden sun."

One of the most interesting poems in the collection is the questioning and subsequently epiphanic "Santa Escolástica" ("Saint Scholastica"). In Santiago on a drizzly April day, the poet allows herself to absorb the dismal atmosphere. "Cemetery of the living," she exclaims, as she contrasts the gloom she sees around her with the city's medieval glory. This leads to her own rephrasing of that tortured question, "Why, since there is God, does Hell prevail?" She enters the Convent of San Martín Pinario in search of comfort. Her female soul begins to feel the sacred majesty of the temple as vividly as it has felt the satisfactions of motherhood. Suddenly, the sun strikes the statue of Saint Scholastica and brings into sharper focus the saint's ecstasy, which in turn produces an ecstasy in Castro, who exclaims exultantly, "There is art! There is poetry! . . . There must be a heaven,/ for there is God."

Kulp-Hill contrasts this joyous poem from *Beside the River Sar* with a poem from *Follas novas* having the same setting, "N'a catedral" ("In the Cathedral"). In the latter, although the sun shines briefly into the dimly illuminated room, the shadows return, and the poet withdraws without consolation. As the contrast between the two poems suggests, Castro's last volume was a testament to hope.

In an age when poets declaimed, Castro had the courage to write honestly and realistically about issues that troubled her. She was unashamed to examine and interpret the feelings of the Galician peasantry, creating from their own forms and phrases a new poetry of rare beauty. As she explored her own hope and hopelessness and pondered the human condition in general, she translated her findings into poetry that speaks to all people.

OTHER MAJOR WORKS

LONG FICTION: *La hija del mar*, 1859 (*Daughter of the Sea*, 1995); *Flavio*, 1861; *Ruinas*, 1866; *El caballero de las botas azules*, 1867; *El primer loco*, 1881.

BIBLIOGRAPHY

Courteau, Joanna. *The Poetics of Rosalía de Castro's "Negra sombra."* New York: Edwin Mellen Press, 1995. A close critical examination of one of Castro's poems. Includes bibliographical references and index.

Dever, Aileen. *The Radical Insufficiency of Human Life: The Poetry of R. de Castro and J. A. Silva.* Jefferson, N.C.: McFarland, 2000. A comparison of Castro's and Silva's poetry. Their works have meaningful differences but share remarkable likenesses in theme, tone, and style, though it is unlikely that they knew of each other's work. Of interest to feminist critics is an interpretation of Castro's literary vocation within a patriarchal society.

Geoffrion-Vinci, Michelle C. *Between the Maternal Aegis and the Abyss: Woman as Symbol in the Poetry of Rosalía de Castro.* Madison, N.J.: Fairleigh Dickinson University Press, 2002. Examines the symbolism of Castro's poetry at length. Discusses her relationship with Manuel Murguía.

Kulp-Hill, Kathleen. *Manner and Mood in Rosalía de Castro: A Study of Themes and Style.* Madrid: Ediciones José Porrua Turanzas, 1968. A thorough critical study of Castro's writing and a bibliography of her works.

_____. *Rosalía de Castro.* Boston: Twayne, 1977. Introductory biography and critical analysis of selected works. Includes an index and bibliography of Castro's writing.

Wilcox, John C. *Women Poets of Spain, 1860-1990: Toward a Gynocentric Vision.* Urbana: University of Illinois Press, 1997. This work on female poets in Spain in the second half of the nineteenth century contains a section on Castro.

Jack Shreve

CATULLUS

Born: Cisalpine Gaul (now in Italy); c. 85 B.C.E.
Died: Probably Rome (now in Italy); c. 54 B.C.E.

PRINCIPAL POETRY

Catullus, 1893 (Elmer Truesdell Merrill, editor)
*Gaius Valerius Catullus: The Complete Poetry, a
New Translation with an Introduction*, 1957
(Frank O. Copley, translator)

OTHER LITERARY FORMS

Catullus (kuh-TUHL-uhs) is remembered only for
his poetry. In the fourteenth century, a manuscript of
his works was discovered; the manuscript contained
116 of his poems, varying from a short couplet to a long
poem of more than four hundred lines.

ACHIEVEMENTS

Catullus is one of the greatest lyric poets of all time.
He lived in Rome when that city was the center of the
known world and when it was rocked to its foundations
by political and social revolution. Catullus was in his
early twenties when, in 62 B.C.E. under the consulship
of Cicero, the Catiline Conspiracy occurred. The poet
lived to see the coalition of Julius Caesar, Pompey, and
Crassus form in 60 B.C.E. and Caesar's subsequent rise
to power. Catullus had been dead only about five years
when civil war broke out between Caesar and Pompey.
Pompey's death at the Battle of Pharsalus occurred
in 48 B.C.E., and Caesar was assassinated in 44 B.C.E.
References to Julius Caesar, Pompey, and Cicero appear in various poems of Catullus. He wrote during
the stormy period when the Roman Empire was established, immediately before the reign of Augustus
(27 B.C.E.-C.E. 14). Catullus bitterly attacked Caesar
and his favorites in early poems but eventually came to
support the Caesarian party. His poetry precedes the
somewhat later literary wave of Vergil (70-19 B.C.E.)
and the Augustan poets.

Catullus was the leading representative of a revolution in poetry created by the *neoteroi* or "new men" in
Rome. Rather than writing about battles, heroes, and
the pagan gods, Catullus draws his subjects from ev-

eryday, intensely personal life. He writes about lovers'
quarrels, arguments, indecent behavior, and his love
for his brother and for his Italian countryside. Whatever he writes is marked by a high level of passion,
rather than by the Augustan ideal of calm detachment.
His poetry is personal, intense, and excited. His language is that of the street: slang, profanity, dialect. His
poems are frequently dramatic monologues in which an
aggrieved suitor addresses his mistress or an injured
party pours malediction on his enemy. The reader must
envision many of Catullus's poems as little one-act
plays, with a persona speaking the lines, a dramatic audience listening to the speech, and a particular situation
in which these words might be spoken appropriately.

Although the content, topics, and language of Catullus's poems were drawn from the seamy streets of
Rome, his poetic forms were not. Catullus studied and
imitated the meters of late Greek literature of the Alexandrian school; probably for this reason, he was called
in ancient times the "learned" Catullus. The late Greek
poets developed complicated metrical patterns that Catullus translated into the Latin language. (This subject is discussed extensively in Merrill's edition of Catullus.)

Catullus was a precursor of the Augustan Age, a
conveyor of the Alexandrian formal tradition into Latin
poetry, with a genius for intense, passionate, personal
poetry. Even in translation, he is funny and obscene, furious and touching.

BIOGRAPHY

Very little biographical information about Gaius
Valerius Catullus is known with certainty. From references in his poetry and from legend, a series of traditional hypotheses about his life have evolved. Ancient
sources indicate that he was born in Cisalpine Gaul. His
family must have been wealthy and powerful, although
he never mentions any family member except his
brother. Catullus was probably a younger son who
went at an early age to Rome to make his way. He
owned a villa at Sirmio in the lake district of northern
Italy and another in the Sabine Hills. It appears that he
lived a life of ease and culture. The only documented
fact about his career is that he traveled to the province
of Bythinia on the staff of the governor Gaius Mem-

mius around 57-56 B.C.E. The likely motive for such a trip would be to earn a fortune, but later unfavorable references in Catullus's poems suggest that the undertaking was not completely successful.

The poems of Catullus are often dramatic, like the sonnets of William Shakespeare: A lover sings the praises of his beloved or heaps scorn on a rival. Although it is not accurate to consider such poems as directly autobiographical, it has become customary to assume that they reflect to some degree real happenings in the life of the poet. If the reader considers the poems to be mainly nonfiction, an emotional tale emerges about love and hate in Rome long ago. The poet falls in love with Lesbia, a married woman. She toys with his affection and keeps him in torment. She is unfaithful to him with many men. The poet attacks his rivals viciously in words, but he is nevertheless enslaved by Lesbia's charms, until he flees from Rome on his venture to Bythinia to escape her treacheries.

Modern scholars suggest that Lesbia is a pseudonym for a real woman, Clodia, the sister of Publius Clodius Pulcher and the wife of Q. Caecillius Metellus Celer, who was consul in the year 60 B.C.E. This hypothesis seems to be supported by several references in the poems and suggests that Catullus really was involved in an affair that followed the outlines suggested in his poems. Sophisticated readers of poetry, however, will hesitate to accept such easy equations of art and reality. It is equally possible that Lesbia and her lover are both merely fictional inventions of a clever writer.

Whether Catullus left Rome to forget his cruel beloved or to get rich, he apparently was unhappy with his experience as a follower of the governor Memmius, who became an object of attack in several of Catullus's later poems. While in Bythinia, he wrote a tribute to his dead brother's grave, and he celebrated in poetry his own return to Italy. In Rome once again, the poet celebrated a new beloved, the boy Juventius, who also proved unfaithful. Catullus viciously attacked a character whom he called Mentula (the word literally means "penis" in Latin) thought to be based on Caesar's associate, Mamurra. Although critical of Caesar, Catullus eventually was reconciled with the Caesarian political group. He died in his thirtieth year.

It was probably an admirer who collected Catullus's poems in a book after his death and divided it into three parts according to the verse forms of the poems. The first group includes sixty poems on various themes, all in iambic or logaoedic rhythm. The middle group includes longer poems and begins with three epithalamia. The third group consists of shorter poems in elegiac meter. Gradually, the poems of Catullus fell out of favor, and he became an unknown figure until the fourteenth century, when Benvenuto Campesino rediscovered the texts, probably in Verona. From that original,

Catullus (Library of Congress)

many copies were made, so that the works of Catullus were well known to the great writers of the Italian Renaissance.

ANALYSIS

Catullus was a master of erotic poetry. Modern attitudes toward sexual love derive from conventions of courtship that can be traced back to Catullus. Some of his sexual poems seem wholesome and agreeable to the modern "liberated" reader; others may seem "unnatural" or obscene. In either case, Catullus was one of the first writers to codify a set of conventions for courtship: the blazon or praise of the beloved, the lover's lament at his unfaithful love, the abasement of the lover captivated by his unworthy beloved, the vilification of the rival for the beloved's affection, the antiblazon or enumeration of the beloved's defects, the comparison of married to adulterous love. These topics or themes have become commonplace in Western literature, but Catullus was one of the first to invent and systematically explore them. The 116 poems of Catullus can be grouped into several categories: those celebrating sexual love, those that taunt and insult, travel and locodescriptive verse, and mythological material such as the stories of Theseus and Ariadne, Peleus and Thetis, and Attis. Although these themes overlap, almost all his verse fits into one or more of these categories.

IN PRAISE OF PHYSICAL LOVE

Examples of his praise for sexual love include poems 5, 7, 8, 51, 70, 86, 87, 109, and others. Poem 5 is rightly famous as the prototype of the address of the lover to his beloved, "gather ye rosebuds while ye may." It is a poem of seduction in which the lover reminds the beloved that life is short, and time is fleeting, and she had better not delay too long in consenting to their union. The lover reminds the beloved that soon they will die and sleep one long eternal night; he asks for a thousand or a hundred thousand kisses. Carried away by the passion of these lines, the reader may fail to notice how contrary this erotic sentiment is to conventional morality. Rather than directing his attention to loftier matters, the lover elevates sexual union to a position of supreme importance. Such an exaltation of love is basic to the courtly tradition that developed later in the Renaissance.

Poem 70 introduces the notion that the beloved is not to be trusted, for lovers' promises are as fleeting as words written in dust or running water. Poem 109 expresses the lover's fervent wish that his beloved speak the truth when she promises to love him. Poem 86 presents a comparison or combat between the beloved Lesbia and another woman called Quintia. The poem is in the form of a blazon and begins by enumerating all of Quintia's outstanding physical features: her complexion, size, and shape. The lover grants that Quintia is physically well made but argues that she lacks personality. Only Lesbia has the inner spark, the charm that can truly be called beautiful. A cruder but nevertheless amusing version of this kind of love poem, sometimes called antiblazon, is poem 43. The lover's rival is called Mentula; Mentula has a girl whom some might call pretty, but the lover systematically examines her nose, feet, eyes, fingers, lips, and tongue, concluding that only a country bumpkin would call such a girl pretty. In every way, Lesbia far surpasses his rival's girl.

To elevate the significance of physical love to that of a religion and to make the beloved a goddess of love turns the lover into a helpless supplicant at the mercy of an unpredictable deity. Poem 8 is the lover's lament. He knows that Lesbia is merely toying with him, and he resolves not to run after her, not to be a foolish slave to desire. The lover rages at his unfaithful mistress—for example, in poems 37 and 58, where he accuses her of becoming a common whore; in poem 38, however, he begs her to take him back again. Strangely, the worse the beloved treats him, the more the lover desires her. Poem 72 explains that Lesbia's behavior breaks the lover's heart but inflames his lust for her. Catullus encapsulates the lover's lament in a couplet, justly called the best two lines of psychological analysis ever written, poem 85. The lover says that he hates and he loves her. If you ask him why, he cannot explain. He simply feels that he is crucified. The final word, *excrucior*, literally "to be crucified," is particularly well chosen because the crossed feelings of love and hate catch the lover when they intersect and nail him, as it were, to a cross.

In addition to his passion for the woman Lesbia, Catullus also celebrates his love for the boy Juventius. The poet's addresses to the boy follow conventions of romantic love similar to those that govern his speeches to Lesbia. Poem 48 celebrates the boy's kisses much as poem 5 does the woman's. Poem 99 tells how the once-sweet kisses of the boy turn bitter because he is unfaithful. Poem 81 mocks the boy for having a new boyfriend, a country hick unworthy of him. Poem 40 threatens a rival who has stolen the affection of the lover's boy. In general, Catullus endorses wine, women (or boys), and song. Poem 27, for example, is a famous drinking song; but, there is always pain close beneath the revelry. Not only does he both love and hate Lesbia, but he is also crucified by conflicting feelings about Rome, about all his acquaintances, and about life in general. He sees the ugliness barely hidden beneath the fashionable woman's makeup, the betrayal lurking behind the hearty greeting of the politicians and lawyers of the capitol, and death everywhere—the death of a pet sparrow, death pursuing golden boys and girls, the death of his beloved brother.

POETIC TAUNTS AND INSULTS

Catullus is also the master of poetic taunts and insults. Seldom has a writer humiliated so many public figures so effectively, so obscenely, so inventively. There are too many poems of this sort to analyze them in detail. Mentula, the supposed rival for Lesbia's favors, heads the list of those in the poet's disfavor. Mentula's virility, wit, poetry, courage, and personal hygiene all come into question. Usually, Catullus uses some common Roman name, the equivalent of English names such as Jimmy or Wayne, as a pseudonym for a historical personage. Modern scholars have spent much effort trying to discover who the characters attacked in the poems really are. No doubt this provided sport for the Roman audience as well, as readers whispered about the true identity of the characters ridiculed or, perhaps, libeled in Catullus's lines.

Sometimes, however, he does not hesitate to name names. Poem 93, for example, is a couplet addressed to Caesar by name, and it says that the poet does not care what the great man thinks. Poem 29 names Mamurra, who was Caesar's prefect in Gaul. The poem accuses Mamurra of looting Gaul for his own profit and refers repeatedly and mockingly to Mamurra as the degenerate descendant of the founding fathers of Rome. After maligning Mamurra's sexual habits and his wasteful fi-

nancial practices, the poem concludes that men like Mamurra have brought Rome to ruin. It is not necessary to know the exact identity of the unfortunate people who suffered the scathing attacks of Catullus. They are better understood as comic types, like caricatures. As such, they show the poet's ability to sketch a portrait of human deviance in a few biting lines. Thallus in poem 25 is the softest, most cunning, most delicate homosexual—and he steals personal belongings from the clothing of people at the public baths. Flavius in poem 6 has a new girl who is too spirited for him. Suffenus in poem 22 is the prolific poet who writes and writes, but who never rises above mediocrity. Furius in poem 23 is the poor man who toadies to the rich and powerful, not realizing that he is better off in poverty than he would be as a client. Egnatius in poem 39 is the ingratiating man who always smiles. In a court of law or a business deal, he remains smiling. Catullus speculates obscenely about how Egnatius polishes his shining teeth. Scatology and references to personal uncleanliness abound in these verses—for example, the attack on Rufus in poem 69. Unfaithfulness and lack of decency in small personal dealings also infuriate Catullus, as in poem 77. Sexual behavior is commonly ridiculed—for example, the poems numbered 88 and 91, which accuse Gellius of incest and other unusual practices. Usually these attacks are framed in the most offensive language imaginable, as the attack on Aemillius in poem 97.

TRAVEL AND RURAL LIFE

A number of the poems are about travel and celebrate the Italian rural life. Poem 10 humorously explains that Catullus did not get rich on his trip to Bythinia. Poem 31 celebrates his return from the barbarian province to his beautiful villa in Sirmio. Even in modern times, this lake-dotted area in northern Italy is a delightful place to visit, but the poem by Catullus is not merely a reflection of the real peace of such a landscape. It is an example of the pastoral convention, a celebration of the virtues of the simple life. Not only is the barbarian province of Bythinia contrasted to the homely peace of Sirmio, but the poem also implies that the country life has a simplicity and virtue lacking in the nasty city. Catullus seems to have a contradictory set of attitudes in this regard. In some poems, his worst insult is to accuse someone in Rome of being a hick or a country bumpkin. At other times, the sexual rivalry and power struggles among greedy Romans seem to turn sour, and he longs for the simplicity and honesty of the farm. Poem 44 is an example of this longing for the rural life. Thus, Catullus turns at times to recall the few moments in his life where decency and faithfulness have appeared—for example, the touching references to his brother's death in poems 65 and 68, and especially the lovely elegy, poem 101.

POEM 64

The most important single poem by Catullus is poem 64, a wedding song or epithalamium for Peleus and Thetis, sometimes called his "little epic." It celebrates the marriage of two sets of mythical characters, Peleus/Thetis and Theseus/Ariadne. The poem actually consists of two legendary stories, one embedded within the other. The outer story concerns the wedding of the man Peleus with the goddess Thetis. According to the myth, from this union was born the great Greek hero Achilles. The inner story concerns Theseus and Ariadne. According to the myth, the island of Crete had exacted a tribute of youths and maidens from Athens who were to be sacrificed to a monster, the Minotaur. Prince Theseus of Athens goes to Crete and, with the help of the Cretan princess Ariadne, slays the Minotaur. He takes Ariadne with him back to Athens but stops along the way at the island of Naxos. There he abandons her and sails to Athens alone.

Ariadne's grief on Naxos is the topic of the embedded story in poem 64. The inner and outer stories are linked together by a clever device. The wedding bed of Peleus and Thetis is decked with an embroidered cloth that depicts the earlier legend of Theseus and Ariadne. As the poet describes the scene of the consummation of the marriage of Peleus and Thetis, he digresses to describe the embroidery, thus juxtaposing and contrasting the two pairs of lovers. Although the language and situation of this poem is much more elegant than the rough "street talk" of the poems concerning Lesbia and of the taunts and insults, there is a certain similarity in subject. The epithalamium celebrates sexual union in extremely frank terms. Both the legend of Peleus and Thetis and that of Ariadne on Naxos involve the mating of a human being with a divinity. Both, therefore, imply that love can elevate humans to superhuman states of being.

Both poems also recognize that the joy of eros is all the more keen because it is fleeting and subject to change. The opening lines of poem 64 tell how Thetis, the daughter of Jupiter and princess of the sea, became enamored of Peleus, the mortal prince of Thessaly. Jupiter himself approves of the match. The wedding takes place in Thessaly, and the poet describes the gathering of the guests and the decoration of the house. Among the decorations of the wedding chamber, there is a wonderfully designed cloth depicting the abandonment of Ariadne on Naxos by her careless lover, Theseus. About half of the poem, from line 50 to line 266, describes the embroidered scene, contrasting the unhappy love of Ariadne to the happy expectations of Peleus and Thetis on their wedding day. The story begins with a lush description of the aggrieved Ariadne wading in the wake of her departing lover's ship. The poet then digresses to tell how Ariadne came to this sorry situation, how Theseus set out from Athens to slay the Minotaur on Crete and free his people from the annual tribute, and how Ariadne helped Theseus slay the Minotaur in its labyrinth and so left Crete with him. Although Ariadne had abandoned her family and friends to follow Theseus, he forgets her and sails away from Naxos. In a long speech, Catullus rehearses a theme common to his Lesbia poems: faithless love. Ariadne cries out her complaint to the faithless Theseus in a brilliant and heart-wrenching dramatic scene, but she realizes that Theseus is so far away that he cannot even hear her.

Ariadne is finally avenged, however. Her complaint echoes to heaven, and Jupiter ordains a terrible revenge. Theseus had promised his father that, if he succeeded in slaying the Minotaur and returned alive from Crete, he would carry new white sails on his return voyage so that his father could see from afar his success, but if he died in the attempt, the sails of his ship would be black. The gods see to it that Theseus's forgetfulness is total; he not only forgets Ariadne but also fails to hoist the new white sails, so that his father, watching from the headland for the return, imagines his son to be dead and commits suicide in despair. Thus, Theseus has cause to grieve for his forgetfulness exactly as Ariadne did. Moreover, the weeping of Ariadne inflames Bacchus, the god of revelry, with love for her.

With luxuriant pomp and procession, he comes to Naxos and takes Ariadne for his own. This apotheosis of Ariadne through love is depicted on the veil that decks the wedding bed of Peleus and Thetis. In addition to this wonderful fabric, other gifts come to the lovers. The centaur Chiron comes down from the mountains with woodland gifts. The Naiads, spirits of streams and springs, bring their greenery. Prometheus, too, who gave humans fire, is a guest. At the wedding party, the three Fates sing, foretelling that a son will be born to the couple, a son who will be the great Achilles. The poem thus implies that the wedding will benefit all of Greece.

Catullus concludes by observing that the gods were once friends and guests at human events, such as this wedding, long ago. Since those ancient times, however, humans have fallen on evil ways—greed, fratricide, incest, lechery of all sorts—and the gods no longer consort familiarly with humankind. This poem of 408 lines is not as massive an accomplishment as the *Aeneid* (c. 29-19 B.C.E.; English translation, 1553) of Vergil, which is the epitome of epic poetry in Latin. On the other hand, jewel-like perfection and economy characterize the little epic of Catullus, making it a glory of the Latin language.

LEGACY

Catullus is a major poet because he transmitted important features of the literary tradition that he received from earlier classical writers and also because he modified tradition and literally invented new styles, themes, and modes of thinking that are still used in modern poetry. The "traditional" Catullus learned from Greek models a number of lyric meters and stanzaic forms. He translated these into Latin, and from his experiments, the later vernacular poets of Europe were able to develop a formal richness in the short poem. He also reworked traditional stories from classical mythology and passed them on, enriched and embroidered more elegantly than they were before passing through his hands. The story of Theseus and Ariadne is ancient and common in classical times, but the modern reader remembers it in the words of Catullus's depiction of Ariadne on Naxos wading after her false lover's departing ship and crying out her grief. If Catullus had done nothing but purvey the poetic forms and stories of Greek culture to modern readers by way of Latin, he would still deserve a major place in literary history. Catullus was more than a merely traditional writer, however. He exhibited a major, original, inventive power in several aspects of his work.

Catullus brought to his poetry an unusual sense of immediate, personal involvement. It is no accident that readers tend to look at his poems as if they were autobiographical. They are written so that it seems certain that they express some lived, deeply felt, personal experience: betrayed love, petty insult, grief at the loss of a brother. Such intense involvement in the poems is created in part by the use of a highly dramatized form of speaking, like the dramatic monologues of Robert Browning. When one reads Catullus, one is compelled to imagine the speaker of the lines as a character in a play. One is forced to construct a persona speaking, and one must imagine the dramatic circumstances under which these words might be uttered. The heightened immediacy of the lines supports Catullus's use of highly colloquial vocabulary and sentence structure. Many students of Latin, approaching Catullus for the first time, are baffled by his language—his use of profanity, slang, neologisms, and sentence fragments. However, to base poetry in language as it is really spoken by ordinary men rather than in some artificial "poetic" dialect was a remarkable achievement, well understood by modern writers.

Catullus invented, too, the introverted concentration of his lyric poetry. His poems almost all turn inward on the speaker's own feeling and attitudes. The speaker may be talking about X, but the poem's real focus is on how the speaker feels about X and not on the ostensible subject of the work. When Catullus writes about the Caesarian party, the reader is interested in how Catullus feels, not about what the Caesarians were or what they did. History tells readers the facts; Catullus understood that poetry tells readers how human beings respond to history.

Because Catullus turned inward and attempted to analyze human emotions, he naturally found himself talking mainly about love and hate. His poems externalize feelings, especially erotic feelings. He used traditional forms of poetry to express attitudes seldom defined before. His poetry, for the first time in Western literature, systematically developed the ideas and conventions of courtly love. When his poems were redis-covered in the Renaissance, writers such as Petrarch saw there a prototype for the conventions of courtly love. Contemporary attitudes toward the sexual rela-tionship are so pervasive and powerful that one seldom stops to consider their origins. Turn on the popular ra-dio stations, however, listen to a few songs, and ask where these ideas come from: Why is erotic love ele-vated to such a high place in the contemporary system of values? Why is faithless love lamented so extrava-gantly? Why is erotic rivalry the source of so much hos-tility and anxiety? Why is the woman given a dominant position in the relationship, like a goddess giving her favors or denying them? Such modern attitudes toward erotic love were, in many cases, first stated in Catullus, transmitted through the courtly love-poets of Europe to emerge scarcely changed in lyrics today.

Catullus's greatest accomplishment was to express intensely personal feelings in traditional poetic forms. Like all the greatest artists, he united a command of tra-dition with an individual talent that caused him to change and expand the possibilities he inherited.

BIBLIOGRAPHY

Arkins, Brian. *An Interpretation of the Poems of Catul-lus*. Lewiston, N.Y.: Edwin Mellen Press, 1999. Surveys Catullus's life and literary influences and offers a reading of his poetry that emphasizes its modernity and accessibility to modern readers.

Dettmer, Helena. *Love by the Numbers: Form and Meaning in the Poetry of Catullus*. New York: Peter Lang, 1997. Offers a reading of Catullus's entire corpus of poetry as a unified body of work orga-nized along thematic, structural, and metrical group-ings.

Fitzgerald, William. *Catullan Provocations: Lyric Po-etry and the Drama of Position*. Berkeley: Univer-sity of California Press, 1995. Fitzgerald interprets Catullus's lyrics and emphasizes his manipulation of the reader's point of view. Does not require

knowledge of Latin. Includes bibliographic refer-ences.

Gaisser, Julia Haig. *Catullus*. Malden, Mass.: Wiley-Blackwell, 2009. A biography of Catullus that looks at his life and his works, particularly his elegies and love poetry.

Quinn, Kenneth, ed. *Catullus: The Poems*. 2d ed. New York: St. Martin's Press, 1977. This scholarly com-mentary is somewhat idiosyncratic but suitable for college-level readers. The Latin text of all poems is presented with introduction and commentary in En-glish. A short bibliographical guide for further study of each of the poems is included.

Skinner, Marilyn B., ed. *A Companion to Catullus*. Boston: Blackwell, 2007. This volume provides lit-erary history and criticism on Catullus, along with advice on how to read his works. His influences and writing style are also discussed. Contains an intro-duction and 27 chapters by Cattullus scholars.

Small, Stuart G. P. *Catullus: A Reader's Guide to the Poems*. Lanham, Md.: University Press of America, 1983. A running narrative, not of the poet's life but of his poetic achievement. Divided by topic, with sane judgments on matters of literary and scholarly controversy. Small supplements a reading of the po-ems by giving topical overviews. Includes bibliog-raphy.

Wilder, Thornton. *The Ides of March*. New York: S. French, 1971. The classic historical novel on the Rome of Cicero, Catullus, Clodius, and his sister—and Julius Caesar, the emperor whose life ended on the title day in 44 B.C.E.

Wiseman, T. P. *Catullus and His World: A Reap-praisal*. New York: Cambridge University Press, 1987. A highly readable reconstruction of the social and political context, informative not only about Catullus but also about late republican Rome and its personalities. Richly documented, with eight pages of bibliography.

Todd K. Bender

CONSTANTINE P. CAVAFY
Konstantinos Petrou Kabaphes

Born: Alexandria, Egypt; April 17, 1863
Died: Alexandria, Egypt; April 29, 1933

PRINCIPAL POETRY

Poiēmata, 1935 (Alexander Singopoulos, editor)
The Poems of C. P. Cavafy, 1951
The Complete Poems of Cavafy, 1961 (Rae Dalven, translator)
Poiēmata, 1963 (George Savidis, editor)
K. P. Kabaphē: Anekdota poiemata, 1968 (Savidis, editor)
Passions and Ancient Days, 1971
Collected Poems, 1975 (Savidis, editor)
Before Time Could Change Them: The Complete Poems of Constantine P. Cavafy, 2001
The Collected Poems of C. P. Cavafy, 2006 (Aliki Barnstone, translator)

OTHER LITERARY FORMS

Except for a few essays on literary topics and short notes on language and metrics to be found in his papers, Constantine P. Cavafy (ko-VO-fee) did not work in any literary form other than poetry. Greek poet George Seferis, in *On the Greek Style* (1966), quotes Cavafy as having said, near the end of his life, "I am a historical poet. I could never write a novel or a play; but I hear inside me a hundred and twenty-five voices telling me I could write history."

ACHIEVEMENTS

Constantine P. Cavafy did not achieve public acclaim during his lifetime. The fortunes of war, however, marooned two English novelists—E. M. Forster and Lawrence Durrell—in Alexandria during World War I and World War II, respectively. Forster had one of Cavafy's best poems, "The God Abandons Antony," translated and printed in his *Alexandria: A History and Guide* (1922) and spread his name among such literary figures as T. S. Eliot, T. E. Lawrence, and Arnold Toynbee, so that after Forster's stay in Alexandria, Cavafy received many European visitors. Durrell mod-

eled aspects of Cavafy in the figures of the brooding old poet of the city and the homosexual physician, Balthazar, important characters in his masterwork *The Alexandria Quartet* (includes *Justine*, 1957; *Balthazar*, 1958; *Mountolive*, 1958; *Clea*, 1960). Thus, the Alexandria that tantalizes the imagination of the modern Western reader is to no small degree the city as imagined by Cavafy.

Cavafy remained almost unknown in Greece until after his death. In 1963, the centenary of his birth was marked by the publication of a collected edition of his works, including both his poetry and volumes of previously unpublished prose and other prose. The 1968 publication of seventy-five previously unpublished poems was the major literary event of the year in Athens.

Adding weight to Cavafy's reputation was W. H. Auden's statement in 1961 (in his introduction to *The Complete Poems of Cavafy*, translated by Rae Dalven) that Cavafy had influenced his writing for more than thirty years. Auden singled out for praise "the most original aspect of [Cavafy's] style, the mixture, both in his vocabulary and his syntax, of demotic and purist Greek," and paid tribute also to Cavafy's rich evocation of Alexandria and of Hellenic culture.

In the early 1880's, when Cavafy began to write, the official language of Greece—the language employed by the government and taught in the schools—was *Katharevousa* or purist Greek, "a language," in the words of Linos Politis in *A History of Modern Greek Literature* (1973), "based on popular speech, but 'corrected' and 'embellished' on the model of the ancient." At the same time, there were in Greece passionate advocates of the demotic or spoken tongue, who believed that it alone should be the language of Greek literature and the Greek state. Although this linguistic controversy persists in Greece, modern Greek writers have overwhelmingly adopted the demotic. The tension between a demotic base and borrowings from purist, classical, and the other evolutionary forms of the language accounts in part for the remarkable vitality of modern Greek poetry—a development in which Cavafy played a significant role. Cavafy himself said, "I have tried to blend the spoken with the written language . . . trembling over every word." The remarkable result was a poetic diction that not only draws on the traditions of

Greek from its entire history but also, on occasion, is able to combine phrases and whole lines of ancient Greek with the modern, demotic language and yet remain entirely clear and understandable to any educated Greek reader.

Cavafy's distinctive language can be appreciated only in the original Greek, but even a reader who knows Cavafy's poems in translation can appreciate one of his principal achievements: the creation, in Auden's words, of a unique "tone of voice, a personal speech . . . immediately recognizable." Cavafy's poetic voice represents a "style of deliberately prosaic quality, simple, concentrated, almost dry, economical, unadorned, divested of every element which would cause it to deviate from the strictest austerity—at its best inevitable," as Petroula Ruehlen puts it in *Nine Essays in Modern Literature* (1965). It is above all Cavafy's *voice* that, in translation, has exercised a powerful influence on contemporary American poetry.

BIOGRAPHY

Constantine Peter Cavafy was born Konstantionos Petrou Kabaphes, the youngest and most beloved son of a wealthy Alexandrian merchant; both Cavafy's father and his mother came from prosperous families in Constantinople. By the time of Cavafy's birth, his father's business in cotton, grain, and buffalo hides had benefited from the Crimean War and the family had settled in a luxurious house in the fashionable rue Cherif in Alexandria. The poet's first seven years were spent in a household accustomed to elaborate balls and parties and the company of wealthy businesspeople and professionals of various nationalities. A generous man of European outlook who had lived for some time in England, Cavafy's father saw to it that the children were tended by an English nurse, a French tutor, and Greek servants. Unfortunately, he died in 1870 without leaving the family well provided for; though the family was always "respectable," and though the Cavafy brothers retained the cachet of a wealthy, upper-class milieu, the family fortune was severely reduced.

In 1872, Cavafy's mother, Haricleia, took the family to Liverpool. Because of the economic crisis of 1876 and the three eldest sons' inexperience and ill-advised speculation, the family farm had to be liqui-

Constantine P. Cavafy (The Granger Collection, New York)

dated in 1879, whereupon the Cavafys returned to Alexandria actually impoverished. Cavafy had thus spent seven formative years, from the age of nine to the age of sixteen, in England, where he acquired an excellent facility with the English language and a lifelong love for the works of William Shakespeare, Robert Browning, and Oscar Wilde. For the rest of his life, Cavafy spoke Greek with a slight English accent and often spoke or corresponded in English with his brothers; in the position he held for thirty years immediately under British superiors in the Irrigation Department of the Ministry of Public Works in Alexandria, he was valued for his ability to teach Egyptian employees the English language.

Upon his return to Alexandria in 1879, Cavafy enrolled for three years in a business school, the Hermes Lyceum. In 1882, political and military disturbances by Egyptian nationalists seeking to end foreign rule and expel foreigners led to the bombardment of the city by

British warships anchored in the harbor. Along with many Europeans, the Cavafy family left, this time for Constantinople and the home of Haricleia Cavafy's father, George Photiades, a wealthy diamond merchant. While living in Constantinople from 1882 to 1885, Cavafy wrote his first poetry and had his first sexual experiences with men. These two activities were to become the chief concerns of his life. He wrote both prose and poetry in French and English as well as in Greek. It was also during this period in Constantinople that Cavafy first became familiar with demotic Greek.

In 1885, Haricleia Cavafy moved the family back to Alexandria for the last time; Cavafy really never left the city again. He took several trips at odd intervals, once visiting France and England and a number of times journeying across the Mediterranean to Athens, but his attachment to Alexandria was profound. When asked late in his life to move to Athens, Robert Liddell reports that Cavafy replied: "Mohammed Aly Square is my aunt. Rue Cherif Pacha is my first cousin and the Rue de Ramleh my second. How can I leave them?" He lived with his mother until her death in 1899, when he was thirty-six, then with his brother Paul, taking in 1907 an apartment on the third floor of 10 rue Lepsius. This apartment was to remain Cavafy's residence until his death twenty-six years later.

In 1891, the death of Cavafy's second eldest brother led him to seek a permanent position in the Irrigation Department, where he had been working part time for three years. At the same time, he began a chronological listing of all his poems to date—a list that shows how many he wrote but did not publish. From 1892, Cavafy's life assumed the routine in which his poetry, work, and personality took their characteristic form. His hours as a bureaucrat were not long, from 8:30 in the morning until 1:30 in the afternoon, but the work was tedious and paid minimally; more often than not, Cavafy came to work as much as an hour late. He was reasonably dutiful, if often too scrupulous about his responsibility for all European correspondence; a "trifle overdeliberate" is the phrase cited in his record for 1913, and his subordinates complained that he was overly strict in requiring fastidiously correct records and translations. Cavafy recognized the cost to his art; Liddell quotes him from 1905: "How often during my

work a fine idea comes to me, a rare image, and sudden ready-formed lines, and I'm obliged to leave them, because work can't be put off. Then when I go home and recover a bit, I try to remember them, but they're gone." He never forgot that he was the son of a rich man. Nevertheless, records show that regular increases in pay and annual leave (finally reaching twelve weeks) marked his path to the position of subdirector of his section. He also supplemented his income by speculation on the Egyptian Stock Exchange, occasionally with great success.

Away from his job, Cavafy's life centered on his apartment at 10 rue Lepsius, where friends and literary figures visited, and on his nocturnal activities in the cafés and shady quarters of Alexandria. While still living with his mother, Cavafy had bribed the servants or persuaded his brothers to ruffle up his bed so that it looked as if he had spent the night at home. Then he had to cross from the respectable section of the city where he lived with his mother to the area of taverns, bars, and brothels. Living alone after 1910, he enjoyed greater freedom; the old Greek quarter called Massalia, to which he had moved, gradually deteriorated, so that at some point a brothel occupied the ground floor in his building. Cavafy did not have a single long-standing relationship during his entire life; his closest friends, Pericles Anastassiades (as of 1895) and Alexander Singopoulos (whom he met in 1915), were both considerably younger. He did not dislike or avoid women, however, counting several among his closest friends.

Cavafy never published his most explicitly erotic poetry during his life. It is clear that he suffered some guilt concerning his sexuality, perhaps in part because of his genteel background and his desire to maintain a certain social standing. A secretive and engaging poseur, Cavafy was extremely vain, about both his looks (cultivating his boyish demeanor past middle age) and his literary reputation, which he often urged others to spread, but he was also a lively and informed conversationalist. His method of distributing his poetry, with its calculated air of mystery, suggests the mixture of arrogance and reticence that characterized both his life and his work. Cavafy died at the age of seventy from cancer of the larynx and was buried in the family plot in the Greek cemetery in Alexandria.

ANALYSIS

To enter the world of Constantine P. Cavafy's poetry is to embrace simultaneously the significance of historical, artistic, and erotic experience, to enter a world with an "atmosphere of refinement and passion . . . just perceptible pathos . . . reserve . . . mystery" in Marguerite Yourcenar's memorable phrasing. This is possible because, as C. M. Bowra points out,

> Cavafy risks no stunning effects. His is a great poetry strictly truthful and circumstantial and realistic, concerned above all to present human nature as it is and to make its presentation entirely convincing not merely to the imagination but to the intelligence. This quiet air, which looks so easy to maintain and must have in fact demanded the greatest self-control and critical judgment, is Cavafy's special triumph.

George Seferis, an important younger contemporary of Cavafy, explains how Cavafy's poetic language makes this possible: "Cavafy stands at the boundary where poetry strips herself in order to become prose." Because he is an "unpoetic" poet, his poetry is both easy and difficult to translate—that is, he rarely employs such devices as internal rhyme, alliteration, simile, or metaphor. Instead, he employs unadorned, factual description. His preference after 1900 for free verse reinforced the deliberately prosaic quality of his poetry.

Cavafy himself classified his poetry thematically into three categories: the historical, the artistic or philosophical, and the erotic, though it is essential to remember that these three kinds of experience often appear in the same poem. Many other divisions are also possible: sequences of poems sharing similar themes, drawn from the same historical period or incident, using the same real or similar imaginary characters. The sum of Cavafy's experience, however, as well as his own statement, make the poet's own classification illuminating.

Cavafy identified both one of the historical periods most important for his work and his own method of using history when he said that the Byzantine historians "cultivated a kind of history that has never been written before or since. They wrote history dramatically." These historians created a sense of the living presence of figures and events, transcending time and assuming eternal significance, just as the Byzantine mosaic artist represented life in timeless, two-dimensional forms. To read about the Alexandrians in 100 B.C.E. today, for example, is to compress the two thousand years between the two epochs and to share the experience of both periods simultaneously. Cavafy's method of dramatizing history is marvelously economical; he need not draw explicit comparisons between the past and present, for he makes the past present by depicting people and events of universal human significance.

"WAITING FOR THE BARBARIANS"

In "Waiting for the Barbarians," for example, one of Cavafy's best-known poems, two imaginary citizens in an unspecified Roman city discuss events in the local senate on a day when the barbarians are coming to take power. No speeches are being given, no laws are being passed. All the political leaders have adorned themselves in their finest attire; bedecked with jewels, they have prepared a scroll to give to the barbarians. The poem is in the form of a dialogue between the first speaker, who asks naïve questions, and the second, apparently as worldly-wise as the first is unknowing, who answers in a dry, flat tone, matter-of-fact to the point of testiness, as if speaking to a child. Lacking any description of events in the third person, the poem creates a sense of live observation with its dialogic form. The naïve questioner is as awed by the splendid throne, garments, and jewelry he asks about as the seemingly more knowing speaker is unimpressed, but the poem's penetrating irony is that both are blind to the truth of their corruption—the first in refusing to see it, as his repeated "why" shows, the second in accepting it so readily with a self-conscious air of world-weary sophistication. Cavafy thus implies that the final truth of a historical situation can never be known, creating a double irony for the reader: The truth is that the truth cannot be known. Nevertheless, on the surface, the poem merely records a simple conversation.

"EXILES"

The dialogue is not as common a form in Cavafy's poetry as the dramatic monologue, which offers him, in Yourcenar's words, "the possibilities of *acting* in every sense of the word . . . to have his own emotions confirmed by another mouth." Two such dramatic monologues are "Exiles," in which the speaker accepts the surface of political or historical events with the culpable naïveté of the questioner in "Waiting for the Barbarians," and "Phihellene," in which the speaker is another self-deluded sophisticate.

Exiled to Alexandria by political events in Constantinople in the ninth century, the speaker of "Exiles" is overly certain that he and his fellow exiles will be able to overthrow the Macedonian usurper Basil, who, in reality, ruled for twenty-two years after killing his co-emperor, Michael III. The activities of the exiles are a kind of game: Their use of fictitious names and their superficial enthusiasm in studying literature both suggest their immaturity. Their confidence that they will overthrow Basil is clearly unfounded, and much of the irony of the poem derives from the speaker's complacency, from his tone of voice.

"PHIHELLENE"

Quite different is the cutting, ironic realism of the speaker of "Phihellene," who thinks he knows all the world's tricks. The speaker is the insignificant monarch of an unspecified territory on the eastern fringe of the Roman Empire; the poem consists of his instructions to a subordinate concerning a coin that is to be minted in his honor. The inscription that will accompany his image on the coin, he specifies, should not be "excessive or pompous—/ we don't want the proconsul to take it the wrong way;/ he's always smelling things out and reporting back to Rome—/ but of course giving me due honor." For the obverse of the coin, he suggests a depiction of a "good-looking" discus-thrower, but above all ("for God's sake," he urges, "don't let them forget"), he is concerned that the inscription testify to his appreciation of Hellenic culture—"that after 'King' and 'Savior,'/ they add 'Phihellene' in elegant characters." The central irony of the poem is the consuming desire of this petty monarch to be celebrated as a man of culture, a desire that has its counterpart in the cultural pretensions of many twentieth century dictators.

HISTORICAL AND POLITICAL PERSPECTIVES

In several poems on Marc Antony, Cavafy further manipulates dramatic situation and point of view to present the unusual perspectives on historical figures for which his poetry is noted. The speaker of "In a Township of Asia Minor" has just dictated a lavishly flattering proclamation in honor of Antony's anticipated victory at Actium. Learning that Octavius has de-feated Antony, the speaker merely instructs his amanuensis to substitute Octavius's name for Antony's, adding "It all fits brilliantly." In "Alexandrian Kings" and "In Alexandria, 31 B.C.E.," Cavafy also shows the superficiality and triviality of politics, here in the third person. The Alexandrians, faced with the parade of Cleopatra's children, who all receive important titles, "knew of course what all this was worth,/ what empty words they really were, these kingships." Just as calmly, they allow a peddler from a nearby village to sell his perfumes for the celebration of Antony's triumph because "someone tosses him the huge palace lie:/ that Antony is winning in Greece" ("In Alexandria, 31 B.C.E.").

In "The God Abandons Antony," Cavafy uses the second person to give Antony advice. Whether the speaker lives in Antony's or Cavafy's time does not matter; he tells Antony right to his face to accept courageously his loss of Alexandria. Antony should not mourn his luck or "say/ it was a dream"; rather, he should "go firmly to the window/ and listen with deep emotion" to the city's "exquisite music," confirming the city's delights and his pleasure in them. Here, Cavafy speaks in the poetic voice of an Alexandrian who has dignity, confidence, and self-knowledge.

ARTISTIC PROCESS AS THEME

In the second major category of his poems, Cavafy shows artists at work and presents some of his ideas on the artistic process. Although Cavafy cannot automatically be identified with the speakers of these poems, it is clear that many of them do, in fact, express his attitude toward his art. The need for craftsmanship and the relationship between art and reality are recurring themes in this group of poems.

Two poems concerning the relationship between art and life are "I've Brought to Art" and "Melancholy of Jason Kleander, Poet in Kommagini, C.E. 595." In the first poem, the poet says he has brought life to art, "desires and sensations . . ./ indistinct memories/ of unfulfilled love affairs," and art has known how "to shape forms of Beauty,/ almost imperceptibly completing life,/ blending impressions, blending day with day." In the second, in the voice of the poet Jason Kleander, he says that art has "a kind of knowledge about drugs:/ certain sedatives, in Language and Imagination," which relieve the pain of the "wound from a merciless knife" that age inflicts.

In many of the poems in this group, Cavafy reveals the sense of secrecy and isolation underlying his art. The first-person speaker in "Hidden Things" says he will be understood only "From my most unnoticed actions,/ my most veiled writing," but that "Later, in a more perfect society,/ someone else made just like me/ is certain to appear and act freely." "Walls," written as early as 1896, indicates just how isolated Cavafy may have felt. His oppressors, identified only as "they," have built walls around him: "But I never heard the builders, not a sound./ Imperceptibly they've closed me off from the outside world." In "The First Step," however, another early poem, he speaks of the necessary difficulty of art: Theocritos rebukes a young poet who says that he has "been writing for two years/ and . . . [has] composed only one idyll"; even the artist who has completed only one work is "above the ordinary world/ . . . a member of the city of ideas." Here, the artist's isolation from the "ordinary world" becomes a badge of pride.

THE EROTIC POEMS

The private world of Cavafy's art is nowhere seen more clearly than in the third division of his work, the erotic poems, the most explicit of which he never published himself. Cavafy perhaps believed that he could publish "Pictured" and "When They Come Alive" within three years of their composition because both justify imaginary erotic experience by the art that it helps to create and nurture. In "Pictured," a writer, discouraged by the slow progress of his work, gazes at a picture of "a handsome boy/ . . . lying down close to a spring." The picture revives the poet's inspiration: "I sit and gaze like this for a long time,/ recovering through art from the effort of creating it." Though it could be argued that there is little art in the picture, the image of the youth has nevertheless inspired the very poem that describes it. "When They Come Alive" is addressed to an unidentified poet (perhaps Cavafy, addressing himself?); the poem begins: "Try to keep them, poet,/ those erotic visions of yours,/ . . . Put them, half-hidden, in your lines." The poem concludes by urging the conscious cultivation of such erotic fantasies.

It is interesting to compare these two poems with another erotic poem, "At the Theatre," written before them but never published in Cavafy's lifetime. Here, erotic reverie is not justified as a stimulus to artistic creation but is rather celebrated for its own sake. Addressed to a young man whose "strange beauty" and "decadent youthfulness" have aroused the speaker's "mind and body," the poem concludes: "in my imagination I kept picturing you/ the way they'd talked about you that afternoon." In "Half an Hour," another poem never published by Cavafy, the speaker recounts a "totally erotic" half hour at a bar in which the sight of "your lips . . . your body near me" were all his imagination needed. As the poet says, "we who serve Art,/ sometimes with the mind's intensity/ can create pleasure that seems almost physical"—as strong a statement of the power of imagination as could be asked for.

Another poem unpublished during Cavafy's lifetime, "And I Lounged and Lay on Their Beds," again justifies debauchery for the sake of art. The poet says that "When I went to that house of pleasure/ I didn't stay in the front rooms where they celebrate,/ with some decorum, the accepted modes of love"; instead, in "the secret rooms," he "lounged and lay on their beds"—a line more suggestive than any fuller description of the experience would be. It was a consummate artistic touch to begin the title with "And," here deliberately ambiguous: It may suggest that much more took place than is explicitly described in the title. In Cavafy's poetry, all experience takes on the sacred value of ancient and mysterious temple rites.

A final poem, "Craftsmen of Wine Bowls," serves to show how Cavafy combined erotic, artistic, and philosophical themes in a single poem. In a dramatic monologue, a silversmith describes how his memory, which he begged to help him, enabled him to see "the young face I loved appear the way it was"—a difficult achievement, because "some fifteen years have gone by since the day/ he died as a soldier in the defeat at Magnesia." Magnesia was the battle that established Rome's supremacy in the Hellenized East; thus, the trouble the silversmith takes to commemorate his fallen love seems justified by the nobility of the soldier's cause. Carved on what is only a small bowl, the figure is of a "beautiful young man,/ naked, erotic, one leg still dangling/ in the water," an appropriate image for Cavafy's delicate, refined, and passionate art.

BIBLIOGRAPHY

Anton, John P. *The Poetry and Poetics of Constantine P. Cavafy: Aesthetic Visions of Sensual Reality.* Newark, N.J.: Gordon & Breach, 1995. Discusses Cavafy's early development and the creation of his own original poetic voice. Includes autobiographical elements and background of ancient Alexandria as a way to further the understanding of the poetry.

Jeffreys, Peter. *Eastern Questions: Hellenism and Orientalism in the Writings of E. M. Forster and C. P. Cavafy.* Greensboro, N.C.: ELT Press, 2005. A critical analysis of the works of Cavafy and E. M. Forster in relation to Hellenism and Orientalism.

Jusdanis, Gregory. *The Poetics of Cavafy: Textuality, Eroticism, History.* Princeton, N.J.: Princeton University Press, 1987. Discusses Cavafy's conception of the poet; his conception of his audience; his formalistic concerns, especially within the context of the redemptive powers of art; and his language and textuality. Explores Cavafy's affiliations with modernism and Romanticism, and his poetics and poetic concerns, especially the role of the poet and the value of art.

Keeley, Edmund. *Cavafy's Alexandria.* Princeton, N.J.: Princeton University Press, 1996. Important study of Cavafy's deployment of the city of Alexandria in his poetry, which demonstrates that from 1911 to 1921 Cavafy developed his own imaginative version of his home city of Alexandria. Suggests Cavafy's image of Alexandria is a various one, including visions of Alexandria as a contemporary homoerotic Sensual City, a Metaphoric City, and a Mythical, Hellenistic City.

Liddell, Robert. *Cavafy: A Biography.* London: Duckbacks, 2002. Gracefully written and appreciative biography of Cavafy and an important resource for all Cavafy scholars. Discusses Cavafy's family background, his early years, his relationship with his mother, his life in Alexandria, his homosexuality, his poetry, and his last years. Numerous illustrations and bibliography.

John M. Lee

GUIDO CAVALCANTI

Born: Florence (now in Italy); c. 1259
Died: Florence; August 27 or 28, 1300

PRINCIPAL POETRY

Le rime, 1527
The Sonnets and Ballate of Guido Cavalcanti, 1912 (Ezra Pound, translator)
The Complete Poems, 1992

OTHER LITERARY FORMS

Guido Cavalcanti (ko-vol-KON-tee) is remembered only for his poetry.

ACHIEVEMENTS

The extant poems of Guido Cavalcanti number fewer than threescore; when taken together, however, they are compelling evidence that he was one of the finest Italian poets of his age. Ezra Pound, Cavalcanti's translator into English, even exalted him above Dante, noting in 1929 that "Dante is less in advance of his time than Guido Cavalcanti." While Pound's enthusiasm for Cavalcanti was perhaps excessive, there is little doubt that, except for Dante, Cavalcanti was the most outstanding member of the famous school of *dolce stil nuovo* ("sweet new style"). Although some critics question the existence of such a school in late thirteenth century Italy, it is generally conceded that a number of poets of the period constituted an informal group defined by common linguistic and thematic concerns. In addition to Dante and Cavalcanti, this group included Guido Guinizzelli, the founder of the school, and several writers of love lyrics: Lapo Gianni, Gianni degli Alfani, Dino Frescobaldi, and Cino da Pistoia.

The major themes of the *dolce stil nuovo* are outlined in Guinizzelli's seminal canzone "Al cor gentil ripara sempre amore" ("To the Noble Heart Love Always Returns"). Foremost is a new concept of nobility, which is no longer tied to birth or social rank but rather to spiritual perfection or moral worth. Second is the identification of love with the noble heart, meaning that love is reserved for the heart of a truly noble soul (as defined above) and that the noble heart is likewise reserved for love. Last is the theme of the spiritualization of woman. Since women inspire love, and love in turn is the cause and product of a noble heart, women may prove to be instruments of moral perfection. Every lady is a potential *angelicata crïatura* (angelic creature), to use Cavalcanti's phrase and to employ terminology characteristic of the *stilnovisti*.

The phrase "the sweet new style" derives from *Purgatorio* (*Purgatory*) in Dante's *La divina commedia* (c. 1320; *The Divine Comedy*, 1802). It is Bonagiunta Orbicciani da Lucca's term for the poetics espoused by Dante, Cavalcanti, and several of their contemporaries. The "sweetness" of the new style refers primarily to the gentleness of the subject matter (love), the purity of the language (vernacular Italian), and the graciousness of the chosen poetic rhythms (implying an avoidance, for example, of harsh rhymes). The "newness" derives from the originality of the poets' inspiration—that is, an inner, emotional need to write verse as opposed to a purely intellectual decision to compose—and from the abundance of new expressions, rather than stereotypical phrases, designed to communicate the psychological state of the poet. Cavalcanti's careful depiction of the various states of his emotions, such as self-pity and bewilderment, is noteworthy for its innovative departure from timeworn clichés. An even more important achievement, however, was the remarkable influence Cavalcanti exerted on his onetime friend Dante, who early in his career referred to Cavalcanti as his *primo amico*, or "first friend," and to whom he dedicated *La vita nuova* (c. 1292; *Vita Nuova*, 1861; better known as *The New Life*). It was Cavalcanti who encouraged Dante to write his poetry in the vernacular instead of in Latin; Dante's decision to follow his friend's advice changed forever the course of Italian poetry.

BIOGRAPHY

Guido Cavalcanti was born in Florence, a few years prior to Dante's birth. The exact year of Cavalcanti's birth has never been established. While some have placed it as early as 1240, Natalino Sapegno and many others believe that the poet was born just before 1260. His father was Cavalcante de' Cavalcanti, a descendant of Guelph merchants and the same figure who appears

next to the Ghibelline Farinata degli Uberti in one of the burning tombs of the heretics in the *Inferno*. Dante's treatment of Cavalcanti's father and father-in-law in this famous episode has led to much speculation about Cavalcanti's own philosophical and religious beliefs and was in part responsible for the depiction of Cavalcanti as a heretic in various stories by Giovanni Boccaccio and others. What is known of Cavalcanti's life comes in large part from the contemporary chronicles of Filippo Villani and Dino Compagni. At an early age, Cavalcanti was betrothed by his father to Beatrice (Bice) degli Uberti, daughter of Farinata. This was essentially a political marriage, one designed, like so many of the time, to put an end to the internecine wars between the Guelphs and the Ghibellines, who supported the papacy and the emperor, respectively. Cavalcanti was among the Guelph representatives at the peace negotiations held by Cardinal Latino in 1280; he took part in the general council of the commune in 1284, together with Compagni and Brunetto Latini, and his friendship with Dante dates from this period. He was a fierce adversary of Corso Donati, leader of the Black Guelphs. Because of his hatred for Donati, he joined the opposing White Guelph faction. His allegiance to that faction led to his exile in Sarzana, Italy, on June 24, 1300. It was on that date that the priors of Florence, of which Dante was one, attempted to resolve the city's political strife by banishing the leaders of both factions. While banished, Cavalcanti contracted malaria. Although he was recalled to Florence soon thereafter, he never recovered, and he died in his native city on August 27 or 28 of the same year. His death was recorded on August 29, 1300, in the register of the dead in the Cathedral of Santa Reparata.

These meager facts about Cavalcanti's life and death shed little light on the poet's personality, which is largely shrouded in legend. Perhaps because Dante attributes *disdegno* (disdain) to him in a verse of the previously cited episode in the *Inferno*, other authors have also characterized Cavalcanti as haughty, aristocratic, and solitary. Dante's portrayal of his supposedly best friend as disdainful has led many to conclude that their friendship sharply diminished at some point during their later years. Some speculate that this happened because of conflicts over literary values, with Dante preeminently interested in ethical understanding and Cavalcanti in aristocratic expression. Others argue that the differences in their perception of love formed the basis for the breakdown of their friendship. A disagreement over political matters is yet another possible explanation, although both Dante and Cavalcanti were White Guelphs, and Dante's permanent exile followed Cavalcanti's temporary exile by only a year or so. Whatever the case, Compagni describes Cavalcanti as a "noble knight" and as "courteous and bold" but also as "disdainful and solitary and devoted to study." Villani writes that the poet was a "philosopher of antiquity, not a little esteemed and honored for his dignity." It is Villani also who outlines the rancor and bitterness that Cavalcanti felt toward Donati, who evidently attempted to assassinate Cavalcanti as he made a pilgrimage to Santiago de Compostela. Boccaccio, in his commentary on the *Inferno*, speaks of Cavalcanti as a "most well-bred man and wealthy and of a lofty intellect." Regardless of who paints the portrait, Cavalcanti always appears as intelligent but a man apart, a solitary person destined to exile by his temperament if not by his politics.

ANALYSIS

Guido Cavalcanti's poetry, like that of other *stilnovisti*, may be viewed, in part, as a reaction to the poetry of Guittone d'Arezzo and his followers. Guittone's mid-thirteenth century poetry was largely imitative of the Provençal tradition: Hermetic in nature, it also emphasized rhetorical, metrical, and verbal complexities. Poets of "the sweet new style," on the other hand, deemphasized technical elements so that aspects such as meter and rhyme were generally subservient to meaning. Also, whereas Guittonian poetry covered a wide range of subjects, Guinizzelli and his disciples focused almost entirely on love and its effects. Cavalcanti, however, should not be seen as a mere conformist to Guinizzelli's dicta, for Cavalcanti in turn distinguished himself from many of his own school. In his concentration on love's psychology, he was philosophically more sophisticated than all other *stilnovisti* except Dante. He introduced, for example, the concept of *spiriti* (spirits) into his poetry to dramatize the conflicting emotions and behaviors that love elicits. The term

"spirit" is a technical term of Scholasticism; it refers, according to Albertus Magnus, to the "instrument of the soul" or the "vehicle of life." Spirits represent the essence of life. They shine in the eyes of the beloved and console the heart of the lover. They are forced to flee, however, when love invades. Their flight results in humankind's metaphorical death. It is not surprising, then, that closely related to the theme of spirits in Cavalcanti's poems is the theme of death.

LYRICAL WORKS

If one facet of Cavalcanti's poetry may be characterized as highly philosophical, the other can be described only as profoundly lyrical. The preoccupation with love and death, for example, results in a melancholy portrayal of the poet's mercurial emotions: Happiness is poignantly juxtaposed to sadness. Tears and sighs become appropriate symbols of the persona's ever-changing state of being because they can stand either for joy or sorrow, pleasure or pain. Love is always the culprit that renders the lover defenseless, a helpless observer. Love causes both agony and ecstasy; eventually, it generates a deep-seated desire for release via death. The poet's sense of helplessness before such an all-powerful conqueror is reflected in the presentation of the lover as spectator. This distancing technique leads to a highly dramatic tension and a beautiful lyric expression. It allows the poet to observe and record the effects of love but does not permit him to intervene.

SONNETS

Cavalcanti's known works include thirty-six sonnets, eleven ballads, two canzones, two isolated stanzas, and one motet. In addition, two ballads of questionable authenticity are occasionally attributed to him. The sonnets, because of their large number, seem to represent the poet's preferred form. The major theme of most of the sonnets relates, not unexpectedly, to the pain and weakness that love inflicts on the lover. Love, however, is not the only argument in the compositions. The sonnets of correspondence, for example, are the most important in the collection from a historical perspective, and they show the range of topics covered. These sonnets were dedicated or written to other men, including the poets Dante, Alfani, Guittone d'Arezzo, Guido Orlandi, and a certain Bernardo da Bologna (about whom very little is known).

The five sonnets addressed to Dante are either responses to rhymes on love by Dante or words of friendly encouragement. "Vedeste, al mio parere, onne valore" ("You Saw, in My Opinion, Every Valor") is a reply to Dante's famous call to love's faithful, "A ciascun' alma presa e gentil core" ("To Every Captured Soul and Noble Heart"). On the other hand, one sonnet to Orlandi, "Di vil matera mi conven parlare" ("Of a Vile Matter I Must Speak"), constitutes a rather caustic personal attack. Another sonnet, addressed to Guittone and entitled "Da più a uno face un sollegismo" ("From Many to One Makes a Syllogism"), falls in the tradition of the harsh literary criticism of Guittone also found in Dante's writings. A sonnet to Nerone Cavalcanti, "Novelle ti so dire, odi, Nerone" ("News I Know to Tell You, So Hear, Nerone"), testifies to the fierce fight between the Cavalcanti and Buondelmonti families.

BALLADS

In the ballads, one finds themes such as that of exile in "Perch'io non spero di tornar giammai" ("Because I Hope Not Ever to Return") and of country delights in "In un boschetto trova' pasturella" ("In a Woods I Found a Shepherdess"). As noted earlier, the theme of death often accompanies or weaves through the prevailing theme of love. This is seen in the ballad "Quando di morte mi conven trar vita" ("When I Must Take Life from Death"). On the poet's pilgrimage to Santiago de Compostela, he stops in Toulouse. There, in the Church of the Daurade, he imagines an encounter with Mandetta, a beautiful woman recalled in the ballad "Era in penser d'amor quand'io trovai" ("I Was Thinking of Love When I Found"). The beauty of Mandetta is also described in the sonnet "Una giovane donna di Tolosa" ("A Young Woman of Toulouse"). The young woman reminds him of his faraway lady, whom Cavalcanti never mentions by name in his poetry. Dante, however, refers to her as Vanna, short for Giovanna, and states in *La vita nuova* that she was also known, because of her beauty, as Primavera, or Springtime.

"MY LADY ASKS ME"

The poet's most famous poem, which is also his most difficult, is neither a sonnet nor a ballad. Perhaps the most-discussed canzone in all Italian literature, "Donna me prega" ("My Lady Asks Me"), a poem of seventy-five lines, has been described by John Colaneri as "an intellectual, philosophical, and somewhat obscure exposition of the essence of love." Most scholars would agree with this description, especially the reference to the poem's obscurity. Interpretations of the work differ widely, drawing variously on Arab mysticism, Averroist thought, Arab-Christian Platonism, Thomist philosophy, and neo-Aristotelianism.

From a technical viewpoint, "My Lady Asks Me" is a virtuoso performance, offering unequivocal proof of the poet's exceptional rhyming ability. The poem is meant to be a treatise on the philosophy of love as well as a highly lyrical composition, however, and in the canzone's opening stanza, Cavalcanti raises the following questions: Where does love exist? Who creates it? What is its virtue, its power, and its essence? The answers to these queries are contained in the remainder of the poem but in a rather complicated philosophical knot.

In most of his poetry, Cavalcanti has a great desire to render visible that within humans that is invisible, such as the movements of the human soul. The poet transforms these actions into images of real beings. Thus, "spirits" (as the term was used in Scholastic philosophy, to designate the vital faculties of humans) were introduced into love poetry. All the *stilnovisti* made use of them for the purpose of artistic representation, but it was principally with Cavalcanti that the systematization of the spirits took place. Indeed, it was primarily because of Cavalcanti that spirits became an integral part of the literary expression of the amorous theme and that they remained there for centuries.

BIBLIOGRAPHY

Ardizzone, Maria Luisa. *Guido Cavalcanti: The Other Middle Ages*. Buffalo, N.Y.: University of Toronto Press, 2002. Ardizzone provides criticism and interpretation of the works of Cavalcanti, along with biographical information.

Cavalcanti, Guido. *The Complete Poems*. Translated and with an introduction by Marc A. Cirigliano. New York: Italica Press, 1992. Features parallel texts in English and Italian of Cavalcanti's poems. Introduction and notes contain discussions of his poetic works and life. Bibliography and index.

_____. *Thirty-three Sonnets of Guido Cavalcanti.* Translated by Ezra Pound. San Francisco: Arion Press, 1991. The introductory essays by Hugh Kenner and Lowry Nelson, Jr., provide useful information on Cavalcanti's works and life.

Dronke, Peter. *Medieval Latin and the Rise of European Love Lyric.* 2d ed. New York: Oxford University Press, 1968. In the chapter on Cavalcanti, Dronke depicts the poet as a master of *stilnovisti* poets. He briefly examines the canzone in the light of contemporary lyric poetry and Scholastic philosophy.

Lind, L. R., ed. *Lyric Poetry of the Italian Renaissance.* New Haven, Conn.: Yale University Press, 1954. An anthology containing several of Cavalcanti's poems, including the famous translation by Ezra Pound of the canzone "Donna me prega." Presents a synthesis of Cavalcanti's theory of love.

Nelson, Lowry. "Cavalcanti's Centrality in Early Vernacular Poetry." In *Poetic Configurations.* University Park: Pennsylvania State University Press, 1992. This short overview places Cavalcanti's work in his own cultural and intellectual contexts and discusses his influence on poets from Dante to Ezra Pound.

Pound, Ezra. *Literary Essays of Ezra Pound.* London: Faber and Faber, 1954. Pound's classic essay "Cavalcanti" offers his view of the poet who influenced him deeply early in his career. He has a scholar's eye as well, for his analysis of "Donna mi prega" is thorough in both senses.

Rebay, Luciano, ed. *Italian Poetry: A Selection from St. Francis of Assisi to Salvatore Quasimodo.* New York: Dover Books, 1969. Besides containing several fresh translations of the poems, the book is a good brief source of background material, particularly on the *dolce stil nuovo.*

Wilhelm, James J. *Dante and Pound: The Epic of Judgment.* Orono: University of Maine Press, 1974. Chapter 4 details Cavalcanti's influence on Dante and Dante's reaction to Cavalcanti, especially as registered in the *Inferno.* Chapter 5 explores Pound's critical attitude toward Cavalcanti and how this differed from his poetic use of him.

Wilkins, Ernest H. *A History of Italian Literature.* Cambridge, Mass.: Harvard University Press, 1954. Eminently readable, easily accessible, this work is a standard assessment of Cavalcanti's achievement, discussing his poetic voice and his emphasis on the psychology of love.

Madison U. Sowell

PAUL CELAN
Paul Antschel

Born: Czernowitz, Romania (now Chernivtsi, Ukraine); November 23, 1920
Died: Paris, France; April, 1970
Also known as: Paul Ancel

PRINCIPAL POETRY

Der Sand aus den Urnen, 1948
Mohn und Gedächtnis, 1952
Von Schwelle zu Schwelle, 1955
Gedichte: Eine Auswahl, 1959
Sprachgitter, 1959 (*Speech-Grille*, 1971)
Die Niemandsrose, 1963
Gedichte, 1966
Atemwende, 1967 (*Breathturn*, 1995)
Ausgewählte Gedichte: Zwei Reden, 1968
Fadensonnen, 1968 (*Threadsuns*, 2000)
Lichtzwang, 1970 (*Lightduress*, 2005)
Schneepart, 1971 (*Snow Part*, 2007)
Speech-Grille, and Selected Poems, 1971
Nineteen Poems, 1972
Selected Poems, 1972
Gedichte: In zwei Bänden, 1975 (2 volumes)
Zeitgehöft: Späte Gedichte aus dem Nachlass, 1976
Paul Celan: Poems, 1980 (revised as *Poems of Paul Celan*, 1988)
Gedichte, 1938-1944, 1985
Sixty-five Poems, 1985
Last Poems, 1986
Das Frühwerk, 1989
Gesammelte Werke in sieben Bänden, 2000 (7 volumes)
Glottal Stop: 101 Poems, 2000

OTHER LITERARY FORMS

The literary reputation of Paul Celan (TSEHL-on) rests exclusively on his poetry. His only piece of prose fiction, if indeed it can be so described, is "Gespräch im Gebirg" (1959), a very short autobiographical story with a religious theme. Celan also wrote an introductory essay for a book containing works by the painter Edgar Jené; this essay, entitled *Edgar Jené und der Traum vom Traume*, (1948; *Edgar Jené and the Dream About the Dream*, 1986), is an important early statement of Celan's aesthetic theory. Another, more oblique, statement of Celan's poetic theory is contained in his famous speech, "Der Meridian" (1960), given on his acceptance of the prestigious Georg Büchner Prize. (An English translation of this speech, "The Meridian," was published in the Winter, 1978, issue of *Chicago Review*.)

ACHIEVEMENTS

Paul Celan is considered an "inaccessible" poet by many critics and readers. This judgment, prompted by the difficulties Celan's poetry poses for would-be interpreters seeking traditional exegesis, is reinforced by the fact that Celan occupies an isolated position in modern German poetry. Sometimes aligned with Nelly Sachs, Ernst Meister, and the German Surrealists, Celan's work nevertheless stands apart from that of his contemporaries. A Jew whose outlook was shaped by his early experiences in Nazi-occupied Romania, Celan grew up virtually trilingual. The horror of his realization that he was, in spite of his childhood experiences and his later residence in France, a German poet was surely responsible in part for his almost obsessive concern with the possibilities and the limits of his poetic language. Celan's literary ancestors are Friedrich Hölderlin, Arthur Rimbaud, Stéphane Mallarmé, Rainer Maria Rilke, and the German expressionists, but even in his early poems his position as an outsider is manifest. Celan's poems, called Hermetic by some critics because of their resistance to traditional interpretation, can be viewed sometimes as intense and cryptic accounts of personal experience, sometimes as religious-philosophical discussions of Judaism, its tradition and its relation to Christianity. Many of his poems concern themselves with linguistic and poetic theory to the point where they cease to be poems in the traditional sense, losing all contact with the world of physical phenomena and turning into pure language, existing only for themselves. Such "pure" poems, increasingly frequent in Celan's later works, are largely responsible for the charge of inaccessibility that has been laid against him. Here the reader is faced with having to leave the dimension of conventional language use, where the poet uses language to communicate with his audience about subjects such as death or nature, and is forced to enter the dimension of metalanguage, as Harald Weinrich calls it, where language is used to discuss only language—that is, the *word* "death," and not death itself. Such poems are accessible only to readers who share with the poet the basic premises of an essentially linguistic poetic theory.

In spite of all this, much of Celan's poetry can be made accessible to the reader through focus on the personal elements in some poems, the Judaic themes in others, and by pointing out the biblical and literary references in yet another group.

BIOGRAPHY

Paul Celan was born Paul Ancel, or Antschel, the only child of Jewish parents, in Czernowitz, Romania (now Chernivtsi, Ukraine), in Bukovina, situated in the foothills of the Carpathian Mountains. This region had been under Austrian rule and thus contained a sizable German-speaking minority along with a mix of other nationalities and ethnic groups. In 1918, just two years before Celan's birth, following the collapse of the Austro-Hungarian Empire, Bukovina became part of Romania. Thus, Celan was reared in a region of great cultural and linguistic diversity, the tensions of which energized his poetry.

Little is known of Celan's early childhood, but he appears to have had a very close relationship with his mother and a less satisfying relationship with his father. Positive references to his mother abound in his poems, whereas his father is hardly mentioned. After receiving his high school diploma, the young Celan went to study medicine in France in 1938, but the war forced his return in the following year to Czernowitz, where he turned to the study of Romance languages and literature at the local university. In 1940, his hometown was

Paul Celan (©A. van Mangoldt)

annexed by the Soviet Union but was soon occupied by the Germans and their allies, who began to persecute and deport the Jewish population. Celan's parents were taken to a concentration camp, where they both died, while the young man remained hidden for some time and finally ended up in a forced-labor camp. These events left a permanent scar on Celan's memory, and it appears that he had strong feelings of guilt for having survived when his parents and so many of his friends and relatives were murdered. After Soviet troops reoccupied his hometown, he returned there for a short time and then moved to Bucharest, where he found work as an editor and a translator. In 1947, his first poems were published in a Romanian journal under the anagrammatic pen name Paul Celan. In the same year, he moved to Vienna, where he remained until 1948, when his first collection of poetry, *Der Sand aus den Urnen*, was published.

After moving to Paris in the same year, Celan began to frequent avant-garde circles and was received particularly well by the poet Yvan Goll and his wife. Unfortunately, this friendship soured after Goll's death in

1950, when Goll's wife, Claire, apparently jealous of Celan's growing reputation as a poet, accused him of having plagiarized from her husband. A bitter feud resulted, with many of the leading poets and critics in France and Germany taking sides. During this period, Celan also began his work as a literary translator, which was to be a major source of both income and poetic inspiration for the rest of his life. He translated from the French—notably the writings of Rimbaud, Paul Valéry, and Guillaume Apollinaire—as well as the poetry of William Shakespeare, Emily Dickinson, and Marianne Moore from the English and the works of Aleksandr Blok, Sergei Esenin, and Osip Mandelstam from the Russian.

In the following years, Celan married a French graphic artist, Gisèle Lestrange, and published his second volume of poetry, *Mohn und Gedächtnis* (poppy and memory), containing many poems from his first collection, *Der Sand aus den Urnen*, which he had withdrawn from circulation because of the large number of printing mistakes and editorial inaccuracies it contained. *Mohn und Gedächtnis* established his reputation as a poet, and most of his subsequent collections were awarded prestigious literary prizes.

Celan remained in Paris for the rest of his life, infrequently traveling to Germany. During his later years, he appears to have undergone many crises both in his personal and in his creative life (his feud with Claire Goll is only one such incident), and his friends agree that he became quarrelsome and felt persecuted by neo-Nazis, hostile publishers, and critics. His death in April of 1970, apparently by suicide—he drowned in the Seine—was the consequence of his having arrived, in his own judgment, at a personal and artistic dead end, although many critics have seen in his collections *Lightduress*, *Snow Part*, and *Zeitgehöft*, published posthumously, the potential beginning of a new creative period.

ANALYSIS

Paul Celan's poetry can be viewed as an expressive attempt to cope with the past—his personal past as well as that of the Jewish people. Close friends of the poet state that Celan was unable to forget anything and that trivial incidents and cataclysmic events of the past for him had the same order of importance. Many of his poems contain references to the death camps, to his dead parents (particularly his mother), and to his changing attitude toward the Jewish religion and toward God. In his early collections, these themes are shaped into traditional poetic form—long, often rhymed lines, genitive metaphors, sensuous images—and the individual poems are accessible to conventional methods of interpretation. In his later collections, Celan employs increasingly sparse poetic means, such as one-word lines, neologisms, and images that resist traditional interpretive sense; their significance can often be intuited only by considering Celan's complete poetic opus, a fact that has persuaded many critics and readers that Celan's poems are nonsense, pure games with language rather than codified expressions of thoughts and feelings that can be deciphered by applying the appropriate key.

MOHN UND GEDÄCHTNIS

Mohn und Gedächtnis, Celan's first collection of poetry (discounting the withdrawn *Der Sand aus den Urnen*), was in many ways an attempt to break with the past. The title of the collection is an indication of the dominant theme of these poems, which stress the dichotomy of forgetting—one of the symbolic connotations of the poppy flower—and remembering, by which Celan expresses his wish to forget the past, both his own personal past and that of the Jewish race, and his painful inability to erase these experiences from his memory. Living in Paris, Celan believed that only by forgetting could he begin a new life—in a new country, with a non-Jewish French wife, and by a rejection of his past poetic efforts, as indicated by the withdrawal of his first collection.

Mohn und Gedächtnis is divided into four parts and contains a total of fifty-six poems. In the first part, "Der Sand aus den Urnen" ("Sand from the Urns"), Celan establishes the central theme of the collection: The poet "fills the urns of the past in the moldy-green house of oblivion" and is reminded by the white foliage of an aspen tree that his mother's hair was not allowed to turn white. Mixed with these reflections on personal losses are memories of sorrows and defeats inflicted on the Jewish people; references to the conquest of Judea by the Romans are meant to remind the reader

of more recent atrocities committed by foreign conquerors.

The second part of *Mohn und Gedächtnis* is a single poem, "Todesfuge" ("Death Fugue"), Celan's most widely anthologized poem, responsible in no small part for establishing his reputation as one of the leading contemporary German poets. "Death Fugue" is a monologue by the victims of a concentration camp, evoking in vivid images the various atrocities associated with these camps. From the opening line, "Black milk of daybreak we drink it at sundown . . ."—one of the lines that Claire Goll suggested Celan had plagiarized from her husband—the poem passes on to descriptions of the cruel camp commander who plays with serpent-like whips, makes the inmates shovel their own graves, and sets his pack of dogs on them. From the resignation of the first lines, the poem builds to an emotional climax in the last stanza in which the horror of the cremation chambers is indicated by images such as "he grants us a grave in the air" and "death is a master from Germany." Although most critics have praised the poem, some have condemned Celan for what they interpret as an attempt at reconciliation between Germans and Jews in the last two lines of the poem. Others, however, notably Theodor Adorno, have attacked "Death Fugue" on the basis that it is "barbaric" to write beautiful poetry after, and particularly about, Auschwitz. A close reading of this long poem refutes the notion that Celan was inclined toward reconciliation with the Germans—his later work bears this out—and it is hard to imagine that any reader should feel anything but horror and pity for the anonymous speakers of the poem. The beautifully phrased images serve to increase the intensity of this horror rather than attempting to gloss it over. "Death Fugue" is both a great poem and one of the most impressive and lasting documents of the plight of the Jews.

"Auf Reisen" ("Travel"), the first poem of the third part of the collection, again indicates Celan's wish to leave the past behind and to start all over again in his "house in Paris." In other poems he makes reference to his wife, asking to be forgiven for having broken with his heritage and married a Gentile. As the title of the collection suggests, the poppy of oblivion is not strong enough to erase the memory of his dead mother, of his personal past, and of his racial heritage. In poems such as "Der Reisekamerad" ("The Traveling Companion") and "Zähle die Mandeln" ("Count the Almonds"), the optimistic view of "Travel" is retracted; in the former, the dead mother is evoked as the poet's constant travel companion, while in the latter, he acknowledges that he must always be counted among the "almonds." The almonds (*Mandeln*) represent the Jewish people and are an indirect reference also to the Russian Jewish poet Osip Mandelstam, whose work Celan had translated. The irreconcilable tension between the wish to forget and the inability to do so completely is further shown in "Corona," a poem referring to Rainer Maria Rilke's "Herbsttag" ("Autumn Day"). Whereas the speaker of Rilke's poem resigns himself to the approaching hardships of winter, Celan converts Rilke's "Lord: it is time" into the rebellious "it is time that the stone condescended to bloom."

The poems in *Mohn und Gedächtnis* are not, for the most part, innovative in form or imagery, although the long dactylic lines and the flowery images of the first half begin to give way to greater economy of scope and metaphor in the later poems. There is a constant dialogue with a fictional "you" and repeated references to "night," "dream," "sleep," "wine," and "time," in keeping with the central theme of these poems. Celan's next collections show his continued attempts to break with the past, to move his life and his poetry to new levels.

VON SCHWELLE ZU SCHWELLE

In *Von Schwelle zu Schwelle* (threshold to threshold), Celan abandoned his frequent references to the past; it is as if the poet—as the title, taken from a poem in *Mohn und Gedächtnis*, suggests—intended to cross over a threshold into a new realm. Images referring to his mother, to the persecution of the Jews, to his personal attitude toward God, and to his Jewish heritage are less frequent in this volume. Many German critics, reluctant to concentrate on Celan's treatment of the Holocaust, have remarked with some relief his turning away from this subject toward the problem of creativity, the possibilities of communication, and the limits of language. Indeed, if one follows most German critics, *Von Schwelle zu Schwelle* was the first step in the poet's development toward "metapoetry"—that is, po-

etry that no longer deals with traditional *materia poetica* but only with poetry itself. This new direction is demonstrated by the preponderance of terms such as "word" and "stone" (a symbol of speechlessness), replacing "dream," "autumn," and "time." For Celan, *Von Schwelle zu Schwelle* constituted a more radical attempt to start anew by no longer writing about—therefore no longer having to think about—experiences and memories that he had been unable to come to grips with in his earlier poems.

SPEECH-GRILLE

Speech-Grille is, as the title suggests, predominantly concerned with language. The thirty-three poems in this volume are among Celan's finest, as the enthusiastic critical reception confirmed. They are characterized by a remarkable discipline of expression, leading in many cases to a reduction of poetry to the bare essentials. Indeed, it is possible to see these poems as leading in the direction of complete silence. "Engführung" ("Stretto"), perhaps the finest poem in the collection and one of Celan's best, exemplifies this tendency even by its title, which is taken from musical theory and refers to the final section of a fugue. A long poem that alludes to "Death Fugue," it is stripped of the descriptive metaphors that characterized that masterpiece, such as the "grave in the air" and "the black milk of daybreak"; instead, experience is reduced to lines such as "Came, came./ Came a word, came/ came through the night,/ wanted to shine, wanted to shine/ Ash./ Ash, ash./ Night."

DIE NIEMANDSROSE

Celan's attempt to leave the past behind in *Speech-Grille* was not completely successful; on the contrary, several poems in this collection express sorrow at the poet's detachment from his Jewish past and from his religion. It is therefore not surprising that Celan's next collection, *Die Niemandsrose* (the no-one's rose), was dedicated to Mandelstam, a victim of Joseph Stalin's persecutions in the 1930's. One of the first poems in this collection makes mention of the victims of the concentration camps: "There was earth inside them, and/ they dug." Rather than concentrating on the horrors of camp existence, the poem discusses the possibility of believing in an omnipotent, benevolent God in the face of these atrocities; this theme is picked up again in

"Zürich, zum Storchen" ("Zurich, the Stork Inn"), in which Celan reports on his meeting with the Jewish poet Nelly Sachs: "the talk was of your God, I spoke/ against him." Other poems contain references to his earlier work; the "house in Paris" is mentioned again, and autumn imagery, suggesting the memory of his mother, is used more frequently. Several other poems express Celan's renewed and final acceptance of his Jewish heritage but indicate his rejection of God, culminating in the blasphemous "Psalm," with its bitter tribute: "Praised be your name, no one."

LATER YEARS

Celan's poetry after *Die Niemandsrose* became almost inaccessible to the average reader. As the title *Breathturn* indicates, Celan wanted to go in entirely new directions. Most of the poems in Celan's last collections are very short; references to language and writing become more frequent, and striking, often grotesque, portmanteau words and other neologisms mix with images from his earlier poems. There are still references to Judaism, to an absent or cruel God, and—in a cryptic form—to personal experiences. In the posthumously published *Snow Part*, the reader can even detect allusions to the turbulent political events of 1968. The dominant feature of these last poems, however, is the almost obsessive attempt to make the language of poetry perform new, hitherto unimagined feats, to coerce words to yield truth that traditional poetic diction could not previously force through its "speech-grille." It appears that Celan finally despaired of ever being able to reach this new poetic dimension. The tone of his last poems was increasingly pessimistic, and his hopes, expressed in earlier poems, of finding "that ounce of truth deep inside delusion," gave way to silence in the face of the "obstructive tomorrow." It is the evidence of these last poems, more than any police reports, which make it a certainty that his drowning in the Seine in 1970 was not simply the result of an accident.

Celan's poetry can be understood only by grasping his existential dilemma after World War II as a Jewish poet who had to create his poetry in the German language. Desperate to leave behind everything which would remind him of his own and his people's plight, he nevertheless discovered that the very use of the German language inevitably led him back to his past and made a new beginning impossible. Finally, the only escape he saw still open to him was to attempt to abandon completely the conventions of German lyric poetry and its language, to try to make his poetry express his innermost feelings and convictions without having to resort to traditional poetic diction and form. Weinrich suggests that Celan, like Mallarmé before him, was searching for the "absolute poem," a poem that the poet creates only as a rough sketch and that the reader then completes, using private experiences and ideas, possibly remembered pieces of other poems. If this is true, Celan must have ultimately considered his efforts a failure, both in terms of his poetic intentions and in his desire to come to terms with his personal and his Jewish past.

OTHER MAJOR WORKS

SHORT FICTION: "Gespräch im Gebirg," 1959.

NONFICTION: *Edgar Jené und der Traum vom Traume*, 1948 (*Edgar Jené and the Dream About the Dream*, 1986); *Collected Prose*, 1986.

TRANSLATIONS: *Der goldene Vorhang*, 1949 (of Jean Cocteau); *Bateau ivre/Das trunkene Schiff*, 1958 (of Arthur Rimbaud); *Gedichte*, 1959 (of Osip Mandelstam); *Die junge Parzel/La jeune Parque*, 1964 (of Paul Valéry); *Einundzwanzig Sonette*, 1967 (of William Shakespeare).

MISCELLANEOUS: *Prose Writings and Selected Poems*, 1977; *Selected Poems and Prose of Paul Celan*, 2001.

BIBLIOGRAPHY

Baer, Ulrich. *Remnants of Song: Trauma and the Experience of Modernity in Charles Baudelaire and Paul Celan*. Stanford, Calif.: Stanford University Press, 2000. Baer sees a basis for comparison of the nineteenth and the twentieth century poets. Bibliographical references, index.

Bernstein, Michael André. *Five Portraits: Modernity and the Imagination in Twentieth-Century German Writing*. Evanston, Ill.: Northwestern University Press, 2000. Compared with Celan are four other German poets and philosophers: Rainer Maria Rilke, Robert Musil, Martin Heidegger, and Walter

Benjamin. Includes bibliographical references, index.

Chalfen, Israel. *Paul Celan*. New York: Persea Books, 1991. A biography of Celan's youth and early career. Includes bibliographical references.

Colin, Amy D. *Paul Celan: Holograms of Darkness*. Bloomington: Indiana University Press, 1991. An overview of Celan's cultural background as well as postmodernist textual analysis.

Del Caro, Adrian. *The Early Poetry of Paul Celan: In the Beginning Was the Word*. Baton Rouge: Louisiana State University Press, 1997. A detailed treatment of the early volumes *Mohn und Gedächtnis* (1952) and *Von Schwelle zu Schwelle* (1955).

Felstiner, John. *Paul Celan: Poet, Survivor, Jew*. 1995. Reprint. New Haven, Conn.: Yale University Press, 2001. Illuminates the rich biographical meaning behind much of Celan's spare, enigmatic verse. Includes bibliographical references, illustrations, map, index.

Hillard, Derek. *Poetry as Individuality: The Discourse of Observation in Paul Celan*. Lewisburg, Pa.: Bucknell University Press, 2009. An examination of individuality in the writings of Celan. Touches on philosophy and the psychology of knowledge.

Rosenthal, Bianca. *Pathways to Paul Celan*. New York: Peter Lang, 1995. An overview of the varied and often contradictory critical responses to the poet. Illustrated; includes bibliographical references, index.

Tobias, Rochelle. *The Discourse of Nature in the Poetry of Paul Celan: The Unnatural World*. Baltimore: The Johns Hopkins University Press, 2006. Provides critical analysis of Celan's poetry in terms of its relationship to the natural world.

Wolosky, Shira. *Language and Mysticism: The Negative Way of Language in Eliot, Beckett, and Celan*. Stanford, Calif.: Stanford University Press, 1995. A useful comparative study that helps to place Celan in context. Bibliographical references, index.

Franz G. Blaha

LUIS CERNUDA

Born: Seville, Spain; September 21, 1902
Died: Mexico City, Mexico; November 5, 1963

PRINCIPAL POETRY

Egloga, elegía, oda, 1927
Perfil del aire, 1927
Un río, un amor, 1929
Los placeres prohibidos, 1931
Donde habite el olvido, 1934
Invocaciones, 1935
La realidad y el deseo, 1936, 1940, 1958, 1964
Las nubes, 1940
Ocnos, 1942, 1949, 1964 (prose poems; English translation, 2004)
Como quien espera el alba, 1947
Variaciones sobre tema mexicano, 1952 (prose poems; *Variations on a Mexican Theme*, 2004)
Poemas para un cuerpo, 1957
Desolación de la quimera, 1962 (*Desolation of the Chimera: Last Poems*, 2009)
The Poetry of Luis Cernuda, 1971
Poesía completa, 1973
Selected Poems of Luis Cernuda, 1977
34 Poemas, 1998
Written in Water: The Prose Poems of Luis Cernuda, 2004 (includes *Ocnos* and *Variations on a Mexican Theme*)

OTHER LITERARY FORMS

Although Luis Cernuda (sur-NEW-dah) is best known for his poetry, he was also a prolific essayist and critic. He published several works in prose, three of which, devoted to criticism, appeared during his lifetime. In his *Estudios sobre poesía española contemporánea* (1957; studies on contemporary Spanish poetry), Cernuda analyzes the most important trends in Spanish poetry since the nineteenth century. He bestows upon Gustavo Adolfo Bécquer the distinction of having reawakened poetry after more than one hundred years of lethargy, and he lauds Miguel de Unamuno y Jugo as the most important Spanish poet of the twentieth century. Cernuda's *Pensamiento poético en la lírica inglesa (siglo XIX)* (1958; poetic thought in English lyricism), a study of the theory of poetry as practiced by nineteenth century British poets, reveals Cernuda's deep appreciation of and attachment to English verse of the Romantic and Victorian periods. Many of Cernuda's essays and magazine and newspaper articles—which appeared originally in such publications as *Caracola, Litoral, Octubre, Cruz y raya, Heraldo de Madrid*, and *Insula*—have been collected in the two-volume *Poesía y literatura* (1960, 1964; poetry and literature) and in *Crítica, ensayos y evocaciones* (1970; criticism, essays, and evocations). *Variations on a Mexican Theme*, often referred to as poetic prose, is an affectionate reflection by the poet on the people of Mexico, their music, their art, their churches, and their poverty and misery. Mexico was the poet's adopted homeland, after some years in what he perceived to be alien environments, and he felt warmed by the Mexicans, their culture, and their climate, so reminiscent of his native Andalusia. *Ocnos* is a meditation on time, a prose poem that becomes the lyrical confession of a poet writing about himself and his art. Because it contains Cernuda's analysis of his work, this volume is a useful companion to his poetry. Cernuda also undertook the translation into Spanish of the poetry of Friedrich Hölderlin, Paul Éluard, William Wordsworth, and William Blake, as well as plays by William Shakespeare. He did not devote much effort to fiction, leaving behind only three short pieces: "El indolente" ("The Indolent One"), "El viento en la colina" ("The Wind on the Hill"), and "El sarao" (the dancing party), all published in the collection *Tres narraciones* (1948; three narratives).

ACHIEVEMENTS

While Luis Cernuda is recognized as an important member of the Generation of '27 (considered by some a second Spanish Golden Age), he did not receive during his lifetime the acclaim and recognition extended to some of his contemporaries, such as Federico García Lorca, Jorge Guillén, Rafael Alberti, and Vicente Aleixandre. Furthermore, Cernuda never enjoyed financial or professional security. His position as a self-exile—he never returned to Spain, even for brief periods, after 1938—might explain his lack of popularity

during the 1930's and 1940's. In addition, his political sympathies (staunchly Republican), his open homosexuality, his reticence, and even the seemingly simple structure and language of his poetry were all factors that may have distanced him from an entire generation of readers. After his death, however, Cernuda's audience has been growing: A number of important critical studies have appeared, a complete edition of his poetry has been published, and a collection of many of his extant essays was issued in 1970—clear indications that Cernuda is being reappraised by a new generation of Spanish poets and critics.

However, as Carlos-Peregrín Otero has observed, it might still be premature to evaluate Cernuda's impact and his role as an innovator in Spanish letters. Cernuda displayed, first and foremost, a commitment to poetry and to the creative act. His work allowed him to express himself and served to sustain him. It was through his poetry that he came to understand himself and the world, and this understanding helped him endure the solitude and melancholy of his alienated and withdrawn existence. Through his writing, he was able to objectify his desire, his passion, and his love and to liberate himself in ways that his social persona never could. He also used his poetry to battle against his obsession with time and its relentless passage. These were the principal themes of Cernuda's works. He expressed them with increasing clarity and simplicity of language, yet, toward the end of his life, his work began to acquire the quiet, meditative tone of a man who is confident in the knowledge that his art, if nothing else, will escape decay.

BIOGRAPHY

Born to a comfortable middle-class family of Seville, Luis Cernuda y Bidón was the youngest of the three children of Bernardo Cernuda Bousa, a colonel of a regiment of engineers, and Amparo Bidón y Cuellar. In Cernuda's poem "La familia" ("The Family"), which appeared in *Como quien espera el alba* (like someone awaiting the dawn), the domestic environment of his youth is portrayed as grave, dark, and rigid like glass, "which everyone can break but no one bends." The poet does not reveal any warmth or affection for his parents or his two sisters. His parents, he adds, fed and clothed him, and even provided him with God and morality. They gave him all: life, which he had not asked for, and death, its inextricable companion. From an early age, Cernuda displayed a timidity and reticence which were to characterize his social interaction throughout his life.

Cernuda first began to appreciate poetry at the age of nine, when he came across some poems by Gustavo Adolfo Bécquer, the nineteenth century Romantic poet whose remains were transferred from Madrid to Seville for permanent interment in 1911, causing excitement among the residents of the city and renewed interest in the poet's work. After completing secondary school in a religious institution, Cernuda enrolled at the University of Seville to study law in 1919. He received his law degree in 1925 but never practiced. His most important experience during his university years was his contact with Pedro Salinas, the eminent poet whose first year as a professor at the university coincided with Cernuda's first year as a student. Their association—at first formal, impersonal, and restricted to the classroom—developed in the course of the next few years, as Salinas encouraged Cernuda and other students to pursue their poetic inclinations. Salinas recommended that Cernuda begin to read French authors, among them Charles Baudelaire, Stéphane Mallarmé, and André Gide. Gide's works helped Cernuda to confront and to reconcile himself to his homosexuality. Through the influence of Salinas, Cernuda was able to publish nine poems in the prestigious magazine *Revista de occidente* when he was only twenty-three. Two years later, in 1927, Cernuda published his first collection, *Perfil del aire* (air's profile). In spite of the coolness with which it was received, with one or two notable exceptions, Cernuda had determined to devote his life to writing, putting an end to any professional indecision he had felt earlier.

Upon the death of his mother in 1928—his father had died in 1920—Cernuda left Seville for good, traveling first to Málaga and then to Madrid, and meeting a number of the writers and poets who would be known as the Generation of '27, among them Manuel Altolaguirre and Emilio Prados (the editors of *Litoral*), Vicente Aleixandre, and Bernabé Fernández-Canivell (future director of the literary magazine *Caracola*, an outlet for Cernuda's poetry). He had met García Lorca in Seville in 1927. In the fall of 1928, through Pedro Salinas, Cernuda was offered an appointment as Spanish lecturer at the École Normale de Toulouse, a position that afforded the young poet the opportunity to spend some time in Paris. During his year in France, he immersed himself in the Surrealist movement and adopted a style and point of view to which he would adhere for the next four years.

The 1930's was a decade of steady productivity for Cernuda, marked by increasing recognition of his gifts among other writers of his generation. At the same time, it was a period of political instability that forced writers to take sides. Cernuda was a staunch supporter of the Spanish Republic and, for a brief period, around 1933, a member of the Communist Party, contributing several political articles to *Octubre*, a magazine edited by Rafael Alberti. In 1934, for a short time, he worked for Misiones Pedagógicas (pedagogic missions), an educational program sponsored by the Republican government to bring culture to remote areas of the country. Cernuda's job was to explain the great masterpieces of Spanish painting, presented to the audience in reproduction. Cernuda spent the first summer of the Spanish Civil War, in 1936, in Paris as a secretary to the Spanish ambassador to France, Alvaro de Albornoz, whose daughter Concha was a friend of Cernuda. Upon his return to Spain, Cernuda joined the Republican popular militia and fought in the Guadarrama. In the winter of 1938, he traveled to England to deliver a series of lectures arranged for him by the English writer Stanley Richardson. A few months later, while returning to Spain through France, Cernuda decided to go into exile permanently, first to Great Britain, where he taught in Surrey, Glasgow, Cambridge, and London, and then to the United States, where he arrived in the fall of 1947. His appointment as professor of Spanish literature at Mount Holyoke College, negotiated for Cernuda by Concha Albornoz, initiated the most stable and financially untroubled period of the poet's life. The New England climate and the isolation of the school, however, made Cernuda restless and caused him to explore the possibility of a teaching post at a university in Puerto Rico. In 1953, after several summers spent in the more hospitable Mexico, he resigned his tenure at Mount Holyoke and settled in Mexico, where he would remain—with only brief returns to the United States to teach at San Francisco State College and the University of California, Los Angeles—until his death from a heart attack in 1963. While in Mexico, he supported himself by his writing and by teaching several courses at the Universidad Autónoma in Mexico City.

ANALYSIS

In the case of Luis Cernuda, it is impossible to separate the poet from the man—his personality from his literary production. As much as Cernuda himself protested that he loathed the intrusion of the person in the poem, he, much more than most of his contemporaries, can be said to have revealed himself through his writing. He offered readers a glimpse of his poetic world from one window only, as Jenaro Talens states, and that window is open to the main character, who is frequently—if not always—Cernuda himself. As a consequence, his poetic production reflects his development as a man and his awareness of himself. This, in turn, tends to focus most analyses of his work along closely chronological lines, as his poetry evolves from the vague and dreamy musings of youth to the bitter acceptance of the relentlessness of time and the inevitability of death.

PERFIL DEL AIRE

Beginning with the first book of poems, *Perfil del aire*—published as a supplement to the magazine *Litoral* and edited by Manuel Altolaguirre and Emilio Prados in 1927—Cernuda embarked upon a journey of self-discovery. In this first collection, the youthful poet presents an indifferent, indolent attitude toward the world; he is there, but he dreams and is surrounded by emptiness. Dreams and walls protect him, provide him with a haven for his loneliness; there, he can savor his secret pleasures and his unfulfilled yearnings. This first major effort, retitled "Primeras poesías" and revised before reappearing in the first edition of *La realidad y el deseo* (reality and desire), was not well received. Cernuda was criticized sharply for imitating Jorge Guillén, and his production was judged unoriginal. More recent criticism, while acknowledging Cernuda's debt to Guillén, dismisses these charges as exagger-

ated, praising this early work for its fine sensibility and for the musical quality of its language.

EGLOGA, ELEGÍA, ODA

The negative reception of his first book encouraged Cernuda to withdraw, at least personally, from what he considered the literary mainstream and, by his own admission, "to wish to cultivate that which is criticized by others." He began work on a second collection, *Egloga, elegía, oda* (eclogue, elegy, ode), a series of four poems patterned after classical and neoclassical models, particularly the works of Garcilaso de la Vega, whose meter and rhyme Cernuda imitated deliberately. Some years later, reflecting on his development as a writer, Cernuda said that, while this second work had permitted him to experiment with classical themes and strophes, its style did not satisfy him, for he was unable to find what he loved in what he wrote. Nevertheless, in *Egloga, elegía, oda*, the poet was able to express more forcefully some of the feelings first introduced in *Perfil del aire*. Vague yearnings have become a compelling attraction to beauty in all its forms; the poet's need to satisfy his desires is confronted by the opposition of desire to such satisfaction. In this set of poems, he begins to remove his cloak of ennui, revealing a strong, sensuous nature. The pursuit of pleasure replaces indifference as the antidote for solitude and sadness. Desiring to express himself in a more daring fashion and to rebel against the constraints of bourgeois society, which misunderstood him and his sexuality, Cernuda gravitated toward the Surrealists. He read the works of Louis Aragon, André Breton, and Paul Éluard, whose poetry he translated into Spanish.

UN RÍO, UN AMOR AND LOS PLACERES PROHIBIDOS

Cernuda's Surrealist stage began, not coincidentally, with his year in France (1928-1929) and resulted in two important works, *Un río, un amor* (a river, a love) and *Los placeres prohibidos* (forbidden pleasures). The most notable technical characteristic of *Un río, un amor* is Cernuda's use of free verse, which was also being adopted during this period by other Spanish poets, such as Aleixandre, García Lorca, and Alberti. Freed of external constraints, Cernuda's verse nevertheless retained a strong sense of meter, and the rhythm of his lines was preserved through accentuation and cadence. He also made use of reiteration, anaphora, and anastrophe. From this period onward, Cernuda began to experiment with longer lines, although they seldom exceeded eleven syllables. In *Los placeres prohibidos*, Cernuda continued to discard technical conventions, alternating between verse and prose poems. Thematically, Surrealism provided Cernuda with the opportunity to liberate himself from social restrictions. Asserting his linguistic and stylistic freedom, he wrote of "night petrified by fists," "towers of fear," "iron flowers resounding like the chest of man," "tongue of darkness," and "empty eyes."

Toward the end of *Un río, un amor*, Cernuda intimates what is expressed openly in *Los placeres prohibidos*; he accepts his homosexuality and admits to being possessed by love. This love takes the form of passionate physical desire, rendered no less glorious and pure because of its carnality; only the outside world tarnishes this love with its opprobrium. In *Un río, un amor*, love produces an emptiness and a vacuum. Man is like a phantom, without direction; he is indifferent to the world, as if he were dead. In *Los placeres prohibidos*, however, love ceases to be the object of dreams; it becomes something real, the primary goal of man's desire, the motive behind all he does and feels: To give in to this love, without reservation, is man's purpose. Its attainment is nevertheless elusive—except for some fleeting moments—and contains an element of pain; herein lies the source of the solitude and the impotence of man.

DONDE HABITE EL OLVIDO

A third work published during this period, *Donde habite el olvido* (where oblivion dwells), closes out Cernuda's Surrealist phase. It was written after a failed love affair, one that the author naïvely had believed would last forever. This accounts for the bitterness of its tone, the poet's desire for death, and the harsh indictment of love, which, once it disappears, leaves nothing behind but the "remembrance of an oblivion." In the fourth poem of this collection, Cernuda retraces his personal history, as if it were a life already lived, replete with regrets and unfulfilled expectations. The first part of the poem exudes optimism, expansiveness, and anticipation, conveyed by the spring moon, the golden sea, and adolescent desire. The light, however, turns

into shadows; the poet falls into darkness and is ultimately a living corpse.

LAS NUBES

With his next major publication, *Las nubes* (the clouds), Cernuda introduced two important new themes into his poetry: historical time, with its specific focus on Spain as the abandoned and beleaguered homeland, and humanity's spirituality and religiosity. Love, the recurring topic of much of Cernuda's work, plays virtually no role in this collection. In "Un español habla de su tierra" ("A Spaniard Speaks of His Homeland"), the poet writes nostalgically of the happy days of the past, before his land succumbed to the conquering Cains. The bitter days of the present find sustenance in the fond memories of years gone by, an idealized past that might someday be re-created, yet to which the poet cannot return. When that day comes, and his homeland is free, it will come looking for him—only to discover that death has come to call first. Ironically, as one critic has pointed out, this poem was prescient in its chronology. In "Impresión de destierre" ("Impression of Exile"), the dislocated narrator—then in London—overhears a fatigued voice announce the death of Spain; "'Spain?' he said. 'A name./ Spain has died. . . .'"

Las nubes also contains the clearest expression of Cernuda's views on traditional religion. While his poetic use of belief in the supernatural has been described as a type of pantheistic hedonism based on Mediterranean mythology, his spiritual quest included attempts to find answers in more traditional Christian imagery by positing the existence of a God through whom humanity can achieve love. Cernuda devoted four poems in this collection to the broad question of the existence of God: "La visita de Dios" ("God's Visit"), "Atardecer en la catedral" ("Dusk in the Cathedral"), "Lázaro" ("Lazarus"), and "La adoración de los magos" ("The Adoration of the Magi"). In the long poem "God's Visit," the protagonist, in a voice filled with anguish, confronts God with the terrible wreckage of what is now the speaker's country, the poet's paradise of years gone by, perhaps destroyed by the casual wave of his hand. As the last hope for renewal, the protagonist begs God to restore to the world beauty, truth, and justice; without these, he warns, God could be forgotten.

"THE ADORATION OF THE MAGI"

More firmly rooted in Christianity is the five-part poem "The Adoration of the Magi," in which Cernuda's debt to T. S. Eliot is clear. The poem opens with a meditation by Melchior on the existence of God, reaching the conclusion that if he himself is alive, God, too, might well exist. This knowledge does not fully satisfy Melchior. To reason the existence of God is not enough; some more evocative proof is needed. The second part of the poem, "Los reyes" ("The Kings"), presents the Magi, each with a distinctive voice which expresses the conflicting visions of a single character: Melchior the idealist, Gaspar the hedonist, and Balthasar the skeptic. Through their intertwined monologues, the pilgrim searches for proof of the existence of God. The next section, "Palinodia de la esperanza divina" ("Palinode of Divine Hope"), is perhaps the most inventive; in it, the author expresses the disenchantment and disappointment felt by the Magi upon arriving in Bethlehem after a long journey and finding nothing but a poor child, a life "just like our human one," after expecting "a god, a presence/ radiant and imperious, whose sight is grace." In the fourth part, "Sobre el tiempo pasado" ("On Time Past"), the protagonist is the old shepherd (Father Time?) who remembers a period in his youth, long past, when three wise men came to look at a newborn child. The old man, however, has no recollection of a god; how can a humble shepherd, whose knowledge of man is so lacking, have seen the gods? The poem closes with a short fifth part, "Epitafio" ("Epitaph"), wherein man, as searcher, is told that he once found the truth but did not recognize it; now he can console himself by living his life in this world, as a body, even though he cannot be free from misery.

PASSAGE OF TIME AS THEME

The publication of *Las nubes* marked a new beginning for Cernuda, the man and the poet. He had departed from Spain; he was approaching the age of forty—an age which, for a man who associated beauty with youth and joy with youthfulness, must have created much anxiety. His prospects for recognition in Spain had been shattered by political events. Cernuda responded to this situation by creating a protagonist with a distinct identity; he created the poet, whose role it was to substitute as the main character for the author and who would, when called upon, assume all responsibility for failure. Thus, Cernuda created what Phillip Silver calls his "personal myth" and entered into the mature stage of his poetic production. Poetry became a means to understand and preserve the past. The need to fulfill a grand passion was discarded; man must resign himself to a world that belongs to the gods, a world in which he cannot partake of paradise. If man can be made into a myth, however, his life will be eternal and his beauty everlasting. In poems such as "Noche del hombre y su demonio" ("A Man's Night and His Demon") and "Río vespertino" ("Evening River") from *Como quien espera el alba*, Cernuda expresses an attitude of acceptance, as if recounting a life already lived. He anticipates, without fear, the inevitability of death. There is but one small consolation: There is no ash without flame, no death without life. In the long poem "Apología pro vita sua" from the same collection, the poet gathers up all the suffering of his existence: his obsessions as a poet, the war, his agnosticism, and his need and hope for a personal, intimate God. From his bedside, the protagonist summons first his lovers to help illuminate his world growing dim, for "Is passion not the measure of human greatness . . . ?" He then calls in his friends to help him renounce the light. As in a confessional, he admits to regrets, but only for those sins which he has not had the opportunity or the strength to commit. He asserts that he has lived without God because he has not manifested himself to him and has not satisfied his incredulity. The protagonist maintains that to die, people do not need God; rather, God needs people in order to live. In an apparent contradiction, a few lines later, he asks God to fill his soul with the light that comes with eternity.

The past, that which has been, and the inevitable passage of time become the dominating theme of the remainder of Cernuda's poetic output. In his mature verses, he recounts his life and his loves with the pessimistic tone of one who knows that they will never come again. Splendor, beauty, passion, and joy are juxtaposed to solitude, old age, and death.

OTHER MAJOR WORKS
SHORT FICTION: *Tres narraciones*, 1948.
NONFICTION: *Estudios sobre poesía española con-*

temporánea, 1957; *Pensamiento poético en la lírica inglesa (siglo XIX)*, 1958; *Poesía y literatura*, 1960, 1964 (2 volumes); *Crítica, ensayos y evocaciones*, 1970; *Prosa completa*, 1975.

BIBLIOGRAPHY

Harris, Derek. *Luis Cernuda: A Study of His Poetry.* London: Tamesis, 1973. A critical study of Cernuda's poetry. Includes bibliographic references.

_____. *Metal Butterflies and Poisonous Lights: The Language of Surrealism in Lorca, Alberti, Cernuda, and Aleixandre.* Anstruther, Fife, Scotland: La Sirena, 1998. An analysis of the use of surrealism in the poetry of Cernuda and other poets. Includes bibliographical references.

Jiménez-Fajardo, Salvador. *Luis Cernuda.* Boston: Twayne, 1978. An introductory biographical and critical analysis of selected works by Cernuda. Includes bibliographic references.

_____, ed. *The Word and the Mirror: Critical Essays on the Poetry of Luis Cernuda.* Rutherford, N.J.: Fairleigh Dickinson University Press, 1989. A collection of critical essays dealing with Cernuda's works.

McKinlay, Neil C. *The Poetry of Luis Cernuda: Order in a World of Chaos.* Rochester, N.Y.: Tamesis, 1999. A brief biographical and critical study. Includes bibliographical references and index.

Martin-Clark, Philip. *Art, Gender, and Sexuality: New Readings of Cernuda's Later Poetry.* Leeds, England: Maney, 2000. A critical interpretation of selected works by Cernuda. Includes bibliographical references and index.

Soufas, C. Christopher. *The Subject in Question: Early Contemporary Spanish Literature and Modernism.* Washington, D.C.: Catholic University of America Press, 2007. This general work on Spanish literature in the early twentieth century has a chapter looking at the themes of absence and experience in the poems of Cernuda and Rafael Alberti.

Clara Estow

RENÉ CHAR

Born: L'Île-en-Sorgue, France; June 14, 1907
Died: Paris, France; February 19, 1988

PRINCIPAL POETRY

Les Cloches sur le coeur, 1928
Arsenal, 1929
Ralentir travaux, 1930 (with Paul Éluard and André Breton)
Le Marteau sans maître, 1934
Moulin premier, 1937
Placard pour un chemin des écoliers, 1937
Dehors la nuit est gouvernée, 1938
Le Visage nuptial, 1938 (*The Nuptial Countenance*, 1976)
Seuls demeurant, 1945
Feuillets d' Hypnos, 1946 (*Leaves of Hypnos*, 1973)
Le Poème pulvérisé, 1947
Fureur et mystère, 1948
Les Matinaux, 1950 (*The Dawn Breakers*, 1992)
Lettera amorosa, 1953
Hypnos Waking, 1956
Cinq Poésies en hommage à Georges Braque, 1958
La Parole en archipel, 1962
Commune présence, 1964
L'Âge cassant, 1965 (*The Brittle Age*, 2009)
Retour amont, 1965 (*Returning Upland*, 2009)
Le Nu perdu, 1971
La Nuit talismanique, 1972
Aromates chasseurs, 1976
Poems of René Char, 1976
Selected Poems of René Char, 1992
This Smoke That Carried Us: Selected Poems, 2004

OTHER LITERARY FORMS

Like many French poets, René Char (shahr) wrote a great number of prose poems, and he is considered one of the finest practitioners in this genre since Charles Baudelaire and Arthur Rimbaud, by whom he was heavily influenced. These works are scattered throughout Char's poetry collections, suggesting that he does not distinguish the prose poem as a separate form. Char published several volumes of essays, including *Recherche de la base et du sommet* (1955; inquiry into the base and the summit) and *Sur la poésie* (1958; on poetry). He also contributed a number of prefaces, introductions, and catalogs for art shows, such as the 1973 Pablo Picasso exhibit in Avignon. Char's lifelong interest in painting is reflected in essays on Georges Braque, Joan Miró, and other contemporary artists; he also was active in other arts, writing the scenario for the ballet *L'Abominable Homme des neiges* (pb. 1956; the abominable snowman), for example, and the play *Le Soleil des eaux* (pb. 1949). Char's work has been set to music by composer Pierre Boulez.

ACHIEVEMENTS

Early in his poetic career, René Char was deeply involved in Surrealism, coauthoring several works with Paul Éluard and André Breton and gaining some recognition for his work. Under that influence, he was encouraged in his taste for the fragment—the incomplete line and "broken" metaphor, which he called *le poème pulvérisé*. These Surrealist techniques led to his being identified with the movement but did not lead to serious individual recognition.

After World War II, Char dedicated his *Leaves of Hypnos* to Albert Camus, a fellow Resistance fighter, who called Char France's greatest living poet, praising his shift from the self-absorption of Surrealism to a more universal view. Char thereby became associated with the rising tide of existentialism and achieved recognition as a major poet. Char also is credited with achieving a new validation for the prose poem, which, though it had a long tradition in France, was still regarded as a stepchild of "real" poetry.

BIOGRAPHY

René-Émile Char was born on June 14, 1907, the son of Émile Char, a manufacturer, and Marie-Thérèse-Armand Rouget of Cavaillon. Char's father, who served as the mayor of L'Île-en-Sorgue, was the son of a ward of the state who had been given the name "Charlemagne," later shortened to "Char-Magne" and, eventually, to "Char." Char spent his childhood in L'Île-en-Sorgue in the Vaucluse region in the south of France.

René Char (©Irisson)

The Vaucluse has a lush landscape ringed with mountains, the beauty of which would later fill his poetry. It is also an area of diverse industries, and the young Char became familiar with men of many occupations, especially craftspeople, peasants, and Sorgue River fishermen. Their rugged independence helped to instill in him a lifelong love of freedom. The boy had begun his education in the public schools when his father died in 1918. He then continued to the *lycée* in Avignon (the closest large city) for his *baccalauréat*. In 1924, he spent some time in Tunisia, where he developed a distaste for colonialism. He returned to study briefly at the École-de-Commerce in Marseilles, leaving from 1927 to 1928 for artillery service in Nîmes. In 1928, he published his first book of poems, *Les Cloches sur le coeur*.

Char sent a copy of his second collection, *Arsenal*, to Éluard, the chief poet of Surrealism, in Paris. Éluard was impressed with Char's work and went to L'Île-en-Sorgue to meet him. They became lifelong friends, and Char moved to Paris, where Éluard introduced him to the leading figures of Surrealism, including Breton. Char cowrote the poem *Ralentir travaux* (works slowed down) with Éluard and Breton and helped found the periodical *La Surréalisme au service de la révolution*. In 1933, Char married Georgette Goldstein (they were divorced in 1949), and a year he later published *Le Marteau sans maître* (the hammer without a master). During the early 1930's, he resided sometimes in Paris, sometimes in L'Île-en-Sorgue, and made several trips to Spain.

By the mid-1930's, the political climate in Europe was changing, and Char broke with the Surrealists in 1934, as Éluard soon would, sensing a need for the kind of action hinted at in *Le Marteau sans maître*: the defense of the oppressed and the fight for justice. In 1935, Char accepted a job as manager of the chalk pits in Vaucluse, but he soon resigned. In 1936, he was seriously ill as a result of blood poisoning, and he spent a year—the same year the Spanish Civil War began—convalescing in Cannes. He published *Placard pour un chemin des écoliers* (sign for a bypath) and *Dehors la nuit est gouvernée* (somewhere night is ruled) in the late 1930's, both titles indicating his growing sense of commitment. As 1939 ended, Char found himself mobilized into the artillery in Alsace, where he fought until the French surrender.

Returning to L'Île-en-Sorgue, Char was suspected by the Vichy police of being a communist because of his association with Surrealism. He fled with Georgette to the Alps and there began his activities as a *maquisard* in the Armée Secrète. Using the name Captain Alexandre from 1943 to 1945, Char became the departmental commander of the Parachute Landing Division of the Second Region of the Forces Françaises Combattantes and deputy to the regional commander of the Free French operations network. He was wounded in combat against the Germans in June, 1944, and after being cared for by Resistance doctors, he continued to Algeria in July, 1944, in response to a summons from the North Africa Allied Council. Subsequently, he was parachuted into France and participated in the battles to liberate Provence. Demobilized in 1945, he received several decorations for his service, including the Croix de Guerre and the Médaille de la Résistance.

From 1939 to the liberation of France, Char did not publish any poetry. When *Seuls demeurant* (the only ones left) and *Leaves of Hypnos* appeared, he became famous. Georges Mounin's critique *Avez-vous lu Char?* (1947; Have you read Char?) praised Char's work and contributed to his success. Char again began to live part of each year in Paris and part in the Vaucluse; he did not, however, participate in the "official" literary life. He generally declined the honors offered to him, although he was made a Chevalier de la Légion d'Honneur and received the Prix des Critiques in 1966, and he argued that poetry should not be considered a means of making a living. He also stood apart from the partisan political involvements which entangled many French writers of the time—especially those who shared Char's leftist sympathies.

One of Char's closest friends was the novelist Albert Camus, who, like Char, linked literature with the struggle toward freedom and human dignity. Char also exchanged letters with the Russian poet and novelist Boris Pasternak and, beginning in 1955, kept in close contact with the German philosopher Martin Heidegger.

Throughout the 1950's and 1960's, the audience for Char's poetry grew, and he was translated into numerous foreign languages. After he became associated with Georges Braque in 1947, Char often published his poetry in beautiful editions, illustrated by celebrated contemporary artists such as Pablo Picasso, Nicolas de Stäel, Louis Broder, and Louis Fernandez. Char also illustrated his poetry himself. His interest in philosophy dominated his later poetry, and beginning in the 1950's, Char saw his role as poet as that of a commentator on society, a revolutionary in the service of humankind. He died in Paris on February 19, 1988.

ANALYSIS

Albert Camus once wrote that René Char's poetry was both ancient and new, subtle and simple, carrying both daytime and night: "In the brilliant landscape where Char was born, the sun . . . is something dark." Camus thus identified one of the predominant characteristics of Char's poetic method: the juxtaposition of opposites. According to critic Robert W. Greene, Char has rejected one of the fundamental concepts of Western thought: the Aristotelian principle that a thing cannot be anything other than what it is at one moment in time. Any poem working within different principles seems obscure and vaporous as Eastern religions which deny the reality of the world. Char, however, deeply admires the fragments of Heraclitus—who believed in the unity of opposites—and sets up oppositions throughout his poetry. Similar concepts can be found in earlier poetry influenced by Eastern thought, such as Ralph Waldo Emerson's "Brahma," in which the slayer is simultaneously the one who is slain. Char's rejection of the identity principle, however, has different implications in its twentieth century context. It reflects the linguistic, subjective philosophies developing in the late nineteenth and early twentieth centuries, and though Char has a tendency toward the fragmentary aphorism (possibly influenced by the fragments of Heraclitus), he grapples with modern problems in a specific way. Thus, as Camus rightly observed, Char's poetry is both "ancient and new."

"COMMUNE PRÉSENCE"

The concluding lines of Char's important early poem "Commune présence" are characteristic in their conjunction of opposites: "You have been created for extraordinary moments . . . Adjust yourself and disperse without regret." Here, a near-heroic proclamation of identity is immediately followed by a line advising assimilation. The following line, "According to a soft hardness," embodies yet another contradiction and illustrates Char's technique of opposing semantic units. It furthermore conveys Char's fundamental view of a world of unsynthesized opposites. Life is simultaneously total resistance and total acceptance. One is reminded of the existentialist assertions that whatever a person does is completely absurd, yet that it is necessary to act as if each moment had meaning. The final two lines of the poem contain a command: "Swarm the dust/ No one will decelerate your union." The penultimate line is a contradiction because a swarm of bees is similar to a cloud of dust only in appearance. Dust moves at random, each mote in its own direction; bees move in rough unison. Dust dissipates into nothingness; bees have a vital purpose. The final line promises that nothing can oppose the eventual union, however— the union that comes from an initial scattering. In political terms, one sees the allusion to humankind as a col-

lection of individual, meaningless units (like dust), which can gain new meaning by union (like a swarm). All those meaningless units (bees, motes, people), added together, become meaning. Metaphorically, darkness becomes the sun.

SURREALIST PERIOD

Char's early association with Surrealism might be regarded as an influence in that direction, or it may be seen as a reflection of what Char already was reaching for in his work. As Camus wrote, "No doubt he did take part in Surrealism, but rather as an ally than as an adherent, and just long enough to discover that he could walk alone with more conviction." This is the general critical appraisal. Anna Balakian, however, asserts that Char carries on the tradition of Surrealism better than anyone else. As Char describes in *Le Poème pulvérisé*, he faces—like Breton and the others—"this rebellious and solitary world of contradictions" and cannot live without the image of the unknown before him. In this vast unknown, this world finally impossible to understand (hence the Surrealist's despair), one can only be an explorer, and poetry is the medium of exploration: words and meaning in conflict. Irrationality is crucial in setting aside the world of illusion and seeing beyond, to the more legitimate world of dreams. *The Nuptial Countenance* has been cited as exhibiting this trait in its mixing of objects that defy classification; it has many resemblances to the works of Breton and Éluard.

Critic Mechthild Cranston argues that Char took two important insights with him when he broke with Surrealism: He saw that the existing world order was in need of reexamination, along with the canons of art, and that violence and destruction would not solve the problems of his generation. The first idea remained with him throughout his career, in his commitment to the Resistance and in his generally leftist politics. The second, however, underwent modification. In Char's Surrealist period, he speaks of the need for violence, catastrophes, and crimes to help create a new concept of art. "Les Soleils chanteurs" mentions specific kinds of violence that will revitalize poetry. Char's poetry of this period is filled with images of chemicals, metals, and machinery, like the works of the Futurists, and has a similar purpose: to destroy the florid, false language of late Romanticism. Char's experience of the real—not metaphorical—violence of World War II changed his orientation. In his poetry published since the war, he abandoned the rhetoric of the Surrealists, achieving a new humility and seeking the simplicity of a child's vision.

LATER POETRY

Char's later poetry is also distinguished by its moral intensity, particularly its commitment to freedom. In Char's view, anything that inhibits human freedom is immoral. The poet's duty is to do battle continually against anything that would restrict humankind's ability to seek meaning. This includes any preconceived ideas, even the idea of liberty itself. One might see in this stance a combination of the didactic nature of Surrealism and the call to action and freedom in existentialism. Like the existentialists, Char attempts to recreate ethics for modern humanity, yet in doing so he invokes the mystery so important to Surrealist art. Thus, for Char, poetry is an existential stance, a becoming, an invitation to return to natural insights and to reject mechanical materialism.

OTHER MAJOR WORKS

PLAYS: *Claire: Théâtre de Verdure*, pb. 1949; *Le Soleil des eaux*, pb. 1949; *L'Abominable Homme des neiges*, pb. 1956 (ballet scenario); *Trois coups sous les arbres: Théâtre Saisonnier*, pb. 1967.

NONFICTION: *Recherche de la base et du sommet*, 1955; *Sur la poésie*, 1958.

MISCELLANEOUS: *En trente-trois morceaux*, 1956 (aphorisms).

BIBLIOGRAPHY

Caws, Mary Ann. *The Presence of René Char*. Princeton, N.J.: Princeton University Press, 1976. Critical interpretation of selected works by Char. Includes bibliographical references and index.

_____. *René Char*. Boston: Twayne, 1977. An introductory biography and critical interpretation of selected works by Char. Includes an index and a bibliography.

Eichbauer, Mary E. *Poetry's Self-Portrait: The Visual Arts as Mirror and Muse in René Char and John Ashbery*. New York: Peter Lang, 1992. An analysis of the relationship to visual art of the poetry of Char

and Ashbery. Includes bibliographical references and index.

Lawler, James R. *René Char: The Myth and the Poem*. Princeton, N.J.: Princeton University Press, 1978. A critical analysis of Char's poetry. Includes bibliographic references.

Minahen, Charles D., ed. *Figuring Things: Char, Ponge, and Poetry in the Twentieth Century*. Lexington, Ky.: French Forum, 1994. A critical study and comparison of the works of Char and Francis Ponge. Includes bibliographic references.

Piore, Nancy Kline. *Lightning: The Poetry of René Char*. Boston: Northeastern University Press, 1981. A short critical study of selected poems. Includes an index and bibliography.

J. Madison Davis

CHARLES D'ORLÉANS

Born: Paris, France; November 24, 1394
Died: Amboise, France; January 4, 1465

PRINCIPAL POETRY

Livre contre tout péché, 1404
Le livre de la cité des dames, 1405 (*The Book of the City of Ladies*, 1982)
Retenue d'amours, 1414
Ballades, c. 1415-1460
Chansons, c. 1415-1460
Songe en complainte, 1437
Rondeaux, c. 1443-1460
The English Poems of Charles of Orleans, 1941-1946 (2 volumes)
The French Chansons, 1986

OTHER LITERARY FORMS

In addition to his poetry, Charles d'Orléans (shahrl dawr-lay-ON) left a long and partly autobiographical speech that he had presented in defense of the duke of Alençon at the latter's trial. The speech, which dates from 1458, contains reminiscences of Charles's captivity and of his early life.

ACHIEVEMENTS

Charles d'Orléans is by any measure one of the preeminent poets of the latter Middle Ages; most critics would in fact rank him second, in France only to François Villon. They would, however, doubtless consider him a rather distant second, and that would represent both an accurate assessment and something of an injustice. He is by no means the literary equal of Villon, one of the world's great poets. However, Charles is often underestimated, not only because he is inferior to Villon but also because, quite simply, he is not Villon.

To many readers, Charles's poetry may seem somewhat dated, in contrast to the timeless texts of his contemporary. Indeed, Charles uses images, formulas, and conventions associated with the literature of courtly love, which enjoyed its greatest vogue during the twelfth and thirteenth centuries. His allegories and personifications have been dismissed as delicate and cultivated playthings, valuable witnesses to an age but of quite limited appeal to modern readers.

It is important, however, to meet Charles on his own terrain and on his own terms; there he is found to be an extraordinary poet. Charles was a wealthy and refined prince; for him and for many of his contemporaries, poetry was both a pastime and an art to be cultivated. A poem might be a witty rejoinder in a literary debate with friends, or it might be an artistic creation of the highest order, an artifact to be sculpted carefully and consciously. In such a system, Charles's use of traditional materials—his allegories and personifications and courtly images—was fully justified. An attentive reading, moreover, reveals that he was by no means a slave to tradition. What he borrowed he was able to renew, and his best poems derive much of their appeal from his subtle re-creation of traditional materials.

Re-creation occurs within the bounds of individual poems as well; there are, for example, few poets more adroit than Charles at leading gracefully into a refrain so as to alter its meaning slightly with each stanza. He is a master of style, of wit, of verbal color, yet he is sometimes considerably more than that. No sooner is the reader lulled by an extended series of abstractions and personifications than Charles suddenly shifts to an unadorned declaration of the pain he felt at his captivity, deprived as he was not simply of love but of his homeland and his freedom.

Charles engaged frequently in poetic contests and games, and poetry was for him avocation as well as art. Under the circumstances, repetition and unevenness are inevitable. More often than not, however, he proves himself to be an extraordinary practitioner of his art—that of the refined and delicate poem that deserves admiration for what it is rather than criticism for what it lacks.

BIOGRAPHY

Charles d'Orléans was born in Paris on November 24, 1394; his father was Louis, duke of Orléans, whose brother was King Charles VI. In 1406, a marriage was arranged between Charles and his cousin Isabelle of

Charles d'Orléans (Hulton Archive/Getty Images)

France. The following year (in November, 1407), his father was assassinated by Jean-sans-Peur, duke of Burgundy, and Charles himself became duke of Orléans. Isabelle died in 1409, and the next year, following an alliance with the count of Armagnac, he married eleven-year-old Bonne d'Armagnac. He spent several years trying to avenge his father's death, doing battle with the Burgundians, concluding more than one unsuccessful treaty, and occasionally seeking the aid of the English.

France's troubles were not limited to the regional struggles that occupied much of Charles's early life; he had, in fact, been born at the midpoint of the Hundred Years' War, and before his twenty-fifth birthday, he was taken prisoner by the English in the Battle of Agincourt (October 25, 1415). He spent the next twenty-five years as a prisoner in England. It was a curious kind of imprisonment; although he was frequently moved from place to place, he was never held behind bars. He was allowed to receive visitors, money, and servants from France, and he had access to various amenities and pleasures, which (according to some reports) may have included female companionship. It was hardly a difficult existence, but Charles was nevertheless separated from his homeland and family, and many of his poems from the period bitterly lament his plight.

Changes in the political and military situation (along with the payment of a substantial ransom and a promise never again to take up arms against the English) secured Charles's release in November, 1440, and as his second wife had died five years earlier, he soon married Marie de Clèves, niece of the duke of Burgundy. For the remainder of his life, he dabbled occasionally in military and political affairs but was largely content to devote his time to poetic pursuits, especially at his castles in Blois and Tours. During the night of January 4, 1465, he died at Amboise, at the age of seventy.

ANALYSIS

The subjects of Charles d'Orléans's poetry are love, his imprisonment in England, and the pain he suffers from both. These are not necessarily discrete subjects; they frequently overlap and merge. For example, in the courtly idiom adopted by Charles, love always entails the lover's loss of freedom. Accordingly, the poet often

appears to have transformed his captivity into an amorous metaphor (without, however, diluting its literal force); he was the prisoner of the English in much the same way that his persona was the prisoner of love. His themes are also related in a more direct way, for his imprisonment deprived him not only of freedom but also of love and pleasure. Thus, even in one of his more clearly patriotic poems, "En regardant vers le pays de France" ("While Looking Towards the Country of France"), where the source of his suffering is his separation from his homeland, his pain is caused in part by the loss of "the sweet pleasure that I used to experience in that country," one of his specific pleasures obviously being that of love.

During his years in England, Charles often lamented the separation from "his lady." Critical efforts to identify that lady (with Isabelle, with Bonne d'Armagnac, or with an English acquaintance) have not met with success; this failure is both inevitable and appropriate. The fact is that courtly convention would be likely to preserve the anonymity of the lady, and also, more to the point, her identity is simply irrelevant. She may thus have been any woman or an amalgam of several women—or she may not even have existed except as an abstraction. Indeed, in some poems she appears to represent not a particular lady but France itself, for Charles uses the same general terms to describe his absence from his lady and his separation from his country. Again, Charles's emotion is his principal focus, and a shifting, ambiguous relation exists between the major causes of it. For a poet like Charles, given to persistent metaphorical associations, his lady and his country easily become almost interchangeable or doubled poetic referents throughout the period of his captivity.

LOOKING HOMEWARD

There are many places where Charles makes explicit reference to his experiences in England. Even though his captors treated him comparatively well, his poems could hardly have conveyed more anguish and melancholy. His best-known work of the period is doubtless the poem "While Looking Towards the Country of France," in which Charles, from Dover, laments his fate and declares: "Peace is a treasure that cannot be praised too highly. I detest war, for it has long prevented me from seeing my beloved France." Later, he was to remark in another context that he would prefer to have died in battle rather than endure his English captivity. Other works express his sorrow at France's lot and his later exultation at the English defeat ("Rejoice, Noble Kingdom of France"). Such passages offer a good deal of interest for reasons both historical and biographical, and even though their artistic value is uneven, some of them are likely to appeal to modern readers more than do Charles's love poems.

LOVE POETRY

On first reading, the love poems may appear dated—and, indeed, some of them are. Charles is generally thought of as a poet of courtly love, and that is the way he began his literary career. At that time, he cultivated (not always with much originality) all the conventions of courtly love inherited from Guillaume de Lorris and Jean de Meung (in *Le Roman de la rose*, thirteenth century; *The Romance of the Rose*, partial translation c. 1370, complete translation 1900) and from others who wrote two centuries or more before Charles. Not only his ideas but also his modes of expression are traditional. Thus, in Ballade 29 he writes: "I do not fear Danger or his followers,/ For I have reinforced the fortress/ In which my heart has stored its goods/ . . . And I have made Loyalty mistress of it." Such passages are often ingenious, but the premises underlying them offer nothing new.

With time, however, his ideas evolved, and later he either turned against courtly love or (according to John H. Fox in *The Lyric Poetry of Charles d'Orléans*, 1969) simply found it largely irrelevant. Thus, while he had earlier noted without much apparent conviction that "Sadness has held me in its power for so long that I have entirely forgotten Joy," his protestations begin to assume a more personal and intense tone. He points out that "the poor souls of lovers are tormented in an abyss of sorrow" (Rondeau 140); he wonders if it is Fortune's desire that he suffer so much (Rondeau 217); he orders Beauty out of his presence, because "you tempt me too often" (Rondeau 236). In some cases, to be sure, the later poems are superficially indistinguishable from the traditional laments of the courtly lover, but one can generally discern a subtle shift of tone, and some texts go further and constitute a clear rejection of courtly premises. For example, replacing the traditional notion

that suffering tempered by hope is adequate recompense for the lover is Charles's insistence (in Rondeau 65) that he can love only if his love is reciprocated, and in Rondeau 160, he states cynically that a medicine can surely be found to help those who are in love.

RETENUE D'AMOURS AND SONGE EN COMPLAINTE

A revealing example of the evolution in Charles's thought is provided by the contrast between his two long poems, *Retenue d'amours* (love's retinue) and *Songe en complainte* (dream in the form of a complaint). The former, written prior to Agincourt, offers a traditional allegorical presentation of a young man's initiation into love: He leaves *Enfance* (childhood) and entrusts his life to Lady Youth. He is afraid, because Youth has long served the God of Love, and Charles has heard many men tell of "the pains that Love makes them endure." Considering himself unable to bear the torment, he is reluctant to expose himself to Love's power. Youth assures him that those who complain are not true lovers who know what joy is and that honor and great good come to those who love. After meeting other members of Love's retinue, he awakens to love in a traditional way: Beauty shoots an arrow into his heart through his eyes. Becoming Love's vassal, he swears to accept the ten commandments of Love (to remain honorable, loyal, discreet, and so on).

More than twenty years later, Charles composed *Songe en complainte*, which serves in one sense as a continuation of the earlier poem, but which also proves to be its converse, its mirror image. Here, noting that his heart requires repose, his purpose is to disengage himself from love, to reclaim his heart, long held captive by the God of Love. Whereas he had earlier emphasized the joy of love and had accepted its pain as a natural, even desirable phenomenon, the older Charles now finds pain too high a price to pay for love and desires release from his vows. His attitude toward love is now melancholy, heavily tinged with skepticism.

The two long poems are important as a dramatic illustration of Charles's evolution, but artistically they are not particularly impressive creations. They are straightforward and (especially in the former case) derivative, and emphasis remains primarily on the elaboration of theme to the virtual exclusion of expressive subtlety and poetic effect. In fact, it could be said, with little injustice to Charles, that his poetic temperament is reductive, not expansive. He is generally more successful in his shorter forms. Thus, the ballades are usually better than the long poems, and the rondeaux are better still. His most successful pieces approach the status of Imagist poems, presenting a single, self-contained, vivid image, generally in the opening lines. The body of the poem is largely an elaboration of this image, often involving the subsidiary images derived from and supporting the principal one. Ironically, the elaboration may at times dilute the power of the image instead of intensifying it. Charles himself must have realized as much; he gradually began to abandon the ballade in favor of the shorter rondeau (a fixed-form poem containing three brief stanzas, usually of four or five lines each, with the beginning of the first stanza serving as the refrain of the other two). The dimensions of this form were ideally suited to Charles's talent and temperament, and his rondeaux present what Fox describes as "an art form at its peak." Many of the themes, images, and personifications used in the long poems find their way into the shorter ones as well, although in the latter Charles molds them to his purposes with greater originality and flexibility.

POETIC TECHNIQUE

Despite the fact that Charles is often considered to have made extensive use of allegory, it is essential to define his technique with more precision. Ann Tukey Harrison correctly suggests that Charles reduces allegories and personifications to metaphors tailored to his purposes. Often the narrative element in his poems is radically diminished or entirely eliminated, leaving him with *Esperance* (hope), *Beauté* (beauty), *Bon Acceuil* (welcome), or some other quality that appears to be a dramatized personification but in fact simply represents an aspect of his own experience. Thus, one of his famous poems, "La Forêt de longue actente" (the forest of long awaiting), provides not the locus of a sustained series of events (as it might have for Guillaume de Lorris, for example) but rather a simple indication of a psychological or emotional state.

Moreover, while Charles may appear to maintain a static set of personifications adopted from earlier tradition, his system is in reality remarkably flexible, each

figure being freely fashioned to the need created by a particular poem and by a particular dramatic situation. Thus, Comfort (for example) may be specific or abstract, ally or foe, as the context dictates. Each figure exists within a rather wide range of possible functions, and as a result, Charles's poetic cosmos is constantly shifting and developing with each text and with each artistic choice.

The stylistic pattern employed in "La Forêt de longue actente" (that is, the conjoining of a natural or architectural object with an abstraction) occurs in many of Charles's poems and pulls them in opposing directions, creating a tension between the concrete and the abstract: the Cloud of Sadness, the Ship of Good News, the Doorway of Thought, the Window of the Eyes. Such formulas are simple stylistic inversions that present a metaphor (thought is a doorway) as an apparent allegory. Charles is clearly fashioning a very personal version of allegory—or, rather, using the appearance of allegory to amplify and deepen the meaning of his images.

Several of Charles's images (castles, forests, ships) suggest confinement or containment, and the temptation to propose a biographical reading is not easily resisted. Obviously, such images reflect the poet's own imprisonment. Such a reading may seem plausible, but it ultimately does an injustice to Charles as a poet, because it reduces the text to an item of biographical evidence. Critical focus must remain on the poem itself, and instead of seeing the text as an index to his life, the critic should regard Charles's experience as material and inspiration for an autonomous series of texts. Some of his poems do indeed speak directly and explicitly of his captivity in England, yet loss of freedom is a familiar metaphor in the tradition of courtly love, to say nothing of love poetry of other ages.

As Charles had first been the willing poetic prisoner of love, and as he had later been imprisoned by the English, he gradually came to see himself as the captive of old age. He began to consider love an inimical force, and for him it was explicitly linked to the aging process. The culmination of this development is found in *Songe en complainte*. He notes that it ill befits an old man to make a fool of himself with regard to love, and he announces that "Love and Old Age are incompatible."

Here the melancholy that characterizes many of his poems takes on a new tone; instead of a gentle melancholy presumably felt by all lovers (and accepted by Charles's persona during his earlier years), this poem offers a note of genuine sadness and almost forlorn resignation. Such an evolution is in one sense typical of his work. There are few themes or images that he either adopts or discards during the course of his career; rather, it is the use of them that changes, the tone of them that evolves. His originality thus lies not in the fashioning of new themes, but in the particular ways his persona comes to react to conventions borrowed from earlier poets.

Charles thus represents the continuation and culmination of a style and a tradition two centuries old or older, but he also represents their renewal. He puts a personal stamp on the allegorical method, and at the same time he manages to raise his poetry—which participates in venerable tradition—above the level of the personal. His poems do not present a broad and elaborate canvas; they are far closer to the refined art of the miniature: diminutive, delicate, intimate. In the rondeau, Charles found his ideal form and cultivated it extensively, leaving a body of work that not only presents unusual historical interest but also preserves a number of small and often exquisite masterpieces.

BIBLIOGRAPHY

Arn, Mary-Jo. *Charles d'Orléans in England, 1415-1440*. Rochester, N.Y.: D. S. Brewer, 2000. A biography of Charles's life while imprisoned in England. Includes bibliographical references and index.

_____. *The Poet's Notebook: The Personal Manuscript of Charles d'Orléans*. Turnhout, Belgium: Brepols, 2008. Examines the history of the manuscript, redating and reordering parts of it. Tables and facsimile pages clarify technical aspects, and a compact disc contains a sortable index of first lines.

Coldiron, A. E. B. *Canon, Period, and the Poetry of Charles of Orleans: Found in Translation*. Ann Arbor: University of Michigan Press, 2000. An analysis of the history and critical reception of Charles's poetry in English translation. Includes bibliographical references and index.

Fein, David A. *Charles d'Orléans*. Boston: Twayne, 1983. Contains a brief biography and careful analysis of the major French poems (with English translations) but omits coverage of the English poems. Fein describes the early ballades as inwardly centered with personified emotions for exploring thoughts and feelings. This pensive, melancholy outlook shifts to outward orientation and irony in the rondeaux.

Mühlethaler, Jean-Claude. "Inversions, Omissions, and the Co-textual Reorientation of Reading: The Ballades of Charles d'Orléans in Vérard's *La Chasse et le de 'part d'amours* (1509)." In *Book and Text in France, 1400-1600: Poetry on the Page*, edited by Adrian Armstrong and Malcolm Quainton. Burlington, Vt.: Ashgate, 2007. Examines Charles's ballades that appeared in Vérard's anthology and discusses his poetry in general.

Spence, Sarah. "Reg(u)arding the Text: The Role of Vision in the Chansons of Charles d'Orléans." In *Chaucer's French Contemporaries: The Poetry/Poetics of Self and Tradition*, edited by R. Barton Palmer. New York: AMS Press, 1999. A translator of Charles's work interprets some of his songs.

Summers, Joanna. *Late-Medieval Prison Writing and the Politics of Autobiography*. New York: Oxford University Press, 2004. Contains a chapter on Charles and the English poems. Charles wrote more than 6,500 lines of poetry while imprisoned, all in a pseudo-biographical mode.

Taylor, Jane H. M. *The Making of Poetry: Late-Medieval French Poetic Anthologies*. Turnhout, Belgium: Brepols, 2007. Contains a chapter discussing Charles and his circle, as well as his personal manuscript.

Norris J. Lacy

ALAIN CHARTIER

Born: Bayeux, Normandy, France; c. 1385
Died: Avignon, France; c. 1430

PRINCIPAL POETRY

The Poetical Works of Alain Chartier, 1974 (J. C.
    Laidlaw, editor)

OTHER LITERARY FORMS

Traditional literary history has judged the poetry of
Alain Chartier (shahr-TYAY) to be less important than
his prose works. This evaluation is based on the fact
that many of the poems are conventional, courtly creations, whereas the prose works deal with substantial
moral and political issues. Modern scholars, however,
have adopted a new perspective on Chartier's poetry,
seeing in it a symbolic extension of the content found in
the prose works. This new approach reveals a continuity and balance in Chartier's works.

Chartier wrote in both Latin and French. His major
prose works in French are *Le Quadrilogue invectif*
(1489; *The Invective Quadrilogue*, late fifteenth century), written in 1422, and *Le Traité de l'espérance:
Ou, Consolation des trois vertus* (1489; *The Treatise
on Hope: Or, The Comfort of the Three Virtues*; late
fifteenth century) written about 1428. *The Invective
Quadrilogue*, composed after the Battle of Agincourt,
is a patriotic allegory in which France exhorts the orders of society—chivalry, the clergy, and the common
people—to seek peace together. Chartier takes a firm
stand in this work, which many critics consider his
most important, for national unity, for the poor, and for
the Dauphin Charles. The author's longest work and
among his last, *The Treatise on Hope*, was inspired by
Boethius. Allegorical and historical figures paint a
vivid tableau of a country distressed by continual conflict and then offer a religious solution to national problems. The treatise is a combination of verse and prose,
with prose predominating.

Chartier's Latin works include official diplomatic
speeches and letters, personal letters to his family and
friends, and *De vita curiali* (1489; *The Curial*, 1888),
the shortest of the prose works. *The Curial*, written first

in Latin, then translated into French, as *Le Curial*, is a
vehement attack on the practices of court life. Because
of the problems presented by the manuscript tradition,
several theories on date of composition and authorship
have been advanced. Scholars are not certain whether
Chartier composed one or both parts.

Above all, Chartier's prose writings are distinguished by their eloquence. Both his contemporaries
and successors appreciated and imitated his conciseness and oratorical style. Modern scholars have appreciated the extent to which he consecrated his literary
skill to addressing the problems of his times. One critic,
Edward J. Hoffman, in his 1942 study, *Alain Chartier:
His Work and Reputation*, sees in Chartier's literary
contribution "a crusading spirit . . . an eloquence born
of sincerity and genuine sympathy, all put to the service
of a high moral purpose: the regeneration of a stricken,
prostrate nation."

ACHIEVEMENTS

Alain Chartier has been called the founder of French
eloquence and one of the first of France's great patriots.
Literary history has admired him most for his patriotism, his humanism, and his erudition. During his lifetime and in the century that followed, Chartier was held
in high esteem for his oratorical and poetic ability.
Then, for many years, he fell out of critical favor and
was rarely mentioned with judgment other than disdain
for the excessively traditional aspects of his work.
Modern critics have benefited from the studies of Arthur Piaget, Pierre Champion, and Gaston Paris, as well
as by the clarification of the confusing and extensive
manuscript tradition. In addition to Hoffman, scholars
such as J. C. Laidlaw, William W. Kibler, and C. J. H.
Walravens have based their evaluations on more reli-
able texts and have viewed Chartier in his historical as
well as his literary context.

BIOGRAPHY

Constructing an accurate biography of Alain Chartier has proved an arduous task for scholars. Biographers have had to deal with many problems—scarce information, variable spellings of the author's surname,
and frequently contradictory references—to propose
an approximate chronology. Account books, political

and diplomatic documents, and the author's own works have been fruitful sources of information.

Chartier was born toward the end of the fourteenth century, probably 1385, into a property-holding family in Bayeux, Normandy, in France. His father was Jean Chartier. Alain was older than his two brothers, Guillaume and Thomas, and preceded them to high office. Thomas was to become a royal secretary and notary; Guillaume, bishop of Paris and royal adviser. Although little information concerning Alain's youth and years as a student is available, it is known that he left his native province to study at the University of Paris. It may be assumed from his scholarly knowledge and ability to write well in Latin and in Middle French that Chartier was an able student and that he received an excellent classical education. In addition to his mastery of language, his works bear witness to a broad knowledge of ancient history, philosophy, and literature.

The artistically nourishing atmosphere of the Anjou court was pivotal in the development of the young Chartier's literary talent, and his courtly love poems must have found an appreciative audience in royal circles. Chartier entered royal duty about 1418 and continued in the services of the Dauphin after the latter was declared King Charles VII. No mention is made of Chartier in royal records after 1429. As royal secretary, it was Chartier's duty to act as spokesperson, deliver speeches, and present credentials during diplomatic missions. His work involved him in negotiations in Hungary, Venice, and Scotland, where he distinguished himself as an orator. Chartier's embassy to Scotland in 1428 is remembered through a famous anecdote. According to the legend, the Dauphiness Margaret of Scotland, daughter of James I and future wife of the Dauphin Louis (later Louis XI), approached Chartier, who was asleep in a chair, and kissed him on the mouth, saying that she did not kiss the man but rather the mouth that had spoken so many virtuous and beautiful words.

Although it is not known if Chartier was a member of the clergy, it is known that he held several ecclesiastical titles, such as canon, curate, and archdeacon, which the French king could have bestowed on a public servant. The emphasis on religion in his works would substantiate his close affiliation with the Church. Furthermore, that he neither married nor had children supports the hypothesis that he became a priest.

Chartier's disappearance in 1429 has been a subject for scholarly research. It is possible that, because of the harshly critical nature of his writings about politics, he fell out of royal favor and was even exiled. It must be remembered that Chartier lived in disillusionment and despair over the moral and political corruption that he had witnessed at first hand. Sensitive to the plight of his beloved country and of his compatriots, Chartier reacted constantly to his times. At the height of his literary career, France was torn by conflict without and within: the Hundred Years' War (1337-1453), the Burgundian-Armagnac civil wars, and the troubled reign of Charles VI. Clearly, Chartier dedicated his life to calling his fellow humans to return to the virtuous ways of the past. Scholars find no evidence to prove that he lived after 1430 and believe that he is buried at the Church of Saint-Antoine in Avignon, France.

ANALYSIS

Alain Chartier was an erudite author, trained in a traditional medieval background that profoundly influenced the formation of his poetic canon. His frequent use of allegory, personification, and courtly themes characterizes his poetry. However, beyond mastery of conventional form and the expression of traditional themes, the poet devoted his scholarship and literary skill to communicating moral ideas to his readers. This aspect of his work issued from his observations of his contemporaries and his participation in the political events of his lifetime. Because he was deeply affected by conflict and suffering, Chartier moved from a purely aesthetic to a more realistic thematic conception.

The 1974 Laidlaw edition of Alain Chartier's poetry is comprehensive in its discussion of the background and manuscript tradition of each poem and also in its review of previous critical editions and bibliography. Students of Chartier will benefit from this work. All the poems discussed in this section are found in the Laidlaw edition.

"THE LAY ON PLEASURE"

Chartier's poetry, though begun in the courtly tradition, illustrates a maturing process and a consequent passage from less serious thematic concerns to moral and political issues. His earliest love poems are traditional in form and at times somewhat awkward. "Le Lai de plaisance" ("The Lay on Pleasure"), dating from about 1414, provides an example of the young poet's early tendency to concentrate on metrical complexity and accurate rhyme scheme rather than on subject matter. Although it is not difficult to identify the poem's theme—thoughts on pleasure on New Year's Day— nor to detect its sad tone, it is nevertheless somewhat perplexing to follow the thematic development through the forty-eight stanzas. The poet presents the subject in a courtly manner in the form of advice on how to be an honorable lover, yet the message is obscured at times by the poet's intention to fulfill all the technical requirements of the lay's fixed form. Chartier engaged in technical exercises with other fixed forms as well. His poetry shows him respecting and occasionally mastering the stanzaic, metric, and rhythmic uniformity of the ballad, the rondeau, and the chanson. Although Chartier was not innovative in the fixed-form genres, his poems possess graceful movement and harmony.

"THE BOOK OF FOUR LADIES"

Chartier's longest poetic work, "Le Livre des quatre dames" ("The Book of Four Ladies"), written after the Battle of Agincourt, about 1416, represents a transition between his idealized poetry and realistic prose. This work holds special interest because, though it was written shortly after the very traditional "The Lay on Pleasure," it contains political ideas that Chartier develops later in his prose. In addition, "The Book of Four Ladies" describes the poet's personal sentiments at some length in a prologue of twelve stanzas. While on a solitary spring walk to forget his sadness over a love affair, the narrator meets four women who in turn reveal their grief at having lost their lovers in battle: One has been killed, one has been captured, another is missing, and the last has fled. It is possible, according to Laidlaw, to speculate on the identities of the women, placing them in the historic context of the conflicts of the Burgundian-Orléanist. Through the lamentations of these women, Chartier expresses far more than grief. He criticizes energetically and eloquently those in power who allowed France to fall into ruin and those who refused to defend their country. Although structur-

ally traditional in its description of an idealized landscape and its plan of debate, the poem is an impassioned patriotic work heralding Chartier's important prose works.

"THE PATRIOTIC DEBATE"

Another poem that gives evidence of Chartier's transition to serious subjects is "Le Débat patriotique" ("The Patriotic Debate"), written sometime between 1416 and 1420. The poetic form is a debate between two noblemen during the course of which the author expresses his scorn for the behavior of the nobility, particularly toward peasants. Thematically, the poem is in the same current as *The Invective Quadrilogue* and *The Curial* because of its attack on the noble class, which, according to Chartier, has lost its nobility of spirit. The poet exhorts members of the privileged classes to return to honor and to earn the respect of those who follow their directions and their examples—it is through valor, not wealth and position, that men acquire distinction. The structural plan of the work, too, reinforces its important message. Hoffman points out that for modern readers, the dramatic, playlike format of this poem is especially realistic and convincing. In addition, he notes, Chartier's vivid vocabulary and energetic movement produce an atmosphere that is radically different from the allegories and didactic debates that characterize many of Chartier's poetic works. Because of the effective manner in which form supports meaning, several critics have ranked "The Patriotic Debate" as one of Chartier's best poems.

Also in the category of moral poetry is "Le Bréviaire des nobles" ("The Breviary for Nobles"), written about 1424. In this work, Chartier is again concerned with honor and virtue, which the poet invites his noble readers to emulate. Although the structure of the poem is completely traditional, it conveys the high moral message that lies at the heart of Chartier's serious writings.

"THE BEAUTIFUL, PITILESS LADY" AND "THE EXCUSE"

It is interesting that Chartier's oeuvre is not chronologically consistent in its development toward greater moral and political expression. One of his most famous and popular poems, "La Belle Dame sans mercy" ("The Beautiful, Pitiless Lady"), written in 1424, shows the poet moving in a different direction. Although many of his love poems became increasingly more realistic and influenced by events in French history, in this poem, the poet looks inward and seems touched by worldly happenings only in the desire to take refuge from them. Here, Chartier seems to reject contemporary reality in favor of creating a more satisfactory, even courtly universe. Strangely enough, however, the poetic world that he envisions is not a happy one. The hero is a sorrowful and scorned lover; the heroine is skeptical and independent. The two of them never succeed in communicating with each other. The portrayal of the cruel heroine angered Chartier's courtly readers to the extent that they demanded, through a noble, proto-feminist institution called the Court of Love, that the poet explain his intentions in belittling both his heroine and love. Chartier answered their accusation in a second poem, "L'Excusation" ("The Excuse"), in which he claimed that Cupid had forgiven him and that he would always serve and respect women. Allusions by other French poets of the period suggest that Chartier was expelled from the poetic Court of Love. This suggestion has not been proved; taken symbolically, however, it can be interpreted as a reflection of Chartier's rupture with the traditional aesthetic system of his day.

OTHER MAJOR WORKS

NONFICTION: *De vita curiali*, 1489 (*The Curial*, 1888); *Le Quadrilogue invectif*, 1489 (wr. 1422; *The Invective Quadrilogue*, late fifteenth century); *Le Traité de l'espérance: Ou, Consolation des trois vertus*, 1489 (wr. c. 1428; *The Treatise on Hope: Or, The Comfort of the Three Virtues*, late fifteenth century).

BIBLIOGRAPHY

Brown, Cynthia J. "Allegorical Design and Image-Making in Fifteenth-Century France: Alain Chartier's Joan of Arc." *French Studies* 53, no. 4 (October, 1999): 385-404. Brown argues that it was the late medieval tendency to allegorize moments of crisis in order to understand and overcome them that set the stage for the construction of Joan's image.

Cayley, Emma. *Debate and Dialogue: Alain Chartier in His Cultural Context*. Oxford, England: Clarendon Press, 2006. Examines the collaborative debating community that existed in France when Chartier was alive and how it is evidenced in his works, focusing on his vernacular verse debates.

Cayley, Emma, and Ashby Kinch, eds. *Chartier in Europe*. Rochester, N.Y.: D. S. Brewer, 2008. Contains essays that place Chartier in the Europe of his time and describe his influence.

Chartier, Alain. *Alain Chartier: The Quarrel of the "Belle dame sans mercy."* Translated and edited by Joan E. McRae. New York: Routledge, 2004. This critical edition of Chartier's well-known work contains a new translation of the poem as well as extensive commentary on the poem and biographical and background information.

Giannasi, Robert. "Chartier's Deceptive Narrator: 'La Belle Dame sans mercy' as Delusion." *Romania* 114 (1996): 362-384. Analyzes the narrator's persona as distinct from that of the author, reading the poem as the rejected lover's revenge fantasy.

Hale, J. R., J. R. L. Highfield, and B. Smalley, eds. *Europe in the Late Middle Ages*. Evanston, Ill.: Northwestern University Press, 1965. This collection of essays provides valuable background information on life in fourteenth and fifteenth century Europe. P. S. Lewis' essay on "France in the Fifteenth Century" supplies helpful information on political and social life at court and makes direct reference to Chartier's work.

Hoffman, Edward J. *Alain Chartier: His Work and Reputation*. Geneva: Slatkine Reprints, 1975. A comprehensive introduction to Chartier's life, works, and critical reputation. As is typical of earlier criticism, Hoffman dismisses much of Chartier's poetry as frivolous and conventional, indifferent to external events.

Hult, David F. "The Allegoresis of Everyday Life." *Yale French Studies* 95 (1999): 212-233. Argues that the major innovation of Chartier's work lies in its interpretive ambivalence, its power to encode or accommodate both realistic and allegorical readings.

Kibler, William W. "The Narrator as Key to Alain Chartier's 'La Belle Dame sans mercy.'" *French*

Review 52 (1979): 714-723. Defends Chartier's poem from charges of escapism and conventionality. Reads it rather as an indictment of the breakdown of the traditional feudal virtues of honesty and honor in French society.

Laidlaw, J. C., ed. *The Poetical Works of Alain Chartier.* New York: Cambridge University Press, 1974. The poems themselves are presented in French, but the extensive introduction surveys Chartier's life and works and analyzes the manuscript tradition in detail. The editor refers to previous critical studies and editions by André du Chesne, G. du Fresne de Beaucourt, Arthur Piaget, and Pierre Champion. The Laidlaw edition has filled gaps and corrected errors of former editions.

Patterson, Warner Forrest. *Three Centuries of French Poetic Theory: A Critical History of the Chief Arts of Poetry in France, 1328-1630.* 2 vols. New York: Russell and Russell, 1966. Volume 1 contains an informative introduction to the historical and intellectual context in which Chartier and his contemporaries wrote. Patterson's entry on Chartier is highly informative. Volume 2 contains examples of Chartier's work in the original French.

Shapely, C. S. *Studies in French Poetry of the Fifteenth Century.* The Hague, the Netherlands: Nijhoff, 1970. Unlike most earlier critics, Shapely argues in his chapter on Chartier that "La Belle Dame sans mercy," read closely and with attention to the full context of Chartier's literary production, offers a moral critique of contemporary cultural mores.

Tilley, Arthur, ed. *Medieval France.* New York: Hafner Press, 1964. A standard text that provides a rapid and readable account of the history, literature, art, and architecture of medieval France. Although the entry on Chartier is brief and the evaluation of his work necessarily attenuated, Tilley's work offers a concise introduction to the principal writers of the early fifteenth century and places Chartier in this context.

Ann R. Hill

CHRISTINE DE PIZAN

Born: Venice (now in Italy); c. 1365
Died: Probably at the Convent of Poissy, near Versailles, France; c. 1430
Also known as: Christine de Pisan

PRINCIPAL POETRY

L'Epistre au dieu d'Amours, 1399 (*The Letter of Cupid*, 1721)
Le Livre du dit de Poissy, 1400
Le Livre de la mutacion de fourtune, 1400-1403
Le Dit de la Rose, 1402
Le Livre du chemin de long estude, 1402-1403
Le Livre du duc des vrais amans, 1405 (*The Book of the Duke of True Lovers*, 1908)
Cent Ballades d'amant et de dame, c. 1410
Le Ditié de Jeanne d'Arc, 1429 (*The Tale of Joan of Arc*, 1977)

OTHER LITERARY FORMS

The oeuvre of Christine de Pizan (krees-TEEN duh pee-ZON) was not limited to poetry but included an impressive number of prose works as well. Composed primarily between 1400 and 1418, these works cover a broad thematic range and bear witness to a powerful and erudite ability; they include letters, short narratives, memoirs, manuals, autobiography, treatises, allegorical psalms, and meditations. Many represent an expansion and development of ideas expressed initially in her poetry; her early poetic commitment to scholarship, political ethics, religious devotion, and women's rights was amplified in the prose works of her maturity.

ACHIEVEMENTS

Christine de Pizan is rightly recognized as France's first woman of letters, professional writer, and feminist. Although scholars of the past acknowledged and respected her ability, modern scholarship has elevated Christine (as she is known by scholars) to a deserved place in world literature. If this recognition has been somewhat tardy, the delay has been the result of the general inaccessibility of her work, spread among dispersed manuscripts. A number of modernized versions from the original Middle French, translations, editions, and critical studies have dramatically heightened interest in her work. Especially remarkable are her learned vocabulary, her knowledgeable use of mythological allusions, and her feminism.

Christine excelled thematically and structurally in both traditional and innovative forms. As an accomplished lyrical poet, she received acclaim from her contemporaries for her conventional courtly poetry. In this category, for example, she demonstrated mastery of the ballade, rondeau, lay, pastoral, and lover's lament. These poems were designed to please the aristocracy at court through an idealized concept of love. Her skill in writing traditional poetry earned the admiration and support of many important members of the nobility, such as the dukes of Orléans, Burgundy, and Berry as well as King Charles V. Although she was composing in the conventional style, Christine often interjected her own personality by describing events in her life, by referring to a noble benefactor, or by expressing her opinions on the important issues of her day. In this regard, the works possess a documentary value.

Although Christine's poetry exhibits a high degree of technical mastery, she was never content with virtuosity for its own sake. Central themes of the necessity for justice and responsibility in government, concern for all women, and religious devotion imbue her writings. As a whole, Christine's works bear witness both to a vast knowledge of history and to a profound moral commitment to the age in which she lived.

BIOGRAPHY

Although Christine de Pizan ranks as France's first woman of letters, she was not of French but of Italian birth. Born about 1365 in Venice, she spent only her first years in Italy, leaving her birthplace when her father received the position of astrologer at the court of Charles V of France. Tommaso di Benvenuto da Pizzano, known as Thomas de Pizan after his arrival in France, brought his family to Paris around 1368, and it was there that Christine had an experience that was to shape the course of her lifework. With her father's encouragement, she received the kind of education usually reserved for boys in the Middle Ages. A precocious child, Christine was eager to learn, and this unique educational opportunity proved to be the single most important factor in her life, for it provided the young artist with the scholarly tools and knowledge on which she was to draw during her entire career. On these early foundations in classical languages, literature, mythology, history, and biblical studies, Christine would build a rich and varied literary edifice. In addition, her educational background influenced her perspective by prompting her to view her subjects in a historical, comprehensive, and ethical light.

Because of her creative talent and her ability to please the court with her poetry, Christine became a favorite and never lacked noble patronage. However, at age fifteen, in 1380, she married not a nobleman but a

Christine de Pizan (Hulton Archive/Getty Images)

court notary from Picardy, Étienne de Castel. According to *L'Avision-Christíne* (1405; *Christine's Vision*, 1993), an autobiographical work, it was a happy marriage, and the couple had three children.

Two extremely unhappy events sharply influenced Christine's life and career before she was twenty-five years old. The first of these was the death of Charles V in 1380 and the subsequent government during the minority of Charles VI. During the regency period of the dukes of Bourbon and Burgundy, Christine's father lost his court position. This demotion meant a loss of prestige as well as severe financial losses from which the scholar and former court astrologer never recovered. A few years later, in 1385, Thomas de Pizan died. Then, in 1389 or 1390, a second, even more devastating, event occurred when Christine's husband died in an epidemic. Thus, her ten-year marriage came to an abrupt end, leaving her with the heavy responsibility of rearing three children alone.

Instead of lamenting the loss of those who had supported and encouraged her literary talents, Christine turned to her art as a source of income as well as a refuge from grief. She was successful in her literary pursuits and regained noble patronage, moving gradually yet not exclusively into prose and producing a wide range of works. Although it is difficult to reconstruct her biography for these years, it is thought that she entered the Dominican convent at Poissy around 1418, the time of the Burgundian massacres. Scholars base this hypothesis on the description of a visit to her daughter at Poissy in "Le Dit de Poissy" (the proverb of Poissy). She did not break the silence of her retreat until 1429, when she composed *The Tale of Joan of Arc*. Thus, Christine concluded her literary career appropriately, honoring a woman who, like herself, had risen above adversity to pursue her goals. The exact date of her death is not known, but she is believed to have died around 1430.

ANALYSIS

The most striking characteristics of Christine de Pizan's work are her breadth of knowledge and her active engagement of the social and political issues of her day. Although these attributes would be considered typical rather than extraordinary in a modern writer,

they are indeed intriguing in a woman living at the turn of the fifteenth century. Clearly, credit for the wealth of knowledge seen in her works must be given to the exceptional education that she received. Nevertheless, an analysis of the artist must include recognition of the artistic sensitivity and the reverence for life that she brought to her career. Because of the broadness of her vision, she transcended the traditional courtly style of poetry in which she was trained and began to include significant personal, political, and moral issues in her poems. Her works weave innovation into traditional background by passing from idealized medieval expression to realistic humanist concerns that are closer in spirit to the Renaissance.

CENT BALLADES D'AMANT ET DE DAME

Christine's first published works in verse reveal her conformity to the literary standards of the era. The aesthetic canon governing late medieval poetry did not accept expressions of individual joy or sorrow but instead required these emotions to be placed in a universal framework. Christine's early works demonstrate not only her respect for the existing literary system but also her mastery of it. In her ballades, lays, and rondeaux, there is a harmonious relationship between form and meaning. An example of the traditional mold can be seen in *Cent Ballades d'amant et de dame* (one hundred ballades of a lover and his lady). In ballade 59, following the social code of the era, the poet advises young lovers to be noble, peaceful, and gracious. Written in decasyllabic lines, the ballade follows the prescribed form in stanzaic composition, regular rhyme, and refrain. The tone is appropriately elevated by the use of virtuous, abstract vocabulary, and verbs in the imperative and subjunctive moods. This ballade is typical of Christine's courtly love poems, which in their grace and elegance meet and even surpass the criteria of the times.

At the beginning of her career, Christine depended on the approval of her patrons, and it was important to please them by adhering to acceptable forms and also to amuse them with clever versatility and occasional flattery. She accomplished this by writing a group of rondeaux, very brief poems in lines of two to four syllables in equally short stanzas. These poems on the chagrin of love are typical of the clever, though sometimes exaggerated, metric exercises with which late medieval poets experimented. Christine also excelled at occasional verse; several of her poems in this category go beyond flattery by conveying a secondary message which in the course of the poem emerges as the main theme. For example, in a series of poems honoring Charles d'Albret, a patriotic high constable, Christine salutes his royal lineage, then hastens to one of her favorite and most important themes, the defense of the honor of women, particularly those in need. Although Christine continues to observe the fixed form of the ballade, she transmits her intense interest in her subject through a passionate tone, a concrete vocabulary, and a rhythmic pattern that dramatically emphasizes key words. The contemporary theme is anchored to ancient history as the poet compares the champion of her sex to the virtuous Roman Brutus.

Many of Christine's poems are centrally concerned with women's rights. It would appear that the genesis of this theme in her work was twofold. First, as a woman who herself had to work for a living, Christine could identify with women who had suffered misfortune, most of whom did not have her advantages. Many times in her works, she pleads for widows and orphan girls. Although Christine's feminism thus had its roots in her own experience, it was also given force by her rejection of widely accepted literary stereotypes of women. She abhorred, for example, the image of her sex in Guillaume de Lorris and Jean de Meung's *Le Roman de la rose* (thirteenth century; *The Romance of the Rose*, partial translation c. 1370, complete translation 1900), in which women are portrayed as greedy, inconstant, and egocentric.

THE TALE OF JOAN OF ARC

Christine's final literary work provides an appropriate conclusion to a survey of her poetic career. In terms of both theme and structure, *The Tale of Joan of Arc* represents a culminating point because in it, the poet restates and unites both forcefully and creatively the concerns that inspired her whole literary career. Of the inspirations, the most prominent is religious devotion. The poem, which extols Joan of Arc's mission to save France, is a pious work, praising God's grace and power. Joan is uniquely qualified to champion France because she is God's handmaiden: "Blessed is He

who created you!/ Maiden sent from God," exclaims the poet in the twenty-second stanza. Two secondary themes, patriotism and political concern, are welded to the religious motif; they also give the poem documentary value.

The poem reflects the attitude of a nation already weary from what was to be known as the Hundred Years' War (1337-1453) yet exhilarated by the victory of Orléans and the coronation of Charles VII at Rheims in 1403. Christine's sense of reality does not allow her to be swept away by optimism. Instead, realizing that there are further civil dangers to be faced, she encourages mutual cooperation between citizens and their king.

The final theme of the poem, yet certainly not the least in importance, is explicitly feminist: The heroine, supported and uplifted by the author's belief that women are able to do all things, confers unity and balance to this hymn of praise. In her enthusiastic expression of admiration for Joan as a woman, Christine employs a range of technical devices that convincingly reinforce her message. Written in sixty-one stanzas of eight octosyllabic lines each, the poem adheres to a traditional stanzaic structure, yet within the stanzas, all formality disappears; marked by exclamations, direct address, rhetorical questions, concrete and picturesque vocabulary, and conversational movement, the style is highly innovative. In this final work, Christine left an eloquent testimony to her accomplishments as a woman and as a poet.

OTHER MAJOR WORKS

NONFICTION: *L'Epistre d'Othéa à Hector*, 1400 (*The Epistle of Othea to Hector: Or, The Boke of Knyghthode*, c. 1440); *Les Epistres sur "Le Roman de la Rose,"* 1402; *Le Livre des fais et bonnes meurs du sage roi Charles V*, 1404; *L'Avision-Christíne*, 1405 (*Christine's Vision*, 1993); *Le Livre de la cité des dames*, 1405 (*The Book of the City of Ladies*, 1521); *Le Livre des trois vertus*, 1405 (*The Book of the Three Virtues*, 1985); *Le Livre du corps de policie*, 1406-1407 (*The Body of Polycye*, 1521); *Les Sept Psaumes allégorisés*, 1409-1410; *La Lamentation sur les maux de la guerre civile*, 1410 (*Lament on the Evils of Civil War*, 1984); *Le Livre des fais d'armes et de chevalerie*,

1410 (*The Book of Fayttes of Arms and of Chivalry*, 1489); *Le Livre de la Paix*, 1412-1413; *L'Epistre de la prison de la vie humaine*, 1416-1418.

BIBLIOGRAPHY

Altmann, Barbara K., and Deborah L. McGrady, eds. *Christine de Pizan: A Casebook*. New York: Routledge, 2003. A collection of essays on various aspects of Christine de Pizan, including her role as defender of women, and analyses of various works.

Birk, Bonnie A. *Christine de Pizan and Biblical Wisdom: A Feminist-Theological Point of View*. Milwaukee, Wis.: Marquette University Press, 2005. While this work deals more with Christine de Pizan's prose, it includes biographical information and discussion of her religious views.

Blumenfeld-Kosinski, Renate. *The Compensations of Aging: Sexuality and Writing in Christine de Pizan, with an Epilogue on Colette*. Paris: Peeters, 2004. Studies sexuality in the works of Christine de Pizan.

Campbell, John, and Nadia Margolis, eds. *Christine de Pizan 2000: Studies on Christine de Pizan in Honour of Angus J. Kennedy*. Atlanta: Rodopi, 2000. A collection of papers on Christine de Pizan, focusing on her poetry and her poetic techniques.

Forhan, Kate Langdon. *The Political Theory of Christine de Pizan*. Burlington, Vt.: Ashgate, 2002. An analysis of the political and social views of Christine de Pizan. Bibliography and index.

Green, Karen, and C. J. Mews, eds. *Healing the Body Politic: The Political Thought of Christine de Pizan*. Turnhout, Belgium: Brepols, 2005. A collection of essays on politics in the writing of Christine de Pizan. Although it focuses on her prose, it sheds light on her poetry.

Kelly, Douglas. *Christine de Pizan's Changing Opinion: A Quest for Certainty in the Midst of Chaos*. Cambridge, England: D. S. Brewer, 2007. This examination of opinion in Christine de Pizan's writings notes that this focus was found in other late medieval French literature.

Kennedy, Angus J., et al., eds. *Contexts and Continuities: Proceedings of the Fourth International Colloquium on Christine de Pizan, Published in Honour of Liliane Dulac*. Glasgow, Scotland: University of Glasgow Press, 2002. A collection of papers from a conference held in Glasgow in July, 2000, on Christine de Pizan. Bibliography.

Richards, Earl Jeffrey, ed. *Christine de Pizan and Medieval French Lyric*. Gainesville: University Press of Florida, 1998. Nine critical essays on the lyrical works, all but one written expressly for this volume and first published here.

Smith, Sydney. *The Opposing Voice: Christine de Pisan's Criticism of Courtly Love*. Stanford, Calif.: Humanities Honors Program, Stanford University, 1990. Smith examines the political and social views of Christine de Pizan, in particular her opposition to the idea of courtly love. Bibliography.

Ann R. Hill

PAUL CLAUDEL

Born: Villeneuve-sur-Fère, France; August 6, 1868
Died: Paris, France; February 23, 1955

PRINCIPAL POETRY
Connaissance de l'est, 1900, 1952 (*The East I Know*, 1914)
Art poétique, 1907 (*Poetic Art*, 1948)
Cinq Grandes Odes, 1910 (*Five Great Odes*, 1967)
Vers d'exil, 1912
Corona Benignitatis Anni Dei, 1915 (*Coronal*, 1943)
La Messe là-bas, 1921
Poèmes de guerre, 1922 (partial translation *Three Poems of the War*, 1919)
Feuilles de saints, 1925
Cent Phrases pour éventails, 1927 (*A Hundred Movements for a Fan*, 1992)
La Cantate à trois voix, 1931
Dodoitzu, 1945
Poèmes et paroles durant la guerre de trente ans, 1945
Visages radieux, 1947
Premiers Vers, 1950
Autres Poèmes d'après le chinois, 1957

Œuvre poétique, 1957
Petits Poèmes d'après le chinois, 1957
Poésies diverses, 1957
Traductions de poèmes, 1957
Poèmes retrouvés, 1967

OTHER LITERARY FORMS

Although the poetry of Paul Claudel (kloh-DEHL) occupies a prominent place in his writings, it was his theater that brought him a worldwide reputation. Gallimard published Claudel's *Œuvres complètes* (1950-1967) in twenty-seven volumes. Claudel stated repeatedly that human drama is not complete unless a supernatural element enriches it and brings to it a vertical sense. From the day of his conversion to Roman Catholicism on December 25, 1886, the Bible became his daily companion. In his poetry, the influence of the Bible manifests itself in an exuberant lyric vein, while in his plays it is evident in his conception of the conflict between good and evil—not so much a question of metaphysics as a struggle that takes place within the soul, among Satan, humankind, and God. Claudel's study of the Bible also resulted in a series of exegetical works that constitute a third important part of his creative artistry. Finally, the numerous volumes of Claudel's correspondence and the two volumes of his journal are indispensable guides to his inner life.

ACHIEVEMENTS

The literary fate of Paul Claudel can be compared to that of Stendhal (Marie-Henri Beyle), who, despite the initial indifference and lack of enthusiasm with which people of his generation received his writings, predicted that his works would be understood and successful by the end of the nineteenth century. Stendhal even dedicated his novel *La Chartreuse de Parme* (1839; *The Charterhouse of Parma*, 1895), not without irony, "to the happy few" who were able to understand his art and thought. Time has proved that Stendhal judged with perspicacity both his own work and the evolution of the literary taste of his country. In the same way, when Symbolism was giving clear signs of its vitality, Ferdinand Brunetière, very skeptical of the success of the new movement, in an article published by *La Revue des deux mondes* on November 1, 1888, dared chal-

lenge all the members of it by saying: "Give us a masterpiece and we will take you seriously." Literary scholar Henri Guillemin is surprised that Brunetière did not recognize the signs that were pointing to the man who was to come: "He was there, the man of masterpiece," he says, and in less than two years Claudel would publish his play *Tête d'or* (pb. 1890; English translation, 1919). However, despite this and many other masterpieces, Claudel remained unknown to the general public until after World War II.

Claudel was too religious for the secular Third Republic of France; his poetry ignored the Alexandrine meter and largely did without rhyme, while his plays dramatized a soul-searching and soul-saving adventure in which the eternal destiny of humankind took priority over psychology. Above all, Claudel did not use the literary language most of the French cherished, and he was accused of writing French poetry in German.

Nevertheless, Claudel persisted on his solitary course, largely undistracted by the literary fashions of the twentieth century. By the end of his life, he was numbered among the preeminent poets and playwrights of modern France.

BIOGRAPHY

Paul-Louis-Charles-Marie Claudel was born in Villeneuve-sur-Fère (Tardenois), France, on August 6, 1868. He was the youngest of three children, with two sisters, Camille and Louise. Their father, Louis-Prosper Claudel, was a civil servant who came to Villeneuve-sur-Fère from La Bresse, a small town in the Vosges region. By nature, he was an unsociable and taciturn person. His profession as civil servant left him little time for his children. Claudel's mother, born Louise Cerveaux, came from a family that had its origins in Villeneuve-sur-Fère. Like her husband, she was an unaffectionate parent; according to Claudel, she never kissed her children. The difficult character of the oldest child, Camille, may have been responsible for the mother's attitude and, indeed, adversely affected all the relationships in the family. In 1882, after many years of following her husband from place to place—Louis-Prosper Claudel had held posts in Villeneuve-sur-Fère, Bar-le-Duc, Nogent-sur-Seine, Wassy, Rambouillet, and Compiègne—Louise Claudel yielded to the pres-

Paul Claudel (Roger Viollet/Getty Images)

sure of Camille and agreed to settle with her children in Paris. Camille was eighteen years of age, Louise sixteen, and Paul fourteen.

Contrary to what one might expect, Paris did not fascinate the young Claudel: The crushing feelings of loneliness and boredom from which he suffered became even more frightening in the big city. Nor did Paris offer a respite from the endless family quarrels. In the restless atmosphere of the country's capital and under the pressure of his anarchist instincts, Claudel at one time contemplated suicide. Fortunately, as he grew into adulthood, he saw the positive side of Parisian life. He discovered the "mystical" beauty of Richard Wagner's music; at the age of nineteen, he was admitted to Stéphane Mallarmé's circle; and while still in the *lycée*, he enjoyed the company of classmates who were to become leading figures in French cultural and political life in the first half of the twentieth century. In 1886, purely by accident, Claudel discovered Arthur Rimbaud, in the June issue of *La Vogue* magazine, when he read Rimbaud's *Les Illuminations* (1886; *Illumina-*

tions, 1932) and *Une Saison en enfer* (1873; *A Season in Hell*, 1932).

On December 25, 1886, Claudel went to Notre-Dame de Paris, and there, during the early afternoon Office of Vespers, his "heart was touched" and he "believed." The nightmares that had haunted his youth were banished; his life and his obvious talent acquired a purpose. A creative enthusiasm inspired him to "evangelize" all the layers of his being. The process of this evangelization was to be reflected in his writings, both poetry and drama; he was to remain forever a poet committed to God and humankind.

After passing the examination for the Ministry of Foreign Affairs, Claudel entered into a diplomatic career that lasted until 1935. His first consular assignment took him to New York City and Boston in 1893. By that time, he had published *Tête d'or* and *La Ville* (pb. 1893; *The City*, 1920). His visit to the United States inspired him to write *L'Échange* (pb. 1901; the exchange), a masterpiece that presents a realistic image of American life and civilization. His diplomatic life took him next to China; between 1895 and 1900, Claudel held posts in Fuzhou, Shanghai, and Hankou. It was at this time that he turned to poetry. Upon his return to France, in 1900, Claudel thought of abandoning poetry and becoming a monk, but he was not accepted in either Solesmes or Ligugé. He decided then to pursue his diplomatic career, which took him back to China.

It was in 1900, on shipboard en route to China, that he met a married Polish woman, "Ysé" (Rose Vetch). They shared an adulterous affair which lasted four years. In 1906, while on vacation in France, Claudel married Reine Sainte-Marie Perrin, daughter of the architect of the Basilica of Fourvière in Lyons. Three days after his marriage, Claudel returned to China, accompanied by his wife. From that year on, Claudel's professional life never knew an eclipse; from China, he went on to Prague, Frankfurt, Rome, and Brazil. Finally, as ambassador, he served in Japan, the United States, and Belgium.

The last years of Claudel's life were filled with honors and recognition. Even the French Academy reversed its 1936 rejection of him, and in 1946, Claudel was elected one of the Immortals of France. Perhaps the most striking symbol of Claudel's success is the fact that, on the night of his death in February, 1955, the Comédie-Française was rehearsing *L'Annonce faite à Marie* (pb., pr. 1912; *The Tidings Brought to Mary*, 1916).

ANALYSIS

One of the outstanding characteristics of Paul Claudel's work is its cosmic dimension. His poetry does not form an exception to this general rule, for Claudel chose as its subject the visible world, enriching it with the invisible things of his faith. He was tempted neither to sacrifice the visible for the sake of the spiritual nor to do the opposite.

When he refers to his poetry in "La Maison fermée" ("Within the House") of *Five Great Odes*, Claudel uses this analogy: "The Word of God is the way that God gives himself to mankind. The created word is that way by which all created things are given to man." The universe of Claudel, one might say, is a human-centered world but certainly not to the exclusion of God. In an analogous sense, the poet is called upon to redeem visible things from the corruption of time and to elevate them, by his created word, to the heights of eternity. "To name a thing," Claudel says in his *Poetic Art*, "means to produce it inextinguishable, for it is to produce it in relationship to its principle, which does not include cessation." In a sense, therefore, the peculiar vocation of the poet is to be a prophet in the etymological sense of the word: He speaks for the visible universe.

However ironic it may sound, one has the impression that Claudel, after his conversion, wanted to "convert his conversion" to his own powerful nature, to the splendor of visible things, and to invite God himself to join him in his celebration of this world. By embracing nature and by calling things by their names, however, the poet determines their place in the intention of their Creator. There is nothing that horrified Claudel more than the idea of a material infinite; he considered it a "scandal of the reason." Speaking of Dante's poetic endeavor, Claudel reminds himself that a true poet does not need "greater stars" or "more beautiful roses" than those that nature furnishes. His task is to use words, those "resonant phantoms," to produce an enjoyable and intelligent picture of the universe.

If it is true that Claudel attained in *Five Great Odes* the summit of his poetic creation, it is because his genius had reached a level of synthesis where painful experiences and poetic inspiration were molded into a harmonious unity. However, this synthesis was achieved only after a lengthy poetic development, beginning with Claudel's assimilation of Rimbaud and Mallarmé.

When, in June, 1886, Claudel discovered in *La Vogue* Rimbaud's *Illuminations* and *A Season in Hell*, he recognized in these poems the sign of his own deliverance. Rimbaud's poetic language fascinated Claudel; the simplest term Claudel could find to describe the fascination was "bewitchment." In an age marked by secularism and aggressive materialism, a young poet dared to speak of the nostalgia of the soul for freedom and of the reality of invisible things. Claudel was not naïve; he could hear blasphemy and cursing in the desperate cries of Rimbaud, but he was happy to inhale that "living and almost physical impression of the supernatural" that the poems of Rimbaud communicated to his soul. Claudel learned much from Rimbaud, not least the daring juxtaposition of images with no clear link among them. Above all, however, Rimbaud made Claudel aware that the material world, when it comes into contact with the spirit, becomes very fragile. Upon reading Rimbaud, Claudel said, he had the impression of hearing the voice of the most authentic genius of his time.

Like most poets of his generation, Claudel was also influenced by Mallarmé. As early as 1887, Claudel was among those who went to listen to the master of the Symbolist movement. It was a great privilege to be admitted to Mallarmé's salon; in the quasi-religious ambience of the Symbolists, to be recognized by Mallarmé was to be consecrated. Little is known of the extent of their personal relationship, but while on his first diplomatic mission in China, Claudel was eager to continue his correspondence with the "master"; he even dared to express his reservations concerning Mallarmé's aesthetic principles. In his "La Catastrophe de l'Igitur," published in *Positions et propositions I* in 1928, Claudel recognizes that Mallarmé was the first poet to place himself in front of an object and ask the question, "What does that mean?" Claudel acknowledges that

Mallarmé's way of trying to infuse the lifeless object with life was worthy of admiration, but he also underscores Mallarmé's failure to give the necessary answer to, or explanation of, his own question.

According to Claudel, if things and objects mean something, the poet has the obligation to speak for them. Mallarmé, on the contrary, hoped to condense in his verse the whole reality of things, by transferring them from the realm of "sensibility" to that of "intelligibility." The difference, then, between Claudel and Mallarmé is that, whereas Mallarmé believed that poetry is the ultimate forum of intelligibility and that there is nothing else to be understood beyond it, Claudel said that through the poetic word, the visible reality becomes a key to another reality, that which is meant by the first one. In other words, and to paraphrase a thought of Claudel, the world is indeed a text that speaks "humbly and joyfully" of its own "absence" and of the presence of its Creator. Claudel rightly calls the adventure of Mallarmé a "catastrophe." One has but to remember the experience of Rimbaud, who, having tried to reach the ultimate and absolute power of the creative word, was forced to abandon poetry altogether, for absolute power pertains only to the absolute Word.

THE EAST I KNOW

The prose poems of *The East I Know*, the composition of which was spread out over a period of ten years, were written under the influence of Mallarmé. Claudel at first called them "impressions," later "poems in prose." In some cases, they are less impressions than precise descriptions of the emotional significance that various elements of the Chinese universe held for him. Some aspects of the descriptiveness that one finds in *The East I Know* do not, it is true, have their origin in Mallarmé; they derive, rather, from one of Claudel's contemporaries, Jules Renard. In 1896, Renard sent a copy of his recently published book, *Histoires naturelles* (1896; *Natural Histories*, 1966), to his friend Claudel in China. It was in this book that Claudel found what he considered the ideal manner of describing nature. He states delightedly that the book is "full of nature"; he also found that Renard's sentences were better balanced than those of Mallarmé. However, Mallarmé's distinctive sentences, composed entirely of subordi-nate clauses (main clauses were indicated by their absence), continued to excite Claudel with their suggestive juxtapositions. Ultimately, *The East I Know* led Claudel to a fusion of the two trends; that is, he had to learn how to harmonize the sentence with the message it contained and the exterior world with the spiritual world of which it offered signs. In achieving this synthesis, Claudel found his voice as a poet.

Claudel's achievement in *The East I Know* is exemplified in "L'Heure jaune" ("The Golden Hour"). The title signifies both the ripeness of the wheat field and the sunset hour. As the poet walks through the wheat field, a path opens in it. Suddenly, the wheat field turns into a table (a bread table) at which the poet can rest. He is invited by God to this universal banquet table, which is illuminated by the sun. Before the sun sets, the poet, raising himself above the table, takes a last look over the universe, which has reached the last phase of its maturity. Indeed, the whole universe has become like the sun, and the only wish the poet can utter is that he not perish before he reaches the "golden hour": "I wander through the lanes of the harvest, up to the neck in gold. . . . All is ripe. . . . Suddenly, to my eyes, the earth is like a sun. Let me not die before the golden hour!"

FIVE GREAT ODES

With *The East I Know*, Claudel completed his poetic apprenticeship. Having done so, he undertook a new genre, the ode. In 1900, he made two important literary discoveries. Thanks to his friend André Suarès, he read Pindar, whose odes he savored for their rhythmic invention and absolute freedom of form. In the same year, while he was seeking admittance to monastic life in Solesmes, his attention was called to the English poet Coventry Patmore, a convert to Catholicism who enjoyed an extraordinary vogue late in the nineteenth century but whose works are scarcely read today. Claudel liked Patmore so much that he translated some of his poems into French. Patmore furthered Claudel's knowledge of the art of the ode; he also taught Claudel how to use the theme of love in poetry—as both a profane subject and a mystical reality expressing the only possible relationship between humans and God. A third element that greatly contributed to the making of *Five Great Odes* was Claudel's visit to the Louvre in 1900, during which he noticed for the first time a Roman sarcophagus with the nine Muses.

These three sources furnished him with sufficient material for the new work. Suddenly, as if a new revelation had filled his being, he realized with exuberant joy that he had something to say, that he possessed the words he needed to speak in the name of the silent universe. It is not surprising that he began to write the first of the odes, "Les Muses" ("The Muses"), in the monastery of Solesmes. He felt at the same time that he was "all alone," "detached, refused, abandoned, without a task, without vocation, an outcast in the middle of the world," yet called to something that he could not fathom. As if in answer to the question that Mallarmé addressed to things, Claudel affirms in the odes that he has found the secret; he knows now how to speak and how to tell what each thing means. It is not a slight change that has occurred: He has regained his voice, has recovered his poetic health, and having been told that he has no religious vocation, is now free to return to his poetic one. He walked out of the monastery in Ligugé, "The Muses" yet to be finished; soon, he boarded a ship to China to resume his diplomatic post. On the ship, he met Ysé, the great love of his life, and he completed "The Muses." The joy that the muse inspired had turned into a question that he would make explicit in his play *Partage de midi* (pb. 1906; *Break of Noon*, 1960): "Why suddenly this woman on the ship?" Claudel could not answer the question; instead, for six years he kept silent. It was not until 1906 that he started to work on the second ode. He wrote about his illicit adventure in *Break of Noon* and ended his relationship with Ysé. The crisis of conscience that had paralyzed him for six years had finally come to a happy resolution. The illicit love had a purpose: Having discovered the "other" embodied in Ysé, Claudel was able to see the world anew, a "world now total" because it was seen with the eyes of the "other" as well as with his own. It was therefore fitting that Claudel should have transformed his love into an imperishable rose.

From the time of his meeting with Ysé, the rose is used in his poetry both allegorically and as a proper name, for Rose was the true name of Ysé. In a sense, his is a "roman de la rose," with the difference that Claudel possessed not so much the rose as the "interdiction."

Because of this restraint, the rose brought him neither happiness nor fulfillment; knowing it was like knowing the "source of thirst." The rose, then, in *Five Great Odes*—it is presented throughout the poem—is a mystical rose with all the symbolism associated with it in the Western literary tradition. Claudel exploits this traditional symbolism and adds to it his own interpretation of the rose's perfume as the very essence of the flower. When inhaled (*respiré*), this perfume gives in an instant a sense of the fullness of eternity. The message of the rose is that, time having been abolished, one lives in eternity.

"THE MUSE WHO IS GRACE" AND "WITHIN THE HOUSE"

In "La Muse qui est la grâce" ("The Muse Who Is Grace"), Claudel continues the theme of the rose, although not without a certain irony. Having spent so many years meditating on the meaning of love, the poet realizes that it would be easier to live without women, but then he must also realize that the Muse herself is a woman—a woman with the face of Wisdom. It is therefore perfectly orthodox to say that in the fifth ode, "Within the House," Claudel substitutes Wisdom for the mystical rose. In doing so, he closed one of the major circles of his poetic and spiritual evolution. The night of his conversion on December 25, 1886, when he went home and opened his sister Camille's Bible, his eye fell on the passage in Proverbs that speaks of Wisdom. Finally, he was led back to this Wisdom through the power of the mystical rose, which is Love.

Wisdom also taught Claudel that Creation is finite. "We have conquered the world," he says in "Within the House," "and we have found that Your Creation is finite." It appears contradictory that, while on one hand Claudel never ceases looking for signs of phenomena to prove that eternity is available to human understanding and is eager to replace the signifying with the signified, on the other hand he berates the idea of indefinite and infinite within the realm of Creation. According to Claudel, if there is a contradiction, it is certainly not going to surface in the right relationship between the world and God; on the contrary, it is always found in the deification of the finite universe. He believes that God so planned the world that everything should return to him. Claudel thus conceives of the universe not as an automatic machine blindly traveling toward an unde-termined goal, but rather as an entity within a perfect circle in which the vocation of the poet is to remind rational as well as irrational beings of the primordial unity their universe must achieve. That is why, in the midst of his joyous celebration in "Magnificat," he raises his voice against Voltaire, Ernest Renan, Jules Michelet, Victor Hugo, and all those who continue to have nightmares or dreams of a self-sufficient, human-created world. In his essay "Introduction à un poème sur Dante" (*Positions et propositions I*), Claudel takes issue with Hugo's cosmology, as expressed in the poem "Plein Ciel" ("Up in the Sky"), in which the Romantic poet imagines "Un Fini sans bornes" ("A Finite Without Limits"). Claudel does not hesitate to call this idea "a scandal for the reason, a disaster for the imagination." In contrast to these figures, he offers the portrait of Christopher Columbus, who, when he sailed to the West to reach India, was not led by any thought of discovery; he was, rather, led by the desire to prove that Earth was a "circle," having its existence within the orbit of God. Thus, Columbus resembles the poet, who by vocation is the "sower of the measure of God," and the symbolism of the last ode's title becomes intelligible: "Within the House" is a perfect "circle," the movement of which is determined by the creative act of God and the redemptive charity of his Son.

LA MESSE LÀ-BAS

The very form of Claudel's verse was biblical in inspiration. He employed from the beginning of his poetic career a form that has come to be known as the *verset claudélien*. Among the influences that shaped this distinctive form, the most significant was the Bible, as Claudel was quick to acknowledge—in particular, the Psalms and the books of the prophets. In the long swell of the Claudelian verset, the cadence and the length of the lines are determined by units of breath, which in turn are conditioned by the nature of the thought that is being expressed. The lyric breath demands a more regular form, and it may even take rhyme and assonance, whereas drama, which is charged with interior struggles and tensions, demands a less regular form.

In 1917, Claudel was charged with a new diplomatic mission, this time to Brazil. The journey there was more painful than previous ones: Claudel had to leave his wife, his children, and his country behind in the midst of a raging war and all its uncertainties. The poem *La Messe là-bas*, written during this period, reflects his sense of exile. There is, however, another equally important theme in the poem—perhaps new at this point in Claudel's life—in the images of bread and wine as they become symbols in a liturgical and sacramental sense.

It should be remarked that the whole poem in its exterior form corresponds to the structure of the Catholic Mass and, as such, is a celebration of Communion. The question, then, can be raised in the following fashion: Communion with whom—and under what species? The first part of the question does not present any major problem; the poet has been separated from his family, and it is fitting that he should attempt to stay in communion with them in some way. On a deeper level, communion is reestablished between the two lovers, Claudel and Ysé. After all, they met on a ship that took both of them into exile, where they were to experience their love for years the desert of their love. On yet another level, Claudel savors communion with Rimbaud, whose poetry reminded him of the voice of the prophet in the desert announcing the breaking of the dawn. Finally, on the deepest level of his thought, Claudel celebrates that Communion with God that Rimbaud was unable to reach, for neither the method of Mallarmé nor the desire of Rimbaud proved capable of containing the absolute, in the poet's word. Faith, on the contrary, assures Claudel that, since God made himself available to the understanding of the human soul in his own Word, the Catholic Mass is the only worthy celebration of this Communion: God instituted the Mass to commemorate his Communion with humankind. That is the reason Claudel selected the frame of the Mass to signify both poetry and communion.

It would be quite absurd to state that in Claudel's symbolism a tree, say, refers to humanity, or that bread represents an invisible celestial food. An object never refers to another object, only to itself. Claudel does not deny that there is something to be signified. In his system, whether aesthetic or spiritual, the physical and the spiritual realms coexist. What Claudel wants to say is that the bread and wine convey something in addition to the reality constituted by their molecular structure; their reality consists also in humanity's hunger and thirst for them. In the same way, one could say that light is provided because of humanity's need to see. Now, human hunger and thirst, if they are authentic, constitute a desire for something absolute—indeed, nothing but the absolute can satisfy them. In the Eucharistic celebration, the bread and wine lend, first of all, their physical appearance, but they are more than that: The word of the poet raises them into that region where the "object" can convey what the human desire is seeking. The poet can tell Ysé that they cannot satisfy their mutual desire and love unless they give priority to the Absolute Who is All in all. Rimbaud is recalled (as Mallarmé might have been) because he, too, was tempted to use the sacramental and liturgical symbolism of the Word without accepting the need for perfect communion.

LOVE BEGETS WISDOM

Claudel believed that every poet enters this world with one purpose. "The thing of beauty" which is ultimately the message of all poets, while gaining shape and identity, traces its own history. In the case of Claudel, this poetic message evolved and developed like a seed—the word is found even on his tombstone—which goes through death and resurrection before producing new life. At the beginning of his poetic career, he gave way to his sentiments of exile: He found himself far from home and from Heaven. At the other end of his career, in a peaceful recognition, he humbly bowed before the solidity of the universe of God. Between these two points, Claudel seems to have run a double itinerary. While he poured all his joys and sorrows into his drama, he reserved for his poetry the history of a rose, as if his life had been a "roman de la rose." In his poetry, however, this rose is transformed into a person, "Rose," who, in turn, having given the poet the joy of loving, is transfigured into a "mystical rose." In Claudel's poetry, love is a blessing when it arrives, but it is also meant to signify the absence of what it promises. Love therefore leads to Wisdom, which alone holds the keys to the mystery of the universe and the destiny of humanity; totality is found neither in woman's love nor in the fascination of the created universe, but in the eternal love of God.

OTHER MAJOR WORKS

PLAYS: *Tête d'or*, pb. 1890 (second version wr. 1895, pb. 1901; English translation, 1919); *Fragment d'un drame*, pb. 1892; *La Ville*, pb. 1893 (second version pb. 1901; *The City*, 1920); *L'Échange*, pb. 1901 (wr. 1893-1894; second version pr. 1951); *Le Repos du septième jour*, pb. 1901 (wr. 1896); *Partage de midi*, pb. 1906 (second version pr. 1948; *Break of Noon*, 1960); *L'Otage*, pb. 1911 (*The Hostage*, 1917); *L'Annonce faite à Marie*, pr., pb. 1912 (second version pr. 1948; revision of *La Jeune Fille Violaine*; *The Tidings Brought to Mary*, 1916); *Protée*, pb. 1914 (second version pb. 1927; *Proteus*, 1921); *La Nuit de Noël*, pb. 1915; *Le Pain dur*, pb. 1918 (wr. 1913-1914; *The Crusts*, 1945); *L'Ours et la lune*, pb. 1919; *Le Père humilié*, pb. 1920 (wr. 1915-1916; *The Humiliation of the Father*, 1945); *L'Homme et son désir*, pr., pb. 1921; *La Femme et son ombre*, pr. 1923 (in Japanese; pb. 1927 in French); *L'Endormie*, pb. 1925 (wr. 1886-1888); *La Jeune Fille Violaine*, pb. 1926 (wr. 1892; second version pb. 1901); *Sous le rempart d'Athènes*, pr., pb. 1927; *Le Soulier de satin: Ou, Le Pire n'est pas toujours sûr*, pb. 1928-1929 (wr. 1919-1924; *The Satin Slipper: Or, The Worst Is Not the Surest*, 1931); *Le Livre de Christophe Colomb*, pb. 1929 (in German; pr. 1953 in French; libretto; music by Darius Milhaud; *The Book of Christopher Columbus*, 1930); *Jeanne d'Arc au bûcher*, pr. 1938 (in German; pb. 1938 in French; English translation, 1939); *Le Festin de la sagesse*, pb. 1939 (wr. 1934); *L'Histoire de Tobie et de Sara*, pb. 1942 (music by Milhaud); *Le Jet de Pierre*, pb. 1949 (wr. 1937); *Le Peuple des hommes cassés*, pb. 1952 (wr. 1927); *Le Ravissement de Scapin*, pb. 1958 (wr. 1949).

NONFICTION: *Jacques Rivière et Paul Claudel*, 1926 (*Letters to a Doubter: Correspondence of Jacques Rivière and Paul Claudel*, 1929); *Positions et propositions I*, 1928; *L'Oiseau noir dans le soleil levant*, 1929; *Écoute, ma fille*, 1934; *Positions et propositions II*, 1934 (*Ways and Crossways*, 1933); *Conversations dans le Loir-et-Cher*, 1935; *Un Poète regarde la Croix*, 1935 (*A Poet Before the Cross*, 1958); *Figures et paraboles*, 1936; *Toi, qui es-tu?*, 1936; *Les Aventures de Sophie*, 1937; *L'Épée et le miroir*, 1939; *Contacts et circonstances*, 1940; *Présence et prophétie*, 1942; *Sei-*

gneur, apprenez-nous à prier, 1942 (*Lord, Teach Us to Pray*, 1948); *Le Livre de Job*, 1946; *L'Oeil écoute*, 1946 (*The Eye Listens*, 1950); *Discours et remerciements*, 1947; *Du côté de chez Ramuz*, 1947; *La Rose et le rosaire*, 1947; *Paul Claudel interroge le Cantique des Cantiques*, 1948; *Sous le signe du dragon*, 1948; *Accompagnements*, 1949; *André Gide et Paul Claudel, 1899-1926*, 1949 (*The Correspondence, 1899-1926, Between Paul Claudel and André Gide*, 1952); *Emmaüs*, 1949; *Une Voix sur Israël*, 1950; *André Suarès et Paul Claudel*, 1951; *L'Évangile d'Isaïe*, 1951; *Francis Jammes-Gabriel Frizeau et Paul Claudel*, 1952; *Introduction au Livre de Ruth*, 1952; *Paul Claudel interroge l'Apocalypse*, 1952; *Le Symbolism de la Salette*, 1952; *J'aime la Bible*, 1955 (*The Essence of the Bible*, 1957); *Conversation sur Jean Racine*, 1956; *Qui ne souffre pas? Reflexions sur le problème social*, 1958; *Darius Milhaud et Paul Claudel*, 1961; *Aurélien Lugné-Poe et Paul Claudel*, 1964; *Au milieu des vitraux de l'Apocalypse*, 1966; *Jacques Copeau-Charles Dullin-Louis Jouvet et Paul Claudel*, 1966; *Journal I*, 1968; *Journal II*, 1969; *Mémoires improvisés*, 1969.

MISCELLANEOUS: *Œuvres complètes*, 1950-1967 (27 volumes).

BIBLIOGRAPHY

Caranfa, Angelo. *Claudel: Beauty and Grace*. Lewisburg, Pa.: Bucknell University Press, 1989. Clearly explains the complex relationship between Claudel's aesthetics and his belief in Catholicism, as expressed both in his plays and in his poetry. The clearest introduction to Claudel's religious beliefs.

Griffiths, Richard. *Claudel: A Reappraisal*. Chester Springs, Pa.: Dufour Editions, 1970. Criticism of Claudel's major works, with bibliography.

Humes, Joy. *Two Against Time: A Study of the Very Present Worlds of Paul Claudel and Charles Péguy*. Chapel Hill: University of North Carolina Press, 1978. Contains an excellent analysis of the two major French Catholic poets of the twentieth century. The paradox in the title of this book refers to the fact that both Péguy and Claudel were more concerned with the representation of the divine in this life and in the next than with meditations on social and political events.

Killiam, Marie-Thérèse. *The Art Criticism of Paul Claudel*. New York: Peter Lang, 1990. This look at Claudel's critiques of art demonstrates how they reflected his aesthetic sensibilities, which found expression in his writings. Bibliography and index.

Longstaffe, Moya. *Metamorphoses of Passion and the Heroic in French Literature*. Lewiston, N.Y.: Edwin Mellen Press, 1999. A historical and critical interpretation of the works of Pierre Corneille, Stendhal, and Claudel.

McInerny, Ralph. *Some Catholic Writers*. South Bend, Ind.: St. Augustine's Press, 2007. Contains an essay on Claudel that discusses the influence his religious beliefs had on his writing and life.

Moses, Nagy. "When the Heart Speaks of Its Reasons: *Cinq Grandes Odes*." *Claudel Studies* 21 (1994): 45-57. This American scholarly journal appears annually and includes excellent essays on Claudel's works. This article contains a thoughtful analysis of his poetic masterpiece.

Paliyenko, Adrianna. *Mis-reading the Creative Impulse: The Poetic Subject in Rimbaud and Claudel*. Carbondale: Southern Illinois University Press, 1997. Claudel found inspiration in the visionary poetry of the late nineteenth century French poet Arthur Rimbaud, but he transformed the agnostic Rimbaud into an orthodox Catholic believer. Palijenko explains that Claudel's clear misreading of Rimbaud's poetry had a profound influence on his own attempt to reconcile modernity and Catholicism in his own poetry.

Waters, Harold. *Paul Claudel*. New York: Twayne, 1970. Remains the best general introduction in English to Claudel's long career as a diplomat and to his plays and poetry. Contains an excellent annotated bibliography of studies on Claudel.

Moses M. Nagy

JEAN COCTEAU

Born: Maisons-Laffitte, France; July 5, 1889
Died: Milly-la-Forêt, France; October 11, 1963

PRINCIPAL POETRY

La Lampe d'Aladin, 1909
Le Prince frivole, 1910
La Danse de Sophocle, 1912
Le Cap de Bonne-Espérance, 1919
L'Ode à Picasso, 1919
Escales, 1920
Poésies, 1917-1920, 1920
Discours du grand sommeil, 1922
Vocabulaire, 1922
Plain-Chant, 1923
Poésie, 1916-1923, 1924
L'Ange Heurtebise, 1925
Cri écrit, 1925
Prière mutilée, 1925
Opéra, 1927
Morceaux choisis, 1932
Mythologie, 1934
Allégories, 1941
Léone, 1945
Poèmes, 1945
La Crucifixion, 1946
Anthologie poétique, 1951
Le Chiffre sept, 1952
Appogiatures, 1953
Clair-obscur, 1954
Poèmes, 1916-1955, 1956
Gondole des morts, 1959
Cérémonial espagnol du phénix, 1961
Le Requiem, 1962

OTHER LITERARY FORMS

Jean Cocteau (kawk-TOH) was a formidable artist in many genres and very prolific. Among his seven novels, little read today, the most important is *Les Enfants terribles* (1929; *Enfants Terribles*, 1930, also known as *Children of the Game*). Among his many plays, some of the most notable are *Orphée* (pr. 1926; *Orpheus*, 1933), *La Voix humaine* (pr., pb. 1930; *The Human Voice*, 1951), *La Machine infernale* (pr., pb. 1934; *The Infernal Machine*, 1936), *Les Parents terribles* (pr., pb. 1938; *Intimate Relations*, 1952), and *La Machine à écrire* (pr., pb. 1941; *The Typewriter*, 1948). In the opinion of many critics, Cocteau's greatest achievements were in the cinema. His masterpieces—which he both wrote and directed—include *Le Sang d'un poète* (1930; *The Blood of a Poet*, 1949), *La Belle et la bête* (1946; *Beauty and the Beast*, 1947), *Les Parents terribles* (1948; *Intimate Relations*, 1952), *Les Enfants terribles* (1950), *Orphée* (1950; *Orpheus*, 1950), and *La Testament d'Orphée* (1959; *The Testament of Orpheus*, 1968). Cocteau also wrote scenarios for ballets by various composers, notably for Erik Satie's *Parade* (1917), for Darius Milhaud's *Le Boeuf sur le toit* (1920), and for *Les Mariés de la tour Eiffel* (1921; *The Wedding on the Eiffel Tower*, 1937), which had music by Les Six. Cocteau also collaborated on two opera-oratorios, *Odipus-Rex* (1927) with Igor Stravinsky, and *Antigone* (1922; English translation, 1961) with Arthur Honegger. Cocteau's nonfiction includes a variety of idiosyncratic autobiographical and critical works.

ACHIEVEMENTS

Jean Cocteau was one of the most remarkable figures in twentieth century art. Extremely versatile, he unified his diverse interests by seeing them as merely different aspects of *poésie: poésie de roman* (poetry of the novel), *poésie de théâtre* (poetry of the drama), *poésie cinématographique* (poetry of the film), and even *poésie graphique* (poetry of drawing). Curiously, with poetry as the metaphorical center of Cocteau's artistic achievement, critics are still uncomfortable with his accomplishments as a poet. Some consider him a central figure through whom the major currents of art in the early 1900's passed, while others regard him as a dilettante, interested only in stylishness and facile demonstrations of his considerable talents, lacking substance under the sparkling facade. Many of his contemporaries were uncertain of his importance because he remained always on the periphery of "serious" art. Looking back, however, it is clear that, at the very least, Cocteau's poetry is another brilliant aspect of one of the most versatile artistic minds of the century and that it has been underrated largely because of the difficulty in grasping Cocteau in all his variety.

BIOGRAPHY

Jean Cocteau was born in a prosperous suburb of Paris to Georges and Eugénie Lecomte Cocteau, a cultivated bourgeois couple who exposed Jean, his brother Paul, and their sister Marthe to the fine arts. When at their suburban home, the children played on the grounds of a nearby castle designed by François Mansart. When in Paris—Cocteau would always consider himself a Parisian above all—his family lived with his grandparents, whose house contained classical busts, vases, a painting by Eugène Delacroix, and drawings by Jean-Auguste-Dominique Ingres. Cocteau's grandfather was a cellist and would often be visited by the renowned violinist Pablo de Sarasate. Some of Cocteau's fondest memories of his early life were of trips to the circus, the ice palace, and the theater, especially the Comédie-Française. Years later, in his own drama, he would attempt to duplicate the lighting or brilliancy of theatrical events in his memory and would discover from lighting technicians that it had been technically impossible to do such things when he was a child. Time had increased the splendor of his memories, including those of the castle and of his grandparents' house. He thus began to perceive his own life as having mythological dimensions, as even his personal experiences had become exaggerated and distorted over time.

In 1899, Cocteau's father committed suicide as a result of financial problems. Cocteau became an indifferent student at the Petit Lycée Condorcet and, later, at the Grand Condorcet. Like many creative personalities, he found the institutional atmosphere oppressive. Besides having a weak constitution, which often led to legitimate absences, he was frequently truant. During his illnesses, he often had his German governess stitching doll clothes for his model theater. One of his closest childhood friends was Réné Rocher, later to become a director, who spent much time with Cocteau and his miniature theaters. After a trip with his mother to Venice, Cocteau began study for his baccalaureate, had his first love affair (with Madeleine Carlier, ten years his senior), and became more involved with the theater—meeting Edouard de Max, who acted opposite Sarah Bernhardt. Quite naturally, with all this to entertain him, Cocteau failed the examination.

On April 4, 1908, de Max sponsored a reading of Cocteau's poetry, by de Max, Rocher, and other prominent actors and actresses, at the Théâtre Fémina. Because the event was attended by many of the elite of Paris, including several leading literary critics, Cocteau became instantly well known. Subsequently, he became acquainted with such literary notables as Edmond Rostand, Marcel Proust, Charles-Pierre Péguy, Catulle Mendès, and Jules Lemaître. He became quite

Jean Cocteau (National Archives)

enamored of Comtesse Anna de Noailles and tried to write poetry like hers, with a refined sensibility and enhanced sensuality. He was one of three founders of a literary magazine, *Schéhérazade*, which was dedicated to poetry and music, and rented a room at the Hôtel Biron, where Auguste Rodin and his secretary, Rainer Maria Rilke, were also staying.

When Cocteau was introduced to the great impresario Sergei Diaghilev of the Ballets Russes, he begged Diaghilev to permit him to write ballets. Diaghilev eventually said "Étonne-moi!" ("Astonish me!"), and Cocteau took this injunction as an order to give shape to the rest of his life's work. His first ballet, *Le Dieu bleu* (1912), was not successful, though Diaghilev produced it for the coronation of George V. Convinced the music was at fault, Cocteau began to associate with Igor Stravinsky, living with him for a while. During this period, Cocteau was also trying to defend himself against the accusation of Henri Ghéon in the *Nouvelle Revue française*, who charged that he was an entirely derivative poet. Around 1914, Cocteau underwent what he called a "molting," breaking free of the influence of Rostand and the Comtesse de Noailles and moving toward his eventual association with Max Jacob and Guillaume Apollinaire.

As World War I broke out, Cocteau attempted to enlist but was rejected for health reasons. Illegally, he became an ambulance driver on the Belgian front, but after being discovered, he was sent back to Paris. These experiences would later form a large part of his novel *Thomas l'imposteur* (1923; *Thomas the Impostor*, 1925). Back in Paris, he met Amedeo Modigliani and Pablo Picasso and introduced the latter to Diaghilev, thereby creating the association that would produce Erik Satie's 1917 ballet *Parade*, with scenario by Cocteau, costumes and set by Picasso, and choreography by Léonide Massine. *Parade* created a scandal with its atonal music and extraordinary set and costumes. Only the presence of Apollinaire, in uniform and wearing a bandage over his head wound, kept the outraged spectators from attacking the creators of the ballet. Cocteau responded vigorously, attacking the musical influences of Claude Debussy, Richard Wagner, and Stravinsky and linking himself with the composers known as Les Six (Georges Auric, Louis Durey,

Arthur Honegger, Darius Milhaud, Francis Poulenc, and Germaine Tailleferre).

In 1919, Cocteau met and fell in love with Raymond Radiguet, who was fifteen, handsome, and a poetic genius—or so Cocteau believed. Radiguet caused Cocteau to reevaluate his aesthetics and move toward a simpler, classic style; thus inspired, he found new energy and created a number of new works, including *Le Grand écart* (1923; *The Grand Écart*, 1925) and the volume of poems *Plain-Chant*. Radiguet, however, died of typhoid in December, 1923, and Cocteau was devastated. Diaghilev tried to shake Cocteau from his despair by taking him on a trip to Monte Carlo. The trip itself did little good, however, and the discovery of opium there proved to be Cocteau's only solace. His addiction eventually provoked his friends and family to persuade him to enter a sanatorium in 1925. There, he came under the influence of Jacques Maritain, the Catholic philosopher, who briefly restored Cocteau's faith in religion. He was able to pick up the pieces of this life and create such works as *L'Ange Heurtebise*, *Orpheus*, and *Children of the Game*. He even patched up his friendship with Stravinsky and wrote the words for Stravinsky's oratorio *Oedipus-Rex*.

In the 1930's, Cocteau seemed inexhaustible, even though he suffered a bout with typhoid in 1931. Plays, poems, songs, ballets, art criticism, and even a column for *Ce soir* poured forth from his pen. He took a trip around the world in imitation of Jules Verne's *Le Tour du monde en quatre-vingt jours* (1873; *Around the World in Eighty Days*, 1873). He became the manager of the bantamweight boxer Alphonse Theo Brown. Perhaps the most important of his activities during this period was his first attempt at *poésie cinématographique*, when he wrote and directed *The Blood of a Poet*.

Cocteau, always controversial, found himself caught between his artistic enemies and new political ones during the Nazi occupation of France. He was viciously attacked in the press. His play *The Typewriter* was banned. He never backed off, however, even when beaten by a group of French fascists for failing to salute the flag.

After the war, Cocteau found himself a "grand old man" of the artistic world, but he refused to rest on his laurels and continued arousing controversy. He traveled and wrote plays, journals, and films. He made recordings and designed frescoes for the city hall at Menton, the Chapel of St. Pierre at Villefranche-sur-Mer, the Chapel of Notre Dame in London, the Church of Saint Blaise-des-Simples in Milly-la-Forêt, and the Chapel of Notre-Dame-de-Jerusalem at Fréjus. He also designed fabrics, plates, and posters. He was made a member of the Royal Belgian Academy and the French Academy in 1955 and received an honorary doctorate of letters from Oxford University in 1956. He died on October 11, 1963, shortly after hearing of the death of his friend Edith Piaf.

ANALYSIS

Jean Cocteau's first three books of poetry enjoyed the kind of success that works that essentially flatter the prevailing literary establishment are prone to have. He was instantly praised and compared to various great poets, present and past, yet never aroused the outrage or bewilderment provoked by significant breakthroughs. Very much a salon poet and dandy, Cocteau had yet to discover his own voice. *La Lampe d'Aladin* contained poems dedicated to the various actors and actresses who had read them at Cocteau's "debut" in the Théâtre Fémina. Like much of the poetry of the early 1900's, the poems of this first volume seem self-serving, overly and insincerely emotional, and very immature, though occasionally some charming cleverness may emerge.

LE PRINCE FRIVOLE

Cocteau's second collection, *Le Prince frivole* (the frivolous prince), is little better than the first. Its title came to be applied to its author, and Cocteau would later refer to the book as elevating him to the "Prince du Ridicule." The creation of poetry here is still an amusing game. Cocteau rather dutifully insists on melancholy in many of the works, but it comes off as posing, even though it may be indicative of an indefinable feeling that all the praise he was receiving was undeserved.

LA DANSE DE SOPHOCLE

After the publication of *La Danse de Sophocle*, the inadequacy of Cocteau's artistic commitment was brought home to him in a review by Henri Ghéon in *Nouvelle Revue française* (André Gide may have had a hand in its authorship). Ghéon pointed out the deriva-tive qualities of Cocteau's three books and implied that the poet was immature, frivolous, and greatly overestimated. Ghéon said that Cocteau was undeniably gifted but that he had not devoted himself to his gift. The review was more important in Cocteau's life than the book itself, though one can see in *La Danse de Sophocle* the beginning of Cocteau's lifelong interest in the eternal truths found in ancient Greek mythology and literature. The review provoked Cocteau to understand "that art and poetry aren't a game, but a descent into a mine, down toward the firedamp and danger."

LE CAP DE BONNE-ESPÉRANCE

Cocteau did not publish another collection of poetry until seven years later, after working for the Ballets Russes, associating with a more radical set of artists, and after his experiences in World War I. Later, when republishing his works, he ignored the earlier three books and dated his beginnings as a poet from *Le Cap de Bonne-Espérance* (the Cape of Good Hope), which was inspired by his association with the aviator Roland Garros. Garros would take Cocteau on daily flights from Villacoublay. He performed numerous acrobatics with Cocteau in the plane, and the poet was inspired by the sensation of flying and the view of Paris from the air. In 1918, after a remarkable escape from a German prison, Garros was shot down and killed. A proof copy of Cocteau's long poem dedicated to Garros was found in his cockpit. In the book, the airplane symbolizes the modern era: It frees humankind from earthly considerations, putting the pilot or passenger into a realm of new visions and solitude, where he can find his soul. At the same time, he faces death.

The poems in *Le Cap de Bonne-Espérance* are extremely sensual, despite the abstract element, and attempt to re-create the physical sensations of flying with fragmented lines and onomatopoeic vowels. These techniques were not original to Cocteau; the typographical effects had been used by Stéphane Mallarmé, Apollinaire, and Pierre Reverdy, and the *lettriste* effects by Pierre Albert-Birot. However, as Adrienne Monnier points out, it was daring of Cocteau to employ these still-radical devices. André Breton, among others, considered the collection not radical enough and had a sour expression the whole time Cocteau was reading it in Valentine Gross's apartment. Cocteau is said to have called his work old-fashioned, in an effort to charm Breton, but many see the reading as the beginning of Cocteau's long battle with the Surrealists. The book also provoked a letter from Proust, who gently asked whether it did not display a certain indiscriminate use of images.

DISCOURS DU GRAND SOMMEIL

Discours du grand sommeil (discourse of the great sleep) consists of eleven poems written between 1916 and 1918 and was inspired by Cocteau's experiences with the Fusiliers Marins, among whom he lived, illegally wearing the Marine uniform until discovered by an officer. A day after Cocteau was ejected from the front, most of the Fusiliers Marins were killed. Cocteau attempted in these poems to end once and for all his role as the "prince of frivolity." Though flippancy was always part of Cocteau's demeanor, he once asserted that it was the bourgeois way of dealing with catastrophe—that what appeared to be frivolity to others was actually Cocteau's way of dealing with his profound sadness. *Discours du grand sommeil*, writes Wallace Fowlie, is "a plunge downward," "a contact with the grim presence of death." The poems are quite effective in conveying the horror of war, of the exhausting marches, the screams of the dying, and the endless suffering. There is also an awakening sense of the soldier as symbolic of the tragedy of human existence and a movement toward a more classical style and attitude. The volume clearly points toward Cocteau's later aesthetic.

VOCABULAIRE

Vocabulaire also reveals a cleaner, purer style than that of Cocteau's youthful works yet still betrays the inordinate influence of the artistic movements of the war years, such as Dadaism, Futurism, Imagism, and cubism. Cocteau's fixation on certain images (such as snow turning to marble) is notable throughout his career. In this collection, the rose appears often, with obvious allusions to Pierre de Ronsard, in clear homage to French classicism. One finds Cocteau in search of himself, struggling as he had since the Ghéon review to achieve originality. The poems consist largely of philosophical speculations on the nature of change and the poet's role in metamorphosis. The endless flow of change is represented by the changes in clouds, aging, swans, the dissolution of salt statues, death, and snow.

Cocteau's private mythology is fully developed here; several poems, such as "Tombeaux" (tombs) and "Oiseaux sont en neige" (birds are in snow), connect homosexuality to the themes of change and death. In these poems, Cocteau seems to be taking stock of his life, trying to find a direction and meaning to it.

POÉSIES, 1917-1920

Under Radiguet's influence, Cocteau was moving toward the tradition of French literature that employs the brief, clear, precise sentence. Cocteau renewed himself with this classicism and rediscovered the themes of classical antiquity. In *Poésies, 1917-1920*, Cocteau introduced a new set of topics, themes, and motifs, such as the clown, circus, angel, sailor, and athlete. Perhaps the most significant poem in the collection is "L'Ode à Picasso" (ode to Picasso), an attempt to grasp the complexity of the painter and artist whom Cocteau often watched at work for hours on end. The poem reveals Picasso as a man possessed by an inner fire, an embodiment of the concept, expressed by Socrates in Plato's *Iōn* (fourth century B.C.E.; *Ion*, 1804), of the madness of the poet. Painting, sculpture, film, and any other expression of art are therefore merely facets of the same thing: *poésie*. Cocteau sees in Picasso a man in constant contact with the Muses, free of mundane considerations. The poem expresses much of what Cocteau would attempt to be, would have the courage to be, after being inspired by Radiguet. The final poem of *Poésies, 1917-1920*, "Mouchoir" (handkerchief), bids farewell to influences of the past and sets the poet out on a voyage into the unknown. To be a poet is thus to move ahead relentlessly, to be uncertain of the results, to follow no one.

PLAIN-CHANT

Plain-Chant reveals in its title a further move toward simplification and, in Fowlie's view, is central to the work of Cocteau. It is classically metered and uses the imagery of Angel, Muse, and Death, symbolism that recurs in much of the rest of Cocteau's oeuvre. The Angel in this lyric poem is clearly Radiguet, and the poem expresses Cocteau's great love for him and also his fear of the death that will inevitably separate them. The Angel is his guide through the mysteries of poetic art and also his protector when the Muse leaves him or Death presses in on him. As Bettina Knapp has observed, however, Death becomes a restorative power, a bridge to another world: "He burrowed within and reached new depths of cognition, with beauty of form and classical restraint." The poem was also strangely prescient, as Radiguet died in 1923, emotionally shattering Cocteau.

OPÉRA

Cocteau's discovery of his identity as a poet under the guidance of Radiguet was not lost in his plummet into despair brought about by the young man's death. The collection *Opéra* mixes Cocteau's visions induced by opium with lucid language and precise control. Even in his agony, he rigorously adheres to a classical detachment, a coolness that enhances the feelings and mythological dimensions of the works. A blending of Christian and pagan mythology points toward Cocteau's extensive revising and adapting of works of classical mythology for the stage and film. "L'Ange heurtebise" in *Opéra* is usually thought to be one of Cocteau's most significant poems. It explores the question of angels, which he had discussed in an essay, *Le Secret professionnel* (1922). The poet is stuck on an earthly plane, struggling to understand a larger reality, while the Angel stands above. The Angel reappears in work after work of Cocteau, inspiring poets and urging them to look on the human predicament with detachment.

LATER YEARS

Cocteau did not cease writing poetry until his death, but most critics seem indifferent to the large number of his works after *Opéra*. Perhaps his work in film and prose detracted from his development in poetry, though Cocteau himself saw all his artistic works as facets of the same creative impulse: It was all poetry to him. His influence on the literary scene waned, perhaps because he had finally found his own unique path, and artists and critics found it difficult to categorize and thus assess the measure of Cocteau's achievement. His variety contributes to the difficulty of an overall assessment: He began each mature collection of poems as if he had only recently become a poet.

At the very least, Cocteau's poetry exhibits many of the primary traits of twentieth century poetry in its clean, precise form, its development of personal mythology, and its exploitation through adaptation of traditional mythological and literary themes. These traits are significant elements of the mainstream of modern poetry, and Cocteau is clearly in the middle of it.

OTHER MAJOR WORKS

LONG FICTION: *Le Potomak*, 1919; *Le Grand Écart*, 1923 (*The Grand Écart*, 1925); *Thomas l'imposteur*, 1923 (*Thomas the Impostor*, 1925); *Le Livre blanc*, 1928 (*The White Paper*, 1957); *Les Enfants terribles*, 1929 (*Enfants Terribles*, 1930; also known as *Children of the Game*); *Le Fantôme de Marseille*, 1933; *La Fin du Potomak*, 1939.

PLAYS: *Le Dieu bleu*, pr. 1912 (ballet scenario; with Frédéric de Madrazo); *Parade*, pr. 1917 (ballet scenario; music by Erik Satie, scenery by Pablo Picasso); *Le Boeuf sur le toit*, pr. 1920 (ballet scenario; music by Darius Milhaud, scenery by Raoul Dufy); *Le Gendarme incompris*, pr. 1921 (ballet scenario; with Raymond Radiguet; music by Francis Poulenc); *Les Mariés de la tour Eiffel*, pr. 1921 (ballet scenario; music by Les Six; *The Wedding on the Eiffel Tower*, 1937); *Antigone*, pr. 1922 (libretto; English translation, 1961); *Les Biches*, pr. 1924 (ballet scenario; music by Poulenc); *Les Fâcheux*, pr. 1924 (ballet scenario; music by George Auric); *Orphée*, pr. 1926 (*Orpheus*, 1933); *Oedipus-Rex*, pr. 1927, pb. 1928 (libretto; English translation, 1961); *La Voix humaine*, pr., pb. 1930 (*The Human Voice*, 1951); *La Machine infernale*, pr., pb. 1934 (*The Infernal Machine*, 1936); *L'École des veuves*, pr., pb. 1936; *Les Chevaliers de la table ronde*, pr., pb. 1937 (*The Knights of the Round Table*, 1955); *Les Parents terribles*, pr., pb. 1938 (*Intimate Relations*, 1952); *Les Monstres sacrés*, pr., pb. 1940 (*The Holy Terrors*, 1953); *La Machine à écrire*, pr., pb. 1941 (*The Typewriter*, 1948); *Renaud et Armide*, pr., pb. 1943; *L'Aigle à deux têtes*, pr., pb. 1946 (*The Eagle Has Two Heads*, 1946); *Le Jeune Homme et la mort*, pr. 1946 (ballet scenario; music by Johann Sebastian Bach); *Phèdre*, pr. 1950 (ballet scenario; music by Auric); *Bacchus*, pr. 1951 (English translation, 1955); *Théâtre complet*, 1957 (2 volumes); *Five Plays*, 1961; *L'Impromptu du Palais-Royal*, pr., pb. 1962; *The Infernal Machine, and Other Plays*, 1964.

SCREENPLAYS: *Le Sang d'un poète*, 1930 (*The Blood of a Poet*, 1949); *Le Baron fantôme*, 1943; *L'Éternel Retour*, 1943 (*The Eternal Return*, 1948);

L'Aigle à deux têtes, 1946; *La Belle et la bête*, 1946 (*Beauty and the Beast*, 1947); *Ruy Blas*, 1947; *Les Parents terribles*, 1948 (*Intimate Relations*, 1952); *Les Enfants terribles*, 1950; *Orphée*, 1950 (*Orpheus*, 1950); *Le Testament d'Orphée*, 1959 (*The Testament of Orpheus*, 1968); *Thomas l'Imposteur*, 1965.

NONFICTION: *Le Coq et l'Arlequin*, 1918 (*Cock and Harlequin*, 1921); *Le Secret professionnel*, 1922; *Lettre à Jacques Maritain*, 1926 (*Art and Faith*, 1948); *Le Rappel à l'ordre*, 1926 (*A Call to Order*, 1926); *Opium: Journal d'une désintoxication*, 1930 (*Opium: Diary of a Cure*, 1932); *Essai de la critique indirecte*, 1932 (*The Lais Mystery: An Essay of Indirect Criticism*, 1936); *Portraits-souvenir, 1900-1914*, 1935 (*Paris Album*, 1956); *"La Belle et la bête": Journal d'un film*, 1946 (*"Beauty and the Beast": Journal of a Film*, 1950); *La Difficulté d'être*, 1947 (*The Difficulty of Being*, 1966); *Journal d'un inconnu*, 1952 (*The Hand of a Stranger*, 1956; also known as *Diary of an Unknown*, 1988); *The Journals of Jean Cocteau*, 1956; *Poésie critique*, 1960.

TRANSLATION: *Roméo et Juliette*, 1926 (of William Shakespeare's play).

BIBLIOGRAPHY

Crowson, Lydia. *The Esthetic of Jean Cocteau.* Hanover: University of New Hampshire Press, 1978. Chapters on Cocteau's milieu, the nature of the real, and the roles of myth, consciousness, and power. Includes introduction and bibliography. This work is for advanced students who have already consulted more introductory works.

Griffith, Alison Guest. *Jean Cocteau and the Performing Arts.* Irvine, Calif.: Severin Wunderman Museum, 1992. This museum catalog includes critical analysis of Cocteau's work as well as information on his contribution to the performing arts. Bibliography.

Knapp, Bettina L. *Jean Cocteau: Updated Edition.* Boston: Twayne, 1989. A thorough revision of Knapp's 1970 volume, which begins with her memory of her introduction to the writing. Knapp pursues both psychological and literary views of Cocteau's work, with chapters following a chronological approach. Includes separate chronology, notes, bibliography, and index.

Lowe, Romana N. *The Fictional Female: Sacrificial Rituals and Spectacles of Writing in Baudelaire, Zola, and Cocteau.* New York: Peter Lang, 1997. Highlights the sacrificial victim common in nineteenth and twentieth century French texts: women. Lowe traces structures and images of female sacrifice in the genres of poetry, novel, and theater with close readings of Baudelaire, Zola, and Cocteau.

Mauriès, Patrick. *Jean Cocteau.* Translated by Jane Brenton. London: Thames & Hudson, 1998. A brief but excellent biography of Cocteau illustrated with many photographs.

Peters, Arthur King, et al. *Jean Cocteau and the French Scene.* New York: Abbeville, 1984. Essays on Cocteau's biography, his life in Paris, his intellectual background, his view of realism, and his work in the theater and movies. Also contains a chronology, an index, and many illustrations and photographs.

Saul, Julie, ed. *Jean Cocteau: The Mirror and the Mask—A Photo-Biography.* Boston: D. R. Godine, 1992. This compilation from an exhibit celebrating the one-hundred-year anniversary of his birth, with an essay by Francis Steegmuller, provides insights into the life of Cocteau.

Selous, Trista. *Cocteau.* Paris: Centre Pompidou, 2003. A retrospective catalog compiled by the Centre Pompidou and the Montreal Museum that offers an illustrated review of Cocteau's creative output. It also includes seventeen essays on Cocteau's life and work.

Steegmuller, Francis. *Cocteau.* Boston: D. R. Godine, 1986. A major biography of Cocteau. Discusses his childhood, the influence of his mother, and fellow poets. Defines him as a "quick-change" artist with a propensity for constant self-invention, discarding old views and activities and assuming new roles or guises with remarkable facility. Twelve appendixes plus numerous illustrations. Includes bibliography, index.

Tsakiridou, Cornelia A., ed. *Reviewing Orpheus: Essays on the Cinema and Art of Jean Cocteau.* Lewisburg, Pa.: Bucknell University Press, 1997. Focuses on Cocteau's film work but is valuable for insight into his general artistry.

J. Madison Davis

TRISTAN CORBIÈRE

Born: Coat-Congar, near Morlaix, France; July 18, 1845

Died: Morlaix, France; March 1, 1875

PRINCIPAL POETRY

Les Amours jaunes, 1873 (*These Jaundiced Loves*, 1995)

OTHER LITERARY FORMS

Tristan Corbière (kawr-BYEHR) is known only for his poetry. Corbière did not publish in any other literary form, but he was a very talented caricaturist.

ACHIEVEMENTS

During his lifetime, Tristan Corbière's poetry received little notice. Although Corbière published only one book of poetry, *These Jaundiced Loves*, and did not write any theoretical works or participate in a *cenacle* (writer's group) or in a poetical movement, his work has played a significant role in the development of French Symbolist poetry. In 1881, his cousin Pol Kalig brought Corbière's work to the attention of Léo Trézenic, who was publishing an avant-garde review with Charles Morice. They showed the poems to the poet Paul Verlaine, one of the review's contributors. Verlaine not only was impressed by Corbière's poetry but also immediately recognized him as one of the major poets of the time. He included Corbière in his *Poètes maudits* (1884; *The Cursed Poets*, 2003) along with Arthur Rimbaud, Stéphane Mallarmé, Gérard de Nerval, Marceline Desbordes-Valmore, and himself under the anagram Pauvre Lelian. Consequently, Corbière's work became known in contemporary poetic circles.

BIOGRAPHY

Tristan Corbière was born Édouard Joachim Corbière, the eldest son of Édouard Corbière and Angélique Aspasie Puyo, on July 18, 1845, at their estate near Morlaix, France. He was named after his father, Édouard, and his maternal grandfather, Joachim Puyo. Corbière's father had been a sailor and was an author of

sea novels and a businessman. Throughout his life, Corbière was tormented by his desire to be a sailor, but his ill health prevented him from realizing his dream. Corbière remained at home until he was fourteen years old, when he became a boarding student at a school in Saint-Brieuc. Corbière missed his family and home, and he did not enjoy school. He spent much time drawing and painting, a talent that was shared by several members of his mother's family. He was particularly good at drawing caricatures. While at school, he began to be troubled by the first symptoms of rheumatoid arthritis. Before long, his health worsened such that he left the school at Saint-Brieuc. He was diagnosed with a rheumatoid arthritis associated with tuberculosis. His parents sent him to Nantes to live with his uncle, a medical doctor. He was enrolled in school at Nantes as a day student but soon had to leave school because of his health. He and his mother went to Provence, where he underwent treatments at Cannes and at Luchon. At the end of 1862, they returned to the family home, Bourboulon, at Morlaix. Corbière began writing less than complimentary poems about various important people of the town.

On the advice of his uncle, Corbière moved into his parents' summer home at Roscoff in the summer of 1863. He spent much time alone, wrote poetry, and lived the life of a sailor to the extent that his health permitted. He wore a sailor's outfit, smoked a pipe, passed time in the port bars that the sailors frequented, and sailed in his small boat along the coastline. He was fond of dogs and always had his water spaniel Tristan with him. Corbière had become friends with a local innkeeper at Roscoff, and there he met several painters from Montmartre, including Jean-Louis Hamon, whom he accompanied to Italy in December, 1869. Corbière returned to Roscoff the following spring.

In the spring of 1871, Corbière met Count Rodolphe de Battine and his mistress Armida-Josephina Cuchiani, an Italian actress. Corbière invited the couple to go sailing with him, but soon he was inviting only Cuchiani, with whom he had fallen in love. In the autumn, the couple returned to Paris, leaving Corbière to his solitude. In 1872, Corbière went to Paris and took a room in Montmartre, not far from Cuchiani's apartment on the

Boulevard Clichy. He changed his appearance, wearing the clothes of a dandy rather than those of a sailor. Corbière went to the theater and attempted to gain the affections of Cuchiani but with little success. In May, 1872, he took both Cuchiani and Battine to Capri to the Hotel Pagano, where he had stayed with Hamon. Returning from Italy, they spent the summer at Douarnenez in Brittany. Once they were back in Paris, Cuchiani showed less and less interest in her poet lover. Disillusioned, Corbière sought out Parisian prostitutes, while Cuchiani remained the muse of his poetry. In 1873, he published his one book of poetry. Financed by his father, the book was published by the Glady brothers. The edition ran to 481 regular copies and 9 deluxe copies. Although Corbière had already published nine of these poems in *La Vie Parisienne*, his collection attracted little attention. The book was mentioned in only three newspaper articles. Corbière was planning to publish another volume of poetry titled *Mirlitons*. However, his health worsened, and his mother took him to the Hôpital Dubois, where he died on March 1, 1875.

ANALYSIS

Tristan Corbière's poetry is a complex compilation of the torment caused by his physical deformity, the restrictions placed on him by his illness, his love of the sea, his admiration for sailors, his love of Brittany, his love of Cuchiani, and the artistic expression of his poetic genius. Through his use of irony and unusual striking imagery, his poetry reflects his love of caricature, his obsession with the marginal, his disdain for bourgeois society, and his resentment at his own state of illness and ugliness. Corbière's poetry remains above all else his own, imbued with an originality of expression and the juxtaposition of contradictory images, ideas, and sentiments.

Corbière lived a very hermetic life. He spent most of his life at Roscoff, wandering about the Breton coasts, sailing along the shore with his only companion, his dog Tristan. He did not participate in poetry circles and interact with other writers who were developing poetical theories. Nevertheless, Corbière is identified as a Symbolist poet and an author significant in the transition from Romanticism to Symbolism. This classification is due primarily to Verlaine's having been made aware of Corbière's *These Jaundiced Loves* and including him in *The Cursed Poets*. Corbière's work does fit into the tradition of Romanticism and its evolution into Symbolism.

The sense of isolation, of being misunderstood and alienated from society (one of the major characteristics of both the Romantic poets and the Symbolists), permeates all of Corbière's poetry. For both the Romantics and the Symbolists, the poet's suffering from isolation had a psychological or emotional base, the result of a *moi* (inner self) that was different and incomprehensible to society in general. It was the reaction of the sensitive soul to the callous, unemotional materialistic world in which the poet lived. Corbière's isolation was the result not only of a sensitive soul unable to acclimate to the world but also of his physical illness and deformity. He readily admitted his ugliness, his noticeable difference. The sailors and villagers of Roscoff referred to him as Ankou (meaning "death" in Breton). His physical appearance was a stumbling block to any love affair; his liaison with Cuchiani brought only sadness and disillusionment, as she preferred the count. His ill health forced him to live most of the time at Roscoff, far from literary circles. Consequently, Corbière's life was in a real sense a continual antithesis: The individual he wished to be and the individual he could be were the exact opposites of each other.

Much of Corbière's poetry transposes his life into poetical form. In his verse, he portrays himself, the Breton coast and sea, and the sailors with whom he passed time in the local taverns, as well as his experiences in Paris and with Cuchiani. His verse also reflects his attitudes and reactions to these milieu. As a poet, he was no longer Édouard Joachim; he became Tristan, connecting himself to the Tristan of Celtic legend, the long-suffering lover of Isolde. However, he also named his dog Tristan, thus equating himself and his dog. The meaning of his creation of the triumvirate of the medieval Tristan, Tristan Corbière, and Tristan the dog remain obscure, as does much of Corbière's verse. Meaning is hinted at, but much is left as enigma.

His self-deprecating descriptions are filled with antithesis and irony. The poems reveal a morbid fascination with death, which is reminiscent of the medieval poet François Villon and also of Edgar Allan Poe, who was particularly appreciated by the French poets of the mid-nineteenth century. His companions in the poems about Brittany are toads, rats, and owls, animals scarcely appreciated by human society and for the most part marginalized. In the last verse of his poem "Le Crapaud" ("The Toad"), he states that he is the toad. The poems depicting Paris describe the city as Corbière found it—unfeeling, unwelcoming, driven by the desire for monetary gain, and providing no consolation to the transplanted Breton poet who posed as a dandy, much as he had posed as a sailor in his native Brittany. The only topics that he never treats in a disdainful manner are sailors and the sea, expressing admiration for sailors and love for the sea in a way that contrasts dramatically with his treatment of other topics.

"EPITAPH"

Corbière's poetry evidences a fascination with language and a strong sense of its musical qualities. Wordplay is important to Corbière. In "Epitaphe" ("Epitaph"), he creates total confusion as he repeats the various grammatical forms of *commencement* (beginning) and *fin* (end) in their various grammatical forms, forming a long sentence filled with repeated sounds and meanings. The rhythm and the rhyme and the alliteration of the verses leads the reader of the poem in an endless circle reminiscent of the Celtic eternal knot.

"THE CONTUMACIOUS POET"

"Le Poète contumace" ("The Contumacious Poet") is a long story poem in which the poet, isolated and alone, spends a night writing a letter that he tears up and casts to the wind as dawn breaks. In the letter, he laments the loss of his love, who is also his muse. This story line is a poetic rendering of Corbière's situation at summer's end, when Cuchiani and the count left Roscoff and returned to Paris, leaving him alone. The poem contains many striking images and descriptions. The first stanzas are devoted to a description of the dilapidated convent where the poet is living. Corbière compares the building to an old woman with a crenelated jaw; the convent's tower has been knocked to

the side over her ear by blows from a fist. One of the passersby is a blue coat containing a revenue collector. The rainbow is described as having been left in cinders by the nights of the poet and his love.

Corbière makes many allusions to other literary works, including Bernadin de Saint-Pierre's novel *Paul et Virginie* (1788) and Robert Louis Stevenson's *Treasure Island* (1881-1882, serial; 1883, book). The poem is also filled with local color as he describes the villagers of Roscoff and the surrounding countryside. Although the poem is permeated with irony, mockery, and a sense of despair, there is an accompanying sense of gentle humor in the descriptions of the donkeys grazing in the convent's ruins, the elderly owls, the attic rats who dance, and the mushrooms that grow on the stairs.

The poet is described in mocking terms as a dried-up, skinny loafer, a used-up playboy with leaden wings. Corbière fills his verse with antithesis. The poet dies in sleep, yet lives in dreams; not knowing how to die, he lives; not knowing how to live, he writes. In the last verse, laughing, he tears up his letter and casts it away.

"A LITTLE DEATH TO MAKE ONE LAUGH"

The poem "Petit Mort pour rire" ("A Little Death to Make One Laugh") addresses the poet after his death as the nimble or playful comber of comets, an image that refuses to be interpreted by the reader but links the poet to the world of symbol and implies the immortality and difference of the poet. Will-of-the-wisps flash from his eyes; his laugh is filled with flowers. Unlike the coffin of the materialist bourgeois, the poet's coffin, a hollow fiddle case, weighs very little—for the poet, a channel of symbolic meaning is translated to another form. For the dullard bourgeois, he is dead; however, this comber of comets has become part of the other world, the world of symbol. The irony of the poem turns on the bourgeois who reject the poet.

BIBLIOGRAPHY

Corbière, Tristan. *The Centenary Corbière: Selected Poems and Prose.* Translated by Val Warner. 1974. Reprint. New York: Routledge, 2003. This translation of Corbière's poetry provides parallel text in French and English, enabling the reader who speaks

French to understand fully Corbière's wordplay. Good introduction for treatment of the context in which the poems were written.

Lunn-Rockliffe, Katherine. *Tristan Corbière and the Poetics of Irony*. New York: Oxford University Press, 2006. Valuable for analysis of how Corbière uses irony. Proposes a method for reading his poetry that makes his irony understandable.

Mithell, Robert L. *Tristan Corbière*. Boston: Twayne, 1979. A good basic biography and analysis of the poet and his works.

Verlaine, Paul. *The Cursed Poets*. Los Angeles: Green Integer, 2001. Important text for understanding Corbière as a Symbolist and how his work entered into the canon of Symbolist poetry.

Shawncey Webb

D

GABRIELE D'ANNUNZIO

Born: Pescara, Italy; March 12, 1863
Died: Gardone, Italy; March 1, 1938

PRINCIPAL POETRY

Primo vere, 1879, 1880
Canto novo, 1882, 1896
Intermezzo di rime, 1884, 1896
Isaotta Gùttadauro ed altre poesie, 1886, 1890
San Pantaleone, 1886
Elegie romane, 1892
Poema paradisiaco—Odi navali, 1893
Laudi del cielo del mare della terra e degli eroi,
    1899
Maia, 1903
Alcyone, 1904 (English translation, 1977)
Elettra, 1904
Merope, 1912
Canti della guerra latina, 1914-1918
Asterope, 1949
Le laudi, 1949 (expanded version of 1899 title, also
    includes *Maia*, *Elettra*, *Alcyone*, *Merope*, and
    Asterope)

OTHER LITERARY FORMS

In addition to poetry, the literary production of Gabriele D'Annunzio (don-NOONT-syoh) encompasses many other genres: short stories, novels, autobiographical essays, political writings, and several plays, in Italian and in French.

The whole of D'Annunzio's production is available in three major editions: *Opera omnia* (1927-1936), *Tutte le opere* (1931-1937), and *Tutte le opere* (1930-1965), which also includes D'Annunzio's notes under the title *Taccuini*. Forty-one volumes of D'Annunzio's collected work were issued under the title *Opera complete* (1941-1943).

ACHIEVEMENTS

Gabriele D'Annunzio dominated the Italian literary scene from 1880 until the end of World War I. His literary work and his personal conduct challenged existing models with such an exuberant vitality that even the less positive aspects of his art and life have been influential, if only for the reaction they have provoked.

Extremely receptive to foreign influences, D'Annunzio, through a series of experiments with new forms and styles of composition, evolved an original poetic language. Replacing traditional grammatical links with paratactic constructions, he forged a style in which assonance, onomatopoeia, and alliteration prevail, achieving enthralling effects of pictorial and musical synesthesia.

Historically, D'Annunzio's most original achievement was to help break the highly academic literary tradition that had been dominant in Italy for centuries and to reintegrate Italian culture into the mainstream of European intellectual life. He was the first modern Italian writer. His literary work in its amplitude and variety served as an invaluable source of motifs, themes, and suggestions for the brilliant generation of poets who came to maturity in the 1920's. As Eugenio Montale has observed, an Italian poet who has learned nothing from D'Annunzio is truly impoverished.

BIOGRAPHY

Gabriele D'Annunzio was born in Pescara, a small port city in the Abruzzi region, on March 12, 1863, to a well-to-do family. He received a solid classical education at the Liceo Cicognini, in Prato, and when he was only sixteen years old, he published his first collection of verses, *Primo vere* (early spring).

In 1881, D'Annunzio moved to Rome, where he registered at the university in the department of Italian literature, but he never completed his university studies. He chose instead to pursue a writer's career, consolidating his fame as a young poetic genius in the literary and aristocratic circles of the capital. During that time, he contributed verses, short stories, and articles to several publications, while enjoying an intense social life punctuated by love affairs, intrigues, and scandals. His second collection of verses, *Canto novo* (new song), was both more accomplished and more personal than its predecessor.

D'Annunzio's Roman period, interrupted by adventurous cruises and occasional sojourns in the Abruzzi region, lasted until 1891. By that time, he had already gained national recognition, sealing his social and literary success with his marriage to Maria Hardouin, duchess of Gallese, and with the publication of a novel. These were fruitful years for D'Annunzio, as witnessed by the production of numerous novels and collections of short stories. D'Annunzio led an extravagant and magnificent life, a life of debts and scandals, of new loves and adventures. At the same time, he maintained an unrelenting rhythm of work. Indeed, all his activities were encompassed and absorbed by a total engagement in literature.

D'Annunzio also nourished political ambitions. In 1896, he published *Le vergini delle rocce* (*The Maidens of the Rocks*, 1898), a novel whose antidemocratic message is emblematic of the writer's political choices. One year later, he entered the political arena and was elected as a representative to the Italian parliament. His activity there was unremarkable until 1900, when, during the controversy over the exceptional laws proposed by Luigi Pelloux's government, he theatrically shifted to the left wing, declaring: "I am going toward life." In the same year, he presented himself as a candidate in the Socialist list but was not elected; with this defeat, D'Annunzio closed his parliamentary experience.

In 1894, D'Annunzio had met Eleonora Duse, the great actress, who played a considerable part in his sentimental life and had a substantial influence on his literary activities. This union of love and art gave rise to a period of great literary achievements. At La Capponcina, a villa in the hilly countryside of Florence, surrounded by horses, dogs, and works of art, D'Annunzio wrote another novel, a number of plays, and the first three volumes of *Le laudi*, which represent the highest expression of his poetic art. His relationship with Duse was interrupted in 1903 by new temptations. After a few years of extravagant expenses, D'Annunzio, driven by his taste for luxury and his passion for cars and planes, was insolvent. In 1909, La Capponcina was seized by the creditors, and one year later D'Annunzio left Italy for France, choosing what he pompously called a "a voluntary exile." There, he split his time between his residence in Arcachon and Paris, where he was soon introduced into the literary and social circles. To this period belong several works in Old French, the most prominent of which is *Le Martyre de Saint Sébastien*, a theatrical text with music by Claude Debussy, which was presented in Paris in 1911.

The French period came to a close at the outbreak of World War I. Faithful to the idea of traditional alliance between France and Italy, D'Annunzio returned to Italy to campaign in favor of Italy's intervention in the war against Germany. D'Annunzio's political speeches were a clamorous success, significantly contributing to the victory of the interventionist party.

Gabriele D'Annunzio (Library of Congress)

As soon as Italy entered the war, D'Annunzio enlisted as a volunteer; he fought first on the front line and then participated in several actions on the sea and in the air. In January, 1916, as a result of a plane accident, he lost his right eye and had to spend three months immobilized and in darkness. During this period of forced inactivity, he painfully scribbled notes that were to become *Il notturno* (1921), a work in prose without a precise narrative line, in which he registered impressions and notations in a stream of consciousness in which past and present are intertwined.

The end of the war and the peace negotiations, quite unsatisfactory for Italy, found D'Annunzio in the role of the poet-prophet, the voice of the people demanding their rights. The polemics over the peace negotiations reached their height when it appeared that the city of Fiume would not be annexed to Italy. With his famous "Marci dei Ronchi," D'Annunzio, at the head of a group of volunteers, entered Fiume and established a temporary government. His action interrupted the diplomatic negotiations between Italy and Yugoslavia; the Italian government first ordered D'Annunzio to leave the city and then sent the fleet to force him out.

Fiume was officially annexed to Italy in 1924. D'Annunzio's action may have had some weight in this decision, but its immediate result was a failure. Meanwhile, in Italy, D'Annunzio's prophetic role had been assumed by Benito Mussolini. D'Annunzio, disillusioned, retired to a large estate on Lake Garda which he renamed Il Vittoriale. There, he spent the rest of his life, surrounded by a rich library and by the mass of disparate objects that he had collected with obsessive passion.

The relations between D'Annunzio and the Fascist government were respectfully cold. The poet, while subscribing to certain principles of fascism, considered Benito Mussolini a poor imitator of his own style; Mussolini, for his part, chose to keep D'Annunzio at a proper distance while bestowing on him honors and subsidies.

When he was not traveling, D'Annunzio led a quiet life at Il Vittoriale, devoting his time to editing his *Opera omnia*. In 1924, under the title *Le faville del maglio*, he gathered and published some of his previous writings; a second volume appeared in 1928. D'Annunzio's *Le cento e cento e cento pagine del libro segreto di Gabriele D'Annunzio tentato di morire* (1935) clearly referred to a strange accident in 1922 (he had fallen from a window) that could have been a suicide attempt. He died in 1938.

Analysis

The "D'Annunzio phenomenon" has stirred a century-long argument between Gabriele D'Annunzio's admirers and detractors, and his reputation has endured alternating periods of favor and disfavor, often related to historical circumstances. Later, under the impetus of a revival both in Italy and abroad, his works were reevaluated in the light of new critical methods.

Considering the number of D'Annunzio's poetry collections, novels, plays, and memoirs, it would be unrealistic to expect a consistent artistic level throughout his oeuvre, but it should be recognized that, in its vastness and diversity, his work is an invaluable documentation of half a century of European intellectual life. In this perspective, it is difficult to isolate certain verse collections from the context of his entire production. The pattern of receptivity and experimentation that characterizes D'Annunzio's poetry can be appreciated only by following the arc of his poetic achievement from *Primo vere* to *Le laudi*, where the voice of the poet reaches the plenitude of his expressive means.

Primo vere

In *Primo vere*, the choice of language, images, and versification is clearly inspired by Giosuè Carducci's model. A second edition of the work in 1880, enriched with fifty-nine new poems, offers greater insight. The delicate musicality of certain verses, and the attention devoted to the description of landscapes as the privileged scenery for love encounters, anticipate the distinctive tone that D'Annunzio was to achieve in *Canto novo*. The driving inspiration of this collection is the poet's yearning for identification with nature. A pervasive pagan sensuality saturates the atmosphere as nature and man vibrate with the same impulses: A woman's breath has the perfume of the forest, and her haunches are like those of an antelope; lovers are entwined like "virgin trees interlacing their branches." The metaphors unify Earth, sea, and man in a vitalistic élan in which all forms merge.

CANTO NOVO

Canto novo establishes the alternation between two themes that constitutes a favorite pattern of D'Annunzio's dialectic: an unresolved conflict between the vitalistic impetus and a fin de siècle introspection and sadness. The tendency to magnify the elegiac and melancholic component in the poet's writings is evident in the prevalent interpretation of the collection's most celebrated poem, "O falce di luna calante" (oh, sickle of waning moon), which has often been read as an expression of weariness and consuming despair; as Barberi Squarotti has noted in *Invito alla lettura di D'Annunzio* (1982), this interpretation takes the poem out of its context in the collection, for the next poem is an invitation to another day of joyous life and love.

INTERMEZZO DI RIME

D'Annunzio's negative note decidedly does prevail, however, in *Intermezzo di rime*, which was later revised and published under the shorter title *Intermezzo*. This new collection presented a sharp change in versification, tone, and inspiration. Influenced by the French Parnassianism, D'Annunzio abandoned Carducci's versification for the traditional meters of sonnets and ballads. The volume also reveals a renewed taste for mythological reminiscence, while the polished elegance of the compositions suggests a new concern with aestheticism. Here, closed gardens substitute for natural landscapes, bucolic pagan eroticism gives way to a refined experimentation with morbid sensuality, and vitalism turns into sadistic cruelty. The entire collection is informed by a spirit of willful transgression. The protagonist, "l'Adolescente," dissipates his vital energies in enervating lust. His attempt to achieve full control of life through the exaltation of the senses results in failure, as the satisfaction of pure sensuality rapidly wears out in disgust.

Several other important themes make their first appearance in this collection: the promenade, a privileged moment for erotic emotions; woman, the luxurious female whose castrating power destroys man's energies; art, the fruit and carrier of corruption; the poet, the supreme artificer, the jeweler chiseling the hard, resistant metal of language. Other, less significant sections of *Intermezzo* reveal a taste for the macabre and the sadistic, quite in fashion at that time.

POEMA PARADISIACO

Following several collections of poems that refined the manner of *Intermezzo*, *Poema paradisiaco—Odi navali* introduced a new style. Here, following the French Symbolists and influenced as well by Giovanni Pascoli's *Myricae* (1891; tamarisks), D'Annunzio proposes a new musicality studiously built on a rhythm of verses broken by enjambments and interrupted by exclamations, questions, and invocations, where rhymes are hidden and assonance prevails. Memory, contemplation, and melancholy govern this poem of gardens (from the Greek *paradeisos*, "of the garden"), where "gardens" signify the closed space of interiority and meditation away from intellectual and sensual turmoil.

Poema paradisiaco evokes the languid melancholy of things that are no more, of sentiments that could have been. The memory of a brief encounter rouses a longing for an opportunity forever lost. The poet recalls flowers that have not been gathered, loves that have not been lived, privileged moments that have not been enjoyed. In "La passeggiata," the poet prefers a sweet and melancholy relation with a woman to the ardor of love, concluding with a subtly ironic comment: "o voi dal dolce nome che io non chiamo!/ perchè voi non mi amate ed io non vi amo" ("You, with the sweet name I do not call!/ because you do not love me and I do not love you"). *Poema paradisiaco* remains one of the fundamental works of nineteenth century Italian poetry for its innovative language and rhythm and for its influence on the following generation of poets.

LE LAUDI

Although all the preceding poetic works of D'Annunzio have provoked contrasting critical opinions, *Le laudi* has by general agreement been recognized as the poet's masterpiece. This vast work was to include seven books dedicated to the seven stars of the Pleiades, but only four books of the projected seven were published during D'Annunzio's lifetime: *Maia, Elettra, Alcyone,* and *Merope*. A fifth book, *Asterope*, published posthumously in 1949, includes the poems that D'Annunzio wrote during World War I.

Maia is mainly devoted to "Laus vitae," a long poem based on D'Annunzio's voyages in Greece in 1898 and 1899. In this poem, he celebrates the creative power of the classical world, comparing the vital drive of Greek civilization with the sterility of contemporary society. Hymns to Hermes, the creator, alternate with descriptions of modern cities where corruption and vice dominate, culminating with a vision of the "Great Demagogue," a mass leader who preaches the destruction of everything that is beautiful and noble. The populace is portrayed as an instinctively violent and somehow innocent animal, exploited by demagogues and sacrificed without pity. Destruction and suffering, the poet-prophet predicts, will be followed by the birth of a new society in which work and beauty will be equally respected and loved.

In these fiery images, D'Annunzio expresses his antidemocratic and aristocratic sentiments, inspired by Friedrich Nietzsche, but the complex system of the philosopher is narrowed down to serve a limited political program. The poem concludes with an invocation to Nature, the immortal Mother, who is the source of creation and renewal.

Elettra, named for the second star in the constellation, is divided roughly into two parts. In the first part, the celebratory and commemorative inspiration of many of the poems and their oratorical manner reveal D'Annunzio's ambition to create a new mythology, to become the epic bard of the new Italian nation. This effort is not always sustained by authentic inspiration, and in many poems rhetoric and artificiality prevail. The second part, "Le città del silenzio," is a celebration of the old Italian cities, silent and forgotten in the enclosure of their glorious past. Evocations of ancient events and descriptions of splendid monuments and palaces dissolve into a subdued musicality tinted with melancholy.

In the third volume of the series, *Alcyone* (which has been translated into English), D'Annunzio reached his highest lyric expression. After the heroic tension of *Maia* and *Elettra* and their fervid affirmations and denunciations, *Alcyone* stands as a pause, a moment of total participation in the joyous blossoming of nature in its fullest season. The book opens with "La tregua" ("The Respite"), an invocation to "il magnanimo despota" (the generous despot), Nietzsche, the master of willpower. After a period of intense commitment to the fight against brutal ignorance, corruption, and vulgarity, the poet asks for a respite. He wants to be rein-

vigorated, forsaking public squabbles for the pure sources of life. The poem concludes with a celebration of pagan nature, the realm of fauns, nymphs, and satyrs.

In the following poems, a series of mythological passages translates the introductory hymn to nature into the apotheosis of poetry. In the poem "Il fanciullo," the divine flute player who modulates the most delicate murmurs of nature is the image of the youthful god of poetry: Here, poetry is the privileged activity where art and nature meet and merge. In "Lungo l'Affrico nella sera di giugno dopo la pioggia," a description of the fresh calm of nature in the twilight after a summer rain evolves into a meditation on the power of poetry. Nature offers itself like ductile clay to the poet, who shapes it into a durable work of art. In the following poem, "La sera fiesolana," this concept evolves into a conception of poetics which is central to an understanding of the collection. The landscape vibrates with a secret urge to express itself; hills and rivers, leaves and drops of rain, all nature utters silent words that only the poet can hear. The voice of nature is the language of poetry itself. "La spica" and "Le opere e i giorni" carry the message even further, affirming that all forms of nature live only as a function of the poetic word, which, by naming them, calls them into existence.

After *Alcyone*, D'Annunzio was chiefly concerned with other literary genres. He seldom returned to poetry and then only for occasional lyric fragments. *Merope*, the fourth book of *Le laudi*, includes ten canzones composed on the occasion of the Italo-Turkish war. These poems do not add anything to D'Annunzio's reputation; the flamboyant rhetoric of the volume betrays its essentially political function.

With *Alcyone*, D'Annunzio's poetic inspiration achieved its fullest expression. The feeling of joyful participation in nature that informed his early verse reappeared in *Alcyone*, decanted, refined, and enriched by the variety of D'Annunzio's painstaking experiments with new forms and techniques and by his unrelenting meditation on poetry. Themes, motifs, and discoveries of the preceding collections merge in *Alcyone*. Mythology, no longer an artificial ornament, is integrated with nature, which speaks through myths and transfers to the poet its creative force. In this world created by poetic language, everything harmonizes in a unique song celebrating the eternal beauty of life and nature in their multiform aspects.

D'Annunzio's art, based on classical culture yet renewed by the European avant-garde, represents the link between traditional and modern forms of poetry. Like all great writers, D'Annunzio created a personal poetic language to give life to his imaginative world; at the same time, his verse transcended personal concerns to serve as a testing ground for modern Italian poetry.

OTHER MAJOR WORKS

LONG FICTION: *Il piacere*, 1889 (*The Child of Pleasure*, 1898); *Giovanni Episcopo*, 1892 (*Episcopo and Company*, 1896); *L'innocente*, 1892 (*The Intruder*, 1898); *Il trionfo della morte*, 1894 (*The Triumph of Death*, 1896); *Le vergini della rocce*, 1896 (*The Maidens of the Rocks*, 1898); *Il fuoco*, 1900 (*The Flame of Life*, 1900); *Forse che si forse che no*, 1910; *La Leda senza cigno*, 1916 (*Leda Without Swan*, 1988).

SHORT FICTION: *Terra vergine*, 1882, 1884; *Il libro della vergini*, 1884; *San Pantaleone*, 1886; *Le novelle della Pescara*, 1902 (*Tales from My Native Town*, 1920); *Le faville del maglio*, 1924, 1928 (2 volumes).

PLAYS: *Sogno di un mattino di primavera*, pr., pb. 1897 (*The Dream of a Spring Morning*, 1902); *La città morta*, pb. 1898 (in French), pr. 1901 (in Italian; *The Dead City*, 1900); *Sogno di un tramonto d'autunno*, pb. 1898 (*The Dream of an Autumn Sunset*, 1904); *La Gioconda*, pr., pb. 1899 (*Gioconda*, 1902); *La gloria*, pr., pb. 1899; *Francesca da Rimini*, pr. 1901 (verse play; English translation, 1902); *La figlia di Jorio*, pr., pb. 1904 (*The Daughter of Jorio*, 1907); *La fiaccola sotto il moggio*, pr., pb. 1905 (verse play); *Più che l'amore*, pr. 1906; *La nave*, pr., pb. 1908 (verse play); *Fedra*, pr., pb. 1909 (verse play); *Le Martyre de Saint Sébastien*, pr., pb. 1911 (music by Claude Debussy, choreography by Ida Rubinstein); *Parisina*, pr., pb. 1913 (music by Pietro Mascagni); *La Pisanelle: Ou, La Mort parfumée*, pr., pb. 1913 (music by Ildebrando Rizzetti and Mascagni); *La Chèvrefeuille*, pr. 1913 (*The Honeysuckle*, 1915).

SCREENPLAY: *Cabiria*, 1914.

NONFICTION: *L'armata d'Italia*, 1888; *L'allegoria dell'autunno*, 1895; *Contemplazione della morte*, 1912; *Vite di uomini illustri e di uomini oscuri*, 1913; *La musica di Wagner e la genesi del "Parsifal,"* 1914; *Per la più grande Italia*, 1915; *La penultima ventura*, 1919, 1931 (2 volumes); *Il notturno*, 1921; *Il libro ascetico della giovane Itali*, 1926; *Le cento e cento e cento pagine del libro segreto di Gabriele D'Annunzio tentato di morire*, 1935; *Teneo te, Africa*, 1936; *Solus ad solam*, 1939.

MISCELLANEOUS: *Opera omnia*, 1927-1936; *Tutte le opere*, 1930-1965; *Tutte le opere*, 1931-1937; *Opera complete*, 1941-1943 (41 volumes); *Nocturne, and Five Tales of Love and Death*, 1988.

BIBLIOGRAPHY

Becker, Jared. *Nationalism and Culture: Gabriele D'Annunzio and Italy After the Reisorgimento*. New York: Peter Lang, 1994. A look at D'Annunzio and his links to Italian fascism that places his works within the history of his time. Bibliography and index.

Bonadeo, Alfredo. *D'Annunzio and the Great War*. Cranbury, N.J.: Associated University Presses, 1995. A scholarly examination of D'Annunzio's role and stance in World War I. Bibliography and index.

D'Annunzio, Gabriele. *Alcyone*. Edited by John Robert Woodhouse. New York: Manchester University Press, 1978. A collection of D'Annunzio's poetry in English with an informative introduction and annotations by the editor. Includes bibliography and index.

Gullace, Giovanni. *Gabriele D'Annunzio in France: A Study in Cultural Relations*. Syracuse, N.Y.: Syracuse University Press, 1966. Biographical and historical account of D'Annunzio's life.

Jullian, P. *D'Annunzio*. New York: Viking Press, 1973. An in-depth biography of D'Annunzio's career.

Ledeen, Michael Arthur. *D'Annunzio: The First Duce*. Rev. ed. New Brunswick, N.J.: Transaction, 2002. An examination of the political beliefs and activity of D'Annunzio. Bibliography and index.

Pieri, Giuliana. *The Influence of Pre-Raphaelitism on Fin de Siècle Italy: Art, Beauty, and Culture*. London: Maney Publishing for the Modern Humanities Reseach Association, 2007. Pieri's discussion of pre-Raphaelitism's influence contains a chapter on D'Annunzio.

Rhodes, A. *The Poet as Superman: G. D'Annunzio.* New York: McDowell, Obolensky, 1960. Narrative biography of D'Annunzio's life in politics and literature.

Valesio, Paolo. *Gabriele D'Annunzio: The Dark Flame.* New Haven, Conn.: Yale University Press, 1992. A critical examination of the works of D'Annunzio. Bibliography and index.

Woodhouse, John Robert. *Gabriele D'Annunzio: Defiant Archangel.* New York: Clarendon Press, 1998. An authoritative biography, presenting D'Annunzio's relationships with the worlds of Italian culture, theater, and politics. Includes extensive bibliographic references.

Luisetta Elia Chomel

DANTE

Born: Florence; May or June, 1265
Died: Ravenna (now in Italy); September 13 or 14, 1321
Also known as: Dante Alighieri Durante Alagherius

PRINCIPAL POETRY

La vita nuova, c. 1292 (*Vita Nuova*, 1861; better
  known as *The New Life*)
La divina commedia, c. 1320, 3 volumes (*The
  Divine Comedy*, 1802)

OTHER LITERARY FORMS

The prose works of Dante (DON-tay) are not usually taken as major literary achievements in themselves, although they provide many useful sidelights and clarifications to a reader of *The Divine Comedy*. Dante titled the work *Commedia*. It was Giovanni Boccaccio, forty years after Dante's death, who called the work *La divina commedia*, the name by which it is commonly known. *Il convivio* (c. 1307; *The Banquet*, 1887) was probably written between 1304 and 1307. An unfinished work of some seventy thousand words

in Italian prose, it is a commentary on three canzones or odes in which the poet proposes a theory of allegory for moral readings of his poetic compositions, so that it will be clear that virtue, not passion, is the topic. A digressive apologia, *The Banquet* is a mine of information about medieval literary culture. *De vulgari eloquentia* (c. 1306; English translation, 1890), a Latin prose work of nearly twelve thousand words, was probably composed in the period from 1304 to 1306. It is believed to be the first study ever written about vernacular language and poetic style and contains fascinating conjectures about the origin of language, Romance linguistics, verse forms, metrics, and poetic sounds. *De monarchia* (c. 1313; English translation, 1890; better known as *On World Government*) is a Latin prose work of nearly eighteen thousand words, probably written in 1312 and 1313; it is a series of arguments for world rule unified under the Holy Roman Empire. Dante's explanations of his ideas about the separate but complementary functions of church and state are particularly valuable. Only a few of Dante's letters survive, but several of them contain seminal passages of Dantean thought.

Many of Dante's lyrics are probably lost forever, but if the eighty or so miscellaneous ones attributed to him are a fair sampling of his efforts, he put his finest in *The New Life*. Many of these smaller poems show only average craftsmanship and are interesting because they reveal a poet who actively participated in his society. Some of the sonnets are exchanges of opinions with friends; six are part of an invective, a contest both socially and intellectually (which was common then), between Dante and Forese Donati. There are love poems to various ladies, some of them real individuals, others clearly allegorical. The lyrics show a very human poet, playful and experimental, heated by anger and love, embittered by exile.

ACHIEVEMENTS

Dante is among the greatest and most influential figures in the long history of Western literature, and no brief summary can do justice to the scope of his achievements. Perhaps his most enduring legacy has been the astonishing supply of signs and symbols for describing and evaluating inner experience that succeeding generations of readers have found in *The Divine Comedy*.

Dante was ultimately a mystic in his approach to God, but he wrote with systematic clarity about every spiritual event, stopping only at the point where language and reason had to be abandoned. Probably the most learned, articulate voice in the Christian West since Saint Augustine, Dante created a powerful mindscape able to reflect every movement of the soul. He did this without subjectivism and narcissism. Dante's vision is both a mirror of the self and a window onto the outside world, the cosmos, and the divine. His inward journey is recounted with great intensity and variety, but with no surprises, for that inner world is no more ambiguous or mysterious than the outer world, and Dante did not confront either world in a metaphysical void. His vision is not a hallucinatory refuge, but a site where the interconnectedness of all things can be rationally presented and the consequent need for spiritual discipline and social duty can be argued.

Dante responded to two primary imaginative impulses. One drove him to put all his experiences into an ordered relationship: eros, history, politics, and faith. Behind these ideal forms and schematizations lies a genuine love of the created world in all its density. Dante insists that experience be known as actual and metaphorical, and that virtue be attained through historical processes. The other impulse moved him continually beyond each part of his creation, always ascending, so that each epiphany becomes a curtain to be drawn back to reveal a higher one. One reads Dante with an awareness of the elaborations of each part and the upward movement of the whole.

Dante was the most important voice in the vernacular love lyric before William Shakespeare. Dante's mastery of lyric form and meter was unparalleled, and he used the intellectually demanding conventions of *dolce stil nuovo* ("sweet new style") with simplicity and ease. Had he taken Holy Orders, he could have given the world a pastoral voice worthy of John Donne or George Herbert. Dante's vocational decision was singular and uncompromising. He decided to be a citizen and a philosophical poet. The pains of citizenship fired the creator in him, so that he ultimately became the grandsire of Italian literature and indeed of much of Western literature written since his time. Dante excelled in the poetry of direct statement, in making

thought melodic. He found ways to energize moral knowledge, so that it could both persuade and delight. He never wrote to be obscure or ambiguous, but it is important to remember that he was addressing keen, well-educated medieval minds. His mastery of narrative technique and symbolic detail encourages some readers to evaluate his art for its own sake, but Dante always wrote to make the reader look beyond his words to the vision that they served.

BIOGRAPHY

Dante Alighieri was a citizen, and his city was Florence. Medieval Italian cities were for the most part independent states, free of feudal allegiances, with power based not on land, but on harbors, commerce, and industry. The nobility within these cities had gradually yielded power to the new bourgeois interests, but the traditional lines of that struggle were still evident, the nobles seeking support from the emperor and the bourgeois and popular elements tending to oppose the empire and join with the pope.

Those in the imperial faction were called Ghibelines, and those in the papal, or at least the anti-imperial faction, were known as Guelphs. The faction one chose to support often had more to do with current and particular needs and where one's friends and enemies were than with hereditary considerations. Dante's Florence was Guelph, which was enough to make rival cities support the Ghibelline cause—not that the Florentine Guelphs were able to live peaceably for long among themselves. A feud between two branches of a family in Pistoia, who called themselves "Whites" and "Blacks," spread to the Florentine upper classes. The Whites attracted the older families and papal supporters, while the Blacks tended to attract the newly rich commercial classes.

Little is known of Dante's youth in Florence. It is clear that he read widely among Provençal and contemporary Italian poets as well as classical Latin writers; his writing also reveals a practical knowledge of music and painting. He may have attended the University of Bologna. He fought in the Florentine army and seems to have enjoyed many friendships throughout his city. The most important event in his life occurred at a May Day festival when he was nine years old. There he first

Dante (Library of Congress)

saw Beatrice Portinari, who was eight at the time. They did not see each other again until nine years later, but Dante's devout fascination with her image and its significance lasted throughout his life. When she died in 1290, Dante diverted his grief by plunging into the difficult politics of the city and the study of philosophy. Between 1296 and 1301, the government of Florence entrusted him with high responsibilities in politics, finances, and diplomacy. His election as one of the city's six priors in the summer of 1300 exemplifies the public trust he enjoyed, a trust he justified when he validated the banishment of his close friend, the poet Guido Cavalcanti.

The year 1300 brought a convergence of several crises, political, spiritual, and economic, in the poet's life. So far as Dante's personal misfortunes are concerned, there are few details in the historical records. The larger event involved Charles de Valois, whom Pope Boniface had invited into Italy to help with the reconquest of

Sicily. Charles was permitted to enter Florence with all his troops, after assurances that he would not take part in the struggle between the Whites and the Blacks. Almost immediately, Charles allowed the Blacks to have the upper hand, at which point they began severe reprisals against the Whites. Dante was in Rome at the time as part of a delegation sent to secure guarantees from the pope that the French forces would not interfere in Florentine politics. Dante was accused in absentia of barratry, extortion, impiety, and disloyalty, accusations that ultimately carried with them the death sentence. Dante never returned to Florence. As an exile, he drew closer to the exiled Whites and Ghibellines, but neither negotiations nor armed conspiracy succeeded in restoring them to power in Florence. Dante became disenchanted and impatient with his fellow exiles, who resented him, and may even have blamed him for the military reversals they were suffering.

A restless Dante may have spent time in at least a half dozen Italian cities and perhaps Paris at one point. He was unable to right things between himself and Florence, so that he might return. When Henry VII was elected emperor, Dante envisioned an Italy unified under the empire, with an end to the destructive rivalry between church and state, but several key cities, aided by Florentine money, resisted Henry. When Dante angrily urged the emperor to conquer Florence, he probably eliminated his last chance of entering the city alive. Florence excluded him from the general amnesty offered to the Whites, and then withstood the emperor's assault; Henry died shortly thereafter. In 1315, probably because it needed talented citizens to help against a rival army, Florence declared itself willing to have Dante return, but he proudly rejected the terms. He was in Verona shortly after that, at work on *The Divine Comedy* under the patronage of Can Grande della Scala and his family. He spent his last days in Ravenna at the court of Guido da Polenta. In 1321, da Polenta sent him on a diplomatic mission to Venice. On his return, Dante fell desperately ill and did not recover. He was buried in Verona wearing Franciscan dress.

ANALYSIS

Dante wrote *The New Life* to give an essential history of his own spirit, which was first aroused, then illuminated by his love for a woman. Here together are the narcissism and ecstasy of youth with the intricate design and perceptions of an older, uncompromising intelligence. The work consists of forty-two passages of prose commentary in which thirty-one poems are set at varying intervals. There are twenty-five sonnets, five canzones, and one ballad. The reader is not meant to abide the prose patiently until he reaches the next poem. Medieval poets believed that it should be possible to state in prose the core idea of any poem they created. Furthermore, no poem existed for its own sake— that is, solely for an aesthetic purpose. The prose keeps the reader in touch with the invisible realities and spiritual implications that were far more important to Dante than personal expression or artistic technique. The poems of *The New Life* describe and deal with romantic and sexual passion. Within the close boundaries and strict internal laws of poetic form, they either exemplify the point Dante is making in prose, or give way to a prose examination of the meanings beneath their surfaces. The poetic voice contains the original turmoil; the prose voice carries the more complete understanding of later personal reflection. The reader is thus able to share in the warmth of the original feelings and the sequence of epiphanies about them.

The topic of *The New Life* is love-suffering, which the poet will complain about but never abandon, for love-suffering is a way of life—indeed, part of the credentials of a noble person. The nobles whom Dante addressed constituted an elite, intelligent group who shared a sensitivity about love and who communicated easily with one another about its subtle doctrines. Traditionally, the medieval love poet did not concentrate on the real presence of the lady so much as on his own feelings about her. The poet would cry out against the upheavals his passions were causing and voice his fear and resentment of her coldness and elevated distance. Despite it all, he would vow to continue his martyrdom. These conventions of refined love were distorted and exaggerated, but they proved fit equipment for capturing the values of romantic experience. They take the reader past appearances into mental and spiritual realities that a camera eye can never see. The new ideas about love, which began emerging less than a century before Dante was born, caused a revolution in the sensibilities of Western European culture. Dante mastered them, then added a revolution of his own. He transcended the devouring egotism of his predecessors by identifying his own erotic drive and the mental processes it stimulated with the Divine Love that beckons to every soul. The lady thus becomes not merely the outer boundary of the lover's consciousness but a mediating presence between self and Deity. No longer a mirror of the poet's feelings, she stands as a window onto the infinite beauty of the Divine Presence and the way of salvation. *The New Life* records Dante's discovery of what he owed to several "God-bearing" ladies whom he encountered on his journey, Beatrice foremost among them.

The work begins with the intelligent and chastened voice of experience: Dante has learned to read the book of Nature, and he knows that the mystical significance of numbers can validate his spiritual discoveries. He has found a *vita nuova*, a new and miraculous life epitomized by the number nine, which the word *nuova* also signifies. Nine is the square of three, a number that, to the medieval imagination, represented perfection and the spiritual life. Dante explains how he first saw Beatrice when she was in her ninth year of life, and not again until nine years later, at the ninth hour of the day. Numbers are the clues to what Heaven has planned for him, so that when Dante writes this book of personal memory, made according to the laws of sequence and cause and effect, the reader is also aware of the perennial present of an unchanging ideal realm. For example, in section 3 of *The New Life*, Dante has a dream that is not only an erotic fantasy but also a prophecy. After he has seen Beatrice for the second time, the God of Love appears in a fiery cloud carrying Beatrice, who is asleep and flimsily clothed. Love wakens her and skillfully makes her eat of Dante's burning heart. Then the God begins to weep and folds his arms around her, and the two ascend heavenward. Dante notes that he had this dream at the first of the last nine hours of the night.

Thus, the historical event of the lady's death, through the significance of numbers, reflects eternity.

The structure of Dante's book of memory suggests infinite harmony and reconciliation, particularly through the numbers three and nine. The thirty-one poems of *The New Life* fall into three groups, each group attached to one of the three canzones, or longer poems. At the center of the second or middle group is a canzone with four poems on either side of it. The first and third groups each have ten poems and one canzone; in the first group, the poems precede the canzone, and in the second, they follow it. Besides the obvious symmetry of the entire structure, there are nine poems in the middle group. If Dante had intended the first poem to be an introduction and the thirty-first to be an epilogue, the numbers nine and one would dominate the plan, although this is only a reasonable conjecture. Of more significance is the merger of numerical sign and literary idea in the middle group: The canzone that is at the exact center of the work refers to Beatrice's possible death with imagery traditionally associated with the Crucifixion of Christ. Thus, the center of the poet's book of memory and the center of Christian history are connected, through the analogy drawn between Beatrice and Christ.

The cast of *The New Life* is small, and the narrative is almost without setting and background. There are really only two actors: the poet and the feminine presence who provides all the imaginative milestones in his life. Some women are useful distractions to prying eyes, so that he can conceal his true love's identity. The death of one of them tunes his grief for the eventual death of Beatrice, as does the death of Folco Portinari, Beatrice's father. If one takes this little history of a pilgrim's soul as an analogy for God's created time, where events can be understood either to anticipate or to look back toward Christ's Passion, death, and Resurrection, one immediately appreciates the suggestiveness of the format. When Dante contemplates the possibility of Beatrice's death, it seems to him that the sun grows dark and violent earthquakes occur. The next dream presents Beatrice following her beautiful friend, Giovanna, just as Christ followed John the Baptist. Her death will be comparably momentous and fruitful for his own life and later ages. Not that these insights en-

abled the poet to bear the actual death of Beatrice; the sonnets and canzones that follow that event are almost all to which a lyric poet can aspire, fusing intellect and pathos so perfectly that readers are reminded how imperfectly united their own souls are; at the same time, they are uplifted by the unity Dante has found. For long moments, the reader can believe that the alleged incompatibility between poetry and philosophy is but a jealous rumor.

As Dante decorates his own love story with signs of what he would come to understand about it in retrospect, he also means to show the progress of his own mind as events teach and shape him. He remembers himself as a self-preoccupied courtly lover, more educated and intellectually demanding than the troubadour poets from whom he learned, but, like them, emaciated by love-suffering, anxious, easily embarrassed, inclined to enjoy nursing his wounds in private, and completely under the rule of his master, Love. When, out of concern for her good name, Beatrice refuses to recognize him, he takes to his bed like a punished child. Then he begins to realize the limitations of this infantile mode. That night in a dream, the god appears and tells Dante that not he, but Love, is at the center of things, equidistant from all points on the circumference. Until he can accept the possibilities of this subtler and more comprehensive definition, the paradoxically painful and pleasurable qualities of his subjective experience will continue to vex him. Then, some town women, gently ridiculing his emaciated condition, suggest logically what Love had put more mysteriously: Happiness can come from the words he uses to praise Beatrice, not the words that concentrate on his own condition. With this nobler theme, his new life begins.

The famous canzone from section 19 that begins "Donne ch'avete intelletto d'amore," or "Ladies who can reason out Love's ways," describes the source of the lady's nobleness and perfection, which make all in Heaven want her with them, so that Heaven itself can be more perfect. On Earth, her glance can banish an evil intention or transform it to a noble one, and the worthy will feel salvation from having looked at her, for God has granted that whoever has talked with her will not come to a bad end. Having shifted his attention to a site outside himself, and having identified Beatrice as an emissary of Divine Love (able like it to create something where nothing has existed), Dante now has a talismanic axiom that will help him meet all future experience—even Beatrice's death, for everything coming to him from her will lead heavenward.

After Beatrice's death, a disconsolate Dante is temporarily distracted by the earthly beauty and compassion of a lady who looks at him sympathetically, but a vision of Beatrice resolves his inner struggle between reason and sensuality, and from then on the image of Beatrice is all he contemplates. The last sonnet of *The New Life* tells how his sigh passed the world's outermost sphere, moved by a new intelligence to the radiance of Beatrice in Heaven. When the sigh tries to report what it saw, its words are too subtle for Dante's comprehension; he is certain only that he hears Beatrice's name again and again. The highest and most serene image of the poet's renewed life is, paradoxically, beyond words. In the final section, Dante tells of a miraculous vision that included sights so profound that he made the resolution to say no more about Beatrice until he could find a suitably elevated vehicle. He closes with the wish that the Lord will grant him a few more years, so that he can compose a work about her that will contain things never said about any woman.

A diary unlike any written before it, *The New Life* was the work of a poet ready for sublime tasks who chose to review the development of his spiritual vision and poetic powers as the first step in the direction of carrying out those tasks. A finished masterpiece in its own right, it also served as a prelude to the greatest sustained poetic achievement in the West since Homer.

THE DIVINE COMEDY

There probably never has been a piece of literary imagination as great in scope, as intricate in relationships among its parts, as fastidiously shaped to the smallest detail as Dante's *The Divine Comedy*. Besides the exacting challenge of maintaining poetic intensity for some fourteen thousand lines, there were the perils of dealing with interpretations of religious doctrine and Holy Writ in a fictional context. Even more perilous was the interpretation of Divine Justice, as it applied to specific historical incidents and individuals. Dante's genius and pious imagination flourished among these boundaries and obstacles. He used the appearances of

the created world to describe the human heart in a theocentric universe. The three-part narrative pictures the soul deprived of God, in hope of God, and with God. Dante needed a design to mirror the unchanging realities beyond time and space, and he needed an action that would be an imitation of the soul's movements toward these realities. The symmetrical design of the entire work reflects divine perfection, as does its three-fold narrative division and three-line stanzas. Each part, *Inferno Purgatorio* (*Purgatory*), and *Paradiso* (*Paradise*), is divided into thirty-three cantos. With the introductory canto, these total one hundred, a number that also traditionally suggested divine unity and perfection.

The world of Dante's *The Divine Comedy* is vertical. The reader always moves downward or upward with the poet: the spiral descent into Hell, the climb up the purgatorial mountain, then up through the various planetary spheres, until the notions of movement up and down are no longer pertinent. The medieval model of the universe was similarly vertical, with Heaven above, Earth at the middle, and Hell below. Everything in God's creation was located at some point or other on a chain or ladder of being, which descended from his divine presence to the lowest form of inert matter. Each being was put at a particular step or degree on this scale, so that it could realize whatever purpose the Creator intended for it, but each thing or being was also understood in terms of what was above it and what was below it. The three realms of Dante's *The Divine Comedy* are vertically related, and each realm has its own vertical plan. The reader is continually urged to compare each spectacle with the one viewed previously and to ponder in retrospect its connection to the spectacle that follows it.

Writing a comedy was also imitating the world, at least as Dante used the term "comedy." In the medieval conception, comedy presented the happy resolution of a difficult situation. Thus, time and history could be seen as parts of a comic action, because Providence, working behind the superficial chaos of Fortune's wheel, would ultimately turn every earthly change to good. Human time and all its pains began with the Fall of Adam, but that Fall looked forward to Christ's redemptive sacrifice. The sacrifice of Christ, who is often referred to as the "Second Adam," made it possible for the pattern of each life to be comic—that is, for humankind to conquer sin and win salvation. Dante's *The Divine Comedy* takes place at the end of Holy Week, during the most spiritually intense hours of the Christian year. For a time, darkness appears to triumph, as the God-Man is slain and buried, but out of seeming defeat comes a victorious descent into Hell and a resurrection that is the archetype of every spiritual rebirth that will come after it. When Dante descends into Hell on Good Friday and reaches Purgatory on Easter morning of the year 1300, the reader contemplates that holier comedy thirteen hundred years before.

The Divine Comedy offers more than structural symmetry and Christian values. It is also an imitation of the swarming variousness of the world of time and space: dreams, boasts, accusations, haunting beauties and catastrophes, wisdom, and reconciliation. The opening words hurry the reader into the narrator's dilemma and impasse, until, ninety-nine cantos later, the vision moves beyond human language and sensation. In his treatment of things invisible, Dante makes the reader touch with understanding almost every texture of earthly existence. To the medieval mind, the world was a book to be read, but a book could imitate the world by being an exhaustive compendium of information about geography, history, the nature of flight, even the spots on the moon. Dante's imagination is alert and curious, not satisfied with building a warehouse of facts. Dante further wishes the reader to visualize and experience the logistics of every step of the journey, feeling the heat, smelling the foulness, seeing different kinds of light and darkness, confronting the monstrosities, and struggling along the broken causeways.

The Divine Comedy is Dante's report of a journey he took into the anagogical realm of existence—that is, the afterlife—to witness the rewards and punishments that God's justice apportions to humankind on the basis of choices freely made in life. Dante himself said this much about his masterpiece. The reader learns while watching him learn, and because of that, even in the *Inferno*, moving toward the center of Earth, the place farthest from God, there is a sense of the intelligence and soul expanding. The journey around which the narrative is constructed is also about the movement of every individual life. It intended to provide equipment for living in a City of God on Earth until the grander city of Jerusalem can be attained.

Although the meticulous physical detail encourages the reader to imagine himself or herself on a journey in time and space, the reader is moving in a mindscape, a spectacle of the sinful human heart. Nowhere in Hell is he or she shown an attitude or act of which every living soul is not capable. Dante's descent involves a lowering of self through the admission of fault and capacity for fault, and the realization that the difference between human sin and Satan's sin is one of degree rather than kind. Self-accusation and contrition make cleansing and regeneration possible, so that the climb to salvation can begin. Dante makes himself fall so that he may rise a stronger man, but his is a controlled fall. The vision of Hell could lead to despair and insane fascination, but with a guide who has been there before, Dante can have this terrible knowledge and survive. Having a second individual on the journey is also a useful narrative strategy, because the guide can interact dramatically with Dante the pilgrim and provide a normative presence, so that Dante the poet need not stultify the narrative with endless digressions about what the pilgrim cannot see.

That Dante should choose Vergil, the greatest of all Latin poets, to accompany him is not surprising. In one way or another, Vergil's writings had nourished every medieval poet. In his epic, the *Aeneid* (c. 29-19 B.C.E.; English translation, 1553), Vergil had described a hero's visit to the underworld, and in that sense had been there once himself. His medieval admirers believed him to be a saint, a moralist, a prophet, even a magician. He was also a pagan and, as Dante strictly reasoned, had not been saved, but he was thought to embody natural wisdom unaided by revelation, which would make him a fit companion for a trip into the region of the damned. Vergil was also a poet of the Empire. He used the story of the fall of Troy to celebrate the founding of Rome and all the achievements of the divinely favored nation that followed it. Vergil predicted an era of world order and prosperity under Roman imperial rule. Many Christians believed that he foresaw in one of his pastorals the coming of the Redeemer and the Christian era. In his essay *On World Government*, Dante had argued that the Empire and the

Church were two discrete but complementary modes by which divine purposes could be realized in human history, one emphasizing reason, the other revelation. Vergil epitomizes both the grandeur and the limitations of that gift of natural reason. He travels with Dante as far as he—that is, reason—can, and then is replaced by Beatrice, who personifies the light of divine revelation denied to pagans.

PART I, INFERNO

The world of *The Divine Comedy* is so wide and various that a comprehensive introduction to it is not possible in a brief essay, but canto 1 of the *Inferno* is a useful place to begin observing how Dante's composition works. It is Maundy Thursday night, the day before Good Friday in the year 1300. The poet's first words are about personal time, the midpoint of life at which he awakened to discover himself in a dark wood, with no idea where the right road was. Because the very first line refers to a stage of life, the reader is not likely to imagine a search through a literal wood for an actual road. A few lines later, as Dante painfully recalls the harshness and recalcitrance of the forest, it becomes clear that he is talking about his own former willfulness. As horrid as this time of error was, says Dante, good came of it. This mixture of fear and optimism sets the tone perfectly for the *Inferno* and for the rest of *The Divine Comedy*. The opening lines involve the reader in the experiences of another being as though they were his or her own (which, in a sense they are). Eschewing biographical or historical detail, Dante presents only the essential, the elementary: At a crossroads in life, another human realized that he or she had lost touch with an important part of himself or herself.

The poet does not know exactly how he lost his way in that wood, but the torpor from which he suffered at the time was obviously spiritual. Struggling out of the wood, he is aware of a steep mountain, and as he looks up at the sun that lights the ways of men, he feels some comfort. Somehow, his awareness of his own poor spiritual state and the grace of a loving God have helped him through a dangerous maze, a place, he notes, from which no one has escaped, once entrapped there. Clearly, the forest is a form of spiritual death, or sin, but all the pilgrim has done so far is avoid the worst. To climb the mountain and achieve the spiritual perfection

it implies, he will need to gain control of the complicated forces within himself.

A quick-stepping leopard first impedes his progress, but a look at the morning sun, as beautiful as it was during the first moments of Creation, restores Dante's hopes, which are again shattered when a lion, head held high, approaches menacingly. Most intimidating is a gaunt, ravenous wolf, which Dante says has conquered many men. The wolf begins to edge Dante back down the path into the dark forest. Dante does not say what each of these beasts symbolizes, but probably they represent types of sinful living. This notion exists because, to the medieval mind, beasts usually stood for the lower or unreasonable parts of the personal hierarchy. The leopard seems to have the flair and energy of youth, the lion the more powerful intellectual pride that can dominate later years, and the wolf the avarice for possessions that comfort advanced years. Any one of these sins could weigh down a traveler throughout life. Dante makes the point that inability to deal with the three brings despair and spiritual disaster. The light of the sun offers encouragement; grace is available, but it has to be used. As he stumbles downward, Dante sees a shadow. Although it seems unaccustomed to speaking, the shadow answers when Dante calls to it for help, just as the way out of the woods appeared when Dante admitted to himself that he was lost. The shadow is Vergil, who stands for the natural good sense that Dante had allowed to lie dormant.

Vergil does not want Dante to take on the she-wolf directly, for she has been the ruin of many. There is another way out of the wood, Vergil says. The person who confronts his or her own demons without a guide or a strategy is inviting failure. Dante first needs to use his reason to understand the nature of unforgiven sin and its punishment. Then he can visit the purgatorial realm, where the vestiges of forgiven sins are removed, and finally a worthier guide will show him the vision of ultimate reward. Vergil also cautions Dante against becoming preoccupied with the sins of his fellow countrymen. In time, says Vergil, a greyhound will come to chase the avaricious wolf from Italy. Whether this greyhound represents a great earthly prince or some divine apocalypse is not clear. The central point of this first canto is that, beginning with his own conscience, then using the legible signs in the book of the natural world and the revival of his own rational faculty, Dante is ready to journey toward whatever perfection he can hope to attain.

The above remarks are not an ambitious reading of obscure material. Dante saw clearly and wrote to be understood. He did, however, believe that it was natural and beneficial to require an audience to be alert to more than the literal in what he said. An extremely sophisticated tradition of biblical interpretation had prepared his audience to do that and to take pleasure in understanding more than surface meanings in a piece of writing. If the created world was a fair field of symbols, and if the revealed word could be read on several metaphorical levels, why not a story of the mind's journey to God? Thus, Dante wrote allegorical fiction, in which what is said is frequently intended to mean something else. The "literal" aspect of allegorical narrative is usually the least important, for it is the sense of the figurative and the symbolic that the author wants to exercise. The reader needs a fine set of interchangeable lenses to see the multiple levels.

Dante's Hell is in the center of Earth, which was thought to be the center of the created world, but in a theocentric universe, Earth was really on the outside looking in. The lowest point in Dante's Hell is therefore the farthest possible point from God; it is frozen, signifying the total absence of human or divine love. This Hell is fashioned from religious tradition and popular belief. Spectacular as some of the punishments are, the chief source of pain is indescribable: the eternal loss of the sight of God.

Although many modern readers reject the idea of eternal punishment, medieval Christian thinkers had concluded that an all-perfect Being had to embody justice as well as mercy. When an individual died, the reign of mercy ended and that of justice began. In this view, the damned have willfully rejected the power of grace, the teachings of the Church, and the Sacraments. If after this, God relented, he would be unjust. Justice also determines the nature of the punishments and the consequent degree of suffering. The punishment Dante imagines for each sin is a symbolic definition of the sin itself, which the sinner has to repeat for eternity. Only the living can learn from this infernal repetition. For all

the uproar and movement in Hell, nothing changes. A medieval definition of change would be the movement of things toward the ideal form that God intended for them; not a single gesture in Hell does that.

Dante's Hell is an inverted hierarchy, with each level revealing a more serious sin below. Hell has nine circles, in addition to an outer vestibule. The upper five circles contain punishments for sins committed through misdirected or uncontrolled emotions; they reflect the perils of natural vitality and appetites, as the image of the leopard suggested. Next, behind the walls of the city of Dis, are crimes that require a stronger determination of the will to disrupt the plan of existence. The violence that appears here (circles six and seven) may be connected with the lion that threatened Dante earlier. The eighth circle is a long sheer drop below this and contains the violators of the various kinds of promise-keeping that make social life possible. The more complicated frauds of treason and betrayal in the ninth and lowest circle may be related to the ravenous wolf. Far more ingenious than the schematic layout of Hell is Dante's ability to keep a sense of spontaneity and discovery in what could have been merely a dutiful walk through a catalog of sin. Dante's skill at variation, which every medieval poet would have coveted, is perhaps the chief source of the poem's excellence. Even in *Purgatory*, where the treatment of each sin runs to a pattern, Dante somehow handles every section uniquely.

One of the sources of variety and sense of forward movement in the *Inferno* is the interaction between Dante and Vergil. Vergil chides, encourages, and revives his pupil as they travel through Hell. The pilgrim Dante becomes stronger and more sure of himself, less frightened by the nightmarish circus about him and more able to despise intelligently the evil he sees. At first, Dante does not believe himself to be fit for such a journey, but when Vergil tells him that Beatrice wills it, he immediately agrees to follow. Two cantos later, in Limbo, the greatest pagan poets are welcoming him to their company. Whenever he has need of Reason, Vergil is always there—even literally at one point—to lift and carry him out of danger. The danger and inhospitableness increase as the two proceed deeper. Everything they see is an inversion or distortion of Charity, the love of God and neighbor in which every Christian act is rooted. At the start, Charon, the underworld boatman, refuses to ferry Dante and Vergil across the river Acheron; in the ninth and lowest circle, Count Ugolino devours the head of the bishop whose betrayal caused the Count and his sons to be starved to death. The reader becomes increasingly aware of Dante's obsession with the two Florences: the City of God on Earth that he wanted it to become and the ungrateful zone of corruption it had been to him. In his darkest hour, Dante was nearer to Beatrice and all that she stood for than Florence would ever be to Jerusalem. Almost until the final instants of *Paradise*, Dante rails against the city that nourished and exiled him.

Somewhat like a gothic cathedral, *The Divine Comedy* is a huge structural support covered with crafted sections of varying size and content, each section somehow finding a place in the totality. A very limited sampling of sections might begin with Upper Hell, where the sins of the incontinent are punished. It may be surprising to find that lust is the first sin viewed here, which makes it the least serious offense in Hell. Medieval moralists tended to treat sexual love as a natural behavior in need of a supernatural perspective. This is quite different from treating sexuality as a taboo, as later ages would. Even so, the reader should consider the mixture of feelings within Dante—who began as a lyric poet in the tradition of erotic courtship—as he watches the souls of the lustful tossed on a roaring black wind, an image of the uncontrollable passion to which they surrendered their reasoning power. They are like flocks of starlings and cranes borne up and down forever, shrieking as they go. The scene conveys the restlessness of human passion and the crowded commonness of the sin itself. The world's most famous lovers are in those flocks: Dido, Helen, Paris, and Tristram. Seeing them, Dante grows dizzy with sympathy.

Two of the lovers are still together, dovelike as they waft along hand in hand. They are Paolo and Francesca, who suffered and died for love at the hands of Francesca's husband. Francesca delivers a courtly lyric celebrating the power of love that brought her and Paolo together, a lyric that ends with the assurance that damnation awaits the one who murdered them. Deeply moved by the lovers' tragedy, Dante asks to know

more. What he hears is not the spell of romance but a rather ordinary process of young lechery: leisure time, suggestive reading, and the knowing glances that precede coupling. Dante has to be true to the old conventions of love here, the ones he transformed in *The New Life*; he also has to maintain the clear-eyed antiromanticism of Christian morality. It is all too much for the pilgrim, who falls into a dead swoon, until he awakes to find himself in the third circle, with the Gluttonous.

Like the Lustful, the Gluttonous have allowed themselves to be controlled and distorted by a natural urge. The image Dante uses to describe the punishment here is startling in the manner of a metaphysical conceit. First, he describes a cold, heavy rain soaking a putrid earth. Cerberus, the three-headed watchdog of the Underworld, is there, each head gorging on the souls of the Gluttonous as they wallow in the mud. To distract the monstrous beast, Vergil throws filthy mud down its throats. Cold rain seems to have no connection with excessive eating, until one considers the motivation that is often behind that excess: self-centered loneliness with indiscriminate sieges of oral gratification. One Ciacco ("Fats"), a fellow Florentine, addresses Dante from the slime. He vents his own alienation and misery, then gives an acid survey of the rottenness that will continue to seep from their native city.

The metaphoric effect is equally powerful in canto 12, when Dante and Vergil enter the pathless wood of the suicides, where the souls have been turned to dead trees that bleed at the touch and are fed on by Harpies, who represent the guilt of self-destruction. Through this same wood run the souls of persons who in life madly spent all they owned. They are being chased and torn to pieces by hunting dogs. Dante's decision to put suicides here among souls who have been violent against themselves seems reasonable. That he should sense a comparable wish for death among those who are impatient to destroy their wealth shows a marvelous awareness of the darker corners of the human situation. Like the cold rain on the Gluttonous, it is a superb reach of intelligence and intuition.

The last four cantos describe the ninth and lowest circle of Hell, which contains the perpetrators of the subtlest, most complicated frauds imaginable. First described are the giants of classical legend who tried to scale Heaven and challenge Jove, and the biblical Nimrod, who directed the attempt to build the Tower of Babel. At the bottom of Hell's pit is the frozen lake Cocytus. There, the traitors, who through intellect and will achieved the most drastic perversion of love, are frozen in unrepentant attitudes of hatred. These are the souls of those who betrayed kin, fatherland, guests, and, lowest of all, those who betrayed their lords. Fed ultimately by all the rivers of Hell, the ice itself may be blood-colored. Tears, a symbol of compassion, freeze instantly there. The famous agony of Count Ugolino of Pisa, who, with his children, starved to death in prison, mirrors perfectly these pitiless surroundings. Ugolino and the others are at Hell's bottom because they violated the promise-keeping that is the root of every social and spiritual relationship, for humans become ethical on the basis of their fidelity to promises of loyalty, hospitality, and the like. The cannibalism that the traitor Ugolino enacts as he devours the skull of the person who betrayed him suggests the ultimate negation of social behavior, where humanity and bestiality are no longer distinguishable.

Satan, the angel once nearest to God, now occupies the lowest extremity of Hell, held in ice up to his chest. This is the summary image of the first third of *The Divine Comedy*. At the center of the heart of darkness is this living death, presided over by the first of God's creatures to defy him. Satan has three faces here, red, yellow, and black, which probably refer to the races of humanity through which his first evil is continued. A parody of the Triune God, his face is the inversion of the spiritual number three. Two batlike wings flap under each face, making a freezing wind that keeps the lake frozen. There is no other movement observable here, unless one includes the tears from those three pairs of eyes, which drip in a bloody mixture from Satan's chins. The draft from his wings evidently freezes all tears but his own. If these tears and blood, which are appalling reminders of the sacramental water and blood that flowed from the side of the Redeemer on the first Good Friday, represent the misery that sin causes, they reveal no contrition whatsoever, for the wings are operated by a will that is still rebellious and an icy egotism that will never cease to oppose God. Even the blindly passionate wind that heaved Paolo and

Francesca about would be a welcome alternative to those hopeless gusts.

Each of Satan's mouths chews on a famous traitor. Situated highest, the mouth of the red face tortures the most notorious traitor of all: Judas Iscariot. In the lower mouths are the two others who make up this Satanic Eucharist, Brutus and Cassius, who subverted God's plan for world empire under Rome by assassinating Julius Caesar. In Dante's conception, sacred and imperial history, although they are separate, are both founded on God's will, and therefore must stand responsible before his justice. In this sense, the things of God and the things of Caesar must ultimately converge. In the midst of these ironies is the supreme irony of Satan's powerlessness, which makes him, for all his gigantic size, ridiculous. He and the giants are mastodons in a museum. Dante and Vergil climb down this hulk out of Hell and see the stars for the first time since early Friday morning.

When Vergil and Dante have climbed down past Satan's navel, they have reached the point farthest from God. What was below is now above them, and Satan appears upside down, a fitting final aspect of the Arch-Rebel. The pair are now in Earth's southern hemisphere, facing an island with a mountain called Purgatory, formed of the land that retreated to avoid Satan when he fell. The Earthly Paradise is on the top of that mountain. It was closed at the expulsion of Adam and Eve, but since Christ's death it has been open to souls purified in Purgatory. Actually, Scripture gives few specific details about Hell, and none at all about Purgatory.

In Purgatory, medieval Christians believed, the residual effects of sins admitted, confessed, and forgiven were removed before the soul entered Paradise. The soul permitted to enter Purgatory was saved and would surely see God someday. Furthermore, these souls could be helped by the prayers of people still on Earth and could enjoy communication with the suffering souls around them. This is quite different from the isolation and hopeless sense of loss in Hell.

PART 2, PURGATORY

If the topic of the *Inferno* is the just punishment of sin, the topic of *Purgatory* is the discipline of perfection. It is a more serenely organized piece of writing, with a pace that is generally more constant. After the terraces of the ante-Purgatory, the mountain has seven cornices, each devoted to purging the stain of one of the deadly sins. Every cornice contains a penance, a meditation, a prayer, a guardian angel, and a benediction. The ascent from one area to another is often accompanied by a brief essay on some topic in natural or moral philosophy. The idea of an ante-Purgatory was probably Dante's own. In its two terraces are the souls of those who delayed repenting until the moment of their death. Having waited too long in life to do what was necessary to be saved, they must wait for some time before they can begin the ascent. In the first terrace are the souls who, although excommunicated by the Church, delayed repentance until the last moments of life. In terrace two are those who delayed similarly, although they always lived within the Church; included here are the souls of the indolent, the unshriven, and the preoccupied.

Saint Peter's Gate is the entrance to Purgatory proper. Three steps of Penance lead up to it: confession, contrition, and satisfaction. At the gate, an angelic custodian inscribes seven *P*'s signifying the Seven Deadly Sins (*peccatum* is the Latin for "sin"), on the forehead of each soul. The letters will be erased one at a time as the soul passes from cornice to cornice. The Seven Deadly Sins were the most widely used description of human evil in the Middle Ages. Somehow or other, every transgression was thought to have come from one of those seven: Lust, Gluttony, Avarice, Sloth, Wrath, Envy, and Pride. Each cornice has a penance appropriate to the stain left by one of those sins. The soul may be made to perform a penitential exercise that symbolically describes the effects of the sin committed, or as counterbalance it may have to perform actions that suggest the virtue directly opposed to the sin. Sometimes souls are assigned to do both.

The meditation in each cornice consists of a whip, or example of the opposing virtue, and a bridle, which is made up of horrid instances of the sin in question. These are followed by a prayer taken from the Psalms or hymns of the Church, then by a benediction (one of the Beatitudes), which is spoken by the angel of the cornice, who then erases a *P* from the soul's forehead. The soul then moves up the Pass of Pardon to the next cornice.

The boundary line for a Hell or Purgatory can be difficult for even a severely legalistic planner to draw. Those souls closest to the entrance of Hell had lost all hope of salvation, though by a narrow margin. In *Purgatory*, those closest to the boundary have avoided that loss by a similarly narrow margin. Dante's Hell begins with the neutrals, those who chose not to choose. They are a faceless mob condemned to chase a whirling standard forever. Next is the Limbo of the unbaptized and virtuous pagans. Dante could not imagine salvation for them, even though their poetry and ideas had nurtured him, but neither could he condemn them for light denied. Thus, the virtuous pagans appear in a dim but pastoral setting, and the poets among them admit Dante to their number. The first terrace of Purgatory also involves fine distinctions, but ones in which the poet is less personally involved. To be excommunicated was not a sin in itself, but a person who was separated from the Church by a sin that called for excommunication, and who put off repentance until the last minutes of life, was grasping salvation by its coattails. Appropriately, these excommunicates and the other late repentants in the second terrace are the only souls in Purgatory who have to undergo a punishment—that is, a wait. All the others are cheerfully engaged in a healing process that will continue until they are ready for Paradise.

Ascending through the cornices of Purgatory is in one way like backing up the spiral road out of Hell. The lowest part of Hell, where the proudest act ever committed is being punished, corresponds to the first cornice, where the stains of pride are being removed. The cornice of Lust, the least of the Seven Deadly Sins, is nearest the top of the mountain, as Lust was farthest from the frozen lake at the bottom of Hell. The descent became increasingly difficult for Dante and Vergil as each circle delivered something more bleak or dangerous. The trek upward in Purgatory is a happy jettisoning of old heaviness, done in the midst of general enthusiasm and encouragement. Instead of Charon, who grudgingly ferried the two across Acheron, an angel of the Lord lightly takes a hundred singing souls across to the island where Mount Purgatory stands. Indeed, the change of mood exhilarates Dante so thoroughly that he all but loses his sense of mission as he listens to the singing of Casella, an old friend and musician.

There are subtle changes in Vergil's presence at this point. He is temporarily eclipsed in the early cantos by the appearance of the astringent Cato, who represents the discipline that will be needed for the lively chores ahead. Moreover, Vergil has not been here before, so although he is still a fount of good sense, he is seeing everything for the first time. He can only partly answer certain questions Dante asks, such as the one about the efficacy of human prayer. Dante will have to wait for Beatrice to explain such matters fully, and interpreters will come forth intermittently to talk about what Vergil cannot be expected to recognize.

Dante and Vergil emerge from Hell on Easter morning at dawn and reach the island shortly after that. They are in the second terrace of ante-Purgatory when the sun begins to set. Night climbing is not permitted, so the two are led to a beautiful valley, where the souls of preoccupied rulers dwell. The cycle of day and night and the natural beauty of the valley indicate their presence still on Earth, in the middle state. The significance of not attempting a penitential climb in the dark is fairly clear, but as night falls, two angels descend to keep watch over the valley. They immediately chase off a serpent who has marauded there. Dante is brilliantly suggestive here. The sentry angels are dressed in green, which is a sign of both hope and penance, but that they should be there at all is puzzling. The point seems to be that, at least in ante-Purgatory, temptation is still a possibility. The fiery swords that the angels bear and the presence of the enemy serpent recall the Fall in Eden, and indeed the theme at the core of this journey is the return to that garden and man's state before he sinned.

The morning dream that Dante has in that valley is also charged with details that add significance to all that will happen. Having his own share of Old Adam's nature, he says, he nods off, and in the first light, the time of holy and prophetic dreams, he sees a golden eagle in midair, about to swoop toward its prey. He thinks of Zeus snatching the boy Ganymede up to Heaven, but then he conjectures that this eagle must always hunt here, so it need not have anything to do with him. Then the eagle comes for him like lightning and takes him up to the circle of fire that surrounds Earth, where they burn together with a heat that wakens him and ends the dream. He finds that Saint Lucy has carried him to Saint Peter's Gate—the beginning of Purgatory proper.

This dream illuminates the rest of the story until the final line, although it is possible to interpret its simpler elements at once. Lucy is one of the three ladies (the other two are Beatrice and the Blessed Virgin) who decided to help Dante out of the dark wood earlier. Lucy personifies the beckoning power of Divine Light by literally transporting Dante to the start of this second phase of his journey. The golden eagle, a bird sacred to Jove and also an emblem of the empire, is doing a comparable thing. Here are two faces of the Godhead, one maternally encouraging, the other ravenously assertive, together making up a richly complicated insight that comes not from a Vergilian lecture or the remark of a dead soul, but from a dream, where the discourse is intuitive and mystical. The progress up the mountain will for the most part involve intellectual and ethical knowledge, but as it is happening the totality of Dante's being will be moving toward a Divine Love that is beyond language and rational understanding, and for which a burning heaven is the most appropriate metaphor. The movement up the cornices will be clear and steady, so uniform as to be tedious at times. It will require the light of day, but the total movement of the self with the Deity is perhaps best reflected in dream light, because Dante is giving his readers not only an encyclopedia of morality but also an imitation of a psychological process.

The removal of the vestiges of sin will render the soul fitter and more able to see the Beatific Vision in its full glory. In Purgatory, all souls are headed homeward, and each step is easier and more satisfying. Innocence, humans' state before sin, is the first destination, and from there a more glorious vision will begin, one that the most artful words can only partially describe.

Signs that Eden is near begin in the sixth cornice, with the Gluttonous. By this time, Publius Papinius Statius, a pagan Latin poet who became a Christian, has joined the party; Dante believes that Vergil's reason and literary art need the supplement of revelation so that everything that is about to happen can be fully appreciated. Vergil had pagan glimmerings of Eden and the prelapsarian state when he wrote of a virtuous Golden Age once enjoyed by humankind, but glimmerings are not enough. Before them in the path, they see a tall tree, watered from above by a cascade. The tree bears ambrosial fruit, but a voice forbids anyone to eat it. Examples of Temperance are then described, which are the goad or whip to counter the vice. The souls of the Gluttonous, all emaciated, suffer from being denied the sweet-smelling fruit, but as one of them tells Dante, they come to the tree with the same desire that Christ brought to the Cross, for both sufferings bring redemption. They see another tree that also keeps its fruit from a gathering of gluttonous souls. A voice tells them to ignore the tree, which is the sort that fed Eve's greed. The connection between the sin of Gluttony and the eating of the forbidden fruit was a point commonly made from medieval pulpits. Particularly noteworthy here is the easy flow of allusions to the Fall of Man and to the suffering on the Cross that compensated for it. The classical story of Tantalus's punishment in the Underworld may have inspired Dante's description of the Gluttonous, but the tree of Eden and the tree of the Cross are clearly the central points of reference here.

PART 3, PARADISE

When the three travelers finally reach the Earthly Paradise, they see not a garden but a forest, a sacred wood wherein dwells the primal innocence that seemed so far away in the dark wood of the *Inferno*, in canto 1. The sacred wood has a single inhabitant, Matilda, who is there to explain these environs and make straight the way of Beatrice, who appears in a spectacular allegorical event called the Procession of the Sacrament. Only eyes that have regained the first innocence are ready for such a vision. Looking eastward, which is by tradition the holiest direction, Dante sees a brilliant light spread through the forest, and a procession led by seven candlesticks to a chanting of "Hosanna." Next come twenty-four elders, heads crowned with lilies, and after them four beasts surrounding the triumphal cart drawn by a griffin, whose birdlike features are gold, and elsewhere red and white. Three ladies, colored respectively red, green, and white, dance in a circle by the right wheel; four in purple dance by the left wheel, led by one who has a third eye. Two old men come next, one dressed as a physician, the other carrying a sword. They are followed by four humbly dressed individuals, and then by a very old man, going in a visionary trance. These last seven all wear red flowers.

Medieval religious processions were usually staged to affirm a crucial matter of doctrine or devotion. The key notion in this masquelike procession is the unity of sacred revelation since the Fall of Man. The twenty-four elders refer to the books of the Old Testament, their lily crowns suggesting pure righteousness. The Benedictus they sing is a reminder that the Old Testament symbolically anticipates events in the New Testament. The four beasts are the beasts of the Apocalypse and the signs of the four Evangelists. The griffin, which is part eagle and part lion, traditionally refers to the two natures of Christ, its gold suggesting divinity, its red and white, humanity. White and red are also the colors, respectively, of the Old and New Testaments, and of the bread and wine in the Eucharist. The ladies by the right wheel are Faith (white), Hope (green), and Charity (red); by the left wheel are the four cardinal virtues: Prudence (with the third eye), Temperance, Fortitude, and Justice. Behind the cart are Luke, Paul, and the Epistles of Peter, James, John, and Jude. The old man is the Revelation of Saint John. The red flowers they all wear signify the New Testament.

Then Beatrice appears on the cart in a red dress and green cloak, her head crowned with olive leaves. At this moment, Dante realizes that Vergil, the man of natural wisdom, is no longer with him. Beatrice, who might as well be called Revelation here, tells Dante to look at the entire procession. All of it is she, Beatrice says. Beatrice's words are the fullest manifestation so far of the significance of one passionate event that occurred when the poet was nine years old. What the God-Man brought into history, she is. The Incarnation that the Old Testament faintly surmised and the New Testament celebrates, she is, with every holy virtue in attendance. The same can be said of the transsubstantiated Host on the altar.

After a rebuke from Beatrice for the wandering ways of his own life, which is perhaps his own rightful dose of the purgatorial suffering he has been content to watch, Dante faints with shame. When he revives, Matilda is drawing him across the stream of forgetfulness. With the memory of evil now gone, he can watch with original innocence as the procession heads toward the Tree of Knowledge, where human sin began. Many medieval writings connected the Tree of Knowledge with the tree on which Christ was crucified. Lore had it that the seeds of the fruit from the first tree were buried on the tongue of Adam and then grew to become the tree of the Cross. Christ was often referred to as the Second Adam, come to reverse the catastrophe caused by the first. Here, the Griffin (Christ) moves the cart with Beatrice (the Word and its Incarnation) past the site on which the temptation and Fall occurred and joins the shaft of the cart to a barren tree, which immediately blossoms. The Griffin then ascends, leaving Beatrice at the roots of the tree. She now represents the Church that Christ at his ascension left behind to care for the humans he had redeemed.

The role of the Empire in God's plan is stressed here, too. An eagle slashes at the tree, just as Roman persecution maimed the Church. Then a gaunt fox appears, probably to represent the heresies of the Church's early history. After the fox has prowled about the cart, the eagle descends again, this time to feather the cart from its own breast. This no doubt represents the symbiotic relationship between church and state in the Holy Roman Empire. That liaison is followed by a dragon that damages the cart, causing it to change into the many-headed beast of the Apocalypse, on top of which is enthroned a whore consorting with giants. The imagery suggests the later corruption of the Church caused by its consorting with earthly powers. Thus, Dante sketches a symbolic history of the decay of the Church that Christ and Peter founded. The point is one he makes directly in many places: that in Christian history, Church and Empire need to maintain separate identities as they pursue God's plan. The atmosphere of these last cantos has been gradually shifting toward Apocalypse, which Beatrice continues by prophesying revenge for what has been allowed to happen to Christendom, but the final canto returns to the theme of a purgatorial journey. Dante now drinks from Eunoe, the water of Good Remembrance, which renders him finally free from the tarnish of an earthly life and ready for a direct vision of the Godhead.

Readers who think of Dante as the poet of Hell often have read only the first third of his masterpiece. The joy that quickens every step of the *Purgatory* makes it an exhilarating sequel to the *Inferno*, but that joy is only a hint of what awaits Dante in the vision of Paradise. The

Inferno and *Purgatory* are preparatory visions, the first stressing the reality of evil and its effects, the second showing that it is possible to remove every one of those effects. *Purgatory* and *Paradise* form the main part of the comedic structure, which leaves the unhappiness of the *Inferno* far behind.

Dante's *Paradise* is a description of Godhead, as much of it as his eyes could register, and as much as his memory could retain. Medieval literary audiences loved well-executed descriptions, and the *Inferno* and *Purgatory* contain some extraordinarily effective ones. Once the poet has left the substantive world, images on which to base descriptions are no longer obvious. Hell and Purgatory are constructed and described according to sinful human actions, which had been traditionally identified and discussed in concrete images. Social history abounds with vivid examples of depravity, but there has never been a great store of fictions or metaphors to describe the state of the soul enjoying Heavenly rewards. Moreover, the step-by-step journey into Hell and up the purgatorial mountain involves a sense of time and space that is inappropriate to the simultaneity of eternity. Thus, the metaphor of the journey does not quite fit a vision of Heaven, although to accommodate human communication and understanding, the vision had to be subdivided and presented in some sequence. Dante reminds his audience, however, that this is only a strategy to help them see.

Until one reaches the presence of God, the Being than Whom none is higher, one has to understand every phenomenon, even heavenly bliss, hierarchically. Every soul in Heaven is completely happy, but even heavenly bliss has its degrees. To describe Paradise, Dante looks outward from Earth to the concentric spheres of the planets and beyond them to the Empyrean, where the Divine Presence begins. Because, moving outward, each successive planet is closer to God, each one can be a gathering point for increasingly elevated forms of blessedness. With the rather technical exception of the souls on the Moon, the imagery Dante uses to describe the souls he meets is nonrepresentational, even approaching abstraction with voices, lights, and patterns. Dante was familiar with the tradition of the cosmic voyage, a literary form that went back to the Stoic philosophers, in which a guide takes a troubled individual to the outer spheres, to provide consolation by demonstrating the littleness of troubled Earth when compared to the grand harmony of all Creation. A powerful counterpoint develops in *Paradise* between accounts of the sordidness of contemporary Italian society and the charity and communion above. Part of the image of Paradise is thus accomplished through negative description, using earthly examples to emphasize what Heaven is not.

The *Inferno* does not start with a poetic invocation. Dante rushes directly into the troubled middle of things. *Purgatory* has an invocation to Calliope, the Muse of epic poetry. It is crucial but perfunctory, and it suits the hopeful premises of that work. The invocation to *Paradise* is a fitting start to a sublime task. It tells what a poet requires to describe his Creator. He starts with the notion that what he has seen is not possible to relate, because when the mind nears that which it has always wanted, memory weakens. Even so, he will sing about that part of it that has remained with him. He calls on Apollo, a god traditionally associated with light, wisdom, and prophecy, to breathe into him and use him like a bellows to utter song worthy of what memory of Paradise he still has left. Dante's audience would have been comfortable with an invocation to a pagan deity, because they believed that many pagan myths were glimpses of Christian light that could be used to make poetry more articulate. As an inspiration to soul and art, Apollo resembles the Holy Spirit, but he also carries all the rich associations of the classical literary tradition.

If Apollo will be generous, Dante continues, he will approach the laurel tree to take those famous leaves, now so neglected by an unheroic and unpoetic age, to create poetry that will ignite better imaginations than his own. From that tree, then, may come light for all future ages. The highly prophetic *Paradise* deserves to be under the keeping of Apollo. The poet approaches the laurel tree sacred to Apollo as he gathers strength to take his pilgrim self from Eden and the last visible traces of earthly things. The tree of tantalizing punishment for the Gluttonous and the tree of the first sin are replaced here by a tree reflecting the highest moral calling of art. As the images of Eden and sin recede, the laurel tree and the tree of Redemption converge. Dante looks at Beatrice looking at the sun, which is both

Apollo's planet and a traditional symbol for God. It is the same sun he saw that morning in the dark wood, but then he was looking through sinful eyes. The eagle, Dante's symbol for the Empire, was thought to be able to look directly into the sun; the suggestion here is that Beatrice, who stands for all revelation, and the eagle are one. It might seem curious that an image of imperial order should be presented at a moment of intimacy between self and Godhead, but Dante will make a similar point throughout *Paradise*: that religious mysticism and social history are different but not antithetical routes to God. The eagle that seized Dante in a dream and took him on high to burn was as much the call of empire as it was a private religious impulse.

Dante is not able to look directly at the sun for long. As he looks at Beatrice looking at eternity, he begins to hear the music coming from the harmonious motion of the heavenly spheres, a sound no mortal has heard since Adam sinned. Instantly, Dante realizes that he has left Earth with Beatrice. The vision that follows, the organization of which is only a metaphor for the ineffable, involves ten Heavens, each of the first seven associated with a planet—Moon, Mercury, Venus, Sun, Mars, Jupiter, Saturn—the eighth Heaven with the zodiac and fixed stars, the ninth the Crystalline Heaven of the *Primum Mobile*, or First Mover, through which motion was imparted to all the other spheres, and beyond that the Empyrean, or realm of God. In the first seven Heavens, the souls are located in the planet with which their earthly activities could be associated, although in actuality each of them is in the Empyrean with God. According to Dante, the first three Heavens are touched by the shadow of Earth. On the Moon, the planet nearest Earth, are those souls who through no fault of their own proved inconstant in vows they had made to God. They were not sinners, only less perfect in salvation. Next is the Heaven of Mercury, filled with souls who lived virtuous lives serving the social order, but who were motivated at least in part by worldly ambition. The sphere of Venus is for those who followed Eros in life but now are delighted to wheel with celestial movement.

In the Heaven of the Sun are spirits whose wisdom furthered the understanding of God on Earth. Mars houses those who gave their lives for the Christian faith, while Jupiter houses the souls of the Just. The second three Heavens (Sun, Mars, and Jupiter) celebrate the virtuous achievements of the active life, but the contemplatives abide above them, in the circle of Saturn. The theme of the eighth Heaven is the Church triumphant, with Christ and the saints in full radiance. The ninth and tenth Heavens, respectively the *Primum Mobile* and the Empyrean, are given to the various direct manifestations of God. They take up the last six cantos, which trail off as even Dante's imagination begins to fade before its task.

The mood of *Paradise* is perfect joy that has no end and leaves not even a trace of unfulfilled desire. The spirits describe that joy by what they do and say. There is a hierarchy of blessedness here, but it exists without anyone feeling envy or deprivation. Just as the courtesy and charity of Purgatory take one above the hatred and cupidity of Hell, so the perfect happiness here lifts one even higher, particularly through the praises for its perfect Source. The points of Christian doctrine and philosophy that are explained to Dante as he moves from Heaven to Heaven with Beatrice are rarefied, some barely fixable in mind or language. To follow these thoughts, the reader must move with Dante past the recognizable specifics of time and place. This commentary can only sample that exquisite brightness. One might begin with the notion that the rewards of Heaven justify everything that humans can know about God's plan. *Paradise* is a celebration and vindication of the Church and all its traditions, and of the plan for justice on Earth through Empire. It is also an opportunity for a citizen poet and visionary to justify himself to the audience of the world.

The Heaven of the Sun provides a satisfying example of Dante's love for the true Faith and the ideal Church. When he and Beatrice ascend to this Heaven, twelve lights carol around them, and one, Saint Thomas Aquinas, speaks. Aquinas belongs with the wisdom and illumination of the Sun. Mastering Aristotelian thought, he put its processes at the service of Christian theology. Among medieval Scholastic philosophers, he was supreme, and as a member of the Dominican Order (whose standard is a blazing sun), he studied and wrote to combat the heresies of unbelievers. Aquinas speaks not to praise a great university scholastic, however, but to praise Saint Francis of Assisi. Saint Francis

was a street preacher, a disciple of the poor, whose spontaneous, instinctive love of God did not move through learned syllogisms. Aquinas tells a lively allegory about Saint Francis and the woman in his life, Lady Poverty. Poverty had been a neglected widow since her first spouse died on the Cross twelve centuries before. Indeed, Poverty and Christ were so inseparable that during the Crucifixion she leapt on the Cross, like a wanton lover. Aquinas compares Francis's taking the vow of poverty to a wedding, an orgiastic celebration at which the guests (Saint Francis's followers) all hasten to follow this couple; as an Order, they will spread preaching and conversion throughout the world. This earthy description of Saint Francis's love for an ideal is no blasphemy: It is a charming reminder of how far the saint actually was from sensuality.

Then a Franciscan, Saint Bonaventure, praises the life work of Saint Dominic, founder of the order to which Aquinas belonged. Dominic, says Bonaventure, was the skillful gardener, sent to cull, trim, and order the plot of Faith and bring it new vitality. It is, like Aquinas's remarks about Francis, a graceful compliment, from lights that glow more brightly as they praise others. The ecstatic preacher and the systematizer of doctrine both work God's will and complement each other. At the same time, the reader cannot forget the diatribes of Aquinas and Bonaventure against the state of those orders.

Dante continually arranges his descriptions of Heaven to portray the idea of perfect happiness, although he relentlessly turns to bitter reminders of what human choice has rendered impossible on Earth. He never puts down the lash of satire for long. If *Paradise* is the happy conclusion of a comedy, it is also filled with astringent reminders that human history is a process of social and moral decay, much like the image of the Old Man of Crete in *Inferno* 14, which starts with a golden head and ends with rotting feet. At points Dante is apocalyptic about this decay, and he foretells destruction for his sinful age. He also implies that one day a strong figure will punish those selfish wrongdoers and usher in an age of justice.

Despite his outcries as an embittered satirist and doomsayer, Dante knows that both sacred and secular history are processes of God's justice, even when they seem to be operating at cross-purposes. In the Heaven of Mercury, Dante interviews Justinian, the Roman emperor and codifier of law, who outlines the historic progress of the Empire. For Justinian, history is the flight of God's sacred eagle. He describes the earliest tribes in Italy, the Punic Wars, and the emperors. Justinian's most startling point is that the highest privilege of Roman justice was the punishment of Christ. The Crucifixion was a legal act, conducted by duly constituted Roman authority, with Pontius Pilate as the agent. It made the Redemption possible. At the same time, as Beatrice will later explain, the legality of the act under Roman law did not remove the need to avenge what had been done to Christ's person, so, somewhat paradoxically, the destruction of Jerusalem was also justified. The path of Divine Justice moved from ancient Rome to the Holy Roman Empire, thanks to Charlemagne, but that magnificent progress has fallen to puny, contemptible heirs, as the Guelphs and Ghibellines of Dante's time continually ruin that justice with their feuding.

Dante's view of the workings of Divine Justice comes with surprises, as when he puts in the Heaven of Jove one Rhipeus, whom Vergil in the *Aeneid* called the most just among the Trojans. Presumably, Rhipeus was a pagan. That he should be in Heaven and the author who wrote about him in Hell is an irony, but Dante means to emphasize the presence of an appetite for justice in the Trojan line even before it settled in Italy.

If the ways of Justice can seem mysterious, Dante had no doubt that they would someday set in balance all the wrongs he had suffered. In Hell, Dante's anger at old enemies sometimes made him spiteful and almost pruriently interested in their pain. He paid particular attention to the part of Hell where barratry, the crime of making personal profit out of public trust, is punished by immersion in a pit of boiling tar. The episode is personal, for Dante was convicted and sentenced to exile on charges of barratry. For all the thrashing about among devils and damned souls in the pit of barrators, not so much as a drop of tar touches the poet. That is his answer to the capricious charges against him.

By placing his fictional journey in 1300, several years before the beginning of the political turmoil in Florence that resulted in his exile, Dante was able to present himself as a pilgrim ignorant of what is to come. This allows the heavenly hosts to refer to his coming suffering as an unjust but transient ordeal. It is a powerful response to his oppressors, because it allows him to assert the righteousness of his own cause and the maliciousness of his enemies through voices that are not to be contradicted, because their foreknowledge comes from the Divine Presence. The highest and most justified reaction to his future sufferings will come when Dante sees how little they amount to in the eye of eternity.

Dante's self-justification in *Paradise* shows a legitimate holy pride in ancestry and a certainty about his own destiny, despite the disgrace that is brewing for him. In the Heaven of Mars, the souls of those who died for the Faith form a cross. One of them, Dante's great-great-grandfather Cacciaguida, reminds him of the simple and virtuous old stock from which he is descended, in a line extending back to ancient Roman times. Cacciaguida hails Dante as a solitary continuation of this earlier nobility, then names clearly what had been hinted about in Hell and Purgatory: exile, poverty, a life at tables and under roofs not his own. Cacciaguida instructs Dante not to temper so much as a word, but to be a gadfly to degenerate Florence as Justice works its way.

Paradise is always ascending toward the vision of God, at which paradoxically it will evaporate, because it is only a human artifact. Actually, Dante is given three manifestations of God's presence. In the *Primum Mobile*, he sees God symbolically as a point of light surrounded by nine rings, each ring representing an order of angels. These nine rings of angels are in pointed contrast to the geocentric world, where the most slowly moving sphere, that of the Moon, is closest to the corruptible center. Here, as Beatrice explains, the fastest and brightest angelic circle, that of the Seraphim, is closest to the point of light. The definition of God as an indivisible point of light may seem unusual, given the traditions of a transcendent, all-encompassing Divinity. Dante was familiar with a definition of God as a sphere whose center is everywhere and whose circumference is nowhere, a concept that neatly implies the traditional idea of God's absolute and indivisible simplicity and his absolute interminability and simultaneity. The image of the point of light and the concentric circles of angels is perhaps as close as the human intelligence can come through symbols to understanding God's essence.

The image of God that Dante is given when he enters the Empyrean is a product of faith and revelation; it is the closest Dante can come directly to God, and this is the image with which *The Divine Comedy* must end. The Empyrean contains the souls of the Blessed on ascending tiers of thrones arranged to form petals of a white rose, as they will appear on Judgment Day. With the rose, a symbol of Divine Love, Dante moves finally beyond time and space in a blinding brightness as a river of Divine Grace pours from an incalculable height. In the center of the rose is a circle of light, the glory of God. It is time now for the final vision, but Dante discovers that Beatrice has left him to take her place among the Blessed. She has sent the great mystic and contemplative Saint Bernard to be his final guide. Doctrine and revelation, which Beatrice represented, have advanced as far as they can. Only ecstasy can go beyond that.

Under Bernard's direction, Dante's journey ends where it was first conceived, for there are the Virgin, and Lucia, whom the Virgin had sent to Beatrice, who in turn summoned Vergil to aid Dante in the descent to Hell. Now Saint Bernard prays for Mary's intercession, so that they can look at God without the instruments of metaphor or symbol. It is, as Dante says, the end of all yearning, satisfying and rendering obsolete the last vestiges of desire in the soul. In one mystical moment, Dante sees all creation held together by love. Then he sees three circles, each one a different color, occupying one space. It is the Trinity. The first two circles (the Father and the Son) reflect on each other, and the third (the Holy Ghost) seems a flame coming equally from the first two. It is a vision beyond logic and intellect. In trying to encompass it, Dante falls, like Icarus, back to his everyday human self. Dante ends with the remark that, whatever the limitations of his own understanding, Love was at the heart of what he saw, that same Love which moves the sun and the stars.

Other major works

NONFICTION: *Epistolae*, c. 1300-1321 (English translation, 1902); *De vulgari eloquentia*, c. 1306 (En-glish translation, 1890); *Il convivio*, c. 1307 (*The Banquet*, 1887); *De monarchia*, c. 1313 (English translation, 1890; also known as *Monarchy*, 1954; better known as *On World Government*, 1957); "Epistola X," c. 1316 (English translation, 1902); *Eclogae*, 1319 (*Eclogues*, 1902); *Quaestio de aqua et terra*, 1320 (English translation, 1902); *Translation of the Latin Works of Dante Alighieri*, 1904; *Literary Criticism of Dante Alighieri*, 1973.

Bibliography

Bloom, Harold. *Dante Alighieri*. Philadelphia: Chelsea House, 2003. A biography of Dante that also examines his works. Bibliography and index.

Gallagher, Joseph. *A Modern Reader's Guide to Dante's "The Divine Comedy."* Liguori, Mo.: Liguori-Triumph, 2000. A canto-by-canto guide to *The Divine Comedy* that is especially helpful for beginning readers of the work. Provides insightful character analysis from a specifically Roman Catholic perspective, along with accessible explanations of Dante's many obscure references. Includes a helpful outline.

Havely, Nick. *Dante*. Malden, Mass.: Blackwell, 2007. Havely looks at the life and work of Dante, focusing on literary and cultural traditions; key themes, episodes, and passages, and on how his work has been received.

Hollander, Robert. *Dante: A Life in Works*. New Haven, Conn.: Yale University Press, 2001. An intellectual biography, drawing on the works of its subject rather than on what little is known (and has already been well covered) of Dante's life.

Jacoff, Rachel, ed. *The Cambridge Companion to Dante*. New York: Cambridge University Press, 1995. An excellent guide to Dante's life, work, and thought. Especially useful for those readers of *The Divine Comedy* who want more information on specific allusions than most footnoted editions supply. Includes fifteen specially commissioned essays that provide both background information and critical commentary and a chronological outline of Dante's life.

Lansing, Richard. *Dante: The Critical Complex*. 8 vols. New York: Routledge, 2003. A collection of criticism and analysis, with volumes looking at Dante's relation to Beatrice, philosophy, theology, history, critical theory, and interpretation.

_____, ed. *The Dante Encyclopedia*. New York: Garland, 2000. An encyclopedia devoted to Dante. Covers his life and works and contains numerous appendixes. Index.

Raffa, Guy P. *Divine Dialectic: Dante's Incarnational Poetry*. Toronto, Ont.: University of Toronto Press, 2000. A study of Dante's worldview as revealed in incarnational images in his poetry.

Reynolds, Barbara. *Dante: The Poet, the Political Thinker, the Man*. 2d ed. Emeryville, Calif.: Shoemaker & Hoard, 2007. A biography of Dante that looks at his political life as well as his poetical life.

Thomas A. Van

JOACHIM DU BELLAY

Born: Château de la Turmelière, Liré, Anjou, France; c. 1522
Died: Paris, France; January 1, 1560

PRINCIPAL POETRY

L'Olive, 1549
Recueil de poésie, 1549
Vers Lyriques, 1549
La Musagnoeomachie, 1550
XIII Sonnets de l'honnête amour, 1552
Les Antiquités de Rome, 1558 (partial translation as *Ruines of Rome*, 1591; *The Antiquities of Rome*, 2006)
Divers Jeux Rustiques, 1558
Poemata, 1558 (in Latin)
Poésie latines, 1558
Les Regrets, 1558 (*The Regrets*, 1984)
Le Poète courtisan, 1559
Œuvres poétiques, 1908-1931 (6 volumes)

OTHER LITERARY FORMS

Joachim du Bellay (dew beh-LAY) is known primarily for his poetry. However, he did write *La Dé-*

fense et illustration de la langue française (1549; *The Defence and Illustration of the French Language*, 1939). In this manifesto, he expressed the aims of the Pléiade, the poetry circle to which he belonged and which was dedicated to developing French as a recognized and acceptable language for poetry.

ACHIEVEMENTS

Joachim du Bellay was instrumental in establishing French poetry as a genre equal to the poetry of the ancients. As a member of the Pléiade, he made significant contributions in both theory and practice to embellishing and purifying the French language. *The Defence and Illustration of the French Language* synthesized the ideas, aims, and rules of writing verse developed by the Pléiade and made them available to the literary community of his time. Du Bellay himself was responsible for establishing the sonnet and the ode in French poetry. He also introduced the satirical poem as a formal poetical genre into French literature with *Le Poète courtisan*. His *The Antiquities of Rome* added yet another genre to French poetry, the poetry of ruins.

BIOGRAPHY

Joachim du Bellay was probably born around 1522 in the family chateau at Liré in Anjou, France. His family belonged to the old nobility and was known for its service both in the Roman Catholic Church and in the army and diplomatic corps. Du Bellay was the son of Jean du Bellay and René Chabot. By the time he was ten years old, both of his parents had died, and he was placed in the care of his older brother René, who apparently paid little attention to him and left him to wander about the family estate. Being of frail health and neglected by his brother, du Bellay spent much of his childhood and adolescence in solitude and began to write poetry. For a time, he considered a career in the army; however, his frail health and his penchant for solitary contemplation led him to abandon the idea of a military career.

Sometime in 1543 or shortly thereafter, du Bellay met the poet Pierre de Ronsard. They became good friends and colleagues in the pursuit of a French poetry genre equal to that of the ancients. In 1546, du Bellay was studying law at Poitiers, where he met several important humanists of the time, including Jacques Peletier du Mans, Marc-Antoine Muret, and Jean Salmon Macrin. Peletier was translating both Greek and Latin authors as well as Italian poets and already involved in proclaiming the French language suitable for literary writing. Du Bellay was very interested in the research and work of these scholars and poets. Encouraged by Peletier, du Bellay wrote poetry in French as well as in Latin, translated Latin poetry into French, and began to develop the classical forms of the ode and the sonnet in French verse. By 1547, Ronsard was also studying in Poitiers. Like du Bellay, he studied classical poetry, but he concentrated more on the Greek poets.

Ronsard convinced du Bellay to go to Paris with him to study at the Collège de Coqueret with the humanist Jean Dorat. There, du Bellay perfected his knowledge of Greek, Latin, and Italian. He also became part of a group of humanist poets that included the master Dorat,

Ronsard, Jean-Antoine de Baïf, Étienne Jodelle, Rémy Belleau, and Peletier. Intent on changing attitudes about poetry and the French language, the group became known as La Brigade and defined itself as devoted to bringing about a revolution in poetry. In 1549, du Bellay published *The Defence and Illustration of the French Language*, which set forth the theory and goals of the group. That same year, du Bellay also published *L'Olive*, a collection of love sonnets, and wrote a poem in honor of the entrance into Paris of Henry II, king of France. His poem for Henry II earned him the protection of the king's sister Marguerite de Valois, who remained his protecterice throughout his career.

In 1553, La Brigade changed its name to La Pléiade, referring to a group of seven Greek poets of antiquity, and du Bellay published a second edition of his theoretical work. He also accompanied his uncle Cardinal Jean du Bellay to Rome, where he served as secretary and manager of his household. Du Bellay remained in Rome through 1557. His sojourn in Rome was a period not only of disillusionment and disappointment, but also of poetic inspiration. He met and became friends with the poet Olivier de Magny. While in Rome, du Bellay wrote his major works, in which he expressed his nostalgia for France, his sadness at the ruin of the Roman Empire, and his disillusionment with the corruption he found in Rome. After returning to France, he published *The Regrets*, *The Antiquities of Rome*, and *Divers Jeux Rustiques*. His health, never good, worsened, and he died on January 1, 1560.

Joachim du Bellay (The Granger Collection, New York)

ANALYSIS

Joachim du Bellay and Pierre de Ronsard are considered the two most important poets of the French Renaissance. Although Ronsard enjoyed a long career as a poet, du Bellay's career was a brief ten years. His first publications appeared in 1549 and his last poetry was published in 1559, shortly before his untimely death at the age of thirty-eight. Nevertheless, du Bellay made significant contributions to French poetry both in theory and in poetic creation.

Du Bellay's *The Defence and Illustration of*

the French Language became the manifesto of the Pléiade. In this work, Du Bellay elucidated the two major aims of the Pléiade, who maintained that medieval French poetry had deteriorated into mediocre genres that lacked the grandeur and significance of the poetry of classical antiquity. The group wished to create French poetry equal to the Latin and Greek poetry of classical antiquity. Du Bellay proposed that French poets write in French rather than in Latin but in imitation of the poets of classical antiquity, using the forms those poets used and the Italian sonnet. Although the sonnet had a long tradition and many practioneers in Italian poetry, du Bellay took the sonnets of Petrarch for his model. The preferred poetical forms for French poetry were to be the sonnet and the ode. Du Bellay also addressed the need to enrich the French poetical language by incorporating words taken from dialects and from other disciplines and by creating new words.

Du Bellay's early poetry illustrates the tenets set forth in the manifesto. In 1549, he published three collections of poetry: *L'Olive*, *Vers Lyriques*, and *Recueil de poésie*. *Vers Lyriques* and *Recueil de poésie* are odes in imitation of Horace, both in form and in subject matter. In *L'Olive*, du Bellay imitates Petrarch, writing poems in sonnet form. By addressing the sonnets in this work to the same mistress, he also incorporates the Italian tradition of the *canzonieri*, a collection of love poems all written to a single woman. This early poetry is a poetry of imitation, a sort of literary exercise that exhibits both the skill of the writer and the appropriateness of French as a language of poetry. However, the individuality of the poet is absent.

Although du Bellay continued to write in these poetical forms, the themes of the poetry that he published after returning from Rome changed dramatically. These poems are no longer mere imitations in French of Latin and Italian poems but are rather the expression of his "moi," of his inner self. Du Bellay filled his poems with the emotions that he felt as he was overwhelmed with homesickness for his native land, as he looked on the ruins of Roman civilization, and as he observed the corruption at the papal court. With *The Regrets* and *The Antiquities of Rome*, du Bellay's poetry becomes a personal expression of the poet while maintaining the style and grandeur of the poetry of classical antiquity.

THE REGRETS

The Regrets, a collection of 191 Petrarchan sonnets, may be seen as a personal diary of du Bellay's time in Rome. Although du Bellay addressed the sonnets of *L'Olive* to an imaginary mistress, a Mlle Viole (the title is an anagram of her name), a number of the sonnets in *The Regrets* are love poems about Faustine, an Italian woman with whom du Bellay had fallen in love. Consequently, the Faustine sonnets portray a real passion experienced by du Bellay. *The Regrets* also contains a number of satirical sonnets in which du Bellay vents his disgust with the hypocrisy and political maneuvering that dominated Roman society. In these sonnets, he began to develop the formal satire that became a French poetic genre with the publication of *Le Poète courtisan*, which satirizes the poet who has used his art to gain favor and wealth.

The rest of the sonnets express du Bellay's misery and sense of exile, loss, and abandonment because he is away from his home in France. With these sonnets, du Bellay introduces the personal patriotic poem into French poetry. In sonnets such as "Heureux qui, comme Ulysse . . ." (happy he who like Ulysses . . .), du Bellay alludes to Ulysses and Jason, heroes of classical antiquity, yet he does not praise their accomplishments but rather concentrates on the happiness they felt upon returning home. The poem continues with a comparison of the grandeur of Rome—its palaces, marble, sea air, the Tiber River—with his ancestral home, the Loire River, and the soft breezes of Anjou. All of these pale in contrast with Rome, but he prefers them, because it is in France that he belongs and finds safety, repose, and joy. The central image of *The Regrets* is of home, whether it is the actual house, the countryside, the smoke from the chimney, or the local river or climate. Du Bellay expresses a sense of dependency on the land where he was born and of never being happy away from it.

THE ANTIQUITIES OF ROME

With *The Antiquities of Rome*, du Bellay created the poetry of ruins. The main theme of his poems is the inevitable destruction of everything created by human beings, whether it be empires, civilizations, or massive marble palaces. The poems express his sadness and regret at seeing the ruins of Rome. Many of the poems also have a tone of irony. The one element of ancient

Rome that remains is the Tiber River, the fluid, ever-flowing, ever-changing river. The recurring images of the poems are ashes, dust, chaos, former grandeur, and present decay. These poems, written at the same time as *The Regrets*, also reflect du Bellay's constant unhappiness and feeling of exile in Rome, He concludes the first sonnet by stating that if time can destroy such solid and durable things as marble buildings, then it will surely end the pain of homesickness.

OTHER MAJOR WORK

NONFICTION: *La Défense et illustration de la langue française*, 1549 (*The Defence and Illustration of the French Language*, 1939).

BIBLIOGRAPHY

Du Bellay, Joachim. *"The Regrets" with "The Antiquities of Rome," Three Latin Elegies and "The Defense and Enrichment of the French Language."* Bilingual edition with translations by Richard Helgerson. Philadelphia: University of Pennsylvania Press, 2006. Contains du Bellay's three major works and good prose translations.

Hartley, David. *Patriotism in the Work of Joachim Du Bellay: A Study of the Relationship Between the Poet and France*. Lewiston, N.Y.: Edwin Mellen Press, 1993. A very useful critical study of du Bellay focusing on one of the most important themes of his poetry, his love and nostalgia for France.

Kenny, Neil. *An Introduction to Sixteenth Century French Literature and Thought: Other Times, Other Places*. London: Gerald Duckworth, 2008. Does not discuss du Bellay extensively but provides a very useful overview of the literary milieu in which du Bellay was writing, as well as information on the other types of literature being developed at the time.

Nauert, Charles G. *Humanism and the Culture of Renaissance Europe*. 2d ed. New York: Cambridge University Press, 2006. Excellent presentation of the role of the classical tradition and the literature of antiquity and of Italy in the Renaissance. Especially good for the Renaissance in sixteenth century France and its influence on French poetry. Bibliographies at the end of each chapter.

Tucker, George Hugo. *The Poet's Odyssey: Joachim du Bellay and the Antiquitez de Rome*. New York: Oxford University Press, 1990. This in-depth study of du Bellay as a poet provides close analysis of the sonnets and pays particular attention to his sojourn in Rome, his reaction to both the politics and the ruins, and their influence on his art.

Shawncey Webb

JOVAN DUČIĆ

Born: Trebinje, Bosnia and Herzegovina, Ottoman Empire (now in Bosnia and Herzegovina); February 5, 1871
Died: Gary, Indiana; April 7, 1943

PRINCIPAL POETRY
Pjesme, 1901
Jadranski sonetti, 1906
Pesme, 1908
Plave legende, 1908 (*Blue Legends*, 1983)
Sabrana dela, 1929-1932 (5 volumes), 1969 (6 volumes)
Lirika, 1943
Izabrana dela, 1982

OTHER LITERARY FORMS

Although Jovan Dučić (DEW-chihch) was preoccupied with poetry, he wrote in several other genres. His travelogues, *Gradovi i himere* (1932; cities and chimeras), contain his impressions gathered during journeys to Switzerland, France, Italy, Greece, Egypt, and other countries. More testimonies to his erudition than reports of his actual experiences, they deal with the history and cultural background of those places rather than with the present. *Gradovi i himere* is the best book of its kind in Serbian literature. A number of historical-cultural essays are collected in the book *Blago Cara Radovana* (1932; *King Radovan's Treasure: A Book of Fate*, 2003). They offer Dučić's views on happiness, love, women, friendship, youth, old age, poets, heroes, and prophets. Dučić also wrote numerous articles on

Slavic writers, his predecessors as well as his contemporaries, in which he presented not only opinions on these writers but also glimpses of his own literary views and accomplishments. Toward the end of his life, he wrote a book about a Serb who went to Russia and became an influential figure at the court of Peter the Great, *Grof Sava Vladislavić* (1942; Count Sava Vladislavić). It is an ambitious pseudohistorical study that reads more like a novel than history. Dučić also wrote numerous essays and articles about cultural, national, social, and political issues of the day.

ACHIEVEMENTS

Jovan Dučić appeared at a crucial point in the history of Serbian literature, at the turn of the century, when the epoch of Romantic and realist poetry was coming to a close and another, usually referred to as *Moderna*, was just beginning. By introducing new themes and sources of inspiration, Dučić was very instrumental in setting Serbian poetry on a new course. He was an aesthete, with a refined taste and an aristocratic spirit. In his poetry, he strove for formal excellence expressed through clarity, precision, elegance, musical quality, and picturesque images. His subject matter and unique style, reflecting the manner of French verse—Parnassian, Symbolist, and Decadent—brought a new spirit to Serbian verse. Unlike previous Serbian poets, who were either Romantically or realistically oriented, Dučić was attracted to esoteric, sophisticated, thought-provoking, and soul-searching themes, creating his own lonely world of imagination and reacting to it in a highly subjective manner. His poetry reveals a sensitive artist with a basically pessimistic outlook. He has sometimes been criticized for this, as well as for his inclination toward art for art's sake. His supreme craftsmanship, however, no one denies. Dučić represents one of the highest achievements in Serbian and in all south Slavic literatures, a fame that increases as time goes on.

BIOGRAPHY

Jovan Dučić was born into a prominent Serbian family in Trebinje, a picturesque little town in Bosnia and Herzegovina, at that time under Turkish occupation, in 1871. As a boy he moved to Mostar, a Herzego-vinian cultural center, and later to Sarajevo. After he graduated, he taught at schools in Bosnia and in Mostar, where he was frequently harassed by Austrian authorities for his nationalist activities. In Mostar, he participated in cultural activities, joined a literary circle, edited literary journals, and began to write poetry. Supported by the Serbian government, he studied liberal arts at the University of Geneva. During his study there and on frequent visits to Paris, he fell under the influence of French culture, particularly that represented by the Decadent and Symbolist poets, which would have a decisive impact on his literary development. Upon his return to Serbia in 1907, he entered diplomatic service and served in that capacity for the rest of his life in various capitals of the world. At the same time, he published poetry and prose works and came to be recognized as one of the leading Serbian writers. He was in Lisbon during World War II and moved to the United States in 1941. Until his death less than two years later, Dučić actively supported the nationalist side of the guerrilla struggle against the Germans in his native country. His book *Lirika* (lyric poems) appeared the day he died. He is buried at the Serbian shrine in Libertyville, Illinois. At his request, his papers and library were sent to his native Trebinje.

ANALYSIS

Jovan Dučić wrote poetry during his entire mature life. His first poems followed in the footsteps of the leading Serbian poet, Vojislav Ilić, at the end of the nineteenth century. Ilić employed a mixture of Romanticism, realism, and neoclassicism, all of which appealed to the young Dučić, especially in view of his patriotic fervor. During his study in Switzerland and prolonged stays in France, Dučić moved away from national regionalism as a result of his falling under the influence of the Parnassians and, later, the Symbolists. Despite some striking similarities to French poets, however, he developed his own style, thus successfully transplanting foreign influences onto a soil uniquely his own. In the latter part of his poetic career, he was free from any foreign influence. Ironically, his own influence on Serbian poets was minimal despite attempts by many to emulate him.

There are three more or less distinct periods in his poetic development. The first (1886-1908) was the period of naïve beginnings, fervent patriotism, love of nature, pronounced musicality, and Romantic sentimentalism. The strong French influence later in this period manifested itself through accentuated pessimism, melancholy, affectation, and a strict attention to form. This development, as literary historian Milan Kašanin sees it, had not only aesthetic but also historical significance, for the French predilection for intellectualism and rationalism replaced in Dučić's poetry the emotion and folkloristic regionalism dominant in Serbian poetry up to that time. Changes in Dučić, in turn, paved the way for historical changes in Serbian poetry in the first decade of the twentieth century.

Dučić carried these and other signs of French influence, notably that of Albert Samain, Henri de Régnier, Sully Prudhomme, Charles Baudelaire, Théophile Gautier, and José-Maria de Heredia, into his second period (1908-1932), but during this period, he was able to transform such influence into a synthesis of his earlier Romantic preoccupations and the French "linear" spirit and discipline. He turned inward, searching for lasting themes and grappling with such perennial problems as humankind's isolation, love, search for faith, and reconciliation with death.

It was not until his third and last period (1932-1943) that he was able to give full expression to this synthesis. Refining it further, he wrote his most mature works, although they consisted more of prose than of poetry. His last poems, some of them undoubtedly his best, return to the simplicity of his earlier period, as if closing the circle.

Dučić wrote a great deal of poetry, but always placing high demands on his craft, he later renounced much of it; in fact, he explicitly forbade the republication of his earliest poetry. As a consequence, his entire authorized poetic output consists of only one medium-sized volume. He was also versatile in his choice of subject matter and in his stylistic approaches. His poems can be grouped according to their overriding themes into patriotic-historical poems, nature poems, love poems, and predominantly meditative poems. Sometimes a poem is limited to one of these themes; more often, however, it combines two or more of them.

PATRIOTIC AND HISTORICAL POEMS

Dučić wrote poems on patriotic and historical themes, undoubtedly under the influence of folk poetry, the Serbian poets still writing in a Romantic vein, and the general patriotic enthusiasm of his countrymen. These early poems are rather bombastic, full of rhetoric, and declamatory, though quite sincere. Later, he moved away from purely patriotic themes and turned to history. Only during the two world wars, especially during World War I, did he return to patriotic poetry, for obvious reasons. Inspired by the enormous suffering, valiant efforts, and glorious exploits of his people, he wrote several excellent poems, of which "Ave Serbia!" and "The Hymn of the Victors" are especially notable.

In somewhat intellectual fashion, Dučić writes not of battles but of the suffering necessary for victory. Love for one's country he calls "a drop of poisonous milk," hinting at its opium-like intoxication. Only that country is blessed "where children unearth a rusted sword" and "paths of greatness lead over fallen heroes." "Glory, that is the terrible sun of the martyrs," he exclaims in praise of the World War I victors. He would raise his voice once again during the second world cataclysm, this time more in anger and despair over the tragic fate of his people, whose end he did not live to see.

His historical poems are in a much lighter vein, devoid of the tragic aura of his patriotic poetry. In the cycle "Carski soneti" (the imperial sonnets) he returns to the glory of Serbian medieval empire, and in the cycle "Dubrovačke poeme" (the Dubrovnik poems) he extolls the virtues and the sunny ambience of the Ragusan Republic, which alone escaped several centuries of Turkish occupation. While the former cycle is unrestrained in its glorification of the pomp and strength of the old Serbian empire, the latter is amusing, humorous, at times irreverent, but above all lighthearted and warm. These poems are read by modern readers only out of curiosity and for amusement, although some of them show Dučić's craftsmanship at its best.

NATURE POEMS

Dučić's poems about nature are both varied and limited in scope. While it is true that he touches upon many phenomena and objects in nature, his approach tends to be somewhat one-sided. This one-sidedness can be seen in his choice of motifs, which are repeated time and again, although in endless variations. Among such often-repeated motifs are the sea, the sun, morning, evening, night, and natural objects that are usually isolated in their surroundings—no doubt reflecting the poet's own isolation and loneliness despite his appearance as a very happy and self-satisfied person. Even the titles of the cycles reveal the concentration on certain motifs: "Jutarnje pesme" (morning poems), "Večernje pesme" (evening poems), and "Sunčane pesme" (sun poems).

Dučić's nature poems are not descriptive per se; rather, description is used primarily to evoke an atmosphere or to underscore the poet's melancholy mood. In the poem "Sat" ("The Clock"), for example, the very first verse sets the desired tone: "A sick, murky day, the sky impenetrable." The tolling of the tower clock contributes to general hopelessness: "Last roses are slowly dying . . . poplars are shedding their last leaves." The entire scene is permeated with "a horrible foreboding and the panic of things." In his treatment of nature, Dučić emulates the Parnassians and the Symbolists, but he also endeavors to "spiritualize" nature, as Pero Slijepčević, a literary historian of Serbian literature, remarks, to present it as something outside and above the poet's perception of it. When a strong musicality is added to his regular versification, the impact of his poem, whether it is read or listened to, is powerful and lasting.

Other poems, such as those in "Sunčane pesme," are almost exactly the opposite: sunny, joyful, invigorating. Thus the poem "April" evokes a fairytale setting: The sky resembles a field covered with roses, the green hill is full of snails, and the sun's gold glitters in mud puddles. The titles of other poems in the Sun cycle—which translate as dawn, a forest, the sun, rain, a pine tree, the wind, and so on—suggest a symphonic picture of nature, as Miodrag Pavlović observes, a picture that nourishes one's imagination and captivates with its seemingly effortless simplicity.

Dučić is a poet of the Mediterranean joie de vivre and closeness to nature, his pessimistic posturing notwithstanding. This fact explains the abundance of sounds and acoustic impressions, with form and color

following closely. As a native of a region close to the Adriatic Sea and having spent most of his life in cosmopolitan centers, he shows little interest in the inland territories of the Balkans and Europe, concentrating on landscapes at or near the sea, both in his poetry and in his travelogues, most of which depict places in the Mediterranean area.

Dučić goes to nature not so much to enjoy it as to meditate in it. Many of his poems depict silence as the most salutary state for the poet's musing about life and the meaning of existence. There he finds "loneliness, in eternal silence, pale, by the river" and "evening waters streaming in quiet sadness, and weeping willows rustling forgetfulness." It is hard to say whether such attitudes stem from affectation or from the need to give his mood adequate expression. Critics have often accused him of affectation and artificiality, but in doing so, they overlook his remarkable ability to create with a few masterful strokes a picture of a landscape capable of moving the reader. Despite certain mannerisms, clichés, and repetitiousness, Dučić's poems about nature are highly ingenious in approach and execution. They belong to the best of their kind in Serbian poetry.

LOVE POETRY

Dučić has been accused of even greater affectation and artificiality in his love poetry, probably because the woman in his poems is seldom a being made of flesh and blood but rather only a vision of an unknown woman, an eternal creature without specific abode or age. She does not exist nor did she ever exist, Dučić admits. Instead of endowing his emotions with a concrete substance, he creates a woman cult, placing her at the altar of an unrealizable dream. She is "the principle that builds and destroys, the God's spirit in every string and line . . . an inexhaustible well of pride and shame . . . an endless desert where the suns of despair rise and set" ("Poem to a Woman"). She is also a constant source of pain and unhappiness, mainly because she does not exist in her own right but only as the poet's chimera: "You have shone in the sun of my heart: for, everything we love, we have created ourselves." Seeing in woman a goddess, a cosmic principle, and destiny, it is not surprising that Dučić cannot find happiness and satisfaction in love. Even though he yearns for satisfaction, he is convinced beforehand of his failure. It is interesting that, as Slijepčević remarks, Dučić never sings about the beginning or the duration of love but only about its end.

It is easy to see only affectation in attitudes such as these, but such an approach does not exhaust the complexity of Dučić's love poetry. The fact is that he did not always advocate such an ethereal relationship. In his earliest poems (later repudiated), as well as in his poems in prose, he does speak of lust, sensual excesses, and even devouring passion. In private life, he was known as an insatiable, often ruthless lover. As he matured as a poet, however, the ideal of a woman beyond reach—but also beyond corruption and decay—slowly took shape: "Remain unreachable, speechless, and distant—for, the dream of happiness means more than happiness" ("Poem to a Woman"). However, despite the withdrawal and lack of confidence, he refuses to dwell on the transience of love, counterposing love to death as one of the few forces that could overcome it. One cycle of his poems is entitled "Poems of Love and Death." By elevating woman to the level of deity, he establishes love as one of the three basic themes of high poetry: God, death, and love. Thus, Dučić's love poetry transcends the Romantic, realist, and Symbolist approach to love, all of which had, at one point or another, taken their turn in shaping his poetic profile. As in his nature poetry, he approaches love in a nontraditional, primarily intellectual way. Love is no longer a manifestation of only feelings but also of thought. In the process, Dučić has created some of the best love poems in Serbian literature, despite some admitted flaws.

Poetry of meditation

Many of Dučić's poems about nature and love show a distinct propensity for meditation, just as many of his purely meditative poems are related to nature and love. Dučić's meditative bent derives not only from his nature but also from his firm belief that only the meditative element and intellectualism could pull Serbian literature out of the confines of narrow regionalism. His time in France and Switzerland, as well as in other parts of the world, only confirmed that belief. He sometimes strained too hard to achieve that goal; nonetheless, some of his meditative poems are genuine artistic achievements.

Dučić never developed his own philosophy, nor was he systematic in expressing his thoughts in his poems. There is no doubt, however, that he was fond of philosophizing and couching his thoughts on many subjects in poetic fashion. Even in his prose works, where his meditativeness is more pronounced, he often expresses his thoughts poetically. From the many poems which are either completely or partially suffused with meditation, several topics clearly emerge. In these works, Dučić frequently addresses God. Even though he sees him in all things, offering his hand "whenever my ship tilts," the poet cannot always suppress doubts about his whereabouts at the time "when a criminal sharpens his knife somewhere" ("Poems to God"). Most of Dučić's references to God are the result of the constant interplay of faith and doubt. Death, "the only thing we did not invent . . . more real than reality . . . the only truth and the only fairy tale, the sum of all symbols" ("Poems of Death"), is also often depicted by Dučić. In accord with his basically pessimistic attitude, he speaks of death as of an inevitable outcome that can be halted temporarily only by love. The experience of love, too, often gives Dučić an opportunity to reflect. Poetry itself is the subject of meditation, as in his famous "My Poetry," in which he pleads with his muse to be beautiful and proud only for him and to ignore the rest of the world as if it were hidden in a mysterious fog. This aptly illustrates his belief in art for art's sake, of which he was the leading proponent in Serbian literature.

Some critics maintain that the reflective poems are the weakest in Dučić's oeuvre. Others believe that this particular characteristic lends his poetry an aura of cosmopolitanism and sophistication that helped Serbian poetry overcome its century-long limitations, as Dučić believed it would. Moreover, far from being trite or superfluous, his meditativeness inspires the reader to do his own thinking.

Blue Legends

Dučić's poems in prose in *Blue Legends* stand out as a curiosity in Serbian poetry, because no other Serbian poet had written prose poems in such a sustained and dedicated fashion. They are also a further testimony to Dučić's versatility and poetic prowess. The thirty-seven poems in this collection cover the ground of his lyric poetry: One finds poems about nature, love, faith, gods, and human behavior in general. The most striking difference lies in the frequent depiction of the ancient world, of pagan and classical antiquity as well as of early Christianity. Dučić, who seldom concerned himself with the present, found in these escapes into the past a convenient idiom to give poetic expression to his thoughts and sentiments. His treatment of love here is much bolder and earthier and his treatment of faith much less reverent than in his lyric poetry; in addition, his conclusions about human nature seem to be more realistic. "The Sun" and "The Little Princess" are generally considered to be the best of these prose poems.

VERSIFICATION, STYLE, IMAGERY

Dučić's style has often been singled out as the most significant and accomplished aspect of his poetry, often at the expense of other qualities. He demanded of himself, as well as of other writers, rigorous attention to matters of style, considering himself to be a craftsperson in a poetic workshop. He constantly revised his works, not hesitating to disown those he did not deem worthy. He remained a student of poetry even when others thought of him as a complete artist, and he had no patience with those who neglected style.

In matters of versification, Dučić shows a remarkable versatility. His most common form is a variation of the Alexandrine, which he used almost exclusively in his later periods (except in the last book published during his lifetime, *Lirika*). He started with hexameter, octameter, and decameter, and settled on the Alexandrine, although he used many variations of these and other meters. All his verses rhyme, but even here there is great variety from poem to poem, even within a single poem. Enjambment is not infrequent. Most of his poems consist of four to six quatrains. He wrote many sonnets; some of the cycles are composed entirely of them.

The texture of Dučić's verse is characterized above all by strong musicality, achieved through a skillful use of vowels, cadence, and resonance, and by avoiding harsh elements such as dissonant consonants, corrupted speech, and provincialisms. The inner rhythm is achieved by strict adherence to the rules of versification, especially those of meter, stress, and caesura, although he sometimes deviates if his highly sensitive ear tells him to do so. This is possible in Serbo-Croatian, where morphological and syntactic rules allow such variations.

The wealth of images and metaphors in Dučić's poetry has often been pointed out. The originality of such figures is undeniable: The armies of night are sailing, and the flags of darkness are waving; a horny moon has entangled itself in the branches of old chestnut trees; his poetry is quiet as marble, cold as a shadow; a sea willow resembles a nymph condemned to become a tree-rustling sadness. Dučić frequently employs personification: A row of black poplars marches through the wheatfield; water fountains are crying; the dawn looks into the window with the childlike eyes of a doe; a snake is taking off its shirt in the blackberry bush. Even with such a wealth of imagery and metaphor, Dučić's verse is always clear and fully expressed, never overloaded with meaning yet never devoid of it. The purity of his language, his striking and bold innovations, and his musical fluidity all contribute to a powerful total effect.

While it is true that many of these characteristics can be traced to the influence of the Parnassians and the Symbolists, it is also true that without his own immense talent Dučić could not have become what he was—a leading poet of his generation, a pathfinder and epoch maker in Serbian literature, and one of the important writers in world literature of the twentieth century. Only the fact that his skillfully composed poetry is extremely difficult to translate has limited his appeal and reputation in the rest of the world.

OTHER MAJOR WORKS

LONG FICTION: *Grof Sava Vladislavić*, 1942.

NONFICTION: *Blago Cara Radovana*, 1932 (*King Radovan's Treasure: A Book of Fate*, 2003); *Gradovi i himere*, 1932.

BIBLIOGRAPHY

Dučić, Jovan. *Songs of the Sun, and of Love and Death*. New York: Serbian Classics Press, 2003. A selection of poems, translated into English, published to commemorate the sixtieth anniversary of his death. Contains an informative introduction by Vasa D. Mihailovich.

Goy, Edward D. "The Poetry of Jovan Dučić." In

Gorski Vijenac: A Garland of Essays Offered to Professor Elizabeth Mary Hill. Cambridge, England: Modern Humanities Research Association, 1970. An expertly written essay by a noted British Slavicist. Goy discusses Dučić's poetry within the framework of European literature as well as his artistic virtuosity.

Holton, Milne, and Vasa D. Mihailovich, eds. *Serbian Poetry from the Beginnings to the Present*. New Haven, Conn.: Yale Center for International and Area Studies, 1988. This collection of Serbian poetry in English provides critical analysis and perspective.

Mihailovich, Vasa D. "Jovan Dučić in America." *Serbian Studies* 4, no. 4 (1988): 55-69. An essay about Dučić's stay in America during 1941-1943, the last two years of his life. It covers his many activities among the Serbs of America. Even though he wrote relatively little poetry at this time, he penned political tracts in support of General Draža Mihailović. The essay chronicles those activities in detail.

Petrov, Aleksandar, ed. *Manje poznati Dučić—A Less Known Dučić*. Pittsburgh, Pa.: American Srbobran, 1994. A valuable publication about lesser known writings of the poet, primarily his poems written during World War II. It contains the editor's informative essay about this period in the poet's life and translations of his last poems.

Puvačić, Dušan. "The Theme of Bosnia and Hercegovina in the Works of Jovan Dučić." *South Slav Journal* 15, nos. 1/2 (1992): 35-43. The author analyzes Dučić's attachment to his native region as expressed in his works. The political background is examined as well as his artistic excellence.

Vasa D. Mihailovich

E

JOSEPH VON EICHENDORFF

Born: Near Ratibor, Silesia (now Racibórz, Poland);
March 10, 1788
Died: Neisse, Silesia (now Nysa, Poland); November
26, 1857

PRINCIPAL POETRY

Gedichte, 1837 (*Happy Wanderer, and Other
Poems*, 1925)
*Neue Gesamtausgabe der Werke und Schriften in
vier Bänden*, 1957-1958

OTHER LITERARY FORMS

Although the reputation of Joseph von Eichendorff
(I-kuhn-dawrf) is based almost exclusively on the lyrical talents which both his poetry and novellas attest, his
poems themselves compose but a small portion of his
entire literary production. Epic poems such as "Robert
Guiscard" and "Julian" are included among his more
eloquent lyrical poems. His first prose work and the first
of his two full-length novels, *Ahnung und Gegenwart*
(1815; presentiment and the present), contains fifty poems that reinforce an already impressionistic, lyrical
style. His second novel, *Dichter und ihre Gesellen*
(1834; the word *Gesellen* is ambiguous: The title means
both "poets and their companions" and "poets and their
apprentices"), is more tightly constructed and reveals a
writer somewhat less conditioned by his proclivities toward poetry. His nine novellas, highlighted by *Aus dem
Leben eines Taugenichts* (1826; *Memoirs of a Good-
for-Nothing*, 1866) and *Das Marmorbild* (1819; *The
Marble Statue*, 1927), do not belie the lyricist and are
strewn with some of Eichendorff's most appealing and
musical verses. The strength of his narrative work lies
not in plot but in allegorical content, landscape descriptions, dream content, and poetic language. Eichendorff's
attempts at drama include *Krieg den Philistern* (pb.
1824; war on the Philistines), the comedy *Die Freier*

(pb. 1833; the suitors), historical plays such as *Der
letzte Held von Marienburg* (pb. 1830; the last hero of
Marienburg), and a dramatic fairy tale. Among his
translations are one-act religious dramas of Pedro Calderón de la Barca, some of the farces of Miguel de Cervantes, and Don Juan Manuel's *Conde Lucanor* (1335).
Eichendorff is recognized also for his accomplishments as a critical historian of German literature and
Romanticism, particularly in *Geschichte der poetischen
Literatur Deutschlands* (1857; history of the poetic literature of Germany). He also wrote numerous treatises
on history, politics, and religion.

ACHIEVEMENTS

Joseph von Eichendorff's reputation as a master
craftsperson among German lyrical poets is beyond
dispute. No literary history fails to list him in the first
rank of German Romantic poets, and such noted poetic
successors as Heinrich Heine, Theodor Storm, and
Hugo von Hofmannsthal enthusiastically acknowledged his major contributions to the genre. Well into
the twentieth century, his work continued to be acclaimed by such literary connoisseurs as Thomas Mann
and Werner Bergengruen. He has been called "the last
knight of German Romanticism," and his works are
said to represent both the climax and the crisis of German Romanticism. The popularity of many of his lyrics
has transformed them into veritable folk songs. Four
of Eichendorff's most memorable poems, "Das zer-
brochene Ringlein" ("The Broken Ring"), "Der frohe
Wandersmann" ("The Happy Wanderer"), "Mondnacht" ("Moonlit Night"), and "Sehnsucht" ("Yearning"), were set to music by Robert Schumann; others
were used by Johannes Brahms, Hugo Wolf, Felix
Mendelssohn-Bartholdy, Hans Pfitzner, and Othmar
Schoeck. His novella *Das Schloss Dürande* (1837; the
castle Dürande) was the basis for an opera by Schoeck.
Memoirs of a Good-for-Nothing is one of the most
widely read German novellas of the nineteenth century
and is often regarded as the quintessential Romantic
novella.

Somewhat less generally conceded, however, is
Eichendorff's status as a religious poet and his function
as a pedagogue and a critic of Romanticism. The didactic intent in his poetry is often overshadowed by the

very obvious accoutrements of Romanticism with which it abounds. The simple musicality of Eichendorff's verses, the frequent repetition of rhymes and images, the limited scope of his themes, the recurrent expression of a simple but sincere piety, and particularly his *Taugenichts* character sometimes earn Eichendorff the label of a naïve, unsophisticated lyricist, albeit a pleasant and refreshingly healthy one. The immediate, conspicuous beauty of his rhythms and melodies may suffice for the superficial reader. A more persistent and careful reading of his verses, however, yields the insight that beyond the aesthetically pleasing exterior of his opus there is a very tenacious and vital religious faith communicated through a rather surprisingly rich range of variations on the Christian theme. Neither a monastic mystic nor a simplistic, uncritical "true believer," Eichendorff was a decidedly world-involved applier of his faith to life and vice versa. His poems testify to his deeply held conviction of the necessary interrelationship between his poetry and his religion, aim to convince the reader of the desirability of such a union, and caution against the dangers of a too subjectively oriented Romanticism which does not permit the freedom to choose and to serve a higher ideal.

BIOGRAPHY

Despite the depiction of incessant wanderings and frequent allusions to "die weite Welt" (the wide world) in the writings of Joseph Freiherr von Eichendorff, the poet himself actually had limited exposure to the world beyond the reaches of his native Upper Silesia in southeastern Germany. His journeys were primarily spiritual ones; even university days in Halle and Heidelberg, a student trip to Paris and Vienna, and eventual civil service posts in Breslau, Danzig, Berlin, and Königsberg did not take him to those distant, exotic, non-German-speaking lands, the *Welschland*, which his work often evokes. His birthplace, the Castle Lubowitz near Ratibor, remained at least the physical mecca to which he periodically returned until the deteriorating financial status of his aristocratic family forced the sale of all its properties in 1822.

By the age of ten, when Eichendorff first read the New Testament and was moved by the story of Christ's Passion, he had already been introduced through the Polish and German folk songs and fairy tales of his native region to the second guiding force of his life, the power of poetry. The poet's deep commitment to the Roman Catholic faith and his love for the music and beauty of words as well as his soon proven facility with them were to sustain him for his entire life, even when professional success as a governmental official was withheld from him and external pressures were overwhelming.

Eichendorff had ample discourse with gifted representatives of the Romantic movement, first in 1807, at the University of Heidelberg, where he heard the lectures of the philosopher Joseph von Görres and where he made the acquaintance of such leading literary figures as Clemens von Brentano, Achim von Arnim, and Adam Müller, and then years later, in Berlin, with Ludwig Tieck and E. T. A. Hoffmann, and in Vienna, with Friedrich von Schlegel. He was, however, to turn eventually from Romanticism and to take it to task figuratively in his poetry and literally in his expository writings. Any tendency to succumb completely to narcissistic Romantic musings on Eichendorff's part was confined to his year in Heidelberg. His conscious awareness of the Dionysian dangers of Romanticism is evident in the larger body of his poetry and is particularly clear in the narrative *Viel Lärmen um Nichts* (1833; much ado about nothing).

After completion of his civil service examinations in Vienna in 1812 and his participation in the Wars of Liberation against Napoleon in 1813 and 1815, Eichendorff married Aloysia von Larisch in 1815. They produced four children. The poet held various bureaucratic posts as governmental councillor in several North German cities until he took an early retirement in 1844 for reasons of ill health. From approximately 1816 to 1855, few details are available about Eichendorff's personal life except for the indirect information revealed in his writing; the diaries he had kept regularly from the age of twelve were not continued into that period. His apparently ineffectual career gained him no special recognition; the sole honor bestowed upon him was the Medal for Science and Art by King Maximilian II of Bavaria.

From the poet's retirement until his death thirteen years later at the home of his daughter Therese in

Neisse, he resided for only brief periods of time in various eastern German cities and in Vienna. In the latter city, his acquaintances included the composer Robert Schumann and the writers Franz Grillparzer and Adalbert Stifter.

Although Eichendorff had a surprisingly wide circle of intellectual, artistic, and politically influential friends in the course of his life, he seems never to have been an overtly influential personal force among them or a dynamic contributor to their social gatherings but was noted rather for his pleasant, unassuming manner and the quiet grace and spirituality of his personality. After his retirement, he turned to the writing of theoretical treatises and translations from Spanish. It seems that the rigors of a profession to which the poet felt no true emotional commitment had to be balanced by the more pleasant practice of poetry; after the duties of that profession no longer had to be met, he could turn from the perspective of age and experience to objective evaluations of the cultural, historical, and literary developments which he had witnessed throughout his life.

Joseph von Eichendorff (Archive Photos/Getty Images)

ANALYSIS

Despite the fact that Joseph von Eichendorff is routinely classified among the German Romantic writers, his affiliation with them is primarily a superficial one. The idyllic nature descriptions, the wandering musicians and students, the nostalgic glance toward home and the glorious past, the veneration of the beloved, and an obvious acquaintance with the religious dogma of Catholicism play such a large role in his work that the temptation arises to accept such a generally accepted label without further question. Unlike many Romantics, however, Eichendorff demonstrated no utter abandonment to an introverted psyche but manifested instead a surrender to a specific, sharply focused ideal beyond the self and repeatedly warned against the perils of subjective self-indulgence. The wandering that is done so frequently in Eichendorff's work is not an aimless roaming, as it might at first appear, but a deliberately chosen pilgrimage to God. When Romanticism failed, in Eichendorff's eyes, to keep its promise to restore humanity's broken relationship with God, it ceased to have validity for the poet.

Eichendorff's poetry and his religious faith were one. Even a random reading of his verses should discourage any attempt to separate the two, despite the fact that his explicitly *geistliche Gedichte* (spiritual poems) do not make up the bulk of his poetic production and represent by no means his masterpieces. In his treatises on literature, Eichendorff himself emphasized the importance not of Christian content in poetry but rather of religious orientation and a permeation of the poetry by religious attitudes. He felt that the talent of a poet should be placed in the service of God and that the Christian atmosphere thus created would permit the concealed but higher meaning of earthly life to manifest itself. When he maintained that all poetry is but the expression or the spiritual body of the inner history of a nation and that the inner history of a nation is its religion, he very clearly established the framework in which his poetry should be read.

Since poetry was not an escape from life for Eichendorff but an indispensable manifestation of the truth and beauty that he found inherent in his religious belief, he believed that the poet himself has a special calling.

As he does among the Romantics, the poet enjoys a lofty position in Eichendorff's view, but instead of having the function of awakening nature in the Romantic sense for aesthetic purposes, Eichendorff's poet has the moral task of awakening human beings themselves and of illuminating and promoting their deepest desire and loftiest aim—that is, the search for and movement toward God. He is to caution against selfish, godless pursuits, encouraging human acceptance of heavenly love. The title of one of Eichendorff's most frequently quoted poems is often overlooked; if cognizance is made of the title "Wünschelrute" ("Divining Rod"), then it becomes clear that the *Zauberwort* (magic word) that is sought in order to set the world singing pertains to the living waters hidden underground which are mentioned in the Gospel of John. The sleeping world will awaken to the everlasting life promised by Christ, if the proper word is found—that is, if the truth of that promise of everlasting life can be articulated.

THE SEARCH FOR GOD

In his poem "An die Dichter" ("To the Poets"), Eichendorff paints a very graphic picture of the ethical responsibilities of the poet: As the "Heart of the World," wandering in the footsteps of the Lord, the poet is to save his fellow men and set them free, for he has been given the power of the word that boldly names the darkness. To name the darkness is to tell the truth and to warn of the dark forces that threaten him who is caught unaware; the nature of that darkness Eichendorff discusses elsewhere. That the poet has an active role in the search for God is obvious in many poems, from the six sonnets produced early in his career, in which he speaks of various aspects of poetry and the poet, to much later ones, such as "Der Dichter" ("The Poet"), in which only the poet, in a mysterious fashion, is the recipient of the deepest beauties of life and the benefactor of the joy that God places in his heart. According to Eichendorff, the poet has special access through God to the truth and beauty of his religion, which he transforms into images and poetry which are reflections of that religion. One is reminded thereby of Friedrich Hölderlin's dictum: "That which endures is produced by poets." The poet's concern is religion within the larger context of human experience. For Eichendorff, poetry is a virtual spiritual personification

and a governing spiritual principle of the life of humankind. The guidance of the poet is therefore essential for ordinary mortals; he is to use his divining rod to locate the living waters of his faith and to articulate them with his songs for the benefit of humankind.

EARTHLY INDULGENCE AND TEMPTATION

Eichendorff's frequently uttered admonition "Hüte dich, bleib wach und munter" (take care, stay awake and lively) is directed against two dangers, that of sensual and aesthetic excess, which he saw as the lure of Romanticism, and that of sterile, middle-class domesticity and the Philistine life. These two hazards are the substance of "Die zwei Gesellen" ("The Two Companions"). The first comrade succumbs to the snares of domestic bliss and is soon imprisoned by hearth and home; the second is seduced by the bewitching sirens of the deep, the enticements of abandoning oneself to eroticism and hedonistic self-indulgence. Interestingly, Eichendorff felt moved to treat the second danger at greater length; he apparently considered it the greater threat and articulated warnings against it more frequently in his poetry, most likely since it was this very indulgence which Romanticism tended to encourage. It is part of the poet's general protest against introversion of the personality. For the narrator of the poem, however, both extremes are distant from God, and he implores God that he be led to him.

Particularly during his student days in Heidelberg, where he was associated with the Romantic movement, Eichendorff concentrated on such poems as "Die Zauberin im Walde" ("The Sorceress in the Forest"), in which the demoniac power of a godless nature and physical beauty are the undoing of a naïve and undisciplined youth. The reader is introduced here to the evil charms of a sultry world where the fresh breezes of God's spirit can gain no entrance. In the poem "Zwielicht" ("Twilight"), the diminishing light of day permits a precarious state in which the usual clear contours are lost and distortions in human relationships are possible. Without the light, which for Eichendorff always means the light of the world, Christ, and consequently also his love, the world is in jeopardy and can be lost in darkness. That God provides the only refuge from earthly sorrows and temptations is clear in "Das Gebet" ("The Prayer"). The pilgrim moving through life, encountering its pleasures and enchantments, experiences through them sorrow as well as joy and has as his only recourse prayer, which overcomes all the evil bewitchments of life when it victoriously reaches God.

POEMS OF MOVEMENT

Eichendorff's poems are poems of movement; when there are no wandering musicians, there are flowing streams, moving clouds, or rustling forests, and always there is at least the flow of song. The two possibilities for movement away from God against which the poet cautions have already been discussed. If one decides to follow either of these choices, one follows, according to Eichendorff, "earthly ponderousness"; if one chooses instead to move toward God, one is reacting to "intimations of Heaven" and opens oneself to God's light and love. Eichendorff speaks about the two influences operating on humans as centrifugal and centripetal forces and sees human life as a constant battleground on which these opposing powers are raging. Centripetal force draws humans away from themselves and toward God as the true center; like the sun, which provides energy for physical life, the divine love of God reaches out to humans and promotes spiritual growth. Humans are free to accept that love and prosper or succumb to centrifugal forces and perish in the abyss of their own earthliness. The movement, then, that is always present in his work can usually be recognized as either of these choices and thus a descent into the darkness of the base individual self and spiritual death or an ascent upward toward the heavenly source of love and eternal salvation. When Eichendorff speaks of love, however, it need not be of divine love; its uplifting power may also be that of human love, which by itself has none of the redeeming features of divine love and which leads to an ever-diminishing world of the self if it is not touched by the light and love of God. Such ill-starred love is treated in poems such as "Verlorene Liebe" ("Lost Love") and particularly in the novella *The Marble Statue*.

"MOONLIT NIGHT"

One of Eichendorff's most famous and beautiful lyrics, "Mondnacht" ("Moonlit Night"), might at first glance appear to be solely a nature poem, even though it is listed among the religious poems in his collected works. Viewed within the framework of the poet's philosophy, the poem clearly appears to be an illustration of God's loving gesture toward his earthly creations. Somewhat in the Homeric manner of not directly describing physical traits of objects but rather depicting subjective reactions to them, Eichendorff here shows the effect of Heaven's kiss upon Earth and nature's response to it. If one takes the sky or Heaven (the German word *Himmel* means both) as a representation of God, then one sees the spirit of God moving across the landscape; the rustling of the forests and the gently waving grain are manifestations of that movement. God's creation, Earth, is visited by him and derives its beauty and holiness from that contact. The poem ends with the human reaction to such an association: The soul of the narrator moves through the quiet countryside in the presence of God's spirit as though it were already flying home.

That homeward journey is in ordinary Christian terms a return to heavenly origins. Eichendorff gives here an exceptionally effective poetic picture of heavenly love, the centripetal pull it exerts on God's creation, the beauty it produces in the physical world, and the spiritual reply to that love in the soul of humans. It is likewise noteworthy that this occurs on a moonlit night; especially with Eichendorff, one must assume that the title of a poem is as important as the text itself and that the moonlight is a significant addition to the poem. Here the light of the moon serves the purpose of illuminating God's moving spirit; were the night not moonbright, the shimmer of blossoms and the billowing of the grain would not be visible to any human observer. What initially appears to be a magnificently executed nature description is thus demonstrated as being a poetic statement of God's love, symbolized by the kiss of Heaven, reaching, like the moonlight, down to his creation, which in turn renders physical as well as spiritual evidence of the efficacy of that love.

RECURRING MESSAGES AND IMAGERY

Eichendorff is sometimes criticized for his repetitiousness and lack of originality, but such objections lose their force with the realization that the poet, in service to his well-defined worldview, is constantly and deliberately reiterating, rephrasing, rearranging, and recombining his relatively few basic concepts in the manner of any dedicated teacher following the tradition of *repetitio est mater studiorum*. Eichendorff is not the aesthete who expresses himself in random variety, casting up beautiful images in a kind of verbal "light show" but rather the pedagogue who is "preaching with other means" the established religious convictions to which his ego and his poetic talents are subordinated and with which they are harmonized. He is a kind of religious philosopher who has achieved an exercise in the sublimation or apotheosis of his philosophy in and through his poetry as well as vice versa. He is used by his poetry and his philosophy as a "musician" of these two muses to create living word entities which embody and transfer to the reader the essence of his philosophy. His poems are thus written "through him" and tend to transcend his personal attributes and abilities as they take on a being and order of their own, culminating in an entity apart from and beyond the poet's own manipulation of words, themes, ideas, and forms.

Since Eichendorff himself spoke of the hieroglyphic language used in his poetry, it would be most profitable to take note of some of his most frequently used words and images. A thorough analysis of the function of such concepts as spring, gardens, *das Bild* ("the image" or "picture"), song, *der Quell* ("source" or "fountain"), water, forests, woman, and light that appear so regularly in Eichendorff's poetry, as well as an investigation of the changing contexts of these motifs, would yield proof of the profundity of his often superficially read poems. Even a quick survey of Eichendorff's poems indicates how frequently light, particularly morning light, is featured in his work. The morning is his favorite time of day and Aurora a favorite allegorical figure.

It may seem surprising that a sound-oriented poet such as Eichendorff emphasizes light so frequently in his work. Although Eichendorff's talent is that of a musician, his sensitivity is not limited to the auditory world; much of the joy he chooses to articulate is that which he experiences through a visual awareness of the beauty of nature. Instead of employing words to paint the detailed splendors of the visually perceptible physical world, however, Eichendorff was better able to sing praises of them. His frequent allusion to light is therefore both his acknowledgment of the spiritual source of

the light which illuminates the wonder of God's creation and a kind of reduction and simplification of multitudinous visual phenomena to one comprehensive symbol. Eichendorff's light is always from above, and when it is not the daylight produced by the sun, it is the light of the moon or the stars, which mitigates and provides relief from the undifferentiated, ambivalent night. Light is for Eichendorff a verification of the Heavenly Father who provides it and of his love for his earthly creatures; it is "des Himmels Kunden" ("tidings from Heaven"), as in the poem "Jugendandacht" ("Youthful Devotion"). In "Der himmlische Maler" ("The Heavenly Painter"), it is God and not the poet who is the painter: God's hand draws the contours of the landscape with the morning light, and as the light makes visible the colors of the countryside, his world is painted and shown in all its glory.

Because Eichendorff was so committed to the idea expressed by his contemporary Clemens von Brentano, that "In dem Lichte wohnt das Heil!" ("in light there is salvation!"), the arrival of light at dawn was an especially welcome occasion for him and the theme of a great many cheerful poems. For Eichendorff, the morning light clarifies the mysteries of the night and erases the worries, fears, and temptations that accompany the night. His morning poems are always expressions of a joyful new beginning; as in the biblical account of the Creation, light means the advent of new life. In Eichendorff's poems, the awakening of nature is heralded by the song of the birds; they seem to acknowledge the source of all light and life as they wing upward toward the heavens. Dawn often coincides with the start of the poet's frequently delineated journeys. Eichendorff was inclined also to write of the other daily transition between light and darkness, the twilight; the time of fading light exemplifies, in contrast to morning hope, an awareness of the bleakness of any diminution of God's light and love.

TECHNICAL AND STYLISTIC DEVICES

Neither in style nor in content does Eichendorff's poetry initially appear to be strikingly innovative; just as the poet's worldview has survived the test of time, so his poetic forms are well practiced and time-honored. For the quintessential poet Eichendorff, however, perhaps more than for poets generally, the poem is itself the message; the "how" of its delivery is as important as the "what" of its content and serves as an additional aspect or reinforcement of the thought contained within it. Eichendorff intimately and intricately links the structure, rhythm, and sounds of the poem to the discourse.

Eichendorff is far more than a facile technician; the standard technical devices he uses are painstakingly chosen to complement the ideas in question, but the full subtleties of such an interrelationship of form and content are exposed only after thorough analysis. With justification, one can say that much of the poet's art conceals itself. Since Eichendorff is a master of *Liedform* ("song form"), in which the entire poem is one organic, melodic unit, his sense of style has been compared to that of Schumann. The cyclical structure the poet often employs involves not only a rephrasing of the initial message at the conclusion of the poem and therefore a full-cycle realization of the essential meaning, but also a counter-reflecting of individual parts internally, so that a wheels-within-wheels effect is created throughout the entire structure. Eichendorff's sonnets and ballads as well as his songs are best rendered orally, so that the sounds of nature he so frequently uses, the liquid rhythms, and the eloquent, poignant melodies, are clearly communicated.

The strength of Eichendorff's work rests therefore not upon superficial novelty but rather upon the quality of his expression and the integrity and skill with which he executed his mission as an artist. What is unique and extraordinary in Eichendorff's writing is the fervor of his belief in the interrelationship of his poetry and his faith and the consistency and emotive power with which he demonstrated that belief in practice. The journeys into "the wide world" which feature so prominently in his work become particularly inviting when it becomes clear that they are ultimately excursions of the soul into regions that promise spiritual nourishment.

OTHER MAJOR WORKS

LONG FICTION: *Ahnung und Gegenwart*, 1815; *Das Marmorbild*, 1819 (novella; *The Marble Statue*, 1927); *Aus dem Leben eines Taugenichts*, 1826 (novella; *Memoirs of a Good-for-Nothing*, 1866); *Viel Lärmen um Nichts*, 1833 (novella); *Dichter und ihre Gesellen*, 1834; *Eine Meerfahrt*, 1835; *Das Schloss Dürande*, 1837 (novella); *Die Entführung*, 1839; *Die Glücksritter*, 1841; *Das Incognito: Ein Puppenspiel*, 1841; *Libertas und ihre Freier*, 1849; *Julian*, 1853.

PLAYS: *Krieg den Philistern*, pb. 1824; *Ezelin von Romano*, pb. 1828; *Der letzte Held von Marienburg*, pb. 1830; *Die Freier*, pb. 1833; *Robert und Guiscard*, pb. 1855 (verse play).

NONFICTION: *Zur Kunstliteratur*, 1835; *Die Wiederherstellung des Schlosses der deutschen Ordensritter zu Marienburg*, 1844; *Zur Geschichte der neueren romantischen Poesie in Deutschland*, 1846; *Über die ethische und religiöse Bedeutung der neueren romantischen Poesie in Deutschland*, 1847; *Brentano und seine Märchen*, 1847; *Die deutsche Salonpoesie der Frauen*, 1847; *Die geistliche Poesie in Deutschland*, 1847; *Die neue Poesie Österreichs*, 1847; *Novellen von Ernst Ritter*, 1847; *Die deutschen Volksschriftsteller*, 1848; *Zu den Gedichten von Lebrecht Dreves*, 1849; *Der deutsche Roman des achtzehnten Jahrhunderts in seinem Verhältnis zum Christentum*, 1851; *Zur Geschichte des Dramas*, 1854; *Erlebtes*, 1857; *Geschichte der poetischen Literatur Deutschlands*, 1857 (2 volumes).

MISCELLANEOUS: *Neue Gesamtausgabe der Werke und Schriften in vier Bänden*, 1957-1958.

BIBLIOGRAPHY

Goebel, Robert Owen. *Eichendorff's Scholarly Reception: A Survey*. Columbia, S.C.: Camden House, 1993. A critical study of Eichendorff's work and the German academic culture of his time. Includes bibliographical references and an index.

Hachmeister, Gretchen L. *Italy in the German Literary Imagination: Goethe's "Italian Journey" and Its Reception by Eichendorff, Platen, and Heine*. Rochester, N.Y.: Camden House, 2002. Examines *Memoirs of a Good-for-Nothing*, which was in part a reaction to Johann Wolfgang von Goethe's *Italienische Reise* (1816, 1817; *Travels in Italy*, 1883), as well as German writers' treatment of Germany.

Lukács, Georg. *German Realists in the Nineteenth Century*. Translated by Jeremy Gaines and Paul Keast. Edited by Rodney Livingstone. Cambridge, Mass.: MIT Press, 1993. Seven essays on major nineteenth century figures in German literature, including Eichendorff, concerning the role of literature in history, society, and politics.

Purver, Judith. *Hindeutung auf das Höhere: A Structural Study of the Novels of Joseph von Eichendorff.* New York: Peter Lang, 1989. In this comprehensive study of Eichendorff's novels in English, Purver argues that the theological and didactic intentions in Eichendorff's work are vitally important.

Radner, Lawrence. *Eichendorff: The Spiritual Geometer.* Lafayette, Ind.: Purdue University Press, 1970. Radner provides a comprehensive critical interpretation of Eichendorff's works.

Saul, Nicholas, ed. *The Cambridge Companion to German Romanticism.* New York: Cambridge University Press, 2009. Contains many references to Eichendorff and his works, including his poems. Also provides perspective on the poet.

Schwarz, Egon. *Joseph von Eichendorff.* New York: Twayne, 1972. A short biography with a bibliography of Eichendorff's work.

Margaret T. Peischl

GUNNAR EKELÖF

Born: Stockholm, Sweden; September 15, 1907
Died: Sigtuna, Sweden; March 16, 1968

PRINCIPAL POETRY

Sent på jorden, 1932
Dedikation, 1934
Sorgen och stjärnan, 1936
Köp den blindes sång, 1938
Färjesång, 1941
Non serviam, 1945
Dikter I-III, 1949
Om hösten, 1951
Strountes, 1955
Dikter, 1932-1951, 1956
Opus incertum, 1959
En Mölna-elegi, 1960 (*A Mölna Elegy*, 1984,
    Muriel Rukeyser and Leif Sjöberg, translators)
En natt i Otoččac, 1961

*Sent på jorden med Appendix 1962, och En natt vid
    horisonten*, 1962
Dikter, 1955-1962, 1965
Dīwān över fursten av Emgión, 1965
Sagan om Fatumeh, 1966
Vatten och sand, 1966
Selected Poems of Gunnar Ekelöf, 1967 (Rukeyser
    and Sjöberg, translators)
Vägvisare till underjorden, 1967 (*Guide to the
    Underworld*, 1980)
I Do Best at Night: Poems by Gunnar Ekelöf, 1968
    (Robert Bly and Christina Paulston, translators)
Urval: Dikter, 1928-1968, 1968
Partitur, 1969
Selected Poems, 1971 (W. H. Auden and Sjöberg,
    translators)
Dikter, 1965-1968, 1976
*Songs of Something Else: Selected Poems of
    Gunnar Ekelöf*, 1982

OTHER LITERARY FORMS

In addition to more than ten volumes of poetry, Gunnar Ekelöf (AY-kuh-luhf) wrote four books of essays: *Promenader* (1941; walks), *Utflykter* (1947; excursions), *Blandade kort* (1957; a mixed deck), and *Lägga patience* (1969; playing solitaire). He also published four books of translations, mostly poetry, from French, German, English, Latin, and Persian: *Fransk surrealism* (1933; French Surrealism), *Hundra år modern fransk dikt* (1934; one hundred years of modern French poetry), *Valfrändskaper* (1960; chosen kinships), and *Glödande gåtor* (1966; a translation of Nelly Sachs's *Glühende Rätsel*). Since his death in 1968, there have appeared two books containing letters, the poet's annotations to some of his own works, and various other materials drawn from Ekelöf's notebooks and manuscripts: *En självbiografi* (1971; an autobiography), selected, edited, and with an introduction by the poet's wife and literary executor, Ingrid Ekelöf, and *En röst* (1973; a voice).

ACHIEVEMENTS

Gunnar Ekelöf is widely recognized as the most original and influential Swedish poet of his generation. His reputation was well established in Scandinavia during his lifetime. Sweden honored him with many national literary prizes; the Danish Academy awarded him its Grand Prize for Poetry in 1964; and in 1966, the Scandinavian Council gave Ekelöf its prize for *Dīwān över fursten av Emgión* (Dīwān over the prince of Emgión). Although Ekelöf never completed his formal education, he was honored by academia. The University of Uppsala gave him an honorary degree in 1958, and in the same year, he was elected a member of the Swedish Academy. His contributions to Swedish literature were recognized: He expressed the voice of modernism and brought a new lyric tone to Swedish poetry. The concerns of Ekelöf's major poems are metaphysical and complex; to make them understood, Ekelöf continually tried to simplify poetic language. He pared away nonessentials—what he called "literary language"—until the tone of his poems became almost conversational. It is not, however, a casual voice that one encounters in the poems; it addresses the reader directly, intensely, and passionately. Scandinavians recognize this voice as belonging to a major poet, and many scholars believe that if Ekelöf had written in a language such as English, he would be regarded as a key international figure in the development of contemporary poetry.

BIOGRAPHY

Bengt Gunnar Ekelöf was born in Stockholm, Sweden, on September 15, 1907. His father, Gerhard Ekelöf, was a wealthy stockbroker, and Ekelöf grew up in big, finely furnished houses. Ekelöf's childhood, however, was not a happy one, despite his comfortable surroundings. His father had contracted syphilis, and his health was deteriorating when Ekelöf was a young boy. Before Ekelöf turned nine, his father died, and Ekelöf was sent away to boarding schools. When his mother, Valborg von Hedenberg, remarried several years later, Ekelöf felt rejected and homeless. Bengt Landgren and Reidar Ekner, the critics most familiar with Ekelöf's biography, point out that Ekelöf's relationship with his parents cultivated and reinforced his role as an "outsider." Ekelöf's failed love relationships—a 1932 marriage to Gunnel Bergström was dissolved after a few months, and an affair during 1933 and 1934 was broken off—reinforced Ekelöf's "outsider" perspective.

Gunnar Ekelöf (©Lufti Özkök)

Ekelöf was particularly fascinated by two subjects as a student: music and Oriental mysticism. In 1926, he spent one semester at the London School of Oriental Studies, and in the next year, he began studies in Persian at the University of Uppsala in Sweden. Ekelöf was often sick as a student, and he never earned a degree, but his studies inspired a lifelong interest in Oriental mysticism and led to his discovery of Ibn el-Arabi's poetry, which moved Ekelöf to write his first poems. The attraction of mysticism for Ekelöf, so compelling when he was young, did not wane as he matured. Strains of mysticism can be found throughout his oeuvre, particularly in the last three collections of original work published before his death: *Dīwān över fursten av Emgión*, *Sagan om Fatumeh* (the tale of Fatumeh), and *Guide to the Underworld*.

In the late 1920's, Ekelöf moved to Paris to study music. Soon, however, his attention shifted from music to the problems of poetic language, as he struggled through an emotional breakdown to write many of the poems which appeared in his first book, *Sent på jorden* (late hour on Earth). After the publication of this initial volume, Ekelöf published new volumes every three or four years, becoming a popular as well as a critically acclaimed poet.

In 1943, Ekelöf married Gunhild Flodquist. Their marriage was dissolved in 1950, and in 1951, Ekelöf married Ingrid Flodquist, who became his literary executor after his death. A daughter, Suzanne, was born to them in 1952. As befitted a poet who sought to dissolve the boundaries of time and place, Ekelöf was a tireless traveler; in the last years of his life, he was increasingly drawn to the Middle East. His travels, particularly his 1965 trip to Istanbul, gave rise to the "eternal wanderers" of his later poetry. In 1968, he died of cancer of the throat. At Ekelöf's request, his ashes were placed in the ancient city of Sardis.

ANALYSIS

To discuss Gunnar Ekelöf's poetry is to discuss more than poetry: His books of poems also document evolving stages of Ekelöf's vision, the quest to resolve the great paradoxes of life and death and the boundaries of time. In his grappling with metaphysical questions, Ekelöf followed the path of the "contemporary mystic," in Eric Lindegren's words, and it is this quest which gives Ekelöf's poetry its distinctive character.

"EN OUTSIDERS VÄG"

In 1941, Ekelöf wrote an essay entitled "En outsiders väg" (an outsider's way), and readers have followed his lead in classifying Ekelöf's perspective as that of an "outsider." Certainly, the Byzantine and ancient Greek settings of his last books of poems are far removed from the life and landscape of his contemporary Sweden. One of the central themes in Ekelöf's poetry is the plight of the individual, both isolated and imprisoned within the conscious ego and subjective will of the "I" and "locked out" from all other people and things. The poet's first duty, Ekelöf has stated, is "to admit his unrelieved loneliness and meaninglessness in his wandering on the Earth." It is paradoxically this awareness, this outsider perspective, that allows the poet to create, for only then is the poet resigned enough to be uninhibited, to write truthfully—and thereby to be of some use to others. In typical Ekelöf fashion, total alienation and dejection are turned upside down to provide the starting point for genuine communication. Ekelöf never veers

from his personal vision, his outsider's way, but at the same time, he never loses his audience. His personal vision is expressed with such uncompromising honesty and conviction that his private questions and dilemmas assume universal significance. Thus, however cryptic and arcane his verse becomes, it is never merely art for art's sake: "It is not art one makes/ But it is oneself."

SENT PÅ JORDEN

By analyzing Ekelöf's volumes of poetry chronologically, one can trace the development of his vision from the desperation and anguish expressed in his early poems to the integration of the individual and the unity of time in a cosmic oneness expressed in the Byzantine triptych. Although *Sent på jorden*, Ekelöf's first volume of poetry, did not receive a great deal of attention when it was published, it has been of enormous consequence for the development of Swedish poetry: *Sent på jorden* ushered in lyric modernism. Ekelöf composed the volume in Paris, supposedly while listening to recordings of Igor Stravinsky:

> I placed one word beside another and finally with a great deal of effort managed to construct a whole sentence. . . . It was the hidden meaning that I was seeking—a kind of *Alchemie du verbe*. . . . [P]oetry is this very tensioned-filled relationship between the words, between the lines, between the meanings.

Like the Surrealists and the Dadaists, Ekelöf sought to exploit the associative and suggestive power of words, but he was not content with mere verbal fireworks; he stressed the arrangement of the whole as he carefully placed "one word beside another."

Ekelöf has called *Sent på jorden* a "suicide book," and many of the poems in the volume express an anguished desperation. The persona of the poems is "dying in [his] own convulsions" as he violently struggles for expression and meaning: "crush the alphabet between your teeth." The persona's identity is ready to shatter as "nerves screech silently in the dying light." Locked up in a room, completely isolated from the outside world and even from the objects of the room itself, the persona can only chant: "I don't want to die, I don't want to die and cannot live . . . it's late on earth." Death offers a solution to the persona's desperation, an annihilation of the self. Thus, death is a tempting liberator, able to free the persona from imprisonment in ego. In "Cosmic Sleepwalker," however, the persona, rather than seeking self-annihilation, dreams of communion with a cosmic mother. The choices for the persona, then, are spelled out in "Apotheosis," the final poem of the collection: "Give me poison to die or dreams to live." The fragmented isolation of the individual, prisoner of the "I," is unbearable. In his first volume, then, Ekelöf defines one of his central themes. He also hints, however, at a resolution for the hysterical persona: a living cosmic oneness, where the individual is a part of a larger whole.

SURREALIST INFLUENCE

In 1934, the same year in which Ekelöf published *Dedikation*, he published a book of translations, *Hundra år modern fransk dikt*. The year before, in 1933, his translations of French Surrealist poems had been published in *Fransk surrealism*. Living in Paris in the late 1920's, Ekelöf was bound to feel the impulses of the various "isms" of the period, and many poems in his early volumes could be termed Surrealist. Ekelöf was attracted to the French Surrealists, particularly Robert Desnos, but ultimately found their methods contrived, artificial, and mechanical. On the title page of *Dedikation*, Ekelöf quotes a poet to whom he was more fundamentally drawn, Arthur Rimbaud: "I say: one must be a seer, one must make oneself a seer." In *Sent på jorden*, Ekelöf asked for "dreams to live," and Rimbaud offered a vision to synthesize life and dreams. Nevertheless, the "apotheosis" that Ekelöf sought in *Dedikation* failed; the glorified dream world of this volume later struck Ekelöf as false, and he rejected it. As Rabbe Enckell has pointed out, the romanticized images and prophetic voice in the volume seem an overcompensation for the desperate tone in *Sent på jorden*.

In *Sorgen och stjärnan* (sorrow and the star), the crucial problem remains the same: "One thing I've learned: reality kills! And something else: That no reality exists except this—that none exists!" In *Köp den blindes säng* (buy the blind one's song), the tone becomes calmer, though the perception is the same. The poet can, however, accept his condition, because it becomes a prerequisite for meaning. Ekelöf himself called *Köp den*

blindes säng a transitional book; what he referred to as "the breakthrough" came with *Färjesång* (ferry song).

FÄRJESÅNG

The persona in *Färjesång* overcomes his desperation, assumes the role of the phoenix, and rises out of his ashes of anguish ready to "write it down." The tone is confident, at times assertive, and even lecturing: "In reality you are no one." The poet—who has experienced true vision—unmasks his readers and exposes the feeble self-deceptions they have invented to give significance and purpose to their lives. "Legal rights, human dignity, free will/ all of these are pictures painted with fear in reality's empty hall." Ekelöf asserts a new understanding of reality "beyond justice and injustice, beyond thesis and antithesis," a reality beyond individual personalities and perspectives. Exposing the meaninglessness of clichés and conventions of daily life, Ekelöf "surrenders" himself, "like the last rat on a sinking ship," in the hope of mystically uniting with all. The climax of the collection, the poem "Eufori" ("Euphoria"), clearly shows how Ekelöf's vision had evolved since the earlier volumes. The tone of the poem is calm. The persona is sitting in his garden, at peace with the natural world around him. The red evening glow, the moth, the candle, the aspen—all are pulsating with life, but in this transcendent moment, they pulsate with more than life: "All nature strong with love and death around you." The poet has a vision of the synthesis of life and death, of the individual consciousness and the awareness of all. In this poem, at least, the poet has an answer for himself and the reader: He can "sing of the only thing that reconciles/ the only practical, for all alike."

NON SERVIAM

The mood is much darker in *Non serviam*. In it the poet is estranged from the comforts of the welfare state: "Here, in the long, well-fed hours'/ overfurnished Sweden/ where everything is closed for draughts . . . it is cold to me." The ugly duckling, the odd one, "Svanen" ("The Swan"), surveys the "anemic blush over endless suburbs/ of identical houses." It is fall in this poem, the land laid waste with "worm-eaten cabbages and bare flowers." In a key poem of this collection, "Absentia animi," rotting mushrooms and tattered butterflies are omens of general oblivion. Echoing *Sent på jorden*, the poem repeats the refrain, "Meaningless. Unreal. Meaningless." The vision from *Färjesång* remains, however, although the intensity of the joyful tone is subdued:

> O deep down in me
> the eye of a black pearl reflects from its surface
> in happy half-consciousness
> the image of a cloud!
> Not a thing that exists
> It is something else
> It is in something existent
> but it does not exist
> It is something else
> O far far away
> in what is beyond is found
> something very near!

In "En Julinatt" ("A July Night"), a poem Ekelöf called central to the collection, the persona yearns for a prenatal state, suggesting "something else . . . beyond" as a state, or condition, of preconsciousness, before the intrusion of "I":

> Let me keep my world
> my prenatal world!
> Give me back my world!
> My world is a dark one
> but I will go home in the darkness
> through the grass, under the woods.

Despising the society and culture that produce "suburbs of identical houses," Ekelöf seems reconciled to the simple elements of nature. Like his predecessor, Edith Södergran, a Finno-Swedish poet he much admired, who declared that "the key to all secrets lies hidden in the raspberry patch," Ekelöf trusts nature's existence, concretely and as a revelation of "something else."

"A Reality [*dreamed*]"

In an essay published in 1941, Ekelöf wrote, "Kinship with the dead—or rather: the dead within one—is in many ways more alive than kinship with one's contemporaries, from whom one is separated by a thick layer of rhinoceros hide." The individual is alone—that is a central theme in Ekelöf's poetry—but teeming with life; the dead remain as integral parts of the individual's ego. In earlier volumes, Ekelöf had exposed the falsehoods of rational philosophies and denied their

reality, but in "En verklighet [*drömd*]" ("A Reality [*dreamed*]"), from the collection *Om hösten* (in autumn), the poet's insight—somewhat akin to Ralph Waldo Emerson's "dream power"—enables him to construct a philosophy of life from his experience of nature. The persona overcomes all limitations, including time, space, and loneliness:

> every landscape, every shift in the landscape, contains
> all possible landscapes
> and this life contains all possible lives:
>
> . . . .
>
> the peopled worlds,
> and the life of the unseen, and the dead.

The 1940's and 1950's

Critics agree that Ekelöf's poetry of the 1940's assured him a place as one of Sweden's greatest lyric poets. The concerns of the poetry are abstract, metaphysical, speculative. Most of the key poems of this period are longer lyrics, varying in tone from the explosiveness of *Färjesång* to the romantic, elegiac tone of *Om hösten*. The poems of the 1950's move in a different direction. Ekelöf simplified his style in an attempt to write depersonalized poetry, and the poems of this decade are generally short, simple lyrics about familiar objects and situations, pruned of all literary baggage to achieve what Ekelöf called "poetry of the factual," or antipoetry. The collections published in the 1950's also reveal a joking, absurd side of Ekelöf's vision. In contrast to the speculative, metaphysical poems of earlier volumes, many of these poems focus on the body: sexuality, eroticism, obscenity. If Ekelöf's antipoetry functions to balance the body-soul relationship by emphasizing feeling and existence here and now, as Pär Hellström's study of these volumes suggests, Ekelöf as seeker still permeates these collections. He continues as a solitary figure, affirming that "I do best alone at night," for then he can listen "to the talk of the eternal wanderers." Eternal wanderers, however, live an existence different from that of ordinary mortals, and many of these poems express a longing for death in the poet's desire to identify with and become a part of timeless existence. The poet's "self-reflecting waters" do not speak "of life but of Lethe's wave"; rebirth is to be found "in the swaddling cloth of death." This fascination with death, however, culminates in a turn toward life-giving uses of the past and tradition. Unable to exist in the isolation of his own ego, unable to accept the social alienation of his contemporary Sweden, Ekelöf turns to "ancient cities" to find his own "future." Thus, the publication of his next volume, *A Mölna Elegy*, marked a transition to the concerns that inform the trilogy that concluded his career.

A MÖLNA ELEGY

In his introductory notes to *A Mölna Elegy*, Ekelöf stated that the poem is concerned with "the relativity of the experience of time"; he hoped, he said, to capture a "traverse section of time, instead of a section lengthwise." In his attempt to analyze "the mood of a certain moment," Ekelöf revealed the complexity of consciousness. The life moment in *A Mölna Elegy* is a moment of mystical insight, with "time running wild" in the consciousness of the persona. The "I" comprises many personalities and undergoes many transformations as the present, past, and future are experienced as independent layers of consciousness. The life of the past—in the memory of the persona's relatives, for example—exists in the present, in the persona's consciousness, as well as in the lives of the dead. Any given moment, then, comprises images from a number of centuries and from various cultures and beliefs—from the past as well as the present. Demarcations of time and space are dissolved, borders between life and death eliminated. All existence is a unity: The reality "beyond" is all of it at once.

"I am of the opinion," Ekelöf once wrote, "that man carries humanity within himself, not only his father's and mother's inheritance but also his cousin's, his second cousins', and further, the animals', plants', and stones' inheritance." As Leif Sjöberg has so convincingly documented, the many "inheritances" which constitute the moment expressed in *A Mölna Elegy* are held together by the "I" of the poem—not only by means of his own observations, but also by means of dead relatives speaking through him, and through allusions to and quotations from dead poets. Ekelöf uses fragmentary allusions, many of them esoteric (such as authentic graffiti and inscriptions in Latin found on tombstones in Pompeii), and borrowings (for example, from Edith Södergran) to document a life and a piece of history.

Ghosts, phantoms, spirits—the "dead ones"—still have a voice, and thus the past continues to live in the present, integral to the speaker's consciousness. People, things, and ideas can be fully comprehended only in the context of their connectedness to the past.

Ekelöf's 1965 trip to Istanbul, where he saw the Madonna icon of Vlachernes, inspired an outpouring of passionate lyrics. Poems came so quickly, Ekelöf wrote to a friend, that, "as far as I can understand, someone has written the poems with me as a medium. . . ." Within a few short months, Ekelöf composed the last three volumes he was to publish in his lifetime.

DĪWĀN ÖVER FURSTEN AV EMGIÓN

The Dīwān trilogy ranges from the Byzantine Middle Ages to an unspecified epoch in the Oriental (that is, Middle Eastern) world to classical antiquity and the Hellenic Age. In accepting the prize of the Scandinavian Council in 1966 for *Dīwān över fursten av Emgión*, Ekelöf stressed that these civilizations of the past can speak to modern times: "I have chosen Byzantium, long since lost, as a starting point from which I should be able to assail the present." His targets are "political decadence" and the "degradation" and "coldness" among persons he observes in modern life. These are familiar themes in Ekelöf's poetry, but they are given a particular intensity in the trilogy, an intensity derived from the controlled, pure passion they express.

In the Dīwān trilogy, Ekelöf has been able to concretize "something beyond" into a female figure, lover-daughter-sister, and finally an all-embracing mother figure. His vision can therefore be expressed in passionate love lyrics, or in what Bengt Landgren has termed "erotic mysticism." The persona in *Dīwān över fursten av Emgión* is captured in battle, imprisoned, tortured, and finally blinded. Locked in darkness, his only means of "escape" and survival is his ability to dream and to remember. The Ekelöf persona recognizes both God and the devil as "tyrants," as exponents of either/or, a world of duality he rejects. Love offers the persona an alternative to "the two locked in combat," a liberation from captivity in ego. The love for the mother figure allows a transition from life to death or the presence of death—or preconsciousness—in the present. The persona's dream power, or vision, enables him to "go home in the darkness" to that "prenatal world" Ekelöf called for in *Non serviam.* "Something else," something beyond, is now seen clearly as a "Mother to no man/ But who has breasts/ With milk for all."

SAGAN OM FATUMEH

The female persona in *Sagan om Fatumeh*, like the male persona in *Dīwān över fursten av Emgión*, suffers horribly. She is apparently deserted by the prince who has fathered her child. For a time she serves in a harem, but eventually she is thrown out on the street. As she becomes an old woman; she has to prostitute herself to survive. Nevertheless, her spirit is never crushed; her visions—the memories of her lover—sustain her. Fatumeh also sustains the prince, for she gives his "soul a shadow"; the love they feel for each other is their realization of the unity of all things, of the soul's awareness of the eternal Mother. Only something that exists can cast a "shadow": The soul exists in its expression of love, as felt between two people, and as a vision of the encompassing love of an Earth Mother. In Fatumeh's final meeting with her beloved, the mystic identification is realized as the lovers are effaced in a cosmic union.

GUIDE TO THE UNDERWORLD

Early in his career, in a poem published in *Färjesång,* Ekelöf described his "underworld":

Each person is a world, peopled
by blind creatures in dim revolt
against the I, the kin, who rules them.
In each soul thousands of souls are imprisoned,
in each world thousands of worlds are hidden
and these blind and lower worlds
are real and living, though not full-born,
as truly as I am real . . .

In *Guide to the Underworld,* the last volume of poetry he published before he died, Ekelöf is able to free these "blind creatures" because the "guide" is free of the ego. He has discovered that, "alone in the quiet night," he can escape the limitations of his own identity and "hover" in his visions, "weightless," "empty," "floating." Life and death, past and present, history and dreams converge and dissolve into each other. In a key poem, "The Devil's Sermon," the persona unites with the Virgin, or Eternal She, in an act of love. Thus, the

persona merges with the universe and is one with the infinite. Ekelöf finally resolves the great paradox—he embraces a reality that is life and death at once:

I wanted both

The part of the whole as well as the whole
And that this choice would involve no contradiction.

OTHER MAJOR WORKS

NONFICTION: *Promenader,* 1941; *Utflykter,* 1947; *Blandade kort,* 1957; *Verklighetsflykt,* 1958; *Lägga patience,* 1969; *Ensjälvbiografi,* 1971; *En röst,* 1973; *Modus Vivendi: Selected Prose,* 1996.

TRANSLATIONS: *Fransk surrealism,* 1933 (with Greta Knutsson-Tzara); *Hundra år modern fransk dikt,* 1934; *Valfrändskaper,* 1960; *Glödande gåtor,* 1966 (of Nelly Sachs's *Glühende Rätsel*).

MISCELLANEOUS: *Skrifter,* 1991-1993 (8 volumes; collected works).

BIBLIOGRAPHY

Adams, Ann-Charlotte Gavel. *Twentieth-Century Swedish Writers Before World War II.* Vol. 259 in *Dictionary of Literary Biography.* Detroit: Gale Group, 2002. Contains a biographical essay on Ekelöf that also analyzes his work.

Fioretos, Aris. "Now and Absence in the Early Ekelöf." *Scandinavian Studies* 62, no. 3 (Summer, 1990): 319. Analyzes the poetic techniques used in "Osynlig narvaro," the fourth entry in *Sent på jorden.*

Shideler, Ross. *Voices Under the Ground.* Berkeley: University of California Press, 1973. A critical study of Ekelöf's early poetry. Includes bibliographic references.

Sjöberg, Leif. *A Reader's Guide to Gunnar Ekelöf's "A Mölna Elegy."* New York: Twayne, 1973. A critical guide to *A Mölna Elegy.* Includes bibliographic references.

Thygesen, Erik. *Gunnar Ekelöf's Open-Form Poem, A Mölna Elegy.* Stockholm: Almqvist & Wiksell International, 1985. A critical study of *A Mölna Elegy.* Includes bibliographic references and an index.

C. L. Mossberg

PAUL ÉLUARD
Eugène Grindel

Born: Saint-Denis, France; December 14, 1895
Died: Charenton-le-Pont, France; November 18, 1952

PRINCIPAL POETRY

Le Devoir et l'inquiétude, 1917
Poèmes pour la paix, 1918
Les Animaux et leurs hommes, les hommes et leurs animaux, 1920
Les Nécessités de la vie et les conséquences des rêves, 1921
Mourir de ne pas mourir, 1924
Capitale de la douleur, 1926 (*Capital of Pain,* 1973)
L'Amour la poésie, 1929
À toute épreuve, 1930
La Vie immédiate, 1932
La Rose publique, 1934
Faciles, 1935
Thorns of Thunder: Selected Poems, 1936
Les Yeux fertiles, 1936
Les Mains libres, 1937
Donner à voir, 1939
Médieuses, 1939
Le Livre ouvert I, 1938-1940, 1940
Choix de poèmes, 1914-1941, 1941
Le Livre ouvert II, 1939-1941, 1942
Poésie et vérité, 1942 (*Poetry and Truth, 1942*, 1944)
Au rendez-vous allemand, 1944
En avril 1944: Paris respirait encore!, 1945
Le Dur Désir de durer, 1946 (*The Dour Desire to Endure*, 1950)
Poésie ininterrompue, 1946
Corps mémorable, 1947
Dignes de vivre, 1947
Le Livre ouvert, 1938-1944, 1947
Marc Chagall, 1947
Poèmes politiques, 1948
Premiers Poèmes (1913-1921), 1948
Une Leçon de morale, 1949 (*A Moral Lesson*, 2007)
Le Phénix, 1951
Poèmes, 1951
Tout dire, 1951
Poèmes pour tous, 1952
Les Derniers Poèmes d'amour de Paul Éluard, 1962 (*Last Love Poems of Paul Éluard*, 1980)

OTHER LITERARY FORMS

Paul Éluard (ay-LWAHR) wrote many critical essays explaining the theories of the Surrealist movement, in which he played so large a part, and delineating his personal aesthetic theories as well. These critical works include the various Surrealist manifestos (many coauthored with André Breton), *Avenir de la poésie* (1937), *Poésie involontaire et poésie intentionelle* (1942), *À Pablo Picasso* (1944), *Picasso à Antibes* (1948), *Jacques Villon ou l'art glorieux* (1948), *La Poésie du passé* (1951), *Anthologie des écrits sur l'art* (1952), and *Les Sentiers et routes de la poésie* (1952). Because the Surrealists were little interested in the limitations of genre, much of Éluard's poetic work falls into the category of the prose poem. His complete works are published in *Œuvres complètes* (1968). Some of his letters are published in *Lettres à Joe Bousquet* (1973).

ACHIEVEMENTS

Paul Éluard was, with Breton and Louis Aragon, a cofounder of Surrealism, one of the principal artistic movements of the twentieth century. Earlier, he had also been instrumental in the Dada movement. As one of the primary theoreticians of Surrealism, Éluard helped to outline its aesthetic concepts in a number of manifestos and illustrated its techniques in his huge output of poetry. He published more than seventy volumes of poetry in his lifetime, many of which reveal his ability to set aside Surrealist theories in favor of poetic effect. As a result, many critics have called him the most original of the Surrealist poets and the truest poet of the group. His love poetry in particular is singled out for praise. Eluard's *Capital of Pain*, *La Rose publique*, and *Les Yeux fertiles* are widely regarded as among the finest products of Surrealism in French poetry.

BIOGRAPHY

Paul Éluard was born Eugène Grindel on December 14, 1895, in Saint-Denis, a suburb of Paris. His background was strictly working-class—his father was a bookkeeper and his mother (from whom he took the name Éluard) a seamstress—and most of his early years were spent in the vicinity of factories in Saint-Denis and Aulnay-sous-Bois. Éluard was a good student at the École Communale, but later, when the Grindels moved to Paris and the boy was enrolled at the École Supérieure Colbert, his scholastic performance declined. His education was cut short by illness, and he was placed in a sanatorium in Davos, Switzerland, when he was sixteen. He returned to Paris two years later and almost immediately entered the army; his experiences in the trenches of World War I crystallized his growing awareness of the suffering of humanity. Suffering from gangrene of the bronchi as a result of poison gas, Éluard spent more time in a sanatorium, reading much poetry, especially the works of Arthur Rimbaud, Lautréamont, and Charles Vildrac. He also read Percy Bysshe Shelley, Novalis, and Heraclitus of Ephesus, and he developed a special feeling for Walt

Paul Éluard (Roger Viollet/Getty Images)

Whitman, whose *Leaves of Grass* (1855) he read many times.

In 1917, Éluard published his first book of poetry, *Le Devoir et l'inquiétude*. The following year, his *Poèmes pour la paix* was published, and he met Jean Paulhan, "impresario of poets," who advanced his career. He also met Breton, Aragon, Tristan Tzara, Philippe Soupault, and Giorgio de Chirico—the writers and artists who would eventually become, with Éluard, the leading figures of the Surrealist movement. Surrealism, however, was preceded by Dada; Éluard, Breton, Aragon, Francis Picabia, Soupault, Marguerite Buffet, and others, according to Tzara, all took part in the public "debut" of Dada in January, 1920, at a matinee organized by *Littérature*, a Dadaist review. The spectacle caused an enormous uproar, and a week later, Éluard joined Breton, Soupault, and others in a public debate at the Université Populaire. Éluard began to publish a review called *Proverbe*, to which all the Dadaists contributed. Wrote Tzara, "It was chiefly a matter of contradicting logic and language."

As Dada moved toward the more rigorous Surrealism, Éluard's name appeared on various manifestos. His poetry changed as a result of his allegiance to Dada and Surrealism; under the influence of the Surrealists' enthusiasm for "automatic writing," his language became freer. He also developed friendships with some of the most influential artists of the time, including Pablo Picasso, Max Ernst, Salvador Dalí, and Joan Miró.

In 1917, Éluard married Gala (Elena Dimitievna Diakanova), whom he had met in Switzerland in 1912; they had a daughter, Cécile, in 1918. Gala turned her affections first toward the artist Max Ernst and later toward Salvador Dalì. Brokenhearted, Éluard disappeared without explanation in March, 1924. Rumors circulated that he had died. In fact, he had sailed on the first available ship out of Marseilles, beginning a mysterious seven-month voyage around the world. He was seen in Rome, Vienna, Prague, London, and Spain, and he visited such distant locales as Australia, New Zealand, the Antilles, Panama, Malaysia, Java, Sumatra, Ceylon, Indochina, and India.

On his return, Éluard once again enthusiastically threw himself into the Surrealist movement, becoming editor and director of the movement's reviews, *La*

Révolution surréaliste and *La Surréalisme au service de la révolution*. Following Surrealist theories, he experimented in his poetry with verbal techniques, the free expression of the mind, and the relation between dream and reality. These inquiries led to *L'Immaculée Conception* (1930; *The Immaculate Conception*, 1990), which he wrote with Breton. That same year, he made a final break with Gala, having met Maria Benz (affectionately called Nusch), who was the subject of numerous works by Picasso. The publication of *Capital of Pain* had established Éluard as an important poet, and with *La Rose publique* and *Les Yeux fertiles*, he became the leading poet of Surrealism.

Éluard's world trip and his memories of proletarian life and of the war had made him sensitive to the political trends of the 1930's. These feelings came to the fore at the outbreak of the Spanish Civil War (1936-1939). The fascist armies in Spain seemed to Éluard the forerunners of a total destruction of the modern concept of freedom. In response, his poetry became more politically oriented. He wrote in *L'Évidence poétique* (1936) that "the time has come when poets have a right and a duty to maintain that they are profoundly involved in the lives of other men, in communal life." He became exasperated with the detachment of his Surrealist colleagues and separated from the group.

In 1939, Éluard once again found himself in the French army, and after the disastrous defeat, he courageously worked for the Resistance in Paris and Lozère, helping to found the weekly newspaper *Lettres Françaises*. He was constantly in danger of arrest, and he and Nusch, whom he had married in 1934, were forced to move every month to avoid the Gestapo. He joined the outlawed Communist Party in 1942 (he had been affiliated with it for nearly fifteen years). He used the pseudonyms Jean du Hault and Maurice Hervent, and the *maquis* circulated his poems underground. One poem, "Liberté," published in 1942 in the Nazi-denounced collection *Poetry and Truth, 1942*, which has been called one of the "consecrated texts of the Resistance." For a brief period, he was forced to hide in an asylum at Saint-Alban. He was deeply affected by the suffering of the inmates and the experience could be seen in his subsequent writings.

After the war, Éluard's life was shattered by the sudden death of Nusch. He sought a solution to his sorrow in his poetry and in extending his love to embrace all humankind. During this period, he was very active in the Communist Party, traveling to Italy, Yugoslavia, Greece, Poland, Switzerland, and the Soviet Union, which awarded him the International Peace Prize. In Mexico, attending the Congress of the World Council on Peace, he met Dominique Lemor, and his love for her did much to restore his moral vision. He married her in 1951, but a heart attack in September, 1952, weakened him, and he died of a stroke that November in his apartment overlooking the Bois de Vincennes, outside Paris.

ANALYSIS

Paul Éluard is regarded by many critics as Surrealism's greatest poet. Dubbed the Nurse of the Stars by Soupault, he was central to the movement from the beginning. Breton once answered the question What is Surrealism? by saying, "It is a splinter of the sparkling glass of Paul Éluard." It is therefore ironic that when Éluard's work is praised, its "non-Surrealistic" elements are generally singled out as having made his work better than that of the poets around him. Critics point out his permanent and universal themes, present even before the birth of Surrealism. He continually explores the themes of love, human suffering, and the struggle of the masses against hunger, slavery, and deprivation. His avoidance of shock and violence, employed programmatically by many of the Surrealists, is also pointed out as evidence of his internal distance from the movement in which he played such a central role. Finally, unlike many of his fellow Surrealists, who regarded the world of dreams as a higher reality, sufficient unto itself, Éluard used dreams to interpret his experience: In his poetry, the dreamworld helps make the "real" world more comprehensible.

Nevertheless, Éluard's poetry can be understood only in the context of Surrealism. His works strongly reflect the Surrealist rejection of nineteenth century values, which had led not to the paradise promised by progressives of that century but to the abject horror of World War I. It was necessary, therefore, to reject the worldview that brought about the enslavement of the human imagination. The enemy was not only order but also the belief in order. Religion and science are both inherently limiting, the Surrealists argued, and fail to take account of the most fundamental element of existence: disorder.

When Éluard found a mystical revelation in six consecutive lines beginning with the letter *p* in Tzara's *Grains et issues* (1935), he was expressing the Surrealist faith in a truth beyond the surface of things, a truth that could be explored only through absolute freedom. Naturally, this freedom must exist in the political sphere as well, that Éluard, like a number of Surrealists, embraced an idealistic vision of communism is not surprising, given the context of the times. Communism preached the destruction of religion and of the bourgeoisie, and it was an avowed enemy of the fascism taking hold all over Europe in the 1920's and 1930's.

Above all, however, the Surrealists turned inward. Love, a privileged theme in their works, is treated as a means of altering consciousness, analogous in its effects to hallucinogenic drugs. Love becomes, paradoxically, both a way of escaping the world and the profoundest way of knowing it. Éluard adamantly holds that all real knowledge comes from love, and his finest poems express a longing for transcendence through sexual love.

"PREMIÈRE DU MONDE" AND "A WOMAN IN LOVE"

In Éluard's works, woman, as the object of love, is a mirror for which men reach; seeing themselves reflected there, they discover "surreality." Woman, in Éluard's poetry, is simultaneously a particular woman (Gala, Nusch, Dominique) and a universal woman, timeless, embodying womanhood and all women. She is a vision of light, and images of brightness, transcendence, and purity are associated with her. The poet, on the other hand, suffers in darkness, isolation, limitation, and impurity. He addresses her: "You who abolish forgetfulness, ignorance, and hope/ You who suppress absence and give me birth . . ./ You are pure, you are even purer than I." In "Première du monde" (from *Capital of Pain*), his woman is the first woman in the world. She is simultaneously held captive by the Earth and possessed by spirit. The light hides itself in her. She is a complex of wheels; she is grass in which one becomes lost; she resembles the stars; she takes upon herself a maze of fire. In another poem, he writes, "I love you for your wisdom that is not mine . . ./ For this immortal heart which I do not possess." In other poems, he relates the image of the mirror to the image of woman so that her eyes become mirrors and she plays a mirrorlike role. Woman is mirror is poetry is woman: Each reflects the other; each is the other. One sees this most strikingly in "L'Amoureuse" ("A Woman in Love," from *Mourir de ne pas mourir*), when the lover becomes one with the beloved: "She has the shape of my hands/ She has the color of my eyes/ She is swallowed in my shadow/ Like a stone against the sky."

SURREALIST INFLUENCES

Éluard's poetic vision of woman is representative of the constant shifting between opposites that characterizes his work. He moves between light and dark, despair and hope, mystery and knowledge. This subtle play between opposites is very much characteristic of Surrealism in general, but Éluard handles it with simple, direct language. Like many great writers dealing with enormously complex and difficult conceptions, Éluard simplifies his language, choosing ordinary words and rearranging them in extraordinary ways. One of his early short poems, "Enfermé, seul" (from *Les Nécessités de la vie et les conséquences des rêves*), illustrates his passionate simplicity: "Complete song/ The table to see, the chair to sit/ And the air to breathe./ To rest,/ Inevitable Idea,/ Complete song."

When Éluard is at his best, this plain language becomes exquisite, as in lines such as: "Dawn fallen like a shower"; "We were tired/ Of living in the ruins of sleep"; "The prism breathes with us"; "The fountain running and sweet and nude." Unlike traditional metaphors, which are based on logical resemblances between things, Éluard's metaphors come out of dreams, revealing the power of the mind to find meaning in "illogical" juxtapositions. The line "She is standing on my eyelids" from "A Woman in Love," for example, could be a literal transcription of a dream: Thus, the poet achieves expression of the previously inexpressible. Like Dalí's famous melting clocks, Éluard's images broaden the vision of the reader. This quality makes Éluard's poetry easy to grasp and yet extraordinarily difficult, immediately meaningful yet provoking endless reflection.

OTHER MAJOR WORKS

NONFICTION: *L'Immaculée Conception*, 1930 (with André Breton; *The Immaculate Conception*, 1990); *L'Évidence poétique*, 1936; *Avenir de la poésie*, 1937; *Poésie involuntaire et poésie intentionelle*, 1942; *À Pablo Picasso*, 1944; *Jacques Villon ou l'art glorieux*, 1948; *Picasso à Antibes*, 1948; *La Poésie du passé*, 1951; *Anthologie des écrits sur l'art*, 1952; *Les Sentiers et routes de la poésie*, 1952; *Lettres à Joe Bousquet*, 1973; *Letters to Gala*, 1989.

MISCELLANEOUS: *Œuvres complètes*, 1968.

BIBLIOGRAPHY

Caws, Mary Ann. *The Poetry of Dada and Surrealism: Aragon, Breton, Tzara, Éluard, and Desnos*. Princeton, N.J.: Princeton University Press, 1970. The chapter on Éluard is a very good analysis of Éluard's views on love and death as they emerge from the poet's continuous fascination with the ineffable that transcends the world of appearances. The emphasis is on Éluard's constant preoccupation with the duality of the world around him.

_____. *Surrealism*. New York: Phaidon, 2004. This art book format survey of Surrealism contains information on Éluard and other poets.

Gaitet, Pascale. "Éluard's Reactions, Poetic and Political to World War Two." *Literature and History* 2, no. 1 (1991): 24-43. Examines Éluard's shift from the destabilizing, antibourgeois doctrines espoused by the Surrealists toward a more conventional use of symbolism, reinforcing traditional values, and a unifying rhetoric during the Resistance era. Gaitet depicts Éluard's poetic output during this era as embracing a more utilitarian, propagandist function, much in keeping with the Communist Party, which he rejoined in 1942.

McNab, Robert. *Ghost Ships: A Surrealist Love Triangle*. New Haven, Conn.: Yale Press, 2004. Describes the love triangle among Max Ernst, Éluard, and Gala, as well as Éluard's disappearance and travels.

Meadwell, Kenneth W. "Paul Éluard." In *Modern French Poets*, edited by Jean-François Leroux. Vol. 258 in *Dictionary of Literary Biography*. Detroit: Gale, 2002. Provides an overview of the life and work of Éluard, with emphasis on collections and poems representing his literary evolution.

Montagu, Jemima. *The Surrealists: Revolutionaries in Art and Writing, 1919-1935*. London: Tate, 2002. This look at Surrealism in both literature and art contains a chapter on Éluard and Max Ernst.

Nugent, Robert. *Paul Éluard*. New York: Twayne, 1974. Approaches Éluard's poetry as the expression of the poet's solitude as well as humankind's solitude and includes a concise chronology and short bibliography of critical works.

Strauss, Jonathan. "Paul Éluard and the Origins of Visual Subjectivity." *Mosaic* 33, no. 2 (2000): 25-46. Offers close readings of passages taken from *Capital of Pain* to demonstrate Éluard's agile usage of the visual and his redefinition of subjectivity in terms of impossible images that can only be expressed through language. This tying of the sensuous to the abstract becomes the cornerstone of Éluard's attempt to create a new theory of subjectivity.

Watts, Philip. *Allegories of the Purge: How Literature Responded to the Postwar Trials of Writers and Intellectuals in France*. Stanford, Calif.: Stanford University Press, 1998. Chapter 4 examines Éluard's poetic output during the Occupation and the period of purge trials in France directly following the end of World War II to show that Éluard's shift from the linguistic and image play of his earlier writings to a strictly metered verse can be seen as a political act calling for the purge of collaborationist writers.

J. Madison Davis

ODYSSEUS ELYTIS
Odysseus Alepoudhelis

Born: Iraklion (also known as Heraklion), Crete; November 2, 1911
Died: Athens, Greece; March 18, 1996

PRINCIPAL POETRY

Prosanatolizmi, 1939
Ilios o protos, mazi me tis parallayies pano se mian ahtidha, 1943

*Azma iroiko ke penthimo yia ton hameno
   anthipolohagho tis Alvanias*, 1945 (*Heroic and
   Elegiac Song for the Lost Second Lieutenant of
   the Albanian Campaign*, 1965)
To axion esti, 1959 (*The Axion Esti*, 1974)
Exi ke mia tipsis yia ton ourano, 1960 (*Six and One
   Remorses for the Sky*, 1974)
To fotodhendro ke i dhekati tetarti omorfia, 1971
To monogramma, 1971 (*The Monogram*, 1974)
O ilios o iliatoras, 1971 (*The Sovereign Sun*, 1974)
The Sovereign Sun: Selected Poems, 1974 (includes
   Six and One Remorses for the Sky, *The
   Monogram*, *The Sovereign Sun*, and various
   selections from his other collections)
Maria Nefeli, 1978 (*Maria Nephele*, 1981)
Ekloyi, 1935-1977, 1979
Odysseus Elytis: Selected Poems, 1981
What I Love: Selected Poems of Odysseus Elytis,
   1986
Ta elegia tes oxopetras, 1990 (*The Oxopetra
   Elegies*, 1996)
The Collected Poems of Odysseus Elytis, 1997
Ek tou plision, 1998
Eros, Eros, Eros: Selected and Last Poems, 1998

OTHER LITERARY FORMS

Principally a poet, Odysseus Elytis (EH-lee-tees),
in the eminently pictorial, imagistic, "architectural" nature of his verse, revealed his other, parallel propensity.
Had he received any formal artistic education, he might
have been a distinguished painter as well. As early as
1935, he produced a number of Surrealist collages; in
1966, he painted some thirty-odd gouaches, all but four
of which he destroyed; and in the years from 1967 to
1974, the period of the dictatorship of the "colonels,"
he produced about forty remarkable collages, nineteen
of which are reproduced in Ilías Petropoulous's book
Elytis, Moralis, Tsarouhis (1974). Elytis's longstand-
ing interest in the arts and his friendship with some of
the most prominent modern artists in Greece and
France have qualified him as an acute art critic as well.

Elytis translated poets as varied as Le Comte de
Lautreamont, Arthur Rimbaud, Pierre-Jean Jouve, Paul
Éluard, Giuseppe Ungaretti, Federico García Lorca,
and Vladimir Mayakovsky. Elytis's prose works include essays and monographs on sympathetic writers
and painters. His most important work in prose, an invaluable companion to his poetry, is *Anihta hartia*
(1974; *Open Papers*, 1995), a work of widely ranging,
often aphoristic reflections, in which Elytis spoke extensively about his poetics and his development as a
poet.

ACHIEVEMENTS

Odysseus Elytis's constantly renewed originality,
his wise optimism, and his glorification of the Greek
world in its physical and spiritual beauty have gradually won for him wide popularity and recognition as
well as several distinctions, honors, and prizes—most
notably the Nobel Prize in Literature in 1979. He won
the National Poetry Prize in 1960 for *The Axion Esti*
and the Order of the Phoenix in 1965. He was honored
with several honorary doctorate degrees from institutions such as the University of Thessaloníki (1975),
University of Paris (1980), and University of London
(1981). In 1989, he was made a commander in the
French Legion of Honor.

BIOGRAPHY

The offspring of a family originating on the island
of Lesbos (or Mitilini), in the eastern Aegean, Odysseus Elytis was born Odysseus Alepoudhelis in Irá-
klion, Crete, in 1911, the sixth and last child of Panyio-
tis Alepoudhelis, a successful soap manufacturer, and
Maria Vranas, of Byzantine extraction. In 1914, the
family had settled permanently in Athens, where Elytis
went to high school, but summers spent in Lesbos,
Crete, and other Aegean islands provided him with
what was to be his poetic world in terms of imagery,
symbols, language, and cultural identity.

Elytis's early literary interests were given an outlet
and direction through his chance discovery of the poetry of Paul Éluard in 1929. From 1930 to 1935, Elytis
attended the law school of the University of Athens but
never graduated. His meeting with the orthodox Surrealist poet Andreas Embirikos in 1935 decidedly enhanced his own Surrealist inclinations. That same year,
Elytis published his first poems in the periodical *Nea
Ghramata*, recently founded by the poet and critic
Andréas Karandonis; under Karandonis's editorship,

Nea Ghramata soon became the rallying center of the new poetry and prose in Greece. Elytis's first collection of poems, *Prosanatolizmi* (orientations), appeared in December, 1939.

Fascist Italy attacked Greece from Albania in 1940, and in 1940-1941, Elytis served as a second lieutenant on the Albanian front, where he almost perished in a military hospital from typhoid. During the Nazi occupation of Greece, his second book of poetry, *Ilios o protos, mazi me tis parallayies pano se mian ahtidha* (sun the first, together with variations on a sunbeam), was published, followed, soon after the liberation, by *Heroic and Elegiac Song for the Lost Second Lieutenant of the Albanian Campaign*. In 1945-1946, Elytis served as director of programming and broadcasting for the National Broadcasting System in Athens. From 1948 to 1952, Elytis lived in Paris, where he studied literature at the Sorbonne, and traveled in England, Switzerland, Italy, and Spain. During this period, he associated with André Breton, Éluard, Tristan Tzara, Pierre Jean Jouve, Henri Michaux, Ungaretti, Henri Matisse, Pablo Picasso, Alberto Giacometti, and Giorgio de Chirico. In 1950, Elytis was elected as a member of the International Union of Art Critics, and in 1953, after his return to Greece, he was elected to the Poetry Committee of the Group of Twelve, which annually awarded prizes for poetry. Elytis served once again as director of programming and broadcasting of the National Broadcasting System in Athens until 1954. From 1955 to 1956, he was on the governing board of the avant-garde Karolos Koun Art Theater, and from 1956 to 1958, he was president of the governing board of the Greek Ballet.

The publication of his two epoch-making books of verse, *The Axion Esti* and *Six and One Remorses for the Sky*, broke Elytis's poetic silence and won for him the National Poetry Prize in 1960. A selection from *The Axion Esti*, set to music by the composer Mikis Theodhorakis in 1964, brought the poet wide popularity.

In 1961, Elytis visited the United States for three months at the invitation of the State Department, and in 1962, he visited the Soviet Union on the invitation of its government. From 1965 to 1968, he was a member of the administrative board of the Greek National Theater.

Odysseus Elytis (©The Nobel Foundation)

In 1967, the government of Greece was toppled by a military coup. For the next seven years, the colonels (as the ruling junta was known) ruthlessly suppressed opposition to their regime, exercising severe censorship and otherwise curtailing civil rights. From 1969 to 1971, Elytis lived in France, primarily in Paris. Following his return to Greece, he published seven poetry books, including *The Monogram*, *The Sovereign Sun*, and *To fotodhendro ke i dhekati tetarti omorfia* (the light tree and the fourteenth beauty), as well as the prose work *Open Papers*. Elytis was awarded the Nobel Prize in Literature in 1979, and in 1980, he received an honorary doctorate from the Sorbonne. He died in Athens, Greece, on March 18, 1996.

ANALYSIS

The suicide of the Greek poet Kostas Karyotakis in 1928 may be said to have marked the end of an era in

Greek poetry, which had long abided in Parnassianism, *poésie maudite*, Symbolism, and *poésie pure*. A spirit of discomfort, decadence, and despair prevailed, intensified by the military defeat suffered by Greece in Asia Minor in 1922. The year 1935 has generally been considered to mark the beginning of a great change in modern Greek poetry—a renaissance in which Odysseus Elytis, along with George Seferis and others, was most instrumental. Rejecting a tired traditionalism, these modernists invigorated Greek poetry by the adoption and creative assimilation of Western trends. The renaissance that they initiated is still flourishing; indeed, twentieth century Greek poetry is as rich as that of any nation in its time.

Adopting Surrealism as a liberating force with his extraordinary lyrical gifts, Elytis brought to Greek poetry a spirit of eternal youthfulness, beauty, purity, sanity, and erotic vigor. His inspiration sprung from nature, particularly from the Aegean archipelago, as well as from the Greek world throughout the centuries. At the same time, however, Elytis's mature vision was shaped by his experiences in World War II, which enriched and deepened his brilliant, careless, pictorial lyricism with historical awareness—an awareness of suffering as an essential and unavoidable part of life, which it is the poet's duty to recognize and transcend. A moderated Platonic idealism, earthly in its roots, characterized most of Elytis's work.

Elytis's early poetry broke new ground in Greek verse. Its youthful, optimistic freshness; genuine, powerful lyricism; and free Surrealistic associations, as well as the graceful richness of its imagery drawn from nature—all conspired to liberate Greek poetry from its Symbolist melancholy and despair. In Surrealism, Elytis found a force of sanity and purity, of liberating newness, but he quickly abandoned the automatism of Surrealist orthodoxy, choosing instead to subject the effusions of his unconscious to formal demands. Inspired by the Apollonian clarity of the Greek sunlight but also including its mystical, Dionysian essence, he thus accomplished an imaginative, creative assimilation, an acclimatization of the positive elements in Surrealism to the Greek world, its reality and spirit.

The physical elements of the Aegean archipelago,

its landscapes and seascapes, provided Elytis with the material for a radiant, sun-drenched poetic realm, a setting in which adolescent youths learn of Eros as the all-mastering, all-penetrating, all-revealing, all-uniting procreative and inspiring force. Elytis identified humans with nature in terms of analogies existing between them: Nature is anthropomorphized in a joyful exchange that no deep sorrow dares to tint.

Throughout his long career, with its constant experimentation, inventive metamorphoses, renovations, and striking changes, Elytis remained faithful to certain fundamental beliefs concerning the objectives of his art:

> The lesson remains the same: it is sufficient to express that which we love, and this alone, with the fewest means at our disposal, yet in the most direct manner, that of poetry.

PROSANATOLIZMI

Elytis's first book, *Prosanatolizmi*, experimental in manner and form, features rhythmical free verse, gently sensual and mostly of imagery set in motion. Although this collection does not delve into thought and emotion, it contains some poems of exquisite beauty and power, including "Anniversary," "Ode to Santorini," "Marina of the Rocks," and "The Mad Pomegranate Tree," which won instant acclaim and lasting popularity, earning Elytis the title of the poet of the Aegean.

ILIOS O PROTOS, MAZI ME TIS PARALLAYIES PANO SE MIAN AHTIDHA

In Elytis's second book, *Ilios o protos, mazi me tis parallayies pano se mian ahtidha*, the idealized "countryside of open heart," the paradise of carefree and unaging youth, the world of an eternal present that ignores the past and hopes in the future, is more consciously mastered and revealed. This early collection demonstrates the poet's conscientious craftsmanship and his sensitivity to the Greek language in all its expressive power, its visual and musical richness and beauty. A more thoughtful tone is apparent here as well.

THE AXION ESTI

The experience of the war, reflected in the long poem *Heroic and Elegiac Song for the Lost Second*

Lieutenant of the Albanian Campaign, permanently altered Elytis's vision. Fourteen years passed between the publication of this wartime elegy and the appearance of Elytis's *The Axion Esti* (its title, meaning "worthy it is," appears in the liturgy of the Greek Orthodox Church as well as in several Byzantine hymns).

The Axion Esti may be viewed as the worldly equivalent of a Greek Orthodox mass, with its three parts corresponding to Christ's life, the Passion, and the Resurrection. The poem is not a Christian epic in the strict sense of the term; it is, however, much indebted to Byzantine hymnology. Its middle section consists of three types of poetic units corresponding to liturgical ones. Eighteen "psalms" alternate, in strictly mathematical, symmetrical order, with twelve "odes" and six "readings." The readings are objective, powerfully realistic prose accounts of representative scenes and episodes of the 1940's, while the psalms, in free verse, are lyrical and thoughtful reactions, and the odes are songlike in their various intricately metrical stanzas. On the whole, the poem is a tour de force in the technical variety of its forms and modes, in the richness of its language and imagery, and in its superbly conscious craftsmanship; it was on this poem in particular that the Swedish Academy bestowed its highest praise in awarding the Nobel Prize to Elytis. In this epic in lyric form, the poet of the impulsive unconscious presented a poetry that is described by Andreas Karandonis as "highly programmed, totally directed to a final goal, and measured in its every detail as if with a compass." Thematically, this epic may be said to have its first conception in Elytis's heroic elegy on the Albanian campaign, for it returns in part to the suffering and the heroism that he witnessed in the war, yet in its epic grandeur and technical variety, *The Axion Esti* widens to embrace the physical and spiritual identity of the Greek nation and the Hellenic world.

Of the three major sections of this poem, the first, "Genesis," is an imagistic and lyrical account of how light, the Aegean sunlight, defined the physical, ethical, spiritual, and psychological characteristics of the Greek world. Parallel to the growth of Greek culture and the Greek nation is the poet's own growth, for in him a personified sun, the divine creator, has its axis. This identification of the poet with the giver of life es-

tablishes the rhythm of the poem, which shifts constantly from the individual to the archetypal, from the microcosm to the macrocosm. The small world of Greece is identical with the "great world," as the "now" is with the "ever."

Following this account of the past, "The Passion"—the centerpiece of the poem, the longest, most stylistically varied, and most significant of the three sections—turns to the present, to the war decade (1940-1949), during which the "created world" is submitted to a major test of suffering. The third and last section, "Gloria," is highly lyrical and prophetic, earthy yet "meteoric," physical yet metaphysical. The disturbed and challenged world is waiting to be restored to its inherent beauty and worth as a "regained paradise," enriched by the lessons learned through hardship.

Speaking of the insistent "search for paradise" in his work, Elytis has remarked: "When I say 'paradise,' I do not conceive of it in the Christian sense. It is another world which is incorporated into our own, and it is our own fault that we are unable to grasp it." Almost always connected with Elytis's notion of paradise are the "girls" ever present in his poetry, embodiments of beauty and inspirers of Eros, both physical and transcendental. Elytis's informing vision was described as a "solar metaphysics," the metaphysics of Greek sunlight. As Elytis remarked: "Europeans and Westerners always find mystery in obscurity, in the night, while we Greeks find it in light, which is for us an absolute. . . . *Limpidity* is probably the one element which dominates my poetry at present," where "behind a given thing something different can be seen."

TO FOTODHENDRO KE I DHEKATI TETARTI OMORFIA

Elytis's solar metaphysics found seminal expression in the collection entitled *To fotodhendro ke i dhekati tetarti omorfia*. These poems depict "the full miniature of a solar system, with the same tranquillity and the same air of eternity, the same perpetual motion in its separate constituent parts." The senses reach their "sanctity," becoming organs of poetic metaphysics and extensions of the spirit. In suggestive dreams, Elytis's "girls" became angelic phantoms, not earthly any more but inhabitants of a paradise that grows melancholy and mysterious. The "light tree" mentioned in the title, which Elytis once saw magically growing in the backyard of his childhood home, is symbolic of the light of life, of revelation and inspiration, of love and communion with the universe; when in his old age he returns in search of it, the tree is gone. In a series of nostalgic, intimate, imaginative recollections of his childhood and youth, he tried to recapture and decipher the meaning of his experience. These poems are apparently progressive stages in the day or week of his whole life, starting from a Palm Sunday morning, progressing to the sunset, then passing into night and the astral metaphysics of his old age. There, with mystical and occult insinuations, all opposites meet and are reconciled.

MARIA NEPHELE

A work that was later regarded to be the summa of Elytis's later writings, *Maria Nephele* was initially received by a curious yet hesitant public. As one critic noted, "some academicians and critics of the older generations still [wanted] to cling to the concept of the 'sun-drinking' Elytis . . . the monumental *Axion Esti*, so they [approached it] with cautious hesitation as an experimental and not-so-attractive creation of rather ephemeral value."

The issue lay with its radically different presentation. Whereas his earlier poems dealt with the almost timeless expression of the Greek reality that were not directly derived from actual events, *Maria Nephele* was based on a young woman he actually met. Moreover, unlike the women from his earlier work, the woman in Elytis's poem had changed to reflect the troubled times in which she lived, becoming a new manifestation of the eternal female. Maria stands opposed to the more traditional women figures of his early poems by serving as an attractive, liberated, restless, and even blasé representative of today's young woman. American youth radicalism hit its apex in the late 1960's, but it took another decade for its force to be felt in Greece. In *Maria Nephele*, the tensions produced from the radicalism interact with some more newly developed Greek cultural realities: increased cosmopolitanism (with its positive and negative aspects), technological advances, and concern with material possessions.

As one critic wrote, the urban Maria Nephele "is the offspring, not the sibling, of the women of Elytis's youth. Her setting is the polluted city, not the open country and its islands of purity and fresh air." The poem consists of the juxtaposed conversations of Maria Nephele, who represents the ideals of today's emerging woman, and Antifonitis, or the Responder, who stands for more traditional views. Maria forces the Responder to confront issues that he would rather ignore. Both characters are sophisticated and complex urbanites who express themselves in a wide range of styles, moods, idioms, and stanzaic forms.

OTHER MAJOR WORKS

NONFICTION: *O zoghrafos Theofilos*, 1973; *Anihta hartia*, 1974 (*Open Papers*, 1995); *I mayia tou Papadhiamandi*, 1976; *Anafora ston Andrea Embiríko*, 1978; *Ta dimosia ke ta idiotika*, 1990; *En lefko*, 1992; *Carte Blanche: Selected Writings*, 1999.

TRANSLATION: *Dhefteri ghrafi*, 1976 (of Arthur Rimbaud and others).

BIBLIOGRAPHY

Books Abroad. (Fall, 1975). A special issue devoted to Elytis. Examines his life and works.

Bosnakis, Panayiotis. "*Ek tou plision*." *World Literature Today* 74, no. 1 (Winter, 2000): 211-212. A critical analysis of Elytis's posthumously published *Ek tou plision* (from close).

Decavalles, Andonis. *Odysseus Elytis: From the Golden to the Silver Poem*. New York: Pella, 1994. These seven essays analyze Elytis's work, interpreting his poetry as it transforms from the personal to the national.

Friar, Kimon. *Modern Greek Poetry: From Cavafis to Elytis*. New York: Simon & Schuster, 1973. Informative introduction, an essay on translation, and annotations to the poetry by the editor. Includes bibliography.

Glasgow, Eric. "Odysseus Elytis: In Memory of a Modern Greek Poet." *Contemporary Review* 270, no. 1572 (January, 1997): 33-34. A brief article written after the poet's death, remembering his life and works.

Hirst, Anthony. *God and the Poetic Ego: The Appropriation of Biblical and Liturgical Language in the Poetry of Palamas, Sikelianos, and Elytis*. New York: Peter Lang, 2004. Hirst examines the role of religion in the works of Elytis, Kōstēs Palamas, and Angelos Sikelianos.

Ivask, Ivar, ed. *Odysseus Elytis: Analogies of Light.* Norman: University of Oklahoma Press, 1981. A collection of critical essays on Elytis's work.

Andonis Decavalles
Updated by Sarah Hilbert

HANS MAGNUS ENZENSBERGER

Born: Kaufbeuren, Germany; November 11, 1929

PRINCIPAL POETRY

Verteidigung der Wölfe, 1957
Landessprache, 1960
Museum der modernen Poesie, 1960
Gedichte: Die Entstehung eines Gedichts, 1962
Blindenschrift, 1964
Poems, 1966
Poems for People Who Don't Read Poems, 1968
Gedichte, 1955-1970, 1971
Mausoleum: Siebenunddreissig Balladen aus der Geschichte des Fortschritts, 1975 (*Mausoleum: Thirty-seven Ballads from the History of Progress*, 1976)
Der Untergang der Titanic, 1978 (*The Sinking of the Titanic*, 1980)
Beschreibung eines Dickichts, 1979
Die Furie des Verschwindens, 1980
Dreiunddreissig Gedichte, 1981
Diderot und das dunkle Ei: Eine Mystifikation, 1990
Zukunftsmusik, 1991
Selected Poems, 1994
Hans Magnus Enzensberger, 1995
Kiosk: Neue Gedichte, 1995 (*Kiosk*, 1997)
Gedichte, 1950-1995, 1996
Gedichte, 1999 (6 volumes)
Leichter als Luft: Moralische Gedichte, 1999 (*Lighter than Air: Moral Poems*, 2000)
Die Geschichte der Wolken: 99 Meditationen, 2003
Gedichte, 1950-2005, 2006

OTHER LITERARY FORMS

Hans Magnus Enzensberger (EHN-zehnz-behr-gehr) has worked in a wide variety of literary forms. His doctoral dissertation, "Clemens Brentanos Poetik" (1961; Clemens Brentano's poetics), completed in 1955, is a central piece of Brentano scholarship. As the founder and editor (now coeditor) of the leftist journal *Kursbuch* (begun in 1965), Enzensberger exercised a substantial influence as a cultural critic on several fronts. Versed in eight languages, he has been a prolific translator of foreign poets and an astute editor of their works. He has written numerous essays and nonfiction works on politics, poetics, and social issues, as well as experimental fiction, drama, and works for radio and television.

ACHIEVEMENTS

Hans Magnus Enzensberger has significantly influenced the course of German intellectual life and letters since he first appeared on the scene in 1957, and his works have been published in many languages. His career has been distinguished by several honors and literary awards. He received the Hugo-Jacobi Prize in 1956, the literary prize of the Union of German Critics for his critical poems in 1962, and the treasured Georg Büchner Prize in 1963. In 1967, the city of Nuremberg honored him with its cultural award for having represented Germany "in a manner so urgently necessary to counteract the clichéd image of neo-German fanaticism within the Federal Republic." Also in 1967, he received the Etna-Taormina International Poetry Prize. He won the Premio Pasolini in 1982, the Heinrich Böll Prize in 1985, the Bavarian Academy of Fine Arts Award in 1987, and the Lifetime Recognition Award from the Griffin Trust for Excellence in Poetry in 2009.

BIOGRAPHY

The eldest of three brothers, Hans Magnus Enzensberger was born in the Bavarian Allgäu and grew up in a middle-class home in Nuremberg. He attended high school from 1942 to 1945, but in 1945, he was inducted into the Volkssturm for militia "cleanup" duty. After the war, he served as an interpreter and bartender for the Royal Air Force, earning his keep as well through the black market. He completed his secondary schooling (the *Abitur*) in 1949 and spent the next five years studying literature, languages, and philosophy in Erlangen, Freiburg, Hamburg, and Paris. His work on Brentano's poetry concluded his university studies. He was later employed as a radio editor in Stuttgart and as a visiting professor in Ulm. In 1957, he traveled to the United States and Mexico; in the same year, he published his first book of poems, *Verteidigung der Wölfe* (defense of the wolves). Returning from Mexico, Enzensberger settled first in Norway. Two years later, a stipend took him to Italy, and later he became a reader for Suhrkamp, the large publishing house in Frankfurt. His second volume of poems, *Landessprache* (country talk), met with great critical acclaim, as did his anthology of modern poetry, *Museum der modernen Poesie* (1960; museum of modern poetry). Several awards and distinctions followed. Enzensberger continued to travel, in 1963 to the Soviet Union and in 1965 to South America, spending the year between these journeys in Frankfurt, where he taught as a visiting professor of poetics. In 1965, he moved from Tjörne to West Berlin and founded the journal *Kursbuch*. In the same year, he

became a professor of poetry at the University of Frankfurt. He was commissioned by the Goethe Institute of the Federal Republic of Germany to conduct lecture tours in 1966 and 1967 to Athens, Ankara, and New Delhi. He went to Wesleyan University as a fellow at the Center for Advanced Studies in 1967 but soon relinquished his fellowship in protest against the Vietnam War. He later traveled through America and the Far East, eventually spending several months in Cuba, where he began work on the epic poem he completed nine years later, *The Sinking of the Titanic*. He traveled to Spain in 1971 with a camera team and held lectures in Japan in 1973, at the behest of the Goethe Institute. He later returned to Berlin, and then to Munich, where he founded and edited the journal *Trans-Atlantik* (1980-1982). In his seventh decade, Enzensberger remained a committed social critic of postwar German society and is regarded as one of Germany's most important literary figures.

ANALYSIS

Hans Magnus Enzensberger stepped onto the literary scene as Germany's angry young man in the 1950's, a time when the Federal Republic of Germany (West Germany) was cashing in on its economic miracle. Enzensberger's anger, which would continue to fuel his verse, was directed against a world controlled by an inhumane technologized civilization and the repressive machinery of power, be it government or industry, politics or the military, or even the mass media of the "consciousness industry." As an independent, abrasive political poet and polemicist, he stands in the tradition of Heinrich Heine and Bertolt Brecht. Gottfried Benn's influence, evident from the beginning, has become more pronounced since the early 1970's. Enzensberger remains the defender of freedom against authority and power, seeking "revision, not revolution."

Enzensberger makes a systematic effort to relate theory and praxis by combining aesthetic and political reflections in his literary works. He fuses literature and history, or historical documentation and literary "fiction," referring to this mixture as *Faktographien* (factographs). Though his concept of literature rests decidedly on a political commitment, this is never so

Hans Magnus Enzensberger (©Lufti Özkök)

explicit in his poetry as to be reducible to a platform of positions. Although Enzensberger, like Brecht, is conscious of the functional value of poetry, its social utility, his aesthetic is fraught with ideological reservations. He rejects monolithic philosophies and political dogmatism, and his position can perhaps be best described as an enlightened and critical skepticism.

EARLY POETRY

Looking for the larger contours in the development of Enzensberger's poetry, it is instructive to speak of three different phases. The first phase includes the volumes *Verteidigung der Wölfe*, *Landessprache*, and *Blindenschrift* (braille). Here, Enzensberger tried to "determine the situation, not to offer prognoses or horoscopes." He sharply criticized current conditions, revealing an aesthetic intelligence and an artistic mastery that had at its command a legion of traditional and modern forms and literary techniques. As a political poet in the vein of Heine and Brecht, Enzensberger did much to resuscitate the political poem. Finally, this phase of his poetry demonstrates his rebellious anger and scorn, as well as his dogmatic skepticism.

In these early volumes, one finds a mixture of Brecht's "public" and Benn's "private" poetry. From Brecht, Enzensberger learned the nature of political poetry and how to put it across, while from Benn he learned a basic method of composition, the notion of "prismatic infantilism," the use of concatenated imagery. Enzensberger's satire is often in the vein of W. H. Auden. In *Blindenschrift*, in particular, Enzensberger exhibits a strong concentration on particulars, a new sort of detail, along with lyrical grace and simplicity.

THE 1960'S AND 1970'S

In Enzensberger's second phase, his poetry receded into the background. These were the years (roughly from 1965 to the early 1970's) when Enzensberger pursued political theory and action and, at one point, polemically called the whole industry of literature into question. He devoted himself to "factual" literature, to the documentary form then very much in vogue in West Germany. He concentrated as well on polemical essays that came to make his *Kursbuch* so controversial.

In the early 1970's, however, Enzensberger returned to poetry. This shift coincided with a renewed interest in the study of history, explicit in recent volumes such as *Mausoleum*, *The Sinking of the Titanic*, and *Die Furie des Verschwindens* (the fury of passing). Here, Enzensberger understands and portrays history in its dialectical dimensions. He locates and concentrates on historical moments during which "the exploitation of science [becomes] the science of exploitation." Frequently, his poetic history of scientific and technological progress focuses on instances of moral regression. It is particularly in these respects that Enzensberger's "philosophy of life" has come to resemble that of Gottfried Benn.

THE SINKING OF THE TITANIC

One of Enzensberger's finest works is his epic poem *The Sinking of the Titanic*, which he himself translated into English in 1980. This poem reveals much about Enzensberger's attitudes toward poetry, toward history, and toward his own growth and change.

Enzensberger began writing *The Sinking of the Titanic* while in Cuba in 1968-1969 but finished it much later, in 1977, in Berlin, after having lost the original manuscript during one of his many travels. While tracing the history of a work's composition is often the task of scholarly research, here it is made part of the poem itself. Enzensberger weaves an intricate and polychromatic fabric in his text, creating a kind of space-time continuum in which the catastrophe of the RMS *Titanic* and his writing about it are simultaneously enacted and represented, explicated and documented, anticipated and recalled, on the various primary, secondary, and tertiary stages that the thirty-three cantos and the sixteen interpolated poems provide.

The structure of the work, as well as its subtitle, "A Comedy," refer directly to Dante's *La divina commedia* (c. 1320, 3 volumes; *The Divine Comedy*, 1802). Enzensberger fuses different historical moments and psychological states to form the distinctive texture of the poem: the historical incident of the 1912 catastrophe; the watershed years of twentieth century German history, from 1918 to 1945; the time of the poem's composition, from 1968 to 1977; temporal excursions to the sixteenth, seventeenth and nineteenth centuries, and to some unspecified future; geographical excursions to the Netherlands, Italy, Havana, and Berlin—all these are portals through which Enzensberger guides

Critical Survey of Poetry

the reader, back and forth. The poet and the reader become eyewitnesses, seeing ideas in motion, people in motion, history re-created.

The power of Enzensberger's poetic imagination creates a fascinating and compelling simultaneity of historical experience and event, fictional vision and scenario. In asides and innuendos, he brings technical issues and compositional problems to the surface of his text. At other times, the tenor of his reflection registers disappointment and resignation, as when he recalls the failure of misguided actions: "Everything we did was wrong./ And so everything was wrong/ that we thought." At other times, he injects ironic self-mockery and persiflage: "A good comrade/ I was not./ Instead of writing about sugar,/ about Socialism on an island,/ I fished dead survivors and dead fatalities,/ non-partisan-like and half a century too late,/ out of the black water."

The intricate configuration of the poem revolves around the *Titanic* as a commonplace symbol for the demise of modern civilization. At the same time, it is important to remember that commonplaces do not sit well with Enzensberger; he is much keener on contradictions, on the "integration of ambivalences," to use a phrase of Benn. Consequently, Enzensberger uses one canto (the sixteenth) to display the hollowness and malleability of the very object that provides his central metaphor—the *Titanic*. This canto is a piece of ironic sophistry, the poetry of the disillusioned Left, and is, like everything else, part of the cargo of Enzensberger's fated ship.

History, being "an invention for which reality provides the stuff," becomes present as it is reenacted in the mind. The twenty-eighth canto concludes: "these people sinking before me, with me, after me, are telephoning/ with one another in my forty-six-thousand-gross-tonnage-head." Enzensberger's poetic figuration of historical fact locates the moving forces of history within the momentum of collective fictions; at the same time, he exposes the radical internalization of contemporary paranoia. Enzensberger, reluctant to "tell the truth," tells instead the truth about truth in this poem. The multiplicity of voices that speak through this work belong not only to the survivors and heirs of the *Titanic*, to those who died tragically then and who die (and live)

tragically now, not only to the books, films, and other commercial enterprises (including the poet's own) that profit from the catastrophe of the *Titanic*, but also to the socially and economically exploited, to radicals with misgivings, and to Enzensberger as he thought and wrote in 1968 as well as Enzensberger as he thought and wrote in 1977. The questions raised by Enzensberger in *The Sinking of the Titanic* will continue to echo in his readers's heads: "How was it in reality? How was it in my poem?/ *Was* it in my poem?"

In 1958, Alfred Andersch said of Enzensberger that he had written "what has been absent in Germany since Brecht: the great political poem." Since that time, Enzensberger's poetry has undergone considerable change, but it has never lacked an underlying political commitment. Enzensberger has shown that "political poetry" need not be artistically retrograde; indeed, for him, a poem is political to the extent that its language constitutes resistance against repression and a means of emancipation from debilitating social forces.

LIGHTER THAN AIR

Lighter than Air, a collection of lyric meditations published in 1999, displays Enzensberger in a lighter mode, as the title suggests. The volume consists of seventy lyric meditations, combining caustic wit with humor as Enzensberger comments on everything from useless products to the inconsequential existence of humankind. Although lighter than some of his other fare, these poems remain concerned with the themes that have always occupied Enzensberger's attention. Enzensberger is typically satiric and sarcastic in his outrage at moral injustices, social inanities, and human self-absorption, as in "Equisetum," which elevates a lowly horsetail to a level of moral superiority over human beings as the plant "bid[es] its time,/ simpler than we are, and hence/ unvanquishable."

OTHER MAJOR WORKS

LONG FICTION: *Der kurze Sommer der Anarchie: Buenaventura Durruits Leben und Tod*, 1972.

PLAYS: *Das Verhör von Habana*, pr., pb. 1970 (*The Havana Inquiry*, 1974); *Die Tochter der Luft: Ein Schauspiel, nach dem spanischen des Calderón de la Barca*, pr., pb. 1992; *Voltaires Neffe: Eine Fälschung in Diderots Manier*, pb. 1996.

NONFICTION: *Clemens Brentanos Poetik*, pb. 1961 (wr. 1955); *Einzelheiten*, 1962 (*The Consciousness Industry: On Literature, Politics, and the Media*, 1974); *Einzelheiten II: Poesie und Politik*, 1963; *Politik und Verbrechen*, 1964 (*Politics and Crime*, 1974); *Politische Kolportagen*, 1966; *Deutschland, Deutschland unter anderem*, 1967; *Staatsgefährdende Umtriebe*, 1968; *Freisprüche: Revolutionäre vor Gericht*, 1970; *Palaver: Politische Überlegungen, 1967-1973*, 1974; *Der Weg ins Freie: Fünf Lebensläufe*, 1975; *Raids and Reconstructions: Essays on Politics, Crime and Culture*, 1976; *Critical Essays*, 1982; *Politische Brosamen*, 1982 (*Political Crumbs*, 1990); *Ach Europa! Wahrnehmungen aus sieben Landern: Mit einem Epilog aus dem Jahre 2006*, 1987 (*Europe, Europe: Forays into a Continent*, 1989); *Dreamers of the Absolute: Essays on Politics, Crime, and Culture*, 1988; *Mittelmass und Wahn: Gesammelte Zerstreuungen*, 1988 (*Mediocrity and Delusion: Collected Diversions*, 1992); *Die grosse Wanderung*, 1992; *Aussichten auf den Bügerkrieg*, 1993; *Civil War*, 1994; *Civil Wars: From L.A. to Bosnia*, 1994; *Diderots Schatten: Unterhaltungen, Szenen, Essays*, 1994; *Deutschland, Deutschland unter anderm: Äusserungen sur Politik*, 1996; *Requiem für eine romantische Frau: Die Geschichte von August Bussman und Clemens Brentano*, 1996; *Baukasten zu einer Theorie der Medien: Kritische Diskurse zur Pressefreiheit*, 1997; *Zickzack: Aufsätze*, 1997 (*Zig Zag: The Politics of Culture and Vice Versa*, 1997); *Nomaden im Regal: Essays*, 2003; *Einzelheiten I and II*, 2006; *Hammerstein: Oder, Der Eigensinn*, 2008.

TRANSLATIONS: *Gedichte*, 1962 (of William Carlos Williams); *Geisterstimmen: Übersetzungen und Imitationen*, 1999.

CHILDREN'S LITERATURE: *Esterhazy: Eine Hasengeschichte*, 1993 (with Irene Dische; *Esterhazy: The Rabbit Prince*, 1994); *Der Zahlenteufel: Ein Kopfkissenbuch für Alle, die Angst vor der Athematik haben*, 1997 (*The Number Devil: A Mathematical Adventure*, 1998); *Wo warst du, Robert?*, 1998 (*Where Were You, Robert?*, 2000; also known as *Lost in Time*, 2000).

EDITED TEXTS: *Gedichte, Erzählungen, Briefe*, 1958; *Museum der modernen Poesie*, 1960; *Allerleirauh: Viele schöne Kinderreime*, 1961; *Poesie*, 1962; *Vorzeichen: Fünf neue deutsche Autoren*, 1962; *Gespräche mit Marx und Engels*, 1973.

MISCELLANEOUS: *Der fliegende Robert: Gedichte, Szenen, Essays*, 1992.

BIBLIOGRAPHY

Demetz, Peter. *Postwar German Literature: A Critical Introduction*. New York: Pegasus, 1970. This basic text remains a useful examination of German postwar authors in the context of their times.

Enzensberger, Hans Magnus. *Hans Magnus Enzensberger in Conversation with Michael Hulse and John Kinsella*. London: Between the Lines, 2002. Contains a lengthy interview with Enzensberger, a career sketch, a comprehensive bibliography, and excerpts from critics and interviewers.

Fischer, Gerhard, ed. *Debating Enzensberger: "Great Migration" and "Civil War."* Tübingen: Stauffenberg, 1996. Papers delivered at the 1995 Sydney German Studies Symposium. Includes bibliographical references.

Goodbody, Axel. "Living with Icebergs: Hans Magnus Enzensberger's *Sinking of the Titanic* as a Postapocalyptic Text." *AUMLA: Journal of the Australasian Universities Modern Language Association, Sydney* 96 (November, 2001): 88-114. The author looks at Enzensberger's use of the *Titanic* as an emblem of modern industrial society and its sinking as a symbol of society's self-destructive tendencies.

Kilian, Monika. *Modern and Postmodern Strategies: Gaming and the Question of Morality—Adorno, Rorty, Lyotard, and Enzensberger*. New York: Peter Lang, 1998. Examines the debate between modern and postmodern thought, including the postmodern notion that "universalizing strategies of modern thought are cognitively and morally wrong," with reference to these German writers. Bibliography, index.

Natan, Alex, and B. Keith-Smith, eds. *Essays on Lehmann, Kasack, Nossack, Eich, Gaiser, Böll, Celan, Bachmann, Enzensberger, East German Literature*. Vol. 4 in *German Men of Letters Literary Essays*. New York: Berg, 1987. A collection of twelve essays, including analysis of Enzensberger in English.

Scally, Derek. "Past Sense and Present Tensions; After Five Decades of Opinion-Giving, Hans Magnus Enzensberger Is No Longer Interested in Playing the 'Answer-o-mat,' He Tells Derek Scally." *Irish Times*, March 15, 2003, p. 61. Enzensberger, once the angry young man of Germany, says that he is no longer interesting in discussing the political state of poetry and is instead happy to act as publisher and encourage other poets.

Schickel, Joachim, ed. *Über Hans Magnus Enzensberger*. Frankfurt am Main, Germany: Suhrkamp, 1970. A hefty biography (more than three hundred pages), including a bibliography of works by and about Enzensberger. In German.

Richard Spuler
Updated by Christina J. Moose

F

J. V. Foix

Born: Sarría, Spain; January 28, 1893
Died: Barcelona, Spain; January 29, 1987

PRINCIPAL POETRY

Gertrudis, 1927
KRTU, 1932
Sol, i de dol, 1936
Les irreals omegues, 1948
On he deixat les claus . . . ?, 1953
Del "Diari 1918," 1956
Onze nadals i un cap d'any, 1960
L'estrella d'en Perris, 1963
Desa aquests llibres al calaix de baix, 1964
Obres poètiques, 1964
Quatre nus, 1964
Darrer comunicat, 1970
Tocant a mà, 1972
Antologia poètica, 1973
Quatre colors aparien el món . . . , 1975
Poemes de pedra, 2006

OTHER LITERARY FORMS

In addition to his poetry, J. V. Foix (fohsh) published a number of works that are impossible to define in terms of conventional genres. Typical of his idiosyncratic manner are his "letters" to Clara Sobirós and Na Madrona Puignau, both invented personages. The Sobirós missive, which appropriately heads both the *Obres poètiques* and the first volume of the *Obres completes* (1974-1990), is a veritable manifesto of Foix's aesthetics. In "Na Madrona," he combines commentaries on contemporary events with a peculiar expression of concern for the ills of his society. In a third epistle, written in 1962 and addressed to Joan Salvat-Papasseit, that most engagé of Catalan poets, Foix, while amicably vindicating the honesty of his own convictions, conveys to his former associate the warm sympathy of a kindred soul, rising, at long last, above all the differences in temperament and upbringing that poisoned their relationship. In *Allò que no diu La vanguardia* (1970; what *La vanguardia* does not say)—the reference is to the noted Barcelonese newspaper—Foix parodies the reporter's jargon, distorting the idiom of the short bulletin and the somewhat longer newspaper column until he attains a magnificent absurdity. In still another vein, he devised a tale of fantasy, *La pell de la pell* (1970; skin's skin), complete with outlandish apparitions and magical transformations of time and place; there are infernal links between this work and *Noranta set notes sobre ficcions ponciones* (1974; ninety-seven notes on fictions à la Ponç), a congeries of paragraph-length meditations and aphorisms, inspired by the paintings of his friend, Joan Ponç.

In *Catalans de 1918* (1965; Catalans of 1918), an ingenuous Foix becomes the James Boswell of a forgotten era. In an intriguing admixture of memoirs and character sketches, he evokes the zeitgeist of the decade between 1910 and 1920. Through autobiographical tidbits (reminiscences—deliciously recounted—of associations, confrontations, collaborations, casual acquaintances, and chance encounters), he introduces an entire gallery of famous and not-so-famous Catalans: revered masters, friends, and colleagues. Foix takes special care to recapture not only the speech of the personages in question but also the ambience that provides an appropriate foil for their cameo appearances. Worthy, too, of special attention is Foix's prolific and influential output as a journalist from 1917 to 1936, before the Spanish Civil War. The numerous articles he contributed to *La publicitat*, a biweekly newspaper he directed from 1931 to 1936, stand out as especially significant, for they attest sensibilities keenly attuned to the critical issues of the day. A select sample of these articles appears in a collection titled *Els lloms transparents* (1969; transparent loins), edited by Gabriel Ferrater.

ACHIEVEMENTS

The domain of the Catalan language comprises most of the eastern sector of the Iberian Peninsula (Catalonia proper, that is, and the Valencian region), the Balearic Isles, the Republic of Andorra, and, to a lesser extent, the French territories of Cerdagne and Roussillon. The Catalan-speaking people boast their own distinctive Romance tongue, a time-honored cultural heritage, and a brilliant literary tradition that goes back to the dawning of the Middle Ages. Thanks to a dramatic resurgence (commonly called the Renaixença) that began in the early 1830's, Catalan literature and art flourished in the twentieth century, despite the cataclysmic convulsions brought about by the Spanish Civil War and the repressive measures imposed by the regime of Francisco Franco.

Together with a number of distinguished contemporary writers, painters, sculptors, and avant-garde artists of all types (Salvador Espriu, Joan Oliver, Mercé Rodoreda, Josep M. Subirachs, Joan Miró, Salvador Dalí, and Antoni Tàpies, to name but a representative few), J. V. Foix stands out as a worthy champion of the best that Catalan culture has to offer to Western civilization. Few Catalan writers can vie with Foix in devotion to motherland, erudition, breadth of vision, and sheer genius for bringing to fruition the highest potential of the Renaixença. Though worlds apart from Espriu in the ultimate resolution and implication of a truly personal and original poetic, Foix, like Espriu, strikes a happy balance between, on one hand, aesthetic sophistication and avant-garde exploration, and, on the other, a sound understanding of the solid, broad infrastructure of the living language of his society. What has earned Foix a rank of special distinction is, above all, his unique talent for articulating through poems, through essays, and, indeed, through his urbane lifestyle and cosmopolitan outlook, the canons of a staunch Catalanism, founded on the principles of moderation and tolerance, transcending chauvinism and partisan affiliation of any kind—canons formulated by Joan Maragall, Foix's illustrious turn-of-the-century predecessor, a thinker who oriented his ideals toward the prospect of a Catalan autonomy within the context of pan-Iberian federalism.

Cognizant of Foix's venturesome, indefatigable quest for ever-novel approaches to the creative process, and of his pursuit of what Northrop Frye and Carlos Bousoño have called, in reference to other writers, the "encyclopedic form" or the *pupila totalizadora*, and what Arthur Terry has termed, apropos of Foix himself,

the *visió còsmica*, some of the more perceptive readers of Foix (Enrique Badosa, Patricia Boehne, Gabriel Ferrater, Pere Gimferrer, Albert Manent, David Rosenthal, and Terry, among others) have drawn parallels between him and such luminaries of twentieth century literature as Ezra Pound, T. S. Eliot, Federico García Lorca, and Fernando Pessoa. Indeed, Foix can mold into a collage of macrocosmic proportions strains issuing from both within and without the mainstream of the autochthonous tradition, techniques borrowed from the *stilnovisti* as well as from the Futurists and the Surrealists, echoes recaptured from the writers of ancient Greece as well as from homegrown classics (Ramon Llull, Ausiàs March, Jordi de Sant Jordi). Foix's overall production, then, projects the epiphany of an innovator endowed with a scrupulous social conscience. His stirring voice frequently has to cry out to bemoan the poet's personal anguish and that of many of his fellow citizens, who, though never having left their own country, have suffered from the malaise that Paul Ilie has perceptively diagnosed as "inner exile."

Because of the prejudicial policies of the centralist Spanish government, limited Catalan readership, and other inimical circumstances, Foix, like practically all his Catalan colleagues, does not enjoy the wide recognition he justly deserves. He does not lack, however, the enthusiastic acclaim of well-informed critics at home and abroad. His name occupies, as it should, a prominent place in the standard histories and anthologies of Catalan literature. He attracted the attention of numerous scholars, and a sizable body of his work has been translated into Castilian, English, French, and Italian. Foix is held in high esteem by the younger Catalan literati, and his influence is detectable among them, especially in the works of Ferrater and Gimferrer, outstanding poets in their own right.

In 1961, Foix was elected to the Catalan Academy (the Institut d'Estudios Catalans), and in 1973, on the occasion of his eightieth birthday, he was awarded the Premi d'Honor de les Lletres Catalanes. On that occasion, two prestigious magazines, *Destino* and *Serra d'Or*, dedicated special issues to him, and his friends published an homage anthology (*Antologia poètica*).

BIOGRAPHY

Josep Arseni Vicenç Foix i Mas, or J. V. Foix, was born of peasant stock. His father came from Torrents de Lladurs, a town in the province of Lérida (Western Catalonia). The second of three children—he shared the household with two sisters—he received the usual schooling and exhibited an unusual, precocious interest in Catalan culture and literary studies. His formal education came to an abrupt end in 1911 after an unsuccessful bout with the study of law. Other occupations were to absorb the young Foix's attention. Following in his father's footsteps, Foix worked in earnest to build for himself a reputation as the premier *pâtissier* in his native town.

In retrospect, Foix presented the intriguing figure of a man with two private lives: One belongs to the bourgeois merchant, who plods a course marked by the work ethic leading to material rewards; the other pertains to the genuine artist fully devoted to a métier that thrives on the values of the spirit. Foix plied his trade by day and wrote at a feverish pace by night. The first fifteen years of his career (beginning, approximately, in the year 1915) were years of particularly intense activity. In *Catalans de 1918*, he provides a captivating account of his numerous sessions in libraries, his contacts with the many aspiring authors of his generation who later became his intimate friends and with established scholars and literati—Fabra, Mosén Jacinto Verdaguer, d'Ors, Carner, and Riba—who were all engaged in the epic task of shaping the future of Catalan culture. From 1917 on, various journals of the avant-garde mushroomed in Barcelona, and Foix contributed articles to all of them and directed some. Himself a central figure of the intelligentsia, he became acquainted with the prominent personalities who were creating a stir in the literary and artistic circles of the Catalan metropolis: Paul Éluard, García Lorca, Tristan Tzara, Dalí, Miró, and Luis Buñuel. Foix relished playing the part of a cultural middleman of sorts, an aesthetician at large. In this role, he introduced, in 1925, the first exhibitions of Dalí and Miró.

Foix's creative surge paralleled and in some cases even anticipated the artistic renewal experienced throughout Europe in the mid-1920's. While the revolutionary tendencies that were fermenting on the Continent were making their sensational impact in Catalonia, especially through the movements of Futurism and Surrealism, and García Lorca was publishing *Romancero gitano, 1924-1927* (1928; *The Gypsy Ballads of García Lorca*, 1951, 1953), Foix was reaping in *Gertrudis* the first fruit of a protracted labor. By 1930, he had completed the main components of those books that many years later would reach the printing press under the titles *KRTU*, *Del "Diari 1918*,*" Sol, i de dol* (alone and in mourning), *Catalans de 1918*, and even some items of *Les irreals omegues* (the unreal omegas).

The advent of the Republic in 1931 and the subsequent five years of autonomy, which encouraged high hopes for the future of Catalan nationhood, enhanced Foix's consciousness of his civic responsibilities. Though he shunned direct involvement in politics, he acquitted himself brilliantly of his self-imposed duties as ideologue in *Revolució catalanista* (1934; the Catalan revolution), a book he coauthored with his friend Josep Carbonell. As a representative of the emerging Catalan state, he attended two international conventions of the PEN Club, held in Belgrade and in Dubrovnik in the early 1930's.

The civil war struck hard at the hopes of those who, like Foix, had set their hearts on tolerance and constructive dialogue. The abolition of the Catalan press, after Franco's victory, brought Foix's journalistic career to a standstill, but censorship could not dry up the fountainhead of his inspiration or stint the vitality of his poetic voice—which, fortunately, found an outlet in numerous books published after the Spanish Civil War. Following Franco's death, Foix had the satisfaction of witnessing a revitalized Catalonia, autonomous once again. He died in Barcelona, Spain, on January 29, 1987.

ANALYSIS

By 1930, J. V. Foix had developed the mainstays of his craft on which he would effect countless variations. In particular, he had perfected his favored techniques of antithesis: the old opposed to the new, the familiar articulated with the exotic, reason contravened by *follia*, fantastical narratives counterbalanced by references to the workaday world, Arcadia admixed with veristic depictions of the Catalan landscape. Other quintessential traits of Foix's resourcefulness readily come to mind: his lyric élan, his profuse language contained within exquisite conciseness of form elaborated to an adamantine luster, his play on perspectivism and the effects of trompe l'oeil, inviting analogies with the visual arts (especially with paintings of Giorgio de Chirico, Dalí, Yves Tanguy, René Magritte, and Miró). Foix's associations with the Buñuel of *Un Chien andalou* (1928) and *L'Âge d'or* (1930) fostered, no doubt, his strong penchant for transforming into devices of literature sudden shifts of focus, flashbacks and flash-forwards, telescopings and superimpositions of images, panoramic shots, foreshadowings, fadeouts, and other cinematic techniques.

Through his mimesis of the oneiric experience, Foix unfolds the wide horizons of a kaleidoscopic, constantly changing universe: He evokes a dreamlike world in a state of flux, brings about mutations upon a protean imagery, develops into full-fledged personal myths symbols rooted in the subconscious. In the final analysis, however, the universe he envisages remains, as Terry has perceptively pointed out, strikingly unified—paradoxical and mysterious though its unity may be. It is because of his convictions concerning an absolute order that governs all things and also because of his compelling drive toward explorations beyond well-trodden paths that Foix, despite his obvious indebtedness to the champions of Surrealism, is not merely another epigone of that movement.

Foix is a bold exponent of the avant-garde, "a poet, magician, speculator of the word," to use his own words, an "investigator of poetry." In his reflections on his own work, Foix employs distinctive terminology—*alliberament* (liberation), "el risc de la investigació estètica" (the risk of aesthetic research), "un joc gairebé d'atzar" (a game of chance, just about), "l'exercici de la facultat de descobrir" (the exercise of the skill of making discoveries)—in order to describe his exploratory, "investigative" imagination. Though keenly aware of the pitfalls lurking in his risky ventures as an avant-garde artist, Foix will not accept a road map or even, at times, general bearings from the Surrealists or from other revered masters. He insists on sallying forth, on his own, into uncharted realms of the imagination, so allured is he by prospects of serendipitous innovations

and by the intuition of elusive *sobiranes certeses* (sovereign certainties).

"WITHOUT SYMBOLISM"

Thus do Foix's, and the reader's, literary adventures begin. At the outset, the author dazzles the reader with an array of colors, odors, sounds, and other sensory perceptions. He frequently projects himself into the persona of the passionate lover, engulfed in one of his usual reveries about his femme fatale. Typical is the prose poem from *Gertrudis*, "Sense simbolisme" ("Without Symbolism"), in which a lover embarks upon a first-person account of a doomed amatory episode. "I abandoned the horse," says the lover, for a start, "that, by the most beauteous blinking of his eyelids, had converted the sun into an ornament for his forehead, and I made sure to take this ornament along with me that night— a very special lantern which guided me, faithfully, to Gertrude's garden." The lover finds his *amada* "tooting" his name "to the pretty cadence of a popular foxtrot." His attempt to embrace her is foiled by "the viscosity of a precise ray of moonlight." Ensuing scenes have the disjointedness of a dream. The sight of Gertrude's tresses stimulates a train of heady olfactory impressions: "The intense odor of the acacias anesthetized us so that we felt on the verge of a fainting spell. By sheer will power, I managed, though, to collect all the odors and enclose them in a case held shut by a ring studded with genuine jewels; and I felt at once revived by my audaciousness at this happy stroke of luck."

Lucky, however, the lover is not, as he soon discovers. In bold images of the type that Carlos Bousoña has labeled *visión*, Gertrude is shown as literally reaching for the stars: "She would unhook the stars one by one and would rinse them, with a shuddering of the infinite, in a pond half green, half silver, and would release them to the toads. . . ." This is clearly the high point of the episode. In contrast with a superwoman endowed with the might of a demiurge, the lover could not be cast in a more demeaning and ridiculous role. He is left to "harmonize" the "infamous croakings" of those denizens of stagnant waters "with the aid of a system of pedals that my beloved, with foresight, had providently arranged." He tries again, to no avail, to possess his beloved.

The distressed lover has little else to do but contemplate his fall from Earthly Paradise. Cognizant of the "heavy threat of the moon," he searches for his horse. The animal, now completely immersed in darkness, its eyes plastered over with "the stimulant of black tar," carries the lover and Gertrude to the rim of an abyss. Another odor—this time the unpleasant smell of the bramble bush—impels him to make a third try for the reward that, once again, proves unattainable. Overwhelmed by gloomy concerns—"torn asunder by fright" when assailed by various nightmarish flashes—the protagonist abandons the horse and tries to return home by taxi, but ends up, instead, in an unknown village. In his last fantasies, he feels a perverse pleasure in "purifying" himself "by gulping down as in a milk shake the smoke of all the chimneys in the neighborhood" and, finally, "in taking refuge beneath the crust of the large cities in order to capture the melody that the people's leaden footsteps create in homage to my littleness."

What order, one may ask, can ever transpire from the lover's stream of consciousness? At issue here is the recognition that "Without Symbolism" (the title proves to be obviously ironic) abounds in symbols that Foix cleverly disguises as principles of an overall design. Design, then, is the fountainhead of the order that an attentive reader will gradually intuit in Foix's composition. In effect, this intriguing piece evolves, organically, from a masterfully carried-out process that enhances the suggestiveness even as it fulfills the potential of a fundamental binary schema. This simple schema stems, in turn, from the atavistic opposition between male and female. To the exaltation of an apotheosized Gertrude, Foix counterposes the debasement of an antihero at the edge of annihilation. If the one shines in all her stellar splendor, the other lurks in the darkness of the netherworld.

"THE PARTISANS OF THE SUN"

Foix, who in another prose poem, "The Partisans of the Sun," constructs a personal mythology on the antagonism between two primeval races—the partisans of the sun, who live in the open and gather at daybreak, and their adversaries, the cave dwellers, who come out only by moonlight—is well aware of the tension between two fields of symbols, the chthonian and the uranic, to borrow the terminology which Rupert C. Allen, Gustavo Correa, and others have employed in their illu-

minating studies of García Lorca: Definitely uranic is the portrayal of Gertrude in the accoutrements of a *donna angelicata*, and unmistakably chthonian the depiction of the lover's persona with the demeanor of a fallen angel. What may interest the reader is the affinity between Foix's and García Lorca's respective versions of stock symbols—the horse, the moon, and various elements of nature—versions that often involve an intermingling of the heavenly and earthly spheres, as when (to mention but a few illustrations from Foix) Gertrude from her lofty position casts the stars into the lowly pond, the menacing moon hangs "heavily" down on the fate of the lover, and the horse loses its association with the sun in order to become a demoniac figure, as lurid as such a common representation of human libido ought to be.

Affinities of this kind detract nothing from the fierce independence and the original genius of the two writers in question. A striking aspect of Foix's innovative spirit is the ambivalent treatment he accords to the Gertrude-lover dyad as a latter-day manifestation of the age-old courtly love tradition, one of the many aspects of medieval literature that has never ceased to fascinate Foix. Insofar as he expatiates on leitmotifs of the quasi-canonized damsel and the virtually doomed young gallant, Foix exhibits a faithful adherence to that tradition. A closer reading, though, brings to light telltale signs of distortions characteristic of parody and even of the burlesque. As he dwells on the veritable chasm that separates the distant, disdainful *belle dame sans merci* and her mournful admirer who stews in the juices of his own morbid passion, Foix appears less interested in revitalizing worn-out topics than in elaborating in his own rendition of the ridiculous Don Juan *manqué*, much in the grotesque vein which Ramón María del Valle-Inclán had developed into a new art form in his revolutionary *esperpentos* of the early 1920's. Foix is quite successful in reconciling the conventions of the past with the fashionable trends of his day. Tradition? Yes, but only up to a point. Not for anything does he declare in one of his more renowned sonnets: "I am excited by what is new and enamored by what is old."

SOL, I DE DOL

With *Sol, i de dol*, Foix's attention shifted directly to the refinement of the outer form of poetry. This sequence of seventy splendid sonnets evinces a control, balance, and precision that many would consider possible only in an author of the classical Renaissance—the Renaissance that the historical and political circumstances of the fifteenth and sixteenth centuries did not allow Catalan literature to experience.

Foix reached the zenith of his mastery, however, in the most complex of his literary modes, which, since it extends toward the farthest stretches of poetic signification, appropriately may be labeled "contextual." Most commonly found in *Les irreals omegues, On he deixat les claus . . . ?* (where did I leave the keys . . . ?), and *Desa aquests llibres al calaix de baix* (these books in the bottom drawer), the "contextual" composition exhibits, instead of a title, an epigraph or a rubric in prose, ranging from three to fifteen lines, followed by a section in verse of variable length, which constitutes the body of the poem proper. By the intertextual articulation of the epigraph (the "pretext," one may say) with the verse component (that is, the "text" proper), Foix creates a "con-text" rich in metaphysical, ethical, and aesthetic connotations. It is not unusual for Foix to challenge his readers to round out the context with their own insights into historical circumstances, merely hinted at either through clues interspersed within the composition itself or by the date included at the end of the piece. Thus, Foix tries to raise the consciousness of his readers about important social issues, even as he engages their full participation in the re-creation of the poem itself.

"I Was Riding at Full Gallop Around the City Walls, Pursued by a Throng of Superstitious Coalmongers"

Civic consciousness, social concern, and a sense of moral outrage are fully evident in Foix's poem "I Was Riding at Full Gallop Around the City Walls, Pursued by a Throng of Superstitious Coalmongers." The broad period the author specifies in the dating of the composition (July, 1929, to October, 1936) was one of the most turbulent in Spanish history. Brutalized victims of a religiosity of the worst kind, foisted on them by a reactionary Big Brother, Foix's *carboners* (coalmongers) have little to do with the *carboneros* whose naïve, innocent, blind faith Miguel de Unamuno y Jugo secretly admired. To Foix, they are the agents of blind passion,

an unthinking multitude as loathsome to him as are their victimizers. The poem calls to mind the unctuousness and bigotry of some, the animosity and resentment of many, and the tensions that seethed within the masses until they exploded in the conflagration of 1936, and Foix's persona cannot but cry out in consternation: "Give me a lamp: —Where is my horse?/ Give me stone-hard coals and luminous pebbles/ Give me night walls in lunar cities." At the end of the poem, the persona attains the dubious distinction of speaking as a prophet of sorts, vexed by suspicions of an ominous handwriting on the wall; thus, Foix—with the prescience of García Lorca's *Poeta en Nueva York* (1940; *Poet in New York*, 1940, 1955), Pablo Neruda's *España en el corazón* (1937; *Spain in the Heart*, 1946), and Pablo Picasso's painting *Guernica* (1937)—cries out against man's inhumanity to man and warns of the danger that humankind will bring on itself the dreadful wrath of the gods.

Other major works

SHORT FICTION: *Allò que no diu La vanguardia*, 1970; *La pell de la pell*, 1970.

NONFICTION: *Revolució catalanista*, 1934 (with Josep Carbonell); *Catalans de 1918*, 1965; *Els lloms transparents*, 1969; *Noranta set notes sobre ficcions poncianes*, 1974.

MISCELLANEOUS: *Obres completes*, 1974-1990 (4 volumes; includes his epistles).

Bibliography

Boehne, Patricia J. *J. V. Foix*. Boston: Twayne, 1980. An introductory biographical study and critical analysis of selected works by Foix. Includes bibliographic references and an index.

Bohn, Willard. *Marvelous Encounters: Surrealist Responses to Film, Art, Poetry, and Architecture*. Lewisburg, Pa.: Bucknell University Press, 2005. Contains a chapter on the Catalan experience, with a discussion of Foix.

Cocozzella, Peter. Review of *Tocant a mà*. *World Literature Today* 68, no. 1 (Winter, 1994): 107. Cocozzella provides a summary in English of Joan R. Veny-Mesquida's introduction in Catalan to *Tocant a mà*. Complementing positivistic analysis with the insights provided by current literary theory, Veny-Mesquida, in a substantial introduction of some eighty pages, calls upon foreign and homegrown pundits—Norman Friedmann, Gerald Prince, Carles Miralles, Maurici Serrahima, Enric Sulla, Ferrater, and Gimferrer, among others—to help him shed light on Foix's engrossing masterpieces.

Rosenthal, David. *Postwar Catalan Poetry*. Cranbury, N.J.: Associated University Presses, 1991. Contains an introduction to Catalan poetry, and a chapter on Foix, followed by chapters on other Catalan poets.

Peter Cocozzella

JEAN FOLLAIN

Born: Canisy, France; August 29, 1903
Died: Quai des Tuileries, France; March 10, 1971

PRINCIPAL POETRY

La Main chaude, 1933
Chants terrestres, 1937
Ici-bàs, 1941
Usage du temps, 1943
Exister, 1947
Les Choses données, 1952
Territoires, 1953
Objects, 1955
Des heures, 1960
Appareil de la terre, 1964
D'après tout, 1967 (*Après Tout: Poems by Jean Follain*, 1981)
Transparence of the World, 1969
Espaces d'instants, 1971
Présent Jour, 1978
A World Rich in Anniversaries: Prose Poems, 1979
Jean Follain: 130 Poems, 2009

OTHER LITERARY FORMS

In addition to his poetry, Jean Follain (faw-LAHN) wrote several nonfiction works, notable among which are *Collège* (1973), an account of his secondary-school experiences in the years immediately following World War I, and a history of Peru, *Pérou* (1964).

ACHIEVEMENTS

Jean Follain was the recipient of several awards for his poetic achievements, including the Mallarmé prize (1939), the Prix Blumenthal (1941), the Capri (1958), and the Grand Prix de Poésie of the French Academy (1970). He was also made a chevalier in the French Legion of Honor.

BIOGRAPHY

Jean René Follain was born in Canisy, France, on August 29, 1903. His maternal grandfather was a notary and his paternal grandfather was a schoolteacher. His father was a professor at the Collège de Saint-Lô in a neighboring town. Follain studied at this institution, where he was awarded a prize for excellence in philosophy. He subsequently wrote one of his finest prose works, *Collège*, about his experiences there.

In 1921, Follain began studies at the law school at Caen and graduated with honors. As a student, he was also interested in the history of the nineteenth century. In 1923, he went to Paris on a probationary basis with a lawyer and in 1927 became a member of the Paris bar and practiced law until 1952.

Meanwhile, Follain became a part of the group of poets and painters that formed around the review *Sagesse*, founded by Fernand Marc, where he published his first poems. There he met André Salmon, Pierre Reverdy, Pierre MacOrlan, Léon-Paul Fargue, Guegen, Armen Lubin, Max Jacob, Pierre Minet, Madeleine Israel, Georges Duveaux, and Alfred Gaspart. In 1932, he collaborated with several of these writers to publish in literary journals such as *Dernier Carre*, *Feuillets inutiles*, and *Montparnasse*. His first poems were published in the *La Nouvelle Revue française*, *Commerce*, *Europe*, and *Les Cahiers des Saisons*. Follain married Madeleine Denis, a painter, in 1934.

In 1952, Follain quit the bar to become a court magistrate in Charleville, where he remained until 1961. Between 1957 and 1967, he traveled quite extensively all over the world to countries such as Thailand, Japan, Brazil, Peru, the United States, the Ivory Coast, and Senegal. In 1969, he made a film for educational television called *Canisy, vu par Jean Follain* (Canisy, as seen by Jean Follain), directed by Michel Nicoletti.

Follain was struck by a car and killed on March 10, 1971, on the Tuileries quay. He had enjoyed an active and distinguished literary career, serving as president of the Friends of Rimbaud; president of the selection committees for the Cazes Prize, the Max Jacob Prize, and the Deux Magots Prize; and assistant secretary general of the French PEN Club.

ANALYSIS

Jean Follain has been hailed as one of the great secret voices of the twentieth century. He addressed humanity's search for a total union between the known surroundings of a fleeting earthly life and the unknown, absolute finalities of death, space, and time. He succeeded in integrating a world of directly observable facts with the complexities of experiences and powers beyond human control. His ability to communicate this message by choosing the proper words and by realizing their full semantic value and power in their proper placement in a sentence constitutes his greatest poetic achievement.

Three major collections of Follain's poetry, *La Main chaude* (the hot hand), *Chants terrestres* (terrestrial songs), and *Exister* (to exist), each introduce a theme or a stylistic component essential to the understanding of Follain's art and repeated in later works. *La Main chaude* introduced Follain's concept of poetry as a continuum of incongruous events, the role of memory, and the ever-present village of Normandy where he spent his youth. *Chants terrestres* presents Follain's preoccupation with words: word choice, syntax, the play of sound, and the power of evocation. *Exister* introduces stylistic patterns that were established for the first time in Follain's poetry and that persisted in later volumes.

LA MAIN CHAUDE

La Main chaude consists of poems whose titles are rather surprising and completely unrelated to one another. They include "Poème glorieux" (glorious poem), "L'Épicier" (the grocer), "Mets" (food), "La Digestion aux cannons" (the digestion of cannons), "La Place publique en été" (the public square in summer), "Ode à l'amour juvenile" (ode to young love), "À la dame

du temps de Borgia" (to the lady of Borgia's time), "Milords" (milords), "Les Belles noyées" (the beautiful drowned ones), "Combat singulier de seigneurs dans la campagne" (the singular combat of lords in the country), and "Appel aux soldats roux" ("Appeal to the Red-haired Soldiers"). At first glance, each poem seems to be a disparate fragment sharing no unity of leitmotif or style with the other poems.

The objective of this collection is to conjure the sense of specific recollections of places, occasions, and objects. Although the poems refer to simple evocations, the familiar is suddenly juxtaposed to unexpected or incongruous words or happenings that shatter known and assumed relationships. The harmony of the collection, then, is achieved from the unity of contrasting spectacles.

Follain's intention in constructing the poems in this manner is not to distort language but to convey the message that the world as perceived and the world of visions are one. He creates a web with simple words whose meanings are unclear. He then compares the web he has created to the Normandy countryside of his youth, where echoes can be discerned from unclear depths and where lights shining on objects create an impression of uncertainty as to whether the lights are illuminating the objects or the grouping of the objects is creating the lights.

Memory has a special role in these poems. It is not simply a link between the past and the present. According to Follain, memory is distinct from the past on which it draws, and it is what makes the past a key to the mystery that stays with people and does not change: the present. The different evocations presented in the various poems of this collection concern the mystery of the present. They recall the concrete details of his youth in Normandy and give them their form, both luminous and removed at the same time. Simultaneously, the form gives the evocations the aura of a ceremony, another of Follain's preoccupations. He compares the evocations of this poetry collection to an unchanging ceremony heralding some inexorable splendor. For Follain, it is a fulfillment not only of a need for ceremony but also of a fondness for the ceremonious, in which each isolated detail is an evocation of the procession of an immeasurable continuum.

CHANTS TERRESTRES

Chants terrestres takes its name from the poem "Chants terrestres" in the collection *La Main chaude*. As in the earlier collection, the poems in *Chants terrestres* bear titles that seem unrelated to one another. They include "La Dame à crieurs de pâtés" (the lady at the pâté-vendor's), "L'Adieu du diplomate" (the diplomat's farewell), and "Le Gant rouge" (the red glove). Again, it is not possible to speak of a unifying thread among the individual poems with regard to a structural plan, a rhythmical pattern, or conventional poetic themes such as nostalgia, death, or regret.

These poems, however, are a testimony to Follain's preoccupation with words. As always, the evocations in the poems reflect his tendency to recall the beloved memories of his native village of Canisy in Normandy. He constructs a world with seemingly simple words that encompass the most minute instances of his life, perpetually in search of the elusive reality of things. Nature and humanity in their most universally accepted forms are seized in sentences in which their substance and truth defy classification or definition. Objects become stratified, and the precision of the lines of verse gives life to inert words so that they, too, become objects. Human life becomes stratified as well. Follain constructs it layer by layer, piece by piece, in such a way that the reader is never really able to distinguish the importance of the events discussed because the most obscure, abandoned, and minute details surface to haunt him in these poems.

EXISTER

In *Exister*, thematic and structural patterns begin to emerge for the first time. In these poems, Follain shows that the emotions experienced in the activities of daily life give rise to complexities or contradictions and can be transcended through disengaged contemplation.

The themes are few and recurring: daily life (especially from Follain's childhood) in contact with the power of time, and the possibility of overcoming its restrictions—work, illness, and violence—through the transcendental forces of love, religion, and contemplation. The style is stark, austere, and simple. Rhetorical devices are seldom used. The depth and power of the text depends on the reader's ability to become an active participant and interpreter of its message on many lev-

els. This is consistent with the goal of modern poetry since Arthur Rimbaud.

Two major and several minor structural patterns emerge. The first major structural pattern deals with emotion and can be presented as follows: emotional response, reversal of emotion, suppression of emotion. For example, in "L'Amirauté" (the admiralty), the first section presents a world that excludes the observer: The windows do not give light, the weather is bad, the town is alien, the building is seen from the exterior. The second section is a complete reversal of the darkness and pessimism of the first part: The building is a place of shelter; it is attractively furnished and comes to be associated with the heart. The second part, then, cancels the initial emotion, and the rest of the poem avoids further emotional reactions. The third section of the poem presages death. The emphasis, however, is on the time of passage into death and not on the physical or mental destruction of the person. The vocabulary is abstract, and there is no evocation of suffering. The fourth part of the poem moves to a totally intellectual level.

This pattern recurs in many other poems of this collection and in subsequent collections. For example, in "L'Amitié" (friendship), pride and human contact are replaced by the frustration of departure and then by detached observation of the external world. In "L'Enfant au tambour" (the child with the drum), the threat of death and the oppressiveness of the garden are succeeded by a contempt for war and by a return to the original scene from an intellectual perspective. In "L'Appel du chevalier" (the call of the chevalier), the boy's tedious work gives way to the heroism of the past and then to a suppression of emotion and consciousness in sleep. This irrelevance of emotion is later evidenced in the poem "Postures" (situations), from the collection *Des heures* (of hours).

The second major structural pattern that emerges in Follain's poetry is as follows: immediate, nonimmediate, conflict, solitude, harmony, essential, and partial harmony. The manifestations of this pattern, however, vary from poem to poem. In "L'Amirauté," it is constructed in the following way: The first section presents a self-contained world that can be easily comprehended by the reader. The second section shows this immediate perception to be only partially valid, and the interplay of elements beyond the observable plays an important role in this section. The poem ends with a shift to the sphere of the timeless and unconditional truth that is beyond the perceived world, in this case, religion. The opposing elements become reconciled.

Examples of the shift from the immediate include the introduction of the elemental forces of wind and night in "L'Appel du chevalier"; the inscription of the hours in the wearing out of the damask in "Paysage des deux ouvriers" (landscape of two laborers); and the wild nature surrounding the enclosure in "Amis d'Austerlitz" (friends from Austerlitz).

Another variation is the sudden interruption of one human activity by another one—for example, work after love in "Indifference du bricoleur" (the handyman's indifference), "Chanson de la maîtresse du boulanger" (song of the baker's mistress), "La Brodeuse d'abeilles" (the embroiderer of the bees); or the inverse, love after work, as in "L'Empailleur d'oiseaux" (the taxidermist of birds) and "L'Anecdote" (the anecdote).

Another technique is the intrusion of psychological elements after establishing an introduction based on the tangible and the concrete, as in "Métaphysique" (metaphysics) and "L'Histoire" (the story). Conflict and solitude appear in many forms. They include the violence of passion and conflict in the kisses of "Les Portraits" (the portraits); solitude in "L'Ennui" (boredom) and "L'Enfant de l'amour" (the love child); torture in "La Matière" ("Matter"); separation in "L'Empailleur d'oiseaux"; the destruction of the flower in "Domaine d'ombre" (the domain of shadow); the duel in "Le Vin du soir" (evening wine); and abandonment in "La Créature" (the creature).

These examples bear witness to the inadequacy of human attempts to live in harmony with the rest of humankind. Harmony or unity may be achieved in a variety of ways. They include love in "Des Hommes" (men); gentleness in "Le Pain" (the loaf); beauty in "La Pyramide" ("The Pyramid"); familiarity in "Parler seul" ("Speech Alone"); benevolence in "La Vie domestique" ("Domestic Life"); reciprocal influence in "L'Existence" ("Existence"); and a communion between nature and the senses in "La Bête" ("The Beast"). Other variations, however, may occur. At times, the reference to harmony is indirect. For example, in "L'Asie" ("Asia"), the man is eating soup.

At first glance, this does not seem to be a universal portrayal of harmony, but it must he noted that in Follain's poetry, food and drink are synonymous with peaceful human interaction. In other cases, conflict and harmony may appear in the same poem—for example, the moans of passion and the soft sounds in "Les Jardins" (the gardens); the conflict between darkness and flames and the harmony that arises from the unity of friends in "Les Amis d'Austerlitz." In still other cases, conflict and solitude are present in the same poem, such as in "Le Vin du soir," as is partial harmony and total harmony (such as compassion and marriage) in "Les Devoirs" (duties), or the loyalty and cooperation between the father and the daughter and the union between the daughter and the leaf in "Aux Choses lentes" (to slow things).

The essential is often represented by references to death (as in "Existence"), which is then linked to the world or universe (as in "Les Portraits," "Le Vin du soir," and "Ineffable de la fin," ineffable to the end), or to religion (as in "Balances," balances, and "Le Pas," the step), or to eternity (as in "Natures mortes," still lifes, and "Les Journaliers," the day laborers), or to timelessness (as in "Le Secret," "The Secret"). This structural pattern directly reflects Follain's sensitivity to humans' need to integrate their earthly surroundings with the absolutes of death, religion, space, and time.

Again, there is a certain variation and flexibility among the elements of the pattern. For example, in the poem "La Brodeuse d'abeilles," the introductory lines present the theme of physical love. The succeeding lines then place the theme of solitude alongside the theme of passion. Follain's intention here is to show the multidimensional aspect of life, represented by people or objects. In this case, it is clearly communicated that the reader cannot perceive this person in a solely physical context. The poem appeals to his sensitivity and depth of perception and comprehension as well as his ability to integrate the deeper meanings of the relationship between two opposing concepts. In this poem, the ability to shift the perspective of the relationship leads to a coherent conclusion of the text. It is suggested that a union or harmony may be attained on an aesthetic level between the *brodeuse* and the physical world represented here by her clothing, her jewelry, and other outward manifestations. This can be realized, however, only when the element of passion or direct physical contact is eliminated entirely.

There are also different rates of progress among the various elements that constitute the pattern. For example, "Enfantement" (child-birth) shows some deviation from the order and progress of the pattern. It begins with the contact with the inaccessible and then moves to the tangible, accessible environment of the city. The person is introduced first and then the description of the city is given. Also, the reversal of emotion precedes rather than coincides with the shift from the immediate. Another example occurs in "Le Sapeur" (the sapper). The progression begins normally from calm observation to the agitation of the fish, which reverses the emotional tone. Next, there is a shift to the remote in terms of the fish being nonhuman and being caught. The next element to be introduced, however, has nothing to do with union or harmony. It shifts back to concrete details, which then leads to the nonimmediate, as represented by the sound of the church bells.

SUBTHEMES

Other, simpler patterns also exist. They appear less uniformly but still serve to indicate general tendencies. The first pattern traces the development from the depiction of the exterior world as a setting for humankind to the presentation of a single person and then to the intangible represented by the soul or God. This pattern occurs in "L'Amirauté," "Domaine d'ombre," and "L'Haine en été" (hate in summer). The development of this pattern is often linked to another one: the introduction of a woman who allows the escape from the immediate, the reference to the soul allowing the reduction of emotional tone and the introduction of the dimension of unity. The latter element of this pattern is especially important because it allows the extension of the poem beyond a point that might otherwise have been final. An example of this occurs in "Apparition de la vieille" (the appearance of the old woman). The harmony brought about by the return of the old woman from the childhood stories seems sufficient to conclude the poem, but a more satisfying conclusion is created by the shift to the intangible—memory—as a culmina-

tion of the movement from the person to the objects associated with her. The same occurs in "Les Uns et les autres" (the ones and the others). The expected conclusion was one that would have preserved the severity of the last lines of verse. Instead, however, it ends with a reference to love, after depicting nature, people, and objects. The effect of this tendency is quite compatible with other aspects of Follain's writing—that is, to show a decrease of humanity's involvement with the exterior world.

The second pattern that emerges is that the poems tend to move from a restrictive view of the world to one that permits penetration into the normally inaccessible, thereby reducing the incommunicability with the world. For example, in "L'Ennui," the poet penetrates into the interior of the body with the song; the body underneath the clothes in "La Mémoire" (the memory) and "Aux choses lentes"; the invisible heart in "L'Amirauté"; and the knowledge of secrets in "Paysage des deux ouvriers."

The third observation to be made is that the poems tend to move from the temporal to the atemporal, which bridges the past and the present.

Finally, the senses alluded to appear in an order of decreasing materialism: touch, sound, sight, scent. At times, this order motivates the harmonious conclusion of the poem—for example, the intense stare in "Aux Choses lentes" or the peaceful visual conclusion of "Pathétique" in contrast to the noise presented in the introduction. Scent is especially associated with the intangible and the essential, as in "Métaphysique" and "La Journée en feu" (the day on fire).

Follain aims at recording the flow of life rather than imposing a form on it. His writing reflects his perception of the duality of life. There is a double inclination to address the known objects of the world and then to subject them to a more abstract vision, thereby giving the reader access to the essential and intangible, which allows him or her to reconcile these two tendencies. Stylistically, the reader must realize that the patterns underlying Follain's poetry do not impose absolute constraints of any kind. The reader is not able to predict accurately what the succeeding line of verse will say. That is because the images and concepts that constitute the text cannot be construed as examples of a single topic. Follain's poetry overflows with semantic excess; the meaning of the lines is not exhausted by their structural relationships. This allows space within the poem for the unpredictable and the spontaneous, thus freeing language and experience from automatization and compelling the reader to take an active part in the creation of meaning.

OTHER MAJOR WORKS

NONFICTION: *Paris*, 1935; *L'Épicerie d'enfance*, 1938; *Canisy*, 1942 (English translation, 1981); *Chef-lieu*, 1950; *Pérou*, 1964; *Collège*, 1973; *Selected Prose*, 1985; *Célébration de la pomme de terre*, 1997.

BIBLIOGRAPHY

Brombert, Beth Archer, et al. *Dreaming the Miracle: Three French Prose Poets*. Buffalo, N.Y.: White Pine Press, 2003. A collection of prose poetry by Follain, Max Jacob, and Francis Ponge. The preface by Peter Johnson places Follain among his fellow poets and analyzes his poetry. Mary Feeney translated the Follain poems and provides a useful introduction.

Cardinal, Roger, ed. *Sensibility and Creation: Studies in Twentieth-Century French Poetry*. New York: Barnes and Noble, 1977. Contains an essay, "Jean Follain: Objects in Time," examining the poetry of Follain.

Caws, Mary Ann, ed. *The Yale Anthology of Twentieth-Century French Poetry*. New Haven, Conn.: Yale University Press, 2004. Contains selected poems by Follain, with an introduction that notes his fame for celebration of everyday things in his poetry.

Follain, Jean. *Jean Follain: 130 Poems*. Translated by Christopher Middleton. London: Anvil Press Poetry, 2009. The translations by poet Middleton span Follain's career and present a broad view of his work.

Gavronsky, Serge, ed. *Poems and Texts: An Anthology of French Poems*. New York: October House, 1969. Translations of selected poems and interviews with Follain and other French poets.

Morgan, Robert. *Good Measure: Essays, Interviews, and Notes on Poetry*. Baton Rouge: Louisiana State University Press, 1993. The poet Morgan includes a close look at some poems by Follain among his many writings on poetry.

Thomas, Jean-Jacques. *Poeticized Language: The Foundations of Contemporary French Poetry*. University Park: Pennsylvania State University Press, 1999. A historical study of French poetry that offers some background and insight into the works of Follain. Includes bibliographical references and index.

Anne Laura Mattrella

UGO FOSCOLO

Born: Zante, Ionian Isles, Greece; February 6, 1778
Died: Turnham Green, near London, England; September 10, 1827

PRINCIPAL POETRY

Bonaparte liberatore, 1797
Poesie, 1803
Dei sepolcri, 1807 (*On Sepulchers*, 1835, 1971)
Le grazie, 1848

OTHER LITERARY FORMS

Ugo Foscolo (FAWS-koh-loh) is best known for his *Ultime lettere di Jacopo Ortis* (1802; *Last Letters of Jacopo Ortis*, 1970), an epistolary novel written after the Treaty of Campoformio (October 17, 1797), in which Napoleon Bonaparte ceded Venice to the Austrians. Napoleon's action shocked Foscolo, who had previously written an ode entitled "A Bonaparte liberatore" ("To the Liberator Bonaparte"). In this autobiographical novel written in the form of letters from the student Jacopo Ortis to his friend Lorenzo Alderani, eroticism and politics (of a strong anti-Gallic strain) are merged. In the same year, Foscolo wrote a tragedy, *Tieste* (pr. 1797), in the style of Vittorio Alfieri, the success of which owed much to its revolutionary democratic spirit.

Between 1804 and 1805, while in France, Foscolo began work on an Italian translation of Laurence Sterne's *A Sentimental Journey* (1768). This translation was finished in 1813 in Pisa and was published as *Viaggio sentimentale di Yorick lungo la Francia e l'Italia* concurrently with an autobiographical work, *Notizie intorno a Didimo Chierico* (1813; news about Didimo Chierico). On January 22, 1809, in support of his nomination for a professorship at Pavia University, Foscolo published an important work titled *Dell'origine e dell'ufficio della letteratura* (about the origin and function of literature), in which he promotes a sociohistorical approach to literature.

Among Foscolo's most important nonlyric works are the tragedies *Aiace* (pr. 1811) and *Ricciarda* (pr. 1813). *Aiace* was not successful at its premiere but has come to be considered one of Foscolo's best works. Foscolo's *Epistolario* (1949-1970; letters) is outstanding, from both a literary and a political standpoint, and is characterized by sincerity even in the most intimate matters. In Switzerland, Foscolo published his speeches under the title *Della servitu d'Italia* (1823; on the servitude of Italy), a work that shows Foscolo's pessimism concerning the then-fermenting Risorgimento, the movement for the unification of Italy.

From 1816 until his death in 1827, Foscolo lived in England and dedicated himself to producing scholarly, critical works such as *Saggi sul Petrarca* (1821; *Essays on Petrarch*, 1823). Through these works, Foscolo helped to initiate in Italy a modern critical awareness of the psychological and sociohistorical background of literature.

ACHIEVEMENTS

Ugo Foscolo was a man of strong commitment and even stronger will, never afraid to follow the path of truth in the pursuit of the ideals he held worthy. Like many Italian writers from Petrarch and Dante on, Foscolo brought a strong thread of classical culture to the Romanticism that dominated the entire European scene during the early 1800's. His personal experiences and his cultural background became the raw material from which he worked all his life. Foscolo's writings, in some sense, summed up much of the achievement and many of the trends of Italian literature of his day (the critical studies of Dante, Petrarch, and Giovanni Boccaccio are notable in this respect), and he stood as a significant milestone for writers of succeed-

ing generations. His burial at the Church of Santa Croce in Florence, where he is entombed among the greatest figures of Italian literary and political history, suggests his place in Italian culture and letters.

BIOGRAPHY

Niccolò Ugo Foscolo was born to parents of mixed heritage; his mother, Diamantina Spaty, was Greek, while his father, Andrea Foscolo, was Venetian. When Foscolo was ten years old, his father died. He and his mother then moved to Venice, where he stayed until 1797, during which time he began to attend political and literary gatherings such as those of the Countess Isabella Teotochi. In this period, he developed an admiration for the revolutionary doctrines of Jean-Jacques Rousseau, Alfieri, and Robespierre while attending classes taught by Melchiorre Cesarotti at Padua University.

In 1797, because of his political ideas, Foscolo was forced to flee to Bologna, where he received the nomination of honorary lieutenant for the French army in Italy. He performed this role as a strict republican until the infamous Treaty of Campoformio, which caused Foscolo to hate Bonaparte so much that he moved to Milan, where he lived from 1797 to 1815. In Milan, Foscolo made the acquaintance of Vincenzo Monti and Giuseppe Parini, and he also pursued love affairs with Teresa Pickler, Isabella Roncioni, and the Countess Antonietta Fagnani Arese.

When, in 1798, the second coalition of the Austrians and Russians reconquered northern Italy from Napoleon (who was at that time in Egypt), Foscolo fought against this action under General Jean-Étienne Championnet, but his open aspiration for Italian independence provoked great hostility from the French. Nevertheless, he went to France for two years (1804-1806) and made the acquaintance of the famous Italian writer Alessandro Manzoni, as well as an English girl, Fanny Emerytt, by whom he had a daughter, Floriana. Returning to Milan in 1806, Foscolo pursued more love affairs and dedicated himself to various writing activities. In 1812, after the presentation of his second tragedy, *Aiace*, in which certain characters were seen as anti-French, the poet was forced to flee to Florence. There, Foscolo involved himself in the circle of the countess of Albany until the Austrians took Milan in 1813. Unable to pledge allegiance to the Austrian government, Foscolo went into voluntary exile in Switzerland in 1815. One year later, he moved to England, where he collaborated in the publication of magazines and journals, gave classes in literature, and was reunited with his daughter, Floriana. He quickly exhausted Floriana's savings, some three thousand pounds, and remained deeply in debt until his death in 1827. Only in 1871 was his body brought to Florence and buried, as requested in his will, in the Church of Santa Croce, next to the tombs of Michelangelo, Machiavelli, Alfieri, and Galileo.

Foscolo's achievements were acknowledged during his lifetime, but it was only after his death that his writings were fully recognized as a milestone in Italian literature. He succeeded in detaching himself from the regionalism of his predecessors. From political realism, he went on to pessimism, though he never espoused the fatalism expressed by his younger contemporary Giacomo Leopardi; Foscolo's was a dynamic pessimism that organized his heroic and lyric behavior. If the function of poetry, as Natalino Sapegno states in his *Disegno storico della letteratura italiana* (1973), is to discover amid the contradictions of this earthly life that universal harmony by which humans restore their own existence, Foscolo, amid a troubled life, found support in his art and created a personal vision of the sublime.

ANALYSIS

The Romantic movement dominated Italian literature during the first half of the nineteenth century, and Ugo Foscolo, along with other writers, such as Vincenzo Monti and Alessandro Manzoni, was part of it, though at a rather different level. Foscolo's personal life and his involvement in the political, social, and literary history of Italy are closely meshed in his poetry.

"SONETTI"

Foscolo's twelve sonnets (known collectively as the "Sonetti"), which combine the strength of Dante and the melancholy of Petrarch, have much in common with his novel *Last Letters of Jacopo Ortis*: the oppressive influence of Fate on politics and personal life, hints of suicide, the pleasures and despair of love, and a sense

of hostility against the invaders of Italy. There is in these sonnets, however, a new sense of nature, a more ironic and melancholic approach to the political problems of Italy, and a more lyric treatment of autobiographical themes such as love, exile, death of loved ones, and exhortations to achieve glory through poetry.

In the sonnet "Te nudrice alle muse" ("You Nurturer of the Muses"), addressed to Italy, Foscolo complains about the proposed abolition of the Latin language, a proposal made by the legislature of the Cisalpina Republic. This sonnet at first appears to be academic and traditional in structure, theme, and style, reflecting the influence of Alfieri and the neoclassical literary forms of the late eighteenth century. There is, nevertheless, an innovative element in this sonnet: the first use by Foscolo of a technique, later perfected in *On Sepulchers*, by which the various sections of a poem are related by larger, "historical" logic rather than by conventional syntactic logic. The two quatrains of this sonnet refer to the past, while, without any apparent connective tissue, the tercets ironically address Italy on the inconveniences that would be caused by the abolition of the Latin language. The logic that related quatrains and tercets reflects the overlying concept that there can be no contemporary Italian language and culture without reference to the language and culture of the past.

The sonnet "E tu?" ("And You?") also contrasts quatrains and tercets: The quatrains have an *abba-abba* rhyme scheme and are historical in content, while the tercets rhyme *aba-cbc* and are erotic in theme and mood. The poet starts by using heroic, quasi-Ossianic terminology to recall the medieval fights in Florence; then, in a more lyric fashion, he praises Florence as the dwelling place of his beloved.

"Ne più" ("Never Again"), another sonnet from this collection, speaks of the tragedy of the exiled Foscolo. The poet, though Italian by birth and education, will never be able to forget that he was born of a Greek mother in the luminous and wooded Zacinto, and that his poetry echoes Homer and Theocritus. Foscolo recalls his island and the myths of Venus and Ulysses with a surge of melody in full rhymes. The first statement nostalgically affirms that he will never again set foot on the sacred shore of his native island and, unlike

Ulysses, will not be granted burial in his native land. The last tercet, however, brings the consolation that, if not his body, at least his song will return to Zacinto: Poetry will be his means of immortality.

The Foscolo of the "Sonetti" reaches a climax of poetic inspiration when he turns from history and mythology to treat his personal life or naturalistically perceived objects. A vein of melancholy emerges in sonnets such as "Perché taccia il rumor di mia catena" ("To Hush the Clangor of My Chain"), "Forse perché della fatal quiete" ("Perhaps Because of the Fateful Quiet"), and "Un dì, s'io non andrò sempre fuggendo" ("One Day, Should I Not Always Flee"). In these sonnets, for example, there are autobiographical references to his unfortunate love for the Florentine Isabella Roncioni and to the death of his brother John, which reminds him of his exile.

The sonnet "Perhaps Because of the Fateful Quiet" is a dialogue with the evening; it moves in a thickly harmonious structure from the proposal of the theme through a central part to the conclusion. Its merit, as Foscolo himself said, lies in producing, through a broken structure, the same effects that musicians achieve through dissonance and painters achieve through shading. The poem starts with monosyllables and bisyllables, pauses at the fourth line in perfect lyric hendecasyllables until the eighth line, and then begins again the tormented rhythmic pattern. In a fashion reminiscent of Edward Young and Giuseppe Parini, Foscolo writes of the evening that is dear to him because it is the image of death; it keeps the secret paths of his heart, promising rest for his ever-warring spirit.

"To Louise Pallavicini Fallen from a Horse"

During the same years in which these sonnets were composed (1800-1802), Foscolo also wrote two *odi*: "A Luigia Pallavicini caduta da cavallo" ("To Louise Pallavicini Fallen from a Horse") and "All'amica risanata" ("To the Healed Friend"), for Antonietta Fagnani Arese. These two odes praise the beauty of and virtually deify the two women to whom they are dedicated. The autobiographical elements and controlled poetic expertise of the sonnets continue in these odes, which are additionally characterized by literary eclecticism and imagery drawn from pagan mythology.

The first ode describes a fall that the beautiful Louise took from a horse and expresses the wish that she will recover and become more beautiful than before. The whole poem is supported by mythic prototypes: Venus stung on the foot while leaning over the dead body of Ado, the "bath of Pallas," the intervention of Neptune against the enraged horse, and finally the fall of Diana into the volcano Etna, followed by her recovery. Though the poem's structure (eighteen stanzas of six lines each) is taken from Carlo Frugoni, and its imagery is inherited from poets such as Ludovico Ariosto, Poliziano, and Alfieri, Foscolo proves his mastery of form, style, and imagination by achieving a certain degree of seriousness in a lyric genre which in eighteenth century Italy had a rather light, occasional status. In Foscolo's work, goddesses care for human suffering and exchange feelings of love with mortal creatures. The highly artificial tone characteristic of occasional verse does not diminish the sense of beauty and serenity which this ode evokes, foreshadowing Foscolo's more mature work in *Le grazie*.

"To the Healed Friend"

The second ode, "To the Healed Friend," usually viewed in relation to the passionate letters that Foscolo wrote to Antonietta Fagnani Arese, is, by contrast, carefully controlled in emotion. The process of deification is more stylized here than in the ode to Louise Pallavicini. The poet begins with a description of the healing of his beloved, again using mythological allusions. The deification reaches its climax when the poet declares that his verses will be the woman's salvation from death and from the jealousy of others. The conclusion reiterates the mood of the earlier sonnet to his native island, "Ne più mai toccherò le sacre sponde" ("I Will Never Touch Again the Sacred Shore") and anticipates the poem *Le grazie* with a recollection of the spirit of Sappho and the sound of Greek poetry. As in the first ode, Foscolo contemplates evil and death only to distance himself from them, to aspire to a higher sense of beauty and eternity.

On Sepulchers

In considering *On Sepulchers*, Giovanni Getto, in *La composizione dei "Sepolcri" di Ugo Foscolo* (1977), observes that the three images—suggesting nature, civilization, and death—presented at the beginning of the poem, represent the complex symbol of *On Sepulchers*'s entire figurative world. The poem draws together all the poetic motifs of Foscolo's earlier work into a new and powerful synthesis. The dialectic of this poem is, ultimately, between death and immortality. If the evils of this life cannot be avoided, immortality may be attained through memory, as evidenced by burial monuments, for after death, the hero will obtain at least this measure of glory. In the various shadings of *On Sepulchers*, Foscolo continuously fuses images and contrasting tones and creates the highly individual syntax that distinguishes his verse.

On Sepulchers is infused with a sense of melancholy, mystery, and historicism. After evoking life, nature, poetry, and hopes broken by death, Foscolo blames the new Napoleonic law for having placed the bones of great men and those of thieves in the same tomb. He remembers then the sensible pagan rituals in honor of the virtuous dead, contrasting them with the superstitious rites of Christianity, which are characterized by a fear of the next world. He then passes to a historical vision in praise of Florence, where Dante and the parents of Petrarch were born, and where Machiavelli, Michelangelo, and Galileo are buried in Santa Croce. The sense of heroism and of the regeneration of the Italian nation comes from a tie between the living and the dead. This is why the heroic spirits of the past inspired Homer, especially the spirit of Hector, the greatest and most unfortunate of all heroes.

For Foscolo, poetry was one of the most pure and significant achievements of humankind. His translations from Homer in the period preceding the composition of *On Sepulchers* inspired him to celebrate the heros of the past in order to unite former times with the present in an ineffable harmony. The occasional, the meditative, the narrative, and the fantastic impulses all converge in this poem. Unlike *Last Letters of Jacopo Ortis*, which echoes the Titanism of Alfieri, and unlike the "Sonetti," which expresses the solitude and the horror of Foscolo's life, *On Sepulchers* testifies to the poet's liberation from his past passions. From the beginning, the reader of *On Sepulchers* has in front of his eyes not a bare tomb but a sepulcher comforted by the tears of the living, because "Hope, the last Goddess, flees the sepulchers." From reason to fantasy, from the past to the present, from the dead to the living, from autobiographical references to the recollection of the great poets and heroes of the past, Foscolo develops his themes like a symphony. The initial rhetorical question in *On Sepulchers*, in which the desolation of death is clearly stated, is finally transformed into the attitude that all people worthy of glory, such as Hector, will have the "honor of tears as long as the sun will shine over human afflictions."

LE GRAZIE

The interrelationship between poetry and the other arts, while present in Foscolo's earlier poetry, becomes central in *Le grazie*. The vision of poetry that eternalizes heroism through emulation of living people, as found in *On Sepulchers*, is here replaced with poetry that focuses on beauty, which educates the human spirit to reveal the secret consonance of the universe.

Aldo Vallone, in *Le Grazie nella storia della poesia foscoliana* (1977), has remarked that the neoclassicism of *On Sepulchers* becomes for Foscolo in *Le grazie* the natural way of composing poetry. The expressive elements contained in this ambitious allegorical and didactic poem, which remained unfinished at Foscolo's death, reveal his absolute mastery of his material. By technical devices such as the usage of certain prepositions, of narrative sections, and of repetition of key words, Foscolo suggests at one moment the shading of the verse, while at another moment he reestablishes equilibrium among the various segments of the poem, producing an effect of musical lyricism.

Composing *Le grazie* while at the villa Bellosguardo, near Florence, Foscolo was inspired by the Venus of Canova and the statuary group of the Graces. The poem also reveals the influence of the neoclassical aesthetics of Johann Joachim Winckelmann, and marks Foscolo's passage from pure to critical lyric. This is not to say that there is any lack of images or lyric pleasure; on the contrary, critical and poetic thoughts are here combined. The philosophical intuition of reality as harmony goes side by side with passion and melancholy.

In the tradition of Homer and Callimachus, three hymns compose *Le grazie*. The first hymn is dedicated to Venus, goddess of beauty, the second to Vesta, goddess of the hearth, and the third to Pallas, goddess of the arts. According to *Le grazie*, aesthetics were born in Greece, and with them civilization began. Italy became the major theater of civilization, and there music, dance, lyric language, greatness of mind, and physical beauty gave rebirth to the Graces—that is, to Harmony. This concept is presented in the second hymn and poetically developed by the image of a sacrifice made by three of the women Foscolo loved: Nencini, with a harp; Martinetti, with a honeycomb; and Bignami, with a swan. The last hymn takes the reader to the middle of an ocean on an ethereal Earth. Pallas, in fact, weaves a veil that exalts youth, love, hospitality, maternal affection, and filial piety. With this veil, she covers the Graces so that they can protect themselves from passion.

The form of the three hymns seems to be less impetuous than that of *On Sepulchers*: Dissonances are softened, and the verse has a smoother and less luminous modulation.

OTHER MAJOR WORKS

LONG FICTION: *Ultime Lettere di Jacopo Ortis*, 1802 (*Last Letters of Jacopo Ortis*, 1970).

PLAYS: *Tieste*, pr. 1797; *Aiace*, pr. 1811; *Ricciarda*, pr. 1813.

NONFICTION: *Orazione a Bonaparte pel Congresso di Lione*, 1802; *Dell'origine e dell'ufficio della letteratura*, 1809; *Notizie intorno a Didimo Chierico*, 1813; *Essay on the Present Literature of Italy*, 1818; *Saggi sul Petrarca*, 1821 (*Essays on Petrarch*, 1823); *Della servitu d'Italia*, 1823; *Discorso storico sul testo del "Decamerone,"* 1825; *Discorso sul testo e su le opinioni diverse prevalenti intorno alla storia e alla emendazione critica della "Commedia" di Dante*, 1825; *On the New Dramatic School in Italy*, 1826; *Epistolario*, 1949-1970 (7 volumes).

TRANSLATIONS: *La chioma di Berenice*, 1803 (of Callimachus's poetry); *Esperimenti di traduzione della "Iliade" di Omero*, 1807 (of Homer's *Iliad*); *Viaggio sentimentale di Yorick lungo la Francia e l'Italia*, 1813 (of Laurence Sterne's *A Sentimental Journey*).

BIBLIOGRAPHY

Cambon, Glauco. *Ugo Foscolo: Poet of Exile*. Princeton, N.J.: Princeton University Press, 1980. A critical study of the works of Foscolo. Includes index.

Franzero, Charles Marie. *A Life in Exile: Ugo Foscolo in London, 1816-1827*. London: Allen, 1977. A biography focusing on Foscolo's life in London.

Magill, Frank N., Dayton Kohler, and Laurence W. Mazzeno, eds. *Masterplots: 1,801 Plot Stories and Critical Evaluations of the World's Finest Literature*. 2d ed. Pasadena, Calif.: Salem Press, 1996. Contains an in-depth analysis of *On Sepulchers*.

Matteo, Sante. *Textual Exile: The Reader in Sterne and Foscolo*. New York: Peter Lang, 1985. A study of Foscolo and Laurence Sterne. Substantial bibliography.

O'Neill, Tom. *Of Virgin Muses and of Love: A Study of Foscolo's "Dei sepolcri."* Dublin: Irish Academic Press, 1981. In-depth study of *On Sepulchers*. Includes bibliographical references and index.

Parmegiani, Susan. *Ugo Foscolo and English Culture*. London: Maney, 2010. Focuses on Foscolo's experiences in England and the effect on his writings.

Radcliff-Umstead, Douglas. *Ugo Foscolo*. New York: Twayne, 1970. An introductory biography and critical analysis of selected works by Foscolo. Includes bibliographic references.

Adriano Moz

GIROLAMO FRACASTORO

Born: Verona, Republic of Venice (now in Italy); c. 1478

Died: Incaffi, near Verona, Republic of Venice (now in Italy); August 6, 1553

Also known as: Hieronymus Fracastorius

PRINCIPAL POETRY

Syphilis sive morbus Gallicus, 1530 (*Syphilis: Or, A Poetical History of the French Disease*, 1686)

Ioseph, pb. 1555 (wr. c. 1540-1545; *The Maiden's Blush: Or, Joseph*, 1620)

OTHER LITERARY FORMS

Foremost among the prose work of Girolamo Fracastoro (fro-ko-STAW-roh) is the treatise *Syphilis* (wr. 1553, pb. 1939). Other scientific pieces include *Homocentricorum sive de stellis* (1538; homocentricity on the stars), *De causis criticorum dierum libellus* (1538; on the causes of critical days), *De sympathia et antipathia rerum* (1546; on the attraction and repulsion of things), *De contagionibus et contagiosis morbis et eorum curatione* (1546; *De contagione et contagiosis morbis et eorum curatione*, 1930), and *De vini temperatura* (1534). Also of interest are three Humanistic dialogues: *Naugerius sive de poetica dialogus* (1549; English translation, 1924), and the unfinished "Turrius sive de intellectione dialogus" and "Fracastorius sive de anima dialogus," which were published posthumously in the *Opera omnia* of 1555.

A play, *La Venexiana* (the Venetian, or Venetian comedy), was discovered in 1928 by Emilio Lovarini, deciphered from manuscript miscellany collected in 1780 by Iacopo Morelli. No other text is known, and no mention was made of the play in its time, although it seems to have been written after 1509. The play was published twice by Lovarini, in 1928 and in 1947. A pseudonym, Hieronymous Zarello, was applied to the work, but the Fracastoro expert Girlando Lentini attested its authenticity in his August, 1948, article, "Non piu anonima la Venexiana," in the *Giornale di Sicilia*. The play was published in 1950 in a bilingual edition with introduction and English translation by Matilde Valenti Pfeiffer. The work has been described by Pfeiffer as "one of the earliest character plays in world literature." Its alternation of long and short episodes during the course of four days and its shift of place and mood anticipate the dramaturgy of William Shakespeare. In five acts, its six characters convey the vulnerability of romantic love. The play moves quickly; the characters are quaint and boldly drawn; the language is unusually pithy and droll. It is a rare document of Venetian life, as its epigraph avers: "Non fabula non comedia ma vera historia" ("Neither fable, nor comedy, but real history").

Another work, "Apocalisse" (apocalypse), extant among Fracastoro's manuscripts as late as 1700, is now lost. W. Parr Greswell notes as well that Fracastoro's "Citriorum epigrammata" and many of his smaller pieces are lost. In referring to Fracastoro's accumulated writings, it is important to note Murray Bundy's observation that "little attempt has ever been made to establish a critical text or to determine chronology."

ACHIEVEMENTS

Girolamo Fracastoro was a Renaissance man in the finest sense of the term. As poet, scholar, scientist, and physician, he embodied the essence of sixteenth century curiosity and Humanistic commitment. Greswell states that "perhaps the productions of no other modern poet have been more commended by the learned, than those of Fracastoro."

Fracastoro's research and writing on infectious diseases drew attention in 1530 when he determined the origin of an epidemic of syphilis in Naples at the time of Charles VIII. It is generally believed that Fracastoro named the disease after the amorous shepherd of Greek mythology, who was punished by the sun god for his infidelity. (Other sources assert that the word derives from *sifilide*, a term in common usage in the local dialect.) A later work, *De contagione et contagiosis morbis et eorum curatione*, dealing with typhus, tuberculosis, and syphilis, developed the concept of infection by transfer of minute organisms from diseased individuals to healthy ones.

In *De sympathia et antipathia rerum*, Fracastoro discussed a concept of *simpatia* different from that of his Humanist contemporaries. For him, it was a *species spiritualis* that unified the world, a cosmological principle that was to be studied naturalistically, one that applied to both anthropological and aesthetic concepts. This concentration of research is also present in *De causis criticorum dierum libellus*. Fracastoro's emphasis in this treatise was so advanced (he located the causes of disease in microorganisms rather than in astral or numerological relationships) as to cause his biographer, Bruno Zanobio, to comment that "the traditional position of philosophy is turned upside down: philosophy is such to the extent that it investigates not abstract but concrete nature."

Fracastoro was renowned as a physician, but his knowledge of astronomy, literature, and philosophy reflected the comprehensive talents of the learned men of his time. Familiar with the new theories made possible by the use of the telescope, he criticized the employment of epicycles and deferents in astronomy and was the first to use the geographical term "pole" when referring to the magnetic extremes of the Earth. In his work *Homocentricorum sive de stellis*, Fracastoro declared that experience was the only valid scientific method, and he furnished illustrations of the movements of celestial bodies, their orbits, the seasons, and the various types of days (civil, solar, and sidereal). The work was apparently known to Giordano Bruno, who included Fracastoro as one of the interlocutors in Bruno's dialogue *De l'infinito universo et mondi* (1583; *Of the Infinite Universe and Worlds*, 1950). The biographer Roberto Massalongo went so far as to assert that the work "paved the way" for the great theories of Nicholas Copernicus. Indeed, Fracastoro was read carefully in the nineteenth century by Alexander von Humboldt, who considered Fracastoro's geological investigations significant enough to classify him with Leonardo da Vinci as a scientist far in advance of his time.

BIOGRAPHY

Girolamo Fracastoro was born around 1478 into a very ancient and honorable patrician family, the son of Paolo Philippo and Camilla dei Mascarelli, of a wellborn family of Vicenza. An esteemed ancestor, Aventino Fracastoro, was a celebrated physician of Scala and a gentleman of Verona; he died in 1368, and his tomb in the Church of San Fermo must have been a constant reminder to the young Girolamo of his noble lineage.

Two oddities regarding Fracastoro's birth and early years have been noted by numerous biographers. At birth, his lips were so tightly sealed that a surgeon's knife was required to separate them. Julius Caesarus Scaliger referred to the event in one of the twenty-seven epigrams in his *Altars in Honor of Fracastoro* (1554), relating that the god of medicine and poetry, Apollo himself, intervened at Fracastoro's birth to create a mouth for the poet. The other extraordinary event was the death of his mother (some say his nurse), who was struck and killed by lightning while holding the young Fracastoro in her arms. There is no further record of the effects of these events on the young poet.

Girolamo Fracastoro (The Granger Collection, New York)

Reports agree, however, that his intellect was early noted and that no expense was spared regarding his education.

Fracastoro entered the University of Padua as an adolescent and exhibited a desire to master every science that occupied his attention, demonstrating a singularly advanced proficiency in mathematics. In addition, he studied literature, astronomy (astrology at that time), medicine, and philosophy, the last with Nicolo Leonico Tomeo and Pietro Pomponazzi. Pomponazzi was a tutor in Aristotle, Averroës, and Alexander of Aphrodisias, and received considerable attention for a paper he wrote that was incorrectly interpreted as calling into question the immortality of the soul.

Upon receiving his degree in 1502, Fracastoro became an instructor in logic and also served as *conciliarius anatomicus*, giving lectures on medicine and anatomy. It was at this time that he met a young medical student named Nicolaus Copernicus. Other colleagues and acquaintances who were to play roles in his literary activities were Alessandro Farnese (later Pope Paul III), Gaspar Contarenus and Ercole Gonzaga (later made cardinals), Giovanni Matteo Giberti (subsequently bishop of Verona), Pietro Bembo (dedicatee of his most significant work of poetry and personal secretary to Pope Leo X), Andreas Navagero (dedicatee of Fracastoro's work on poetics and a national historian and ambassador), and the brothers Marcus Antonius, Joannes Baptista, and Raymundo della Torre (all utilized as characters in Fracastoro's literary "dialogues").

Fracastoro married young, possibly in 1500; his wife, Elena, who was apparently five years older than her husband, died in 1540. They had five children, four sons and one daughter, only two of whom survived their father. During the period of national strife after the League of Cambria, Fracastoro took refuge in the Republic of Venice, where he enjoyed the patronage of General Alviano, serving as personal physician and as an instructor in the informal academy that Alviano had established in Pordenone. Niccolò Machiavelli commented on the precarious situation of the Venetian and Veronese states at this time. German, Spanish, French, and Swiss troops were all garrisoned in the area at one time or another, and plague was rampant. Soon after the defeat of the Venetian forces, Fracastoro retired to the villa in Incaffi and alternated residence between there and Verona, some fifteen miles distant. The villa was a peaceful retreat, frequented regularly by writers, scientists, philosophers, and artists. Fracastoro himself has described it in the eulogy for Marcus Antonius della Torre:

> Here acts, absolv'd from modish fashion's school
> Nor moves in measur'd steps, nor stands by rule
> But drinks at pleasure, and reclines at ease
> No laws to trammel, no fops to tease.

Between 1509 and 1530, Fracastoro actively practiced medicine and continued his research in botany, cosmography, and infectious diseases. Fracastoro was an eminent physician, serving Catherine de Médicis, and was once called to serve as court physician to Marguerite of Navarre. The early version of *Syphilis: Or, A Poetical History of the French Disease* (not to be con-

fused with Fracastoro's treatise on the same subject) was completed by 1525, and Fracastoro's retirement to study and to write coincides with its publication in 1530 (his first work to issue from a printing press). By that time, he was no longer happy to be recognized primarily as a physician, though it was in this capacity that he was subsequently called on by Pope Paul III (Alessandro Farnese) to serve as medical adviser (*medicus conductus et stipendiatus*) to the Council of Trent in 1545.

At the time, the pope was very concerned about both security and the political ramifications of holding the Council in Trent; his preference was Bologna. Fracastoro's assessment of the danger of epidemic convinced the authorities of the wisdom of the change. Fracastoro's influence on the decision to move the council from Trent to Bologna suggests the stature of his professional opinion. In 1546, Fracastoro was made a canon of Verona. Though always interested in politics, he never held public office.

Fracastoro died of cerebral apoplexy on August 6, 1553. He had predicted such a death, which occurred without the attendance of either physician or priest. Earlier, he had saved the life of a nun who was suffering from the same affliction by application of a remedy of his own devising. Ironically, his servants failed to understand his motions calling for medical aid in his own case, and he is said to have died quite resigned to his fate. Though there is some controversy concerning his place of burial, his body reputedly rests in the ruins of the parish church of Saint Eufemia, near the villa in Incaffi; the church itself has been destroyed. Soon after his death, an effigy in bronze was placed in the Benedictine cloister near Verona. In Verona itself, south of the Porta Vittoria, is a *cimitero* with monuments to the city's greatest citizens. Fracastoro's name can be found most prominently over the alcove designated number one. In 1559, a statue of Fracastoro by Danese Cataneo was erected in the Piazza dei Signiori, near those of Catullus, Napos, Macer, Vitruvius, and Dante.

ANALYSIS

Girolamo Fracastoro flourished in the atmosphere of the Italian Renaissance, when the diminished influence of theological study gave way to an increased interest in science and nature. The contemplative attitude was gradually replaced by a more aggressive operative one. Nature was viewed as an autonomous reality with its own laws before which supernatural intervention was of minimal use. Humans were forced to rely on their capacity for progressive understanding of the principles that regulated the natural world.

SYPHILIS

Such were the ideas that made up the narrative poem *Syphilis*, on which rests Fracastoro's literary fame. Written in 1521 and dedicated to Bembo, the poem consists of thirteen hundred verses in Latin hexameter (not verses in the contemporary sense of stanzas, but blocks of copy in his handwritten manuscript); in the words of Bruno Zanobio, it "represents a magnificent paradigm of formal sixteenth century virtuosity in refined Latin of a didactic quality reminiscent of Vergil's *Georgics* (37-30 B.C.E.). The work reveals the author's early concept of *seminaria* (microorganisms), a concept that he derived from the pre-Socratic philosopher Democritus by way of the *semina morbi* of Lucretius's *De rerum natura* (c. 60 B.C.E.; *On the Nature of Things*, 1682), available to Fracastoro in a 1515 translation by his friend Andreas Navagero.

It is significant to note the exercise of poetic license in the application of some scientific terms. Meter altered the use of terminology in these cases: *contages* was used for *contagio* (contact or touch); *seminaria* for *semina* (seeds); *achores* for *pustula* (sores, infections). This was the case earlier, when Lucretius used *pestilitas* for *pestilentia* (pestilence or plague). Fracastoro's *seminaria* differ from traditional *semina*, however, and it is difficult to know if the author foresaw the actual existence of microbes. The inability at the time to distinguish between organic and inorganic and the belief in spontaneous generation would probably have prevented Fracastoro from assigning to his *seminaria* the characteristics of microorganisms as they are known today.

Fracastoro developed the concept further in a prose treatise, also entitled *Syphilis*, which was completed in 1553 but not published until 1939. Zanobio interprets Fracastoro's work on syphilis to be his new premise for the construction of a philosophy of nature: "Nature creates and destroys and gives misery and happiness, and it is useless to appease the gods. Science, whose power alone can give joy, dictates man's actions." Fracastoro's most significant contribution to the scientific side of syphilography was *De contagione et contagiosis morbis et eorum curatione*, published sixteen years after the poem *Syphilis*. Leona Baumgartner and John F. Fulton observe that in his concept of animate contagion, Fracastoro was "a precursor of [Louis] Pasteur and [Robert] Koch."

The poem *Syphilis* was an immediate success and earned extravagant praise from many sides. Bembo announced that the work equaled that of Lucretius and Vergil. Jacopo Sannazzaro, a contemporary and a cruel critic of anyone who threatened to challenge his own supremacy, commented that it surpassed his *De partu virginium* (1527; of Virgin birth), a work twenty years in process. It was neither the first nor the last poem on the subject, but it was the longest, the most serious, the most eloquent, and by far the best publicized.

An early version of the poem was completed by 1521; the date has been established through Fracastoro's mention of Pope Leo as being still alive (the pope died in 1522). The author first presented the work to Bembo in a two-book version. Bembo suggested changes, among which was the deletion of a myth on the origin of mercury as a remedy. He thought it too obvious an imitation of Aristaeus in Vergil's *Georgics*. Fracastoro rejected most of the suggested changes but did expand the work to three books.

The earliest extant version, published in 1530, is referred to as the "Verona text." In this text, two verses are omitted, while the lines beginning "Quo tandem . . ." and "Aetheris inuisas . . ." have been entered, apparently in Fracastoro's own hand, on the "authorized" or "Rome text" of the following year. This change is not found in other contemporary editions, and there were no other changes in seven subsequent editions published in the author's lifetime. The omitted lines are not included in the *Opera omnia* of 1555 but are in the one of 1574. The poem is found in more than one hundred editions; it has appeared many times in Latin editions, eleven Latin versions of which are in the *Opera omnia*. Many bilingual editions exist, with several editions in English. It has appeared in six languages.

SYPHILIS, BOOK 1

Book 1 of *Syphilis* begins with a consideration of the "varied chances of things" that appear responsible for the dread disease. The author observes "how number governs moved things and things moving," a possible reference to the theories of Pythagoras and Heraclitus. Fracastoro, as a protobacteriologist, determines that the "origin of the affliction" is to be found in the air; the *semina morbi* (diseased seeds) are *semina coeli* (germs of the heavens). References to seeds, germs, atoms, and corpuscles can be traced to the writings of Lucretius and Epicurus, but Fracastoro makes the observation that this affliction strikes only the *humanum genus* (human race), Vergil's *ingens genus*, the race having mind and reason.

"Into Italy, it broke with the Frenchmen's war and after them it was named [*morbus Gallicus*]." Although the disease did not at that time carry the onus of immorality it subsequently assumed, it was referred to by the Italians as "the French disease," by the French as "the Neapolitan evil," by the Germans and English as "the French pox and Bordeaux evil," in Holland and North Africa as "the Spanish pox," in Portugal as "the Castilian disease," in Persia and Turkey as "the Christian disease," in Russia as "the Polish disease," and in Poland as "the German disease."

Italy at the time of the poem's composition was torn by conflicts with Louis XII of France and Maximilian of Germany. The country was suffering from plague, famine, and war. It is not surprising, then, that the author should designate Mars as influential in the country's misfortunes: "Venus and Mars the dire/ Against all humans, planets would conspire/ . . . when they converge at some spot in the skies." Giovanni Boccaccio in his *Decameron: O, Prencipe Galeotto* (1349-1351; *The Decameron*, 1620) had referred to the influence of celestial bodies that resulted in the Black Death. Guy de Chauliac, a famous fourteenth century French surgeon, had attributed the plague to the conjunction of Saturn and Mars on March 22, 1345, in the fourteenth degree of Aquarius: "Two centuries before this, in the skies/ Saturn and Mars would lock their silent cars." Fracastoro himself drew an astrological parallel to the syzygy of the same planets in the sign of Cancer: "Jupiter calls a congress of the stars/ Evoking Saturn and the war god Mars . . . he calls the Crab . . . to open the dou-

ble doors of heaven's halls." By the "god's decree . . . to the air is this new poison given, the effluvium of homicide." With the introduction of Sirius, the air carries "the seeds of poison everywhere." Here, the author invents a new god who has no basis in classical mythology and is indeed a fictitious character offering prophecy. Such an expediency was often resorted to by fifteenth and sixteenth century writers.

Fracastoro, however, writes as a physician, a man of science, and he proceeds to reveal the difficulties of his investigation. The halting speech of the poet results from the delay with which the heavens confront the scientist as he seeks to link the disease to the things that cause it. "Making no advance," he fears that much "hangs on the play of chance." As he proceeds to "comb the symptoms," he finds that the disease is at home both in hovel and in court. Its symptoms are never quite the same. "Its form and seed vary everywhere/ Knowing no bounds and limits, peoples, states . . . it flashes through the air." He does, however, ascertain that it survives four months of incubation, "shutting the moon's disc four times." To more dramatically delineate this "hideous leprosy," Fracastoro describes the personal plight of a handsome youth of Brescia: "Gone is the brilliance of his youth and spring/ Dying by inches his soul sinks. . . ." This graphic depiction is extended to include the suffering of Fracastoro's native land as well as the personal grief he feels with the premature death of his friend Marcus Antonius della Torre. Wright refers to this final section of book 1 as "some of the finest verse ever done by Fracastoro, indeed by any Latin poet of the period." The following invocation to Italy has been deemed by Mario Truffi as the equal of Petrarch and Giacomo Leopardi:

> Dear land, my land, that only yesterday
> Hoped for the happiness of peace profound.
> O soil of heroes! God's land! Holy ground,
> Where is your ancient treasure? Torn away.
> Your breasts, prodigious for Adige's flood,
> Gave you fecundities so passing good.
> Today, O Italy, what colors drear
> Depict your suffering, your ills, your fear?
> Trembling are all the strings of my poor lute
> To tell of your misfortunes, but are mute.
> Garda, go hide your shame amidst your reeds.
> Laurels no longer seek your water's needs.

Fracastoro demonstrates dramatic concern on many levels. One analogy connects the desolate River Adige and Lake Garda, into which it flows near his home, with the desecrated blood of his nation: "The Adige bathes in new sterility, having lost its ancient force." Another parallel is drawn between the decline of the country and the death of della Torre: "Noble Anthony passes and naught can save him from the tomb, still in the bloom of spring, O Italy!" Fracastoro finally resorts again to the poetic muse to save his country: "The mellow lyre of old Catullus hand/ Might stir your woods again, O Fatherland." This allusion to classical poetry would not have been lost on the author's contemporaries. Bembo related that the work "makes me think the soul of Vergil has passed into [Fracastoro]."

SYPHILIS, BOOK 2

Book 2 of *Syphilis* includes, as did book 1, the customary encomiums to Bembo ("armed in his humility, whose sheer ability is equal to the grandest name") and to Pope Leo X ("Prince, whose fame is more than great"), that they might turn a willing ear to the poet's voice. It also pays tribute to Sannazzaro, the "Christian Vergil," as "Fornello's god, a new poet's voice/ That made old Vergil's epic heart rejoice."

Soon, "in fear and trembling," Fracastoro "takes up his pen" to prescribe medication and treatment. His prescriptions are many and varied—some, clearly, dated folk remedies and others still in use today. One of the first is "Spain's ornament, the pride of Italy," the lemon tree. "Beloved of Venus," it acquired its power through the tears Venus shed for Adonis, which were "shut within the golden rind a gift/ Of heav'nly virtues, energetic, swift." There follow in rapid succession both exotic and common reliefs: myrrh of Arabia, frankincense from Libya, and apopanax from the Nile, as well as cinnamon, bittercress, cassia, cucumber, turpeth, saffron, mint, thyme, ladysmantle, briony, chicory, hartstongue, and hops, these last as common "pharmacopia of the day." In addition, one finds salves and ointments made from oil, wool fat, honey, goose fat, linseed paste, starwort, and narcissus. Other applications include copper and potassium nitrates and oxides of lead, antimony, and storax. Considering that bloodletting was also part of the cure, the activities prescribed are strange: hunting, a form of tennis, and wood chopping—"Be active if you wish to keep alive."

The use of mercury is traced at this point to a mythological origin. The Syrian shepherd Ilceo has incurred the wrath of Diana and Phoebus for killing a favorite deer. He has been stricken with a disease for which no remedy exists under the sun. The goddess Calliroe appears to him, however, and directs him to a nymph, Lipare, who leads him to a cave below Mount Etna wherein is found a stream in which flows a liquid metal (quicksilver). It is interesting to note that this substance, mercury, was known for its medicinal properties to Aristotle as *arguron chuton*, and to Pliny the Younger as *argentum vivum*. Such treatment was also applied in the intervening centuries by Rhazes and Avicenna.

The Ilceo myth probably represented a nonclassical reference for Fracastoro. The name is not found elsewhere, and Bembo thought it a poor choice of material. It is of interest to note, however, that it is this section of the work that Greswell chose to excerpt in the *Memoirs of Angelus Politianus, Joannes Picus of Mirandula, Actius Sincerus Sannazzarius, Pietrus Bembus, Hieronymous Fracastorius, and the Amalthei* (1801). Wright observes that the author's language becomes less poetic in the closing section of the book, after the telling of the myth, as Fracastoro relates the therapeutic marvels of the common herbs as skin treatment.

SYPHILIS, BOOK 3

Truffi finds the third book of *Syphilis* to be the "best from the poetic side." In this section, Fracastoro praises Christopher Columbus for his explorations in the New World ("yoking the mountains in a mighty quest"); Fracastoro was the first to use Columbus's achievement as poetic material. Fracastoro's Columbus desperately invokes the moon to reveal land to him and his fatigued mariners. There then appears a sea nymph, who directs him to the island of Ofiri (Haiti, scene of the first European landing in the Americas on December 6, 1492). The sailors anger the gods by shooting forest birds sacred to Apollo, whereupon they are cursed. This episode parallels scenes in the *Odyssey* (c. 725 B.C.E.; English translation, 1614) and in Vergil's *Aeneid* (c. 29-19 B.C.E.; English translation, 1553). The remedy for their affliction is to be found in "seeking aid from the same forest they profaned."

The "aborigines" whom they encounter on the island are descendants of the Atlanteans, the cursed remnants of an ancient race, who are afflicted with a disease that demonstrates "a living path/ Of what the gods invented in their wrath." Fracastoro relates their plight through the legend of Sifilo (Syphilis). During a particularly long and devastating drought, Syphilis, a shepherd for King Ilceo, inveighed against the sun god and instead venerated King Ilceo. Syphilis advocated similar conduct on the part of others until they, "braving gods, denying gods, devastating temples fair," convinced Ilceo of his own glory, and the King, in "mad joy and blinded thus, commanded that each state receive him as a god." It was at this point that the "island paradise received the evil of a subtle seed. . . . He who wrought this outrage was the first, and after him this malady is called Syphilis, and even the King escaped not its attack."

Upon consultation, the nymph America advised a sacrifice. Initially, Syphilis was designated, but through the intercession of Juno (recalling the legend of Iphigenia and the biblical story of Isaac), a substitution was made—in this case, a black cow's blood to appease Terra (Tellus, Latin deity of the earth) and a white heifer to change Juno's mood. The blood of the beast created "fecund seeds in Tellus's vast breast," which became the *lignum-sanctum* (Guaiacum tree) from which was extracted the syphilis cure: "the lignumsanctum you must/ Cull, lest disaster fall on every one/ For a bird-murder and an outraged sun." Thus, it was determined that "Every year a shepherd symbolizes/ The victim; ancient are the sacrifices." The author ends his work by appealing to Apollo (and to Bembo) that his poem be remembered, "as descendants may one day wish to read of signs and appearance of the disease."

Again, it should be noted that there was in Fracastoro's time no hint of immorality involved with the disease. To the contrary, Fracastoro asserts in his poem that the disease "hatched from a poison that no vice has wrought," though he does refer to it as venereal (from Latin *venereus*, love) in the prose adaptation written later.

NAUGERIUS SIVE DE POETICA DIALOGUS

In *Naugerius sive de poetica dialogus*, the focus of Fracastoro's aesthetics is revealed. According to Zanobio, Fracastoro determined that neither content nor form rendered the essence of the poetic but rather "intuition, the universal present in all things and expressing itself in the judgment that regulates them." Bundy sees this as "the view of a pagan of the Renaissance quite in sympathy with the frank aestheticism of the majority of contemporary [1924] artists." John Addington Symonds praised Fracastoro's writing from a literary standpoint, suggesting that it "recalls the purity of phrase of Catullus." Bundy further notes that Fracastoro's use of the dialogue is Ciceronian in both form and substance, in that Fracastoro employed the later Latin variation on Plato of using less dramatic, more real characters, as did Fracastoro's contemporaries Giovanni Pontano, Sperone Speroni, Antonio Minturno, and Gimabattisto Gyraldus. Ciceronian as well is the "absence of philosophical first principles directing the course of the dialogue; [Fracastoro] is frankly eclectic rather than a great original thinker."

Fracastoro's *Naugerius sive de poetic dialogus* not only presents a theory of the poetic but also presents it as "consummate art" itself. According to Bundy, "The symmetry, the beauty of external form, illustrates the ideal which he sets forth." Bundy further asserts that in this work Fracastoro was one of the first writers of the Renaissance to formulate in elegant manner a concept close to Aristotle's intentions in his *De poetica* (c. 334-323 B.C.E.; *Poetics*, 1705) and that *Naugerius sive de poetica dialogus* "is one of a few Renaissance treatises which insists upon an aesthetic standard." Wilmer Cave Wright has commented that to be immortal, one needs only to write a treatise telling poets what the aim of poetry is. The poets, of course, will not read the work, but it will be mandatory reading for all subsequent historians of criticism.

THE MINOR POEMS

Of Fracastoro's works of poetry other than *Syphilis*, Truffi notes "the poem on the death of della Torre, that to G. B. della Torre, to Rainerio, to Bishop Giberti, to Marguerite de Valois (Queen of Navarre), to Francesco della Torre, to Alessandro Farnese, to Pope Giulio III and minor poems all praiseworthy for their purity of style and classicity of verse." The eulogies for Marcus Antonius della Torre are included in various versions of the collected works; the "minor poems" are less commonly available. Henry Wadsworth Longfellow included two of them in his anthology *The Poets and Poetry of Europe* (1896), commenting that Fracastoro wrote "A few poems in the mother tongue which show liveliness and facility of poetical composition." One, "To a Lady," retains the familiar hexameter and identifies the woman's "all perfect symmetry" as the eternal model of beauty wherein love finds its future home. In "Homer," the Horatian motto *ut pictura poesis* is employed by the author to indicate how, through the depiction of "sunny banks and grottoes cold," Homer became "the first great painter of scenes of old." Fracastoro is said to have written a madrigal, "Madrigal al sonno" (to slumber), on the occasion of his wife's death. The "Madrigal al sonno" is a hymn on the power of narcotics to alleviate suffering, written in the vernacular and lacking the weight of Fracastoro's Latin verse. "Alcon seu de cura canum venaticorum" (Alcon, or: how to take care of dogs for the hunt) is a short poem about the training of dogs for the hunt, known to have been among Fracastoro's favorite pastimes. The poem is included only in works appearing later than the sixteenth century, and Emilio Barbarani rejects it as spurious, mainly because it was not included in the volume of the author's poetry that was organized in 1555.

As a major writer of the Italian Renaissance, Fracastoro exhibits the comprehensive thinking of the period. He was equally at ease in the speculative and in the applied fields of science and art. Though securely based in the classical form of his predecessor, Vergil, Fracastoro's poetry embraced common topics and rendered them with grace and sensitivity. His versatility lends a particular vitality to his writing that will assure his work a permanent place in the respect and esteem of future generations.

OTHER MAJOR WORKS

PLAY: *La Venexiana*, pb. 1928 (wr. after 1509; English translation, 1950).

NONFICTION: *De vini temperatura*, 1534; *De causis criticorum dierum libellus*, 1538; *Homocentricorum sive de stellis*, 1538; *De contagionibus et contagiosis morbis et eorum curatione*, 1546 (*De contagione et contagiosis morbis et eorum curatione*, 1930); *De sympathia et antipathia rerum*, 1546; *Naugerius sive de poetica dialogus*, 1549 (English translation, 1924); *Syphilis*, wr. 1553, pb. 1939.

MISCELLANEOUS: *Opera omnia*, 1555 (includes "Turrius sive de intellectione dialogus" and "Fracastorius sive de anima dialogus").

BIBLIOGRAPHY

Fracastoro, Girolamo. *Fracastoro's "Syphilis."* Translated with introduction, text, and notes by Geoffrey Eatough. Liverpool, England: Francis Cairns, 1984. Written mainly from the point of view of a literary scholar who stresses Fracastoro's poetic achievements. Contains a detailed analysis of the poem *Syphilis*. Includes a computer-generated word index.

Gould, Stephen Jay. "Syphilis and the Shepherd of Atlantis." *Natural History* 109, no. 8 (October, 2000): 38-42. Gould discusses the "Syphilis sive morbus Gallicus" by Fracastoro and the genome of syphilis.

Greswell, W. Parr, trans. *Memoirs of Angelus Politianus, Joannes Picus of Mirandula, Actius Sincerus Sannazarius, Petrus Bembus, Hieronymus Fracastorius, Marcus Antonius Flaminius, and the Amalthei*. Manchester, England: Cadell and Davies, 1805. An early biography of Fracastoro, based primarily on an even earlier life by F. O. Mencken. It is concerned primarily with Fracastoro as a literary figure. Especially good on reporting on his contemporaries' opinions about him. Contains notes and observations by Greswell.

Hudson, Margaret M., and Robert S. Morton. "Fracastoro and Syphilis: Five Hundred Years On." *Lancet* 348, no. 9040 (November 30, 1996): 1495-1496. The authors pay tribute to the physician who spread knowledge of the origin, clinical details, and available treatments of syphilis throughout a troubled Europe.

Pearce, Spencer. "Nature and Supernature in the Dialogues of Girolamo Fracastoro." *Sixteenth Century Journal* 27, no. 1 (Spring, 1996): 111-132. Fracastoro was one of the first philosophers of nature during the Italian Renaissance. In his dialogues, Fracastoro attempts to construct a philosophical anthropology in which humanity's supernatural vocation may be accommodated within the rational framework of a philosophy of nature.

Pfeiffer, Matilde Valenti. Introduction to *La Venexiana*. New York: S. F. Vanni, 1950. Pfeiffer's introduction offers some historical information on the discovery of the play and Emilio Lovarini's conjecture that the play was written by Fracastoro.

Rosebury, Theodor. *Microbes and Morals: The Strange Story of Venereal Disease*. New York: Ballantine, 1973. Two chapters are devoted to Fracastoro, dealing specifically with syphilis as a medical problem. This book presents the best semipopular treatment of the origins of syphilis and whether it was brought from the Americas by the sailors of Columbus.

Simmons, John G., ed. *Doctors and Discoveries: Lives That Created Today's Medicines*. New York: Houghton Mifflin, 2002. Contains a biography of Fracastoro and a discussion of his poem.

H. W. Carle

G

FEDERICO GARCÍA LORCA

Born: Fuentevaqueros, Spain; June 5, 1898
Died: Víznar, Spain; August 19, 1936

PRINCIPAL POETRY

Libro de poemas, 1921
Canciones, 1921-1924, 1927
Romancero gitano, 1924-1927, 1928 (*The Gypsy Ballads of García Lorca*, 1951, 1953)
Poema del cante jondo, 1931 (*Poem of the Gypsy Seguidilla*, 1967)
Llanto por Ignacio Sánchez Mejías, 1935 (*Lament for the Death of a Bullfighter*, 1937, 1939)
Primeras canciones, 1936
Diván del Tamarit, 1940 (*The Divan at the Tamarit*, 1944)
Poeta en Nueva York, 1940 (*Poet in New York*, 1940, 1955)
Collected Poems, 2002 (revised edition)

OTHER LITERARY FORMS

The publisher Aguilar of Madrid issued a one-volume edition of the works of Federico García Lorca (gahr-SEE-uh LAWR-kuh), compiled and annotated by Arturo del Hoyo, with a prologue by Jorge Guillén and an epilogue by Vicente Aleixandre. In addition to the poetry, it includes García Lorca's plays, of which the tragic rural trilogy *Bodas de sangre* (pr. 1933; *Blood Wedding*, 1939), *Yerma* (pr. 1934; English translation, 1941), and *La casa de Bernarda Alba* (pr., pb. 1945; *The House of Bernarda Alba*, 1947) are world famous and represent García Lorca's best achievement as a poet become director-playwright. To portray all the facets of García Lorca's artistic personality, the Aguilar edition also includes his first play, *El maleficio de la mariposa* (pr. 1920; *The Butterfly's Evil Spell*, 1963); an example of his puppet plays, *Los títeres de Cachiporra: La tragicomedia de don Cristóbal y la señá Rosita* (pr. 1937; *The Tragicomedy of Don Cristóbal and Doña Rosita*, 1955); selections from *Impresiones y paisajes* (1918; impressions and landscapes), García Lorca's first published prose works, in which his genius is already evident in the melancholic, impressionistic style used to describe his feelings and reactions to the Spanish landscape and Spanish life; several short prose pieces and dialogues; a number of lectures and speeches; a variety of representative letters to friends; texts of newspaper interviews; poems from the poet's book of suites; fifteen of his songs; and twenty-five of his drawings.

Although the Aguilar edition reflects a consummate artist, still missing from its pages are a number of other works: a five-act play, *El público* (fragment, pb. 1976; *The Audience*, 1958), and the first part of a dramatic biblical trilogy titled "La destrucción de Sódoma" (wr. 1936; the destruction of Sodom), on which García Lorca was working at the time of his death. Lost are "Los sueños de mi prima Aurelia" (the dreams of my cousin Aurelia) and "La niña que riega la albahaca y el príncipe preguntón" (the girl who waters the sweet basil flower and the inquisitive prince), a puppet play presented in Granada on January 5, 1923. "El sacrificio de Ifigenia" (Iphigenia's sacrifice) and "La hermosa" (the beauty) are titles of two plays whose existence cannot be substantiated.

Reportedly, García Lorca also collected a group of poems titled "Sonetos del amor oscuro" (sonnets of dark love), the title suggesting to certain critics the poet's preference for intimate masculine relationships. Until the 1960's, most of the works evaluating García Lorca centered on the events of his life and death and were only interspersed with snatches of literary criticism. Since his death, thematic and stylistic studies by such noted scholars as Rafael Martínez Nadal, Gustavo Correa, Arturo Barea, Rupert C. Allen, and Richard L. Predmore have served to illuminate García Lorca's symbolic and metaphorical world.

ACHIEVEMENTS

The typically Spanish character of his plays and poetry, enhanced by rich and daring lyrical expression, have made Federico García Lorca one of the most universally recognized poets of the twentieth century. His tragic death in 1936 at the hands of the Falange, the Spanish Fascist Party, in the flower of his manhood and literary creativity, merely served to further his fame.

The first milestone of García Lorca's short but intense career was the publication of *The Gypsy Ballads of García Lorca*, which solidly established his reputation as a fine poet in the popular vein. His dark, brooding, foreboding ballads of Gypsy passion and death captured the imagination and hearts of Spaniards and foreigners, Andalusians and Galicians, illiterate farmers and college professors. Critics saw in García Lorca's poems the culmination of centuries of a rich and diverse Spanish lyric tradition. For example, Edwin Honig has noted that García Lorca's poetry took its inspiration from such diverse sources as the medieval Arabic-Andalusian art of amorous poetry; the early popular ballad; the Renaissance synthesis in Spain of classical traditions, as exemplified by the "conceptist" poetry of Luis de Góngora y Argote; and the *cante jondo*, or "deep song," of the Andalusian Gypsy.

Living in an era of vigorous cultural and literary activity, called by many Spain's second golden age, García Lorca clearly maintained his individuality. His innate charm and wit, his strong and passionate presence, his *duende*, or "soul," as a performer of Andalusian songs and ballads, and his captivating readings of his own poetry and plays drew the applause and friendship of equally talented writers and artists, such as Rafael Alberti, Pedro Salinas, Jorge Guillén, Vicente Aleixandre, Salvador Dalí, and Luis Buñuel.

The poet reached the peak of his popular success in the late 1920's. Both his *Songs* and *The Gypsy Ballads of García Lorca* were published to great critical acclaim. In the same period, he delivered two memorable lectures, the first at the *cante jondo* festival organized jointly with composer Manuel de Falla in Granada, and the second at the festival in honor of Góngora's tercentenary. His play *Mariana Pineda* (pr. 1927; English translation, 1950) was produced in Barcelona, and the following year he founded and published the literary journal *Gallo*. Despite these achievements, however, García Lorca suffered a grave spiritual crisis, to which he alludes in his correspondence but never really clarifies. This crisis led him to reevaluate his artistic output and turn to new experiences and modes of expression.

The result of García Lorca's soul-searching can be seen in his later works, especially *Poet in New York* and *Lament for the Death of a Bullfighter*. In the former, García Lorca fully unleashes his imagination in arabesques of metaphor that on first reading appear incomprehensible. *Poet in New York* is a difficult and frequently obscure work that has been viewed as a direct contrast to his earlier poetry. However, as Predmore has so painstakingly demonstrated, these poems extend rather than depart from García Lorca's established preference for ambiguous and antithetical symbolism.

The two threads that run throughout García Lorca's work are the themes of love and death: They lend a poetic logic and stability to what may otherwise appear chaotic and indecipherable. A study of these themes in García Lorca's poetry and plays reveals a gradual evolution from tragic premonition and foreboding, through vital passion repressed and frustrated by outside forces, to bitter resignation and death. Throughout his life, García Lorca's constant companion and friend was death. The poet Antonio Machado described this intimacy with death in his lament for García Lorca:

> He was seen walking with Her, alone,
> unafraid of her scythe.
>
> . . . .
>
> Today as yesterday, gypsy, my Death,
> how good to be with you, alone
> in these winds of Granada, of my Granada.

García Lorca's gift of imagination, his genius for metaphor and volatile imagery, and his innate sense of the tragic human condition make him one of the outstanding poets of the twentieth century. With his execution in Granada in 1936 at the outbreak of the Spanish Civil War, the frustrated personas of his poetry and plays, who so often ended their lives in senseless tragedy, materialized in his own person. In García Lorca, life became art and art became life. Combining the experience of two cultures, he addressed in both, the Andalusian and the American man's primal needs and fears within his own interior world.

BIOGRAPHY

Federico García Lorca was born on June 5, 1898, in Fuentevaqueros, in the province of Granada. His father, Don Federico García Rodríguez, was a well-to-do landowner, a solid rural citizen of good reputation. After his first wife died, Don Federico married Doña Vicenta Lorca Romero, an admired schoolteacher and a musician. García Lorca was very fond of his mother and believed that he inherited his intelligence and artistic bent from her and his passionate nature from his father. It was in the countryside of Granada that García Lorca's poetic sensibility took root, nourished by the meadows, the fields, the wild animals, the livestock, and the people of that land. His formative years were centered in the village, where he attended Mass with his mother and absorbed and committed to memory the colorful talk, the folktales, and the folk songs of the *vega* (fertile lowland) that would later find a rebirth in the metaphorical language of his poetry and plays.

In 1909, his family moved to Granada, and García Lorca enrolled in the College of the Sacred Heart to prepare for the university. This was the second crucial stage in his artistic development: Granada's historical and literary associations further enriched his cultural inheritance from the *vega* and modified it by adding an intellectual element. García Lorca wanted to be a musician and composer, but his father wanted him to study law. In 1915, he matriculated at the University of Granada, but he never was able to adapt completely to the regimentation of university studies, failing three courses, one of them in literature. During the same period, he continued his serious study of piano and composition with Don Antonio Segura. García Lorca frequented the cafés of Granada and became popular for his wit. In 1916 and 1917, García Lorca traveled throughout Castile, Léon, and Galicia with one of his professors from the university, who also encouraged him to write his first book, *Impresiones y paisajes*. He also came into contact with important people in the arts, among them Manuel de Falla, who shared García Lorca's interest in traditional folk themes, and Fernando de los Ríos, an important leader in educational

Federico García Lorca (Getty Images)

and social reforms, who persuaded García Lorca's father to send his son to the University of Madrid.

In 1919, García Lorca arrived in Madrid, where he was to spend the next ten years at the famous Residencia de Estudiantes, in the company of Rafael Alberti, Jorge Guillén, Pedro Salinas, Gerardo Diego, Dámaso Alonso, Luis Cernuda, and Vicente Aleixandre. There García Lorca published his first collection of poems, *Libro de poemas*, and became involved with the philosophical and literary currents then in vogue. In 1922, García Lorca returned to Granada to conduct with Manuel de Falla a Festival of Cante Jondo.

The years from 1924 to 1928 were successful but troubled ones for García Lorca, marked by moments of elation followed by depression. During these years, García Lorca developed a close friendship with Salvador Dalí and spent several summers with the Dalí family at Cadaqués. He published his second book of poems, *Songs*, in 1927 and in that same year saw the premiere of *Mariana Pineda* in Barcelona and Madrid. In December of 1927, García Lorca participated in the famous Góngora tricentennial anniversary celebrations in Seville, where he delivered one of his most famous lectures, "The Poetic Image in Don Luis de Góngora." Gradually, García Lorca's fame spread, and his *The Gypsy Ballads of García Lorca* became the most widely read book of poems to appear in Spain since the publication of Gustavo Adolfo Bécquer's *Rimas* (*Poems*, 1891; better known as *The Rhymes*, 1898) in 1871. During the period from May to December of 1928, García Lorca suffered an emotional crisis that prompted him to leave Spain to accompany Fernando de los Ríos to New York. After spending nine months in the United States, a stay that included a visit to Vermont, García Lorca returned to Spain by way of Cuba with renewed interest and energy for his work. The clearest product of this visit was *Poet in New York*, one of his greatest books of poems, published four years after his death.

After his return to Madrid in 1930, García Lorca turned his focus increasingly to the dramatic. In 1932, under the auspices of the Republic's Ministry of Education, García Lorca founded La Barraca, a university theater whose aim was to bring the best classical plays to the provinces. In the same period, he saw the successful staging of *Blood Wedding* and *El amor de don Perlimplín con Belisa en su jardín* (pr. 1933; *The Love of Don Perlimplín for Belisa in His Garden*, 1941). His achievements in Spain were capped by another trip to the New World, this time to Argentina, where *Blood Wedding, Mariana Pineda*, and *La zapatera prodigiosa* (pr. 1930; *The Shoemaker's Prodigious Wife*, 1941) were staged and received with great enthusiasm. The years 1934 and 1935 saw the writing of the *Lament for the Death of a Bullfighter* and the premieres of at least four new plays. By 1936, García Lorca had decided to return to Granada for the celebration of his name day and also to bide his time until the political turmoil in Madrid abated. During his stay, the civil war broke out, and amid the fighting between the Nationalist and the Popular forces in Granada, García Lorca was detained and executed on August 19, 1936, in the outskirts of Víznar. His body was thrown into an unmarked grave.

ANALYSIS

In imagery that suggests an "equestrian leap" between two opposing worlds, Federico García Lorca embodies a dialectical vision of life, on one hand filled with an all-consuming love for humanity and nature and, on the other, cognizant of the "black torso of the Pharaoh," the blackness symbolizing an omnipresent death unredeemed by the possibility of immortality. The tension between these two irreconcilable forces lends a tautness as well as a mystery to much of his poetry.

"ELEGÍA A DOÑA JUANA LA LOCA"

A recurring theme throughout García Lorca's work that is expressive of this animating tension is that of thwarted love, repressed by society or simply by human destiny and ending inevitably in death. This obsession with unfulfilled dreams and with death is evident in the poet's first collection. In a moving elegy to the Castilian princess Juana la Loca titled "Elegía a doña Juana la Loca," García Lorca details in fifteen stanzas the lamentable fate of a woman driven to madness by her unrequited love for her husband, Felipe el Hermoso. Throughout the poem, García Lorca addresses her as a red carnation in a deep and desolate valley, to whom Death extended a bouquet of withered roses instead of flowers, verses, and pearl necklaces. Like other great tragic heroines of Spanish literature, such as Isabel de Segura and Melibea, and those of García Lorca's own creative imagination, she is a victim of fate.

The themes of violent passion and death, later more fully expressed in *The Gypsy Ballads of García Lorca*, are latent in the description of Juana as a princess of the red sunset, the color of blood and fire, whose passion is like the dagger, whose distaff is of iron, whose flax is of steel. Here, metallic substances are symbols of death; Juana lies in her coffin of lead, and within her skeleton, a heart broken into a thousand pieces speaks of her shattered dreams and frustrated life.

"BALLAD OF THE LITTLE SQUARE"

In contrast to the bleak symbolism of these works, children and their world interested and delighted García Lorca, and he futilely sought in their charm and innocence a respite from the anguish of existence. In another poem from his first collection, "Balada de la placeta" ("Ballad of the Little Square"), the poet is listening to children singing. In a playful dialogue, the children ask the poet what he feels in his red, thirsty mouth; he answers, "the taste of the bones of my big skull." The poet's consciousness of death's presence mars his contemplation of youthful fun. Although he might wish to lose himself in the child's world, he clearly recognizes in a later poem, "Gacela de la huida" ("Gacela of the Flight"), that the seeds of death are already sown behind that childish exterior: "No one who touching a newborn child can forget the motionless horse skulls." Still, he tries to reject the physical destruction, the putrefaction of death that he so vividly describes in "Gacela de la muerte oscura" ("Gacela of the Dark Death") and in the *Lament for the Death of a Bullfighter.*

"THE SONG OF THE HORSEMAN"

García Lorca was a master of the dramatic ballad, full of mystery, passion, and dark, sudden violence. His tools were simple words and objects culled from everyday living, which contrasted with and intensified the complex emotions underlying the verse. García Lorca's mastery of the ballad form is exemplified in "Canción de jinete" ("The Song of the Horseman"),

from *Songs*. The horseman's destination is the distant city of Córdoba. Although he knows the roads well and his saddlebags are packed with olives, he fatalistically declares that he will never reach Córdoba. García Lorca never tells a story outright; he makes his audience do the work. Thus, Death is looking at the horseman from the towers of Córdoba, as he cries "Ay! How long the road! Ay! My valiant pony! Ay! That death should wait me before I reach Córdoba." How? Why? Who? Where? These questions are left to the imagination.

"SOMNAMBULE BALLAD"

It is through the figure of the Andalusian gypsy that García Lorca best conveys his personal vision of life. With his characteristic techniques of metaphorical suggestion and dramatic tension, enriched by an artist's palette of colors, García Lorca in *The Gypsy Ballads of García Lorca* treats his usual subject matter of love and death, passion and destruction, with great lyrical fantasy. The refrain "Green, how much I want you green" establishes the enchanted atmosphere of the famous "Romance sonambulo" ("Somnambule Ballad"), where everything possesses the greenish cast of an interior world: "Green wind, green flesh, green hair." The best known of García Lorca's ballads, it only implies the story behind the death of a pair of lovers: his the result of a wound that runs from his chest to his throat, hers from drowning in the sorrow of having waited for him so long in vain.

The themes of passion and violence are underscored by the theme of liberty, denied to the lovers by fate and a false social order. The gypsy girl's death is already intimated in the first stanza, where she is described as having a shadow on her waist, with green flesh, hair of green, and eyes of cold silver that cannot see. On a first reading, the two lines "The ship upon the sea/ and the horse in the mountain," which precede the description, seem to be a discordant and senseless addition to the narrative. To understand their function, the reader must see them in relation to the theme of liberty. Humans are imprisoned by their passions, by destiny, death, a sense of honor, and social institutions. In contrast, the images of the ship upon the sea and the horse on the mountain suggest total freedom. The horse, which in García Lorca's work often represents male virility, prefigures the gypsy's attainment of the freedom that is his by nature. The image of the ship, on the other hand, has a long tradition of symbolizing liberty, especially in the Romantic period; its interpretation here, as such, is logical and expected. The description of the stars as white frost and the mountain as a filching cat foreshadows the violence of the characters' deaths.

Thus, "Somnambule Ballad" offers a profusion of surrealistic and seemingly disconnected images governed by a vigorous inner logic. In this, it is representative of García Lorca's finest works. The repetition of key images—of green, cold silver, the moon, water, and the night—unifies the poem. The gypsy girl and the gypsy are together in death and cannot hear the pounding of the drunken civil guard on the door. Death has granted them freedom, and all is as it should be: "The ship upon the sea, and the horse on the mountain." Using the local color and ambience of gypsy life, García Lorca gives voice to his own frustrations and those of humanity in general. Fettered by passion, destiny, and social norms, humanity's only escape is through death.

POET IN NEW YORK

The strange poems of *Poet in New York* are the work of a mature poet. In New York, García Lorca, who had loved life in all its spontaneity, who had grieved over the death of gypsies, their instinctive and elemental passions suffocated, was confronted with the heartless, mechanized world of the urban metropolis. In *Poet in New York*, the gypsy is replaced by the black person, whose instinctive impulses and strengths are perverted by white civilization and whose repression and anguish is embodied in the figure of the great King of Harlem in a janitor's suit. The blood of three hundred crimson roses that stained the gypsy's shirt in "Somnambule Ballad" now flows from four million butchered ducks, five million hogs, two thousand doves, one million cows, one million lambs, and two million roosters.

The disrespect for life in this landscape of vomiting and urinating multitudes is portrayed in the death of a cat, within whose little paw, crushed by the automobile, García Lorca sees a world of broken rivers and unattainable distances. Alone, alienated, and frustrated in his endeavors, humans cannot appeal to anyone for help, not even the Church, which in its hypocrisy and heathen materialism betrays the true spirit of Christianity. The poet sees death and destruction everywhere. His own loneliness and alienation, described in "Asesinato" ("Murder"), recall the haunting words and melody of the *cante jondo*: "A pinprick to dive till it touches the roots of a cry."

LAMENT FOR THE DEATH OF A BULLFIGHTER

Considered by many to be García Lorca's supreme poetic achievement, *Lament for the Death of a Bullfighter* is the quintessence of the Spanish "tragic sense of life." In this lament, García Lorca incorporated aspects of a long poetic tradition and revitalized them through his own creativity. Based on a true incident, as were most of García Lorca's poems, the elegy was written on the death of his good friend Ignacio, an intellectual and a bullfighter, who was gored by a bull and died in August of 1934. The bullfight is elevated by García Lorca to a universal level, representing humanity's heroic struggle against death. Death, as always in García Lorca's poetry, emerges triumphant, yet the struggle is seen as courageous, graceful, meaningful.

The elegy is divided into four parts: "La cogida y la muerte" ("The Goring and the Death"), "La sangre derrameda" ("The Spilling of the Blood"), "Cuerpo presente" ("The Body Present"), and "Alma ansente" ("Absent Soul"). In general, the poem moves from the concrete to the abstract, from report to essay, from the specific to the general. Part 1 describes the events, the chaos, the confusion, the whole process of death in a series of images appealing to all the five senses. Phones jangle, the crowd is mad with grief, the bulls bellow, the wounds burn. What dominates is the incessant and doleful bell, reminding the poet, with each repetition of "at five o'clock in the afternoon," of the finality of death, worming its way into Ignacio's being, hammering its way into the public mind and into the poet's consciousness. The macabre sights and smells of death are detailed in all their colorful goriness: the white sheet, a pail of lime, snowy sweat, yellow iodine, green gangrene. Time ceases for Ignacio as all the clocks show five o'clock in the shadow of the afternoon. Refusing to look at Ignacio's blood in the sand, García Lorca vents his anger and frustration at seeing all that beauty, confidence, princeliness, strength of body and character, wit, and intelligence slowly seeping out as the moss and the grass open with sure fingers the flowers of Ignacio's skull.

The poet's initial reaction of shock and denial slowly softens into gradual acceptance. Using the slower Alexandrine meter in "The Body Present," García Lorca contemplates the form of Ignacio laid out on a sterile, gray, cold stone. The finality of death is seen in the sulphur yellow of Ignacio's face and in the rain entering his mouth in the stench-filled silence. García Lorca cannot offer immortality. He can only affirm that humankind must live bravely, and that death too will one day cease to exist. Hence, he tells Ignacio to sleep, fly, rest: Even the sea dies. Death, victorious, challenged only by the value of Ignacio's human experience, is dealt with in the last part. By autumn, the people will have forgotten Ignacio, robbed by death and time of the memory of his presence. Only those like the poet, who can look beyond, will immortalize him in song.

Lament for the Death of a Bullfighter expresses the fundamental attitude of the Spaniard toward death: One must gamble on life with great courage and heroism. Welcoming the dark angels of death, the "toques de bordón," or the black tones of the guitar, the poet is paradoxically affirming life. This is humanity's only consolation.

García Lorca's evolution as a poet was characterized throughout by this movement toward an all-encompassing death. Synthesizing a variety of themes and poetic styles and forms, García Lorca embodied, both in his life and in his verse, modern humans' struggle to find meaning in life despite the overwhelming reality of physical and spiritual death.

OTHER MAJOR WORKS

PLAYS: *El maleficio de la mariposa*, pr. 1920 (*The Butterfly's Evil Spell*, 1963); *Mariana Pineda*, pr. 1927 (English translation, 1950); *La doncella, el marinero y el estudiante*, pb. 1928 (*The Virgin, the Sailor, and the Student*, 1957); *El paseo de Buster Keaton*, pb. 1928 (*Buster Keaton's Promenade*, 1957); *La zapatera prodigiosa*, pr. 1930 (*The Shoemaker's Prodigious Wife*, 1941); *Bodas de sangre*, pr. 1933 (*Blood Wed-*

ding, 1939); *El amor de don Perlimplín con Belisa en su jardín*, pr. 1933 (*The Love of Don Perlimplín for Belisa in His Garden*, 1941); *Yerma*, pr. 1934 (English translation, 1941); *Doña Rosita la soltera: O, El lenguaje de las flores*, pr. 1935 (*Doña Rosita the Spinster: Or, The Language of the Flowers*, 1941); *El retablillo de don Cristóbal*, pr. 1935 (*In the Frame of Don Cristóbal*, 1944); *Así que pasen cinco años*, pb. 1937, (wr. 1931; *When Five Years Pass*, 1941); *Los títeres de Cachiporra: La tragicomedia de don Cristóbal y la señá Rosita*, pr. 1937 (wr. 1928; *The Tragicomedy of Don Cristóbal and Doña Rosita*, 1955); *Quimera*, pb. 1938 (wr. 1928; *Chimera*, 1944); *La casa de Bernarda Alba*, pr., pb. 1945 (wr. 1936; *The House of Bernarda Alba*, 1947); *El público*, pb. 1976 (wr. 1930, fragment; *The Audience*, 1958).

NONFICTION: *Impresiones y paisajes*, 1918; *Selected Letters*, 1983 (David Gershator, editor).

MISCELLANEOUS: *Obras completas*, 1938-1946 (8 volumes).

BIBLIOGRAPHY

Anderson, Reed. *Federico García Lorca*. London: Macmillan, 1984. Anderson's study focuses on García Lorca's dramatic art. The book has a fine overview of García Lorca's relationship to Spanish literature in general as well as insightful discussions of the early and mature dramas.

Binding, Paul. *Lorca: The Gay Imagination*. London: GMP, 1985. Binding's is a fine study focusing on García Lorca's work as it is an outgrowth of the poet's sexuality. Binding has a sympathetic sense of the modern temperament, and his readings, particularly of García Lorca's mature works, are excellent.

Bonaddio, Federico, ed. *A Companion to Federico García Lorca*. Woodbridge, Suffolk, England: Tamesis, 2008. Provides biographical information and critical analysis. Contains a chapter on poetry.

Delgado, Maria M. *Federico García Lorca*. New York: Routledge, 2007. A biography that looks at the life, politics, and mythology surrounding the poet and dramatist. Also looks at his legacy.

Gibson, Ian. *Federico García Lorca*. New York: Pantheon Books, 1989. A monumental biography that goes to the heart of García Lorca's genius with brilliant prose and telling anecdotes. Meticulously reconstructs the poet's periods in New York, Havana, and Buenos Aires. Vividly re-creates the café life of Spain in the 1930's and the artistic talents that were nurtured there. Evokes the landscapes of Granada, Almeria, Cuba, and Argentina celebrated in the poetry.

Johnston, David. *Federico García Lorca*. Bath, England: Absolute, 1998. Asserts that García Lorca, rather than celebrating, is more concerned with deconstructing the essentials of Spain's culture of difference. Claims that the poet's most radical ultimate intention was the deconstruction of a civilization and the redefinition of the individual's right to be, not through the language of ethics or of the law but in terms of a natural imperative.

Mayhew, Jonathan, ed. *Apocryphal Lorca: Translation, Parody, Kitsch*. Chicago: University of Chicago Press, 2009. Literary criticism of García Lorca's works. Mayhew contrasts the perception of the poet in the English-speaking world to that in the Spanish-speaking world. He notes the poet's legacy among American poets.

Morris, C. Brian. *Son of Andalusia: The Lyrical Landscapes of Federico García Lorca*. Nashville, Tenn.: Vanderbilt University Press, 1997. In six chapters and an epilogue, Morris identifies the presence of Andalusian legends, traditions, songs, and beliefs in García Lorca's life and works.

Sahuquillo, Angel. *Federico García Lorca and the Culture of Male Homosexuality*. Jefferson, N.C.: McFarland, 2007. Examines García Lorca's life and works from the perspective of his sexuality.

Stainton, Leslie. *Lorca: A Dream of Life*. New York: Farrar, Straus and Giroux, 1999. Stainton, an American scholar who lived in Spain for several years, writes of García Lorca's sexuality, his left-wing political views, and his artistic convictions. Her detailed account is strictly chronological. García Lorca's work is described but not analyzed.

Katherine Gyékényesi Gatto

GARCILASO DE LA VEGA

Born: Toledo, Spain; 1501
Died: Nice, France; October 13, 1536

PRINCIPAL POETRY

Las obras de Boscán y algunas de Garcilasso de la Vega repartidas en quatro libros, 1543
Las obras del excelente poeta Garcilasso de la Vega, 1569
Obras del excelente poeta Garci Lasso de la Vega con anotaciones y enmiendas del Licenciado Francisco Sánchez . . . , 1574
Obras de Garci Lasso de la Vega con anotaciones de Fernando de Herrera, 1580
Garcilaso de la Vega: Natural de Toledo, Principe de los Poetas Castellanos, de Don Thomas Tamaio de Vargas, 1622 (*The Works of Garcilaso de la Vega surnamed the Prince of Castilian Poets*, 1823)
Obras de Garcilaso de la Vega, ilustradas con notas, 1765
Garcilaso: Works, A Critical Text with a Bibliography, 1925
Garcilaso de la Vega: Obras completas, Edición de Elías L. Rivers, 1964
Garcilaso de la Vega y sus comentaristas: Obras completas del poeta acompañadas de los textos íntegros de los comentarios de El Brocense, Fernando de Herrera, Tamayo y Vargas y Azara, 1966
The Complete Love Sonnets of Garcilaso de la Vega, 2005
Selected Poems of Garcilaso de la Vega, 2009 (bilingual edition)

OTHER LITERARY FORMS

Garcilaso de la Vega (gahr-see-LAH-soh day lo VAY-guh) is remembered only for his poetic works.

ACHIEVEMENTS

Garcilaso de la Vega revolutionized Castilian poetry, playing a unique role in Spanish literature and achieving a notable place in European literature as well. In accomplishing this poetic revolution, Garcilaso may rightly be called the first modern Spanish poet. Although the fifteenth century in Spain had seen efforts to introduce into Castilian poetry the Italian hendecasyllable, attempts such as those of the Marquis of Santillana, who composed a collection of "Sonetos fechos al itálico modo" (sonnets made in the Italian way), had not been successful. Equally unsuccessful had been the use of a non-Italianate hendecasyllabic line by the fifteenth century poets Juan de Mena and Francisco Imperial.

Garcilaso's perfection of the Castilian hendecasyllable, successful cultivation of both Italianate verse forms and metrical innovations, and his use of classical models, all contributed to a poetry of intimate sentiment, delicate metaphor, conceptual content, and musicality. Religious themes, so important in the poetry of even the late Middle Ages in Spain, are completely absent in his verse, which crystallized the introduction into Spain of the essentially secular values of the Renaissance. From fifteenth century Spanish poetry, Garcilaso retained a certain predilection for wordplay, along with the favorable influence of the Catalan poet Ausias March. While at times expressively manipulating syntax, Garcilaso created a poetic diction soon regarded as a model of lucid simplicity for the Spanish language.

In international terms, Garcilaso is also notable for having preceded by many years the introduction of Italianate forms and sentiment into both English and French poetry. His use of pastoral poetry to express interiorized sentiments, of interest to the student of comparative literature, also represents a notable contribution to the development of this international literary mode.

Garcilaso's poetry, all of which was published posthumously, was rapidly accorded classic status, and editions of his poems with copious annotation and commentary appeared within the sixteenth century. The first of these was the edition by the esteemed scholar Francisco Sánchez de las Brozas, initially published in 1574. The important poet Fernando de Herrera first published his annotated edition in 1580. Additional annotated editions were published by other editors in the seventeenth and eighteenth centuries. The 1543 edition

included most of the sonnets currently known to be Garcilaso's or attributed to him, all the other poems in Italian meters, and one poem in a traditional Castilian verse form. Subsequent editions have gradually been enlarged by adding more sonnets, other compositions in Castilian verse forms, and several Latin poems, as well as some letters and the poet's will. Virtually all dating of his compositions is conjectural, and the numbers commonly assigned to specific poems do not correspond to their presumed order of composition.

Garcilaso's poetry in some sense became the model and inspiration for virtually all poetry written during the nearly two centuries of Spain's Golden Age and for much of Spanish poetry up to the present day. Although the traditional Castilian verse forms were championed by poets such as Cristóbal de Castillejo and his followers in the sixteenth century, the influence and acceptance of Garcilaso's innovations was so pervasive that it has been said that every Spanish poet "carries his Garcilaso inside himself." Garcilaso's own compositions in the traditional verse forms—and his Latin poetry—illuminate the development of his Spanish poetry in the new style but are not themselves of primary interest in defining or understanding his art. The poetical canon left by Garcilaso provided the inspiration and basis for both of the somewhat antithetical schools or styles of poetry that were to evolve later in the Golden Age. The statement of ideas without metaphorical adornment and Garcilaso's retention of wordplay and puns from medieval Spanish poetry evolved ultimately into the dense, conceptual style exemplified by Francisco Gómez de Quevedo y Villegas, while Garcilaso's manipulation of word order, sense of color, and use of metaphor were reflected in Luis de Góngora y Argote's hyperbatons, polychromatic palette, and extravagant imagery.

Garcilaso pioneered the use of six distinct verse forms in Spanish poetry. The Spanish sonnet, composed of fourteen hendecasyllabic lines divided into two quatrains and two tercets, possessed a fundamentally different structure from the sonnet subsequently developed in English by William Shakespeare. The *estancia* combined lines of eleven and seven syllables in a pattern established in the poem's first strophe and then repeated in the subsequent strophes. The *lira*, so called because of its use in an ode whose first line contained this word (meaning "lyre"), was a particular form of the *estancia*, which became standardized. The *tercetos* consisted of three-line stanzas of eleven-syllable lines, with the first and third lines rhyming, and the middle line rhyming with the first and third lines of the next stanza. The *octava real* was a stanza of eight hendecasyllabic lines, rhyming *abababcc*. Garcilaso also introduced into Spanish the use of blank verse.

BIOGRAPHY

Garcilaso de la Vega's brief but active life might serve as a model for that of the multitalented Renaissance man. Born in 1501 of a family with influence in the court of Ferdinand and Isabella and with several well-known authors in its antecedent generations, Garcilaso died in 1536 of wounds received in Provence while he was fighting for Emperor Charles V.

Garcilaso entered the emperor's service in 1519 or 1520, was first wounded in battle in 1521, and he participated in several important campaigns, for which he

Garcilaso de la Vega (©CORBIS)

was awarded the prestigious Order of Saint James in 1523. During his accompaniment of the court in the subsequent years of the decade, his friendship with the poet Juan Boscán developed. This relationship was of profound significance for Garcilaso's literary career; when, for example, his friend Boscán was persuaded by the Venetian ambassador to employ the Italian hendecasyllable in Castilian verse, Garcilaso did likewise, changing Spanish poetry forever. It has been suggested that his sonnets 31 and 38 were written in this period.

In 1525, Garcilaso married Doña Elena de Zúñiga, a lady-in-waiting to Charles V's sister, Princess Leonore. The following year, he met and became infatuated with Isabel Freyre, who came to Spain from Portugal with Doña Isabel de Portugal when the latter married Charles V. Although his marital relationship apparently never saw expression in his poetry, Garcilaso's love for Isabel Freyre, seemingly unrequited, became a central poetic theme. The "Canción primera" ("First Ode") and sonnets 2, 15, and 27, probably from this period, express the poet's emotional state and his amorous devotion to an unnamed lady. The first numbered of his "Canciones en versos castellanos" ("Songs in Castilian Verse Forms"), on the occasion of "his lady's marriage," was presumably composed in response to Isabel Freyre's wedding. While with the retinue of Charles V in Italy, where the monarch had gone in 1529 or 1530 to receive the Imperial crown, Garcilaso apparently composed his "Canción cuarta" ("Fourth Ode") and sonnet 6, perhaps reflecting his anguish over the affair with Isabel.

In 1531, however, Charles V withdrew his favor, banishing Garcilaso to a small island in the Danube River because he had persisted in supporting a marriage opposed by the royal family. Sonnets 4 and 9 and the "Canción tercera" ("Third Ode") reflect the poet's unhappiness during this period. Thanks to the intervention of the duke of Alba, however, the island confinement was altered to banishment to Naples, where the poet gained a position of confidence with the viceroy, earned the praise of Cardinal Bembo, and, as reflected in his sonnets 14, 19, and 33 and in the famous "Canción quinta, a la flor de Gnido" ("Fifth Ode, To the Flower of Gnido"), made the acquaintance of several other important Neapolitan literary figures. During this period, he also studied the classics and met the expatriate Spanish author Juan de Valdés, who mentioned Garcilaso in his *Diálogo de la lengua* (wr. c. 1535, pb. 1737; dialogue of the language). Garcilaso's "Egloga segunda" ("Second Eclogue"), probably composed shortly after his brief trip to Spain and return to Naples in 1533, praises the House of Alba, while the "Egloga primera" ("First Eclogue") and sonnet 10, both apparently composed during the period 1533-1534, reflect the death at that time of Isabel Freyre. It is reasonable to assume that during this time in Naples, the poet composed his several Latin poems and stopped composing in the old Castilian verse forms.

During 1535 and 1536, Garcilaso returned to the emperor's service. Sonnets 32 and 35 suggest that Garcilaso was wounded in an encounter with the Moors in an expedition to Tunis in 1535. With the emperor's entourage in Sicily after returning from Tunis, Garcilaso composed his "Elegía primera" ("First Elegy"), for the recent death of the brother of the duke of Alba, and the "Elegía segunda" ("Second Elegy"), addressed to his friend Boscán. The "Egloga tercera" ("Third Eclogue"), generally regarded as the poet's last work, was written when Garcilaso was again part of the emperor's court and in full favor, as Charles V decided to move against the French. It was while participating in this campaign that the poet was killed.

Boscán, Garcilaso's lifelong friend, gathered Garcilaso's poems, intending to publish them with his own. Upon Boscán's death in 1542, his widow carried out the project, realizing its publication in 1543.

ANALYSIS

While Garcilaso de la Vega took much inspiration from Italian and classical models, he did not merely imitate them; rather, he assimilated and transformed these influences in the development of his own distinctive poetic voice.

"SECOND ECLOGUE"

This development is particularly evident in Garcilaso's eclogues. The "Second Eclogue," his longest composition, fully initiated the pastoral mode in his po-

etry. The poem possesses a balanced structure in which motifs and differing stanzaic forms—*tercetos*, *estancias*, *rima al mezzo* (interior rhyme)—are arranged in a symmetrical pattern centered on lines 766 through 933, which portray in dialogic form a chance encounter between the shepherd Albanio and Camila, his childhood playmate, who has earlier rejected his translation of their childhood friendship into love. On being rejected once more by Camila, after his hopes have been raised, Albanio goes mad. This central scene is preceded by a prologue in which Albanio laments his sad state; by several *estancias* inspired by Horace's *Beatus ille*; and by a section of dialogue between Albanio and Salicio in which Albanio recounts the story of his love for Camila, her negative response, and his present desire to kill himself. The dialogue, modeled on an episode in Jacopo Sannazzaro's *Arcadia* (1501-1504), is punctuated by an exchange in Petrarchan *rima al mezzo* in which Camila the hunter appears at the fountain where she first rejected Albanio and recalls the unpleasant incident.

Following the central scene between Camila and Albanio, a passage in *rima al mezzo* presents the struggle of Salicio and Nemoroso, another shepherd, to control the crazed Albanio. The following passage is in *tercetos*; with Albanio subdued, Nemoroso tells Salicio that Severo, a sage enchanter who had cured him, has come to Alba and can cure Albanio of his love woes. A brief dialogic *rima al mezzo* then leads to a lengthy panegyric by Nemoroso to the House of Alba. A short dialogue in *estancias* reaffirms the certainty of Albanio's eventual cure, and as dusk falls, the two shepherds discuss their leave-taking and the disposition of Albanio.

The "Second Eclogue" departs from the refinement of Vergilian bucolics and displays characteristics that separate it from the more perfected form that Garcilaso was to achieve in his "First Eclogue" (which, despite its designation, was composed after the "Second Eclogue"). The tranquility and idealization of nature and human feelings are disturbed by a number of familiar or rustic expressions and proverbs, concentrated in the dialogue between Albanio and Salicio that precedes Camila's appearance. These exchanges acquire an almost comic character that has caused some critics to regard them as constituting a dramatic farce in themselves. The poet engagingly steps outside the poetic conventions of the pastoral mode by having Albanio question Salicio's advice with the query, "Who made you an eloquent philosopher/ being a shepherd of sheep and goats?" There is a considerable amount of jocularity elsewhere in exchanges between Albanio and Salicio and in Nemoroso's initial resistance to helping Salicio subdue the crazed Albanio. Although it has been assumed that Albanio represents Garcilaso's friend and mentor the duke of Alba, a number of details suggest that Albanio is more plausibly Bernardino de Toledo, the duke's younger brother, whose death in 1535 occasioned Garcilaso's "First Elegy." Though somewhat distracting, these elements contribute to the originality of Garcilaso's poetic creation.

The "Second Eclogue" is also rich in conceits and various forms of wordplay. Some of these devices are reminiscent of Petrarch, while others have their antecedents in Castilian poetry of the fifteenth century. In its representation of Albanio's love as an anguished state, the poem recalls the Petrarchan influence evident in Garcilaso's earlier works.

"FIRST ECLOGUE"

In "First Eclogue," Garcilaso attained perfect balance and equilibrium, a consistent and refined tone, idiom, and sentiment, and the definitive expression of the central amorous relationship in his life, the love for Isabel Freyre. A four-stanza prologue and dedication to the duke of Alba introduces two shepherds, again Salicio and Nemoroso, who lament respectively and in succession, each in twelve stanzas, their disappointments in love. The two successive speeches are separated by a one-stanza transition, and culminated by a single stanza conclusion, so that the poem as a whole comprises thirty fourteen-line stanzas.

In the two shepherds and their lamentations, the poet has represented himself ("Salicio" is an anagram of Garcilaso, while "Nemoroso" is a coinage based on the Latin root *nemus*, closely related in meaning to Spanish *vega*, a meadow) and expressed in a perfectly balanced duality the two essential elements of his relationship with Isabel Freyre: its failure, followed by her marriage to another, and her death. The lamentations begin at daybreak and end as the sun sets and the shep-

herds return with their flocks. Unity is achieved in the use of a single verse form throughout, the *estancia* (here a fourteen-line stanza of eleven- and seven-syllable lines); in the two shepherds' embodiment of the poet; and in the restriction of the action to a single day's time. Without calling attention to itself, an exquisite and seemingly effortless design governs the entire poem, which in its structure is similar to that of Vergil's "Eighth Eclogue."

The poem's opening six lines establish the delicacy and balance of the pastoral mode, exemplifying Garcilaso's expressive manipulation of word order to yield consonance of form and meaning. The first two lines, "The sweet lamentation of two shepherds/ Salicio jointly and Nemoroso," introduce the duality of the shepherds, separating and balancing them at the beginning and end of the poetical line. Here, the use of the first of many carefully positioned modifiers begins to create the idealized, gentle, tender ambience that defines the eclogue. The opening lines contain no active verbs, instead using infinitives, participles, and verbs of being. This construction suggests that the sheep are forgetful of their grazing, attentive rather to the shepherds' "savory song," a dreamlike oblivion and perfect harmony between nature and man. In an abrupt change, the next line addresses the duke of Alba, expressively heightening the contrast between the idyllic pastoral environment and the affairs of state or martial concerns that preoccupy the dynamic man of action.

The evocation of the duke's military activities in the succeeding stanzas touches a theme that was an important part of the poet's life and that finds expression in other of his poems, most notably the "Second Elegy." This poem, apparently written to Boscán from Sicily in 1535, expresses the poet's distaste for the petty politics of the emperor's retinue. Garcilaso depicts himself as a tender lover trapped in Mars's service, envying Boscán's tranquil, secure family life, and scorning the hypocrisy and ambition of those who surround the "African Caesar." The poem's opening lines, remarking on Vergil's presence in Sicily, through Aeneas, confirm Garcilaso's active awareness of Vergil during this period.

The stanza of the "First Eclogue," which connects the dedication to the duke with the beginning of Salicio's lament, returns to the idyllic natural setting. A characteristic hyperbaton represents the gradually rising sun, first rising above the waves, then above the mountains, and finally directly revealed at the beginning of the stanza's third line to introduce at daybreak the reclining Salicio. The pasture in which the shepherd is at his ease is crossed by a gurgling brook whose pleasant sound harmonizes with the music of the shepherd's sweet complaint. Assonant rhyme in addition to the usual consonantal rhyme, and internal rhyme in one verse, lend the passage a delicate musicality. As the clear brook flows unimpeded and burbling to accompany the shepherd's song, so too does the stanza, continuous, unimpeded, and without rigorous syntax.

The stanza that begins Salicio's complaint, addressed to the absent Galatea, who has not returned his love, is reminiscent of the plaints of several of Vergil's shepherds and provides a strident contrast to the sonorous passage preceding it. The shepherd first berates Galatea as harder than marble to his complaints and colder than ice to the fire that consumes him. The bitterness of these sentiments becomes death in the absence of the one who could give him life with her presence, then shame and embarrassment at his own pathetic state, then incredulity at the lady's refusal to command a soul that has always given itself to her, until it dissolves in the stanza's last line in the flowing tears bidden to emerge abundantly and without sorrow. This final line becomes a refrain at the end of the remainder of Salicio's stanzas, with the exception of the last one. Following stanzas contrast the permanence of the shepherd's sorry state with the daily changes of a delicately evoked nature, questioning the justice of his situation and reproachfully recalling his lady's falseness and deception.

While Salicio's unrequited love for Galatea recalls Garcilaso's disappointment in his love for Isabel Freyre, the shepherd Nemoroso's lament for his lost love, Elisa, recalls Garcilaso's mourning at Isabel's death. Nemoroso's lament confirms in a general way, though without many specific borrowings, Garcilaso's profound familiarity with Petrarch and his ability to equal or surpass the Italian model in his own poetry. Nemoroso's theme, the loved one's death, is also traditionally regarded as the subject of Garcilaso's famous sonnet 10,

"Oh dulces prendas, por mi mal halladas" (O sweet favors, found to my woe), and sonnet 25. Sonnet 10, expressing the poet's grief on finding a token of his departed love, and contrasting the joy that love once brought him with the sadness it presently causes, is reminiscent of both Vergil and Petrarch. The sonnet is recalled in the "First Eclogue" when Nemoroso describes the consoling tears engendered by a lock of Elisa's hair, always kept at his bosom.

Nemoroso's song begins with an evocation of nature, distilled into select details each refined with adjectival description into exquisite perfection ("running, pure, crystalline waters," "green field," "fresh shade"). The natural setting is self-contained, turned in upon itself and vaguely anthropomorphic as green ivy winds its way among trees that see themselves reflected in the water. The harmony between man and his thoughts and an idealized natural surrounding is disturbed only by the suggestion of present sadness and by the last line's reference to joy-filled memories, implying that joy is past.

The following stanzas recall the happy times the lovers shared and mourn their brevity; in imagery that anticipates the Baroque violence of Góngora, the shepherd expresses his passion, his rage, and his desolation. In the final stanza of Nemoroso's lament, anger and despondency yield to a quiet prayer to the now-divine loved one to hasten the coming of the shepherd's death so that they may enjoy tranquilly together and without fear of loss the eternal fields, mountains, rivers, and shaded flowery valleys of the third sphere. Natural beauty is thus raised to a cosmic plane; in Salicio's plaint, the imagery that concludes the lament recalls its opening lines.

The dreamlike poetic moment of the two shepherds' lamentations is ended in the eclogue's final stanza. Looking at the pink clouds and sensing the creeping shadows that reverse the process of sunrise described at the poem's opening, the two shepherds awaken from their reverie and conduct their sheep home, step by step. So, too, does the reader leave an exquisite and incomparably evoked poetic world of true sentiment, delicate appreciation of nature, and harmony between man and his surroundings, representative of Garcilaso's enduring contribution to Spanish literature.

BIBLIOGRAPHY

Cammarata, Joan. *Mythological Themes in the Works of Garcilaso de la Vega*. Potomac, Md.: Studia Humanitatis, 1983. A critical analysis of Garcilaso's use of folklore and mythology. Includes bibliographical references and index.

Fernández-Morera, Dario. *The Lyre and the Oaten Flute: Garcilaso and the Pastoral*. London: Tamesis, 1982. A critical study of selected works by Garcilaso. Includes bibliographical references and index.

Garcilaso de la Vega. *Selected Poems of Garcilaso de la Vega: A Bilingual Edition*. Translated by John Dent-Young. Chicago: University of Chicago Press, 2009. This translation divides the poems into sonnets, songs, elegies, and eclogues, providing a short introduction to each.

Ghertman, Sharon. *Petrarch and Garcilaso*. London: Tamesis, 1975. Ghertman analyzes and compares the linguistic styles of Petrarch and Garcilaso.

Heiple, Daniel L. *Garcilaso de la Vega and the Italian Renaissance*. University Park: Pennsylvania State University Press, 1994. Heiple analyzes Garcilaso's work and its place in the history of Italian renaissance literature. Includes bibliographical references and index.

Helgerson, Richard. *A Sonnet from Carthage: Garcilaso de la Vega and the New Poetry of Sixteenth-Century Europe*. Philadelphia: University of Pennsylvania Press, 2007. Helgerson starts with a sonnet to Juan Boscán from Garcilaso and proceeds to examine Garcilaso's effect on the poetry of Europe.

Torres, Isabel. "Sites of Speculation: Water/Mirror Poetics in Garcilaso de la Vega, Eclogue II." *Bulletin of Hispanic Studies* 86, no. 6 (2009): 877-893. Examines Garcilaso's "Second Eclogue," noting water and mirror images in the poem.

Theodore L. Kassier

THÉOPHILE GAUTIER

Born: Tarbes, France; August 30, 1811
Died: Paris, France; October 23, 1872

PRINCIPAL POETRY

Poésies, 1830 (English translation, 1973)
Albertus: Ou, l'Âme et le péché, 1833 (enlarged edition of *Poésies*; *Albertus: Soul and Sin*, 1909)
La Comédie de la mort, 1838 (*The Drama of Death*, 1909)
España, 1845
Poésies complètes, 1845
Émaux et camées, 1852, enlarged 1872 (*Enamels and Cameos*, 1903)
Dernières Poésies, 1872

OTHER LITERARY FORMS

Théophile Gautier (goh-TYAY) was an immensely prolific writer with a widely diversified range of interests and concerns. Although he considered himself primarily a poet, he earned his living as a journalist for some forty years, contributing art, theater, and literary criticism to various newspapers and journals. Gautier's art criticism is often eloquent and perceptive, anticipating the achievement of Charles Baudelaire. As an art critic, Gautier is notable for his early and passionate defense of such contrasting contemporary painters as Eugène Delacroix and Jean-Auguste-Dominique Ingres and for introducing the French public to the works of such Spanish masters as Bartolomé Murillo, Diego de Velázquez, Jose de Ribera, Francisco de Zurbarán, and Francisco de Goya. Gautier's theater criticism is especially voluminous, and, although only a small part of it is of continuing interest for its wit and stylistic verve, it is a remarkable quotidian document of the Parisian theatrical scene of the mid-nineteenth century. In addition to theater criticism, Gautier wrote a number of plays—some as a collaborator—none of which holds the stage today, even as a curiosity. More successful were his scenarios for a number of popular ballets, including the enduring favorite *Giselle: Ou, Les Wilis* (1841; *Giselle: Or, The Wilis*, 1970).

Of greater interest are Gautier's works of literary

criticism. *Les Grotesques* (1844; *The Grotesques*, 1900) is a collection of studies of then little-known French authors of the fifteenth through the mid-seventeenth centuries, originally published as a series of individual newspaper articles under the collective title "Exhumations littéraires." The authors discussed (among them François Villon, Cyrano de Bergerac, and Théophile de Viau) were generally ignored or considered as *naïfs* in the early part of the nineteenth century, and Gautier played an important role in the rise of their reputations. Additionally, Gautier wrote several perceptive, if somewhat biased, appreciations (amounting to monographs) of such contemporaries as Gérard de Nerval, Honoré de Balzac, and Baudelaire, and he began *Histoire du Romanticism* (*History of Romanticism*, 1900), which remained unfinished because of his death but was published posthumously in 1874.

Gautier was also a passionate traveler, and he left a number of perceptive and entertaining travelogues of visits to Spain, Italy, the Middle East, and Russia. In the best tradition of travel literature, these works are more than simple guidebooks; they are accounts of the intellectual and spiritual voyages of an artist through the sometimes exotic sensibilities of foreign cultures.

The most significant literary genre to which Gautier contributed other than poetry was fiction—not only novels but also a considerable number of short stories, tales, and novellas. Many of these shorter works were originally published in newspapers and journals, and they typically deal with the fantastic (a popular subgenre of the early nineteenth century, exemplified by the tales of E. T. A. Hoffmann and Edgar Allan Poe) or present exotic evocations of the Orient (not the Far East, as the modern reader might assume; for Gautier, the Orient was the Middle East). Of particular note is an early collection of tales, *Les Jeunes-France: Romans goguenards* (1833; liberally translated as "the new French generation," a title referring to a popular name accorded to the second generation of French Romantic writers and painters). Significantly, Gautier was one of the first Romantics to cast a critical look at Romanticism, and three of the six tales in *Les Jeunes-France* are delightful out-and-out parodies of Romantic emotional excess and literary paraphernalia.

Gautier also wrote three novels: *Mademoiselle de Maupin* (1835-1836; *Mademoiselle de Maupin: A Romance of Love and Passion*, 1887), *Le Roman de la momie* (1856; *The Romance of the Mummy*, 1863), and *Le Capitaine Fracasse* (1863; *Captain Fracasse*, 1880). To some extent, all three are variations of the popular historical romance as exemplified by the novels of Sir Walter Scott or, in France, by Alfred de Vigny's 1826 novel, *Cinq-Mars* (English translation, 1847). *The Romance of the Mummy* is somewhat overburdened by minute technical detail, a quality that, along with a plot of more than usual improbability, has relegated the work to almost complete oblivion. *Mademoiselle de Maupin* is, on the other hand, possibly the best-known title in the Gautier canon. Its titular heroine (loosely based on an actual seventeenth century personality) is bisexual, not only an accomplished singer but also an adroit swordswoman who frequently dons male attire. The novel has been criticized for the flatness of its two other major characters, Albert and Rosette, as well as for a seeming reversal in the development of the heroine. Gautier quickly divested himself of the traditional apparatus of the historical novel and used the work as a vehicle for the exploration of the problem of identity: In one sense, the union of male and female in the person of the heroine serves as a metaphor for human perfection.

Finally, in *Captain Fracasse* (another manifestation of the early nineteenth century predilection for the early seventeenth century, the age of Louis XIII and Richelieu), in the tradition of Vigny's *Cinq-Mars* and Alexandre Dumas, père's *Les Trois Mousquetaires* (1844; *The Three Musketeers*, 1846), Gautier again appropriated the apparatus and structure of the historical romance, in which complications are typically happily resolved. Gautier endows this "literary machine" with a number of ironic twists that play with the idea of the illusions and uncertainties of human existence, undermining the assumptions of the genre even as he demonstrates a dazzling mastery of its conventions. *Captain Fracasse* is considered by many critics to be Gautier's prose masterpiece.

ACHIEVEMENTS

Théophile Gautier was one of the most influential, as well as one of the few successful, poets of the second generation of French Romantics. His early poetry clearly demonstrates his debt to the greats of the first generation, but it did not take long for Gautier to establish his own voice and develop his own aesthetic (eclectic as it was). By mid-century, Gautier had become a leading literary figure, influential in his own right. His formulation of the theory of art for art's sake, in which the value of art is determined solely by its capacity to create beauty, regardless of ethical or utilitarian considerations, was profoundly influential and produced ramifications beyond the borders of France (a major instance being the aesthetic movement of late nineteenth century England, represented by such writers as Walter Pater, Algernon Charles Swinburne, and Oscar Wilde).

As the doctrine of art for art's sake eliminated ethics and social function as criteria for the making and criticism of art, it also tempered the vague notion of imagination with a concept of art as craft and discipline. In one literary review, Gautier was to state, "Art is beauty, the eternal invention of detail, the correct choice of words, the painstaking care of execution; the word 'poet' literally signifies 'maker.' . . . Everything which is not well made does not exist." As the prime spokesman for this reexamination of aesthetic principles, he evolved a concept in which literature might emulate the plastic arts (particularly sculpture) by being "chiseled," "polished," and "objective." This notion was strongly advocated in Gautier's verse collection *Enamels and Cameos*, but it was more consistently developed and perfected by the generation of poets who succeeded Gautier, the Parnassians (particularly Charles-Marie Leconte de Lisle and José-Maria de Heredia).

No major poet was more generous in acknowledging a debt to Gautier than was Charles Baudelaire. The latter's masterpiece, *Les Fleurs du mal* (1857, 1861, 1868; *Flowers of Evil*, 1909), was dedicated to Gautier: "the impeccable poet, the perfect magician . . . my very dear and most venerated master and friend." Certain of Baudelaire's concepts of the feminine ideal, death, and the "spleen of Paris" are easily traced back to the poetry of Gautier. There are similar debts in the works of such poets as Paul Verlaine, Stéphane Mallarmé, and Paul Valéry.

Not the least of Gautier's accomplishments was purely personal, for he was renowned for his friend-ships with many of the leading cultural and artistic personalities of his day, including Victor Hugo, Delacroix, Nerval, Baudelaire, Hippolyte Taine, the Goncourts, and Maxime Du Camp. At Gautier's death, more than eighty poets from all over Europe contributed to a commemorative volume of poems in recognition of his place in French letters and his passionate commitment to art and beauty.

Assessing Gautier's poetic achievement is problematic. If he was overpraised by his contemporaries and no longer seems the "impeccable poet" of Baudelaire's dedication to Gautier in *Flowers of Evil*, he is surely underestimated today. His place as a transitional figure is clear; the influence of both his poetry and his ideas on the course of French literature is undeniable; his influence outside his native country in the nineteenth century was not inconsiderable. In the history of Western culture, few have argued as eloquently as Gautier the notion that art is humanity's supreme achievement, ennobling people, lifting them above the petty pursuits and scarring disappointments of human existence.

BIOGRAPHY

Pierre-Jules-Théophile Gautier was born on August 30, 1811, in Tarbes, a small town in southern France at the foot of the Pyrenees. His father, a minor government official, was transferred with his family from this provincial home on the frontier of Spain to the cosmopolitan bustle of Paris in 1814, when Gautier was not quite three years old. Tarbes made an indelible impression on Gautier, who himself traced his wanderlust and his perpetual fascination with the exotic to a desire to recapture the idealized world of his early life at Tarbes.

In Paris, after an unsuccessful attempt to conform to the regimen of a boarding school, Gautier was enrolled as a day pupil at the Collège Charlemagne. There, his scholastic career prospered. His parents, particularly his father, were strongly supportive of their son's interests, and Gautier was encouraged to develop an early talent for sketching by studying art in the studio of the painter Louis Édouard Rioult. Gautier's years of study in the studio were to be of the greatest importance in his development as a writer.

While enrolled at the Collège Charlemagne and simultaneously studying with Rioult, Gautier met and befriended the precocious young writer Gérard de Nerval (who published his first collection of poetry at the age of seventeen and, in his twentieth year, published a translation of *Faust: Eine Tragödie* (pb. 1808, 1833; *The Tragedy of Faust*, 1823, 1838) much admired by Johann Wolfgang von Goethe). Nerval was one of the chief organizers of the pro-Romantic claque that was to attend the premiere of Victor Hugo's drama *Hernani* (English translation, 1830) at the Théâtre-Français on February 25, 1830, and he enlisted Gautier's assistance as the head of a subsquad of Hugo supporters. The evening was destined to become a watershed in French theatrical history; it served to mark the "official" recognition of the Romantic movement in France. Gautier left a warm and lively account of that evening, which the French refer to as the "battle of *Hernani*." The long-haired, outrageously attired young Romantics (Gautier would be known throughout his life for the *gilet rouge*, or red waistcoat, he wore that evening) applauded and cheered their hero, Hugo, while the old-guard neoclassicists hissed him down. The performance could barely proceed for the noise and interruptions, but somehow the new Romanticism triumphed.

Gautier and Nerval soon became involved with a group of young literary hopefuls who together formed a literary club, the *petit cénacle* (so called to distinguish it from the original *cénacle* of the first-generation Romantics: Hugo, Alphonse de Lamartine, Vigny, and Alfred de Musset). This "little club" was a flamboyant and colorful group, most of the members of which are now forgotten. In July, 1830, under the influence of his fellow members, Gautier's first collection of verse, *Poésies*, appeared, containing poems that were clearly imitative of the established poets of the first generation. It was not long, however, before Gautier began to write poetry and fiction critical of Romantic excess, and both *Albertus* and the short-fiction collection *Les Jeunes-France* are examples of this ironic, satirical vein.

The life span of the *petit cénacle* was quite short, but another, even more Bohemian and intellectually stimulating, "club" developed around a group of writers and artists who took up communal living in a slum area

Théophile Gautier (Hulton Archive/Getty Images)

near the Louvre, in a cul-de-sac called the Impasse du Doyenné. Among Gautier's comrades there were Nerval, Delacroix, Dumas, and Arsène Houssaye (the future director of the Théâtre-Français). It was among these artists that Gautier composed *The Drama of Death, Mademoiselle de Maupin*, and *Les Jeunes-France*, and his years among them were to mark the end of the more carefree, youthful stage of his career.

It soon became necessary for Gautier to take on the burden of providing for the financial security and comfort not only of himself but also of a number of dependents (including, at one time or other, his father and two sisters, two mistresses—Eugénie Fort and Ernesta Grisi—and three illegitimate children). In 1836, he accepted the post of art and theater critic for the Parisian newspaper *La Presse* (his first article was devoted to some paintings of Delacroix), thus inaugurating a long and often wearisome career as a journalist. Over the years, he contributed to several leading newspapers and journals, including *Le Figaro, Le Moniteur universel*, and *Le Revue des deux mondes*. Although he became a highly influential critic, Gautier never really enjoyed the work, ever resenting the time lost from the composition of poetry.

In 1840, Gautier made a trip to Spain on a quasi-business venture to buy rare books and artifacts to be resold at higher prices in France. The enterprise turned out to be a financial disaster, but it proved to be an inspirational gold mine for the poet—the travel book *Voyage en Espagne* (1843; *Wanderings in Spain*, 1853) and a collection of verse, *España*, were derived from this experience. The trip tempered Gautier's rather idealistic vision of Spain, but it failed to cure him of his desire to travel. Future travels took him to Italy, the Middle East, North Africa, and, twice, to Russia. Each major trip resulted in a travel book, which, besides serving the purpose of a guidebook, served as a record of Gautier's perceptions and personal development.

During the last twenty years of his life, Gautier was involved with a number of mistresses, most seriously with Ernesta Grisi, the famous contralto, who was mother of his two daughters. Gautier had earlier become infatuated with Ernesta's sister, the celebrated ballerina Carlotta Grisi. His love for Carlotta was unrequited, but they remained lifelong friends; for her, he created the title roles in the ballets *Giselle* and *La Péri* (1843). It was Ernesta, however, who provided the background of domestic peace in which Gautier could work freely. He soon became a Parisian literary lion and received the title of Chevalier de la Légion d'Honneur. He became a favorite of the literary salons, particularly those of Madame Sabatier, of the actress Rachel (Elisa Felix), and of Princess Mathilde. The last named was to prove a most generous friend and benefactor, appointing Gautier as her personal librarian at a time of great financial difficulty for the poet, who was nearly destitute and suffering from the privations of the Franco-Prussian War. Over the years, Gautier developed many binding friendships both within and outside the literary world and became well respected for his affection, concern, even-temperedness, and generosity. Rarely has a literary figure received such tributes for both artistic and personal qualities. The most important artistic endeavor of his last twenty years was the composition of a final collection of poems, *Enamels*

and Cameos. After contending with a variety of illnesses, including several heart attacks, Gautier died in Paris at the age of sixty-one and was buried in the cemetery of Montmartre.

ANALYSIS

The typical twentieth century critical estimation is that Théophile Gautier is a transitional figure in French poetry, although this was not the judgment of his own time, for he was highly, perhaps extravagantly, praised by his contemporaries. Today, Gautier is often viewed as a second-generation Romantic whose earliest work is excessively imitative of the previous generation and whose mature work anticipates the poetic achievement of later, greater poets and of entire literary schools. It is a curiosity that Gautier is better known today as a spokesperson for an aesthetic doctrine, art for art's sake—which he never systematized and only fitfully realized—than for his poetry itself.

That particular aesthetic was years in developing. If Gautier was incapable, even to the end, of setting aside all the Romantic "baggage" of his early years, there always existed in him a detached, ironic, objective observer who bridled at subscribing wholeheartedly to Romantic subjectivity or Romantic political and social involvement. The idea that a work of art should exist in a vacuum, as some kind of cold, clear object without reference to extraneous and irrelevant religious, political, and social meanings, was first clearly stated in Gautier's work in the preface to the novel *Mademoiselle de Maupin*. This concept of art for art's sake was not original with Gautier, who was himself uncomfortably conscious of the vagueness of such grand abstractions as beauty, form, and art: In subsequent pronouncements, he attempted to grapple with these abstractions and to concretize them. For all this, Gautier was still a child of the Romantic era (a fact he would fondly recall until his death), and as a boy of nineteen, he exuberantly entered the literary scene, consciously treading in the giant footsteps of the noted first-generation French Romantic poets: Hugo, Lamartine, Vigny, and Musset.

POÉSIES

Gautier's first book of verse, *Poésies*, is characterized by a precocious formal virtuosity. Stock Romantic themes, such as love and the impermanence of life, abound in this first collection, although as early as the second edition of 1833 (which enlarged the scope of *Poésies* from forty to sixty poems), the detached, satiric observer characteristic of Gautier's mature verse can be detected—most notably in the long narrative poem "Albertus: Ou, l'Âme et le péché" ("Albertus: Soul and Sin"), after which the 1833 collection is named. With typical Romantic whimsy and ambiguity, Gautier termed the poem a "theological legend." The work recounts the tale of a witch who, by transforming herself into a beautiful woman, lures the titular hero into selling his soul for a single night of pleasure. Upon sealing the bargain, she reverts to her normal state and drags Albertus off to a witches' Sabbath. The discovery of the hero's mangled body in a forest clearing the following morning presumably demonstrates the wages of sin.

Even a brief summary suffices to indicate the customary Romantic fascination with the occult, the macabre, and the grotesque. In this poem, however, Gautier, much in the manner of Goethe and Lord Byron (to whom "Albertus" is unmistakably indebted), casts an ironic glance back on the clichés and excesses of Romanticism, the enthusiastic abandon that often merely gave way to bathos. In spite of the evident enjoyment and skill with which he creates the Romantic milieu (certain passages give early witness to Gautier's undeniable descriptive genius), there is at the same time an ironic undercutting of the emotional atmosphere of Romantic horror. Gautier would refer to "Albertus" and to *The Drama of Death* as examples of his *maladie gothique* (gothic illness). While acknowledging their descriptive verve and the formal and prosodic talent they evidence, a modern reader is likely to view these early works as occasionally enjoyable compendia of motifs and preoccupations of the Romantic era.

THE DRAMA OF DEATH

The Drama of Death (a miscellany of fifty-six poems composed between 1832 and 1838) possesses, as do all Gautier's collections to some extent, no particular thematic unity. Like *Poésies*, *The Drama of Death* displays the poet's mastery of a variety of verse forms; also noteworthy are the early glimpses of Gautier's developing aesthetic, particularly in the poems concerning Michelangelo, Petrarch, Albrecht Dürer, and Ra-

phael, which celebrate the enduring triumphs of art. Other poems, especially the three-part title poem, confirm Gautier's obsession with death. Some of these death poems are somberly eloquent in their struggle to balance the states of being and nonbeing; more often, they demonstrate a morbid fascination with the gruesome physical mutation caused by death or the idea of animate interment, such as "Le Ver et la trépassée" ("The Worm and the Dead Woman"), which is cast as a ghoulish dialogue between a young bride-to-be, mistakenly buried alive, and a worm, her rather unexpected spouse. Indeed, the theme of death pervades Gautier's oeuvre, but in early Gautier works, one might describe it as an obsession, often purely physical, without resolution. The psychology of this obsession was of tremendous consequence for Gautier's aesthetic, ultimately leading him to prefer the enduring to the mutable—to prefer, as he stated, "marble to flesh"— and to value art over life itself.

ESPAÑA

The mature phase of Gautier's career as a poet began with the collection of forty-three miscellaneous poems titled *España*. This collection was viewed as a kind of poetic companion volume to the 1843 travelogue *Wanderings in Spain*: Both convey the traveler-poet's absorption in the topography and the art and culture of the Iberian Peninsula; both relate a search for the ideal (which Spain had always represented to Gautier) tempered by experience. Gautier's descriptive genius, the immense technical vocabulary characteristic of his entire canon, more consistently comes to the fore in this collection than in any of its predecessors.

The poem "In deserto" (in the desert) subtly exemplifies Gautier's growing mastery of his art while revealing the contradictions that often distinguish his poetic practice from his poetic theory. Through a rapid accumulation of images, Gautier paints a vivid portrayal of the stark central wilderness of Spain. Each subsequent image is calculated to reinforce the effect of aridity and desolation. In the first ten lines, there is a topographical description of a wasteland of rocky mountains and stretches of desert, rendered in a technical vocabulary capable of fine distinction: "Les monts aux flancs zébrés de tuf, d'ocre et de marne/ . . . le grès plein de micas papillotant aux yeux/ . . . L'ardente solfatare avec la pierre-ponce" ("The mountainsides striped like the zebra in tuff, ochre and marl/ . . . Sandstone replete with mica sparkling to the eye/ . . . The glowing volcanic vent with its pumice stone").

The sun rises to a noonday glare over a world incongenial to the gentle, fragile forms of life:

> Là, point de marguerite au coeur étoilé d'or
> Point de muguet prodigue égrenant son trésor;
> Là, point de violette ignorée et charmante,
> Dans l'ombre se cachant comme une pâle amante

> (There, no daisy with heart of golden stars
> No lavish lily of the valley stringing out its pearls,
> There, no charming and unnoticed violet
> Hiding in the shadows like some pale lover.)

In this landscape, only the smooth-skinned viper and the scaly lizard are at home. In a final image, a solitary eagle is seen atop a mountain peak, silhouetted against the raw and riotous colors of sunset. The effect of the whole is of a photograph focused to the sharpest clarity, and if this were the sum of Gautier's intention, the poem would be an unqualified success. Instead, he chooses to complicate the effect by the inclusion of a single metaphor. It seems as if Gautier were uncomfortable with the sharp, objective lines of the photographic image, and a subjective note is introduced when, suddenly, a narrator appears to remark that the rocks, boulders, and sandy expanses "are less arid and dead to vegetation/ Than my rocklike heart to all feeling." The reader recognizes the comparison immediately as a rather overworked, sentimental image pieced together from conventional Romantic vocabulary.

In the midst of a hard-edged descriptive "composition of place," this subjective note is a solitary leftover of what John Ruskin would term the "pathetic fallacy," in which the external world appears as a projection of the poet's inner reality. Is the unusual and stark position of the image so early in the poem (one would conventionally expect it in the conclusion) a coup of perception or a miscalculation? Does it, perhaps, signal some realization on the poet's part of a certain "inhumanness" in an aesthetic that increasingly stresses surface and gesture over the subjectivity of inner meaning? To a modern reader, this "rocklike heart" probably seems gratuitous, and the poem as a whole discloses the

Gautier whom critic Wallace Fowlie calls a "prisoner of appearances," restricted in his role as "spectator of the visible world of objects, landscapes, and animals." That it was perplexing for Gautier to "look within" is a characteristic made more clear in another poem from *España*, "À Zurbarán."

Gautier frequently required the stimulus of some existing artifact for poetic inspiration. He developed for this purpose the concept of the *transpostion d'art*, in which an art object (a painting, a piece of statuary, even a building) could be created anew in words, recomposed, as it were, by the poet. Some of Gautier's finest achievements are in this genre. "À Zurbarán," for example, is a powerful evocation, not of a single canvas by the sixteenth century Spanish master, but of that superascetic religiosity that thrived in the age of the Inquisition and that imbues so much of Francisco de Zurbarán's work. Thus, Gautier singles out Zurbarán's monks and penetrates to the very essence of their spirituality, formed by the harsh discipline of fasting, hair shirts, and flagellation. The poet is dumbstruck by the display:

> Croyez-vous donc que Dieu s'amuse à voir souffrir
> Et que ce meurtre lent, cette froide agonie
> Fassent pour vous le ciel plus facile à s'ouvrir?

> (Do you then believe that God is amused by suffering,
> And that this prolonged death, this gelid agony
> Will make the gates of heaven more easy to open?)

Along with the poet's sense of revulsion, however, is a recognition of the strange, unearthly strength in the physical presence of these ascetics: "Pourtant quelle énergie et quelle force d'âme/ Ils avaient, ces chartreux, sous leur pâle linceul" ("All the same, what energy, what spiritual power/ They had, those brothers, beneath their colorless shrouds").

The mere reproduction or evocation, even recomposition, of the Zurbarán canvases is not, however, Gautier's principal intent. The subject of the poem is, rather, the inability of the narrator to reconcile two extremes of emotion: revulsion and admiration. How can he balance his "Mais je ne comprends pas ce morne suicide" ("But I do not comprehend this gloomy suicide") with his vision of "Le vertige divin, l'enivrement de foi/ Qui les fait rayonner d'une clarté fiévreuse" ("The divine vertigo, the intoxication of faith/ Which makes them shine with a febrile brightness"). Toward the conclusion of the poem, the real source of this dilemma is revealed when the narrator (with the eyes of a painter) expresses his personal difficulty in conceiving of a totally spiritualized life, in which the physical world is a mere tribulation to be put up with—indeed, a matter of little import:

> Forme, rayon, couleur, rien n'existe pour vous,
> À tout objet réel vous êtes insensibles,
> Car le ciel vous enivre et la croix vous rend fous.
>
> (Form, light, color, nothing exists for you,
> To every physical object you rest insensible,
> For heaven intoxicates you and the cross has made
>   you mad.)

How could the poet who once described himself as "un homme pour qui le monde extérieur existe" ("a man for whom the external world exists") understand such transcendent spirituality, such unworldliness? For Gautier, the solid ground of reality lay exclusively in the perceived object, and he saw in the plastic arts the true medium for achieving permanence and endowing life with value. Literature, too, might approach the plastic, both in subject matter and in treatment. This was to be the goal of his final collection of verse, and the theory of art for art's sake was to be its foundation.

ENAMELS AND CAMEOS

Gautier's poetic practice was not always aligned, however, with his theoretical views, as is clear from the contents of *Enamels and Cameos*—nor, for that matter, was his poetic theory consistently formulated. All the same, as the critic P. E. Tennant has pointed out, Gautier was consistent about stating four basic principles: First, beauty is defined by clarity of form (the *forma* of classical aesthetics), and form and idea are inseparable; second, pure art is autonomous, not to be held accountable to social, political, or religious evaluation; third, art is not natural but, rather, artificial—divine of effect, perhaps, but made by man; and, fourth, although a certain irrational state ("inspiration") is functional in the creation of art, pure art is the product of calculation and hard work.

The appearance of *Enamels and Cameos* in 1852 was a turning point in French literature, marking the shift from Romantic lyricism to a more aesthetic, objective manner in which art would exist in a world of its own, apart from the mundane personal or social concerns of everyday life. Gautier labored over and corrected the contents of the collection for the last twenty years of his life, eventually enlarging its scope from the eighteen poems of the first edition to the forty-seven poems of the final edition of 1872. Once again, there is no rigorous thematic unity or structure (Richard Grant, in his study *Théophile Gautier*, makes a case for a loose thematic structure), nor is the disposition of the individual pieces of particular significance—with the exception of "L'Art" ("Art"), which Gautier specified as the final poem. As the title of the collection suggests, and as Gautier himself stated, the goal was "to treat small subjects in a restricted manner."

All but four of the poems are in octosyllabic quatrains, for Gautier had come to favor the more intimate eight-syllable line to the rhetorical twelve-foot Alexandrine. The almost exclusive repetition of a single stanzaic form does not preclude a surprising variety of subject matter—on the contrary, it emphasizes a richness of rhyme and a certain structural solidity.

Gautier does not wholly abandon the big Romantic themes; rather, he treats them in miniature. For example, a number of poems in the collection are openly personal in the Romantic manner: "Le Château du souvenir" ("The Castle of Remembrance") is clearly autobiographical, and several other poems celebrate Gautier's affairs with various mistresses. However, though Gautier avails himself of the confessional mode introduced by the Romantics, his "personal" poems are in fact curiously impersonal, conveying little sense of the familiar or intimate; in them, life is preserved in cameo.

Gautier's two best-known poems are included in *Enamels and Cameos*: "Symphonie en blanc majeur" ("Symphony in White Major") and "Art." The latter is an openly didactic piece and a clear poetic statement of Gautier's concept of literature as plastic art, its final stanza making this exhortation to his fellow poets: "Carve, burnish, build thy theme,—/ But fix thy wavering dream/ In the stern rock supreme."

"Symphony in White Major" is a tour de force of

thematic variation, and a comparison with "In deserto," from the collection *España*, a poem that shares the same fundamental technical procedure, reveals the measure of Gautier's progress as an artist. Like "In deserto," "Symphony in White Major" is an evocation of a landscape, but the landscape evoked is that of a woman's body. That the woman of the poem existed in real life (she was the striking beauty Marie Kalergis, a student of Frédéric Chopin and a friend of Franz Liszt) is of little consequence. Gautier's aim is not a photographic image in the manner of "In deserto" but the re-creation, for the reader, of the associations and sensations produced within the artist by the sight of the woman.

There is clearly something not entirely human about such perfect beauty, for the first image is of a *femme-cygne* (swan woman) "from the Rhine's escarpments high." What follows is not so much a direct description of the woman's body as an enumeration of images, similes, and metaphors that relate the unique essence of her beauty: its pure, glacial whiteness. Much in the technique of the "transposition d'art," Gautier has analyzed the woman's beauty in order to retrieve its essential components, reconstructing not flesh and blood, but rather an effect:

> Of the marble still and cold,
> Wherein the great gods dwell?
> Of creamy opal gems that hold
> Faint fifes of mystic spell?
> Or the organ's ivory keys?
> Her wingèd fingers oft
> Like butterflies flit over these,
> With kisses pending soft.

It is a beauty that calls forth worship: "What host, what taper, did bestow/ The white of her matchless skin?" The woman's beauty is, in some sense, an abstraction of beauty itself. The heroine is barely present; the greater part of the poem avoids specific reference. Certainly, the final stanza refers directly back to the source of the artist's fantasy. Even here, however, personal experience is transformed and the passion of love expressed only indirectly. How much more satisfying is this ambiguity than the blunt, awkward "rocklike heart" of "In deserto":

> What magic of what far name
> Shall this pale soul ignite?
> Ah! who shall flush with rose's flame
> This cold, implacable white?

The technical and conceptual advances evident in "Symphony in White Major" can be found throughout *Enamels and Cameos*. There are inconsistencies with Gautier's aesthetic ideal of the cool, clear, nonsubjective work of art (his Parnassian successors, Leconte de Lisle and Heredia, would more consistently realize the goal of literature as a plastic art), but few readers have denied the integrity of the craftsman who labored over these poems. The poems may not affect the reader in his or her emotional being, but they please the intellect with their fluctuating colors, their wealth of rhyme, and their perfection of form.

OTHER MAJOR WORKS

LONG FICTION: *Mademoiselle de Maupin*, 1835-1836 (2 volumes; *Mademoiselle de Maupin: A Romance of Love and Passion*, 1887); *Fortunio*, 1838 (novella; English translation, 1915); *Le Roman de la momie*, 1856 (*Romance of the Mummy*, 1863); *Le Capitaine Fracasse*, 1863 (*Captain Fracasse*, 1880); *Spirite: Nouvelle fantastique*, 1866 (novella; *Spirite*, 1877).

SHORT FICTION: *Les Jeunes-France: Romans goguenards*, 1833; "Omphale," 1835 (English translation, 1902); "La Morte amoureuse," 1836 ("The Beautiful Vampire," 1926); "Une Nuit de Cléopatre," 1838 ("One of Cleopatra's Nights," 1888); "Le Roi Candaule," 1844 ("King Candaules," 1893); *Nouvelles*, 1845; *Un Trio de romans*, 1852; *Avatar*, 1857 (English translation, 1900); *Jettatura*, 1857 (English translation, 1888); *Romans et contes*, 1863.

PLAYS: *Une Larme de diable*, pb. 1839; *Giselle: Ou, Les Wilis*, pr. 1841 (ballet scenario; *Giselle: Or, The Wilis*, 1970); *La Péri*, pr. 1843 (ballet scenario); *Le Tricorne enchanté*, pr. 1845; *La Fausse Conversion*, pr. 1846; *Pierrot posthume*, pr. 1847; *Pâquerette*, pr. 1851 (ballet scenario); *Gemma*, pr. 1854 (ballet scenario); *Théâtre de poche*, pb. 1855; *Sacountala*, pr. 1858 (ballet scenario); *Yanko le bandit*, pr. 1858 (ballet scenario).

NONFICTION: *Voyage en Espagne*, 1843 (*Wander-*

ings in Spain, 1853); *Les Grotesques*, 1844 (2 volumes; *The Grotesques*, 1900); *Salon de 1847*, 1847; *Caprices et zigzags*, 1852; *Italia*, 1852 (*Travels in Italy*, 1900); *Constantinople*, 1853 (*Constantinople of To-Day*, 1854); *Les Beaux-Arts en Europe, 1855*, 1855-1856 (2 volumes); *L'Art moderne*, 1856; *Honoré de Balzac: Sa Vie et ses œuvres*, 1858; *Histoire de l'art dramatique en France depuis vingt-cinq ans*, 1858-1859 (6 volumes); *Abécédaire du Salon de 1861*, 1861; *Trésors d'art de la Russie ancienne et moderne*, 1861; *Loin de Paris*, 1865; *Quand on voyage*, 1865; *Voyage en Russie*, 1867 (*A Winter in Russia*, 1874); *Ménagerie intime*, 1869 (*My Household of Pets*, 1882); *Tableaux de siège*, 1871 (*Paris Besieged*, 1900); *Histoire du Romanticism*, 1874 (*History of Romanticism*, 1900); *Portraits contemporains*, 1874 (*Portraits of the Day*, 1900); *Portraits et souvenirs littéraires*, 1875; *L'Orient*, 1877; *Fusains et eaux-fortes*, 1880; *Tableaux à la plume*, 1880; *Les Vacances du lundi*, 1881; *Guide de l'amateur au Musée du Louvre*, 1882 (*The Louvre*, 1900); *Souvenirs de théâtre, d'art, et de critique*, 1883; *Victor Hugo*, 1902; *La Musique*, 1911; *Critique artistique et littéraire*, 1929; *Les Maîtres du théâtre français de Rotrou à Dumas fils*, 1929; *Souvenirs romantiques*, 1929.

MISCELLANEOUS: *The Works of Théophile Gautier*, 1900-1903 (24 volumes).

BIBLIOGRAPHY

Gosselin Schick, Constance. *Seductive Resistance: The Poetry of Théophile Gautier*. Atlanta: Rodopi, 1994. Schick's exhaustive study begins with an analysis of the intertextual repetition of Gautier's poetry, the citations, imitations and transpositions that make evident the poetry's displacement of the significant and the personal into aesthetic simulacra. The study covers each of Gautier's five major collections and deals with the contextuality, the fetishism, and the eroticism revealed in a miscellany of poems.

_____. "Théophile Gautier's Poetry as 'Coquetterie posthume.'" *Nineteenth-Century French Studies* 20, nos. 1/2 (1992): 74-84. Insightful study of the treatment of death in Gautier's late poetry. Describes the maturity that was generally lacking in his early poetry.

Grant, Richard B. *Théophile Gautier*. Boston: Twayne, 1975. Albeit somewhat dated, this book still remains one of the best introductions in English to the writings of Gautier. It includes an annotated bio-bibliography of primary works in French, English translations, and critical studies in both French and English.

Henry, Freeman. "Gautier/Baudelaire: *Homo Ludens* Versus *Homo Duplex*." *Nineteenth-Century French Studies* 25, nos. 1/2 (1996/1997). Baudelaire dedicated his 1857 book of poetry *Flowers of Evil* to Gautier. This essay examines how both poets created complex poems that permit several levels of interpretation.

Kearns, James. *Théophile Gautier, Orator to the Artists: Art Journalism in the Second Republic*. London: Legenda, 2007. Examines Gautier's role as an art journalist and critic.

Koestler, Kathleen. *Théophile Gautier's "España."* Birmingham, Ala.: Summa, 2002. Provides critical analysis of *España* that touches on the poet's doubts about the efficacy of language.

Majewski, Henry F. "Painting into Text: Theophile Gautier's Artistic Screen." *Romance Quarterly* 47, no. 2 (Spring, 2000): 84-102. Examines one important aspect of the complex intertextual signs informing Gautier's poetry. He proposes to study the function of painting in Gautier's poetry as a kind of artistic screen.

Theodore Baroody

STEFAN GEORGE

Born: Büdesheim, Germany; July 12, 1868
Died: Minusio, Switzerland; December 4, 1933

PRINCIPAL POETRY
Hymnen, 1890
Pilgerfahrten, 1891 (*Pilgrimages*, 1949)
Algabal, 1892 (English translation, 1949)
Die Bücher der Hirten-und Preisgedichte, der Sagen und Sänge und der hängenden Gärten,

1895 (*The Books of Eclogues and Eulogies, of Legends and Lays, and of the Hanging Gardens*, 1949)

Das Jahr der Seele, 1897 (*The Year of the Soul*, 1949)

Der Teppich des Lebens und die Lieder von Traum und Tod, mit einem Vorspiel, 1899 (*Prelude, The Tapestry of Life, The Songs of Dream and Death*, 1949)

Die Fibel, 1901 (*The Primer*, 1949)

Der siebente Ring, 1907 (*The Seventh Ring*, 1949)

Der Stern des Bundes, 1914 (*The Star of the Covenant*, 1949)

Das neue Reich, 1928 (*The Kingdom Come*, 1949)

The Works of Stefan George, 1949 (includes the English translations of all titles listed above)

OTHER LITERARY FORMS

Of the books written by Stefan George (gay-AWR-guh), only *Tage und Taten* (1903; *Days and Deeds*, 1951) does not contain any poetry. The volume is a collection of miscellaneous small prose: sketches, letters, observations, aphorisms, and panegyrics. It was expanded to include the introductory essay from *Maximin, ein Gedenkbuch* (1906; memorial book for Maximin) for the eighteen-volume edition of George's complete works, *Gesamt-Ausgabe*, published between 1927 and 1934. In addition to his original works, George published five volumes of translations and adaptations: *Baudelaire, Die Blumen des Bösen* (1901; of Charles Baudelaire); *Zeitgenössische Dichter* (1905; of contemporary poets); *Shakespeare, Sonnette* (1909; of William Shakespeare) and *Dante, Die göttliche Komödie, Übertragungen* (1909; of Dante). *Zeitgenössische Dichter* contains George's translations of poetry by Algernon Charles Swinburne, Jens Peter Jacobsen, Albert Verwey, Paul Verlaine, Stéphane Mallarmé, Arthur Rimbaud, and others. Editions of George's correspondence with Hugo von Hofmannsthal and Friedrich Gundolf were published in 1938 and 1962, respectively.

ACHIEVEMENTS

Most of Stefan George's works were consciously addressed to a carefully selected and limited reader-ship, and until 1898, his lyric cycles were published only in private, limited editions. Poems that appeared in early issues of *Blätter für die Kunst* (leaves for art) were initially ignored in Germany because of the journal's limited circulation, the general obscurity of its contributors, and the poets' lack of connections with accepted literary circles. However, George's early poems and translations were received very favorably by poets and critics in France and Belgium. In 1898, the first public edition of *The Year of the Soul*, still his most popular cycle of poems, brought George the beginnings of broader recognition. Subsequent collections won him increasing acclaim for his originality and artistic virtuosity, until in 1927, he became the first, if reluctant, recipient of the Frankfurt/Main Goethe Prize. By 1928, when his collected works appeared, George was recognized internationally as the most gifted of the German Symbolist poets and the most influential renewer of the German language since Friedrich Nietzsche.

George's important contributions to modern German poetry resulted from his efforts to revitalize and elevate decaying artistic standards. His efforts in cultivating a new literary language took into account contemporary literary influences from other national literatures. While pursuing his goals, he actively encouraged other German poets, including Hofmannsthal, Leopold von Andrian, and Karl Wolfskehl, to strive for a new idealism focused on truth, originality, and self-examination, rejecting the identification of poetry with the personality of the poet and his experiences that had long characterized the nineteenth century imitators of Johann Wolfgang von Goethe.

In 1933, when the Nazis endeavored to distort and exploit his artistic ideals, George refused their offers of money and honor, including the presidency of the German Academy of Poets. Nevertheless, after his death, misinterpretation of his ideas and attitudes regarding artistic and intellectual elitism established a link with Nazi ideology that reduced his literary stature and for many years deprived him of his rightful place in German literary history. Above all else, George was a poet of uncompromising artistic integrity, whose attempts to give German poetry a new direction of humanism and idealism were prompted by profoundly moral and ethical motives.

BIOGRAPHY

Stefan Anton George was born in Büdesheim near Bingen in the Rhine district of Germany. His ancestors were farmers, millers, and merchants. When George was five years old, his father, a wine dealer, moved the family to Bingen. Bingen had a lasting impact on the poet's imagination, and its landscapes informed much of his early poetry. In 1882, George began his secondary education in Darmstadt. He received broad humanistic training and excelled in French. While in school, he taught himself Norwegian and Italian and began translating works by Henrik Ibsen, Petrarch, and Torquato Tasso. When he was eighteen, he began writing poetry and published some of his earliest lyrics under the pseudonym Edmund Delorme in the journal *Rosen und Disteln* that he had founded in 1887.

Upon leaving school in 1888, George began the travels that later characterized his lifestyle. He went first to London, where he became acquainted with the writings of Dante Gabriel Rossetti, Swinburne, and Ernest Dowson, whose poems he later translated and published in German. In Paris, in 1889, he met the French poet Albert Saint-Paul, who introduced him into the circle of Symbolist poets surrounding Mallarmé. In this group of congenial literary artists, which included Verlaine, Francis Vielé-Griffen, the Belgian Albert Mockel, and the Polish poet Wacław Rolicz-Lieder, George found needed personal acceptance and friendship as well as important poetic models. Verlaine and Mallarmé became his acknowledged masters and provided him with a sense of his own poetic calling.

After returning to Germany, George studied Romance literature for three semesters in Berlin. During this time, he experimented with language and even developed a personal Lingua Romana that combined Spanish and Latin words with German syntactical forms. In 1890, he published his first book of poems, *Odes*, in a private edition. Two years later, with Carl August Klein, he founded *Blätter für die Kunst*, which served as an initial focus for his circle of disciples and remained a major vehicle for his ideas for twenty-seven years.

Other encounters with contemporary writers and artists, with his own disciples, and with other personal friends had decisive formative influence on George's career. In 1891, he began a productive if frequently stormy friendship with Hofmannsthal, whom he viewed as his only kindred spirit among modern German poets. When Hofmannsthal refused to commit himself exclusively to George's literary ideas, their association broke off in 1906. George's only significant relationship with a woman, a friendship with Ida Coblenz (later the wife of Richard Dehmel), began in 1892 and influenced many of the poems in *The Year of the Soul*, which he originally intended to dedicate to her. After their association ended in disappointment for George, he limited his emotional involvement to young male disciples, among whom Gundolf and Maximilian Kronberger had profound impact on his mature poetry. Although George was gay, his relations with his young disciples may have been platonic. Affection for Gundolf moved George to direct his creative attention toward molding German youth, while Kronberger, a beautiful adolescent who died of meningitis in 1904, provided him with a model for the divinely pure power of youth as an absolute force of life.

Stefan George (Hulton Archive/Getty Images)

By 1920, most of George's poetic works had been completed. He spent his remaining years actively guiding his youngest disciples, working more as a master teacher than as a poet. When his health finally failed, he moved to Minusio near Locarno, Switzerland, where he died on December 4, 1933.

ANALYSIS

In the preface to the first issue of *Blätter für die Kunst*, Stefan George defined artistic goals for the journal that gave direction to his own poetry for the rest of his career. With its high literary standards, its personally selected group of contributors, and its carefully formulated program, *Blätter für die Kunst* was intended to be a force in the creation of a new German poetry. Its express purpose, specifically reflecting George's perception of his own poetic calling, was to foster a newly refined and spiritual form of literature based on a rejuvenation of classical ideals and a revival of pure literary language. Poetry thus engendered was to be a manifestation of a new way of feeling, furthering the quest for permanent values while rejecting any idea of literature as simple diversion, political instrument, or vehicle for naturalistic social criticism. George's ultimate goal was to provide artistic leadership for a generation that would build a new humanistic society embodying Platonic ideals of goodness, truth, and beauty. Everything that George wrote was directed toward the accomplishment of these purposes.

Intimate association with the French Symbolists in Paris was the formative experience of George's career. It provided him with models for his approach and technique, ideas concerning the poet's role in life, and a starting point for the lifelong exploration of his own poetic nature and its delineation in his works. From Baudelaire, Mallarmé, and Verlaine, he learned to view poets as mediators between phenomena and literary art who describe their perceptions using symbolism that is understood completely only by the poets themselves. Through their symbolic creations, the poet thus isolate themselves in a world to which their own spiritual identity provides the key, a key that the reader must seek in the poem. In this regard, it is important to understand that George completely rejected the idea of identity between the poetic and the personal self. The progressive revelations in his lyrics of the poet's role in life are therefore idealizations rather than reflections of experience.

A clearly defined process of strengthening, refinement, and crystallization of the poet's role emerges in the cycles that document George's development. His *Odes*, which belong within the frame of traditional idealism, examine such themes as the tension between reason and feeling, change as a basic force in life, and unhappy love and death; therein is revealed a personal struggle with self-examination and doubt. In *Algabal*, however, there is a new sense of personal validity; the title figure symbolizes the exclusive artist who creates a private realm in isolation from nature. A further objectification of poetic self appears in the prologue to *The Tapestry of Life*, in the figure of an angel. This alter ego of the poet appears not as a heavenly messenger but as a representative of life, announcing the colorful fabric of the artistic yet puzzling order of existence. George's attempts to refine and perfect the revelation of his poetic identity culminate in the Maximin poems of *The Seventh Ring* and *The Star of the Covenant*, in which Maximin becomes the ultimate symbol for the desired perfect fusion of body and spirit in self-awareness.

Central to George's view of the social role of the poet was the idea that the poet enjoys the special position of "master" within a circle of devoted disciples. This principle, which he saw modeled in the salon of Mallarmé, had significant impact on his poetry and the conduct of his personal life. The relationship of the poet to his disciples is reflected in poems dedicated to close friends and associates in *The Books of Eclogues and Eulogies, of Legends and Lays, and of the Hanging Gardens* and other cycles. It is also evident in the consistent emergence of the symbolic poet as a teacher figure. This casting of the poet in the role of educator is readily visible in poems from *The Year of the Soul* and in the "Zeitgedichte" ("Time Poems") section of *The Seventh Ring*, in which the poet-teacher gives specific directions to his contemporaries, suggesting appropriate models for them to emulate. Developed to its ultimate in *The Kingdom Come*, the poet's role as teacher becomes that of a prophet who judges the age and sounds a warning.

From the standpoint of technique and approach, George considered the revitalization, refinement, and purification of literary language to be the most important aspect of his creative task. He protested against the debasement of language, advocating a revival of pure rhyme and meter with precise arrangement of vowels and consonants to achieve harmony in a distinctly musical poetic form. Creation of language became a basic principle of his writing. He followed the pattern of Mallarmé and rejected everyday words. Stressing the importance of sound and internal melody in his poems, he formed new, musically resonant words and imbued his verses with rich vowels, assonances, alliteration, and double rhymes. George's perception of the spoken and the written word as embodiments of the reality of the world extended even to a regard for the importance of the visual impression created by printed forms. To offer language that was unusual in this respect, he developed a special typeface and modified traditional orthography and punctuation for his publications. George undertook all these measures because he believed that language alone can open hidden levels of mind, soul, and meaning.

While progressively modifying French Symbolist and other external influences to suit his own purposes, George succeeded at least partially in creating the new German poetry toward which he was striving. Patterning his poems after Baudelaire's perception of the symbolic structure of existence, he created works that reflected his personal attitudes of austerity and self-denial, while celebrating the ethical supremacy of the spirit over material existence. The poetic cycle became his characteristic form, and each of his collections exhibits the basic unity that it demands. In addition to genuine originality in the coining of words and in imagery, George's poems typically feature colorful calmness of motion, sensually intense metaphors and symbols, and remarkable simplicity. The unaffected wording and ordering of lines in *The Year of the Soul*, for example, anticipate certain tendencies in Surrealism, while the smoothly flowing verses of the "Gezeiten" ("Tides") section of *The Seventh Ring* and the utter clarity and lack of ambiguity in the poems of *The Star of the Covenant* reflect the complete creative control of words that George consistently demonstrated in his po-

etry. It is perhaps in that rare mastery of personal poetic language that George made his greatest contribution to German literature.

Even George's earliest, less successful cycles reflect searching attempts to define his poetic self. From the exploratory *Odes*, which focus on artistic experiences and on the mission and position of the artists in the world, George moved in *Pilgrimages* toward a more distinctly personal approach to self-examination, styling himself a wanderer in a manner somewhat akin to Goethe's poetic perception of himself. Not until *Algabal*, however, did he present a clearly cohesive symbolic representation of his own special nature.

ALGABAL

As George's first highly characteristic work, *Algabal* offers vivid examples of the new kind of poetic creation for which the poet pleaded in the first issue of *Blätter für die Kunst*. The poems of *Algabal* are replete with samples of the musical language that became such a critical part of George's works as a whole. In uniquely worded verses characterized by sonorous repetition of melodic vowel combinations, the poet transforms carefully chosen elements of reality into symbols for his internal world. In so doing, he gives them a different kind of existence, creating new levels of artistic revelation. He develops the central complex of symbols from the life of Elagabalus, the youthful Roman emperor and priest of Baal whose promotion of physically beautiful favorites and open homosexual orgies brought about his assassination. Transforming his eccentric model into Algabal, the lonely king of a personally created subterranean realm, George creates a haunting symbol for his poetic identity.

The first section of the cycle, "Im Unterreich" ("In the Subterranean Kingdom"), focuses on Algabal's domain as a major symbol for a new level of creative feeling. In an overwhelming intensity of visual impression, the components of external nature are transformed into precious gems that flash in bright colors, illuminating from within an edifice to which the light of day does not penetrate. Similarly, the natural smells of outside reality are replaced by peculiar, musty fragrances of amber, incense, lemon, and almond oil that infuse the artificial world. The most profound symbols of "In the Subterranean Kingdom" are the lifeless birds and plants of

Algabal's garden. Amid stems and branches made of carbon, the black flower appears as a symbol for art, a conscious contrast to Novalis's blue flower of romantic longing.

In the other sections of *Algabal*, "Tage" ("Days"), "Die Andenken" ("The Memories"), and "Vogelschau" ("View of Birds"), George tightens the symbolic focus to elucidate the unique personality of the ruler of the underground palace and garden. Verses that stress the self-examination aspect of the creative process reveal George's perception of himself as a poet whose nature compels him to return alone to an ancient age in which other values predominate. New symbols are formed to treat traditional literary themes. Juxtaposed to the black flower of artificial life, for example, are images of death in vivid reds and greens. "View of Birds," the final poem of the cycle, underscores the idea that it is only through the poet's actively formative power of perception that life is given to the artistically constructed poetic world.

THE YEAR OF THE SOUL

Among all George's collections of poetry, the most popular yet least typical is the key cycle of his middle period, *The Year of the Soul*. Two factors in particular distinguish the poems of this group from his other major works. *The Year of the Soul* is George's only book that centers on love between man and woman. It is an important document of his relationship with Coblenz. His poetic treatment of that ultimately unhappy emotional involvement contrasts markedly with the harmoniously warm and human love poems that he wrote for young men in *The Seventh Ring* and other later cycles. *The Year of the Soul* also differs from other George volumes in style and technique. The decorative stylization of diction and the boldness of ornamentation in nature imagery suggest a connection with the intentions and motifs of *Jugendstil*, whereas the pronounced simplicity of form that characterizes most of George's poetry reflects his tacit rejection of the *Jugendstil* tendency in art.

The poems of *The Year of the Soul* frame exploration of the problems of unfulfilled love in carefully controlled images of external reality. Modifying the traditional German nature poem, George symbolizes nature by a cultivated park that is organized and created by the gardener/poet. The park landscapes that he evokes offer individual natural phenomena as symbols for private experience and moods of the soul.

The first and most important of the book's three major sections presents the essence of the volume in concentrated form. It is divided into three subcycles, "Nach der Lese" ("After the Harvest"), "Waller im Schnee" ("Wanderer in the Snow"), and "Sieg des Sommers" ("Triumph of Summer"), each of which constitutes a rounded unit in its own right. Beginning with autumn, the poet employs the rhythm of the seasons to illuminate changing moods—hope, suffering, reflection, and mourning in an ever-renewing confrontation with the self. Special emphasis on color accents the varying moods evoked by the nature images, intensifying the dialogue between "I" and "you," newly perceived Faustian aspects of the poet's own soul which appear in the guise of the poet and a fictitious female object of his love. The motifs of "Wanderer in the Snow" augment the tension between the poet and the accompanying "you" as the wanderer traverses a winter of bitterness, austerity, and mourning. Sheer hopelessness radiates from the lines of the seventh poem, in which the poet declares that despite his faithful attention and patience, his love relationship will never bring him so much as a warm greeting. In "Triumph of Summer," a transition from the harsh emptiness of winter imagery to the anticipated warmth of summer promises a new approach to spiritual fulfillment. The ten poems of this segment dwell on the idea of joint creation of a "sun kingdom" with the "you" of the previous sections. The "sun kingdom," a symbol for the ideal realm for which George longed throughout his career, remains, however, a transitory vision as summer's end becomes a symbol for final parting.

The poems of the two other major parts of *The Year of the Soul*, "Überschriften und Widmungen" ("Titles and Dedications") and "Traurige Tänze" ("Sad Dances"), focus more precisely and personally on problems and themes introduced in the preceding section. In verses dedicated to friends, the poet again assumes the role of teacher, instructing his disciples concerning the inner spiritual encounter with love. Lyrics written specifically for Coblenz give additional substance to the symbolic portrayal of George's painful love affair, while the beautifully songlike stanzas of "Sad Dances" elevate the volume as a whole to a single powerful symbol for his private experience of *Weltschmerz*.

THE SEVENTH RING

In 1907, George published the richest, most ambitious, and most complex collection of his career. *The Seventh Ring* represents the high point and culmination of his poetic development. It is especially fascinating for its presentation of a significant spectrum of George's stylistic possibilities, themes, and poetic perceptions, together with its clear revelation of his ultimate goals. In addition to the ever-present poems dedicated to members of his circle, the cycle contains the most important elements of the new tendencies that appeared in George's poetry after 1900. To be sure, the two later volumes, *The Star of the Covenant* and *The Kindgom Come*, are important for what they reveal of the final perfecting of ideas that are central to *The Seventh Ring*. Nevertheless, the sometimes sterile rigidity and flatness of *The Star of the Covenant* and the lack of uniformity in *The Kingdom Come* (which encompasses all of George's lyric creations written after 1913) render those two books anticlimactic.

Although *The Seventh Ring* is somewhat uneven in form, a fresh poetic emphasis on principles of mathematical order is evident in the highly visible relationships between special numbers, internal symbolism, and the formal organization of the work. There are obvious connections among the title, the division of the poems into seven groupings, the seven biblical creative periods, and the year of publication, 1907. In addition, the number of items in each subcycle is a multiple of seven, while the constitution of individual poems and their integration into units are governed by specific numerical factors. Especially important is the placement of the "Maximin" section. Positioned fourth in conscious reference to the year of the death of Maximilian Kronberger, the verses that he inspired form the thematic as well as the structural nucleus of the symmetrical collection.

Viewed in its entirety, *The Seventh Ring* is George's most comprehensive attempt to define his own position within his age. The "Time Poems" at the beginning permanently establish the poet in the chosen roles of teacher and judge that characterize all his later writings. They attack the follies of the era, providing points of reference and standards against which to measure them as well as models for emulation in building a new, ideal, Hellenistic society. Goethe, Dante, Nietzsche, and Leo XIII are among the examples of great human beings whom George glorifies. In "Tides," which contains some of the most impressive love poetry in the German language, George reveals as nowhere else the intensity and inner meaning of his feelings for Gundolf and Robert Boehringer. Through the same lyrics, however, he comes to terms with the fact that those relationships have been replaced in importance by the more transcendent encounter with Maximin.

The so-called Maximin experience is commonly recognized as the key to George's mature poetry. In the "Maximin" section of *The Seventh Ring*, George transforms the life of his young friend into a symbol for the manner in which eternal, divine forces are manifest in the modern world. Deification of Maximin enables him to create a private religion as part of his quest for permanent values in the Hellenic tradition. The god Maximin is the embodiment of a primeval force, a universally present Eros. In lyrical celebrations of Maximin's life and death, George transforms the characteristic dialogues with self of earlier poems into conversations with divinity. In so doing, he elevates himself to the rank of prophet and seer. His prophetic calling then opens the way to new themes of chaos and destruction. While developing these themes, the poet creates the visions of Germany's fall that accompany the further revelation of Maximin's character in the other sections of *The Seventh Ring* and in *The Star of the Covenant* and *The Kingdom Come*.

OTHER MAJOR WORKS

NONFICTION: *Blätter für die Kunst*, 1892-1919 (12 volumes); *Tage und Taten*, 1903 (*Days and Deeds*, 1951); *Maximin, ein Gedenkbuch*, 1906.

TRANSLATIONS: *Baudelaire, Die Blumen des Bösen*, 1901; *Zeitgenössische Dichter*, 1905 (of contemporary poets); *Dante, Die göttliche Komödie, Übertragungen*, 1909; *Shakespeare, Sonnette*, 1909.

MISCELLANEOUS: *Gesamt-Ausgabe*, 1927-1934 (18 volumes; poetry and prose).

BIBLIOGRAPHY

Bennett, Edwin K. *Stefan George*. New Haven, Conn.: Yale University Press, 1954. A succinct critical study of George's works with a brief biographical background. Includes bibliography.

Goldsmith, Ulrich K. *Stefan George*. New York: Columbia University Press, 1970. Biographical essay with bibliographic references.

Metzger, Michael M., and Erika A. Metzger. *Stefan George*. New York: Twayne, 1972. Biography of George includes a bibliography of his works.

Norton, Robert E. *Secret Germany: Stefan George and His Circle*. Ithaca, N.Y.: Cornell University Press, 2002. This biography of George looks at him as a poet, a pedagogue, politician, and prophet. George and his circle were a very powerful political force in Germany, and he was viewed as the prophet and savior of the nation. One section is devoted to his poetry.

Rieckmann, Jens, ed. *A Companion to the Works of Stefan George*. Rochester, N.Y.: Camden House, 2005. Contains essays on George's poetics, his early works, his links to aestheticism, his relation to Friedrich Nietzsche and Nazism, his sexuality, and his literary circle. Also features a list of his works.

Underwood, Von Edward. *A History That Includes the Self: Essays on the Poetry of Stefan George, Hugo von Hofmannsthal, William Carlos Williams, and Wallace Stevens*. New York: Garland, 1988. A very useful monograph on the comparative poetics of the four poets. Bibliographical references, index.

Lowell A. Bangerter

GUIDO GEZELLE

Born: Bruges, Belgium; May 1, 1830
Died: Bruges, Belgium; November 27, 1899

PRINCIPAL POETRY

Dichtoefeningen, 1858
Kerkhofblommen, 1858
XXXIII Kleengedichtjes, 1860
Gedichten, gezangen, en gebeden, 1862
Liederen, eerdichten et reliqua, 1880
Driemaal XXXIII kleengedichtjes, 1881
Tijdkrans, 1893
Rijmsnoer, 1897
Laatste verzen, 1901
Poems/Gedichten, 1971
The Evening and the Rose, 1989 (bilingual edition)

OTHER LITERARY FORMS

Although known primarily as a poet, Guido Gezelle (kuh-ZEHL-uh) also wrote numerous essays on language, literature, art, and Flemish culture. These works were published during his lifetime in such Flemish journals as *Reynaert de vos*, *'t Jaer 30*, *Rond den heerd*, *Loquela*, and *Biekorf*. In addition, he published in 1886 a Flemish translation of Henry Wadsworth Longfellow's *The Song of Hiawatha* (1855) and, in 1897, a Flemish translation of Monsignor Waffelaert's Latin treatise *Meditationes theologiae* (1883). These translations, as well as his poetry and surviving letters, appear in the nine volumes of *Jubileumuitgave van Guido Gezelle's volledige werken* (1930-1939).

ACHIEVEMENTS

Although Guido Gezelle is one of Flanders's greatest poets and holds a prominent place in Netherlandic literature by being one of its leading nineteenth century poets and a significant forerunner of modern Dutch poetry, he won his fame primarily after his death. Some of his former poetry students helped to promote his art.

Especially instrumental in doing so was Hugo Verriest, who followed in Gezelle's footsteps by becoming a teacher and a priest. Verriest brought Gezelle's poetry to the attention of his own brilliant student Albrecht Rodenbach, a leader of a student group interested in preserving Flemish culture. While at the University of Louvain, Rodenbach became acquainted with Pol De Mont, a student-writer who had important connections with an artistic movement in Holland. This group of young artists, who called themselves the Men of the Eighties, was interested in setting new trends by breaking with the literary conventions of the past. They admired Gezelle and made the North (Holland) receptive to his poetry. De Mont was also involved with a group of artists in the South (Flanders), called Van Nu en Straks (of today and tomorrow). One of their goals coincided with that of the Men of the Eighties—that is, they wished to break with their past. Furthermore, they wished to revive Flemish consciousness in general and were, in fact, very successful in so doing. In their journal, *Van nu en straks*, they printed numerous articles on Flemish history, economy, and politics, as well as on Gezelle's poetry, giving it the highest praise.

Because this journal gained subscribers from all over the world, Gezelle's name was circulated far and wide. His poetry was printed not only at home but also abroad, and it became an inspiration to younger poets of note, especially Prosper van Langendonck and Karel van de Woestijne in the North. They picked up Gezelle's play with rhythm and sound, as well as his fresh and artistic use of the Flemish idiom. In a real sense, they not only owed Gezelle a literary debt but also helped to promote his art in their own modern verse.

In his later years, Gezelle was elected founding member of the Royal Flemish Academy (1886), awarded an honorary degree from the University of Louvain (1887), honored with the papal decoration "Pro Ecclesia et Pontifice" (1888), knighted in the Order of Leopold (1889), and appointed to the Society of Dutch Letters in Leiden (1890). However, a higher level of recognition came after his death. Then, sculptors carved his statue, streets received his name, anthologies printed his verse, and translators recast some of his poems in various languages. Thus, Gezelle after his death accomplished what he had set out to do in his youth—to liberate Flanders and to inspire a "school" of writers. These writers, as well as Gezelle, are still read and studied in the twenty-first century.

BIOGRAPHY

Born in Bruges on May 1, 1830, the year the kingdom of Belgium was established, Guido Gezelle was to become an important leader of and spokesperson for the Flemish literary revival. Having inherited his father's literary sensibility and his mother's strong Roman Catholic devotion, Gezelle was destined to become a poet-priest. After he graduated in 1846 from Sint Lodewijkscollege in Bruges, he continued his training in theological studies at the Minor Seminary in

Roulers (1846-1849) and at the Major Seminary in Bruges (1850-1854). He was ordained to the priesthood on June 10, 1854.

In August, 1854, he was appointed to teach sciences and languages at the Minor Seminary in Roulers. Quickly thereafter, in 1857, he was promoted to professor of poetry, a position he held until August, 1859. These two years were marked by unusual creativity. Gezelle formed a eucharistic confraternity with some of his students in an effort to revive medieval devotion to Jesus Christ through adoration of Christ's Sacrament of Love. This confraternity provided both his students and himself with a poetic-mystical atmosphere enabling Gezelle to pursue his poetic goal—namely, to revive a kind of medieval Flemish "school" of poetry in an age when French was more prestigious and Flemish poetry virtually nonexistent. Gezelle was successful in encouraging some of these students to become poets, and during these years, he produced several collections of poetry himself: *Kerkhofblommen* (churchyard flowers), *Dichtoefeningen* (poetic exercises), *XXXIII Kleengedichtjes* (thirty-three small poems), and *Gedichten, gezangen en gebeden* (poems, hymns, and prayers).

Despite these early achievements, Gezelle met with criticism from all sides. His pedagogical approach ran counter to the rigid format of his day. By his unstructured classroom methods, he threatened an educational system that stressed adherence to uniformity of methods and conformity to previously set standards. Moreover, his close ties with students belonging to the confraternity raised eyebrows among those of his religious superiors who considered suspect any friendship between students and clergy. Hence, in 1860, Gezelle was relieved of his teaching assignment in Roulers and sent to Bruges. There, he was appointed director of the New English College and given a teaching assignment at the Anglo-Belgian Seminary. Gezelle's highly ineffective supervision of the college led to its demise within the year, while his teaching methods at the seminary continued to alienate colleagues and superiors alike. In 1865, Gezelle was discharged from all teaching duties and assigned the lesser post of curate at St. Walburgis parish in Bruges.

Gezelle's parochial duties as curate were so time-consuming that they brought his first poetic phase to an abrupt stop. Gezelle did, however, become active as a journalist, encouraged by his bishop, who recognized Gezelle's writing talents. After a period as a regular contributor to *Reynaert de vos*, a humorous political weekly based in Antwerp, he wrote for and then became editor of *'t Jaer 30*, an ultraconservative weekly concerned with local politics, which, under Gezelle's editorship, acquired a strong pro-Catholic and pro-Flemish tone. Finally, in 1865, he started his own journal, *Rond den heerd*, which contained everything from proverbs and jokes to essays on saints' lives, language, and the arts. In time, however, Gezelle's double workload as curate and editor became so exhausting that he began to suffer from increasingly bad health. Also, because he lacked sufficient time to scrutinize articles submitted to *'t Jaer 30*, he allowed into print too many pieces characterized by inflamed political rhetoric and a libelous tone. In addition, he was a poor manager of funds. Embroiled in political and financial problems, he suffered a mental collapse in 1872.

Gezelle was discharged from his parochial and editorial duties in Bruges and sent for recuperation to the quiet town of Courtrai in 1872. There he was assigned less time-consuming work as curate of the Church of Our Lady. Surrounded by friends and admirers of his verse, Gezelle slowly recovered and gradually resumed his poetic work. In 1873, he became a regular contributor to the *Westvlaamsch idioticon* (West Flemish lexicon). Gezelle poured all his energies into this language study in an effort to revive the Flemish idiom, which had suffered from the increasing Frenchification in Flemish life and culture. This language study also spurred on his desire to restructure completely his early poetry collections and to publish them as his complete works in 1877. In addition, in 1880, he produced a collection of somewhat inferior poems, *Liederen, eerdichten et reliqua* (songs, elegies, and relics), and in 1881, he founded the language journal *Loquela*.

As a result of his renewed poetic and language interests, Gezelle in time won acclaim from all sides and received several honors. Moreover, his bishop gradually relieved Gezelle of all pastoral duties to provide him with the time required for private study and writing.

These circumstances became the stimulus for Gezelle's second burst of poetic activity. He reached the peak of his poetic career with the publication of *Tijdkrans* (time cycle) in 1893 and *Rijmsnoer* (string of rhymes) in 1897. In their language, impressionism, intricate cyclical structuring, and pure Flemish diction, these collections are the crowning achievement of his life. After his death on November 27, 1899, a final volume of poems was compiled, *Laatste verzen* (last poems).

Aɴᴀʟʏsɪs

While teaching poetry at the Minor Seminary in Roulers (1857-1859), Guido Gezelle began to pursue his goal of reviving Flemish literature, in particular poetry. He encouraged his students to become poets, and he also produced several volumes of poetry.

Dɪᴄʜᴛᴏᴇꜰᴇɴɪɴɢᴇɴ

With *Dichtoefeningen*, Gezelle made his literary debut. This collection contains the first public announcement of his literary-patriotic goal—to create a medieval Catholic and Flemish poetic program. In "Aanroeping" ("Invocation"), he establishes that its sources of inspiration are to be Christ, Mary, and nature. Its purpose is to render praise through the Flemish idiom, and the poet's role is to convert the sounds and sights supplied by nature into verbal music and painting. In "Principium a Jesu" ("Beginning in Jesus"), Gezelle amplifies his views of inspiration by emphasizing that the poet has a greater responsibility than merely to paint and echo nature's sights and sounds: He also has the ethical obligation to reflect Christ in his lines, thereby to instill Christian praise. To do so, Gezelle believed that the poet himself must first be sanctified through grace so that he might rightfully return nature's gifts to their source. Through the Christian muse, the poet can thus transform his own verbal music into Christian song. Poetry in this sense becomes a concomitant of grace as the poet cooperates with inspirational grace to return his poetic product to its ultimate source, Christ.

The earliest poems in *Dichtoefeningen* are essentially displays of the poet's own virtuosity as he chimes in his lines nature's sounds and vividly depicts nature's sights. Examples are "Boodchap van de vogels" ("Message from the Birds") and "Pachthofschildering"

("Farmyard Sketches"). The later poems turn these poetic exercises into spiritual exercises regarding the lessons residing in nature—lessons that lead the poet into the self and, hence, to a discovery of God. The poem "Het schrijverke" ("The Water Strider") is a meditation on an insect. The poet is puzzled by what the bug writes on the water as it skids along its surface. The bug teaches the lesson that it writes the name of God. The intellectual knowledge the poet gains from the bug's actions provides the basis for the experiential knowledge he acquires in "O 't ruisen van het ranke riet" ("Oh, the Rustling of the Slender Reed"). Here, the poet learns not only to intuit the meaning of the reed's "sad song" as the "sweet song" heard by God but also to hear his own sad pleas echoed in the rueful rustling of the reed. This self-identification with nature leads to further self-discovery in "De waterspegel" ("The Water Speculum"), where the poet sees reflected in creation not only his own image but also that of God, its "wonderous Artist." In "Binst het stille van de nacht" ("In the Quietness of Night"), he recognizes that, unlike the natural phenomena surrounding him, the poet himself assumes a very special place in creation, for he must do more than learn from, identify with, and admire nature and its Creator. The poet must also through his own verbal music transmit the spirit of God. The poem "Aan de leeuwerk in de lucht" ("To the Skylark in the Air") is the poetical and spiritual culmination of *Dichtoefeningen*. The poet no longer is the medium through which nature flows back to its original source, God; here, he transcends nature as his ecstatic poetic flight surpasses that of the lark. Through his ascent, the poet, unlike the lark, can ultimately bathe in God's peace.

GEDICHTEN, GEZANGEN, EN GEBEDEN

Gedichten, gezangen, en gebeden is a bittersweet collection containing poems about the ecstasies of Gezelle's triumphs and the agonies of his sadness experienced primarily during his Roulers years. It is the most personal of his collections, for the first time introducing the themes of sin, guilt, and friendship. In a significant way, this collection presents both the public and private voices of the poet-priest on the various meanings of the cross. A number of these poems celebrate the Eucharist. Some of these follow the tripartite division of

Ignatian meditational exercises, in which the memory prompts the imagination to see, the intellect analyzes what the imagination sees, and the will moves the affections to respond to God.

In "Bezoek aan het Allerheiligste" ("Visiting the Holy of Holies"), for example, as the persona partakes of the Eucharist, he pictures God's presence in Rome, Jerusalem, and Flanders. The imagination sees God descending everywhere, which prompts his intellect to ask why God would leave his angels to dwell here below. The answer, however, lies beyond the persona's grasp and only emphasizes the limitations of human intellect. This in turn leads the persona's will toward adoration, to plead for God's acceptance and to resolve to become more worthy of God's grace. While the persona in this poem is driven to his knees, in another meditation poem on the Eucharist, "Wie zijt gij" ("Who Art Thou"), he is moved to look up at the skies, to trace God in the stars, and to lift himself in songs and joy.

Others of the public poems were commissioned by Gezelle's bishop for the edification of Flemish-speaking people. The most moving of these are the Jesu poems, most notably "Jesu waar't de mens gegeven" ("Jesus, Were It Giv'n to Man"), "Jesu," and "Jesu liefste Jesu mijn" ("Jesu, Dearest Jesu Mine"). Though inspired by Gezelle's own sense of inadequacy, guilt, and shame, these poems are nevertheless public in intent. In them, as J. J. M. Westenbroek points out in *Van het leven naar het boek* (1967), the poet speaks foremost as the public priest, seeking to move others to pray. All of them have a two-part structure, the first part usually describing how sinful humans resist God's grace, the second part depicting Christ as the patient wooer of ungrateful humans. Strongly Christ-centered prayers, they are intended to move humans to reflect on their guilt and sin and therefore to sue for grace. The soul-searching and penitent response these poems elicit belong to the essence of prayer.

The poetical highlights of *Gedichten, gezangen, en gebeden*, according to Westenbroek, are three poems addressed to Gezelle's closest friend, Eugeen van Oye. They trace the various stages of that friendship between 1858 and 1859, when van Oye was wavering about his future vocation and Gezelle fervently tried to retain him for the priesthood. In "Een bonke kersen kind" ("A

Bunch of Cherries, Child"), Gezelle uses the cherry cluster as a symbol in the opening and closing frame of the poem. The cluster of ripened cherries evokes an outburst of sensual joy at the beauties of creation as shared with the friend, but it also serves as a warning that such joys must not serve as selfish delights but should be returned with thanks to their source. The temptation alluded to pertains to giving in to sensual pleasures as ends in themselves. In "Rammentati" ("Remember"), written after van Oye's decision to forego the priesthood, the earlier joy is replaced by the poet's fears and deep concern about the boy's spiritual welfare. The poem is a series of warnings to "remember" that the secular world is filled with much greater temptations than the sensual delights afforded by nature. Though not pressing van Oye to forego his secular ambitions, Gezelle instead seeks to fortify him for his journey into secular life by giving him concerned advice so that he might ultimately reach his heavenly home. In "Ik mis u" ("I Miss Thee"), written after van Oye had left the college, the poet pours out his grief over the boy's absence. A retrospective poem, it recalls various moments when van Oye was still one of his protégés. The poet misses his voice amid the chapel choristers and the poems he used to bring to his room, but most of all at the altar rail when the poet-priest used to feed him with Christ. Whereas "Remember" ended with warnings, this poem ends with uncomfortable questions: whether van Oye will remain steadfast in the faith, and whether Gezelle will ever see him again, even after death.

In the final analysis, nearly all the contents of *Gedichten, gezangen, en gebeden* are focused on the cross, whether expressed as devotion to the Sacrament, the poet's own suffering in taking up Christ's cross, or his priestly care for students. In all instances, they are indeed poems, songs, and prayers.

XXXIII KLEENGEDICHTJES

Toward the end of his Roulers days, Gezelle began to experiment with a new poetic form. The timing was not accidental. When it seemed inevitable that he would be separated from his confraternity, Gezelle could no longer rely on those student-poets allied with the confraternity to form the basis for his literary-patriotic platform. Hence he turned to a new poetic

form that would have meaning in and of itself, rather than by virtue of the specifically Flemish-Catholic cause he wished to promote. Bernard F. Van Vlierden, in *Guido Gezelle tegenover het dichterschap* (1967), points out that by this time Gezelle was steeped in Arabian literature and had discovered some extremely brief poems. Some of them were condensations and crystallizations of rich thought, others no more than an interplay of sheer rhythm, cadence, and sound, splendid examples of *poésie pure*. Gezelle imitated and adapted this concise form and gave it its first expression in *XXXIII Kleengedichtjes*. All these poems are quite brief, some only two lines of assonantal and alliterative chiming, chiseled artifacts of melody and sound, the meaning of which resides in the beauty of language itself. The majority, however, are short prayers. In fact, by the very title he chose for this collection, Gezelle explains that he meant to show the interrelatedness of poetry and prayer. The word *kleengedichtje* means "small poem," while the closely related word *kleingebedje* means "spiritual aspiration." Such brief, intense poems, Gezelle believed, are by their very nature nonverbal responses that arise from the heart, rather than the mind—outbursts that well up from the depths of one's being as it feels attuned to the rhythm and harmony of life itself. The *XXXIII Kleengedichtjes* thus demonstrate that poetry resides in prayer and that prayer resides in poetry.

Along with Gezelle's interest in this new poetic form came his desire to achieve an ideal structural form for the collection as a whole. Although it has no tight internal structure, *XXXIII Kleengedichtjes* is nevertheless a cohesive unit because all its poems are brief and all demonstrate the interrelatedness of poetry and prayer. Furthermore, Gezelle purposely included thirty-three poems, not only because the number equaled the years of Christ's life, but also because it is a perfect number. Gezelle had already shown his fondness for perfect numbers when he had used the triad in the title of the earlier collection *Gedichten, gezangen en gebeden*. (This triad device is repeated later in the title *Liederen, eerdichten et reliqua*.) He had also already incorporated a unit of thirty-three poems in *Gedichten, gezangen en gebeden*. These, in fact, became the model for *XXXIII Kleengedichtjes*.

DRIEMAAL XXXIII KLEENGEDICHTJES

Not until 1881, however, when Gezelle wrote *Driemaal XXXIII kleengedichtjes* (three times thirty-three small poems), did he arrive at the circular pattern that characterizes the structure of the later *Tijdkrans* and *Rijmsnoer*. This expanded edition of *XXXIII Kleengedichtjes* consists of three units of thirty-three poems. Each unit has an internal structure, beginning with the poems on the cross and ending with poems about heaven. What dominates each unit, then, is the cross, whether as the cross of passion or the cross of triumph that opens the way to heaven. In its circularity, each unit resembles a set of Rosary prayers. Interestingly, as Gezelle explained in an article in *Rond den heerd*, the Flemish custom on Rosary Sunday was to pray a special Rosary of thirty-three Hail Marys in memory of Christ's life. In a sense, the *Driemaal XXXIII kleengedichtjes* repeats the circularity of the Rosary three times, to emphasize thereby the perfection of the overall structural pattern itself. The collection ends, appropriately, with the explanation of the number symbolism. In the last poem, "Die drieëndertig jaar" ("Who Three and Thirty Years"), Gezelle dedicates his heart, his hope, and all these poems thirty-three times to Christ.

TIJDKRANS

In many of the *XXXIII Kleengedichtjes*, Gezelle shows his interest in the poetical nature of language itself. This interest was an outgrowth of the philological study he was engaged in at the time and that resulted in his language journal *Loquela* in 1881. Both this philological interest and his growing concern with structural patterning paved the way for his last two, and greatest, collections, *Tijdkrans* and *Rijmsnoer*. In these final works, Gezelle demonstrates with great success the poetic potential of the Flemish language, and he did so in the perfect structural form these collections possess.

Written long after his emotional breakdown, *Tijdkrans* voices entirely new concerns. Here, Gezelle is no longer interested in imitating nature but rather in deciphering what it ultimately means. Whereas in his youth, as in *Dichtoefeningen*, he was drawn to the happy lark, in *Tijdkrans*, he feels much more drawn to the sad nightingale, identifying with its mournful song.

As he wonders if it sings of its own banishment, he is moved to reflect on his own life as a constant grave and to think of this earth as exile from the better world to come. The nightingale is mentioned several times in *Tijdkrans*, and in its song, Gezelle repeatedly hears expressions of his own sadness and chronic discontent. Having suffered from repeated setbacks in his youth, occasioned by somewhat envious colleagues and superiors who considered him a failure as a teacher, college director, and editor, he had gradually came to distrust humankind and to feel trapped by society itself. Hence, in *Tijdkrans* he feels constantly pursued by a vague enemy force he labels the world, and he lashes out at it repeatedly, accusing it of having pestered him too long. One major motif that emerges in *Tijdkrans*, then, is that life is constant strife, and the poet throughout adopts a combative stance to fend off both real and imagined attacks.

Such paranoia resulted in Gezelle's need for protection. Given his gloomy outlook, however, he could hardly turn to humankind for comfort. Hence, in *Tijdkrans*, he often repeats his wish to die and, thus, to escape to eternity for safety and freedom. In these poems, he is increasingly drawn away from the world, seeks solitary communion with nature, and ultimately through contemplation finds peace solely in God. Nature becomes the medium for those contemplative flights, and the best time to commune with it is at night, when the threatening world of humanity is asleep. Not only by night but also by day nature provides comfort in various ways, for it teaches worthwhile lessons that inevitably direct the poet's attention to God. Through nature Gezelle discovers, for example, the protection of God's omnipresence and constancy, for whether he poetically plumbs the depths of the ocean or scales the heights of the firmament, God is always there. Nature also provides the comfort of the Resurrection by its perennial renewal of springtime beauty and summer growth. Furthermore, it also instructs humanity how to live, for nature never does more than what it is appointed to be. As "O wilde en onvervalste pracht" ("Oh, Wild and Unadulterated Splendor") points out, simple flowers neither deceive nor pretend but in their untainted splendor reveal their naked truth, that they are what they appear to be. Humans, by contrast, deceive, disguise, and dissemble. In its constancy of praise, beauty, and purpose, then, nature becomes the poet's faithful protector and friend.

The greatest protector and friend in *Tijdkrans*, however, is eternity itself. It alone offers the poet ultimate permanence and, hence, protection from the ravages of time. While Gezelle longed for this permanence outside time, he also strove for it while alive and still part of time. This he did through the structural pattern he adopted for *Tijdkrans*. As its title suggests, *Tijdkrans* is concerned with time. In it, Gezelle not only writes about time, but he also directs himself against time by imposing on the collection a structural pattern that surpasses time. Within the boundaries of its three separate parts—"Dagkrans" (day cycle), "Jaarkrans" (year cycle), and "Eeuwkrans" (eternity cycle)—Gezelle was able to lock into permanent place all those poems concerned with time. The year described in "Jaarkrans" is much more than a specific year, consisting of specific hours, days, and months; it essentially pertains to all years as they repeat the cyclical and oscillating patterns of the various months and seasons. Thus the year cycle in *Tijdkrans* is actually the time cycle of the collection as a whole. Moreover, the permanence of this universal year is absorbed by the permanence of eternity discussed in "Eeuwkrans." *Tijdkrans* thus possesses a meaningful progression of ideas throughout—the various stages of the typical day in "Dagkrans" spill over into the seasonal rhythms of the typical year in "Jaarkrans"; and both the day and the year in their predictable recurrence of hours, months, and seasons anticipate the static constancy of eternity in "Eeuwkrans." "Eeuwkrans," then, becomes the meaningful backdrop for both "Dagkrans" and "Jaarkrans"; for the stability inherent in the ever recurrent flux of time is absorbed in the permanence and constancy of eternity itself. In the structural pattern adopted for *Tijdkrans*, then, Gezelle was able to conquer the enemy time.

RIJMSNOER

Gezelle's last collection, *Rijmsnoer*, contains 216 poems, of which 204 were composed during the four-year span from 1893 to 1897, and reflects an inner peace he had found. While the majority of these poems are about nature, Gezelle no longer uses nature as the medium through which to voice his complaints. Rather,

nature has become the symbol of God's grand design, and the poet simply bathes in the sheer joy of that design. Gezelle no longer reiterates his wish to die, nor does he express a chronic discontent with the world and dissatisfaction with the enemy time. Rather, in *Rijmsnoer*, he has found full satisfaction in the harmony that nature provides.

Paralleling the structure of *Tijdkrans*, *Rijmsnoer* also contains three basic sections—a short introduction of eight poems, called "Voorhang" (proscenium); a very large middle movement of 139 poems, divided into twelve units devoted to the months of the year; and a short conclusion of 8 poems, titled "Aanhang" (appendix). Dominating the entire collection is the large middle movement. It is essentially an amplification of "Jaarkrans," the middle panel in *Tijdkrans*. Unlike the collection *Tijdkrans*, however, which includes a separate section devoted to eternity ("Eeuwkrans") and which by implication gives meaning to its middle panel "Jaarkrans," the middle panel of *Rijmsnoer* is suffused with Gezelle's awareness and assurance of eternity. Thus, in *Rijmsnoer*, the tension between time and eternity is nearly erased.

The most significant image in *Rijmsnoer* is the sun. For Gezelle, sunlight had become a symbol of eternal light. It not only makes flowers grope toward it, especially when the sun is darkened by clouds, but it also teaches people to reach toward light, especially when the shadows and clouds of daily existence seem to block out God's light. In a real sense, then, *Rijmsnoer* is filled with sun worship, the worshiper-poet progressing from seeing through a glass darkly to beholding God the Sun face to face. Living, for Gezelle, had in these final years become a ceaseless act of praying, a moving away from physical sight to increasingly greater spiritual insight. He had, as he says in "Zonnewende" ("Sun Searching"), come to see "with eyes closed" and "to breathe in the light of the sun." He had learned to conquer not only time but also death. He had come to experience within himself that like the sun, which appears anew each day, he too, despite the darker aspects of life and death, will eventually rise again and ultimately "shine eternally" ("Mortis Imago"/"Image of Death"). The culmination of this long search for light finds expression in "Ego Flos" ("I Am a Flower"),

Gezelle's last great mystical poem, incorporated in *Laatste verzen*. Written shortly before his death, this poem pictures the poet as God's special flower and celebrates his one day surpassing all earthly flowers by growing in the full light of the Sun.

REVIVING FLEMISH LITERATURE

Ironically, though *Tijdkrans* and *Rijmsnoer* never refer even once to Gezelle's patriotic goal of reviving Flemish literature, it is precisely these two collections that stimulated that revival, especially after the poet's death. These collections were at first neither admired nor clearly understood, but later they were praised for their innovativeness in language and style. No longer resorting to those monotonous rhymes, conventional stanzaic patterns, and didactic techniques that characterize some parts of the earlier *Dichtoefeningen* and *Gedichten, gezangen en gebeden*, the collections *Tijdkrans* and *Rijmsnoer* from beginning to end are truly inspired rather than consciously made. Their poems are fluid and varied, unforced and free, quickening and slowing their pace in accordance with the natural rhythms of colloquial speech. They are daringly innovative in their language as well. In them, Gezelle stretched his own Flemish idiom to its very limits, coupling contemporary words to medieval roots, transforming verbs into nouns and nouns into verbs, or simply combining different parts of speech. Through these two collections in particular, Gezelle became recognized far and wide.

OTHER MAJOR WORKS

TRANSLATIONS: *The Song of Hiawatha*, 1886 (of Henry Wadsworth Longfellow's poem); *Meditationes theologiae*, 1897 (of Monsignor Waffelaert).

MISCELLANEOUS: *Jubileumuitgave van Guido Gezelle's volledige werken*, 1930-1939 (9 volumes).

BIBLIOGRAPHY

Gezelle, Guido. *The Evening and the Rose: Thirty Poems*. Rev. ed. Translated by Paul Claes and Christine d'Haen. Antwerp: Guido Gezellenootschap, 1999. This bilingual translation of Gezelle's poetry provides perspective on the poet.

Hermans, Theo. *A Literary History of the Low Countries*. Rochester, N.Y.: Camden House, 2009. Contains substantial discussion of Gezelle as well as translations of a number of his works.

King, Peter. *Gezelle and Multatuli: A Question of Literature and Social History*. Hull, England: University of Hull, 1978. A critical assessment of the works of Gezalle and his contemporary Multatuli, also known as Eduard Douwes Dekker. Includes bibliographical references.

Thys, Walter. *Intra an extra muros: Verkenningen voornamelijk in de Neerlandistiek en het comparatisme*. Delft: Eburon, 2008. This multiple-language work contains an essay on Flemish literature, which examines Gezelle and his role in its revival.

Van Nuis, Hermine J. *Guido Gezelle, Flemish Poet-Priest*. New York: Greenwood Press, 1986. A brief biography and critical study of Gezelle's life and work.

Van Roosbroeck, G. L. *Guido Gezelle: The Mystic Poet of Flanders*. Vinton, Iowa.: Kruse, 1919. A short study of Gezelle's place in the history of Flemish literature.

Hermine J. van Nuis

GIUSEPPE GIUSTI

Born: Monsummano, Tuscany (now in Italy); May 12, 1809
Died: Florence, Italy; March 31, 1850

PRINCIPAL POETRY

Poesie, 1877, 1962
Le più belle pagine di G. Giusti, 1934

OTHER LITERARY FORMS

The prose writings of Giuseppe Giusti (JEWS-tee), though inferior to his poetic ones, must be regarded, nevertheless, as a complement to them, for like his verses, they bear the mark of constant, painstaking rewriting and polishing. While his writings in prose suffer from a belabored style, his poetry retains its appearance of streamlined spontaneity despite numerous revisions.

When Giusti's *Epistolario* (1904, 1932, 1956; correspondence) was published in its complete form, it confirmed his place in Italian literary history as a significant regional writer. Giusti's letters epitomize the distinct flavor of the Tuscan language as it was spoken by the common people of his time. In the vernacular that he cultivated with pride, perhaps even with a certain arrogance, Giusti depicted vignettes of everyday life in contemporary Tuscany.

A similar spirit informs *Raccolta dei proverbi toscani, con illustrazioni cavata dei manoscritti di G. Giusti ed ora ampliata ed ordinata* (1853; illustrated collection of Tuscan proverbs from G. Giusti's enlarged and rearranged manuscripts), published three years after Giusti's death by his closest friend, Gino Capponi. The proverbs are a repository of Tuscan folkloric wit and wisdom, but like Giusti's letters, they suffer at times from the linguistic excesses to which he was prone. "Memorie inedite" (unpublished memoirs), later published as *Cronaca dei fatti di Toscana* (1890; chronicle of events in Tuscany), as well as the introductory essay to *Della vita e delle opere di Giuseppe Parini* (1890; about Giuseppe Parini's life and works)—an introductory anthology of Parini's poems edited by Giusti himself—give a much better portrayal of him than do most of the letters or the sparse fragments of his autobiography.

Cronaca dei fatti di Toscana emerges as a truthful portrait of the author, as well as a faithful description of the political upheaval of 1847, when the Tuscan people were first given hope for resurgence by Pius IX's liberal concessions. Describing the Lucca festivals in those days of euphoric anticipation, Giusti interpreted them as a spontaneous popular symbol of the aspirations to freedom that the people of the region entertained. Turning out in droves "to rejoice at the ceasing of evil and at the beginning of good," men, women, children, and elderly folk from the countryside poured into the city. They came as out of a stifling closet into the fresh air, their parish priest leading them, waving their flags and carrying flowers while singing joyfully.

Although his choice of poems for the Parini anthology was far from excellent, in the accompanying essay, Giusti reveals his affinity with that great Lombard poet, especially his appreciation for Parini's universal satire.

Giusti, too, was to satirize the vices and corruption of society at large, rather than focusing on individuals in order to vent personal grudges. Another important aspect of his essay on Parini is his correct evaluation of eighteenth century Italian literature as the seedbed for the peninsula's resurgence in the nineteenth century. Nevertheless, even in his obvious admiration for, and agreement with, Parini's philosophical outlook, Giusti—as a "native" Tuscan writer—could not repress his sense of superiority over Parini in matters of language.

ACHIEVEMENTS

Giuseppe Giusti was a key poet of the Italian Risorgimento, and although the label of "minor poet" has been applied to his name, it does not minimize the important role he played in the literature and history of nineteenth century Italy. His greatest gift as an author was his keen common sense, exemplified in his use of the satiric traditions of his native Tuscany. While his regional standing may have limited his range, it also contributed to his instantaneous recognition and fame throughout the peninsula, as his *scherzi* (jokes) were circulated in manuscript form long before they became available in print. *Scherzi* are satirical poetic compositions, often in short, quick-moving verses in the tempo of lively musical compositions also named *scherzi* by early nineteenth century composers. Structured in a great variety of meters and lengths, the *scherzi* were written to satirize events, mores, and public figures. Giusti's rapidly growing fame reinforced his belief that it was by the poetic word that he could contribute to his country's liberation.

With their sarcastic needling of police spies, princes, ministers, and courtiers, Giusti's *scherzi* became weapons of liberalism and symbols of the Italians' patriotic aspirations to unity and freedom. Although Niccoló Tommaseo, and even his friend Alessandro Manzoni, found Giusti unduly sardonic in matters of linguistic pride and purity, it was to Giusti that Manzoni went for advice to give the final, polishing touches to the language of his immortal novel *I promessi sposi* (1827, 1840-1842; *The Betrothed*, 1828, 1951). Manzoni's elegant Florentine language in that novel was to become the model for Italian prose.

Thus, if by his almost fanatical devotion to the Tuscan vernacular Giusti limited the scope of his poetic aspirations, he nevertheless helped to awaken the national conscience to the need for political and linguistic unity.

BIOGRAPHY

Giuseppe Giusti was born on May 12, 1809, in Monsummano, near Pescia in the Val di Nievole, of a well-to-do family. Giusti began his studies with a local priest, whose coarse and aggressive manners had a considerable influence on the boy's aversion for school. Reacting against his father's ambitious plans for him, the young Giusti continued to be a reluctant pupil in his brief residencies in boarding schools in Florence and in Lucca and in a Pistoia seminary. When his father sent him to study law at the University of Pisa in 1826, the greatest attraction for the recalcitrant scholar was the Café of the Hussar along the Lungarno, where students gathered in informal merrymaking. It was in that carefree atmosphere that the poet began to be formed, as among his peers Giusti observed the various types and characters he was to make universal in his verse. The satirist in him did not fail to note with humor the hypocrisy that infiltrated even that joyful circle of student gatherings; it was from those early experiences, for example, that he later drew one of his most famous poems, "Gingillino" (1844-1845; "The Trifler").

Because of difficulties with his family, as well as a brief incident with the police, Giusti did not obtain his law degree until 1834, when he was twenty-five years old. His legal career, nevertheless, proved to be quite perfunctory; indeed, he gave it up before he had even started, lacking interest in the profession altogether. In 1836, he met Gino Capponi, who became his best friend and whose serenity was a positive influence on Giusti. Nevertheless, because of continuing family difficulties and a lack of physical vitality (only much later discovered to be the result of tuberculosis), he began to suffer from nervous disorders, alternating periods of depression and recovery.

A journey to Rome and Naples, where Giusti was welcomed enthusiastically by liberals in intellectual circles, did not help his recovery and indeed may have worsened his ill health. Sporadic short excursions took him outside Tuscany, to La Spezia and to Milan, where he was a guest of Manzoni for a month. Between 1846 and 1847, Giusti lived alternately in his paternal home and at the Capponi residence in Florence.

When the Civic Guard was formed, Giusti happily joined it with the rank of a major. Having become officially recognized as a "very Tuscan writer," in 1848, he was named a resident member of the prestigious Crusca Academy. The same year, after the 1848 Revolution, he briefly held political office as a deputy in the first and second Tuscan legislative assemblies of Borgo Buggiano. With Capponi, he promoted the liberal cause, seeking a friendly agreement between the grand duke and the people, disregarding past grudges. In 1849, shortly before the restoration of the grand duke, Giusti was elected to the Constituent Assembly for the short time that it existed.

Giusti's satirical poems, needling the unemployed spies, the police *birri*, and the civil servants who were conveniently being retired, belong to this period of political upheaval, when the downfall of the old society was rapidly taking place. "A Leopoldo II" (1847; "To Leopold II") is a poem in which Giusti tried to see that ruler as a true prince and as a father of his region. It was an ephemeral enthusiasm, however, which was soon to be deflated by the grand duke's flight and the demagogues' seizure of power; when Leopold returned, he was accompanied by the Austrians.

Accused of having betrayed the cause of the people, disillusioned and bitter, Giusti at first sought refuge with his family at Pescia and Montecatini, and later at his friend Capponi's in Florence, where he died on March 31, 1850, of tuberculosis, the silent disease that had been undermining his health all along. Though deeply saddened by the failure of the Constituent Assembly and the triumph of reactionary forces, Giusti never lost hope for Italy's resurrection—for its Risorgimento.

ANALYSIS

Giuseppe Giusti's poetics should be sought in his concrete approach to life: Without searching for past utopias or making gigantic leaps into the future, Giusti's poems concentrate both in time and space on the present, on the topography, history, and mores of contemporary Tuscany. In one of his short prose writings, aptly titled "Dell'aurea mediocrità" (about golden mediocrity), Giusti evaluates human life in terms of a median condition residing between Heaven and Earth. Humanity's horizon should be sought, he suggests, at eye level, between the sky and the land, where the concreteness of life lies.

This amused acceptance of things as they are, not as they should be, had its roots in Giusti's native Tuscan traditions. Although his satirical mode has been traced to all sorts of Italian and foreign satirists, humorists, and caricaturists—his style has been compared, for example, to that of the lighthearted French folk poet Pierre Jean de Béranger—his primary inspiration was the homely Tuscan folklore that extolled the virtues of moderation.

"THE BOOT"

The folkloric element in Giusti's verse is evident in the early poem "Lo stivale" ("The Boot"), written in 1836. Headed by an epigraph taken from Dante's rhymes, it is written in stanzas of six hendecasyllabic lines. The Boot is the narrator; it stands for Italy, whose safety resides in that unity that Dante so strongly advocated. Describing the Boot from top to toe, Giusti recalls the Boot's history and its ravaging by many who sought to rule it—"from one thief to the next." It is true, the Boot once "galloped" by itself and ruled the Roman world, but wanting too much, it fell flat on the ground. While sketching the long, harrowing history of the peninsula, Giusti directs his sarcasm particularly against the papacy. "The priests harmed me most/ that truly malevolent race and indiscreet." In the end, the Boot asks only to be refurbished and given a solid form by a competent boot maker, yet should such a man of courage and energy appear, he would, as usual, "be kicked in his seat."

NOTABLE SCHERZI

Among Giusti's most famous *scherzi* of this first period are "L'incoronazione" ("The Coronation"), written in 1838, and three others, all of 1840: "Il brindisi di Girella" ("Girella's Toast"), "Umanitari" ("The Humanitarians"), and "Il Re Travicello" ("King Travicello"). "The Coronation" was written on the occasion of the coronation of the emperor of Austria as king of Italy, but the satire is actually directed against Leopold II—

the emperor's brother—during whose tenure as grand duke of Tuscany the atmosphere in the region became more stagnant than ever. Identified in this poem as "il toscano Morfeo" ("Tuscan Morpheus") for the somnolence he caused among his subjects, Leopold became proverbially symbolic of complacency and ineptitude in government.

"Girella's Toast," "The Humanitarians," and "King Travicello" address what Giusti called, with much contempt, "our deepest wounds"—that is, the proliferation of cosmopolitanism, the opportunism of the weathercocks (those ready to change their loyalty to enter the ranks of the latest conqueror), and the obsequious role so many Italians played in order to gain favor, giving their allegiance to harsh or inept monarchs such as the dull-witted King Travicello. All those vices had to be eliminated if the country were to be rebuilt. Cosmopolitanism in particular went against Giusti's grain, for he believed that the Italians, being so divided among themselves, were hardly ready for the international scene.

It was this aversion to cosmopolitanism that prevented Giusti from siding with either the classicists or the Romantics in the battle between the two factions that had begun to rage in 1816, when he was a small boy. His posture on this all-important issue of his time was typically Giustian: He wanted to follow a middle road, preserving a balance between the old and the new. This eventually happened, though Giusti failed to understand how much the future of Italian independence was to be indebted to the spreading and absorption of European ideas within the peninsula.

"THE LAND OF THE DEAD"

"La terra dei morti" (1842; "The Land of the Dead") is Giusti's answer to a poem by the French poet Alphonse de Lamartine, "La Dernier chant du pèlerinage d'Harold" (1826; "The Last Song of Harold's Pilgrimage"), which had been reprinted in 1842. Recalling Lord Byron's exploits on behalf of the Greek struggle for independence from Turkey, Lamartine had contrasted Hellenic heroism with the Italians' resignation to their position as slaves of foreign rulers—a servility that lowered them to "human dust," the inhabitants of "the land of the dead." In 1826, Lamartine's insult to the Italian people had provoked strong reactions and had even embroiled him in a duel; since then, Giusti had been fueling his own patriotic sentiments. In "The Land of the Dead," he employed a seven-syllable line that imparted a spirit of urgency to the verse. There are great patriots in Italy today, Giusti replies to Lamartine, men such as Manzoni, Giuseppe Niccolini, and Gian Domenico Romagnosi, heirs to past glories. Will the ruins and monuments, vestiges of former greatness, be the Italians' cemetery or that of the barbarians, the invaders of the peninsula? Judgment Day will not be late in coming when the country is resurrected to life.

"THE SNAIL"

One of Giusti's most popular satirical poems, "La chiocciola" ("The Snail"), neatly sums up his outlook on life. In fast-moving lines of five syllables, "The Snail" dispenses the poet's Tuscan wisdom—a wisdom embedded in wit and practicality. Observing a snail during a walk in the country, Giusti realizes how far superior it is to a human. A peaceful, home-loving, moderate creature, it never leaves its house in search of adventures or exotic foods. Unlike so many "teaching owls," who in fact can teach nothing to their peers, the snail excels above other living creatures. Even the hangman should take notice of this "exemplary" animal, which has been given by nature the prodigious ability of regrowing its head. Giusti's characteristic humor is particularly evident in the refrain: "Hail to the snail."

"THE TRIFLER"

Much has been written about "The Trifler," an unusually harsh and relentless tirade against the "squandering" Tuscan bureaucrats that is quite unlike most of Giusti's satiric compositions. Gingillino is the symbol of all triflers, the host of civil servants who make up the slothful, spineless, and corrupt bureaucratic complex. As a baby, a child, a student, and finally as a graduate and an adult, Gingillino is "educated" to join the dalliers. He promptly learns to put into practice the dishonest teachings of peers and superiors and, in turn, goes on to flatter and please everybody by his deceit and sloth, but particularly the mighty, those in high places, in order to gain their favors.

"The Trifler" is a powerful, extended satire comprising 701 lines, including a prologue. The following

stanzas, in various meters, consist of lines ranging from four to eleven syllables. This structural variety is meant to convey the various vices and tricks the dishonest bureaucrats must learn to master. From this large crowd of "demons," among whom even Judas would look like an inexperienced buffoon, the poet emerges, crazed and melancholy, wandering alone in the night's solitude to enjoy "the chaste embrace of your beauty, my deceived country."

"IN SANT' AMBROGIO'S"

Giusti's later poems, epitomizing the hopes and aspirations of the Italian people, belong to the years from 1846 to 1848. They are statements of the evolution of historical events to their dramatic apex; they also represent the poet's spiritual growth, greatly enhanced by his physical decline. Perhaps none of Giusti's compositions belonging to this last period of his life has been more quoted, lauded, and anthologized than "Sant' Ambrogio" (1846; "In Sant' Ambrogio's"). It is a poem that blends the lyric and satirical strands of Giusti's verse, relating an episode that the poet had witnessed when, in 1845, he was visiting Manzoni and his family in Milan. Doubtless Manzoni's religious fervor must have been felt by Giusti, whose Christian charity may well have been revived by his illness as well.

With subtle irony, the poet pretends to recount the incident with all due respect to a high-placed official of the Buon Governo—the Tuscan grand duke's police establishment—which regarded the poet's "little satires of no count" as dangerously anti-Austrian and subversive. Wandering about with Manzoni's son, Filippo, in Milan, he finds himself in the ancient fourth century Church of Saint Ambrose, the patron saint of the Lombard city.

At first, the poet is seized by a sense of revulsion, seeing the church invaded by a crowd of blondish, mustachioed, foul-smelling foreign military men, standing at attention before God. When the priest is about to consecrate the Host, the famous chorus "Va pensiero" ("Go forth my thought") is sounded by horns. The chorus, taken from Giuseppe Verdi's opera *I Lombardi alla prima crociata* (the Lombards in the First Crusade), has always been well known for echoing in its sad strains the unfulfilled aspirations of an oppressed people. No longer quite like himself, the poet is suddenly overcome by compassion for the Croatian and

Czechoslovakian soldiers, who are forced to be away from their countries and their loved ones. "Those poor people" stand watch over the Italians, says Giusti. They are slaves of the emperor of Austria, serving among people who hate them; they are the tools of a monarch who fears seditious revolts and loss of power. The spontaneous fraternal compassion of the patriotic poet heightens as the foreign soldiers begin a German chant. Is it not possible, Giusti asks, that in their souls, they resent "il principale" (the master) as much as the Italians do? "I may as well flee," he concludes; "otherwise I am liable to embrace a corporal."

Giusti's short life as a man and as a writer represents a landmark in Italian letters precisely because he was in tune with his times. Greatly desiring Italy's liberty, he nevertheless resisted fanaticism and intolerance, and his compassion and humor reflected the character of his people at their best.

OTHER MAJOR WORKS

NONFICTION: *Cronaca dei fatti di Toscana*, 1890; *Della vita e delle opere di Giuseppe Parini*, 1890 (includes poems by Parini); *Epistolario*, 1904, 1932, 1956.

MISCELLANEOUS: *Raccolta dei proverbi toscani, con illustrazioni cavata dei manoscritti di G. Giusti ed ora ampliata ed ordinata*, 1853; *Tutti gli scritti editi ed inediti di G. Giusti*, 1924 (includes all of his prose and poetry).

BIBLIOGRAPHY

Adami, Stefano. "Giuseppe Giusti." In *Encyclopedia of Italian Literary Studies*, edited by Gaetana Marrone, Paolo Puppa, and Luca Somigli. Vol. 1. New York: Routledge, 2007. Analyzes his satirical poetry and provides important biographical details.

Horner, Susan. *The Tuscan Poet Giuseppe Giusti, and His Times*. Cambridge, Mass.: Macmillan, 1864. A biography of Giusti with some historical background.

Riall, Lucy. *Risorgimento: The History of Italy from Napoleon to Nation-State*. New York: Palgrave Macmillan, 2009. Describes the Risorgimento, revealing the political context in which Giusti functioned.

Tusiani, Joseph. *From Marino to Marinetti*. New York: Baroque Press, 1974. An anthology of forty Italian poets including Giusti translated into English with some biographical notes on each.

Carolina D. Lawson

JOHANN WOLFGANG VON GOETHE

Born: Frankfurt am Main (now in Germany); August 28, 1749

Died: Weimar, Saxe-Weimar-Eisenbach (now in Germany); March 22, 1832

PRINCIPAL POETRY

Neue Lieder, 1770 (*New Poems*, 1853)
Sesenheimer Liederbuch, 1775-1789, 1854 (*Sesenheim Songs*, 1853)
Römische Elegien, 1793 (*Roman Elegies*, 1876)
Reinecke Fuchs, 1794 (*Reynard the Fox*, 1855)
Epigramme: Venedig 1790, 1796 (*Venetian Epigrams*, 1853)
Xenien, 1796 (with Friedrich Schiller; *Epigrams*, 1853)
Hermann und Dorothea, 1797 (*Herman and Dorothea*, 1801)
Balladen, 1798 (with Schiller; *Ballads*, 1853)
Neueste Gedichte, 1800 (*Newest Poems*, 1853)
Gedichte, 1812-1815 (2 volumes; *The Poems of Goethe*, 1853)
Sonette, 1819 (*Sonnets*, 1853)
Westöstlicher Divan, 1819 (*West-Eastern Divan*, 1877)

OTHER LITERARY FORMS

The unique significance of the contribution to German letters made by Johann Wolfgang von Goethe (GUR-tuh) lies in the fact that his best creations provided models that influenced, stimulated, and gave direction to the subsequent evolution of literary endeavor in virtually every genre. Among more than twenty plays that he wrote throughout his career, several have special meaning for the history of German theater. *Götz von Berlichingen mit der eisernen Hand* (pb. 1773; *Götz von Berlichingen with the Iron Hand*, 1799) was a key production of the Storm and Stress movement, mediating especially the influence of William Shakespeare on later German dramatic form and substance. With *Iphigenie auf Tauris* (first version pr. 1779, second version pb. 1787; *Iphigenia in Tauris*, 1793), Goethe illustrated profoundly the ideals of perfected form and style, beauty of language, and humanistic education that characterized German literature of the classical period. His famous masterpiece *Faust: Eine Tragödie* (pb. 1808, 1833; *The Tragedy of Faust*, 1823, 1838), with its carefully programmed depiction of the spiritual polarities that torment the individual, rapidly became the ultimate paradigm for the portrayal of modern humanity's fragmented nature.

Goethe's major narratives, including *Die Leiden des jungen Werthers* (1774; *The Sorrows of Young Werther*, 1779), *Wilhelm Meisters Lehrjahre* (1795-1796; *Wilhelm Meister's Apprenticeship*, 1825), *Die Wahlverwandtschaften* (1809; *Elective Affinities*, 1849), and *Wilhelm Meisters Wanderjahre: Oder, Die Entsagenden* (1821, 1829; *Wilhelm Meister's Travels*, 1827), are powerful illuminations of fundamental human problems. The monumental saga of Wilhelm Meister established the pattern for the German bildungsroman of the nineteenth century, and it also had a substantial impact on Romantic novel theory.

A large portion of Goethe's oeuvre is nonfiction. He completed more than fourteen volumes of scientific and technical writings, the most important of which are *Versuch die Metamorphose der Pflanzen zu erklären* (1790; *Essays on the Metamorphosis of Plants*, 1863) and *Zur Farbenlehre* (1810; *Theory of Colors*, 1840). His historical accounts, specifically *Campagne in Frankreich, 1792* (1822; *Campaign in France in the Year 1792*, 1849) and *Die Belagerung von Mainz, 1793* (1822; *The Siege of Mainz in the Year 1793*, 1849), are vividly readable reports of firsthand experience. Writings that reveal a great deal about Goethe himself and his perception of his artistic calling are his autobiography, *Aus meinem Leben: Dichtung und Wahrheit* (1811-1814; *The Autobiography of Goethe*, 1824; better known as *Poetry and Truth from My Own Life*), and the many published volumes of his correspondence.

ACHIEVEMENTS

Johann Wolfgang von Goethe's overwhelming success as a lyricist was primarily the result of an extraordinary ability to interpret and transform direct, intimate experience and perception into vibrant imagery and symbols with universal import. In the process of overcoming the artificiality of Rococo literary tendencies, he created, for the first time in modern German literature, lyrics that were at once deeply personal, dynamically vital, and universally valid in what they communicated to the reader. Beginning with the poems written to Friederike Brion, and continuing through the infinitely passionate affirmations of life composed in his old age, Goethe consistently employed his art in a manner that brushed away the superficial trappings and facades of existence to lay bare the essential spirit of humankind.

In his own time, Goethe became a world figure, although his immediate acclaim derived more from his early prose and dramatic works than from his lyrical writings. Even after the turn of the nineteenth century, he was still recognized most commonly as the author of *The Sorrows of Young Werther*, the novel that had made him instantly famous throughout Europe. Nevertheless, the simple power, clear, appealing language, and compelling melodiousness of his verse moved it inexorably into the canon of the German literary heritage. Much of his poetry was set to music by the great composers of his own and subsequent generations, and the continuing popularity of such creations as "Mailied" ("Maysong") and "Heidenröslein" ("Little Rose of the Heath") is attributable at least in part to the musical interpretations of Franz Schubert and others.

The real importance of Goethe's lyric legacy is perhaps best measured in terms of what it taught other writers. Goethe established new patterns and perspectives, opened new avenues of expression, set uncommon standards of artistic and aesthetic achievement, assimilated impulses from other traditions, and mastered diverse meters, techniques, and styles as had no other German poet before him. His influence was made productive by figures as different as Heinrich Heine and Eduard Mörike, Friedrich Hölderlin and Hugo von Hofmannsthal, Stefan George and Rainer Maria Rilke. As a mediator and motivator of the literary and intellectual currents of his time, as a creator of timeless poetic archetypes, as an interpreter of humanity within its living context, Goethe has earned an undisputed place among the greatest poets of world literature.

BIOGRAPHY

Three aspects of Johann Wolfgang von Goethe's childhood contributed substantially to his development as a literary artist. A sheltered existence, in which he spent long hours completely alone, fostered the growth of an active imagination. A complicated attachment to his sister Cornelia colored his perceptions of male-female relationships in ways that had a profound impact on the kinds of experience from which his works were generated. Finally, contrasts between his parents in temperament and cultural attitudes gave him an early awareness of the stark polarities of life on which the central tensions of his major literary creations are based.

While studying law in Leipzig between 1765 and 1768, Goethe began to write poems and simple plays in the prevailing Anacreontic style. Although some of these productions relate to his infatuation with Kätchen

Johann Wolfgang von Goethe (Library of Congress)

Schönkopf, an innkeeper's daughter, they are more the product of his desire to become a part of the contemporary intellectual establishment than a direct outpouring of his own inner concerns. Among the important figures who influenced his education and thinking during this period were Christoph Martin Wieland, Christian Fürchtegott Gellert, and Adam Friedrich Oeser.

The experiences that resulted in Goethe's breakthrough to a distinctly individual and characteristic literary approach began when he entered the University of Strasbourg in 1770. Encounters with two very different people during the winter of 1770-1771 sharply changed his life. Johann Gottfried Herder introduced him to the concepts and ideals of the Storm and Stress movement, providing him with new models in Homer and Shakespeare and moving him in the direction of less artificial modes of expression. Of equal consequence for the immediate evolution of his lyrics was an idyllic love affair with Friederike Brion that ended in a parting, the emotional implications of which marked his writings long afterward.

On his return to Frankfurt in 1771, Goethe was admitted to the bar. During the next five years, he fell in love with at least three different women. A painful involvement with Charlotte Buff, the fiancé of his friend Johann Christian Kestner, was followed by a brief attraction to Maximiliane Laroche. In April, 1775, he became engaged to Lili Schönemann, the daughter of a wealthy Frankfurt banker. Of the three relationships, only the interlude with Maximiliane Laroche failed to have a significant impact on his art. *The Sorrows of Young Werther* derived much of its substance from Goethe's experiences with Charlotte Buff, while the powerful internal conflicts generated by his feelings for Lili gave rise to a small group of very interesting poems.

When the engagement to Lili became intolerable because of its demands and restrictions, Goethe went to Weimar, where he settled permanently in 1776. For the next ten years, he served as adviser to Carl August, duke of Weimar, whom he had met in Frankfurt in 1774. A broad variety of political and administrative responsibilities, ranging from supervision of road construction to irrigation, from military administration to direction of the court theater, left Goethe little time for serious literary endeavor. The resulting lack of personal fulfillment coupled with the prolonged frustrations of an unhappy platonic love affair with Charlotte von Stein caused him to flee to Italy in search of artistic and spiritual rejuvenation. While there, he perfected some of his most significant dramatic works.

The combination of exposure to Roman antiquity, classical Italian literature, and a uniquely satisfying love alliance with the simple, uneducated Christiane Vulpius formed the basis for renewed poetic productivity when Goethe returned to Weimar. In *Roman Elegies*, he glorified his intimate involvement with Christiane in imagery of the Eternal City. A second, more disappointing trip to Italy in 1790 provided the stimulus for the less well known *Venetian Epigrams*.

In 1794, Goethe accepted Friedrich Schiller's invitation to collaborate in the publication of a new journal. There followed one of the most fruitful creative friendships in the history of German letters. Among the famous lyrical compositions that emerged from their relationship were the terse, pointed forms of the epigram war that they waged against their critics in 1796, and the masterful ballads that were written in friendly competition in 1797. Goethe regarded Schiller's death, in 1805, as one of the major personal tragedies of his own life.

The two specific experiences of later years that provided the direction for Goethe's last great productive period were exposure to the works of the fourteenth century Persian poet Hafiz and a journey to the places of his own childhood. While in Frankfurt in 1814, Goethe fell in love with Marianne von Willemer, the wife of a friend. The Hafiz-like dialogue of their intense spiritual communion is the focus of *West-Eastern Divan*, in which Goethe reached the culmination of his career as a lyricist. After it was published, only the final work on his immortal masterpiece *Faust* remained as a substantial task to be completed before his death.

ANALYSIS

In his famous letter to Johann Wolfgang von Goethe of August 23, 1794, Schiller identified the addressee as a writer who sought to derive the essence of an individual manifestation from the totality of natural phenomena. More particularly, he saw Goethe's goal as the literary definition of humankind in terms of the organization of the living cosmos to which it belongs. Only to the extent that Goethe viewed himself as representative of humanity in general does Schiller's assessment offer a valid approach to the understanding of his friend's lyric poetry. The focus of Goethe's verse is less humankind in the abstract than it is Goethe himself as a distinct, feeling, suffering, loving, sorrowing, longing being. From the very beginning, his works assumed the character of subjective poetic interpretations of his specific place in society, the implications of direct encounters with nature and culture, and the significance of concrete interpersonal relationships. He later described his creative writings as elements of a grand confession, pinpointing the fact that a major key to them lay in the penetration of his own existence.

Goethe's development as a lyric poet is clearly a continuum in which internal and external events and circumstances contribute to sometimes subtle, sometimes obvious modifications in approach, technique, and style. It is nevertheless possible to recognize a number of well-defined stages in his career that correspond to important changes in his outward situation and his connections with specific individuals. The predominant tendency of his growth was in the direction of a poetry that reaches outward to encompass an ever-broader spectrum of universal experience.

The Anacreontic creations of Goethe's student years in Leipzig are, for the most part, time-bound, occasional verse in which realistic emotion, feeling, and perception are subordinated to the artificial conventions and devices of the time. Typical motifs and themes of the collection *New Poems* are wine, Rococo eroticism, the game of love with its hidden dangers, stylized pastoral representations of nature, and a peculiarly playful association of love and death. Individual poems often move on the border between sensuality and morality, mirroring the prevailing social patterns. Especially characteristic is the employment of language that magnifies the separation of the world of the poem from experienced reality. In their affirmation of the elegant facades, the deliberate aloofness, the uncommitted playfulness of Rococo culture, these lyrics document Goethe's early artistic attitudes, even though they reveal little of his unique poetic gift.

STRASBOURG PERIOD

Under the influence of Herder in Strasbourg, Goethe began to move from the Decadent artificiality of his Leipzig songs. A new appreciation for the value of originality, immediacy of feeling, unmediated involvement in nature, and directness of approach is apparent in creations that are notable for their vivid imagery, plastic presentation of substance, force of expression, and power of language and rhythm.

Two types of utterance dominate the verse of this period. Highly personal outpourings of the soul, in which the representation of love is more passionate, serious, and captivating than in the Leipzig productions, are couched in formal stanzas that arose from Goethe's fondness for Friederike Brion. Free-verse poems that focus on Storm and Stress ideals of individuality, genius, and creativity reflect the lyrical influence of Pindar and the dramatic legacy of Shakespeare in their form and tone. In what they reveal of Goethe's worldview, the love poetry and the philosophical reflections are deeply intertwined. Without love, Goethe's perception of life is empty; without the depth of awareness of individual responsibility in creation, love loses its strength and vitality. Love forms the basis for the experience of nature, while the external surroundings with their beauties, tensions, conflicts, and potential for joy give full meaning to love.

The most important new feature of the Strasbourg poetry is the visible emphasis on existential polarities in the description of the poet's relationship to people and things. Love and suffering, defiance and submission, danger and ecstasy are juxtaposed in the portrayal of a world of change, growth, and struggle. In endless variation, Goethe offers the intimate revelation of loneliness, longing, and lack of final fulfillment that are the fundamental ingredients of life viewed as a pattern of restless wanderings. The very acts of searching, striving, creating, and loving are communicated with an energy and a spiritual intensity that carries the reader along in a rush of emotional participation in universal experience.

THE LILI POEMS

Among Goethe's most interesting early works are the sometimes tender, often intensely painful lyric documents of his courtship of Lili Schönemann. Few in number, these writings illustrate the poet's cathartic use of his talent in a process of self-analysis and clarification of his position with respect to external events. At the same time, they underscore a growing tendency to come to grips with and master life through his art. Consisting of occasional pieces that are connected by recurring themes related to the tension between the attractions of love and the devastating torments of an accompanying loss of freedom, the Lili poems combine visions of joy with ironically biting yet dismal portraits of despair. A gem of the period is the famous "Auf dem See" ("On the Lake"), a vivid projection of both physical and spiritual flight from oppressive love, written in Switzerland, where Goethe had taken temporary refuge from the demands of life with Lili.

WEIMAR PERIOD

During Goethe's first years in Weimar, the frustrations of an unsatisfying association with Charlotte von Stein, the all-consuming responsibilities of the court, and his own inability to overcome completely the break with Lili contributed to his lyrics a new preoccupation with themes of melancholy resignation and self-denial. The heavy moods that characterize his works of this period inform short meditative poems as well as longer philosophical reflections, mournful love songs, and a few haunting ballads. Especially profound are two eight-line stanzas, each titled "Wanderers Nachtlied" ("Wanderer's Night Song"), in which the poet longs for and admonishes himself to courage, comfort, hope, belief, and patience. "Warum gabst du uns die tiefen Blicke?" ("Why Did You Give Us the Deep Glances?"), the most powerful of his poems to Charlotte von Stein, presents love as a mystical mystery. The two dramatic ballads, "Erlkönig" ("Elf King") and "Der Fischer" ("The Fisherman"), emphasize humanity's psychological subjection to the demonic power of its own impressions of nature.

ITALIAN JOURNEY

The experience of Italy completely changed Goethe's poetry. Among the most important developments that the journey inspired were the abandonment of suggestion and tone in favor of pure image, the transition from lyrical song to epic description, and the replacement of extended elaboration of worldview with terse epigrams and short didactic verse. During Goethe's classical period, his ballads achieved perfected form, while his depictions of nature attained their final goal in brightness and joyful plasticity. Where earlier poems feature colors that flow softly together, or points of color that invoke mood and an impression of the whole, the works created after 1790 are dominated by structure and the placement of objects in space. Ideas are presented in classical meters, especially hexameter, and as a result confessional poetry loses much of its melody.

ELEGIES, EPIGRAMS, AND BALLADS

Three groups of poems are particularly representative of the new directions in Goethe's lyrics: *Roman Elegies*, the epigrams, and the classical ballads. In their rich mural presentation of the poet's life in Rome, the *Roman Elegies* document the author's increasing tendency to circumscribe his own existence in verse, while their form, style, and combination of classical dignity with inner lightheartedness reflect the direct influence of Ovid, Catullus, and Propertius. The poems of *Venetian Epigrams* were similarly motivated by direct exposure to elements of classical Italian culture. They are especially notable for their rich imagery and their realism in depicting the emotional intensity of the poet's longing for Germany. In structure and style, they were models for the more famous epigrams written by Goethe and Schiller in 1796. Unlike the elegies and epigrams, Goethe's powerful ballads of 1797 arose out of materials that he had carried within him for a long time. The lyrical and melodic aspects that are absent from the other forms remain strong in rhythmic creations that emphasize passion and excitement while developing themes related to the classical ideal of pure humanity. Goethe viewed the ballad as an archetypal lyric form. His "Die Braut von Korinth" ("The Bride of Corinth") and "Der Gott und die Bajadere" ("The God and the Bayadere") are among the greatest German ballads ever written.

POETRY OF LATER YEARS

The erotic poetry of Goethe's old age had its beginnings in a group of sonnets that he wrote to Minchen Herzlieb in 1807. During the seven years that followed their creation, he wrote verse only occasionally. At last, however, the combination of stimuli from the deeply meaningful love affair with Marianne von Willemer and exposure to the works of Hafiz moved him to compose his greatest poetic accomplishment, *West-Eastern Divan*. In the framework of a fantasy journey of rejuvenation, Goethe entered a friendly competition with Hafiz while simultaneously declaring his own newly regained inner freedom. The central themes of the collection include longing for renewal of life, recognition of the need for spiritual transformation, coming to grips with Hafiz as a poet, love, wine, worldly experience, paradise, looking upward to God, and looking downward to the human condition. In some of the poems, Goethe returned to a kind of Anacreontic love poetry. In the heart of the cycle, he made of Hatem and Suleika timeless archetypal models for man and woman bound in the love relationship.

After *West-Eastern Divan*, Goethe wrote only a few poems of consequence. Among them, "Uworte, Orphisch" ("Primeval Words, Orphic"), in which he attempted to develop the core problems of human existence in five eight-line stanzas, and "Trilogie der Leidenschaft" ("Trilogy of Passion"), a tragic document of the state of being unfulfilled that was inspired by his final love experience, attained the power and stature of earlier lyrics. In these two creations, Goethe pinpointed once more the essence of his own spiritual struggle between the light and the night of human existence.

"WELCOME AND FAREWELL"

While living in Strasbourg and courting Friederike Brion, Goethe created for the first time sensitive love poetry and descriptions of nature that exude the vitality of immediate experience. Perhaps the most characteristic of these works is the famous "Willkommen und Abschied" ("Welcome and Farewell"). The substance of the poem is a night ride through the countryside to Sesenheim and a joyful reunion with Friederike, followed by a painful scene of parting when morning comes. Significant elements include a new and plastic rendering of nature, fresh and captivating imagery, and melodic language that is alive with rhythm and motion. A special power of observation is demonstrated in the poet's representation of that which cannot or can hardly be seen, yet the scenery is not portrayed merely for its own sake; rather, it is symbolic, for the uncanny aspects of the ride through the darkness are overcome by a courageous heart that is driven by love. Landscape and love thus become the two poles of the poem generating an inner tension that culminates in a peculiar equation of the beloved with the world as a whole. The portrayal of Friederike is especially notable for its psychological depth, while the expression of Goethe's own feelings of passion and eventual guilt lends the entire picture qualities of a universal experience of the heart.

"PROMETHEUS" AND "GANYMED"

Deeply personal yet broadly valid content is also typical of the so-called genius poems of Goethe's Storm and Stress period. The intensity of emotional extremes is particularly vivid in the sharply contrasting hymns "Prometheus" and "Ganymed," which reflect the poles of Goethe's own spirit even more strongly than do his dramas. In depicting the two mythological titans, the poet concentrated on the creation of dynamic archetypes. "Prometheus" is a hard, even harsh portrait of modern humanity. The speaker of the lines is loveless and alone. Emphasis is placed on "I"; the focus is inward and limiting. In his defiant rejection of Father Zeus and the attendant process of self-deification, Prometheus champions the value of individuality and independence. Important themes of his declaration of emancipation from gods who are less powerful than humans include faith in self, belief in the power of action, knowledge of the difficulty and questionability of life, and the divinity of humans' creative nature. The tone of "Ganymed" is completely different. In the soft language of a prayer, the title figure proclaims his total submission to the will of the Father and his desire to return to the divine presence. A new side of Goethe's religiosity is revealed in the transformation of his sensitivity to nature into a longing for God's love. The central concern is no longer "I" but "you"; the direction is outward toward the removal of all boundaries in a coming together of deity and humankind. In the manner in which they play off the real world against the ideal realm, "Prometheus" and "Ganymed" are especially representative of the existential polarity lyrics that Goethe wrote during the pre-Weimar years.

ROMAN ELEGIES

Roman Elegies, the major lyrical product of Goethe's first Italian journey, comprises twenty confessional hexameter poems knit tightly together in a cycle that documents the poet's love for a fictitious young widow (Christiane Vulpius in Roman disguise). Two primary thematic configurations dominate creations that are among Goethe's most beautiful, most sensuously erotic works. The story of the tender love affair with Faustine, integrated into the Italian framework, is played off against the problems associated with renewal and adaptation of antiquity by the modern poet. Within this context, love becomes the key that makes entry into the Roman world possible.

Lively, direct reflection of the writer's enthusiasm for Rome sets the tone for the cycle. At the center of the introductory elegy, which forms an overture to the love adventure, there is a longing for the beloved who gives the city its true character. This yearning is followed in the next segment by a cynical glance backward at the boredom of Weimar society, which is in turn contrasted with the first report of the developing amorous relationship. An attempt to idealize the new situation, focusing specifically on the rapidity with which Faustine gives herself, leads to the elaboration of the described experiences in the light of ancient mythological gods. Through the creation of a new goddess, "Opportunity," as a symbol for the woman he loves, Goethe effectively connects the motifs of the sequence with classical themes. The fifth elegy provides the first high point in the poetic chain with its projection of the spirit of the author's existence in Rome as a blend of antiquity, art, and the erotic, which mutually illuminate, intensify, and legitimize each other to yield a true "life of the gods." Other important sections of the cycle touch on questions of jealousy, gossip about the lovers, a Homeric idyll of the hearth, and a variety of encounters with Rome and its traditions, history, and secrets. Elegy thirteen is especially interesting for the tension that it establishes between the demands of lyric art and those of love for Faustine. A dialogue between Amor and the poet develops the idea that the former provides plenty of material for poetry but does not allow enough time for creative activity. Colorful pictures of the joys of love culminate in imagery of the couple's morning awakening together in bed. There is grand irony in the fact that the lament about not having enough time to write becomes a magnificent poem in itself.

Throughout the collection, love is the focus of polar conflicts on several levels. The intense need for unity with Faustine in the physical alliance is juxtaposed to the act of self-denial that provides the quiet enjoyment of pure observation and contemplation in the creative process. Within the social frame, the fulfilled love that is sought and attained cannot be brought into harmony with reality. Fear of discovery necessitates disguise of the beloved, deception of relatives, secret meetings, and isolation from the surrounding world. In the final elegy, however, Goethe is forced to conclude that the beautiful secret of his love cannot remain hidden for long because he himself is incapable of remaining quiet about it. The result is a many-faceted revelation of love as a timeless human situation.

BALLADS

Careful examination of Goethe's most representative ballads reveals a clear progression from verse stories in which humans are at the mercy of a potentially destructive, magically powerful natural world to lyric accounts that proclaim the supremacy of the human spirit over the restrictions of mortal experience. Influenced by the popular pattern established in Gottfried August Bürger's "Lenore," Goethe's early ballads such as "Elf King" and "The Fisherman" describe the fatal resolution of inner conflicts in terms of individual surrender to seductive impressions of external reality. Later, philosophically more complex works ("The Bride of Corinth" and "The God and the Bayadere") portray death as a process of transcendence that purifies the individual while preparing the soul for joyful fulfillment on a higher plane of existence.

"Elf King" is somewhat similar to "Welcome and Farewell" in its representation of a night landscape's malevolent lure as it impresses its terror on the minds of those who encounter it. The substance of the narrative is the homeward night ride of a father and son; the darkness gives uncanny form and life to things that would appear harmless by day. The boy, who is ill with fever, believes that he hears the elf king enticing him, describes what he sees and feels to his father, and dies of fright when the older man's reassurances fail to convince him of the falseness of his delirious vision. Rhythmic language that conveys the beat of the horse's hooves through the countryside, immediacy created by dialogues involving the child, the phantom elf king, and the father, and moods evoked by contrasts between light and shadow, intimate fear and pale comfortings, all contribute to the psychological intensity of a presentation in which the poet attempted to find accurate formulation for the fantastic, indefinite problem of human destiny.

In "The God and the Bayadere," a confrontation with death is handled much differently. The legend of the prostitute who spends a night providing the pleasures of love to the god Siva in human form, only to awaken and find him dead on the bed, is a forceful lyrical statement about the redeeming properties of love. Denied her widow's rights because of her way of life, the bayadere makes good her claim by springing into the flames that arise from the funeral pyre. In response to this act of purification, Siva accepts the woman as his bride. Strong Christian overtones exist in the first stanza's emphasis on the god's humaneness and in the obvious parallels to the relationship between Christ and Mary Magdalene. The poem's thrust is that the divine spark is present even in a degraded individual and that even the lowest human being can be transformed and exalted through the cleansing influence of pure love.

WEST-EASTERN DIVAN

A major key to the literary productions of Goethe's old age is found in the notion of personal fulfillment through direct sensual and spiritual enjoyment of life. The implications of that approach to experience are most thoroughly and splendidly elaborated in *West-Eastern Divan*, a carefully constructed collection of verse that attempts to blend and join the artistic legacies of East and West in a book about love in all its manifestations. Both the pinnacle of Goethe's lyric oeuvre and one of the most difficult of his creative works, *West-Eastern Divan* is a conscious declaration of the validity of humanity's unending search for joy in the world.

As revealed in the opening poem, the focal metaphor of the volume is the Hegira, which Goethe uses as an image for his flight from oppressive circumstances into the ideal realm of foreign art. Two central relationships dominate the twelve sections of his dream journey to the Orient. On one level, the individual poems are portions of a playful fantasy dialogue between Goethe and his Eastern counterpart Hafiz. The object of their interchange is a friendly competition in which the Western poet seeks to match the achievements of a revered predecessor. Conversations between two lovers, Hatem and Suleika, develop the second complex of themes, derived from elements of the love experience shared by Goethe and Marianne von Willemer.

"Buch des Sängers" ("Book of the Singer"), the most important of the first six cycles, sets the tone for the entire work. In the famous poem "Selige Sehnsucht" ("Blessed Longing"), Goethe explored the mystery of how one gains strength through the transformation that occurs as a result of sacrifice. Borrowing from a ghazel by Hafiz the motif of the soul that is consumed in the fire of love like a moth in a candle flame, he created a profound comment on the necessity of metamorphosis to eternal progress. The uniting of two people in love to generate the greatest possible joy is made to stand for the longing of the soul to be freed from the bonds of individuality through union with the infinite. The antithesis of "Blessed Longing" is presented in "Wiederfinden" ("Reunion"), a creation of extremely vivid imagery from "Buch Suleika" ("Book of Suleika"), the eighth and most beautiful section of *West-Eastern Divan*. Based on Goethe's separation from Marianne and their coming together again, the poem develops the idea that parting and rediscovery are the essence of universal existence. In a uniquely powerful projection of creation as division of light from darkness and their recombination in color, Goethe produced new and exciting symbols for love's power, rendered in lines that form a high point in German lyric poetry.

OTHER MAJOR WORKS

LONG FICTION: *Die Leiden des jungen Werthers*, 1774 (*The Sorrows of Young Werther*, 1779); *Wilhelm Meisters Lehrjahre*, 1795-1796 (4 volumes; *Wilhelm Meister's Apprenticeship*, 1825); *Die Wahlverwandtschaften*, 1809 (*Elective Affinities*, 1849); *Wilhelm Meisters Wanderjahre: Oder, Die Entsagenden*, 1821, 1829 (2 volumes; *Wilhelm Meister's Travels*, 1827).

SHORT FICTION: *Unterhaltungen deutscher Ausgewanderten*, 1795 (*Conversations of German Emigrants*, 1854); *Novelle*, 1826 (*Novel*, 1837).

PLAYS: *Götz von Berlichingen mit der eisernen Hand*, pb. 1773 (*Goetz of Berlichingen, with the Iron Hand*, 1799); *Clavigo*, pr., pb. 1774 (English translation, 1798, 1897); *Götter, Helden und Wieland*, pb.

1774; *Erwin und Elmire*, pr., pb. 1775 (libretto; music by Duchess Anna Amalia of Saxe-Weimar); *Claudine von Villa Bella*, pb. 1776 (second version pb. 1788; libretto); *Die Geschwister*, pr. 1776; *Stella*, pr., pb. 1776 (second version pr. 1806; English translation, 1798); *Iphigenie auf Tauris*, pr. 1779 (second version pb. 1787; *Iphigenia in Tauris*, 1793); *Die Laune des Verliebten*, pr. 1779 (wr. 1767; *The Wayward Lover*, 1879); *Jery und Bätely*, pr. 1780 (libretto); *Die Mitschuldigen*, pr. 1780 (first version wr. 1768, second version wr. 1769; *The Fellow-Culprits*, 1879); *Die Fischerin*, pr., pb. 1782 (libretto; music by Corona Schröter; *The Fisherwoman*, 1899); *Scherz, List und Rache*, pr. 1784 (libretto); *Der Triumph der Empfindsamkeit*, pb. 1787; *Egmont*, pb. 1788 (English translation, 1837); *Faust: Ein Fragment*, pb. 1790 (*Faust: A Fragment*, 1980); *Torquato Tasso*, pb. 1790 (English translation, 1827); *Der Gross-Cophta*, pr., pb. 1792; *Der Bürgergeneral*, pr., pb. 1793; *Was wir bringen*, pr., pb. 1802; *Die natürliche Tochter*, pr. 1803 (*The Natural Daughter*, 1885); *Pandora*, pb. 1808; *Faust: Eine Tragödie*, pb. 1808 (*The Tragedy of Faust*, 1823); *Des Epimenides Erwachen*, pb. 1814; *Faust: Eine Tragödie, zweiter Teil*, pb. 1833 (*The Tragedy of Faust, Part Two*, 1838); *Die Wette*, pb. 1837 (wr. 1812).

NONFICTION: *Von deutscher Baukunst*, 1773 (*On German Architecture*, 1921); *Versuch die Metamorphose der Pflanzen zu erklären*, 1790 (*Essays on the Metamorphosis of Plants*, 1863); *Beyträge zur Optik*, 1791, 1792 (2 volumes); *Winckelmann und sein Jahrhundert*, 1805; *Zur Farbenlehre*, 1810 (*Theory of Colors*, 1840); *Aus meinem Leben: Dichtung und Wahrheit*, 1811-1814 (3 volumes; *The Autobiography of Goethe*, 1824; better known as *Poetry and Truth from My Own Life*); *Italienische Reise*, 1816, 1817 (2 volumes; *Travels in Italy*, 1883); *Zur Naturwissenschaft überhaupt, besonders zur Morphologie*, 1817, 1824 (2 volumes); *Die Belagerung von Mainz, 1793*, 1822 (*The Siege of Mainz in the Year 1793*, 1849); *Campagne in Frankreich, 1792*, 1822 (*Campaign in France in the Year 1792*, 1849); *Essays on Art*, 1845; *Goethe's Literary Essays*, 1921.

MISCELLANEOUS: *Works*, 1848-1890 (14 volumes); *Goethes Werke*, 1887-1919 (133 volumes); *Goethe on Art*, 1980.

BIBLIOGRAPHY

Armstrong, John. *Love, Life, Goethe: Lessons of the Imagination from the Great German Poet*. New York: Farrar, Straus and Giroux, 2007. Goethe's works are analyzed and his life examined in this comprehensive volume. Armstrong discusses a wide range of Goethe's writings, including his lesser known works, and gives a close study of his personal life. Knowing German and English, he provides translations of several key passages, while keeping his writing style plain and clear. This volume offers readers a better understanding of Goethe's writing, and the circumstances that inspired it.

Atkins, Stuart. *Essays on Goethe*. Columbia, S.C.: Camden House, 1995. Essays on the apprentice novelist and other topics, by the preeminent Goethe scholar.

Boyle, Nicholas. *Goethe: The Poet and the Age, Volume I: The Poetry of Desire (1749-1790)*. Oxford, England: Clarendon Press, 1991. A monumental scholarly biography. See the index of Goethe's works.

_____. *Revolution and Renunciation (1790-1803)*. Volume 2 in *Goethe: The Poet and the Age*. New York: Oxford University Press, 2000. This second volume covers only the next thirteen years of Goethe's life. Boyle's extensive discussion of the Wilhelm Meister novels and Goethe's drama *Faust* is set amid a period of radical political and social change, fallout from the French Revolution.

Kerry, Paul E. *Enlightenment Thought in the Writings of Goethe: A Contribution to the History of Ideas*. Rochester, N.Y.: Camden House, 2001. An examination of the philosophy that filled Goethe's writings. Bibliography and index.

Swales, Martin, and Erika Swales. *Reading Goethe: A Critical Introduction to the Literary Work*. Rochester, N.Y.: Camden House, 2002. A critical analysis of Goethe's literary output. Bibliography and index.

Wagner, Irmgard. *Goethe*. New York: Twayne, 1999. An excellent, updated introduction to the author and his works. Includes bibliographical references and an index.

Weisinger, Kenneth D. *The Classical Facade: A Nonclassical Reading of Goethe's Classicism*. University Park: Pennsylvania State University Press, 1988. The works covered by this interesting volume all come from the middle period of Goethe's life. In his analysis, Weisinger searches for a kinship between *Faust* and Goethe's classic works. The author asserts that all these classic works share a nonclassic common theme: the disunity of the modern world.

Williams, John R. *The Life of Goethe: A Critical Biography*. Malden, Mass.: Blackwell, 1998. An extensive examination of the major writings, including lyric poems, drama, and novels. Includes a discussion of epigrams, aphorisms, satires, libretti, and masquerades. Discusses Goethe's personal and literary reactions to historical events in Germany, his relationship with leading public figures of his day, and his influence on contemporary culture. Suggests that Goethe's creative work follows a distinct biographical profile. Includes large bibliography.

Lowell A. Bangerter

EUGEN GOMRINGER

Born: Cachuela Esperanza, Bolivia; January 20, 1925

PRINCIPAL POETRY

Konstellationen Constellations Constelaciones, 1953

33 Konstellationen, 1960

5 mal 1 Konstellation, 1960

Die Konstellationen les Constellations the Constellations los Constelaciones, 1963

Das Stundenbuch, 1965 (*The Book of Hours, and Constellations*, 1968; includes translations from *Konstellationen*)

Worte sind Schatten: Die Konstellationen, 1951-1968, 1969

Einsam Gemeinsam, 1971

Lieb, 1971

Eugen Gomringer, 1970-1972, 1973

Konstellationen, Ideogramme, Stundenbuch, 1977

Vom Rand nach innen: Die Konstellationen, 1951-1995, 1995

OTHER LITERARY FORMS

As the leading theoretician of concrete poetry in Europe, Eugen Gomringer (GAWM-rihn-gehr) has also published essays, manifestos, and lectures, including the important and provocatively titled *Poesie als Mittel der Umweltgestaltung* (1969; poetry as a means of shaping the environment). In addition, most of his theoretical texts were reprinted in his best-known collection of poems, *Worte sind Schatten*. Gomringer has also promoted the school of concrete poetry as an editor of journals and collections. In 1953, he cofounded the journal *Spirale* and served as the editor of its literary section. In 1960, he founded the Eugen Gomringer Press in Frauenfeld, Switzerland, serving as the editor for eleven issues of the journal *Konkrete Poesie/Poesia concreta*, which was published in Frauenfeld from 1960 to 1964. Gomringer has always been fascinated by nonrepresentational painters and artists whose "concrete" works he sees as being intimately connected to his own; in 1958, he edited a collection of essays in honor of the fiftieth birthday of sculptor, designer, and abstract painter Max Bill, and in 1968, he published monographs on the works of Josef Albers and Camille Graeser. He also collaborated with artists on books with "concrete" artistic themes.

ACHIEVEMENTS

In 1953, in Bern, Switzerland, Eugen Gomringer published his first concrete poems in his newly founded magazine *Spirale*, earning himself the title the "Father of Concrete Poetry." Although another group of concrete poets (the "Noigandres" group) had organized in Brazil at about the same time, Gomringer's first poems appear to have predated those of the Brazilians, and it was Gomringer's poems and theoretical texts that served as the basis for the spread of this new school in Europe. More important, Gomringer's linguistic ingenuity showed the German-speaking world that literary innovation and creativity were still possible in the aftermath of the (linguistic) destruction of the Third Reich. He demonstrated that it was perfectly legitimate, and even a matter of great urgency, to question the adequacy of the building blocks of any new literature—namely, the language itself. Gomringer was recognized for his efforts with the Punta Tragara Premio per la Poesia Concreta in 2007 and the Bavarian Order of Merit in 2008.

Gomringer's influence was enormous in Germany, Austria, and Switzerland. The experimental poet Helmut Heissenbüttel has openly admitted his indebtedness to Gomringer; indeed, the whole Stuttgart school of poets who gathered around the aesthetician Max Bense (including Heissenbüttel, Franz Mon, and Claus Bremer) would hardly have been conceivable had it not been for Gomringer's pioneering work. In Austria, the poets Friedrich Achleitner and Gerhard Rühm, who formed the nucleus of the short-lived but important neo-Dadaistic cabaret Die Wiener Gruppe (the Viennese group), were friends of Gomringer and transmitted his ideas to their own countrymen, including nonmembers of the group, such as the poets Ernst Jandl and Friederike Mayröcker. In Gomringer's own Switzerland, usually rather conservative in literary matters, his work acted as an impetus or signal for a new beginning. Although there was no Swiss concrete school as such, poetic creation, which had been in the doldrums since the end of the war, began to accelerate, and one can discern Gomringer's influence in the poems of Kurt Marti, Peter Lehner, Ernst Eggimann, Hans Schumacher, and others. Even German-speaking writers whose primary interest is prose owe a debt to Gomringer, for he taught them to experiment with language within their texts. This is not to say that any of these authors slavishly copied Gomringer's works, but they did change or alter their language so that it would more adequately confront a highly industrialized and technological society. This broad trend toward linguistic restructuring lasted about twenty years and is one of the central components of postwar German literature.

BIOGRAPHY

Although he was born in Bolivia, Eugen Gomringer received his secondary education in the German-speaking part of Switzerland and studied economics and art history at universities in Bern and Rome. His study of art brought him into contact with modern nonrepresentational painting, which he emulated in his first poems in the early 1950's. At a meeting in 1955 with other poets who wrote in a similar fashion, Gomringer decided to term these poems "concrete." From

1954 to 1958, he served as secretary for Bill, who was then the director of the Hochschule für Gestaltung (institute of design) in Ulm, West Germany, a descendant of the famous Bauhaus school. Bill, who was also the head of the departments of architecture and product design at the institute, was greatly affected by constructivist principles and frequently used elementary shapes with almost mathematical precision in his paintings and sculptures. Gomringer was in turn influenced by Bill's works. It was also in Ulm that Gomringer met other artists of the abstract school, such as Albers and Friedrich Vordemberge-Gildewart, as well as the influential professor of semiotics Bense and the poet Heissenbüttel.

After his stay in Ulm, Gomringer embarked on a decade of intense creative activity. He began publishing collections of the poems that he had been writing in the previous years, and he founded his own press and his own magazine, *Konkrete Poesie/Poesia concreta*, in 1960. He served as business manager for a Swiss labor organization, the Schweizerischer Werkbund, from 1962 to 1967, and he began working as a design and advertising consultant for various firms, including a large department store and (since 1967) the famous Rosenthal concern.

The 1960's marked the high point for Gomringer's creative output and for the concrete school that he had fostered. By the end of that decade, one could discern several signs indicating that the peak of the movement had passed. Instead of writing poems, Gomringer began writing monographs and essays. An *Anthology of Concrete Poetry* appeared in 1967 (edited by Emmett Williams), firmly establishing Gomringer's role in the movement, and an English translation of some of Gomringer's works appeared in 1968 (*The Book of Hours, and Constellations*, edited by Jerome Rothenberg). Gomringer published an anthology of his poems and theoretical writings in 1969 (*Worte sind Schatten*) and edited two anthologies of concrete poetry in 1972. In that same year, Gomringer made a lecture tour through South America that perhaps served as his official farewell to the concrete movement, for since then he has done little creative writing. He has devoted most of his energy to his design and advertising career and taught the theory of aesthetics at the art academy in Düsseldorf

from 1976 to 1990. In 2000, he founded the Institut für Konstruktive Kunst und Konkrete Poesie in Rehau.

ANALYSIS

Although Eugen Gomringer's principal inspiration derived from the visual arts, he was also attracted in his university years to poets who emphasized the visual aspects of their works. He admired Arno Holz, who arranged the lines of his poems symmetrically on either side of an imaginary "central axis" running down the middle of the page. He enjoyed the idiosyncratic vocabulary and typography of Stefan George, and he was fascinated by the condensed elliptical style of Stéphane Mallarmé and the typographical pictures of Guillaume Apollinaire's *Calligrammes* (1918; English translation, 1980). These affinities, along with concrete poetry's resemblance to the reductive and destructive tendencies of late expressionism and Dada, have led some scholars to see a direct link between prewar and postwar linguistic experimentation—a misleading connection, for Gomringer does not share the philosophical tenets (the search for the inner essence of humanity that lies beyond the grasp of reason) or the elements of shock and negation found in this earlier poetry. Instead, Gomringer affirms the economic recovery of postwar Europe and rejoices in technological progress. He argues that the modern industrial world requires a level of communication that is direct, simple, abbreviated, and universally intelligible. The irrationalism of the prewar years has no place in his work. In Gomringer's view, poetry today should resemble the signs in a large international airport, where travelers speaking a variety of languages must be able to find their way with a minimum of confusion. Poetry should be like contemporary advertising copy—straight to the point and easy to remember.

Gomringer chose to call his poetry "concrete" because his poems disregard the syntactical relationships of traditional verse. Isolated words are placed on a paper in such a way that the visual arrangement contributes to or even constitutes the field in which thoughts can move. The concrete poem is thus neither a statement nor a description but an assemblage of words that forms an object. That is, it is not an assertion about something, but rather its own concrete reality; it is not an abstraction from reality but a concrete object made of the reality of language. The development of this new form paralleled developments in what is generally called the "abstract" art of the first half of the twentieth century. A large group of abstract painters (Wassily Kandinsky, Paul Klee, Piet Mondrian, Hans Arp, and Kurt Schwitters, to name only a few) created aesthetic constructions that, like Gomringer's poetry, satisfy a natural desire for order. The aesthetic harmony characteristic of both the concrete poem and the abstract work of art is, however, basically different from the harmony of the natural world, and only the arrangement of the materials on the canvas or on the paper can make this harmony visible. Many of these artists claimed, too, that since they were dealing with the essential elements of reality, their paintings were not "abstract" at all but rather "concrete," much more concrete than traditional mimetic art. Theo van Doesburg wrote a manifesto in 1930 about concrete art, Bill termed an exhibit of his works in 1944 "concrete," and Kandinsky always maintained with great tenacity that his paintings were the only truly concrete works to have been created.

To call attention to the unique form of his poems, Gomringer uses the term "constellation." He defines a constellation as a grouping of a few different words on a page in such a manner that the relationship between the words does not arise through syntactic means but through the material, concrete, and spatial presence of the words themselves. Thus, the reader is permitted to select, by experimenting and playing with the text, the interpretation that suits him best. The poet establishes the field of language from which meaning will emerge, but the reader is invited—indeed, obliged—to participate in the creation of the poem. Nothing is taught, narrated, or described: The poem is an autonomous product.

Such a process points to the most radical aspect of Gomringer's oeuvre. Through a confrontation with the language of the concrete poem, Gomringer hopes, the reader will gain a new relationship to the objects of the real world, because these objects are reflected in and represented by language. These new relationships should lead to insights about the tyranny of language over thought—that is, the reader should realize that inherited language systems are no longer adequate to

communicate ideas in a highly technological age and that a new universal language must be developed in order to facilitate the understanding of complex, specialized data. Concrete poetry promotes the development of this language by designing models from various languages and testing their efficacy on the global community. In this search for a universal language, he anticipated later developments in the science of linguistics, such as generative-transformational grammar and theories of universals.

WORTE SIND SCHATTEN

Gomringer's most representative collection, *Worte sind Schatten*, includes examples of the four categories into which his constellations can be divided: visual constellations, or ideograms, whereby the arrangement of the words on the page constitutes the main impact of the poem; audiovisual constellations, which can be read either silently or aloud; constellations in foreign languages (Spanish, French, English, and Swiss-German); and constellations in book form, which require the reader to turn several pages to see the poem develop visually before his eyes, much like a film. The constellations in all categories generally employ a small number of words restructured or varied in the poem by means of combinations and permutations.

The visual texts have no real beginning and no real end, because words or letters are arranged on the page, not necessarily in lines, to form a linguistic picture. The eyes of the reader must roam about the page until they have grasped the poem, both words and picture, as an entity. In this category, one finds a poem that contains the numeral 4 printed several times to form the shape of the Roman numeral IV (much like some types of computer pictures), a poem in which the letters of the word "wind" are arranged in a seemingly haphazard pattern on the page, perhaps to suggest leaves being blown by the wind, and the famous "Schweigen" poem, in which the word *schweigen* (silence) is printed fourteen times to form a box on the page with a space in the middle, the "silence" of the poem. Such poems are usually tautologies, in that the "picture" is an illustration of the semantic content of the word being used.

The audiovisual constellations are for the most part printed in traditional verse form—that is, individual lines and stanzas are recognizable even though the lexicon has been greatly reduced. An example is the poem titled "Vielleicht" (perhaps):

vielleicht baum
baum vielleicht
vielleicht vogel
vogel vielleicht
vielleicht frühling
frühling vielleicht
vielleicht worte
worte vielleicht.

(The other words translate to "tree," "bird," "spring," and "words.") The poem suggests the extent to which names for things are arbitrary, imprecise, or inaccurate.

Gomringer's constellations in foreign languages are similar in structure to the audiovisual poems, leading some scholars to view both categories as only truncated imitations of traditional verse. An example is a poem in English, "You Blue," which can be interpreted, variously, as a comment on the color spectrum, on racial discrimination, or on the scale of human emotions: "you blue/ you red/ you yellow/ you black/ you white/ you."

The constellations in book form are perhaps the most innovative of Gomringer's works. An example of this type of poem is *5 mal 1 Konstellation*. Here, Gomringer prints various combinations of the words *mann* (man), *frau* (woman), *baum* (tree), *kind* (child), *hund* (dog), *vogel* (bird), *berg* (mountain), *land*, *wind*, *haus* (house), *wolke* (cloud), and *see* (sea or lake). Each word has a set position on the page, but all the words are not printed until the final page: Sometimes only an individual word appears, and at other times the words are in groups of two, three, or four. Each page is like a part of a landscape painting, and when the pages are turned, the landscape seems to come to life. In another of these book-poems, *1 Konstellation: 15*, words and letters appear and disappear within a grid of fifteen squares printed in the center of the page. When one leafs through the poem, these words and letters seem to jump and skip about, much like the figures in an animated cartoon. A final example, *The Book of Hours*, is both the most profound and the longest (forty-three pages) of the poems, and it requires the most meditation on the part of the reader. Using a minimal vocabulary of twenty-four words, such as *freude* (joy), *wort* (word), *frage* (question), *ziel* (goal), *geist* (spirit), and the possessive adjectives *mein* and *dein* (my, your), Gomringer provides the reader with a quasi dialogue consisting of almost every possible combination of these words—for example, "dein geist, mein geist"; "dein geist, mein wort"; and "dein mein geist." The poem invites religious and philosophical interpretation on many levels.

THE LIMITS OF CONCRETE POETRY

A further analysis of these and similar poems is not possible, for as Gomringer states repeatedly, his concrete poems do not make a statement about reality but are their own reality. This brings one to the central dilemma of Gomringer's work: If the concrete poem has no content or theme and reaches fruition only when the reader projects his own meaning onto it, how can the reader hope to gain new information about the technological and scientific world from it? Does not the reader only interpret the poem in the light of knowledge already present in his own consciousness? The lack of syntactic structures in the poem, which supposedly allows words to form new relationships, does not appear to be an adequate device to overcome this handicap, because the reader can never escape the traditional semantic categories assigned to the words in natural language. Thus, Harald Hartung, in his book *Experimentelle Literatur und konkrete Poesie*, criticizes the words used in *The Book of Hours* arguing that they are but clichés taken from premodern and pretechnological nineteenth century poetry, of little value today.

Gomringer's followers (Heissenbüttel among them) recognized this predicament and attempted a more realistic solution. They reasoned that to change one's view of the world, which is filtered through language, one must change all the features of language, including syntax and morphology. Even these experiments were not successful, however, because the authors did not take into account the fact that communication must be based on some type of accepted norm. Drastic unilateral adjustments to the norm without the agreement of the other members of the language community can rarely have a tangible effect.

Gomringer's constellations have also been criticized for other reasons. It has been charged that, by avoiding social and political issues, the poems tend to affirm rather than censure the established order. Moreover, the detailed a priori theoretical matrix makes the poems elitist to a degree; the average reader, unaware of the manipulations he is "supposed to" perform, will dismiss the poems as unintelligible babblings. Finally, the reductive nature of the form is perhaps its most serious and inescapable liability: Solutions to complex contemporary problems cannot be achieved within such a simplistic format. Precisely because it offers an oversimplified aesthetic, concrete poetry still attracts a small number of practitioners, but Gomringer's more lasting legacy will be found in the work of writers who have turned his linguistic innovations to larger purposes—including writers who have no direct acquaintance with his work, who have nevertheless absorbed the critical attitude toward language that he fostered.

OTHER MAJOR WORKS

NONFICTION: *Manifeste und Darstellungen der Konkreten Poesie, 1954-1966*, 1966; *Camille Graeser*, 1968; *Josef Albers: Monographie*, 1968; *Poesie als Mittel der Umweltgestaltung*, 1969; *Der Pfeil: Spiel—Gleichnis—Kommunikation*, 1972 (with Anton and Joachim Stankowski); *Modulare und serielle Ordnungen*, 1973 (with Paul Lohse); *Konkretes von Anton Stankowski*, 1974 (with Anton Stankowski); *Theorie der konkreten Poesie*, 1997; *Zur Sache der Konkreten*, 2000.

EDITED TEXTS: *Max Bill*, 1958; *Konkrete Poesie: Deutschsprachige Autoren*, 1972; *Visuelle Poesie*, 1972.

BIBLIOGRAPHY

Dencker, Klaus Peter. "Visual Poetry, What Is It?" In *Translations: Experiments in Reading*, edited by Donald Wellman, Cola Franzen, and Irene Turner. Cambridge, Mass.: O.ARS, 1986. A comparison study of pattern poetry and concrete poetry genres, and an analysis of the theories of Gomringer.

Gumpel, Liselotte. *"Concrete" Poetry from East and West Germany*. New Haven, Conn.: Yale University Press, 1976. A critical and historical study of experimental poetry in Germany. Includes bibliographic references and an index.

Hanson, Louise. "Is Concrete Poetry Literature?" In *Philosophy and Poetry*, edited by Peter A. French and Howard K. Wettstein. Boston, Mass.: Blackwell, 2009. Examines concrete poetry and tries to determine whether it is literature or perhaps visual art.

Linnemann, Martina E. "Concrete Poetry: A Post-War Experiment in Visual Poetry." In *Text into Image: Image into Text*, edited by Jeff Morrison and Florian Krobb. Amsterdam: Rodopi, 1997. A comparative study of the concrete poetry of Gomringer and Claus Bremer.

Melin, Charlotte, ed. *German Poetry in Transition, 1945-1990*. Hanover, N.H.: University Press of New England, 1999. This bilingual edition introduces the works of nearly one hundred poets, including Gomringer. Discusses concrete poetry and Gomringer in the introduction and presents his poem "Worte sind Schatten."

Robert Acker

LUIS DE GÓNGORA Y ARGOTE

Born: Córdoba, Spain; July 11, 1561
Died: Córdoba, Spain; May 23, 1627

PRINCIPAL POETRY

Fábula de Polifemo y Galatea, 1627 (*Fable of Polyphemus and Galatea*, 1961)

Obras en verso del Homero español, 1627 (includes *Fábula de Polifemo y Galatea* and *Soledades*)

Soledades, 1627 (*The Solitudes of Don Luis de Góngora*, 1931; also as *The Solitudes*, 1964, Gilbert Cunningham, translator)

Obras poéticas de D. Luis de Góngora, 1921 (3 volumes; based on the Chacón manuscript of 1628)

Selected Poems of Luis de Gongora y Argote, 2007 (bilingual edition)

OTHER LITERARY FORMS

During the Golden Age of Spain, drama was the most prestigious literary form. Lope de Vega Carpio had developed Spain's national *comedia*, and Luis de Góngora y Argote (GAWNG-kuh-ro ee or-KOH-tay), like almost every other Spanish writer, tried his hand at theater. Góngora's plays met with little success. He completed two *comedias*: *Las firmezas de Isabela* (pr. 1610) and *El doctor Carlino* (pr. 1613). A third play, "Comedia venatoria," was left unfinished. Góngora's plays were unsuccessful because of their excessive difficulty; he was primarily a lyric poet, and therein lies his importance. Ironically, his greatest achievement in poetry constituted his main fault in drama: The dialogue was so complicated that the audience was unable to follow the plot, and the long lyrical sequences in the plays diverted attention from the main action.

ACHIEVEMENTS

The figure of Luis de Góngora y Argote has prompted critical polemics for the last three centuries. For a long time, critics divided his poetry into two categories: the easy-to-understand popular poems and the *culteranos*, complex works that are difficult to comprehend because of distorted syntax and a new poetic language. To quote a famous expression, Góngora became known as Prince of Light, Prince of Darkness. Research indicates, however, that his poetry developed in one constant line, culminating in the integration of opposing stylistic tendencies. The year 1613 marked the beginning of a literary controversy, yet unresolved, when the first manuscript copies of *Fable of Polyphemus and Galatea* were distributed at court. Literary circles in Spain were shocked, and opinion was drastically divided. On one hand, Góngora's ardent admirers proclaimed him to be the prince of poets. On the other hand, his enemies accused him of destroying both language and poetry. It is important to mention that among his severest critics were two of the leading Spanish poets of the Golden Age: Lope de Vega and Francisco Gómez de Quevedo y Villegas. With *Fable of Polyphemus and Galatea* and the first part of *The Solitudes*, distributed in 1613, Góngora nevertheless became the central figure of Spanish poetry. The impact of his complex style, *culteranismo*, was so powerful that even his worst enemies were ultimately influenced by his poetry.

Góngora's reputation fluctuated in succeeding centuries. His Baroque vision horrified the classicist souls of the eighteenth century, who held him responsible for the decadence of Spanish poetry. Nevertheless, they admired the "easy" Góngora, the Prince of Light. This attitude prevailed during the nineteenth century as well. The revaluation of Góngora's *culteranismo* did not begin until the end of the nineteenth century, when the French Symbolists, especially Paul Verlaine, praised Góngora's poetry as a brilliant attempt to create musicality and perfection. The most significant revaluation of his work, however, was initiated in 1927, when a group of young Spanish poets and critics joined to celebrate the third centennial of his death. The enthusiasm following the celebration led to the creation of the Generation of '27, the most brilliant group of Spanish poets since the time of Góngora. Critics today credit Góngora with perfecting the poetic language in Spanish. His work did not constitute a break with Renaissance models, but rather a culmination of its ideals. In the words of scholar Dámaso Alonso, Góngora was Europe's foremost seventeenth century lyrical poet. A young generation of international critics seems to agree with Alonso's judgment.

BIOGRAPHY

Luis de Góngora y Argote was born in Córdova, Spain, on July 11, 1561. He was the son of Francisco de Argote and Leonor de Góngora. His use of his mother's surname before his father's, not an unusual practice in Spain, was a result of economic considerations and a desire to carry a more euphonic name (Góngora was extremely fond of proparoxytonic words). It seems that, coming from an aristocratic family, his father originally intended to make his son a lawyer and to place him, through various political connections, in the court of the Habsburg rulers. Consequently, the young Góngora was sent to study at Salamanca, where he never completed his studies because he spent most of his time writing poems, flirting, and gambling. Góngora nevertheless was able to learn Latin, Greek, and classical literature and mythology. His maternal uncle, who held a hereditary position at the Cathedral of Córdova, convinced the young poet to enter the church. Góngora became a deacon and in 1585 inherited his uncle's position; he was not ordained as a priest until almost thirty years later.

Luis de Góngora y Argote (Hulton Archive/Getty Images)

The young poet was uncomfortable in his role as a churchman. There is a letter extant from the bishop of Córdova accusing Góngora of not fulfilling his ecclesiastical duties and of preferring bullfights to the chorus. Góngora was also accused of writing profane poetry. He replied sarcastically to these accusations, and a small fine was imposed on him. Thereafter, Góngora devoted himself to writing poetry, and his name became famous throughout Spain, especially because of his romances, which are included in many of the important collections of the time, such as the *Flores* of Pedro de Espinoza and the important *Romancero general* of 1600.

In 1613, with his *culteranos*, he became the central, if controversial, figure of Spanish poetry. The polemics and debates that his poems aroused, together with their success, moved him to abandon his native Córdova to settle in Madrid in 1617. His hopes of obtaining favors from the government proved futile, and this circumstance, combined with his passion for gambling and a luxurious lifestyle, soon consumed his limited capital.

Sad, destitute, and frustrated, he returned to Córdova in 1627, where he died on May 23 of that year.

ANALYSIS

Romances and *letrillas* constitute two important forms of popular Spanish poetry. The romance is customarily written in octosyllabic lines (although other metric forms are sometimes used). The rhyme is assonantic, or imperfect, meaning that after the tonic vowel, all other vowels are equal. This poetic mode has no stanzas, and only the even lines rhyme, usually with one assonance carried throughout the entire poem. The *letrillas* are generally written in octosyllabic lines and grouped in stanzas of either four, eight, or ten lines. The rhyme is consonantic, or perfect, meaning that all sounds after the tonic vowel are identical. The *letrilla* usually has a refrain. Both the romances and the *letrillas* were originally intended to be sung.

It would be a mistake to consider the romances and *letrillas* written by Luis de Góngora y Argote as "popular" or "easy" poems. His first dated poem (1580) is a romance; his last, dated 1626, is also a romance. This poetic form was basic to Góngora's work. Although the themes of the romances vary, they generally follow traditional Spanish subjects. Góngora wrote amatory, mythological, satirical, religious, and Moorish romances. Within the Moorish convention, some of his best romances correspond to the theme of the *cautivo*, the Christian prisoner of the Moors, who dreams of his homeland. It is important to remember that this theme is also present in many other authors. For example, having once been a *cautivo* in Africa, Miguel de Cervantes included this theme in a long fragment of *El ingenioso hidalgo don Quixote de la Mancha* (1605, 1615; *The History of the Valorous and Wittie Knight-Errant, Don Quixote of the Mancha*, 1612-1620; better known as *Don Quixote de la Mancha*). Hence, the situation described in the romances of captives is genuine. Góngora was able to re-create lyrically a popular feeling in a superior manner.

The *letrillas* are also numerous and cover a wide range of subjects. Many of them are satirical and were intended to make people laugh. It is interesting to note, though, that some of Góngora's most accomplished creations in this genre are not sarcastic but deal with religious themes. Indeed, his *letrillas* devoted to the Yuletide are among his best poems.

"THE FABLE OF PYRAMUS AND THISBE"

It is impossible to consider in detail the romances and *letrillas*. They total 215 compositions, with approximately forty-four additional ones attributed to the poet. One of the romances, however, deserves special attention: "Fábula de Píramo y Tisbe" ("The Fable of Pyramus and Thisbe"). The perfect conjunction of the two "styles" that critics noted in Góngora's poetry, it is a *culterano* poem in a popular form. Góngora took a mythological theme and inverted the topos into a cruel parody. This parody is also stylistic: Góngora took his own literary devices and converted them into a new form. "The Fable of Pyramus and Thisbe" is not "easy"; presupposing an extensive knowledge of mythology and Spanish Renaissance culture, the poem is a net of references, imagery, and ideas that captures in its lines the epitome of the Spanish Baroque. A work of 508 lines, it is a virtual encyclopedia of literary figures. The most prominent are metaphors of the first, second, and third degrees, metonymies, catachreses, and hyperboles. A typical example of the style of the poem is found in the description of Thisbe. Góngora follows all the Renaissance topoi of beauty: Her face, for example, is a crystal vase containing carnations and jasmines. The inversion of the topos follows immediately. Because her face is made of flowers, her nose should also be floral, but it is described as an *almendruco*, a small almond. The ending *-uco* in Spanish (the base word is *almendra*) carries a pejorative connotation. This example shows the vision that Góngora is trying to capture in the text: It is a contrasting world of light and shadows, of beauty and ugliness—a Baroque worldview.

OCCASIONAL SONNETS

Góngora was the author of at least 166 sonnets; some fifty more are attributed to him. The sonnets, like the romances, span his entire literary life. It is important to remember that the sonnet form had not only a literary function in the Golden Age, but also a social one. Poets were expected to write for various special occasions, and most of the time, the sonnet was the chosen form; it was short and had a flavor of enlightenment and culture. Thus, Góngora often was compelled to write occasional sonnets. Many such poems were written for spe-

cial festivities, such as births, weddings, and hunting parties, or were merely encomiastic compositions to celebrate sayings or actions of the nobility. Góngora managed to overcome the limitations imposed on him, composing masterpieces based on these stock themes. Not all his sonnets, however, were occasioned thus; many were born in the soul of the poet and offer lyrical expressions of his persona.

It is impossible to consider the sonnets individually, but the "Inscripción para la tumba de El Greco" ("Epitaph for the Tomb of El Greco") deserves mention. Critics have noted that there is a relation between Góngora's poetry and El Greco's art. Both responded to a distorted vision of the world that was typical of the Baroque period. Góngora's admiration for El Greco's painting is easy to understand in the light of his poetry. Both artists were successful in creating a new code and a new mode of expression.

Góngora frequently employed traditional Renaissance topoi. The carpe diem and *brevitas vitae* themes combine in a sonnet written in 1582 to create a typically Baroque worldview. The poet describes a beautiful woman in the spring of her life; the Baroque spirit emerges in the last stanza, when the poet asserts that the gold of her hair will become silver, that the freshness of her face will become a crushed violet, that beauty, youth, and the lady herself will become "earth, dust, smoke, shadow, nothingness."

FABLE OF POLYPHEMUS AND GALATEA

Fable of Polyphemus and Galatea is Góngora's masterpiece. The text is a re-creation of Ovid's fable of Acis and Galathea. Góngora transforms the 159 Latin hexameters into sixty octaves. The poem also contains an introduction of three octaves, for a total of sixty-three octaves (504 hendecasyllabic lines). The argument of the poem is basically the same as Ovid's: The horrible Polyphemus loves Galathea, a beautiful nymph, but she falls in love with the young and beautiful Acis. In a jealous rage, the Cyclops grabs a gigantic rock and crushes Acis under it. The young lover is changed into a river by Galathea's mother, Doris.

In *Fable of Polyphemus and Galatea*, Góngora created a completely new poetic language. The border between everyday and lyrical language had never before been so clearly delineated. Góngora found his tools in the rhetorical devices of the classical Roman and Greek writers, learning from them not only a new vocabulary but also a new syntax. His use of this new grammar offered the best means of giving the language a new "sound": He intended that only a highly educated and select few would be able to understand his work. The main syntactical innovation introduced by Góngora was the hyperbaton. This grammatical inversion had indeed been used before in Spanish but never taken to the extremes to which Góngora carried it. He consistently separated the noun from its adjective and the subject from its object; furthermore, as in Latin, he placed the verb at the end of the sentence. In addition to these grammatical anomalies, Góngora introduced hundreds of neologisms. A further complication was his use of words whose meaning had evolved through the centuries. Góngora used these words in their original metaphorical sense. He was able to develop a complete code of metaphors, based on mythology and private associations. Once the code was established, he constructed his images accordingly, creating such difficult texts that even the learned Spanish speaker needed a prose "translation" of the poem. Hence, the first critics and commentators did exactly that, and in the twentieth century, Alonso's work in reviving Góngora began with a prose version of the most complicated poems.

In spite of its difficulties, *Fable of Polyphemus and Galatea* is not unintelligible. Góngora's art is completely organized and follows a rigorous pattern. Even the most difficult passages respond to a logic that takes notice of the most minute details. The obvious conclusion is that even in his "darkest" moments, Góngora is still the Prince of Light. *Fable of Polyphemus and Galatea* shines with the magical light of inner order and beauty. It reveals a Renaissance attitude hidden behind a Baroque mask.

THE SOLITUDES

Góngora originally conceived *The Solitudes* as four books, each being a long eclogue. Unfortunately, he completed only the first and a part of the second. Undoubtedly, the unfavorable reception of *Fable of Polyphemus and Galatea* and the *Soledad primera* (*First Solitude*) prompted his abandonment of the project. In the words of A. A. Parker, Góngora was too proud to cast any more pearls before swine. Although

the poem is incomplete, Góngora left a substantial fragment. The *First Solitude* is composed of 1,091 lines, and the unfinished *Soledad segunda* (*Second Solitude*) of 979 lines. The external form of *The Solitudes* is the *silva*, a stanza combining seven- and eleven-syllable lines in a free pattern. After the rigid mode in which he composed *Fable of Polyphemus and Galatea*, Góngora probably thought that he could express himself more eloquently in a flexible stanza. Indeed, *The Solitudes* carry the difficulties of *Fable of Polyphemus and Galatea* to an even higher degree.

The argument of the poem is almost nonexistent. A young man survives a shipwreck and reaches the shore, where he is greeted by shepherds. The next morning, he sets out on a walk and meets a group of people celebrating a rural wedding. The rest of the poem describes the festivities that follow the ceremony. At sunset, the newly married couple goes off to enjoy their first night together. The *Second Solitude* begins the next morning, when the young pilgrim meets a group of fishermen on the banks of a river. He accompanies them to a nearby island, and again there is a description of the rest of the day. Throughout the following morning, the group observes a hunting scene. Góngora was probably near the completion of the *Second Solitude* when he stopped abruptly. It has been suggested that Góngora planned to write "solitudes" of the country, of the shore, of the woods, and of the desert. The first two books follow a similar pattern: the journey; the arrival, followed by a soliloquy, festivities, a chorus; and, finally, evening games in the *First Solitude* and hunting in the *Second Solitude*.

It is clear that the nature of the poem is not heroic but lyrical. What Góngora accomplished was to create a world that was both parallel to and removed from nature. In many ways, this new world was better than nature itself. At first, *The Solitudes* may appear to be superficial, without a "message" and preoccupied with only the technical aspects of poetry. However, after the difficulties of the text are overcome, one sees that the poem offers an optimistic view of the world: Things are intrinsically beautiful. The world is infused with light. Nature is perceived in an instant and is captured in its purest form. Góngora, the magician of sounds and colors, became a daemon with the power to create a new world.

OTHER MAJOR WORKS

PLAYS: *Las firmezas de Isabela*, pr. 1610; *El doctor Carlino*, pr. 1613.

BIBLIOGRAPHY

Chemris, Crystal Anne. *Góngora's "Soledades" and the Problem of Modernity*. Woodbridge, Suffolk, England: Tamesis, 2008. Chemris argues that *The Solitudes* represent a reaction to the transition in worldviews from the Baroque era to the Renaissance.

Collins, Marsha S. *"The Soledades," Góngora's Masque of the Imagination*. Columbia: University of Missouri Press, 2002. Collins provides extensive analysis of *The Solitudes*, with the intent of making the poetry understandable to the modern reader by creating a conceptual map with which to navigate the poetry.

De Groot, Jack. *Intertextuality Through Obscurity: The Poetry of Federico García Lorca and Luis de Góngora*. New Orleans: University Press of the South, 2002. Compares and contrasts the poetry of Góngora and Federico García Lorca, looking at how Góngora influenced the later poet.

Foster, David William, and Virginia Ramos Foster. *Luis de Góngora*. New York: Twayne, 1973. A standard biography. Contains a good annotated bibliography, including entries for several studies in English.

Góngora y Argote, Luis de. *Selected Poems of Luis de Góngora*. Translated by John Dent-Young. Chicago: University of Chicago Press, 2007. This bilingual translation of Góngora's shorter poems, the *First Solitude, The Fable of Polyphemus and Galatea*, and "The Fable of Pyramus and Thisbe," contains commentaries on the poems that provide a wealth of information.

McCaw, R. John. *Transforming Text: A Study of Luis de Góngora's "Soledades."* Potomac, Md.: Scripta Humanistica, 2000. An extensive critical interpretation of *The Solitudes*. Includes bibliographical references.

Wagschal, Steven. *The Literature of Jealousy in the Age of Cervantes*. Columbia: University of Missouri Press, 2006. Examines the theme of jealousy in early modern Spanish literature. The two chapters on Góngora look at the beautiful and sublime as well as myth and the fractured "I."

Woods, Michael. *Gracián Meets Góngora: The Theory and Practice of Wit*. Warminster, England: Aris & Phillips, 1995. A critical study of the use of humor in the works of Góngora and Baltasar Gracián y Morales. Includes bibliographical references and indexes.

Francisco J. Cevallos

GOTTFRIED VON STRASSBURG

Born: Alsace(?), Holy Roman Empire (now Alsace-Lorraine, France); flourished c. 1210
Died: Place and date unknown
Also known as: Godfrey of Strawbourg

PRINCIPAL POETRY

Tristan und Isolde, c. 1210 (*Tristan and Isolde*, 1899)

OTHER LITERARY FORMS

The only surviving works attributable to Gottfried von Strassburg (GOT-freed vawn STROS-boorg) are poems. Scholars believe Gottfried composed other poetry besides *Tristan and Isolde*, but they disagree about which surviving poems can be attributed to him. It is thought, however, that he composed several shorter works in the tradition of the *Minnesänger*, German lyric poets whose principal subject was love.

ACHIEVEMENTS

Gottfried von Strassburg is known for a single poem, but that work is one of the most significant among surviving poetry of the Middle Ages. *Tristan and Isolde* has been called the greatest courtly love poem extant. Written in an intricate style filled with irony and allusion, the poem celebrates the virtues of human love and cautions against its perils. What is particularly noteworthy is Gottfried's ability to graft onto the story of Tristan and Isolde a sophisticated commentary on the influence of love; his observations display a keen psychological insight into the nature of this human drive. Furthermore, his recurring critique of the literature of his own day suggests something about the nature of literary practice at the end of the twelfth century.

BIOGRAPHY

Little is known about Gottfried von Strassburg's life, although there is no doubt about his authorship of *Tristan and Isolde*. Contemporary sources mention "Gottfried" as the poem's author, often referring to him as "Meister" and appending "von Strassburg" to his given name. These scant details, as well as internal evidence from *Tristan and Isolde*, make it possible to reconstruct a sketch of his career. The date of Gottfried's birth is unknown, but it is thought that he was probably born in Alsace. The wide array of learning he displays in *Tristan and Isolde* suggests he was educated in the classics, rhetoric, literature, music, and possibly law and theology. He was probably not a nobleman, but instead was a member of the patrician class of bureaucrats that handled administrative tasks in the city of Strassburg, which in the twelfth century was a growing urban center on the Rhine River. The date of Gottfried's death is also uncertain, but scholars have been able to determine the date of composition of *Tristan and Isolde* to be around 1210. Because the poem remained unfinished—all of the thirty surviving manuscript versions break off in the middle of the tale—consensus among scholars is that Gottfried died before he could complete it.

ANALYSIS

Like most medieval poets, Gottfried von Strassburg chose to adapt existing works rather than invent new ones. Whether a poem was composed for oral recitation or reading, it was considered good form for poets to take a story already familiar to their audience as their subject and embellish it, demonstrating their artistry by rhetorical flourish or new thematic interpretations. For example, the "matter of Britain"—largely stories dealing with King Arthur—was retold and reinterpreted frequently. Similarly, the story of Tristan and Isolde had existed in many versions for hundreds of years be-

fore Gottfried decided to make it the subject of his long romance. The tale has its origins in Celtic folklore and became part of the medieval romance tradition sometime during the eleventh or twelfth centuries. As is evident in Gottfried's *Tristan and Isolde* and other versions of the story, details of Tristan's life and adventures have parallels in the Arthurian tradition; later writers, especially Sir Thomas Malory in *Le Morte d'Arthur* (1485), go to great lengths to integrate the story into the Arthurian cycle. The story of Tristan and Isolde is emblematic of the courtly love tradition: A handsome, noble, highly skilled knight falls hopelessly in love with a woman he can never marry, and she often returns his affection. What might in other ages be considered either tragic or immoral becomes, in the hands of skilled medieval poets such as Gottfried, a noble passion that, in extreme cases, is held up as an ideal with religious overtones.

TRISTAN AND ISOLDE

Relying principally on the version of the legend presented in the work of Thomas of Britain (twelfth century), Gottfried re-creates the story of Tristan in Middle High German, using rhyming couplets as his basic poetic form. His unfinished work extends for approximately twenty thousand lines. A prologue written in quatrains provides a moralizing commentary on human behavior that also serves to recognize Gottfried's patron, Dieterich, whose name is spelled out in the first letters of a succession of stanzas. Gottfried begins the narrative proper with the story of Tristan's parents, relates Tristan's life as an orphan, and describes the exploits that eventually take him to the court where Isolde resides. His lengthy description of the effect of a love potion drunk by Tristan and Isolde on their way to the court of Tristan's uncle King Mark, where Isolde is to become Mark's bride, is followed by episodes describing the lovers' efforts to pursue their passion without discovery, their brief interlude of undisturbed bliss in the Cave of Lovers, and Tristan's banishment from Mark's court.

Despite his reliance on previous versions of the Tristan legend for details of his story, the originality of Gottfried's work is undeniable. Even a cursory reading reveals his familiarity with matters of law, hunting, poetry, and classical literature. Gottfried uses his wide knowledge to invest his poem with gravitas. Furthermore, a significant difference between Gottfried's account of the Tristan legend and those of Thomas of Britain and other poets is his focus on the interior lives of the characters. Although the poem shares with other romances a certain episodic quality and contains sections of narrative describing the actions of the hero in combat, most of Gottfried's work concentrates on the feelings of the lovers as they try to understand what is happening to them. Additionally, the poet uses the structure of his work to reinforce his thematic aims: Scenes and characters are carefully balanced so that readers are able to see Gottfried's commentary on love unfold in all its complexity. The sense of cause and effect generated by the poem gives it affinities to modern fiction.

Thematically the poem can be described as an extended commentary on the conflict between love and duty. Tristan and Isolde share a perfect love, but one that cannot be enjoyed openly, since both have other obligations—Tristan as Mark's vassal and kinsman, Isolde as Mark's wife. The poem explores in great detail the nature of passionate, human love, finding it to be filled with conflicts that can drive a devoted lover to the brink of madness. The strange coexistence of pleasure and pain in the love relationship is what intrigues Gottfried most, and throughout the poem, he gives numerous examples of the way love makes Tristan and Isolde alternately blissful or despondent. The contrasting emotions generated by love are paralleled in the poem by a number of other contrasts. For example, Tristan is both a loyal knight and an inveterate liar, while Isolde is a paean of virtue and a continual source of temptation (both for her husband and her lover). *Tristan and Isolde* celebrates courtly love as superior to the knightly virtues that the hero also possesses. Gottfried emphasizes this distinction by the relative length of his accounts of Tristan's exploits as a lover and a fighter: The scenes of love are described in detail and often interrupted with more generalized commentary on the nature of love itself, while those in which Tristan demonstrates his skills as a fighter are often glossed over.

Gottfried uses a number of literary devices to call attention to his principal themes. Notable among them is his use of irony. Often what seems to be a good act has unintended consequences. Sometimes Tristan and Isolde are the beneficiaries of these ironic occurrences, at other times they suffer from them. Several critics have suggested that Gottfried is ahead of his time in employing symbolism in his tale, for example in using light and dark imagery to suggest the contrast between the purity of his fated lovers with the sordid behavior of those who would expose them to King Mark. Gottfried makes frequent use of reification, describing human emotions and actions such as love, jealousy, deceit, or surveillance as if they were active agents working on behalf of or against the interests of his protagonists. Most notable among these is his depiction of Love, which is frequently described as a huntsman, a falconer, or a physician. There is a strong implication that Love is capable of conquering men and women and holding them in thrall, much as a medieval lord might control his subjects who have no power to escape his clutches.

Gottfried also employs allegory, a common medieval device, most notably in his lengthy allegorical description of the Cave of Lovers, the sylvan grotto where the lovers retreat after Mark banishes them both from court. For a brief time, Tristan and Isolde live in this ideal retreat, needing only each other's company for sustenance. The physical properties of the cave—its ceiling, windows, door, and bedchamber—are equated to the properties of love—constancy, integrity, simplicity, kindness, good breeding, humility, and, above all, honor. In some ways the Cave of Lovers is like the Garden of Eden, where innocence prevails. Such a reading helps justify Gottfried's evident approval of Tristan and Isolde and his condemnation of the world outside the cave, where everyone is intent on destroying their happiness. This notion is reinforced by his portrayal of Mark's passion for his wife as purely sensual, while Tristan's seems to rise above the purely physical level.

Certainly the most important literary device used in the poem, and the one that has generated the most critical controversy, is the love potion. Gottfried makes no attempt to deny the literal power of the potion to imbue Tristan and Isolde with undying passion. Once they drink the potion, they are powerless to escape its effects. A more modern reading of the poem would suggest that the potion is intended as a visible symbol of the emotion it engenders. This reading seems to be borne out by the fact that Gottfried centers his interest on the lovers' feelings and takes great pains to describe their interior lives. When he does recount their efforts to deceive King Mark or others, he almost always includes some description of the inner drive that motivates their deception.

Finally, Gottfried inserts a number of digressions or "excursions" in which he builds up a special relationship with his readers. On more than one occasion, he mentions that his work is intended for those discerning readers who can understand the curious and complex nature of love—that is, those who would appreciate the courtly love tradition that he celebrates in the poem. In extended comments on the nature of literature, he offers a critique of contemporary writers in which he praises a number of them and demeans his chief rival, Wolfram von Eschenbach, author of the highly popular romance *Parzival* (c. 1200-1210; English translation, 1894). Gottfried's recurrent comments are a veiled argument that he should be regarded as a major literary figure, a claim that history has certainly accorded him.

BIBLIOGRAPHY

Batts, Michael S. *Gottfried von Strassburg*. New York: Twayne, 1971. Provides an overview of the Tristan legend, a critical reading of Gottfried's poem, analysis of his style, and a synopsis of other interpretations of the work.

Bekker, Hugo. *Gottfried von Strassburg's "Tristan": Journey Through the Realms of Eros*. Rochester, N.Y.: Camden House, 1987. Detailed reading of the poem, focusing on the narrator's asides, interruptions, and excursions, which Bekker argues help focus on one of Gottfried's main purposes, to illustrate the journey through the various aspects of human love.

Chinca, Mark. *Gottfried von Strassburg: "Tristan."* New York: Cambridge University Press, 1997. Provides a summary of the poem, commentary on its structure and relationship to the Tristan tradition, critical analysis, and details about the original manuscript and scholarly editions.

Hasty, Will, ed. *A Companion to Gottfried von Strassburg's "Tristan."* Rochester, N.Y.: Camden House, 2003. Twelve essays discussing the artistry, themes, and critical reception of the poem; several examine the poem's relationship to other medieval literary works.

Hatto, A. T. "Introduction." *Gottfried von Strassburg: "Tristan."* Rev. ed. New York: Penguin Books, 1967. Discusses the major themes of the work and problems involved in translating Gottfried's medieval German into English; this volume includes the best modern English translation of the poem.

Jackson, W. T. H. *The Anatomy of Love: The "Tristan" of Gottfried von Strassburg*. New York: Columbia University Press, 1971. Extended analysis discussing the intellectual background, poetic structure, and use of language in conveying what Jackson believes is a countercultural view of love for Gottfried's age.

MacDonald, William C. *Arthur and Tristan: On the Intersection of Legends in German Medieval Literature*. Lewiston, N.Y.: Edwin Mellen, 1991. Explores parallels between the Tristan story and Arthurian legends in the work of Gottfried and other medieval German writers.

Sneeringer, Kristine. *Honor, Love, and Isolde in Gottfried's "Tristan."* New York: Peter Lang, 2002. Examines the concept of honor as it was understood by Gottfried's audience; explains how the poet uses structural devices to highlight the transcendent quality of love.

Laurence W. Mazzeno

GÜNTER GRASS

Born: Danzig (now Gdańsk, Poland); October 16, 1927

PRINCIPAL POETRY

Die Vorzüge der Windhühner, 1956
Gleisdreieck, 1960
Selected Poems, 1966
Ausgefragt, 1967 (*New Poems*, 1968)

Poems of Günter Grass, 1969 (also in a bilingual
    edition as *In the Egg, and Other Poems*, 1977)
Originalgraphik, 1970
Gesammelte Gedichte, 1971
Mariazuehren, Hommageàmarie, Inmarypraise,
    1973 (trilingual edition)
Liebe geprüft, 1974 (*Love Tested*, 1975)
Die Gedichte, 1955-1986, 1988
Novemberland: dreizehn Sonette, 1993
Novemberland: Selected Poems, 1956-1993, 1996
    (bilingual edition)
Letzte Tänze, 2003
Dummer August, 2007

OTHER LITERARY FORMS

Günter Grass (gros), already attracting attention in
Germany for his poetry, burst onto the worldwide literary scene in 1959 with his wartime fantasy novel, *Die
Blechtrommel* (1959; *The Tin Drum*, 1962). He would
develop a loyal following for his long fiction, which,
like his poetry, juxtaposes startling imagery against
passages of lyric beauty. Some of the better-known
novels are *Katz und Maus* (1961; *Cat and Mouse*,
1963), *Hundejahre* (1963; *Dog Years*, 1965), *Der Butt*
(1977; *The Flounder*, 1978), *Die Rättin* (1986; *The Rat*,
1987), and *Mein Jahrhundert* (1999; *My Century*,
1999). In the 1960's, Grass added drama to his repertoire with absurdist, politically charged plays. He fu-
eled controversy by publicly supporting Willy Brandt
as German chancellor, wrote the candidate's speeches,
and spoke in support of the Social Democrat platform.
Much of Grass's work from the 1970's onward has
been nonfiction—essays, speeches, memoirs, and lectures—encompassing literature, history, and politics as
they affect Germany. Despite success in other venues,
Grass has regularly returned to writing poetry, which
provides an opportunity to test out on a small scale
ideas that might be appropriate for larger works.

ACHIEVEMENTS

Günter Grass first earned recognition for his poetry,
winning a minor prize in 1955. This honor paled in comparison to the critical acclaim that greeted his initial
novel, *The Tin Drum*, which was showered with awards
and became a best seller. Grass collaborated on the

screenplay for the 1979 film version, which won an
Academy Award for Best Foreign Language Film. Most
of Grass's literary awards are for works in genres other
than poetry. He has garnered top literary awards and
honors, including the Preis der Gruppe 47 (1958), the
Literature Award of the Association of German Critics
(1960), France's Foreign Book Prize (1962), the Georg
Büchner Award (1965), the Fontane Prize (1968), the
Carl von Ossietzky Medal of Honor (1968), the Premio
Internazionale Mondello (1977), the Viareggio-Versilia
Prize (1978), the Alexander-Majakowski Medal,
Gdańsk (1979), the Antonio Feltrinelli Prize (1982),
the Karel Capek Prize (1984), the Leonhard Frank Ring
(1988), the Thomas Mann Award for Literature (1990),
the Sonning Award (1996), the Prince of Asturias
Award for Letters (1999), and the Ernest Toller Award
(2007). He was also granted honorary doctorates at Harvard University and Kenyon College. In 1999, Grass received the Nobel Prize in Literature for his body of work.

BIOGRAPHY

Günter Wilhelm Grass was born in Danzig (now
Gdańsk, Poland), a largely German-populated port on
the Baltic and a protectorate under the League of Nations from 1920 until its absorption into the Third
Reich in 1939. He was the son of Protestant grocer Wilhelm "Willy" Grass and his Catholic wife, Helene
Knoff Grass. Günter and his younger sister were raised
as Catholics. At the rise of the Nazi Party, Grass joined
the Hitler Youth. At the age of fifteen, he volunteered
for German submarine service but was turned down.
However, in 1944, he was drafted. While serving with a
tank division, he was wounded at Cottbus and subsequently captured. He recovered in an American hospital and was briefly interned in a prisoner-of-war camp
before being released in 1946. He soon afterward reunited with his family.

After the war, Grass worked as a potash miner,
black marketer, and jazz-band drummer before landing
a job carving tombstones as an apprentice stonecutter.
He subsequently studied art at the Düsseldorf and
Berlin academies of art (1948-1951 and 1953-1956)
and, at the same time, began writing. In 1954, he married Anna Schwartz, and they would have four children
(in the 1970's, Grass fathered two other children out of

wedlock, by two different women). After winning a poetry prize, he was invited to join the Group 47, which included such well-known German writers as Heinrich Böll, Martin Walser, Hans Werner Richter, and Uwe Johnson. Under the group's auspices, Grass published his first collection of poems and drawings, *Die Vorzüge der Windhühner* (the advantages of windfowl), which in subject matter and surrealistic style would anticipate much of his later work After living in Paris for a time, he attracted worldwide attention in 1959 with the release of his first novel, *The Tin Drum*. He was elected to the German Academy of Arts in 1963.

While earning a reputation as the conscience of postwar Germany, Grass has issued a constant stream of written work across a range of genres. In addition to multiple works of poetry, he has also written numerous plays, novels, political speeches, and scholarly essays. When not writing, he often travels and teaches, and he has lectured at educational institutions such as Harvard University, Yale University, Smith College, and Kenyon College. In 1966, he was writer-in-residence at Co-

lumbia University. In 1978, Grass and his wife were divorced, and he married Utte Grunert in 1979. From 1983 to 1986, he served as president of the Berlin Academy of Arts. His memoir *Beim Häuten der Zweibel* (2006; *Peeling the Onion*, 2007) revealed for the first time that Grass was a member of the notorious Waffen-SS during World War II.

ANALYSIS

Before he became a world-renowned novelist, Günter Grass wrote poetry that presaged, echoed, or underscored the tones and themes of his fiction. His poetry and fiction both owe a debt to Franz Kafka for their concise, parable-like nature.

From the beginning of his career, Grass demonstrated a unique poetic voice that offered readers and listeners several overlapping personas. The sensitive, wide-eyed teenager of World War II—who witnessed terrible things that left indelible impressions on his psyche—is seldom absent. The cynical critic is lurking, too, extrapolating on small observations to broach more complex issues of greater import, to ask questions for which there are no answers, and to hope for the best while expecting the worst. The radical liberal sometimes shows up to rant. Grass the humorist is often present: His wit is sometimes sardonic, tinted black, prurient, or crude, but comic relief has helped soften audience reaction as he deftly negotiates between the extremes of anarchy and servility. The most obvious presence is the craftsperson: Grass at his best has an uncanny ability to blend a few precise words with memorable images to produce symbols that extend into metaphors. His early verse in particular is notable for its concision: Grass pares language to its essence, resulting in epigram-like pieces (ostensibly about food or common objects or ordinary events) of surreal brevity with multiple layers of meaning.

Grass's poetry, often enhanced by the author's evocative drawings and etchings, generally touches on one of several broad subjects. A constant thread is autobiography, life as filtered through the poet's consciousness, where the everyday has the potential to illuminate the universal. National history is also a major concern. Grass muses about the effects of the devastation wrought on Danzig, where he grew up, and of the de-

Günter Grass (Mottke Weissman/Courtesy, D.C. Public Library)

molition of Germany, and speculates on how events from the past shape the present and inform the future of his countrymen and of the world at large.

The poetry of Grass can be appreciated on several levels. Casual readers can enjoy the author's sly turns of phrase, the quickly sketched visions that open up into panoramas of possibility, and the rhythm (and occasional rhyme), especially in bilingual editions. Depth of understanding can be increased from an examination of the meaning beneath the surface; the similes, metaphors, and allusions reveal new facets. Complete enjoyment of Grass's poetry comes with specialized knowledge: the ability to grasp linguistic puns and wordplay in the original German and a familiarity with German history and politics.

NOVEMBERLAND

Novemberland, which collects nearly forty years of Grass's work, contains fifty-four poems, including the thirteen-sonnet series called "Novemberland 1993." The formal, traditional sonnets focus on significant events from German history that happened to fall in November. In the second poem of the series, "Novemberland," Grass deals with three events that took place on November 9: the Beer Hall Putsch when Adolf Hitler unsuccessfully tried to seize power in Munich, Bavaria, and Germany (1923); *Kristallnacht*, the night when the windows of Jewish businesses were smashed (1938); and the razing of the Berlin Wall as a precursor to the reunification of Germany (1989), which Grass vehemently opposed. Unlike most other poems in the collection, the "November" series is serious, with little overt humor, and moralistic in tone. Grass rails against talk shows, complains about taxes, criticizes the destructiveness of neo-Nazis, and compares the workings of the German government to a carnival. Grass contrasts the old Germany with the new and reacts with anger or sorrow to the problems associated with reunification.

Grass's trademark—grotesque, Dali-esque images, captured with a few poignant strokes—is present throughout the collection. In "Family Matters," museum patrons can see aborted fetuses floating in glass jars while the unborn embryos contemplate their erstwhile parents' fate, and in "The Jellied Pig's Head," Grass presents a recipe for jellied pig as a means to con-

demn those who lack the courage to take a moral stance. In this collection, Grass employs simple symbols; for example, in "The Flag of Poland," a desiccated apple stands for the loss not only of innocence and childhood, but also of human immortality in the Garden of Eden. In "Nursey Rhyme," children's laughter becomes sinister and treasonous in what the poet views as Germany's repressed society. Other poems such as "Prophet's Fare" offer extended political allegory or spotlight troubles associated with emigration, mostly in blank verse. As a collection, *Novemberland* gives readers a healthy dose of the highly compacted abstract concept with multitudinous meanings, which Grass is a master at creating.

LETZTE TÄNZE

Letzte Tänze (last dance), a trilingual volume (German, English, and Celtic) featuring illustrations by Grass, is highly autobiographical. Two contradictory themes dominate the collection, both indicated by the title. The word "last" suggests the poet's awareness that at the age of seventy-six—his age when this book was published in 2003—he is approaching the end of his life. Like the elderly everywhere, he waxes nostalgic, reminiscing about the way things used to be in the good old days. Regrets and missed opportunities are relived in agonizing detail, and fond occasions take on a rainbow aura. Memory is faulty and selective, and small incidents from the past loom larger because of the impact they had on the individual. However, the word "dances" indicates that Grass is not finished yet. Dancing, the pure joy of moving unrestrained to different musical beats, provides physical stimulation, which in turn—on the theory that a sound mind resides in a sound body—boosts mental activity. The very process of writing about something as exuberant as dance, Grass seems to say, is enough to keep one young in the twilight years.

Despite the narrow constraints of his overarching theme, Grass covers a variety of subjects with an impish, sometimes vulgar, touch. In this collection, the poet subtly acknowledges his acceptance of his public responsibility as Germany's moral compass (a position that would be severely undermined several years later by his revelation that he served, albeit briefly, in the hated SS). Though his role as cultural arbiter is a serious one, Grass insists on being allowed to exercise the playful side of his powerful intellect and to be excused if he steps on a few sensitive toes as he whirls in dance.

OTHER MAJOR WORKS

LONG FICTION: *Die Blechtrommel*, 1959 (*The Tin Drum*, 1962); *Katz und Maus*, 1961 (*Cat and Mouse*, 1963); *Hundejahre*, 1963 (*Dog Years*, 1965); *Örtlich betäubt*, 1969 (*Local Anesthetic*, 1969); *Aus dem Tagebuch einer Schnecke*, 1972 (*From the Diary of a Snail*, 1973); *Der Butt*, 1977 (*The Flounder*, 1978); *Das Treffen in Telgte*, 1979 (*The Meeting at Telgte*, 1981); *Danziger Trilogie*, 1980 (*Danzig Trilogy*, 1987; includes *The Tin Drum*, *Cat and Mouse*, and *Dog Years*); *Kopfgeburten: Oder, Die Deutschen sterben aus*, 1980 (*Headbirths: Or, The Germans Are Dying Out*, 1982); *Die Rättin*, 1986 (*The Rat*, 1987); *Unkenrufe*, 1992 (*The Call of the Toad*, 1992); *Ein Weites Feld*, 1995 (*Too Far Afield*, 2000); *Mein Jahrhundert*, 1999 (*My Century*, 1999); *Im Krebsgang*, 2002 (*Crabwalk*, 2003); *Das Danzig-Sextett*, 2005 (includes *Die Blechtrommel*, *Katz und Maus*, *Hundejahre*, *Der Butt*, *Unkenrufe*, and *Im Krebsgang*).

PLAYS: *Hochwasser*, pr. 1957 (revised pb. 1963; *Flood*, 1967); *Stoffreste*, pr. 1957 (ballet); *Beritten hin und zurück*, pb. 1958 (*Rocking Back and Forth*, 1967); *Gesellschaft im Herbst*, pr. 1958; *Noch zehn Minuten bis Buffalo*, pb. 1958 (*Only Ten Minutes to Buffalo*, 1967); *Onkel, Onkel*, pr. 1958 (revised pb. 1965; *Mister, Mister*, 1967); *Fünf Köche*, pr. 1959 (ballet); *Die bösen Köche: Ein Drama in fünf Akte*n, pr., pb. 1961 (*The Wicked Cooks*, 1967); *Mystisch-barbarisch-gelangweilt*, pr. 1963; *POUM: Oder, Die Vergangenheit fliegt mit*, pb. 1965; *Die Plebejer proben den Aufstand*, pr. 1966 (*The Plebians Rehearse the Uprising*, 1966); *Four Plays*, 1967 (includes *The Flood, Mister, Mister, Only Ten Minutes to Buffalo*, and *The Wicked Cooks*); *Davor: Ein Stuck in dreizehn Szenen*, pr., pb. 1969 (partial translation as *Uptight*, 1970; *Max*, 1972); *Theaterspiele*, 1970 (includes *Noch zehn Minuten bis Buffalo, Hochwasser, Onkel, Onkel*, and *Die bösen Köche*); *Die Vogelscheuchen*, 1970 (ballet).

SCREENPLAY: *Katz und Maus*, 1967 (with others).

RADIO PLAYS: *Zweiunddreissig Zähne*, 1959; *Goldmaeulchen*, 1963 (staged 1964).

NONFICTION: *Der Inhalt als Widerstand*, 1957; *O Susanna: Ein Jazzbilderbuch: Blues, Balladen, Spirituals, Jazz*, 1959 (with Herman Wilson); *Die Ballerina*, 1965; *Dich Singe ich, Demokratie*, 1965; *Fünf Wahlreden*, 1965; *Reder über das Selbstverständliche*, 1965; *Der Fall Axel C. Springer am Beispiel Arnold Zweig: Eine Rede, ihr Anlass, und die Folgen*, 1967; *Briefe über die Grenze: Versuch eines Ost-West-Dialogs*, 1968 (with Pavel Kohout); *Günter Grass: Ausgewählte Texte, Abbildungen, Faksimiles, Bio-Bibliographie*, 1968; *Über das Selbstverständliche: Reden, Aufsätze, offene Brief, Kommentare*, 1968 (partial translation as *Speak Out: Speeches, Open Letters, Commentaries*, 1969); *Über meinen Lehrer Döblin und andere Vorträge*, 1968; *Kunst oder Pornographie? Der Prozess Grass gegen Ziesel: Eine Dokumentation*, 1969 (with Kurt Ziesel); *Die Schweinekopfsülze*, 1969 (with Horst Janssen); *Speak Out: Speeches, Open Letters, Commentaries*, 1969; *Der Schriftsteller als Bürger: Eine Siebenjarhesbilanz*, 1973; *Die Bürger und seine Stimme*, 1974; *Günter Grass: Ein Materialienbuch*, 1976; *Denkzettel: Politische Reden und Aufsätze (1965-1976)*, 1978; *Die Blechtrommel als Film*, 1979 (with Volker Schlöndorff); *Werkverzeichnis der Radierungen*, 1979; *Aufsätze zur Literatur*, 1980; *Günter Grass: Katalog zur Ausstellung in Winter 82/83 der Galerie Schürer, CH-Regensberg—Ausstellung über das Zeichnerische, grafische und plastiche Werk*, 1982; *Zeichnen und Schreiben: Das bildnerische Werk des Schriftstellers Günter Grass*, 1982 (with Anselm Dreher; *Graphics and Writing*, 1983); *Zeichnungen und Texte 1954-1977*, 1982 (with others; *Drawings and Words, 1954-1977*, 1983); *Ach, Butt, dein Märchen geht böse aus: Gedichte und Radierungen*, 1983; *Radierungen und Texte, 1972-1982*, 1984 (with others; *Drawings and Words, 1972-1982*, 1985); *Widerstand lernen: Politische Gegenreden, 1980-1983*, 1984; *Geschenkt Freiheit: Rede zum 8 Mai 1945*, 1985; *Günter Grass: Werk und Wirkung*, 1985 (with Rudolf Wolff); *On Writing and Politics, 1967-1983*, 1985; *Günter Grass: Mit Selbstzeunissen und Bilddokumenten*, 1986 (with Heinrich Vormweg); *In Kupfer, auf Stein*, 1986; *Ausstellung anlässlich des 60: Geburtstages von Günter Grass*, 1987; *Günter Grass: Graphik und Plastik*, 1987 (with Walter Timm); *Günter Grass: Mit Sophie in die*

Pilze gegangen, 1987; *Günter Grass: Radierungen, Lithgraphien, Zeichnungen, Plastiken, Gedichte,* 1987; *Calcutta: Zeichnungen,* 1988; *Zunge zeigen,* 1988 (*Show Your Tongue,* 1988); *Meine grüne Wiese: Kurzprosa,* 1989; *Skizzenbuch,* 1989; *Deutscher Lastenausgleich: Wider das dumpfe Einheitsgebot,* 1990 (*Two States—One Nation?,* 1990); *Deutschland, einig Vaterland? Ein Streitgespräch,* 1990 (with Rudolf Augstein); *Günter Grass: Begleitheft zur Ausstellung der Stadt-und Universitätsbibliothek Frankfurt am Main, 13 Februar bis 30 März 1990,* 1990; *Ein Schnäppchen namens DDR: Letzte Reden vorm Glockengeläut,* 1990; *Schreiben nach Auschwitz: Frankfurter Poetik-Vorlesung,* 1990 ("Writing After Auschwitz," in *Two States—One Nation?,* 1990); *Totes Holz: Ein Nachruf,* 1990; *Nachdenken über Deutschland,* 1990-1991 (with others); *Gegen die verstreichende Zeit: Reden, Aufsätze und Gespräche, 1989-1991,* 1991; *Günter Grass, vier Jahrzehnte,* 1991; *Vier Jahrzehnte: Ein Werkstattbericht,* 1991; *Meine grüne Wiese: Geschichten und Zeichnungen,* 1992; *Rede vom Verlust: Über den Niedergang der politischen Kultur in geeinten Deutschland,* 1992 ("On Loss," in *The Future of German Democracy,* 1993); *Rede über den Standort,* 1993; *Schaden begrenzen, oder auf die Füsse treten: Ein Gespräch,* 1993 (with Regine Hindebrandt); *Angestiftet, Partei zu ergreifen,* 1994; *Die Deutschen und ihre Dichter,* 1995; *Gestern, vor 50 Jahren: Ein deutsche-japanischer Briefwechsel,* 1995 (with Kenzaburō Ōe; *Just Yesterday, Fifty Years Ago: A Critical Dialogue on the Anniversary of the End of the Second World War,* 1999); *Der Schriftsteller als Zeitgenosse,* 1996; *Fundsachen für Nichtleser,* 1997; *Auf einem anderen Blatt: Zeichnungen,* 1999; *Fortsetzung folgt: Literatur und Geschichte,* 1999; *Für-und Widerworte,* 1999; *Vom Abenteuer der Aufklärung: Werkstattgespräche,* 1999 (with Harro Zimmerman); *Wort und Bild: Tübinger Poetik Vorlesung & Materialien,* 1999 (with others); *Ohne Stimme: Reder zugunsten des Volkes der Roma und Sinti,* 2000; *Fünf Jahrzehnte: Ein Werkstattbericht,* 2001; *In einem reichen Land: Zeugnisse alltäglichen Leidens an der Gessellschaft,* 2002; *Briefe, 1959-1994,* 2003; *Freiheit nach Börenmass; Geschenkte Freiheit: Zwei Reden zum 8 Mai 1945,* 2005; *Beim Häuten der Zweibel,* 2006 (*Peel-*

ing the Onion, 2007); *Steine wälzen: Essays und Reden, 1997-2007,* 2007; *Die Box: Dunkelkammergeschichten,* 2008; *Unterwegs von Deutschland nach Deutschland,* 2009.

EDITED TEXTS: *Dokumente zur politischen Wirkung,* 1971 (with others); *Gemischte Klasse: Prosa, Lyrik, Szenen & Essays,* 2000.

MISCELLANEOUS: *Ein Ort für Zufalle,* 1965 (illustrations and text by Ingeborg Buchmann); *Cat and Mouse, and Other Writings,* 1994; *Werkausgabe,* 1997 (16 volumes); *The Günter Grass Reader,* 2004 (Helmut Frielinghaus, editor).

BIBLIOGRAPHY

Braun, Rebecca, and Frank Brunssen, eds. *Changing the Nation: Günter Grass in International Perspective.* Würzburg, Germany: Königshausen & Neumann, 2008. Grass scholars from various countries examine his work with an emphasis on its international stature.

Grass, Günter, et al. *The Günter Grass Reader.* New York: Houghton Mifflin Harcourt, 2004. This volume features a wide range of work from Grass's career, including excerpts from novels, short fictional pieces, essays, and poems, some published for the first time in English.

Grimm, Reinhold, and Irmgard Elsner Hunt, eds. *German Twentieth Century Poetry.* New York: Continuum, 2001. This bilingual collection includes the work of sixty modern German poets in chronological order, including Berthold Brecht, Hugo von Hofmannsthal, Franz Kafka, Rainer Maria Rilke, Nelly Sachs, and Grass. Contains biographical information on each poet.

Hutchinson, Peter. "Politics and Playfulness in Günter Grass's Sonnet Cycle 'Novemberland.'" *The German Quarterly* 78, no. 2 (May 19, 2008): 224-239. This article focuses on Grass's "Novemberland" sonnets, with particular attention paid to the poet's use of humor to poke fun at politics and politicians.

Kampchen, Martin. *My Broken Love: Günter Grass in India and Bangladesh.* New York: Viking Books, 2001. An interesting study of Grass's travels to and sojourn in Southeast Asia, featuring an analysis of the work produced during and after his visit.

Keele, Alan Frank. *Understanding Günter Grass*. Columbia: University of South Carolina Press, 1988. Provides a good introduction to Grass's works for the general reader. Covers the novels through *The Rat*.

Ohsoling, Hilke. *Günter Grass: Catalogue Raisonne. Volume 1—The Etchings*. London: Steidl, 2008. Profusely illustrated, this series of books examines the drawings, etchings, lithographs, watercolors, and sculptures that Grass created for his books of fiction and poetry. Other volumes deal with the poet's artistic efforts in other media.

O'Neill, Patrick. *Günter Grass Revisited*. New York: Twayne, 1999. Presents a sound overview of Grass's works. Includes chronology, select bibliography, and index.

Preece, Julian. *The Life and Work of Günter Grass: Literature, History, Politics*. New York: Palgrave Macmillan, 2004. A thorough study of the writer, analyzing a full range of his work in a political and historical context, with special emphasis on his literary influences.

Taberner, Stuart. *The Cambridge Companion to Günter Grass*. New York: Cambridge University Press, 2009. Essays cover Grass's entire body of work, with special emphasis on his literary style in relation to his life.

Jack Ewing

GUILLAUME DE LORRIS *and* JEAN DE MEUNG

Guillaume de Lorris
Born: Lorris(?), France; c. 1215
Died: Unknown; c. 1278
Also known as: Guillaume de Loury

Jean de Meung
Born: Meung-sur-Loire, France; c. 1240
Died: Paris, France; 1305
Also known as: Jean de Mehun; Jean de Meun;
  Jehan Clopinel

PRINCIPAL POETRY

Le Roman de la rose, thirteenth century (*The Romance of the Rose*; partial translation c. 1370, complete translation 1900)

OTHER LITERARY FORMS

Guillaume de Lorris (gee-YOHM duh LO-rees) is not known to have written anything other than the first portion of *The Romance of the Rose*. Jean de Meung (zhon duh MUHNG), perhaps in connection with a scholarly career, undertook translations from a number of Latin works. He rendered Vegetius's fourth century *Epitoma rei militaris* as *L'Art de chevalerie*; also extant is Jean's translation of the letters of Abélard and Héloïse, but his versions of Giraud de Barri's *The Marvels of Ireland* and Saint Aelred of Rievaulx's *De spirituali amicitia* (early twelfth century) have not survived. This latter work had a discernible influence on *The Romance of the Rose*, particularly in the view of friendship presented by the character Reason. Jean was influenced most, however, by one other work he translated, Boethius's *De consolatione philosophiae* (523; *The Consolation of Philosophy*, late ninth century). Boethius, as a character in his own work, is instructed in points of Neoplatonic metaphysics by Philosophy, and Jean adopts both this instructional mode and much of Philosophy's teachings in his portrayal of Reason.

Manuscript tradition assigns to Jean two other poems, a *Testament* (thirteenth century) and *Codicil* (thirteenth century). This ascription is uncertain, but it is worth mentioning that the *Testament* contains a retraction of certain "vain little poems," probably not intended to include *The Romance of the Rose*. As is also the case with Geoffrey Chaucer, such a retraction is problematic at best, and critics tend to divide into two camps, either questioning the sincerity of such last-minute penitence, or else imparting thereby a greater moral seriousness to even the apparently playful aspects of the author's works.

ACHIEVEMENTS

Guillaume de Lorris and Jean de Mueng's *The Romance of the Rose* is a major work of Old French literature and of the allegorical genre. Its popularity was immediate and widespread (as attested by the more than three hundred manuscripts that still survive), and the poem exerted a strong influence at least down to Elizabethan times. By 1400, interest in the poem had developed into a "quarrel," or debate, with one faction (including Christine de Pizan) decrying the misogyny and lasciviousness in the poem, and the other faction upholding the poem's aesthetic worth and moral soundness. Probably the most illustrious medieval author to be influenced by *The Romance of the Rose* was Chaucer, who translated part of the poem into Middle English. Dean Spruill Fansler considered Jean to have been Chaucer's "schoolmaster," in that Chaucer's first exposure to authorities such as Boethius and Ambrosius Theodosius Macrobius was doubtless through *The Romance of the Rose*. Chaucer's first major poem, *Book of the Duchess* (c. 1370), is a dream allegory much indebted to Guillaume in its descriptive passages. Subsequently, *The Romance of the Rose* became for Chaucer but one of many Continental influences, but it is worth noting that Jean's portrait of the Old Woman is echoed in Chaucer's Wife of Bath. A major contemporary of Chaucer, the anonymous Pearl-Poet, makes explicit reference to *The Romance of the Rose*, and the poem exerted a structural influence on his dream allegory *Pearl* (c. 1400).

The popularity of *The Romance of the Rose* continued into the Renaissance; as Alan Gunn notes in *The Mirror of Love: A Reinterpretation of "The Romance of the Rose"* (1951), twenty-one editions of the poem were printed between 1481 and 1538. Edmund Spenser, particularly in *The Faerie Queene* (1590, 1596), is the major figure of this period to have reaped benefits from a reading of Jean. From him, according to scholar Rosemund Tuve, Spenser learned how "to use large images in a huge design, philosophically profound if allegorically read."

In the following centuries, interest in the poem waned as allegory in general fell into disfavor. In the twentieth century, beginning perhaps with C. S. Lewis, critics and readers have once again found in *The Ro-*

mance of the Rose a work of complex artistry. Interpretations of the poem vary widely, however—so much so that scholars may even be said to have entered into a new "quarrel of the Rose."

BIOGRAPHY

Most of what is known of both authors of *The Romance of the Rose* is inferred from their works alone. Midway through the poem, the God of Love mentions two of his most faithful servants, Guillaume de Lorris and Jean Chopinel ("the lame") of Meung-sur-Loire. From the statement (line 10,588) that Jean de Meung will continue Guillaume's work forty years later, critics have worked back to a date of around 1230 or 1235 for Guillaume's portion and 1275 for that of Jean. Jean is otherwise known to have lived in Paris from 1292 until 1305. Presumably, he had left Meung-sur-Loire, a small village southwest of Orléans, for the intellectual climate surrounding the recently established University of Paris.

An illustration from The Romance of the Rose *(thirteenth century).* (Hulton Archive/Getty Images)

ANALYSIS

A sense of allegory has not been completely lost to the modern reader, who is likely to have come on instances in George Orwell's *Animal Farm* (1945), if not in John Bunyan, Spenser, or medieval morality plays. Guillaume de Lorris imparted a major impetus to the popularity of one subgenre of allegory, the dream allegory. In contrast, to understand Jean de Meung's "exploded" approach, it is worth referring to the more encyclopedic style of allegory that Boethius had anticipated and that was developing shortly before Jean's time in, for example, the *Complaint of Nature* by Alanus de Insulis. One other convention that may prove to be a barrier for the modern reader of *The Romance of the Rose* is that of courtly love, which was found earlier in Provençal lyrics and their reinterpretation of Ovid's *Ars amatoria* (c. 2 B.C.E.; *Art of Love*, 1612), and in the romances of Chrétien de Troyes. The relationship of this convention to medieval reality is widely disputed, but its signs are obvious enough: The Lover is struck by Cupid's arrows and undergoes a physically debilitating "lovesickness," which can be relieved only by the Lady's favors.

The first and most obvious feature to note about the text proper is that it is the work of two authors. Guillaume's portion, lines 1 through 4058, was left unfinished. In some manuscripts, a quick and inartistic close was provided, presumably by some enterprising scribe. Jean's massive continuation (to line 21,780), however, became a lasting part of the poem. The fact of dual authorship raises questions about the unity of the work—that is, whether Jean understood Guillaume's intentions.

THE ROMANCE OF THE ROSE

Guillaume establishes the pattern of versification for *The Romance of the Rose*. Ambrosius Theodosius Macrobius, author of *In somnium Scipionis* (c. 400, *Commentary on the "Dream of Scipio,"* 1952) is cited as an authority. Since Macrobius categorized merely erotic dreams as meaningless "insomnia," some commentators have inferred that Guillaume must have intended his readers to delve beneath the first, erotic level of the dream allegory that follows.

One night, the author, "in the twentieth year of his life," fell asleep and dreamed what he would call *The Romance of the Rose*, in which may be found "the whole art of love." It is Love who commands him to retell the dream, in a poem undertaken "for she who is so precious and so worthy to be loved that she should be called Rose." These remarks can be examined closely for clues to the interpretation of what follows. If the dream is told at the urging of Love, it seems unlikely, as Lewis pointed out, that Guillaume intended to close with a "palinode" (or repudiation) of Love. The dedicatory remark indicates a clear affinity between the Rose and "the Lady," but a more precise allegorical interpretation is not given.

The Dreamer wakes to a fine May morning, dresses, and goes out from the town, led on by the sweet singing of birds. (The lyrical landscape through which he walks becomes a commonplace used by other writers in dream allegories.) He follows a river to a garden enclosed by high walls, on which are depicted the first of the allegorical figures: Covetousness, with her clawed hands; Old Age with her mossy ears; and so on. (Symbolic details such as these recall the iconographic details of medieval paintings.) Apparently, these figures signify those qualities banned from the Garden of Delight and perhaps from the courtly life in which young love may bloom. Inside the wall, the figures will be animated, and yet the static, pictorial sense with which Guillaume begins his allegory is consistent with the generally decorous tone of his work.

The Dreamer, hearing birdsong from within the garden, seeks out a doorway, on which he knocks and which eventually is opened by Idleness. She exhibits all the qualities of beauty that are commonplaces in medieval literature, including sweet breath and clear skin (which is likely to have been rather rare in medieval reality). The Dreamer wanders on to the next group of allegorical figures: Diversion, Joy, Courtesy, and their company of dancers. All are lovely, elegant youths dressed in the most delicate fashions. Surpassing them, however, is the God of Love in his robe of many flowers, with all manner of birds flocking about him. The sweetness of these scenes and the sylphlike creatures who frolic about in them may fail to charm modern readers, especially those who encounter the poem in two English translations: Charles Dahlberg's prose version or Harry W. Robbins's very pedestrian pentameters. Readers who cannot approach the Old French might take a look at these passages in the Middle English version, or in Frederick S. Ellis's Victorian version, which goes a long way toward reproducing "the harmony . . . such as would cheer the saddest wight,/ And wake his soul to sweet delight."

The entrance of the God of Love gives way to another of Guillaume's decorative allegories, this time involving the God of Love's twin bows and ten arrows (named for encouragements and discouragements to love: Beauty, Despair, and so forth). This sort of schematic allegory appears in passages in Spenser's work but does not become a major part of Jean's repertoire in his continuation of the poem.

The Dreamer wanders off again, cataloging the varieties of fruit, trees, animals, and flowers he sees, until he arrives at the Fountain of Love, where Narcissus died. In the bottom of this pool, he sees twin crystals in which are reflected all of the garden, including, finally, a single rosebud that he must possess. At this moment, he is struck by Love's (encouraging) arrows; he becomes Love's vassal and is instructed in his commandments. It is in this section that Guillaume's poem is most clearly an art of love, and yet the simultaneous involvement of the Narcissus myth has yielded conflicting interpretations. The crystals are seen either as the Lady's eyes, reflecting the whole garden of her love, or as the Lover's own eyes, the narcissistic point of view from which his love will spring. In this view, what is ostensibly an art of love gives way on a deeper level to an allegory of misdirected (because it is not divine) love.

At this point in the text, the Dreamer becomes the Lover, and his quest of the Rose begins. The Lover attempts a direct approach with Fair Welcome but is snubbed by Danger. Reason instructs him of his folly, but the Lover tries again, counseled by Friend and Venus, and obtains a kiss. Jealousy erects a castle enclosing the Rose and imprisoning Fair Welcome, with the Old Woman set to guard him. The Lover laments this ill turn of Fortune's wheel. It is worth remarking that in these passages Guillaume's allegorical methods begin to incorporate monologues offered by various advisers, a technique that will be the dominant mode employed by Jean.

CRITIQUES OF JEAN'S CONTRIBUTION

In analyzing Jean's portion, it is perhaps best to begin with a short synopsis of his allegorical plot. Reason and then Friend reappear to give advice, after which the God of Love summons his barons for an assault on the castle. False Seeming and Abstinence overcome the gatekeeper Foul Mouth, whereupon the Old Woman panders to Fair Welcome. Danger interferes again, however, and Fair Welcome is again imprisoned. Venus, Nature, and Genius are enlisted as helpers; Venus shoots a flaming arrow through an aperture in the tower, through which the Lover then passes with his pilgrim's staff. After a few assaults on a narrow passage, the Lover scatters seed on the rosebud, plucks it, and then awakens from his dream.

Lewis believed that Jean was an inept allegorist and points to the redundant appearances of Reason, Friend, and Danger. He also faults Jean for lapsing out of allegory into "literal narration" in the Old Woman episode, but here he is clearly too prescriptive in his ideas of allegory. The development of allegory, as John V. Fleming argues, was in the direction of increased exemplification and thence to verisimilitude; William Langland's figures likewise slip over into the literal, and even Chaucer's seemingly realistic characters are in part allegorical representations of the occupations for which they are named.

More challenging are Lewis's other charges, that Jean has no sense of structure, is a popularizing "encyclopedist," and is uninspired even in his satires. These charges stem from the various "digressions" and soliloquies (not represented in the plot synopsis above) that stretch out Jean's portion to its unassimilable length. The advocates for the various approaches to love summon up wide-ranging sets of arguments that recall the exhaustiveness of Scholastic theologians and the comprehensiveness of the encyclopedic poets immediately preceding Jean. All manner of authorities are cited, any number of exemplary tales are retold, and a great deal of practical advice is dispensed. Guillaume had indeed cited Macrobius, told the tale of Narcissus, and given the ten commandments of love, but in nothing like the proportions exhibited by Jean.

To the charge that Jean was a popularist, Gunn counters that Jean in various passages asserts that his intentions are literary, not didactic, and that his is a handbook of love, and not of the various other disciplines from which illustrative matter is drawn. Jean fulfills his desire to popularize Boethius via a separate translation, rather than in the derivative passages in *The Romance of the Rose*. Gunn's defense of Jean's aims as being aesthetic rather than didactic, however, probably tips the balance too far in the opposite direction. Partway through her discourse, Reason states: "Your country is not on earth. You can easily learn this from the clerks who explain Boethius's *The Consolation of Philosophy* and the meanings which lie in it. He who would translate it for the laity would do them a service." Shortly thereafter, the Lover interjects, "Ah, lady, for the king of angels, teach me by all means what things can be mine." Jean probably did not intend his work to be read as an encyclopedia, but as a Boethian work that, while not without aesthetic intentions, could be mined for *sententiae* or authoritative statements—and not only concerning love, for Reason here addresses the riches of the spirit.

As for the quality of Jean's satire, Lewis was clearly too dismissive of its merits, stating that of Jean's two main targets, women and churchmen, "neither is a novel subject for satire." Lewis was disgruntled, as most modern readers tend to be, by Jean's "general vice of diffuseness," which lulls one into inattentiveness through each "gallop of thousands of couplets." By taking a cue from the Dreamer, however, and strolling leisurely through Jean's labyrinthine garden, the reader will discover some flowers of wit. One of the more extended satires of women is found in Friend's discourse, and one may also find there many cynical observations on opportunistic love. The discourse of False Seeming has been read more profitably not as a vague satire on clerics, but as a specific attack on the contemporary development of the mendicant orders of the church. In addition to these satires, there can be found many amusing instances of an irony whereby Jean undercuts a speaker's view, or wherein the Lover exhibits a comical obtuseness. (Tuve's study singles out and illuminates many such passages.)

The charge that Jean's work is lacking in structure can best be considered in conjunction with the question of the poem's unity. Jean's narrative follows a more as-

sociative logic than that of Guillaume, with one subject leading to another in what sometimes seems like a nightmare of digressiveness. It is inconceivable that Guillaume would have gone on at such length. The two sections are also quite different in tone and allegorical method. In Guillaume's section, the tone is decorous, as emblematized in his pictorial, iconographic approach to allegory. With Jean, the tone is abstract and anarchical, as embodied in the *psychomachia* ("soul-battle" or war of abstractions) of the assault on the castle, and didactic, as achieved by means of the Boethian technique of instruction. The differences are everywhere evident, but can Jean's section be read as in any way fulfilling Guillaume's?

Two main structural metaphors have been advanced as justifying the shifts that occur in Jean's section. The first of these is the threefold progress with which the Church fathers interpreted the Fall: the suggestion to the senses (Satan), delight of the heart (Eve), and consent of the reason (Adam). The Dreamer had already been seduced by the sensations of the garden, then shot through with the passions of Love; Jean, in addressing the third, intellectual seduction, sensibly enough takes an approach by way of the debates of the scholarly world. The second traditional framework cited is that of the *gradus amoris*, or five "steps of love"; Guillaume provides the four preliminaries, and Jean gathers all his faculties to address the final, climactic phase. These arguments depend on the assumption of traditions so pervasive as to preclude explicit references to them within the text—traditions simply taken for granted. While this assumption remains debatable, what can perhaps more easily be agreed upon is that Jean's section in itself is unified enough to provide at least a sustained commentary on Guillaume; a problem nevertheless remains in interpreting the precise stance taken by Jean on any of the individual issues he raises.

This problem recurs when one considers whether Jean's allegory is capable of a thoroughgoing religious interpretation or is ultimately secular in its outlook. It is by no means obvious how a reader should weight the various philosophies presented by the allegorical figures. The two figures who seem to have the most authority are Reason and Nature. Those who favor a Boethian solution to the poem's metaphysics feel that

Reason comes closest to being Jean's spokesperson. Nature, however, outweighs Reason at least in the sheer bulk of text assigned to her, and so Jean has been said to advocate her brand of secular regeneration. That the poem closes with the attainment of the Rose lends support to this interpretation; Jean is then seen as a free-thinker, ahead of his time, or as a clerkly satirist of the pretensions of courtly love. A perhaps more attractive view asserts that Jean ironically undercuts every philosophical system presented in the poem, leaving a series of negations and partial truths that the Lover, of his very (fallen) nature, cannot but fail to integrate. A parallel to Jean's technique can be found in the *via negativa* of some kinds of Scholasticism.

Running somewhat counter to these intratextual battles is the view, argued most extensively by Fleming, that *The Romance of the Rose* was not seen by its contemporaries as invoking any serious tensions with received Roman Catholic thought. One medieval reader of the poem had declared that Dante's *La divina commedia* (c. 1320; *The Divine Comedy*, 1802) was a "copy" of *The Romance of the Rose*, and manuscript illuminations likewise seem to gloss the poem theologically. The poem was well received at first in conservative religious circles, and only toward the end of the Middle Ages did the "quarrel" as to its moral effects arise. In Fleming's view, Jean left himself open to such misinterpretation by letting some characters run on to such lengths that readers lost sight of his more orthodox pronouncements.

This stance has as its major strength an honest attempt to read the poem through the eyes of its contemporaries rather than from a twentieth century point of view. It is by no means certain, however, that medieval "criticism" had as its goal the impartiality to which modern critics ideally aspire. There is ample evidence of a countertendency to draw numerous contradictory readings from a given allegorical work, as a kind of speculative exercise. Furthermore, it seems presumptuous to dismiss the "quarrel" as belonging to an age that had forgotten how to read allegory correctly. The comparison to *The Divine Comedy* points equally to that work's greater sense of integration of courtly and religious ideals. In the end, it seems necessary to grant to *The Romance of the Rose*, as to Chaucer's *The Canterbury Tales* (1387-1400) and Langland's *The Vision of William, Concerning Piers the Plowman* (c. 1362, A Text; c. 1377, B Text; c. 1393, C Text; also known as *Piers Plowman*), a profound and ultimately unresolvable ambiguity that reflects the questing and uncertain spirit of a sophisticated age.

BIBLIOGRAPHY

Arden, Heather M. *The Romance of the Rose*. Boston: Twayne, 1987. A general introduction to the work, including detailed outline and plot summary, discussion of cultural and literary contexts, and a review of critical approaches. Includes a chronology and a selected annotated bibliography.

Brownlee, Kevin, and Sylvia Huot, eds. *Rethinking "The Romance of the Rose": Text, Image, Reception*. Philadelphia: University of Pennsylvania Press, 1992. A collection of thirteen essays by distinguished critics of the poem, most written expressly for this volume. Three focus on Guillaume de Lorris, two on Jean de Meung, two on manuscript illuminations, and six on the early reception of the poem inside and outside France.

Christine de Pizan and Jean de Montreuil. *Debate of "The Romance of the Rose."* Translated and edited by David F. Hult. Chicago: University of Chicago Press, 2010. Translations of documents related to the debate over *The Romance of the Rose* and other writings by Christine de Pizan that put it into context.

Heller-Roazen, Daniel. *Fortune's Faces: The "Roman de la Rose" and the Poetics of Contingency*. Baltimore: The Johns Hopkins University Press, 2003. A critical analysis of *The Romance of the Rose* that focuses on the relation of the second part to the first: whether it was intended to complete the poem or to stand as a separate work.

Hult, David F. *Self-Fulfilling Prophecies: Readership and Authority in the First "Roman de la Rose."* New York: Cambridge University Press, 1986. Offers a detailed analysis of Guillaume de Lorris's section of the work and argues that it is not fragmentary but finished, a complete artistic whole.

Huot, Sylvia. *"The Romance of the Rose" and Its Medieval Readers: Interpretation, Reception, Manuscript Transmission*. 1993. Reprint. New York: Cambridge University Press, 2007. Addresses the reception of *The Romance of the Rose* by French-speaking readers from the late thirteenth to the early fifteenth century, primarily through close study of the manuscript tradition.

Kay, Sarah. *The Romance of the Rose.* London: Grant & Cutler, 1995. A brief critical guide to the backgrounds and the most important formal and thematic approaches for study of the poem.

Kelly, Douglass. *Internal Difference and Meanings in the "Roman de la rose."* Madison: University of Wisconsin Press, 1995. Argues that the controversies and divergent critical interpretations raised by the work are best considered as the result of divergent meanings developed in the book itself: Different textual levels offer different meanings to different readers.

Luria, Maxwell. *A Reader's Guide to the "Roman de la Rose."* Hamden, Conn.: Archon, 1982. An introductory book for the general reader or student, including a survey of major critical approaches. Includes outlines, summaries, and glossaries to help orient readers; a number of sources and analogues; and a selective research bibliography.

Paul Acker

Jorge Guillén

Born: Valladolid, Spain; January 18, 1893
Died: Málaga, Spain; February 6, 1984

Principal poetry

Cántico: Fe de vida, 1928 (revised 1936, 1945, 1950; *Canticle*, 1997)
Maremágnum, 1957 (translated in *Clamor*, 1997)
Clamor: Tiempo de historia, 1957-1963 (3 volumes; includes *Maremágnum*, *Que van a dar en el mar*, *A la altura de las circunstancias*; *Clamor*, 1997)
Que van a dar en el mar, 1960 (translated in *Clamor*, 1997)
A la altura de las circunstancias, 1963 (translated in *Clamor*, 1997)

Cántico: A Selection, 1965
Homenaje, 1967 (*Homage*, 1997)
Affirmation: A Bilingual Anthology, 1968
Aire nuestro, 1968 (includes *Cántico*, *Clamor*, and *Homenaje*; *Our Air*, 1997)
Y otros poemas, 1973
Final, 1981
Horses in the Air, and Other Poems, 1999

Other literary forms

Jorge Guillén (gee-YAYN) is a literary theorist and translator as well as a poet. His critical work *Language and Poetry* (1961) was first published in English translation, appearing in Spanish as *Lengua y poesía* the following year. Guillén edited *El cantar de los cantares* (1561; *The Song of Songs*, 1936), a translation of the Song of Solomon by Luis de León, and the Aguilar edition of the works of Federico García Lorca; in addition, he published volumes of correspondence and essays on García Lorca and Gabriel Miró.

Guillén's translations of poetry into Spanish are included in *Homage* under the heading "Variaciones"; among them are three of William Shakespeare's sonnets; "Torment," by the Portuguese Antero Tarquínio de Quental; poems by Arthur Rimbaud; "The Lake Isle of Innisfree," by William Butler Yeats; several poems by Paul Valéry; and others by Jules Supervielle, Saint-John Perse, Archibald MacLeish, and Eugenio Montale.

Huerto de Melibea (pb. 1954; the orchard of Melibea) is a short poetic drama re-creating the Fernando de Rojas tragedy *Comedia de Calisto y Melibea* (1499; commonly known as *La Celestina*; *Celestina*, 1631); it was later incorporated into *Clamor* in *Our Air*.

Achievements

The most classical and intellectual member of the Generation of '27, Jorge Guillén is widely regarded as one of the greatest Spanish poets. The clean beauty of his lyrics has been recognized by contemporaries as diverse as García Lorca and Jorge Luis Borges. He has been called the Spanish equivalent of T. S. Eliot and Valéry. His greatness as a poet stems from the high quality of his verse rather than from the influence he has exerted.

Guillén's "Salvación de la primavera" ("Salvation

of Spring") has been called one of the greatest love poems of the Spanish language. In the wake of a century of Spanish poetry that lacked interest in pantheism, Guillén and his friend Pedro Salinas are credited with creating a mode of poetry whereby hidden reality is disclosed by the contemplation of simple things.

Guillén was awarded the Etna-Taormina International Poetry Prize in 1961, and he received numerous other awards as well, including the Award of Merit Medal from the American Academy of Arts and Letters (1955), the Bennett Literary Prize (New York, 1976), the Miguel de Cervantes Prize (Alcalá de Henares, Spain, 1977), and several Italian literary prizes.

BIOGRAPHY

Jorge Guillén was the oldest of four children born to Julio Guillén Sáenz and Esperanza Alvarez Guerra, both of Valladolid. In "Patio de San Gregorio," Guillén recalls his childhood as both happy and difficult, filled with duties, studies, and games. He attended high school in Valladolid and at the Maison Perreyve of the French Fathers of the Oratory in Fribourg, Switzerland. He pursued his university studies at Madrid and Granada, and he graduated in 1913. Thereafter, he secured a teaching position at the Sorbonne, and he worked as a correspondent for the newspaper *La libertad* from 1917 to 1923. He received his doctorate from the University of Madrid in 1924, writing his dissertation on the "Fábula de Polifemo y Galatea" (1627; *Fable of Polyphemus and Galatea*, 1961) of Luis de Góngora y Argote.

In 1921, while in Paris, Guillén married Germaine Cohen, who bore him two children: Teresa in 1922 and Claudio in 1924. Germaine died in 1947, and in 1961, while in Bogotá, Colombia, Guillén married Irene Mochi Sismondi. Guillén reconciles his two marriages in the poem "Pasiones" ("Passions"), where he represents Germaine as France and Irene as Italy and proceeds to vow undying love for both countries, citing a vigorous confrontation with the future as the most effective way of keeping the past alive. The "In memoriam" section of *Clamor*, which became the central section of *Our Air*, is devoted to his love for Germaine, and the "El centro" ("The Center") section of *Homage* is devoted to his love for Irene.

Guillén assumed his first professorial chair at the University of Murcia in 1926. Three years later, he was offered a lectureship at Oxford, and from 1931 to 1938, he was a professor at the University of Seville. After being imprisoned in Pamplona for political reasons in 1938, he fled Spain, crossing the bridge between Irún and Hendaye on foot. He went to the United States, taught at Middlebury College in Vermont for one year, spent the following year at McGill University in Montreal, and then moved to Massachusetts, where he taught at Wellesley College until 1957. He taught one final year as Charles Norton Eliot Professor at Harvard, retiring in 1958.

In 1982, Guillén's native city of Valladolid staged a weeklong tribute to him; scholars and fellow poets from Spain and from abroad came to honor the venerable poet, who had published his most recent volume, *Final*, at the age of eighty-eight. On February 6, 1984, Guillén died of pneumonia in Málaga, Spain.

ANALYSIS

Jorge Guillén was stigmatized early in his career as a cold, intellectual poet, and although that is almost the opposite of the truth, it took a long time for his reputation to recover. He strove after the ideal of *poesía pura* (pure poetry) and sought to distill from experience its barest essence, weeding from his verse the incidental and the ornamental.

Guillén's concern for *poesía pura* was obviously influenced by Juan Ramón Jiménez and Valéry, while his pantheistic view of nature reveals the influence of José Ortega y Gasset. There was no such view of nature among the poets of nineteenth century Spain, and the radiance and intensity in Guillén's work are reminiscent of the Neoplatonic tradition of the sixteenth century poet Luis de León. In technique, Guillén was influenced by Francisco Gómez de Quevedo y Villegas (especially in the trenchant wit of his epigrams, which Guillén called *tréboles*) and Juan Meléndez Valdés, the great Spanish lyricist of the eighteenth century. In Guillén's classical Spanish rhythms and packed metaphors, he reveals the influence of Góngora, and there are also traces in his work of the creationism and Surrealism of the Chilean Vicente Huidobro.

Fond of assonance and short lines, Guillén uses a wide variety of meters. Often he uses the *décima* (with stanzas of ten octosyllabic lines) to express in simple form his ecstasy before the miraculous panorama of nature in a balance of rhythm, thought, and feeling. Contrary to the Spanish practice, he capitalizes the first word of each line of his poetry, and many of his poems have a circular structure, harking back in the last line to a keyword in the first.

Nouns that stress essence predominate in Guillén's poems, and his lexicon is basic and relatively spare. As fond as he is of onomatopoeia, he uses nearly as many nouns that are expressive of sound (such as *baraúnda, batahola, guirigay, algarabía*) as he does verbs. In "Alamos con río" ("Poplars with River"), for example, *arrullar* (to coo) appears as "Poplars that are almost music/ Coo to him who is lucky enough to hear." In addition, Guillén is fond of elliptical sentences and exclamations, colloquial expletives (such as *zas* and *uf*), and rhetorical questions. Although his poetry is not easy reading, his vocabulary is not difficult.

Guillén was well grounded in Spanish and world literature; quotations of and allusions to all periods abound in his work. His pieces are often headed by untranslated epigraphs in English, German, French, Italian, or Portuguese. He also makes moderate use of classical allusions, although often without encumbering the poetry with specific names.

CANTICLE

Many years of Guillén's poetic career were devoted to refining his *Canticle*, first published in 1928. The original collection included a mere 75 poems; in 1936, the poet added 50 more. The edition of 1945 contains 270 poems, and the 1950 volume contains 332.

First and foremost in *Canticle*, which, strictly speaking, is a "canticle" or "hymn of praise," Guillén wishes to communicate his ecstasy at the very existence of the created world. In the short poem "Beato sillón" ("Blessed Armchair"), for example, it is the armchair that gratefully puts him in touch with the physical universe and that allows him to transcend it ("The eyes do not see,/ They know"). He does not need magic to attain these heights, for he is fortunate enough to be able to savor the incidental properties of a world that, for him, is "well-made."

In *Canticle*, Guillén celebrates the perfection of the universe, ever grateful for its never-ending miracles. In

a ten-line poem titled "Perfección" ("Perfection"), the poet submits to the beauty of one sunny day at noontime. He senses that the attributes of nature (the dense blue of the firmament "over-arching the day" and the sun at its zenith) reveal a superior order, which he perceives in architectural terms ("All is curving dome"). The sun reigns over the firmament, and its counterpart on Earth is the rose, humankind's perennial symbol of divine beauty. This moment so affects the poet that he feels time stop in a vision of the completeness of the planet. A corollary to this attitude is that death, as part of that natural order, is not to be feared, for without death, the perfect order of the universe would be impossible.

CLAMOR

After the overwhelming optimism of *Canticle*, it comes as somewhat of a relief, as G. G. Brown notes, to see that the poet is capable of recognizing some of the more negative features of life in his next volume, *Clamor* (in Spanish, the word *clamor* has more the connotation of "plaint" or "cry" than it does in English). Here, Guillén undertakes to describe the baseness of a Satanized world, even alluding to the horrors of the Spanish Civil War, a subject previously avoided in his work. As the poet grew older, he found it more difficult to savor nature in self-absorbed tranquillity. Guillén himself, however, insisted that *Clamor* is not a negation of *Cántico*, but rather a further perceptual step.

In *Clamor*, there are such titles as "Dolor tras dolor" ("Pain After Pain"), "Zozobra" ("Anguish"), and "El asesino del planeta" ("The Murderer of the Planet"); the vehement political statement of "Potencia de Pérez" ("Power of Pérez"); and references to Avernus, pollution, the vulgarity of television and pornography, nuclear holocaust, and the biblical Cain, the first murderer. (In a much later poem, Guillén uses the neologism *cainita* to describe the agony of his struggle in Spain before he chose to become an exile). A unique feature of *Clamor* is Guillén's insertion among the poems of his *tréboles* (literally "shamrocks" or "clover"), three-line or four-line statements that variously resemble epigrams, haiku, and other brief forms (for example, "Yours is the dawn, Jesus/ Watch how the sun shines/ In an orange-juice sky").

HOMAGE

In *Homage*, there is somewhat of a reconciliation between the rapture of *Cántico* and the bitterness of *Clamor*, as the poet seeks consolation from art, which allows some of his earlier optimism to resurface. In the section "Al Margen" ("Marginal Notes"), Guillén documents his reactions to many of the world's great thinkers and writers, from Sappho to César Vallejo. Guillén expresses his appreciation of Aristophanes for making him laugh ("While I laugh, I do not die"), of the converted Spanish Rabbi Sem Tob for his wisdom, of the erudition of Alfonso Reyes, and of the Italian Communist Antonio Gramsci ("From the prison there flashes before the astounded/ Like a revelation, that incredible/ capacity for injustice that is man's"). There are also some less charitable observations (concerning Arthur Schopenhauer, for example). At the end of this section, under the heading "Al margen de un Cántico" ("Marginal Notes on a Cántico"), Guillén includes five poems of commentary glossing his own earlier poems, thereby reserving a place for himself in his own literary history.

This section is followed by the love poems of "The Center," written to Guillén's second wife, followed in turn by the section "Atenciones" ("Attentions"), which consists of verse portraits of writers ranging from Juan Ruíz to Rubén Darío. "Attentions" includes a five-poem cycle that honors the memory of José Moreno Villa, Salinas, García Lorca, Emilio Prados, and Manuel Altolaguirre. The final section of *Homage* includes Guillén's translations of an impressive number of poems from world literature, as well as sundry poems of his own.

LOVE AND LOVERS

It comes as no surprise that a poet who is keenly aware of the miraculous should frequently concentrate on the nature of love. For Guillén, the love between man and woman suggests the larger relationship between humans and the cosmos and allows one to become greater than one is, to transcend the confines of time and space, of history and geography. In addition, love can give the assurance that death itself has been transcended, synchronizing the lovers with the natural cycle of the world. Moreover, the lover can be the salvation of the beloved by protecting that person from "phantoms" that might keep the beloved from communicating with his or her own inner vitality.

For Guillén, the body of a woman is the epitome of perfect creation. In "Desnudo" ("Nude"), for example, the poet observes that the female body needs no embellishment, no backdrop to improve its perfection, for that perfection consists not in its "promise" but in its "absolute presence." Another example of a sensuous achievement is the epithalamium "Amor dormido" ("Love Asleep"). The poet and his beloved are together in bed, bathed by moonlight. He contemplates her as she sleeps. Without waking up, she embraces him, and the poet feels himself transfigured, drawn into the realm of her dream.

WOMEN

Guillén has a special tenderness for the company of women, and his students at Wellesley became the subjects of a number of affectionate poems such as "Muchachas" ("Girls"), "Poesía eres tú" ("You Are Poetry"), "Nadadoras" ("Swimmers"), and "Melenas" ("Hair"). He is emphatic about the need for a man to become a man in the total sense, through the welcome intercession of a woman, and in a short poem, "El caballero" ("The Gentleman"), Guillén writes contemptuously of the typical Spanish café scene ("All men, terrible world of men/ Life that way could not be uglier"). Here, he employs a humorous neologism, *machedumbre* (composed of *macho*, meaning "male," and *muchedumbre*, meaning "crowd") to convey precisely how ridiculous and unthinkable such a world without women would be for him. The strong convictions that Guillén holds on this subject lead him to pontificate, in a later poem, "Sucesos de jardín" ("Garden Happenings"), that "He who never embraces [the other sex] is ignorant of everything."

Despite the foregoing quotation, Guillén is generally successful in avoiding clichés and seldom indulges in arrant nostalgia. In "Su persona" ("Her Person"), for example, the poet chides himself for attempting to feast on the memory of an old love, a figment of mist not anchored concretely in his current physical reality. He refuses to allow "phantoms" to convert him into a phantom, and love as a memory is condemned as a "fictitious delight." According to Guillén, one can relive and enjoy the past most profitably by continuing to savor new experiences rather than by wallowing in memories.

HUMOR AND RELIGION

Humor and self-deprecation are not alien to Guillén. In "Perfección de la tarde" ("Afternoon Perfection"), for example, the poet depicts a garden setting in lofty imagery, complete with alliteration and ecstatic utterances. In the midst of this garden idyll, however, a robin's dropping lands smack on the poet's bald pate, and the poet stands humbled in his pomposity.

Guillén himself has characterized *Canticle* as a "dialogue between man and the world," wherein "man affirms himself in affirming creation," and there is a noticeable absence of traditionally religious subject matter in this volume. In *Clamor*, there is clearly a greater emphasis on the message of Christianity, as in "Epifanía" ("Epiphany")—in whose manger scene the helpless infant "says in silence: I am not a king,/ I am the way, the truth and life"—and in "Viernes santo" ("Good Friday"): "A centurion already understands./ The three Marys weep. Sacred Man./ The Cross." A poem in *Homage*, "La gran aventura" ("The Sublime Adventure"), may provide a more balanced view of Guillén's religious stance. In this poem, he speculates whether the creation of humans by God or the creation of God by humans is the worthier marvel, concluding that in either case, there is no escape from the miracle of creation—that "the earth is a sublime adventure."

Guillén's achievement as a poet stems from his rare ability to seize a fragment of time and transform it into a single, simple jewel of articulation. When his lapidarian stance became obsessive and threatened to dehumanize his poetry, he dared to change and strove for means to make his work more human. Nor was he oblivious to evil and suffering; rather, he sought to be attentive to the "well-made world" while in the shadow of the other, "badly made world." The words that Guillén once wrote in a dedicatory passage to his readers were true of himself as well: He was eager to share life like a fountain and to realize that life more fully through the power of words.

OTHER MAJOR WORKS

PLAY: *Huerto de Melibea*, pb. 1954.

NONFICTION: *En torno a Gabriel Miró*, c. 1959; *Federico en persona: Semblanza y epistolario*, 1959; *Language and Poetry*, 1961 (*Lengua y poesía*, 1962).

BIBLIOGRAPHY

Havard, Robert. *Jorge Guillén, Cántico*. London: Tamesis, 1986. A critical study of Guillén's *Canticle*. Includes bibliographic references.

MacCurdy, G. Grant. *Jorge Guillén*. Boston: Twayne, 1982. An introductory biography and critical study of selected works by Guillén. Includes bibliographic references.

Machado, Antonio, Pablo Neruda, Federico García Lorca, and Jorge Guillén. *Cuatro Poetas: Poems of Antonio Machado, Pablo Neruda, Federico García Lorca and Jorge Guillén*. Translated and edited by Albert Rowe. Ilfracombe, Devon, England: Original Plus, 2004. This bilingual edition gathers some of the best-known poems by Guillén and three other poets. Contains a brief but detailed biography of each poet with some analysis.

McMullan, Terence. *The Crystal and the Snake: Aspects of French Influence on Guillén, Lorca and Cernuda*. Anstruther, Fife, Scotland: La Sirena, 2002. Contains two essays on Guillén, examining, in particular, the influence of Paul Valéry on his work.

Matthews, Elizabeth. *The Structured World of Jorge Guillén: A Study of Cántico and Clamor*. Liverpool, England: F. Cairns, 1985. Matthews analyzes Guillén's *Canticle* and *Clamor*. Includes bibliographic references.

Miller, Martha La Follette. "Self-Commentary in Jorge Guillén's *Aire Nuestro*." *Hispania* 65, no. 1 (March, 1982): 20-27. A critical study of Guillén's works.

Sibbald, K. M., ed. *Guillén at McGill: Essays for a Centenary Celebration*. Ottawa, Ont.: Dovehouse, 1996. A collection of critical essays on Guillén's works. Text in English and Spanish. Includes bibliographical references.

Soufas, C. Christopher. *The Subject in Question: Early Contemporary Spanish Literature and Modernism*. Washington, D.C.: Catholic University of America Press, 2007. Contains a chapter analyzing the poetry of Guillén and Vicente Aleixandre and provides context for understanding Guillén's poetry.

Jack Shreve